Care free PLANTS

Carefree PLANTS

A Guide to Growing
the 200 Hardiest, Low-Maintenance,
Long-Living Beauties in Canada

With Canadian Consultant Trevor Cole

Reader's
Digest

Reader's Digest Association (Canada) ULC
Montreal

CARE-FREE PLANTS

CANADIAN PROJECT STAFF
Consultant and Writer: Trevor Cole
Senior Editor: Pamela Johnson
Senior Designer: Andrée Payette
Copy Editor: Gilles Humbert

PROJECT STAFF
Senior Editor: Delilah Smittle
Senior Designer: Judith Carmel

Project Editors:
Tovah Martin
Barbara Pleasant

Consulting Editor:
Rosemary Rennicke

Writers:
Richard E. Bir
C. Colston Burrell
Lina Burton
Judy Glattstein
Peter Loewer
Betty Mackey
Tovah Martin
Barbara Pleasant
Guy Sternberg
Amy Ziffer

Copy Editor:
Anne B. Farr

Proofreader:
Vicki Fischer

Gardening Consultants:
Stephanie Cohen
Mike Courtney

Fact Checker:
Thomas Scully

Contributing Designers:
Martha Grossman
Eleanor Kostyk
Carol Nehring

Illustrators:
Carolyn Bucha
Dolores R. Santoliquido

Photo Researchers:
Alexandra Truitt
Jerry Marshall

Indexer:
Lina Burton

READER'S DIGEST ASSOCIATION (CANADA) ULC
Vice President Book Editorial:
Robert Goyette

THE READER'S DIGEST ASSOCIATION, INC.
President and Chief Executive Officer:
Tom Williams

Executive Vice President, RDA & President, North America: Dan Lagani

Executive Vice President, RDA & President, Allrecipes.com: Lisa Sharples

Executive Vice President, RDA & President, Europe: Dawn Zier

Library and Archives Canada Cataloguing in Publication

Care-free plants: a guide to growing the 200 hardiest, low-maintenance, long-living beauties in Canada / Canadian consultant, Trevor Cole. – 1st Canadian ed.

Includes index.
ISBN 978-1-55475-085-6

1. Landscape plants. 2. Low-maintenance gardening.
I. Cole, Trevor J. II. Reader's Digest Association (Canada)

SB407.C37 2005   635.9
C2004-906431-2

Address any comments about *Care-free Plants* to:
    Editorial Director
    Reader's Digest Books Division
    Reader's Digest Association (Canada) ULC
    1100 René-Lévesque Blvd. W.
    Montreal, QC H3B 5H5

ABOUT THIS BOOK

Who doesn't yearn for a property filled with lush and colorful plants? Naturally, you want to look out your windows and see paradise, but, if you are like most of us, you can't help wondering if you can spare the time and effort needed to create your own Eden.

That's where this book comes in. The fact is that you *can* have a fantastic garden and also have the time to relax and enjoy it. If you plant wisely, you can be the proud owner of a wonderful garden that you can develop in your spare minutes without also developing an aching back or a groaning pocketbook. When you match care-free plants to the conditions of your site, gardening becomes a cinch. We've thought of every situation. No matter where you live, you'll find suggestions for plants that will thrive in your yard. No matter if you garden in a sunny spot by a windy beach or a thoroughfare, or in a shady, swampy niche, the following pages will offer you schemes that feature the easiest-to-grow, most rewarding, most foolproof, and most problem-free plants for your site. To help you further, we've included an encyclopedia section, in which you'll find descriptions of 200 care-free annuals, perennials, bulbs, shrubs, trees, groundcovers, and vines for your garden.

We've designed combinations for every situation, from the sunniest and driest to the shadiest and wettest location, and for every type of soil. If you want to customize your care-free combinations, you'll find lots of additional plant choices in the "Other Bedfellows" boxes that accompany each situation. The recipes for success in the following pages use plants that are beautiful and readily available in addition to being easy to grow. Flip through the following pages. You'll find money-saving tips and seasonal advice. You'll learn the formula for a low-upkeep lawn as well as a restful pond-side planting. And we'll tell you how to do it all quickly, simply, and effectively. What's the secret to great gardening? Learning to work smart, not hard, with Care-Free Plants.

HOW TO USE THIS BOOK

Combinations

In this section, we will help you get started by defining your garden conditions. If you're not quite sure what you have underfoot, leaf through the pages of this section, read the descriptions of what constitutes a soggy site and how many hours of sun qualify a space as a "sunny site." Then plant accordingly.

Our lists of plants that tolerate filtered, part-day shade and other conditions are great to get you started, but we go one step further. Rather than leaving you groping in the dark wondering which plants are compatible, we provide a hard-hitting package that combines shrubs, trees, bulbs, vines, annuals, and perennials to furnish height, breadth, and a display that lingers over the longest possible time span. Annuals, bulbs, shrubs, and trees work in tandem to keep the garden dancing through the seasons. We also recommend other horticultural hard-hitters, allowing you to mix and match, and make it work for you.

Need to know more? Cross-reference the Combinations in Part One with the Encyclopedia in Part Two, and you'll find every plant fully described and pictured. This is foolproof gardening at its best.

Encyclopedia

Here's where you'll find out about the easy-care plants we mention in Part One. We've dug up all the dirt on 200 of the easiest plants available to let you ease your aching back. And we recommend the best varieties for every application.

The plant encyclopedia presents a substantial list of annuals from ageratum to zinnia, perennials from anise hyssop to yucca, vines that climb, trail, or dangle; bulbs, hardy and tender, including the lesser-known varieties; shrubs and trees great or small for a focal point or for a bed. Each is listed alphabetically by common name followed by botanical name. All the data is conveniently at your fingertips; the profile for each plant includes its preferred soil pH, soil type, light requirements, quirks, where it grows best, lifespan, potential pitfalls, propagation, and critter resistance.

Containers
Lawns
Maintenance

Here's where we tackle the challenges inherent in keeping a landscape prime and pretty throughout the seasons. Whether you're making a container garden, grappling with crabgrass, or preparing to prune, you'll find what you need to get the job done without blood, sweat, or tears.

Everyone can garden in containers: all you need is a porch, deck, or windows. We show how to choose the right container and foolproof plants, from common to courageous. You'll also find suggestions for other container bedfellows, soil mixes, watering strategies, feeding, and grooming.

Most gardeners grapple with grass, and in this chapter you'll find virtually everything you need to make lawn maintenance a snap. Discover the best grasses for your region, exactly what grass needs to look prime, and how to make mowing easier. Find suggestions for fertilizing and guidelines for optimal mowing heights. And when grass isn't the best answer, choose from our list of care-free groundcovers and give your lawn mower a break.

In the pages of the maintenance chapter you'll find advice on planting, feeding, watering, weeding, mulching, pruning, grooming, propagating and controlling pests. A calendar helps reduce future work by timing tasks.

Glossary

Part of care-free gardening is leaving nothing unexplained. So in our glossary, you'll find complete, every-day-language definitions for all of the useful gardening terms that you'll find scattered throughout this book.

Climate
Zone Map

This Zone map divides Canada into 9 hardiness Zones based in part on the average minimum winter temperature in each region. Studying it will help you decide whether a plant will survive season after season in your garden.

Care-Free Plants helps you work garden wonders with practically no sweat. In our book, there's no "mission impossible," as far as gardening is concerned.

CONTENTS

PART ONE

CHAPTER ONE

PLANTS FOR SUN-DRENCHED PLACES

All plants operate on solar power because of their unique talent for converting light into energy through a process called photosynthesis. So rejoice if you have a garden site with plenty of sun, because you're well on the way to having a garden that can support many kinds of foliage and flowering plants.

In gardening, full sun is usually defined as 10 to 12 hours of direct sun each day, and many of the most colorful flowering plants that you can grow, thrive in full sun. To measure how much sun an area receives, visit the spot in the morning, at noon, mid afternoon and late afternoon. On each visit, mark the portion of soil that receives sunlight with spray paint or a sprinkling of baking flour. This way you can total up the hours of sunlight an area receives each day in various seasons, making it easier to select plants that will thrive there.

But you must take into consideration that full sun can vary in intensity. Full sun in northern latitudes is less intense than full sun in the southern ones, which are closer to the equator. Cloud cover, which is usually heaviest in lower altitudes and in the East, also diminishes the intensity of the sun. For this reason, gardeners in southern Ontario and British Columbia often can, and should, grow plants described as needing full sun in sites that receive an average of only 6 to 7 hours of full sun per day. Other factors also hold sway. For example, soil type and moisture, as well as daytime and evening temperatures also influence a plant's sun tolerance. We have considered all options. Throughout this chapter as well as the rest of the book, we've specified which plants thrive when grown in full sun in cooler gardens, yet appreciate partial shade in hot, sunny regions, and under special environmental conditions.

This chapter features garden ideas for six different sun-and-soil combinations for year-round performance and beauty. No matter what your situation has to offer, you'll find care-free ideas for design and color combinations, and you'll discover many plants that will suit your garden's needs.

Plants for Good Soil

FOR MOST PLANTS, A GARDEN SITE THAT OFFERS RICH, loamy soil and full sun is the best of all possible worlds. Nearly everything you plant will thrive in this situation with little additional care, but to capitalize on the situation, consider growing care-free plants that have multiple endearing traits. For example, lavender and dianthus boast beautiful flowers and intoxicating fragrance. And their soothing gray-green foliage lets them and other silver-leaved plants, such as artemisia and dusty miller, combine well with any other plants. Silver-leaved plants can be paired with bright blooming perennials and shrubs, employed as a quiet, cooling presence along a sunny sidewalk, or cut and woven into indoor container bouquets.

Snapdragons, hollyhocks, larkspur, fragrant sweet peas, and other upright-growing flowering plants, which are sometimes called spire plants, bring excitement to the garden with their vertical shapes and are best used to create a colorful backdrop for small bulbs or any shorter, dainty plants. If red is your passion, you can indulge in Oriental lilies, red-leaved Japanese maples, or all types of roses. If you want a green, velveteen lawn to showcase your collection of garden plants, this sunny situation will support your ambitions there, too. With full sun and good soil, you really can have it all.

THE LOWDOWN ON LOAM

Garden soil can have a character or texture that is somewhat sandy or basically like clay, or it can be ideal: a fertile, well-drained combination of sand, clay, and silt known as loam. Sandy soil is made up of large mineral particles. The loose, crumbly texture of sandy soil is easy to dig, so it drains quickly, discouraging fungal root rot, but plant nutrients are quickly leached from the soil with each rain. Whereas clay particles are much smaller, giving the soil a heavier, water-holding texture. Clay soil retains nutrients, but drains poorly and is hard to till. Either type of soil can be transformed into fertile loam with generous additions of organic matter. Compost is the finest form of organic matter to work into soil to improve its texture and fertility, but any material derived from decomposed plants, such as rotted hay, grass clippings, shredded leaves, peat moss, or rotted sawdust, will improve soil by boosting its organic content.

For an early summer sunny combination that can't miss, frame pink roses with blue-flowered lavender and pincushion flowers, silvery annual dusty millers, and blue pansies. Edge the planting with evergreen dwarf boxwood shrubs for year-long greenery.

OTHER BEDFELLOWS — Ageratum, akebia, alstroemeria, anise hyssop, artemisia, aster, balloon flower, barberry, blanket flower,

Silvery lamb's ears and cooling, blue-flowered salvias exert a calming influence on the hot-pink roses in this sunny summer garden. The billowing salvias are placed where they can disguise the bare lower canes of the tall roses.

Because the transformation from less-than-perfect soil to fertile loam involves billions of microscopic soil-borne life forms, which slowly break down organic material into water-soluble nutrients that plants can absorb through their roots, this process takes time. You can make vast improvements in your soil by digging in a 10 cm (4 in) thick layer of compost in one fell swoop, but it's better to allow 2 years for this miracle to take place. Before starting a new bed, dig and amend your soil. The first season, plant it with annuals, which will be pulled up at the end of the season. Dig it again in fall, incorporating more organic matter, and by the second spring you will have soil that is the envy of gardeners everywhere.

If you, like most gardeners, already have established beds, or if you can't devote the time to digging in amendments, applying a layer of compost annually as a mulch on the soil's surface is the truly care-free way of keeping your soil healthy. Rain and earthworms do the work of incorporating the organic matter into the soil over a season or two, which is exactly what you might expect from a simple strategy that follows nature's blueprint.

KNITTING THE GARDEN TOGETHER

Unplanted earth is an invitation to weeds, so pay close attention to spacing plants in the garden. Space large plants by 1 and 1/2 times their mature width. Fill the gaps between young upright plants with smaller, spreading companions like hardy geraniums or creeping veronica. In spring, the spaces between late-blooming perennials, such as coreopsis and rudbeckia, can be filled with early-flowering bulbs like snowdrops and daffodils. At the front of the bed, use low, spreading annuals like ageratum or bugleweed to visually tie clumps of plants together and shade out weeds. As the big plants mature and spread, you can easily dig up the filler plants and move them to a sunnier home.

begonia, bluebeard, borage, butterfly weed, daffodil, dusty miller, fan flower, grape hyacinth, golden rain tree, hyacinth, lamb's ear, larkspur, lobelia, love-lies-bleeding, magic lily, morning glory, Oriental poppy, perilla, plectran- thus, red hot poker, rose, Russian sage, salvia, spider flower, squill, tithonia, wishbone flower, wisteria, yellowwood.

Plants for Cool Summers

COOL SUMMERS ARE A JOY FOR PEOPLE AND PLANTS alike. Some of the advantages of gardening in northern latitudes or at higher elevations in mountainous regions include low humidity and delightfully cool summer days that seldom exceed 27°C (80°F). Additionally, many coastal areas benefit from cooling lake or ocean breezes.

In these locales, if you have a sunny garden site and you crave a sumptuous traditional flower garden, you're in luck. Color balance is a crucial factor of garden design, and many people quickly discover that they have favorite colors when it comes to foliage and flowers. In sunny sites bright, saturated colors usually show up best, whereas white and light pastels are easily lost in the sun's glare. Towering mauve-flowered foxgloves, deep pink and red hollyhocks, and the huge, fragrant magenta or deep pink flowers of peonies are the pride of sunny gardens in early summer. High summer belongs to colorful annuals, combined with pink phlox, warm-hued daylilies, and lavender-blue catmint. Late-summer color is often even stronger, with the deep blue flowers of monkshood, the golden flowers of rudbeckia, and the vivid pink flowers of turtlehead blooming just ahead of those of bright yellow sneezeweed. In autumn, cool blue and purple asters bring the blue of the sky down to earth and unite it with warm-hued gold and burgundy chrysanthemums and trees ablaze in brilliant seasonal red and gold.

STRETCHING COOL SUMMERS

Though temperatures in the cool-summer areas of the country are perfect for summer gardening, because plants are less likely to wilt under the sun's glare and the soil is more likely to retain sufficient moisture for plant roots, the season often seems painfully short. Frosty nights may persist well into spring, delaying planting until summer is nearly under way. Invest in perennials, shrubs, and hardy bulbs. These plants, which are in the ground and ready and waiting for spring are a reassuring presence, making it easier to wait for warm planting weather before setting out summer annuals.

Fortunately, there are a number of cold-tolerant annuals that can be planted before the last frost has passed. Some of these are calendula, dusty miller, lobelia, pansy, snapdragon, and sweet alyssum. Yet because bedding plants are often grown in heated greenhouses, they fare best in the garden when they become accustomed to outdoor conditions gradually, over a period of 2 weeks. This process, called hardening off, initially involves setting potted plants outdoors in a sunny, protected spot for a few hours each day for a week. Then, the week prior to planting, allow them modest exposure to chilly winds and cool nights, but bring them indoors if hard

In a sumptuous, cool-summer flower garden, white-flowering doublefile viburnum creates a background for trellised clematis and sweet peas. Anchoring the bed, a peony is edged in yellow-green lady's mantle and fragrant, white-flowered sweet alyssum and blue lobelia.

OTHER BEDFELLOWS
Aster, bluebeard, borage, buddleia, calendula, candytuft, catmint, centaurea, chrysanthemum, cosmos,

Cool, sunny, garden sites prolong the flowering of early-summer bloomers like roses, lady's mantle, and catmint.

freezes threaten. By this time, their stems will have become sturdy and new leaves will be a bit thicker and more frost-tolerant. The move into cold soil and chilly air will only cause a modest shock to the plants' roots.

RAISED BEDS AND BERMS

Sometimes plants in cold-winter climates are ready to go into the garden in spring, but the soil remains too clammy and wet for planting. So gardeners face frustrating delays. Building raised beds or berms may give you a head start on the planting season, because they warm up and dry out faster than lower-lying garden areas. Raising the soil level even 10 cm (4 in) can offer the additional advantage of superior drainage for plant roots. Indeed, the combination of great drainage and cool-summer weather brings out the best in several stellar perennials, such as artemisia, catmint, and veronica, which require excellent drainage to reach their full care-free potential.

COPING WITH WINTER COLD

Though cool summers are splendid, winters in northern latitudes and high altitudes are often long and cold, so plants grown there must have exceptional hardiness. Use the hardiness ratings (see Zone maps on the endsheets, at either end of this book) for your locale as a guide when shopping for plants. Also look for protected areas in your yard, called microclimates. Microclimates exist in spaces protected from freezing winds by walls, fences, or dense evergreen planting, and also are places where a masonry wall or rock outcropping may absorb and hold the sun's heat, elevating the surrounding temperatures. You can use these warm spots to grow plants rated one or two Zones warmer than your area's Zone.

To help garden plants get through freezing winters, use mulches. The insulation provided by a generous layer of mulch placed over the root zones will protect perennials and shrubs from cycles of soil freezing and thawing, which can heave the plants out of the ground, leaving the roots exposed and vulnerable to freezing and dehydration. Mulching is especially helpful in mild-winter areas where there is no consistent snow cover. The best winter mulches are fluffy organic ones like leaves, hay, straw, and evergreen boughs. If you use leaves chop them with a shredder or lawn mower. The chopped leaves will offer good insulation and are less likely to blow around.

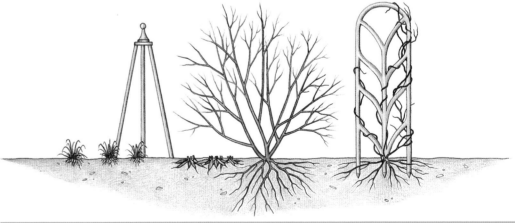

Look to the Future

Peonies and shrubs persist for decades, and their roots should not be disturbed. Leave room between these permanent plantings for growing annuals. In spring, the vacant spaces allotted to summer annuals will give you room to carefully move about, pruning shrubs and removing debris.

crocus, daffodil, daylily, dianthus, dusty miller, euonymus, euphorbia, flowering cherry, forsythia, geranium, golden chain

tree, grape, gypsophila, hens and chicks, holly, hollyhock, iris, Japanese maple, juniper, lily, lilac, monkshood, Oriental

poppy, ornamental cabbage, ornamental grasses, pansy, pincushion flower, rose, smokebush, snapdragon, statice, tulip.

Plants for Hot Summers

A heat-beating combination mixes orange-flowered trumpet vine and globe amaranth 'Strawberry Fields' with blue-flowered ageratum, a dwarf Chinese holly, yellow-flowered butter daisies, daylily 'Stella de Oro', and iris leaves.

GARDENING IN THE SEARING SUMMER SUN is always a challenge. Not only do plants wilt in the heat, but gardeners also suffer! But hot summers don't mean that you can't have a colorful garden. Numerous care-free plants with tropical temperaments crave high temperatures and strong sunlight.

The wisest approach is planning in advance to make sure that neither you nor your garden stumbles into the scorching season unprepared. Most climates with hot summers also have long spring and fall seasons, which offer the ideal conditions for working outdoors. Instead of waiting until summer's hot breath is just around the corner, get as much digging and planting done as you can fit into the shorter, cooler days of spring and fall. And when the dog days do arrive, enjoy gardening in the cool hours of the morning or evening.

You won't be the only one to benefit from shifting your schedule to suit the seasons. Your plants will also appreciate your advance planning. Plants set out in fall or early spring are spared the stress of starting out in a hot summer with skimpy roots that cannot take up moisture as fast as it evaporates through their leaves. When perennials and shrubs show new green growth in spring, rapid root growth is also taking place below ground. So, every spring day that a plant can spend in the garden contributes to the growth of a deep, extensive root system that it will need to pull moisture from the soil in the hot days ahead.

SIZZLING COLORS FOR HOT GARDENS

Flowers that are white or pastel colored are much harder to see in the glare of strong summer sunlight than those that are rollicking shades of red, bright yellow, orange, bright pink, or purple. Flowers that are easy to spot in intense sunlight include those of sulfur cosmos, four-o'clocks, and hot-colored zinnias. Don't be afraid of putting plants like these into a sunny garden, but do limit your color scheme to a few coordinating colors, because the brighter the colors are, the more noticeable they will be if they clash. When working with orange, combine it with its complementary color, which is deep purple. Use flowering and foliage plants in yellow shades, such as butter daisies, 'New Gold' lantana and 'Marguerite' ornamental sweet potato vine to help blend together bright flowers. Tone down the intense magenta of flowers, such as rose campion and some hardy geraniums, by combining them with plants that have neutral, silvery gray

OTHER BEDFELLOWS Alstroemeria, artemisia, blanket flower, bluebeard, boxwood, buddleia, butterfly weed, canna,

leaves, such as dusty miller and artemisia. Care-free evergreens, such as juniper and mugo pine, also have a calming influence on bright bloomers, and they not only make great companions and provide a neutral background for setting off flower colors, but they also maintain their fresh greenery through winter, when they become the main attraction of the border.

If your winters are mild, you have the opportunity to grow cool-season annuals from fall to spring. Annual dianthus, dusty miller, pansies, and snapdragons are sold as fall bedding plants in warmer climates, and planting them can keep your garden colorful nearly year-round. In cool-winter areas, look for flowering cabbage and kale, which can survive mild freezes. You'll find the cold-hardy annuals mentioned above in early spring. Adding a few of them to planters and window boxes can add one or two months of color to the growing season.

WONDERFUL WATER MISERS

A number of care-free plants, including buddleia, purple coneflower, and yucca, which grow well in hot-summer areas, have the added talent of being drought tolerant. Because hot summer sun saps moisture from plants, seek these and others, such as ornamental grasses, portulaca, and stonecrop, which are rarely thirsty at the end of a summer day. These natural water misers all share a few traits. When shopping for them, look for plants with succulent leaves, which store water; plants with small leaves or finely dissected leaves, which have less surface area exposed to evaporation; and plants with silver or gray leaves, which reflect excess light. Plants with abundant thorns, or fuzzy leaves shade themselves, reducing evaporation from the leaves.

Before buying, read descriptions of plants on nursery tags and in mail-order catalogs carefully to learn their origins. Those from areas with soil and climate that are similar to yours should adapt. Deep-rooted prairie plants, such as purple coneflower, are incredibly drought tolerant. Salvias and yuccas, which are native to the Southwest, are equally able to thrive in hot, dry situations, as are artemesias and other herbs from Mediterranean countries. Summer-flowering bulbs from South America and South Africa, as well as Australian plants like phormiums are also superb performers for hot-summer gardens.

Watering your garden will be necessary sometimes, even if you grow plants that can take the heat. So make use of strategies to limit the time and water your garden requires. Place plants close together, including tall plants or trellised vines, so that they will cast some welcome shade on shorter neighbors. Concentrating your summer garden in a compact space also makes it easier to reach it with a hose. Or use soaker hoses, which are the most efficient and economical way to get water into the soil with minimal loss to evaporation. But remember that using mulch alone can conserve a great deal of soil moisture by slowing evaporation and keeping the soil cool.

REGIONAL ADVICE
When to Water

In arid climates, water in the evening to increase nighttime humidity around your plants, which helps them recover from wilting days. In humid climates, irrigate first thing in the morning, and avoid watering leaves, so that the garden and plants will be dry by night. Dry nighttime conditions deter fungal leaf diseases.

Vivid flowers, which aren't lost in the sun's glare, show to best advantage in a sunny garden. Use just a few hues like the red, orange, and blue combination shown here, to avoid clashing colors. Be generous with greenery to soften the effect and unite the picture.

Carolina jessamine, cleome, cockscomb, coreopsis, crocosmia, euonymus, euphorbia, geranium, gladiolus, golden chain tree, goldenrod, hops, hyacinth bean, Joe Pye weed, juniper, lacebark pine, lantana, lavatera, love-lies-bleeding, magic lily, morning glory, nasturtium, portulaca, purple coneflower, red hot poker, rudbeckia, salvia, stonecrop, verbena, zinnia.

Plants for Dry Soil

EVERY GARDEN IS DRY SOMETIMES, but in some climates and with some soil types, moisture is always at a premium. Scant rainfall typical of many places in the West, as well as in areas where late-summer droughts create temporary desert conditions, sets the stage for a garden created with dry soil in mind. The same gardening techniques that serve desert gardeners apply to areas with sandy soil, which dries out quickly no matter how much rain falls, and they can also be used to good effect on a slope that is difficult to water because of runoff. In these and other types of dry, sunny sites, you can still have a colorful garden by using plants that are adapted to these conditions and by using the special planting techniques described here.

DODGING THE DROUGHT

Summer is always the most stressful season in a dry garden, but you may be amazed at how easy it is to succeed at growing "off-season" plants, which are quenched by winter rains. Even in high deserts, spring-flowering bulbs like crocuses, daffodils, and tulips will blissfully bloom in spring with little or no supplemental water during their most active period of growth, which is from late fall to late spring. Later, when Mother Nature turns up the heat and turns off the water, these plants quietly go dormant before the hot summer season. In dry climates with mild winters, take advantage of cold-tolerant annuals that can be grown from seed sown outdoors in fall, such as larkspur, poppies, and even cosmos. They'll need supplemental watering until they germinate, unless the season is wet, but any soil holds water longer at the end of the year than during summer.

PLANTS FOR PARCHED PLACES

All gardens need supplemental water once in a while, but growing plants that are natural water misers, such as cotoneaster, stonecrop, and yucca, keeps this need within practical limits. Look to nature for clues to help you find promising plants. Prairies and mountainsides as well as arid parts of the world have contributed a wealth of beautiful plants that will thrive in a garden like yours.

And they are not all cacti! Garden-worthy plants with succulent, water-holding leaves like portulaca and stonecrop are specially adapted to dry environments because their thick leaves work like small water reservoirs. Silver-leaved plants, such as artemisia, Russian sage, and sun rose, reflect excess light, and the downy hairs on the leaves and stems of these and other plants shade and insulate them from the evaporative power of the sun. Deeply rooted perennials and grasses are good choices. Choose shrubs with small, waxy leaves, such as cotoneaster. Among annuals, those with papery "petals," which are really modified leaves called bracts, such as globe amaranth and zinnia, keep their fresh appearance through days of baking heat (for additional drought-tolerant plants, see pages 17 and 319).

SUNKEN BEDS

Raised beds are a valuable asset in poorly drained or infertile soils, but you should take the opposite route for the plants you'd like to pamper in an arid garden. Beds that are slightly sunken are designed to collect

Lacebark pine and fountain grass form a wind-resistant background for this drought-tolerant garden. Try yarrow 'Coronation Gold', barberry 'Crimson Pigmy', purple coneflower, aster, sedum 'Autumn Joy', and the bright flowers of ground-hugging, annual portulaca.

OTHER BEDFELLOWS
Artemisia, blanket flower, blue star, butter daisy, butterfly weed, coreopsis, cotoneaster, crocus, dianthus, dusty

Burgundy Japanese barberry, pennisetum grass, and purple-flowered verbena make a lush dry-soil planting.

filter through and enter the soil. Large bark nuggets, rounded river rock, or other coarse mulch materials are good choices. Take care not to build up a thick layer, however. Plants adapted to dry conditions resent being smothered in mulch. A generous inch (3 cm) of mulch, spread evenly over the bed in spring, will do the trick.

TIMELY TRANSPLANTING

Even drought-tolerant plants need water during the first few weeks after transplanting, because their ability to survive with scant moisture depends in part on the presence of mature, far-reaching roots. There are several ways to reduce the time you must spend insuring that your dry-site garden is care-free from the very beginning.

Before removing a plant from its container, make sure that the soil in the pot is saturated. In addition to reducing transplanting trauma, wet roots slip free from pots more easily than dry ones. As a result, fewer roots are injured during transplanting, and every root is plumped up with water as you set the plant in place.

Whenever possible, set out new plants in the evening, so that they will not be immediately challenged by the drying effects of hot sun. Also look for periods when some cloud cover, or perhaps even rain, is in the weather forecast to undertake major planting projects, such as planting a large bed or setting out shrubs and trees.

If you must set out plants in bright, breezy weather, you can get them off to a strong start by covering them with temporary shade. Anything that filters sunlight will do, such as covering plants with bed sheets or a wooden lattice propped up by stakes. Cardboard boxes, weighed down with a stone, are great for popping over small shrubs or young annuals, and upside-down flower pots make good shade covers for small perennials. Remove the shade covers after 3 days, because as soon as the plants begin to grow, they will crave sunlight.

Root's-eye View

The secret to survival for plants weathering droughts is having deep, water-seeking roots. Long-lived shrubs and trees become more drought resistant the longer they are in the ground. Locate annuals and perennials where you won't dig into and damage the root masses of the woody plants each time you replant or divide these more transient neighbors.

rainfall and cast cooling shade over the soil. After lowering the soil level by 10 cm (4 in), prepare a sunken bed the same way you would any other new planting site. Loosen the soil and amend it with compost. Besides making the soil more hospitable to plant roots, organic matter helps buffer the effects of chemical imbalances, such as excessive salt, which often builds up in dry-climate soils, and it also neutralizes acid or alkaline soil, conditions that can be harmful to many garden plants.

Mulching is the key to care-free gardening in dry soils. Choose a porous mulch that encourages water to quickly

miller, euphorbia, geranium, globe amaranth, goldenrod, grape, hens and chicks, iris, juniper, lavender, love-in-a-mist, mugo pine, ornamental grasses, ornamental onion, periwinkle, poppy, portulaca, purple coneflower, rudbeckia, Russian sage, sedum, sneezeweed, stonecrop, sun rose, thyme, tulip, verbena, white pine, yucca, zinnia.

Plants for Moist Soil

DO YOU HAVE A LOW, SUNNY SPOT that never seems to be dry enough to dig? Don't despair. While wet soil can be murder on plants that demand great drainage, there are plants that prefer this unusual niche. You can also plant moisture-loving trees as a care-free way to slowly change the nature of the site by removing some of the moisture from the soil and by introducing shade, as seen in the illustrated combination on this page. In nature, trees often shade moist sites, and there is a wealth of shade- and moisture-loving perennials, shrubs, and other plants that have adapted to these conditions. So planting trees in a wet site opens up a whole new world of planting possibilities. Another care-free option is to simulate a low meadow, as might occur along the banks of a stream that floods often in winter and spring, introducing some of the plants that are native to these areas.

The abundance of moisture in this type of site can also help some marginal plants to tolerate strong sunlight, because no matter how intensely the sun shines, the roots of plants always get the moisture they need. So, this is a good place to grow moisture-loving plants that adapt to either full sun or partial shade. Some of these include aster, bee balm, and small trees like dogwood and Japanese maple. Arrange plants according to height, with the taller ones at the back of a bed, and capitalize on differences in plant texture. For example, a background clump of tall, dusty pink-flowered Joe Pye weed partners well with the brighter pink flowers of shorter perennials like bee balm or astilbe. And the tall strappy leaves of moisture-loving yellow flag iris flatter any plant in its company, including ground-hugging bugleweed or the vivid colored leaves of sun-tolerant varieties of coleus.

As the seasons pass, you will undoubtedly discover that some plants like this niche so well that they prosper with little care. Where winters are mild, dainty, colorful, spring-flowering primroses often flourish. Put tall garden phlox to work filling the garden with color through the second half of summer. And annuals may surprise you by reseeding themselves and coming back year after year. If you plant spider flower or periwinkle, learn to identify the seedlings, which will often appear in late spring near where the parent plants grew the year before. On a cloudy day, thin the seedlings by gently digging and transplanting the volunteers to a moist place where you want them to bloom later in the summer.

MAKING A GARDEN

Naturally wet soil can be an ideal garden situation for adapted plants. The soil is often high in organic matter, and quite fertile as well. The only thing

A site with moist soil and full sun can be fertile ground for a colorful garden. Here, decorative, multi-trunked small river birches grow alongside pink-flowered garden phlox, blue-flowered spiderworts and balloon flowers, and pink-and-white wax begonias. The green dwarf winged euonymus at the right will become a blaze of red foliage in fall, when most other plants are past flowering.

OTHER BEDFELLOWS — Aster, astilbe, bee balm, borage, bugleweed, bullbay magnolia, campanula, canna, clethra, coleus,

Adequate moisture makes it possible for plants like these, which prefer partial shade, to flourish in sun. Here, the mauve flowers of astilbe and the chartreuse flowers of lady's mantle are calmed by the soft, green fronds of ferns.

Can-Do Cannas

In warm climates, wet soil causes many plants to rot, but not cannas. These nearly indestructible flowering beauties can even tolerate standing water for short periods. A mass of cannas is an easy fix for a sunny wet spot. They are not hardy, so you need to dig and store the rhizomes indoors where it stays above freezing in winter.

missing from wet soil is abundant air, and plant roots need air to survive. Without it, there is the danger of fatal root rot. So, as you envision a garden for a wet, sunny site, do plan to cultivate the soil with a digging fork before planting. If you must, wait for the opportunity to cultivate the soil in a season when it is somewhat dry, because digging wet soil often results in compacted clumps that reduce soil drainage further. Late summer and fall is the dry season in many areas, so this may the best time to create this type of a garden. However, nurseries usually offer the best selection of plants in spring. If necessary, buy your plants in spring and keep them in containers until the soil becomes dry enough to cultivate.

A MEADOW ALTERNATIVE

In nature, streams and rivers often scour open flood plains clean in spring, and then a variety of perennial wildflowers sprout, and annual ones germinate from seeds, turning the area into a meadow. A number of beautiful care-free plants will prosper for many years in this type of situation. Some are asters, blanket flower, lanceleaf coreopsis, garden phlox, goldenrod, Joe Pye weed, meadow rue, purple coneflower, rudbeckia, and a few types of ornamental grasses, particularly switch grasses. As a bonus, you may be able to add late-season color to such a meadow garden by sowing annual cosmos from seed in late spring.

This type of meadow is typically mowed once a year, in early winter, after the plants have shed mature seeds, and the birds have feasted on them through the long winter. During the growing season, you can keep a wildflower meadow area from looking unkempt by neatly mowing its margins. You can also mow pathways that meander invitingly through the meadow. Another way to make a wildflower meadow fit into an urban neighborhood by looking less wild is to install a decorative fence that sets it apart from the rest of the landscape.

Look to the Future

River birches are small, decorative trees that provide the kind of high shade preferred by many moisture-loving perennials, and the tree roots will absorb excess soil moisture. A few years after planting birches, introduce perennials like astilbe, ferns, black cohosh, hosta, and turtlehead.

coreopsis, dogwood, false cypress, forget-me-not, garden phlox, goldenrod, hornbeam, iris, Joe Pye weed, lady's mantle, magic lily, meadow rue, obedient plant, perilla, periwinkle, primrose, purple coneflower, red-osier dogwood, sneezeweed, spider flower, spiderwort, sweetbay magnolia, turtlehead, viburnum, wax myrtle, winterberry holly, wisteria.

Plants for Pondside Planting

THE REFLECTION OF CLOUDS ROLLING BY, the lazy hovering of a dragonfly on gossamer wings, and the chorus of frogs create a unique ambience in a pondside garden. If you are lucky enough to have a pond, or have the ambition and budget to build one, you will marvel at the diversity of beautiful plants that thrive in its company, their colors and textures accentuated with remarkable clarity in close proximity to water.

When choosing plants for the area around a pond or other water feature, such as a creek, keep in mind that you are really creating two scenes. One is a garden scene as seen from land, which features containers and garden plants, and the other scene is a garden vignette in reverse, as seen reflected in the water. The latter changes during the day as the sun moves across the sky, resulting in a revolving scene as mirrored by the water.

ADDING CONTAINERS

As you landscape around your water feature, leave a few unplanted places that are big enough to accommodate large containers that can be filled with flowering annuals. Colorful annuals grown in containers near the water's edge could include any of these: coleus, dusty miller, fan flower, licorice plant, moss verbena, pansy,

petunia, Swan River daisy, sweet alyssum, and sweet potato vine. Experiment with color all you like, but feature plants that have fine leaf texture or a cascading habit. These traits make plants especially handsome when they are positioned near water. Perennials with interesting textures can also make fine container subjects for sunny ponds. For example, low containers planted with species of short, waving ornamental grasses or a flock of succulent hens and chicks offers riveting contrasts and reflections when placed near the water.

BACK AND FRONT

Water features are irresistibly attractive to people and also to small wildlife, so if you are building your own, it's wise to situate it in a place where the feature can be viewed from many directions. At the same time, a pond or stream will appear more natural, and will reflect more than one dramatic scene, if it has a back and a front. Think tall when choosing plants for the back, or far side of a water feature. Imagining these plantings as a backdrop for the water and shorter plantings. In a very sunny site, tall ornamental grasses and tall perennials like Joe Pye weed, are good choices for background plants, especially if you are also planting shrubs. During the first years,

Plan a pond-side planting for colorful reflections. Here, a red-leaved Japanese maple and green Chinese juniper mix with pink-flowered Japanese anemones and silvery lamb's ears. Creeping thyme and bugleweed are set off by pots of purple-flowered verbena.

OTHER BEDFELLOWS Artemisia, astilbe, begonia, blue-beard, candytuft, cardinal flower, coreopsis, daffodil, daylily, dianthus,

while the shrubs are growing, the ornamental grasses and perennials can help fill the vacant space.

Be careful when choosing trees to grow near a water feature. Leaves, twigs, or fruits that fall into a pond must eventually be removed by hand, especially if fish live in the pond. But if tree litter is limited to autumn only, you can temporarily cover a small pond with bird netting to capture debris before it fouls the water. Keep scale in mind when choosing pond-side trees. If you have a small pond, choose a tree with small stature, such as a flowering cherry like 'Okame', which does not set fruit, a Japanese maple, or star magnolia.

DRESSING THE EDGES

The lowest bank of a pond where water is likely to overflow after heavy rains, is a prime spot for growing plants that tolerate temporary flooding. Some good choices include groundcover bugleweed and flowering perenni-

als like bee balm. Many primroses and some iris species can grow in nearly boglike conditions, and their upright stature is beautiful when mirrored on the water's surface.

Along the high banks of streams or ponds, which remain dry when the lower banks overflow, consider creating a gravel beach. Tuck clumps of low-growing, gray-green foliaged dianthus, or ground-hugging, fragrant creeping thyme into planting pockets between the stone. Add a swaying clump of ornamental grass or succulent, flowering sedums. Indeed, because man-made ponds are most often edged in stone, you have an excellent opportunity to grow plants there that like nothing better than to nestle in between the sun-warmed stones. Prime plant possibilities for a pond-side rock garden include candytuft, hens and chickens, moss phlox, and sun rose. Mulching these plants with small pebbles creates a clean, natural look that is especially attractive in close company with water.

Moisture-loving plants turn a pond bank into a colorful garden. Here a Japanese maple provides partial shade for candelabra primroses, hostas, and lady's mantle. A purple phormium thrives in drier soil a short distance from the shore.

fan flower, flowering cherry, foxglove, garden phlox, goldenrod, holly, hosta, iris, lady's mantle, meadow rue, monkey flower, ornamental grasses, pansy, periwinkle, petunia, phormium, primrose, red-osier dogwood, spiderwort, star magnolia, summersweet, sun rose, swan river daisy, sweet alyssum, thyme, veronica, wisteria.

PLANTS FOR SHADE

All plants need light to grow. But you don't need full sun to nurture a dazzling array of care-free plants. In nature, many woodland wildflowers, bulbs, small trees, shrubs, and other plant treasures have adapted to grow where trees block out some sun. Many plants commonly grown in full sun can also adapt to partial shade, or may need it to survive hot climates.

But all shade is not created equal. Shade can be partial or very dense. In nature, partial shade occurs along the edges of forests and in open woods. Densely shaded places with little or no direct sun are found in deep woods. In your backyard, the equivalent of partial shade would be the dappled shade beneath a shade tree, or you may have dense shade, where the sun is blocked for several hours a day by a wall or fence. Plants that thrive in these types of shade need only about 4 hours of sun a day. They get the required quota as the sun moves in its daily cycle, causing structures in your yard to cast alternating patterns of sunlight and shadow over your plants.

The amount of shade your plants receive is also influenced by seasonal sun and growth cycles. When grown beneath deciduous trees, some plants take advantage of full sun in late winter and early spring for a quick burst of growth early in the season, before trees leaf out. But when light levels in that same site during the summer are low, bulbs and plants like bleeding heart, called spring ephemerals, go dormant until the following spring. Shrubs and small trees that grow well in partial shade, such as azalea, hydrangea, and dogwood, are perfectly attuned to this seasonal rhythm of changing light, and also flower early in the year.

Whether the shade in your garden comes from trees or buildings, and no matter what climate or soil conditions you face, with the good advice you'll find in this chapter, you'll be amazed at how many care-free plants are truly made for the shade.

Plants for Filtered Light

ONE OF THE CHALLENGES OF TURNING a shady spot into a lush, colorful garden is to compose a mixture of plants that will grow together happily without root competition. After all, where sun is scarce, not only must plants vie for light, but there's usually competition for moisture and nutrients below ground.

The trick to having a care-free shade garden lies in matching plants to the site. Many plants, such as leafy hostas and colorful foxgloves and astilbes, thrive in filtered or partial shade. Their shallow or fleshy roots are adapted to share space with the roots of shade-loving neighbors. Here you'll find design and growing tips for getting a number of plants to thrive in filtered light.

VERTICAL LAYERING

The most successful approach to designing a care-free garden in filtered or partial shade is to arrange the plants so that their foliage grows in layers, according to their heights. This kind of layering exists along the edge of a natural woodland, where tall trees give way to smaller ones like dogwoods, then to shrubs like viburnums and azaleas, and finally to perennials, annuals, and groundcovers. Besides being a highly hospitable situation for plants that are adapted to share light and root space, this design allows small, showy plants to be showcased against the backdrop of taller ones. This kind of layering also creates an ideal habitat for birds, drawing a greater number of species to your garden, because in nature, each species occupies a specific layer, which limits competition for food and nesting places.

FILTERED AND PARTIAL SHADE

Filtered and partial shade are different ways of blocking sunlight, but the end result is that plants in each situation receive about the same amount of light. Filtered shade can be found beneath any open canopy that provides dappled sunlight throughout the day. The source of filtered shade might be the overhead boughs of a loose limbed or small-leaved tree, such as dogwood, silverbell, or stewartia, or perhaps very tall, widely spaced evergreen pines. Filtered shade is also found beneath a pergola, an arbor, or beside a picket fence or lattice panel. Plants grown in filtered shade often show a full, mounded shape and rarely stretch toward the sun, because they receive a steady, yet intermittent, light supply all day long.

The same plants that grow in filtered shade also often thrive in partial shade, a situation in which buildings, walls or thick tree canopies; or closely spaced trees and shrubs block light for all but 3 to 4 hours daily. The best kind of partial-shade situation for gardening is usually found on the east side of a house or along a woodland edge, where plants receive sunlight in the cooler hours of the morning and are shaded and protected from the hot afternoon sun. Morning sun dries dew from plant leaves promptly, which reduces fungal diseases, and it gives plants a short but intense period of exposure to

Making the most of a fence, care-free chocolate vine climbs its pickets. In the partial shade of the vine grow tried-and-true pink-flowered peony, airy lavender-flowered meadow rue, yellow-green lady's mantle, and frosty silver-leaved dead nettle. An evergreen hardy camellia, at right, will produce pink flowers in winter.

OTHER BEDFELLOWS Astilbe, azalea, bergenia, bleeding heart, Boston ivy, bugleweed, caladium, calla lily, camellia, clethra,

To put pizzazz in your dappled-shade garden, combine care-free perennials like columbine with the spires of foxgloves and shrubby, flowering rhododendrons. These plants make wonderful bedfellows for filtered light.

Eastern Exposures

Morning sun helps dry dew from leaves, which limits problems with fungal diseases. Especially in humid climates, look for sites with an eastern exposure when planting mildew-prone plants like bee balm and garden phlox. The combination of morning sun and afternoon shade suits them perfectly.

Root's-eye View

To prevent competition, underplant a deep-rooted, sun-loving tree, such as oak, with a shallow-rooted, shade-tolerant smaller tree, such as dogwood. The open tree limbs will admit sufficient light to shallow-rooted, shady shrubs, such as azalea, and ground-hugging perennials like hostas and epimediums.

sunlight, followed by a long recovery period in the afternoon. This is a situation that can help you grow a wider selection of plants than you normally could if you live where summers are hot, because many plants that grow in full sun in cooler climates can wilt and eventually die if exposed to full sun in hot areas.

TURNING A CONCEPT AROUND

Don't give up on sites that are shaded in the morning and sunny in the afternoon. This is often an ideal niche for plants that are usually grown in full sun, yet can adapt to partial shade. Some of these include begonia, pansy, phormium, and summer-flowering bulbs, such as lily and gladioli, along with perennials like ornamental grasses, yucca, and sedum. In hot-summer climates you may have great success if you try growing perennials that prefer full sun in cooler summer conditions, such as catmint and veronica, by planting them in a spot where they receive full sun only in the afternoon.

THE UNDERGROUND STORY

Underneath it all, thirsty tree roots are always competing with garden plants for water and nutrients. Trees with many surface roots, such as birches, beeches, maples, and apples, are the worst offenders. If you're planting beneath a shallow-rooted tree, consider planting dry-soil-adapted groundcovers like vinca or epimedium. Or build a shallow berm or raised bed. Keep the bed at least 1.8 m (6 ft) from the trunk of the tree to prevent damage to the trunk and shallow roots. Line the floor of the bed with thick, perforated plastic to keep tree roots from invading your bed. To avoid root competition altogether, create shade gardens under tree species with deeper roots, such as oak, hickory, or other nut trees.

cohosh, columbine, cyclamen, daylily, dogwood, English ivy, epimedium, euonymus, ferns, foamflower, foxglove, fuchsia, garden phlox, goatsbeard, hosta, hydrangea, impatiens, Japanese anemone, Japanese maple, lungwort, mahonia, mountain laurel, pachysandra, phormium, redbud, red buckeye, rhododendron, spiderwort, stewartia, trillium, yellowwood.

Plants for Dense Dry Shade

In most densely shaded sites, either large trees or buildings block the sun. And any barrier than can block sun can also stand in the way of rainfall, which explains why dense shade and dry soil go hand in hand. Your task is to find drought-tolerant plants that require scant light and moisture. It's a design bonus if they also brighten dim garden spots with colorful blossoms or leaves. If you also use a couple of light-reflecting tricks to supplement sunlight, all that's left for you to do is to irrigate as needed.

BRINGING LIGHT INTO DARKNESS

The best plants for making a dark spot appear brighter are those with pale, light-reflecting colors. White flowers and variegated or lime-green foliage will not only enliven dense shade, they will also make the site seem spacious. Choose plants like variegated Solomon's seal, hostas with white-edged leaves, and silvery-leaved dead nettle for the light-reflecting quality of their leaves. Shiny evergreen leaves like those of epimedium also brighten dark shadows by reflecting light that filters through the trees. Colored flowers for lightening dense shade include those of pastel-flowering hellebores and spring bulbs.

If your shady garden bed is next to a wall or fence, painting the backdrop white or a light color will reflect light onto the plants. Another light-reflecting feat is achieved by disguising mirrors behind openwork gates or window frames, and then hanging them on a wall or nearby fence. The reflection of light from the mirrors brightens the garden bed and makes the space seem larger. A bird bath, basin, or small pond will also reflect the sky like a mirror, brightening the shade.

PLANTING BETWEEN TREE ROOTS

Under the soil's surface, around the trunk of a tree, the roots are thick and woody, almost like underground branches. The good news is that you can plant shade-loving, drought-tolerant bulbs, groundcovers, and perennials in small pockets of enriched soil between these mature roots with little risk of damage to the tree. Here's how it's done. Using a sturdy trowel, dig out a pocket of soil at least twice as big as the root ball of the new plant. If possible, be even more generous. Add a few handfuls of compost and mix it thoroughly with the existing soil. Remove the plant from its container and loosen the soil around the root ball. Place the loosened soil ball of the plant in the hole, set the growing point, or crown, level with the surrounding. Fill the hole around the plant with soil, firm the soil around the plant's roots, and water well. Cover the planted area with a 5 cm (2 in) thick layer of compost as a mulch to conserve moisture.

MAINTAINING MOISTURE

It's a jungle down below. The roots of many trees are most numerous close to the surface where they compete with the roots of smaller garden plants for the limited water that manages to trickle through the canopy to the ground below. And, although many plants can tolerate temporary drought after they have developed mature roots, young and tender plants almost always need supplemental water to get them off to a strong start while they are growing an adequate root system. The most efficient way to provide supplemental moisture to a dry-shade garden is to outfit it with a soaker hose. Simply arrange the hose on the ground so that it snakes

Woodland native azalea teams up with crocus, squill, snowdrops, frosty looking dead nettle and burgundy bugleweed to make the most of the dry soil and shade under a tree.

OTHER BEDFELLOWS
American holly, asarum, barberry, bugleweed, coleus, columbine, crocus, cyclamen, daffodils,

around your plants, and then cover it with loose mulch to hide it from view. Turn the hose on for several hours or overnight about once a week during dry weather, or more often if temperatures are very hot. The moisture will seep deeply into the soil with no runoff, fostering the development of deep, water-seeking roots. With the development of deep roots, your young plants won't wilt during brief dry periods.

About 2.5 cm (1 in) of water per week is the standard recommendation for supplemental watering. Measure the water by setting a shallow tin can or other container on the ground where the irrigation water will drip into it. When the container collects water to the recommended depth, you can stop watering. Note the time it takes to provide the right amount of water, and in the future, water for the same time period with each watering, and you won't have to measure again.

SEASONAL SOAKING

When dry shade is due to the close company of trees, dry soil typically prevails from spring to fall, when tree roots take up the most soil moisture and the branches overhead shed rain like a giant umbrella. Not surprisingly, many plants that are native to woodland areas, including asarum, columbine, wood aster, and dainty blue-flowered phlox, are perfectly attuned to the seasonal changes in sunlight and soil moisture typical of their ancestral forest habitat. These and other adapted plants are top choices for a care-free garden in dry shade.

Nature can be unpredictable, and even these plants can be set back when drought comes at unexpected times, particularly early spring. During unusually dry springs, be prepared to provide water to make up for rain that fails to fall. For these plants, which are often willing to accept dry soil in summer, moisture in late winter and spring is essential for a happy and healthy life.

ELEMENTS OF DESIGN

Keep in mind that every centimeter does not have to be occupied by plants. In fact, the visual contrast between foliage and soil-covering surfaces of stone, wood, or pebble mulch, as well as seating areas and garden art always creates visual interest and excitement in the garden. Dry, shady garden spots are no exception. Because such areas

are usually sheltered from the elements, they are excellent spots for placing a bench, an artful stone, a bird feeder, or statuary. Indeed, adding something as simple as a pair of stools made of log rounds can instantly turn a dark, dry place into an inviting outdoor room.

If your problem spot is a narrow side yard, you can make it feel more accessible and spacious by emphasizing low-growing plants, such as asarum, epimedium, or hostas, planted along the edges of a walkway. Another strategy that makes narrow corridors more appealing is to add several containers planted with shade-tolerant annuals like coleus and impatiens, or hardy flowering perennials like astilbe and hydrangea.

Drought-tolerant shade plants with variegated and golden leaves, or pale flowers, make dim nooks seem bright and spacious. Hostas, ornamental grass, and white-flowered hydrangea work their magic here.

English ivy, epimedium, annual geranium, golden hakone grass, grape hyacinth, hellebore, hepatica, hollyhock, hosta, hydrangea, lantana, licorice plant, mountain laurel, mugo pine, ornamental grasses, snowdrop, Solomon's seal, squill, squirrelcorn, stonecrop, tulip, sweet woodruff, wood aster, woodland phlox.

Plants for Moist Shade

A WOODLAND CARPETED WITH WILDFLOWERS in spring is an unforgettable sight. Rich, moist soil coupled with dappled shade can foster not only native woodland treasures but also shade-loving plants from around the world. Woodlands and forests in Europe, Japan, and China have given us some of the most beautiful plants we can grow in our shady, moist gardens.

A cluster of small trees can offer a protective canopy for your treasures, and even a single tree can allow you to grow a few shade-loving plants. Or tuck woodland beauties like Solomon's seal, forget-me-not, and bleeding heart into soil along the east side of your house, where morning sun is plentiful but there is protection from scorching afternoon sun. Better still, install an arbor or pergola and plant your shade plants beneath it, where they will be sheltered from the midday sun.

PLANNING FOR SEASONAL CHANGE

Many shade- and-moisture-loving plants flower early in spring when sun and moisture are plentiful. This is because in nature, rain is typically abundant in late winter and spring, but conditions dry radically as summer begins. And dwindling rainfall isn't the only change. Trees clothed with leaves block out light while simultaneously absorbing a great deal of moisture from the soil. The result is that places that are moist and partially shaded in early spring become shadier and drier as the season progresses.

It is easy to create a woodland garden that is lush with greenery and flowers in spring. However, the same places where blue woodland phlox, trilliums, and miniature daffodils flower in spring may look barren by midsummer without heat-tolerant recruits.

You can count on spreading foliage perennials like hostas and ferns to emerge in late spring in time to hide the yellowing foliage of spring bulbs as they begin to go dormant, and you can be sure that the hostas and ferns will maintain their good looks throughout the rest of the growing season. Heucheras are also valuable for this purpose, along with short, shade-loving grasses, such as golden hakone grass.

Do plan to provide supplemental water to your shade garden should a drought cut off its natural water supply. Although hostas, hellebores, and other shade-loving perennial plants are surprisingly drought tolerant, weather is always unpredictable, and is sometimes inhospitable. Droughts can last for several weeks, and can even come in the spring, when rain is usually adequate. Because this particular gardening niche depends on ample water in spring, strategic watering with sprinklers or soaker hoses during spring droughts can ensure its health and resilience through the rest of the season.

BOLD BACKGROUNDS

In a shade garden that is viewed from one vantage point, the entire scene will appear more lush and have greater visual depth if you employ trees and shrubs as background plants. For example, dogwoods underplanted with azaleas make a background that is packed with dazzling flower color in spring. Or you can mix in shrubs that produce colorful berries in autumn, such as viburnum or winterberry holly. Small spiraea, dwarf summersweet, or hydrangea can add color to a shady shrub border in midsummer, and the glossy evergreen leaves and blue berries of mahonia are invaluable for providing much-needed interest in winter. If your shady spot already has a fence or wall, soften its appearance by training a long-lived vine to grow upward until it spills across the top of the structure.

Trees cast welcome shade on a care-free collection of rhododendrons, pink- and white-flowered bleeding hearts, and leafy Solomon's seal, lungworts, hostas, ferns, and sweet woodruff.

OTHER BEDFELLOWS Asarum, astilbe, azalea, begonia, bergenia, bleeding heart, blue star, bugleweed, caladium, camellia,

Hostas, ferns, and azaleas make wonderful bedfellows for moist garden sites with filtered light.

choices to provide a long season of color. Shade-loving perennials that bloom in spring and have lasting foliage interest, such as columbine and lungwort, can be combined with species that flower later on the scene, for example, Japanese anemone and monkshood.

If you are confused by the design concept of using plant textures, simply think of texture as leaf or flower size. Contrast plants that have large leaves or flowers against those that have petite ones. For example, if you use oak-leaf hydrangea as a background plant, its large, broad leaves can be counted on to appear even larger in company with the feathery flower spikes and cut leaves of astilbe, or the puffy sprays of meadow rue flowers. If the background plant has small leaves, as found in most azaleas, choose foreground plants with bold foliage, such as that of bergenias, hostas, or turtleheads.

ADD COLOR WITH CONTAINERS

Most shade-and-moisture-loving perennial and woody plants look their best when allowed to develop into undisturbed colonies. Disturbing their roots can slow the growth progress and compromise their ability to tolerate drought. Set aside special places where you want to grow shade-tolerant annuals, such as impatiens or tender summer bulbs like caladiums, where you can plant them without digging into the roots of permanent plantings. Better yet, grow these and other colorful plants in containers, and either sink the pots into the garden or set them on the ground among your hostas and ferns.

Using containers broadens your plant palette, because you can use plants that prefer more light when they are young, such as browallia, wishbone flower, or coleus. Start them in a sunny spot, and then shift the pots to the shade garden when the plants approach their peak. If moved to a shady location when they begin to flower, many annuals actually bloom longer than they would if left in a brighter spot. In fact, even annuals that normally need at least a half day of sun, such as dusty miller, flowering tobacco, petunia, and salvia, seem relieved to be moved into shade in midsummer. Should they sulk or stop flowering, simply move them temporarily back to better light. Flowers in pastel shades, like pink and blue, or even white flowers show best in partial shade, though occasional bursts of red can be a welcome surprise.

Climbing hydrangea is ideal for growing on a heavy stone or brick wall, or you might employ the less-weighty Dutchman's pipe on a wooden fence. You can also emphasize the vertical presence of a wall by growing upright plants in strategic places. This is a task for which the tall flower spires of foxgloves are supremely suited.

With a background in place, you are set to embrace the varying leaf textures of foreground perennials, which range from the light and airy divided leaves and feathery flowers of astilbe and goatsbeard, to large-leaved black cohosh and turtlehead. You can easily fine tune your

campanula, cohosh, coleus, columbine, dead nettle, dogwood, Dutchman's pipe, fern, forget-me-not, foxglove, garden

phlox, goatsbeard, golden hakone grass, heuchera, Japanese anemone, lungwort, mahonia, meadow rue, mountain laurel,

primrose, red buckeye, red-osier dogwood, silverbell, snowbell, summersweet, turtlehead, viburnum, winterberry holly.

Plants for Wet Soil

CONTINUOUSLY MOIST SOIL OPENS A WHOLE WORLD of possibilities for shade gardeners who are naturally drawn to mossy glens. In nature, you'll find wet, shaded sites along the banks of a tree-lined pool or stream, or in a low spot where rainwater collects after running down slopes. You may find soggy soil near a seasonal stream at the base of a steep slope, or where two gentle slopes converge. The soil is usually fertile in such spots because there is a natural accumulation of organic matter and all the water a plant could need. When shade is part of the bargain, there are many ways to turn a wet spot into a rich tapestry of color and texture, by adding bold, beautiful shade plants. Your challenge is to discover care-free plants, such as turtlehead, yellow flag iris, ferns, and woodland phlox, and to combine them with simple structures that will make the area equally hospitable to humans.

EASING ACCESS

Before you begin making a garden in a wet spot, plan a pathway that is designed to assure safe footing. A series of steppingstones may be sufficient to get you from one place to another, or you might set steppingstones into a wider, more stable path lined with gravel. Another option is to build a elevated boardwalk that, surrounded by the foliage of your garden plants, appears to float mysteriously across the wetland. Choose a building material that works harmoniously with other materials present in your landscape. For example, you might build a brick walkway to echo the walls of a brick home. Or choose stone if there is a stone patio or wall nearby, or if natural stone

outcroppings are part of the scene. Then, after the hardscaping is in place, experiment cautiously when choosing plants, using promising ones on a small scale at first.

DESIGNING DRIFTS

When you find a plant species that thrives in your wet, shady spot, add several of them. Many plants adapted to moist shade are very willing, on their own, to spread into lush colonies. Give them free reign to grow into drifts. Small drifts of slow-to-spread epimedium, lungwort, or turtlehead mimic the way they grow in nature. Remember that it's easier to care for a mass planting of one or two species than to tend to the whims of an assortment.

Between clumps of plants, allow open space to facilitate air circulation. Pathways that thread through a moist shade garden act as channels for health-giving light and air, and they even become drainage ditches during heavy rains. This decreases the likelihood of fungal diseases, which thrive in damp, stagnant air and standing water. You also may need to thin stems from time to time to open the center of shrubby plants to light and fresh air.

KEEPING SOIL SOFT

Not only does wet soil drain slowly initially, but it is easily compacted by footsteps or even the pressure of pounding rain. To address both of these problems, consider building raised beds or natural-looking berms in a wet-shade garden. Plants appreciate the extra root space and improved drainage created when a bed is a few centimeters above surrounding moisture-laden soil. You can

In summer, a low damp place in shade is brightened by the pink flower plumes of astilbes, the shaggy magenta flowers of bee balm, and potted impatiens. Shrubby clethra and ground-hugging primroses will steal the scene in spring, when it's their turn to burst into flower.

OTHER BEDFELLOWS — Asarum, astilbe, azalea, bee balm, begonia, bergenia, caladium, canna, cohosh, coleus, cowslip,

construct raised beds from various materials, including boards, landscaping timbers, brick, stone, or concrete blocks. In a wet site, it's a good idea to excavate a few centimeters of soil first, and then line the base of the bed with an 8 cm (3 in) deep layer of gravel. The gravel helps drain away excess water and forms an oxygen-rich zone for roots. After installing the frame, fill the bed with native soil mixed with compost and sand to further improve its texture and drainage. For a more natural appearance, build shallow berms using the same techniques described above.

WORKING WET SOIL

Whether you are simply making minor contour changes in your wet site, such as making a path, or taking on a larger project, such as constructing raised beds, it's impor-
tant to work when the soil is relatively dry. Digging in very wet soil is unpleasant, and the soil tends to compact into hard clumps. A care-free reality is that naturally fertile soil that stays constantly moist may not require deep digging or the addition of soil amendments to make it hospitable to plants. If this is the case, simply place plants into planting holes rather than cultivating a large bed.

Whenever you are working in a damp or wet area, keep a pair of short boards handy to use as standing platforms while you plant, weed, or trim your garden plants. The boards will keep mud off your shoes and distribute your weight, reducing soil compaction. Having two boards, so that you can stand on one while moving the other to your next position, makes it easy to move between closely spaced plants without stepping on soil.

REGIONAL ADVICE
Plastic Lumber

Building raised beds of wood is common, but in many areas even treated wood eventually becomes termite bait. Using a new material called plastic lumber, which is used for decking, solves this problem. Because it's made from a blend of recycled plastic and sawdust, it's also moisture resistant.

Root's-eye View

Many plants that thrive in moist conditions have shallow roots. Surface roots reduce the risk of root rot, because they grow where air is available and soil is likely to dry periodically. But having all the roots near the soil's surface makes them vulnerable to drought damage. Protect roots by covering the soil around shady plants with a moisture-retaining organic mulch, such as compost or leaf mold.

A swath of chartreuse-flowered lady's mantle plants, and yellow iris thrive in a low, wet garden area. The planting mimics the way that wetland plants reproduce to form colonies, or drifts, in nature.

dogwood, Dutchman's pipe, Dwarf cattail, English ivy, epimedium, fern, foamflower, forget-me-not, goats beard, golden hakone grass, hosta, Japanese maple, Joe Pye weed, lady's mantle, lungwort, meadow rue, pachysandra, red twig dogwood, rhododendron, Siberian iris, sweet potato vine, turtlehead, vinca, wishbone flower, woodland phlox, yellow flag iris.

CHAPTER THREE

PLANTS FOR WINDY SITES

Enjoying breathtaking views and a sense of seclusion are just a few of the highlights of living and gardening on a hillside. But the same breezes that cool you on hot days can torment plants when the wind gains strength and whips everything, shredding leaves, limbs, and toppling pots. City gardeners with rooftop or terrace gardens face a similar challenge, as do seaside and lakeside gardeners, and even those with gardens that overlook an empty field. If the wind where you live sometimes nearly blows you off your feet, imagine what it can do to your plants.

The care-free way to cope with a windy site is to grow plants that can stand up to or bend with the wind. When selecting wind-worthy plants, look for those with small leaves on flexible stems like forsythia, roses, and catmint, which all bend in the wind. Ornamental grasses, designed by nature to endure the full force of a prairie storm, are also mainstays in windswept sites. Avoid plants with broad, easily tattered leaves or brittle, breakable branches. When it comes to wind resistance, stature is also important. Ground-hugging plants like dianthus, sedum, petunia, and groundcovers like epimedium and sweet woodruff form a carpet that allows the wind to roll right over them without damage. When battling garden winds, you can also make your garden more care-free by filtering the wind with windbreaks of trees and shrubs. You can also diffuse its force with strategically placed picket fences or lattice panels, which break the force of the wind while allowing air circulation, a deterrent to fungal diseases.

The following pages reveal special techniques for gardening in wind, including tips for thwarting its attendant problems, such as wind laden with salt spray, whether from the ocean or winter road salt. Keep your eyes open for natural sources of inspiration, then fill in the blanks with our palette of care-free, wind-tolerant plants.

Plants for Windy Sites

GENTLE BREEZES ARE ALWAYS WELCOME in the garden, but persistent, strong winds are another thing altogether. There's no doubt that strong winds stress plants, often snapping branches, tattering leaves, and sometimes stunting their growth. Beyond that, strong wind can keep small wildlife like birds and beneficial insects from visiting your garden, and the wind also has an exhausting effect on gardeners. If you crave relief from the wind, your key to a care-free garden is having a well-planned windbreak.

A windbreak is usually an arrangement of plants that breaks the force of the wind. Wind can come in different guises. Frigid blasts from the North accompanied by wind-driven snow can desiccate plant leaves, ruin the appearance of plants, and sometimes even kill plants. But windbreaks composed of several layers, or rows, of plants, which are called shelterbelts, can reduce wind so effectively that homes protected by them may require up to one-third less supplemental heat in winter. In a good shelterbelt, plants are planted in rows according to their heights, with short plants facing the full brunt of the wind, backed up by a row of intermediate-sized plants, which are in turn backed by tall evergreen trees, which are the closest to the house or garden. When strong winds encounter such a shelterbelt, they are lifted up and over the windbreak, so that the house and landscape rest in a protected pocket. And, although shelterbelts were designed to deflect freezing winter wind, they can also be sited where they will deflect salty ocean breezes or blasts from seasonal windstorms.

A proper shelterbelt requires a substantial amount of ground space. But even a scaled-down version that allows some wind to filter through can improve growing conditions in a windswept yard, and it will benefit the house as well. For example, a row of ornamental grasses planted in front of a row of mixed shrubs, backed by an intermittent planting of tall evergreen and deciduous trees is diverse and natural looking, and it can reduce the force of wind by more than half. Windbreaks that include dense evergreens will also become secure shelters for birds in cold weather.

COOL WINDBREAKS FOR HOT PLACES

Hot summer winds leave gardens parched, and they can toast plant leaves to a crisp, but planting a dense windbreak that stops wind altogether can trap heat and turn the landscape into an oven. Where summers are hot, design a windbreak that includes deciduous trees or shrubs to provide summer shade and to break the force of the wind as it passes through their limbs. Leaving gaps between the shrubs will allow wind to pass through the branches at a reasonable speed, which will deter fungal diseases that thrive on stagnant air. And, the dappled shade cast by the shrubbery can protect nearby garden plants that need shelter from the summer sun.

GO ANYWHERE GRASSES

Ornamental grasses can help turn any windblown site into a handsome care-free garden. These hardy, drought-tolerant, and adaptable plants form tight clumps that not

A care-free garden can also be a windbreak. White pines and junipers offer protection for fountain grass, rose-colored sedum 'Autumn Joy', red-flowered sun rose, and red-tinged hens and chickens.

OTHER BEDFELLOWS   Ageratum, akebia, anise hyssop, artemisia, aster, barberry, blanket flower, blue star, boxwood, bugle-

A windproof bed can be designed as a windbreak, as here, where the force of the wind is broken by a row of conifers. The flexible stems of pennisetum grass and petunias bend in the wind, adding graceful motion to the garden.

only resist wind but also actually transform it into a visual delight as the wind coaxes from them graceful motion and whispering sound. Popular species of ornamental grass, such as maiden grasses and fountain grasses, are easy to grow, and happily, spring-flowering bulbs and wind-resistant annuals and perennials like begonias, sedums, and hens and chicks will thrive at their feet.

LESSONS OF THE WIND

Become attuned to the rhythms of the wind. Wind is often much quieter during the night than it is during the daylight hours, which has important implications for you and for your plants. It's usually more comfortable to work in your garden in the still hours of the early morning or evening. And, if you like to cut flowers for indoor arrangements, the freshest blossoms are available first thing in the morning, after they have had a full night of recovery from the previous day's drying effects.

Take a cue from the flexible stems and thin-bladed leaves of grasses when judging which types of plants will be less than care-free in windy sites, namely those with stiff stems and broad, flat leaves such as tithonia and canna. Plants with large leaves should also be avoided in a windy garden, because they work like wind-catching sails, often pulling at the plants until they end up tattered and prostrate on the ground. If you really want to grow them, plant these vulnerable plants in a protected place next to a wall, fence, or other windbreak.

You may also find that staking tall plants is more trouble than it is worth. Instead of bracing stiff-stemmed spire plants, such as gladiolus and hollyhocks, choose plants with a low, spreading growth habit, for example, creeping veronicas often work better than upright forms. Also look for flexible plants with small leaves like ground-hugging portulaca, which maintains its handsome good looks even when hot winds blow.

weed, butterfly weed, catmint, columbine, coreopsis, cotoneaster, crocus, daffodil, daylily, dianthus, false cypress, forsythia, geranium, goldenrod, Japanese maple, lacebark pine, lamb's ear, lavender, mahonia, ornamental grasses, poppy, portu-laca, purple coneflower, redbud, rose campion, rose, rudbeckia, serviceberry, smokebush, wax myrtle, yarrow, yucca.

In areas with salt breezes, juniper and wax myrtle make good foundation shrubs. Flower beds can hold salt-tolerant perennials including spiky yuccas, and yellow-and-red flowering lantanas, blanket flowers, and daylilies.

Plants for Salt Spray

WHETHER SILHOUETTING A ROCKY COASTLINE or a sandy beach, seaside gardens enjoy a gorgeous setting and views. But they appear deceptively calm and peaceful in contrast to the waves and sounds of the ocean and the starkness of the beach environment. In reality, seaside gardens take the brunt of the elements that are part and parcel to their ocean setting. Careful thought must go into their creation. Wind is often a constant presence, and placid weather can quickly turn into a raging gale as storms move over the water, with nothing to buffet their force. Tough, care-free plants are mandatory. If they can't resist wind, they'll be turned into confetti. If they won't tolerate salt spray, they'll be desiccated and possibly killed.

Actually the brunt of salt-laden breezes might not be felt over the entire property. On the leeward side of your house, out of the reach of wind and salt, you can grow a wider range of plants, including flowers in containers that will be sheltered from hostile elements. This would also be the best place to locate a special raised bed or berm composed of salt-free soil to serve as a home for favorite plants. Study your garden to learn its subtleties. The easiest way to learn where salt spray is most intense is to check your windows. If the panes are constantly clouded with salt deposits, it's an excellent clue to the severity of the problem. Cleaner panes mean that plants will be subjected to less wind and salt.

CUTTING DOWN ON SALT

In addition to salt spray, salt buildup in the soil is a seaside gardener's biggest problem. Surprisingly, inland gardeners in cold climates can face the same problem when they try gardening near streets or sidewalks that are salted to melt snow and add traction in winter. If you live right at the edge of the dunes or on a street where traffic splashes salted snow spray into your yard, your plants will have to contend with salty soil and salty air. Many plants are sensitive to salt, which can dry out roots, damage leaves, and even kill the plant. The first signs of salt damage are scorched, brown, crispy leaf margins. Another symptom of salt stress is wilting even though the soil is moist. Fortunately, there are many plants that are somewhat salt tolerant. And rain and irrigation water moves so rapidly through the porous, sandy soil found in most seaside gardens that salts are quickly leached away, unlike regions that are more arid or that have poorly drained soil, where salts can accumulate in the soil. You can do your part to help the situation. Even without the leaching action of rain, simply enriching the soil with organic matter will help buffer the effects of salt on plant roots.

Airborne salt is a subtle enemy of plants. Even gentle sea breezes carry salt that settles on garden foliage. Plants that are protected with waxy, thick, or succulent leaves, which are impervious to salt, are well adapted to the rigors of life by the sea or in an area splashed with road salt. Rugosa roses have proven themselves over generations of seaside gardening. Their thick, leathery leaves are not only resistant to the damaging effects of salt spray, but are also just as resistant to insect pests and diseases that plague other roses. Sedums and the seaside or roadside seem to go together like sand and waves. These durable, adaptable plants tolerate heat, drought, salt spray and

OTHER BEDFELLOWS   Akebia, anise hyssop, artemisia, aster, blue star, bluebeard, butterfly weed, catmint, coreopsis, cosmos,

In a garden that weathers the vagaries of salty ocean air, as the season ends the rusty tones of sedum 'Autumn Joy' and aster are brightened by the pink-flowers of rugosa rose and annual geranium.

REGIONAL ADVICE
Protecting Evergreens

In cold climates, protect evergreens from harsh winter winds and salt spray by enclosing them in burlap in early winter. Attach burlap to wood stakes driven into the ground to form a fabric box around shrubs, without touching them. Remove the burlap in early spring.

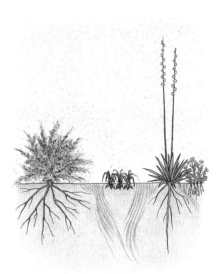

Root's-eye View

To help water flow through the soil quickly, carrying away excess salt in the process, space plants widely. Generous spacing also aids in the rinsing of foliage, which happens naturally every time it rains. Allow elbowroom between clump-forming plants like daylilies, and let low, sprawling plants like hardy geraniums fill the unplanted areas.

every conceivable abuse. Many plants with felted leaves, such as artemisia and lavender are also resistant to salt spray. The leaf hairs intercept the salt before it reaches the leaf surface, keeping it from burning the leaves.

NATIVE RESTORATION

Because beach erosion is such a prevalent problem, many seaside communities provide homeowners with lists of specially adapted plants recommended for local planting. These lists usually include some native plants that are best procured at local nurseries, but they are well worth seeking out. Beaches are such unusual planting niches that selected natives are often required to anchor a successful beachside garden, which can then be embellished with more tender or exotic beauties.

REDUCING ROADWAY SALT INJURY

You don't have to live by the sea for your plants to experience salt damage. Where winter temperatures don't generally fall below -29°C (-20°F), road clearing can involve heavy loads of salt, which can be carried to plants by wind or splashed on them by fast-moving cars. Near roads or sidewalks that are salted frequently in winter, plant only salt-tolerant species, such as juniper, lilac, mugo pine, or rugosa rose. In high-traffic areas, plant medium-sized perennials from the list below, which won't obscure visibility. In spring, as soon as the snow melts, thoroughly rinse salt off plants with a spray of water from a hose. Then flood the soil around the plants' root zones to leach out accumulated salt. From spring to fall you can brighten these beds with colorful annuals.

crocus, daffodil, dianthus, dusty miller, euphorbia, geranium, goldenrod, gomphrena, lamb's-ears, lavender, lilac, morning glory, mugo pine, ornamental grasses, petunia, pines, plectranthus, poppy, portulaca, purple coneflower, rose campion, rugosa rose, rudbeckia, smokebush, sneezeweed, statice, sweet alyssum, thrift, trumpet vine, verbena, yarrow.

CHAPTER FOUR

PLANTS FOR HILLSIDES AND INCLINES

Slopes are tough places to garden. Rain runs off a slope quickly, so the soil is often dry, and erosion from rain and wind can cause mudslides. So, how do you cope with a slope? Solutions depend on the steepness of the slope. Extremely steep slopes may be best topdressed in stone, but a rocky hillside need not be bare. Plants that are adapted to this kind of terrain can be tucked between stones, transforming a rocky outcrop into a beautiful garden.

Luckily, not all slopes are dangerously steep. If you can find places where you can stand while you plant or weed, fast-growing groundcover plants are a good choice. Not only do groundcovers hold the soil firm, but their leaves and stems break the impact of heavy rain, allowing water to soak into the soil, rather than eroding it. A moderate slope devoted to one species of groundcover is easiest to maintain. But adventuresome gardeners can combine a tapestry of groundcovers with varying textures. Underplant the groundcovers with tough, spring-flowering bulbs for an additional splurge of color.

Mingle ornamental grasses and deep-rooted perennials or wildflowers on a gentle slope to create a rustic meadow. A decorative fence that separates the meadow from manicured yard areas will tie it into a suburban setting.

In this chapter, we'll delve further into these solutions, but there are a few practical issues to address before launching into a project on a slope. First, be sure to follow the essential rule for working on a slope: begin at the bottom of the slope and work your way upward to avoid creating an avalanche as you work. After setting out, new plants will need to be mulched to hold the soil in place and prevent weeds from sprouting until the plants can spread to cover the bare soil. Straw-textured mulches knit themselves together and stay in place over bare soil better than loose mulches like bark nuggets. And finally, to make a hillside garden even more care-free, install soaker hoses beneath the mulch to provide young plants with water for their first season.

Plants for Rocky Hillsides

IF YOU CAN'T BEAT IT, ENHANCE IT. A rock garden is a great way to handle a sloping front yard, or to artfully plant any hillside. Rock gardens showcase the natural beauty of stone as well as plants. A well-constructed rock garden will look as if it has been there forever, especially once the rocks are clothed in care-free plants. You can choose any style for your rock garden, from an informal tumble of stones to a simple garden built around existing ones. If you need to stabilize the slope, add small, stacked-stone retaining walls backfilled with good soil. They'll serve the additional purpose of creating more planting pockets for plants, particularly suited to those that require perfect drainage.

Choose local stone so that it blends in seamlessly with the surroundings, especially if you are adding rock to an existing outcrop. Consider the options. Weathered, uncut stone gives a more natural look, while cut stone creates a more formal mood. Garden artistry enters in when you mix and match a variety of plants with the stone. The most successful formula is to balance nearly equal areas of stone and plants, so that the soft textures of the foliage and the flowers are framed and flattered by the heavy, smooth surfaces of stone.

PLACING ROCKS

In order to make the most of an existing stone outcrop, first, clear away all of the unwanted vegetation. Then add additional stones if needed to create a balanced look, starting at the bottom of the slope and working upward. Choose the largest, heaviest rocks for the base of the slope, and work upward, decreasing the size of the rocks as you go. This is a trick of perspective that makes use of the way things at a distance naturally look smaller than the same objects would if they were close by. Putting successively smaller rocks at the top of the hill will increase its perceived height. To make the stones as stable and natural looking as possible, dig out places for the stones and position them so they are half buried in the soil. When working with stones that are somewhat flat in shape, place them so that they tilt backward toward the slope. This trick encourages water to flow back into the soil behind the stone where it will benefit plants tucked into planting pockets.

SOIL FOR ROCK-GARDEN PLANTS

From a plant's point of view, the outstanding characteristic of a rock garden is the superior soil drainage it provides. So it stands to reason that most rock-garden plants thrive when planted in a mixture of one part soil, one part rich compost, and one part coarse sand. Mix the soil for

Creeping cotoneaster controls erosion at the top of this hillside. Below, nooks are colored by deep-pink flowered dianthus, yellow-flowered sun rose, yellow-flowered stonecrop, white-flowered candytuft, yarrow 'Summer Pastels' bugleweed.

OTHER BEDFELLOWS   Artemisia, bellflower, blanket flower, bluebeard, butterfly weed, candytuft, catmint, clematis, columbine,

REGIONAL ADVICE
Rock Gardens in Shade

In areas with moist seasonal weather and ample trees, consider a shady rock garden. Plants that form a tapestry of green on a shady slope include ferns, asarum, hellebores, small hostas, and trilliums. Add containers of impatiens or begonias for bright summer color.

Steps made from cedar logs carve an inviting path to the house in this hillside, front-yard garden. Hardy, drought-resistant, low shrubs and perennials soften the rocky terrain and reduce erosion.

planting pockets in advance, so it will be ready as you place the stones. Use the amended soil to make little beds or to fill nooks and crannies where you will later place plants. Wedge the soil mix into deep crevices or broad pockets between stones, poking about with a spade handle or metal rod to eliminate hidden air pockets.

Many rock-garden plants creep or cascade, forming low carpets of color between stones. To avoid a patchwork look, group similar-looking plants together so they'll interweave as they mature. Shrubs can become an integral part of the scene. But, when planting shrubs among stones, keep the root ball level and the crown of the shrub upright. Small planting pockets are perfect places for clusters of little bulbs like miniature daffodils, squill, or grape hyacinths. Where the layer of soil is shallow, such as atop large stones, plant the area with shallow-rooted, hardy succulents, such as stonecrop and hens and chicks. Most

rock-garden plants eagerly spread to fill in vacant places, but until they do, you will need to patrol the area periodically and pull weeds by hand. As your plantings mature, occasional trimming of plants to keep the scene neat, and the stones visible, becomes an important yet enjoyable task of nurturing a hillside rock garden.

FINISHING TOUCHES

After the rock garden is planted, water it gently to keep from dislodging plants, and water it thoroughly. It takes several passes with a hose outfitted with a sprinkler head to wet the soil in crevices between the rocks. Afterward, apply a 2.5 cm (1 in) thick mulch of pea gravel or fine pebbles. This type of mulch allows water to filter through freely to plant roots, but it does a good job of holding soil and roots in place. It also keeps foliage high and dry, and that's just what rock-garden plants prefer.

WHAT TO LOOK FOR:
Small Leaves, Large Flowers

The best-looking rock garden plants have small leaves and a fine texture, yet they produce comparatively large flowers. These characteristics help them to contrast beautifully with the stone. In addition, they appear naturally stunted, the same way they would look if they were growing on a wind-swept mountain.

coreopsis, creeping phlox, crocus, daffodil, epimedium, euphorbia, geranium, grape hyacinth, hellebore, hens and chicks, heuchera, honeysuckle, hosta, hyacinth, Japanese maple, juniper, lamb's-ears, lobelia, ornamental grasses, portulaca, rock rose, rose, rose campion, snowdrop, squill, statice, thrift, thyme, trillium, tulip, verbena, yucca.

Ground-covers for Hillsides

PLANTS THAT RAMBLE AND SCRAMBLE over the ground are great problem solvers for inclines that are too steep to mow but not too steep to plant. At their best, groundcovers form a thick carpet of foliage that excludes weeds, retains moisture, and protects the soil against erosion.

Simplicity is the design key to getting stellar results from groundcovers grown on sloping ground. The beauty of a carpet of bugleweed or moss phlox comes from the solid mass of flowers it produces when it is in bloom. After the flowers have passed, the consistency of the foliage texture and color kicks in to extend the show. Slopes planted with broad bands of only a few species of plants are also much easier to maintain than a mixed collection of different plants. Trimming, feeding, and weeding can be done quickly and efficiently.

THE TEXTURES OF GROUNDCOVERS

Plant texture provides clues that you can use when deciding what plant to put where. Visually, the fine texture of plants with small leaves causes them to appear to be farther away than they actually are. The coarse texture of plants with thick stems and larger leaves, appear closer to a viewer than they actually are. So, if you place plants with bold textures, such as bergenia or hens and chicks,

This hillside is braced by creeping junipers, blue oat grass, daffodils, daylilies, rudbeckias, and lilac-flowered thyme.

in the foreground of your slope and position fine-textured plants, such as candytuft or dianthus, to the rear, the optical illusion that you created will make the area appear larger and more expansive. If you reverse the combination of textures, the hill will actually look less steep than it actually is. You can actually create the same optical illusion described above, by combining plants with warm and cool colors. Warm colors advance and cool colors recede. For instance, if you set plants with blue-green foliage, such as hostas, or blue flowers, such as ageratum, at the back of a bed, or at the top of a hill, the blue colors will blend into the sky at the horizon line, causing a bed to look deeper than it actually is, and it will also cause a hill to appear greater than its height. If you want to make the hill look shorter, put plants with ruddy foliage, such as barberry, or plants with yellow, orange, or red flowers, such as rudbeckia or daylilies, toward the front of the planting.

Use plants with highly visible, upright, straplike foliage, such as ornamental grasses and daylilies, to their best advantage. They contrast handsomely with creeping juniper and other spreading shrubs. Also keep in mind that some vines make good groundcover plants, particularly clematis and honeysuckle.

Another point to ponder is how you'll handle the inevitable transition area, where the plant textures and heights change, which occurs at the bottom of the slope where the groundcovers merge with lawn grass or some type of garden bed. Because the area at the base of a slope is often moist and well endowed with organic matter, it's an excellent place to grow perennials that form a low hedge, such as hardy geraniums, rudbeckia, or even groundcover roses, which have been bred to have a low, spreading habit and to bloom intermittently.

PLANTING GROUNDCOVERS ON SLOPES

It's frustrating to cultivate the erosion-prone soil on a slope. Taking a gentle approach is the best idea. Clean away existing vegetation by hand or smother it by covering the soil with black- or clear-plastic sheeting for two or three months, a process called solarization. If you cannot take the time to weed or solarize, kill the vegetation with a commercial herbicide, following label directions

OTHER BEDFELLOWS Artemisia, asarum, bergenia, bugleweed, candytuft, catmint, clematis, cotoneaster, creeping

A rocky hillside can become a showcase for care-free flowering groundcovers like sedums. To show plants to best advantage, plant them, as they grow in nature, in natural-looking groupings called drifts.

carefully (for information on safe usage and storing chemicals, see the maintenance chapter). If there is insufficient topsoil on your hillside to plant in, you should spread as much good topsoil on it as necessary to form a smooth planting bed. Immediately plug in new plants, firm them in well, and apply a thick layer of straw mulch on the soil around the new plants. Straw is less likely to blow or wash away than other mulches, and it reduces evaporation while the plants are growing new roots. Irrigate as often as needed to keep the soil lightly moist for at least a month, or until the plants show signs of new growth. How do you know when a plant is established? New growth above ground usually reflects the development of strong roots below the soil. If you are in doubt, you can gently tug on the stems. A plant that is established resists being pulled out of the ground.

KEEPING A CLEAN CARPET

Although mulch deters many weeds, a few always manage to gain a foothold. Weed plantings as often as needed for the first two seasons. After the first season, consider using an herbicide to control weeds, but read the label carefully to make sure the product is safe to use around groundcovers. After the second season, the plants should spread into a carpet that few weeds penetrate.

Maintenance is easy. In spring, use a balanced, controlled-release fertilizer, remove debris, and renew gaps in the mulch. In time, the plants will weave into a community that is naturally care-free.

Look to the Future

Gardening on slopes isn't easy, so plan to do it as seldom as possible. It's wise to use long-lived groundcover plants that get bigger and better with time, such as creeping juniper. As the juniper spreads, it will cover space initially occupied by perennials. This long-lived, drought-tolerant, densely growing shrub never needs trimming, making the slope easier to maintain.

phlox, crocus, daffodil, daylily, dead nettle, dianthus, English ivy, epimedium, euphorbia, ferns, geranium, grape

hyacinth, hens and chicks, honeysuckle, hosta, Japanese spurge, juniper, lady's mantle, lamb's-ears, ornamental grasses,

pachysandra, red-osier dogwood, rose, rudbeckia, snowdrops, stonecrop, sweet woodruff, thyme, vinca.

Plants for Hilly Meadows

Late summer ornamental grass, cosmos, and rudbeckia will be followed in spring by daffodils and poppies, then blanket flower, coreopsis, and meadow rue.

DO YOU MOW A HILLSIDE OVER AND OVER, with little to show for your efforts? If so, consider transforming the area into a care-free wildflower meadow. A single annual mowing, in fall or spring, is usually sufficient to maintain such a meadow. And meadow plants growing on a slope present an impressive picture that changes constantly as different species come in and out of bloom. Meadow gardens are always packed with intrigue. And the show is a never-ending display of different plant combinations, usually pairing flowering plants with clump-forming grasses.

The display is even more gratifying because very little site preparation goes into creating a meadow. When you seek out plants that thrive naturally in your climate and soil, the job becomes easy. After planting them once,

many wildflowers multiply or reseed with no assistance on your part. You can use your saved time and energy to experiment with other flowers to add to the palette, fine-tuning your collection with each passing season.

YARD-SIZED MEADOWS

They're somewhat wild and woolly by nature, so wildflower meadows are best located a short distance from your house, separated from it by a swath of neatly mown turf. There's other advantages to setting off your meadow with a trim lawn. It serves as an open area, allowing you to stand back and admire the view. It also acts as a buffer zone for wildlife, which are naturally drawn to wildflower meadows. A short fence also helps to set apart a wildflower area. Fences lend a sense of importance, too, making the meadow look like an intentional garden rather than a happy accident.

Start small with a wildflower meadow, and expand your space as you need more room for a growing collection of plants. Many of the flowers listed here have such strong constitutions that they seldom fail when given an opportunity to grow.

ADOPTING WILDFLOWERS

Prepare the site for planting by eliminating weeds and creeping grasses. You can pull or dig out weeds, but disturbing the soil often stimulates even more weeds by breaking the roots of perennial weeds, which can sprout new plants from the pieces. So, it is usually easiest to spot-treat unwanted vegetation with an all-purpose contact herbicide like glyphosate. Leave tuft-forming grasses in place to help protect the soil from erosion. After the unwanted plants die, usually within 3 weeks, rake the open patches of ground and begin planting perennial and annual flowers, along with any additional small ornamental grasses that suit your scheme.

For fast results, start with purchased plants of colorful, flowering native perennials, such as coreopsis, gold-

OTHER BEDFELLOWS
Artemisia, aster, bee balm, blue star, borage, bugleweed, candytuft, catmint, columbine, coreopsis, creeping

enrod, purple coneflower, and rudbeckia. These flowers can be started from seed, but the seedlings often take two years to reach blooming size. Meanwhile, they may be overtaken and lost in the exuberant growth of other plants in a wildflower meadow. By contrast, container-grown nursery plants of these and other hardy perennials often bloom the first summer after being set out in early spring.

Some gardeners prefer to stick with only native plants, but you will get much more color, over a longer season, by inviting imported bulbs and annuals into your meadow. For early spring excitement, plant daffodils in large natural-looking drifts, and stud the edges of your meadow with smaller bulbs, such as crocus and grape hyacinth. The fading foliage of these and other spring-flowering bulbs will be hidden from view by perennials and annuals that appear later in the spring.

A few self-seeding annuals, notably cosmos, poppies, and larkspur, are often used as leading color plants in a wildflower meadow. Although these annuals do shed seed by the millions, much of it is eaten by birds or carried away by rain. So, to make sure you have all the color you desire, it is usually best to sow at least a few new packets seed each year. Experiment with other informal annuals that can be grown from seed, such as rose campion, but do not try to add hybrid annuals normally used for formal beds and borders, such as petunias and begonias, to a wildflower meadow. Their large, bold flowers often look out of place among the delicate wildflowers, and they rarely reseed with success.

MOWING YOUR MEADOW

In the interest of neatness, and to control tree seedlings and other woody weeds that inevitably pop up, a meadow should be mowed at least once a year, preferably in late fall. This job may be too rough for a mower, but it is easily tackled by a gas-powered weed trimmer equipped with a blade. Allow the debris to lie on the ground through winter as a mulch. Seeds may germinate under its protection, and it will prevent soil erosion. In early spring, rake open patches, loosen the top 1 cm (1/2 in) of soil with a hoe, and plant seeds of annuals like poppies, cosmos, and larkspur.

A hillside planted as a meadow garden is a riot of color from spring to fall, as flowering perennials and selfseeding annuals take turns blooming in ever changing color combinations. Garden maintenance amounts to an annual mowing.

phlox, crocus, daffodil, daylily, dianthus, epimedium, four-o-clock, foxglove, hardy geranium, goatsbeard, goldenrod, grape hyacinth, Joe Pye weed, larkspur, ornamental grasses, purple coneflower, rose campion, rudbeckia, shrub rose, sneezeweed, snowdrops, species tulips, spiderwort, squill, sweet woodruff, turtlehead, yarrow.

CHAPTER FIVE

PLANTS FOR ALL SEASONS

From the opening of the first spring snowdrop to the last autumn aster, gardeners strive to keep their gardens beautiful and interesting all year long. There may be a week during the growing season when even the best garden slips into a lull. But it's possible to create a garden that performs virtually nonstop throughout the seasons, including winter, when many plants are at rest.

This chapter explores strategies for decking each season with color, fragrance, and form, from early spring until winter shrouds the garden in muted shades. The constants of this quiet season will be plants with interesting forms or textures that look good even when dormant, evergreens whose subtle golds, greens, or burgundys contrast with wheaten shades of dormant perennials, and a few winter bloomers whose fragrance and color foretell spring.

But while the garden is actively growing, the reliable elements will be flowering plants that bloom over and over, tying spring, summer, and fall together. Week after week, these plants become the crucial background players for perennials and shrubs, which are chosen for succeeding bloom times so that you can enjoy nonstop, if short-lived, bursts of color.

Think beyond blossoms, and plant for foliage harmony. Daylilies and irises, for example, are popular because they put on a show-stopping floral display. But they also enliven the garden from spring to fall with handsome, strappy leaves, which rise from the ground like green fountains. Also consider the subtle, season-long beauty of plants with colored or variegated leaves, which can brighten shady spots that are inhospitable to flowering plants.

When searching for multiseason plants, we have not only considered flowers, but also foliage, fruits, seed heads, fall color, bark texture, and winter silhouette. It's these subtle attributes of the care-free plants featured in this chapter that will step out to transform an ordinary garden into a showplace of four-season beauty.

Plants for Early Spring

THE SURE CURE FOR A GARDENER'S WINTERTIME BLUES is a vibrant spring garden. Fortunately, blooming is the first thing on the agenda for many plants when they emerge from winter dormancy, so early-spring color is not difficult to create in any type of garden.

Begin with easy-to-grow spring-flowering plants for guaranteed success. Combine spring-flowering bulbs with shrubs. Add spring-blooming trees, such as flowering cherry and dogwood, and it's a cinch to orchestrate a garden blooming in harmony. There is a bonus to all this spring splendor. The hidden benefit is that the garden becomes an enchanting place to carry on the activities of preparing for the coming growing season. Spring is a time of digging and dividing crowded perennials, setting out summer annuals, and planting new shrubs and trees. And, because the spring scene was planned and planted months ago, it's the result of late-summer and fall backaches that seem like ancient history when you're rewarded with flowers in spring. Like magic, garden plants are poised to take off as soon as days lengthen and the soil begins to warm.

CHOOSE THE MOOD

Spring-flowering bulbs are the stars of the early-spring garden. Follow your personal taste and the style of your garden when deciding whether to grow them in naturalized drifts or in formal arrangements. Most gardeners like to use small bulbs, such as crocus, snowdrops, and squill, as surprises, casually tucking them into the soil around shrubs and small trees. On the other hand, hyacinths and tulips have a uniformity that lends them to formal front-yard displays. You can extend the show by coupling these and other spring bulbs with cold-tolerant pansies in similar or complementary colors.

THE COLORS OF SPRING

When choosing shrubs and bulbs for early spring color, be careful where you plant white-flowered varieties. When white blossoms are injured by frost, they invariably turn an unsightly brown, and they show every small bruise and bite. The same damage is usually less noticeable on pink or lavender blossoms. There are exceptions, such as white bridal wreath spiraea and the flowers of serviceberry, which always manage to look fresh and pristine, but in general, choose varieties with colored flowers when it comes to early azaleas, tulips and lilacs. Any color in the rainbow is welcome after a long stretch of drab winter days, so experiment. The evergreen groundcover bugleweed, grape hyacinth, and other spring bloomers mix and match easily with the vivid yellow flowers of daffodils or brightly colored tulips. You can also choose bulbs with flowers in Easter-egg pastels. If your garden includes spring-flowering shrubs like yellow forsythia or pink azaleas, lighten the scene with drifts of flowering groundcovers, such as white-flowered candytuft or lilac-flowered moss phlox. And after long winter months of longing for spring, who can help plucking a few early blossoms to enjoy indoors? For this very reason, try to grow a few extra daffodils, hyacinths and tulips to cut and bring indoors to enjoy in a vase of water. To avoid gaps in the

A home landscape is awash in the spring colors of ornamental cherry and star magnolia trees, lilac and forsythia shrubs, and flowering crocus, grape hyacinth, squill, and miniature daffodil bulbs.

OTHER BEDFELLOWS
Akebia, azalea, boxwood, bugleweed, camellia, candytuft, clethra, crown imperial, dead nettle,

Spring gardens usher in the growing season with a rich combination of flowering bulbs, shrubs, and trees.

flower garden, you can plant extra bulbs at the rear of a bed where the harvested blossoms won't be missed.

FLOWERING BOUGHS

Many spring gardens are built around flowering trees, and with good reason. When a flowering cherry, dogwood, star magnolia, or redbud is covered with colorful blossoms, they always steal the show. And even if your yard is small, you can probably find a good place for one of these compact, spring-blooming beauties. You can cut branches from flowering trees and shrubs to use in your indoor arrangements. They combine beautifully with the flowers of bulbs, and you can mix in bits of greenery from emerging vines to fill the vase. When flowering cherry or forsythia branches are gathered just as the flower

buds are opening, they will usually keep for more than a week in a vase if you crush the stem base.

One of the first spots to consider is the area just beyond one of the front corners of your house. When small trees or large shrubs are situated so that they visually pull the corner of the house outward, they often make the house appear larger and also visually tie the house to the surrounding landscape. As long as they are set at least 4 to 5 cm (12–15 ft) away from exterior walls, they will not block views or crowd the structure.

Do not assume that you need to flank both sides of your house with matching trees unless you want a strongly formal look. Instead, choose two different plants for these strategic corner positions, such as a flowering cherry on one side balanced with a bushy smokebush on the other. Nonflowering trees with showy foliage or interesting bark, such as Japanese maples and river birches, are also fine trees to feature in your spring landscape.

LATE-WINTER SUN

Take advantage of the sun that filters through the branches of large, deciduous trees before they leaf out. Later in summer, the area underneath will be a lush shade garden. But now it can be a temporary display area for spring-blooming perennials, shrubs, and bulbs. The late-winter sun that filters through the bare branches is often sufficient to nurture hellebores and early daffodils. Daffodils are made for the shade, but plant tulips in sunnier sites. Their blossoms will twist to face south or west if they lack light. The edge of wooded areas is also the perfect place for azaleas and rhododendrons. Surround these shrubs with woodland phlox, trillium, and Solomon's seal. They will set the stage for strategically placed hostas and large deciduous ferns. These shade lovers emerge in time to hide the fading foliage of spring bulbs, allowing them to yellow and slip into dormancy unnoticed.

Root's-eye View

Plant spring-flowering bulbs beneath spring-flowering shrubs and trees in any color combinations you like. Sharing root space is no problem for these plants, which are designed by nature to grow together. Be sure to let the bulb foliage die down rather than mowing it, so they can continue to store food.

REGIONAL ADVICE
Bulbs for Fall

Where winters are not too cold (Zone 4 and warmer), try some of the fall-flowering crocus. The flowers appear in late fall, last for several weeks, and are amazingly cold tolerant. After a hard frost, they lie on the ground and seem dead, but soon straighten up and recover when the sun shines.

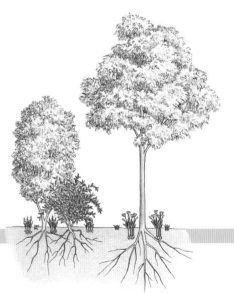

dogwood, Dutchman's pipe, epimedium, ferns, forget-me-not, fuchsia, golden chain tree, heuchera, holly, hyacinth, juniper, lacebark pine, lamb's-ears, Oriental poppy, pansy, primrose, redbud, red-osier dogwood, serviceberry, silverbell, snowbell, snowdrops, Solomon's seal, spiraea, star magnolia, sweet woodruff, trillium, tulip, witch hazel, wood hyacinth.

Plants for Early Summer

EARLY SUMMER IS A TIME OF BOUNTY IN ANY GARDEN. A full canopy of leaves on trees and shrubs form lush clouds of green overhead, and sunny beds boast an abundance of beautiful blossoms. The list of early-summer bloomers is a long one. The starlets of the early-summer garden are hardy perennials that spend spring growing new stems and leaves in preparation for a bright flush of flowers. However, personal preferences strongly affect which plants figure most prominently in your garden at this time. Peonies and irises are a mainstay in many gardens, accompanied, perhaps, by pink or blue campanulas and clematis. Roses can be counted on to perfume the early-summer air. Other gardeners may prefer more unusual plants such as foxtail lilies with their 2.4 m (8 ft) spikes of white, yellow, or orange flowers, flowering onions with globes of mauve flowers on stiff stems, or the alpine clematis that don't need hard pruning and have delicate white, pink, or rose flowers.

Early summer in the garden is a time of flowers and fragrance. Here, red roses, yellow petunias, and white-flowered sweet alyssum nestle at the base of a honeysuckle-entwined lamppost.

If you need a wide variety of sizes, shapes, textures, and flower colors summer after summer without replanting, you should collect perennials. The simplest way of filling your early-summer garden with care-free color is to infuse the garden with two or three perennials that bloom simultaneously. They need not stand side by side. In fact, a more pleasing picture might be staged by sprinkling the flowering perennials among other plants that are not yet in bloom, and won't compete for attention.

FRAMING FEATURE FLOWERS

When featured flowers are framed against green foliage plants, or late blooming perennials, they often look more refined than when they stand alone, or cheek-by-jowl with other showy flowering plants. Try using silvery leaved plants like lavender to frame a bright flowering plant like a bush of red roses. Plants with pale gray or bluish foliage, such as lavender, artemisia, lamb's ears, rose campion, and Russian sage, always make good framing plants for snappier neighbors. Or, set your flowering plants off by surrounding them or backing them with plants that have striking, dark foliage, such as dwarf boxwoods, liriope, dark burgundy black cohosh, or even smokebush.

CARE-FREE ANNUAL EDGINGS

Plan to grow an abundance of annuals in climates that are very hot in summer or very cold in winter, because both extremes limit the number of perennials that will thrive there. Annuals, because they only live during the growing season, aren't affected by winter's worst weather. And in summer, many annuals like nothing better than blooming for weeks on end, unaffected by heat, humidity, and strong sun. Annuals will provide nonstop color in high-visibility beds and containers, and they can even thrive in the dry, hot strips of soil abutting driveways, sidewalks, and median strips.

Put annuals to work unifying the landscape, no matter where you live. Each summer, install a handful of annuals in your yard in the same way you might use colorful ribbon to decorate a wrapped gift. Edge beds with ribbons of flowering annuals. Or run them in small drifts through existing perennial flower beds. But be sure to save a few annuals for planting in containers. The design idea here is to repeat the use of the same annuals in

OTHER BEDFELLOWS Astilbe, bee balm, bergenia, blue star, borage, browallia, calendula, calla lily, campanula, catmint,

Early summer is a peak season in the garden for shaggy, pink-flowered bee balm, petunias, and roses, as well as many other flowering perennials, groundcovers, and shrubs.

REGIONAL ADVICE
Pinch Late Bloomers

In areas where asters and chrysanthemums won't bloom until September or October, pinch back the stems in July to half their length to make the plants compact. They will bear twice as many flowers in fall, and won't need staking to hold their heads high.

different parts of your yard, echoing threads and splashes of color throughout the landscape, making the garden look and feel like a cohesive unit.

When choosing annuals, look for those that have a long flowering time for your climate. Some like it cold. Flowering cabbage, lobelias, pansies, and sweet alyssum are good candidates where temperatures remain cool in fall and early spring, or where summer night temperatures remain low. Moderate summer climates are ideal places to grow garden standbys like petunias and impatiens. Where summers are very hot, choose heat-tolerant annuals like ageratum, caladiums, annual grasses, narrowleaf zinnia, or any wax begonia. The color range in annuals is so great that you can have fun experimenting with different color combinations and plant shapes from year to year while maintaining the same perennials and shrubs. Annuals are so inexpensive that you can even experiment with those that are marginally suited to your area. Sometimes you can find a spot for a container of annuals that is sheltered from the sun, or from brisk, chilly winds, expanding the number of plants that you can grow.

ADDING HEIGHT

If there seems to be something missing in your summer garden that you can't quite put your finger on, perhaps what you really need is more vertical interest. Plants that rise high, such as vines grown on arbors or upright trellises, shrubs with an upright habit like columnar junipers, or even a climbing rose attached to a post or pillar, give your eyes a welcome break from looking down into the garden. As you raise your head to admire vertical plants, you can't help taking in the view of the wonderful tree canopies and the brilliant blue sky, which you might otherwise miss. Vertical plants make maximum use of ground space, so they are especially functional in a small garden. And, in addition, fast-growing annual vines like canary vine, morning glory, and scarlet runner bean can give an instant look of maturity to new beds.

WHAT TO LOOK FOR:
Mix-and-Match Colors

Want to change the accent colors in high-visibility beds? It's a cinch when you install a bush of red roses as the dominant plant. Annuals with blue, yellow, or white flowers will always compliment red roses. Just be sure to avoid crowding the rose, which needs abundant fresh air and sunshine to deter disease.

clematis, coleus, columbine, coreopsis, daylily, dead nettle, dianthus, dusty miller, euonymus, ferns, foxglove, fuchsia, garden phlox, gayfeather, geranium, goatsbeard, heuchera, hollyhock, hops, hosta, impatiens, Japanese maple, lady's mantle, lamb's ears, larkspur, lavatera, lily, lobelia, meadow rue, ornamental onion, rose, scarlet runner bean, smokebush.

Plants for Mid to Late Summer

STRESS ESCALATES IN THE DOG DAYS OF LATE SUMMER for both gardens and gardeners. Even if you live in a climate that luxuriates in cool nights, the days are long and often dry. In much of the country, late-summer days are hot, and nights are sultry. Many areas also suffer from prolonged droughts this time of year. The best plan is to join forces with the season rather than fighting it. So relax your pace in late summer, and enjoy the many care-free plants that grow best when it's hot.

Having plenty of color in a late summer garden calls for advance planning, especially if your garden is built around bulbs and perennials. Although daylilies, monkshood, rudbeckia, and several other perennials provide bright mid- to late-season blooms in cooler gardens, in hotter areas, colorful plants for late summer are more limited. Look for heat-tolerant annuals, succulent perennials, those perennials that are native to hot, arid climates, and the few late-blooming shrubs that are available in nurseries. There are also some welcome surprises in store for gardeners this time of year. When you plant magic lilies, you'll see flowers appear within days of a deep, soaking rain in mid to late summer. In general, however, late summer is often a lull time in gardens. Summer's perennials are past their flowering peak. Some long-performing annuals that you would think you could count on, such as marigolds, temporarily cease flowering during intense heat waves, only to resume with the first break in a late-summer heat wave. And fall-blooming asters, chrysanthemums, and golden-rods are waiting in the wings, ready to respond to the shorter days of autumn by covering themselves with purple and golden blossoms. The best way to bridge the flowering gap is to fill the gaps in your garden with long-blooming, heat-tolerant annuals.

SCORCH-PROOF ANNUALS

Heat-tolerant annuals, such as cockscombs, sulfur cosmos, and zinnias can provide a rainbow of late-summer color, and gomphrenas are always willing to produce colorful papery flower bracts in the hottest weather. In sun or partial shade, annual salvias will respond to fertilizer and supplemental water by sending up a fresh flush of flower spikes.

In fact, nearly all annuals planted in spring, whether in beds or in containers, will be in need of a little pampering by late summer. Spend a little extra time with them, pinching off spent blossoms and old stems, and giving them all a deep drench with a water soluble, balanced fertilizer. The results can be dramatic, including improved leaf color within 2 days, and a fresh flush of flowers 2 to 3 weeks later.

SOME LIKE IT HOT

Although they can succumb to the barest hint of frost, plants that have tropical origins are custom-made for the sultry season. Plants from hot climates, such as lantana, canna, caladium, tithonia, and sweet potato vine, grow rapidly and flower abundantly in the heat that causes other plants to wilt and stop flowering. In warm climates, these and other tender perennials are routinely grown in the ground year-round. But in Canada's cold-winter climate these plants are treated as annuals, or dug up at the end of the season and overwintered indoors. Grown in sunny beds of moist soil, or in pots of

Light up a late-summer garden with a golden rain tree, blue-flowered butterfly bushes, obedient plants with lilac flowers, yellow zinnias, and mounds of blue-flowered ageratum.

OTHER BEDFELLOWS Artemisia, blanket flower, bluebeard, canna, castor bean, chrysanthemum, cockscomb, cosmos, daylily,

Late summer is time of bold colors in the garden, with exuberant perennials, such as golden-flowered black-eyed Susan and goldenrod, carmine-flowered stonecrop, and deep-purple asters spilling out of their beds.

moist soil, caladiums will light up any shady or partially sunny place, and the cascading stems and chartreuse or deep purple leaves of sweet potato vine is the finishing touch for a container garden composed of several species of summer-flowering annuals.

To derive maximum performance from tropicals, be sure to water them often enough to keep the soil slightly moist during their summer growth period Fertilize them with every other watering, using a balanced, water-soluble fertilizer mixed at half strength, according to the package label. And don't forget that several popular bedding plants are tropicals, too, including impatiens and annual geraniums. Indulged with an extra ration of care, these heat-tolerant plants can pull you and your garden through the hottest season.

BECKONING BUTTERFLIES

Late summer is the season for butterflies and for gardeners who enjoy watching their antics. High on the list of nectar flowers are butterfly bush and lantana, but any nectar is good nectar to a thirsty butterfly. Joe Pye weed flowers often get plenty of visitors. And the show isn't over at dusk. Wait until dark to enjoy night-flying moths in search of the evening flowers of four-o-clocks and fragrant flowering tobacco.

To make your garden even more hospitable to butterflies, stock it with plants that produce flat blossoms, which are easy for butterflies to land on. Plants with daisy-shaped flowers, which make late-season butterfly havens include blanket flowers, cosmos, purple coneflowers, rudbeckias, and zinnias.

WHAT TO LOOK FOR:

Cut and Come Again

Buddleia and zinnia are good examples of cut-and-come-again plants, because the more flowers you cut, the more they flower. Annuals respond similarly, so keeping your flower vases filled will also keep plenty of color in the late-summer garden.

flowering tobacco, four-o'clock, geranium, gladiolus, globe amaranth, gypsophila, hornbeam, hosta, hydrangea, Japanese

anemone, Joe Pye weed, lantana, magic lily, morning glory, ornamental grasses, perilla, phormium, pincushion flower,

portulaca, purple coneflower, rudbeckia, Russian sage, salvia, smokebush, spider flower, stonecrop, tithonia, veronica.

Plants for Fall

AUTUMN SIGNALS THE START of the garden's slow saunter toward winter. Plants and gardeners alike welcome the return of cooler weather and lower humidity. It's a time when some flowering plants finally get exactly what they've been waiting for: the short days and cool temperatures that trigger asters, chrysanthemums, and goldenrods to cover themselves with blossoms. Smart gardeners take advantage of the crisp, cool weather by planting spring-flowering bulbs, digging beds for the next season, and fertilizing lawns.

Active bloomers are few in the fall, though some spring-blooming perennials like candytuft and veronica will rebloom in autumn if they've enjoyed a stress-free summer. Some annuals including marigold and impatiens, often push out a strong showing of blossoms at season's end. Where autumns are long and warm, reblooming roses get in on the act, too. In colder areas, roses will set brilliant red or orange fruits, called hips, which are a winter taste treat for birds.

But the garden isn't the only game in town for color. Mesmerized by maples and spellbound by parrotias, you will find yourself looking skyward every chance you get, watching the colors of autumn grasses and trees change against a background of bright blue October skies.

GLORIOUS GRASSES

Several types of turf grasses dazzle the eye in the autumn landscape. If your lawn features species such as bluegrass, perennial ryegrass, or any type of fescue, it should awaken from its summer dormancy and green up beautifully in the moderate temperatures of fall. But it may need a little help. In many areas autumn is a dry season, so supplemental water may be needed to help your lawn during its late-season growth spurt. Early fall is also an excellent time to fertilize any lawn. In addition to promoting vibrant green color, a fall feeding with a controlled-release lawn fertilizer helps the grass store nourishment for the cold weather ahead. Finally, any type of lawn grass benefits from the removal of fallen leaves. Leaves allowed to settle atop your grass, block sunlight and fresh air, which are essential to its health.

Ornamental grasses laden with showy seeds bend and sway, dramatizing the brisk winds of autumn. And they persist far beyond the first few freezes. Even after the leaves of ornamental grasses fade from green to buff, don't trim them back. Besides being pretty, the long grass leaves help insulate the base of the plants from extreme cold and shelter the shallow roots as well. In many areas it is best to delay pruning until late winter, or just before new growth begins to emerge from the plants' crowns.

BLUSHING FOLIAGE

The same processes that make trees turn red and gold lead to changes in the leaf colors of some perennials and shrubs. As these plants sense the coming of winter, the green coloration in their leaves fades to reveal shades of yellow, orange, and red. Forsythias will glow in a soft shade of buttery yellow, while viburnums will turn to

Red-leaved euonymus and red chrysanthemums usher in fall with yellow goldenrod, sneezeweed and buff eulalia grass.

OTHER BEDFELLOWS
Autumn crocus, artemisia, aster, bluebeard, camellia, celosia, chrysanthemum, cosmos, dogwood, dusty

In fall's palette, leaves lose green pigment, and reveal red, orange, and gold. Flowers are purple and gold.

bronze. Many Japanese maples that were a gentle bronze color all through summer will turn to crimson red, and compete for your attention with the brighter red leaves of winged euonymus.

Several perennials follow suit, turning bronze in response to long, cool nights. When autumn ferns, bergenia, epimedium, or hardy geraniums blush bronze, any nearby plants with silvery foliage will seem lighter and brighter in contrast. Even though you may have appreciated artemisia, dusty miller, lamb's ears, and Russian sage all summer, their platinum foliage will become breathtaking with the advent of fall. For all plants, autumn becomes a time of second glances.

Look around for places where you can plug in the combination of the intriguing coarse texture and the kaleidoscope colors that comes with cold-tolerant ornamental cabbage and kale. If you're not sure where they will look best, pot each in a roomy container at least

15 cm (6 in) wide, and experiment with placement. Containers are especially practical in very cold climates because these plants are severely damaged when temperatures drop below about -5°C (25°F). Whisk them indoors when killing frost threatens, and take them outside again during the day. But do leave them out when it's chilly. The leaf colors of these ornamental coles become increasingly vivid in response to night temperatures that are consistently below 10°C (50°F). And, of course, don't overlook the punch of color that cold-tolerant pansies can contribute to flower beds, window boxes, and containers. They can even survive being buried in snow, emerging to bloom anew with each thaw.

BITTER BERRIES

In autumn, you won't be the only one enjoying nature's bounty. This is the season when many shrubs and trees produce colorful berries, and birds take full advantage, harvesting each berry in its time. From a bird's point of view, ripening doesn't necessarily happen immediately. For some shrubs, such as hollies, the right time may not be until spring. Some fruits, such as those of serviceberry, are snapped up as soon as they ripen, but others must mellow for weeks or months before they become palatable to birds. Half the entertainment as autumn slips into winter comes from noting when shrubs such as cotoneasters and viburnums are stripped of their berries. Last of all are the bitter berries of junipers and hollies, which actually begin to ferment before birds accept them. But until then, the berries remain for your pleasure.

THE SNEEZING SEASON

If you suffer from seasonal allergies in the fall, don't blame your sneezes on the season's outstanding flowering plants, such as aster, goldenrod, and sneezeweed. The culprit is usually ragweed pollen, which hits the air at the same time these flowers bloom. In fact, this is probably how sneezeweed got its name. A terrific upright perennial that covers itself with yellow blossoms in late summer and early fall, sneezeweed is a fine partner for asters in shades of purple and pink. But even without sneezeweed at its side, a clump of purple asters makes an ideal accent in the autumn landscape, especially if you import a few pumpkins to display near your entryway.

REGIONAL ADVICE
Guaranteed Grasses

Ornamental grasses vary so much in hardiness, size, and shape that the best way to get to know which is best for your garden is to visit area public gardens to study local favorites. Note the species and cultivar names, and while they're fresh in your mind's eye, decide where you will plant them next spring, and mark the spot.

WHAT TO LOOK FOR:
Short-Day Standouts

The strongest fall bloomers form buds and flowers in response to the lengthening nights of autumn. In addition to asters, chrysanthemums, goldenrod, and sneezeweed, cosmos and marigolds often clothe themselves with blossoms as days become shorter.

miller, geranium, golden chain tree, gomphrena, holly, honeysuckle, hornbeam, Japanese anemone, Japanese maple, lantana, monkshood, ornamental grasses, pansy, parrotia, red buckeye, river birch, rose, rudbeckia, Russian sage, salvia, silverbell, snowbell, stewartia, sun rose, sweet autumn clematis, tithonia, turtlehead, viburnum, yellowwood.

Plants for Cold Winters

EVERY CLIMATE HAS ITS PROBLEMS. In many regions, winter comes early and stays late, much to gardeners' chagrin. This may explain why gardeners in cold climates often create beautiful gardens. They may be the result of long winter nights spent planning and dreaming.

But don't wait until summer to enjoy your garden. There's entertainment out there even when it's shrouded with snow and whipped by frigid winds. Trees and shrubs offer dramatic silhouettes through every season, but the shapes of their limbs and the texture of their bark are most pronounced after leaves drop in fall. Evergreens become even more endearing when they're the only verdure in sight. Combined with plants that hold their form through winter, weatherproof garden features, such as fences, walls, statuary and pillars offer reassuring evidence that both you and your garden are waiting patiently for spring. Meanwhile, a bird feeder well stocked with sunflower seeds or suet, and a variety of shrubs with berries and seed-laden, dormant perennials will assure plenty of appreciative winged visitors.

STRETCHING THE SEASON

For any gardener frustrated by a short season, one of the simplest coping strategies is to stretch the season as far as possible. In autumn, cover late season performers with boxes, blankets, or nonwoven season-extending fabric, or floating row cover, to help them survive the first few frosts. Lobelia, pansies, and other diehard annuals will continue to bloom until snow blankets the ground. In addition, many container-grown flowering plants can be cleaned up, pruned back, and brought indoors, where they will continue to color sunny window sills for several weeks. Given sufficient light, you can coax zonal geraniums to bloom indoors throughout winter months.

Outside, stock your landscape with ornamental grasses that form buff-colored silhouettes that remain attractive well into winter. To insure that spring comes as early as possible, make liberal use of the small spring-flowering bulbs that appear before the last snow has gone, such as crocus, snowdrops, and squill. When you go outdoors in late winter to admire buds forming on forsythias and flowering cherries, it doubles the excitement to find flowering bulbs pushing up around your feet.

Evergreens that withstand prolonged periods of extreme cold include junipers and spruces in assorted shapes and sizes. These are invaluable for keeping the garden furnished through winter months. For a unified look, work with two or three species that offer slight variations in form and texture. If your landscape includes other hardy evergreens, pair them with contrasting shrubby junipers, which come in varying shades of green.

SEASONAL SHELTER

Snow is a cold-climate garden's best insulation. But you never know when snow will come, how much insulating cover it will give, or how long it will stay. To keep

A winter landscape is enlivened by evergreen columnar junipers and mugo pines, and brilliant red-osier dogwood. In summer the scene will be refreshed by pink-flowering peonies and blue-flowered monkshood.

OTHER BEDFELLOWS   Asarum, aster, bergenia, birch, black cohosh, cotoneaster, crocus, daffodil, dead nettle, dianthus,

your dormant plants safe from winter harm if the snows don't come, and to increase its insulating effects, cover dormant plants with loose evergreen boughs after cleaning up the garden in late fall. When you remove the boughs in spring, don't be surprised to see tender green shoots breaking through the soil slightly ahead of schedule.

Stone walls, thickets of shrubs, and other short barriers also provide the garden with extra protection from wind while providing visual interest when the rest of the landscape is buried in snow.

CHILLY CONTAINERS

Cold-climate gardeners often become experts at growing plants in containers. These range from window boxes that hold huge cascades of petunias and other trailing plants to barrel halves brimming with nasturtiums and various other tender or hardy plants. While the summer show of container-grown annuals is always outstanding in the neighborhoods of the north, comparable wonders take place indoors over the winter months, as smaller containers are called into service to hold bulbs forced into bloom on sunny window sills. Tulip, hyacinth and daffodil bulbs sold in the fall are easy to grow in containers, and bulbs potted up in the fall will bloom in late winter or early spring, provided they are given a suitable regimen of temperature, water and light. Hyacinths are especially endearing bulbs to force because of their intoxicating fragrance. Additionally, hyacinths have sturdy stems and are less prone to falling over than the long-stemmed tulips and daffodils usually grown in pots.

You can use any type of container for forcing bulbs, although tulips and large-flowered daffodils grow best when planted in deep pots, with at least 8 cm (3 in) of soil below the bulbs, and 10 cm (4 in) of soil over the bulbs. However, it is possible to coax small daffodils and hyacinths into bloom by planting them in shallow dishes with a mixture of soil and pebbles tucked up to the necks of the bulbs, taking care not to cover the growing points of the bulbs.

These bulbs are so forgiving that many gardeners use any containers they have on hand for forcing bulbs. Later, when the plants are ready to be displayed in high-visibility spots indoors, the recycled planting pots can be tem-porarily slipped into more decorative brass or ceramic containers for display indoors while they are flowering.

For the first six weeks after planting any hardy spring-flowering bulbs in containers, keep the soil barely moist, and store the planted containers in a cool place, such as a garage or unheated porch that stays above freezing, or put the pots into a plastic bag, seal the bag and store it in the refrigerator. Although you may see no signs of life from the bulbs, the roots are actively growing. After 6 weeks, when shoots of green do appear, move the pots to a bright location, but keep them cool. Continue to water the soil regularly, and enjoy the show as the leaves give way to dramatic flower spikes. After the flowers fade, keep on watering until the foliage starts to die down. Then stop watering and allow the bulbs to dry. They can be planted in the garden immediately or in the fall. They probably won't bloom the first year but will after that.

REGIONAL ADVICE
Tough Bulbs

In fall, reward yourself in advance for surviving winter. Plant little bulbs where the snow melts quickly in early spring. Scatter crocus, snowdrops, and squill along the edge of a lawn, a pathway, or close to the edge of a patio or deck where you are sure to notice them.

A winter border can be a colorful sight. Here, the brilliant stems of red-osier dogwood are highlighted by the evergreen, winter-flowering perennial called stinking hellebore, and evergreen ivy.

Dutchman's pipe, English ivy, euphorbia, false cypress, ferns, forsythia, geranium, goatsbeard, goldenrod, grape hyacinth, hellebore, holly, hyacinth, hydrangea, ironwood, juniper, meadow rue, ornamental grasses, pachysandra, periwinkle, pine, redbud, rose, serviceberry, snowdrops, squill, summersweet, tulip, viburnum, white pine, yellowwood, yucca.

Plants for Mild Winters

Wintergreen barberry and a kousa dogwood anchor a foundation planting. Silvery dusty millers and blue pansies color the bed in cool months. French hydrangea and larkspur highlight summer.

COASTAL BRITISH COLUMBIA enjoys a climate the rest of us can only envy, with little or no snow and, for the southern portions, hardly any frost, where gardening can continue year-round. Winter is a season of ample rainfall and cool temperatures that can be enjoyed in the company of numerous garden plants. Although many plants do slip into dormancy where winters are mild, there are plenty of evergreen trees, shrubs, and even perennials, as well as hardy annuals that will keep the garden vibrantly alive with greenery and flowers through the slow season.

If you are developing a new landscape, winter may not be slow at all. In a mild-winter climate, autumn is the preferred planting season for perennials and evergreens large and small. When planted in the autumn, these plants will benefit from cool temperatures and winter rains. By the time warm weather returns the following summer, they are comfortably settled in with strong, deep roots established in the soil. In addition, some perennials, such as daylilies and coreopsis, are best divided in autumn when they become crowded after several years in the same spot. When divided at the right time, by spring they will be well rooted and ready to bloom.

THE ELEGANCE OF EVERGREENS

Where winters are mild, landscapes offer design lessons in contrast. In addition to the coniferous evergreens that can be grown in colder parts of Canada, the mild winters of coastal British Columbia enable gardeners to enjoy a wide selection of broad-leaved evergreens that will not always survive in other parts of the country. Their foliage adds to the pallet of textures in the winter garden, but many also have attractive flowers or fruit.

Rhododendrons are widely grown and their broad, dark green leaves make a good back-drop for the seed heads of grasses that persist well into winter. The many varieties of camellia have smaller, lighter leaves and will flower in winter and early spring. Both Japanese and English hollies brighten up the winter garden with their bright berries and often variegated foliage, while the evergreen winter daphne fills the air with its heady fragrance from mid-winter onward.

One of the best evergreen groundcovers for this region is bearberry, especially the variety 'Vancouver Jade'. This forms a dense mat, is resistant to salt spray, and is a good choice for coastal gardens. Dwarf boxwoods, evergreen azaleas, and other broadleaf evergreens thrive where winters are mild. Or use needled evergreens, such as junipers or mugo pine to create a similar effect.

WILLING WINTER BLOOMERS

If you have acid soil and partial or filtered shade to accommodate them, camellias can be counted upon to color up winter in mild climates. Many varieties bloom best in late fall, after the weather has cooled down and you are likely to be spending more time in your yard where you can enjoy their large, rose-shaped, white, pink, or carmine blossoms. In woodland areas, consider growing cyclamen around the base of the trees for the off-season charm of their little winged flowers, and let spring come early with the blooming of evergreen hellebores. Evergreen leatherleaf mahonia is a mainstay in many gardens with mild winters, both because it holds its foliage year-round and because its yellow flowers appear before winter has come to an end.

Add fragrance to your winter garden with witch hazels. These woody plants can be grown either as shrubs or

OTHER BEDFELLOWS — Azalea, barberry, boxwood, bugleweed, camellia, candytuft, Carolina jessamine, cotoneaster, daffodil,

small trees. Even one of these filtered-shade loving plants, stationed among larger deciduous trees, is enough to provide delicate yellow flower color and a pervasive perfume in the season when it's least expected.

HAIL HALF-HARDY ANNUALS

In any mild-winter climate, there are a handful of cold-hardy annuals waiting to be discovered for wintertime entertainment. Consider planting dusty miller, dianthus, flowering cabbage and kale, pansies, and snapdragons. You can find them in garden centers as autumn bedding plants in areas where they'll flourish long after autumn has come and gone. They may bloom little during the shortest days of winter, but will provide great color again in early spring. When in doubt about the staying power of not-quite-hardy plants, such as snapdragons, plant them in a sheltered place. A wall or building can absorb heat during the day and warm nearby plants at night. Such a sheltered spot also shelters plants against damage from harsh winter winds.

In mild-winter climates, you can also use winter to practice and refine your outdoor seed-sowing skills. Annuals like larkspur and poppies should be sown in winter. Neither is a good candidate for transplanting, because of their low survival rate, yet both are easily grown from seed sown outdoors in late autumn or early winter. Unless every seed germinates and the seedlings are terribly crowded, wait until early spring to thin them. Invariably, a small percentage will be lost over winter to hungry rabbits or root rot in cold, wet soil.

With a liberal sprinkling of broad-leaved and needled evergreens and hardy perennials that retain their leaves in mild winters, gardens in mild climates can remain quite colorful all through winter.

dead nettle, dogwood, English ivy, euonymus, false cypress, flowering cabbage, forsythia, grape hyacinth, hellebore, hens and chicks, holly, Japanese maple, liriope, magnolia, mahonia, ornamental grasses, pansy, phormium, river birch, rose, Stewartia, stonecrop, viburnum, vinca minor, wax myrtle, witch hazel, wood hyacinth, yucca.

PLANTS FOR EXTREME SOIL

Some lucky gardeners are blessed with deep, friable, fertile soil. They are fortunate enough to have inherited soil with a loose, crumbly texture that makes it easy for plant roots to stretch out in all directions, absorbing all of the moisture and nutrients they need. But most gardens have more humble beginnings. But be assured that no matter what kind of soil you have, you can choose a number of garden-worthy plants that will thrive there, and no matter what sort of soil you have at the outset, simply improving it by incorporating organic matter sets the stage for a successful garden.

Don't let yourself be intimidated by the scientific aspects of soil improvement; it's really quite simple. The most important thing you need to know is your soil's level of acidity or alkalinity, which is called its pH value, and the value is measured on a pH scale that runs from 0 to 14, with 7.0 representing neutral soil. Most garden plants thrive in neutral to nearly neutral soil. Strongly acid soils have a low pH, with ratings on the pH scale usually between 4.0 and 6.0. The pH ratings for alkaline soils are higher than neutral, usually ranging between 7.5 and 8.0. In general, soils in high rainfall-areas tend to be acidic, whereas arid regions often have alkaline soil.

If the pH is too far one way or another on the scale, plants are unable to absorb essential nutrients, even if those nutrients are in the soil. So, if you notice yellowing leaves or pale leaves with darker green veins or other signs of poor growth or nutrition, consider using a soil pH test, either an over-the-counter kit, or take soil samples to a commercial laboratory to test (check your telephone book's yellow pages under "laboratories" or "soil testing"). But don't despair if your soil's pH is extreme. Even in extreme soil, a beautiful, care-free garden is within the realm of possibility. In other areas of your landscape where you don't want to invest the time and labor to alter your soil's pH so that you can grow plants that are not adapted to your soil, simply choose from among the no-fuss plants we describe in this chapter, which are adapted to grow in your garden's unique soil conditions.

Plants for Acid Soil

Acid soil is fertile ground for a shade-loving flowering dogwood, rhododendrons, columbines, hostas, ferns, and wood hyacinths.

To LEARN HOW PLANTS THAT THRIVE IN ACID SOIL fit into their natural environment, explore a natural forest. The same forces that shape and nurture a forest create acid soil. Copious rain that filters through the trees and soaks the ground below leaches alkaline minerals, such as limestone sediment, from the soil, neutralizing it. At the same time the natural mulch of evergreen needles or the tannin-filled leaves of trees like oaks, which blanket the forest floor, contribute acidity to the soil as they begin to break down. So, unless a forest happens to be sitting atop a hefty deposit of crumbled limestone, the natural pH of its soil will be in the acidic range.

One look at a forest proves that acidic soil can support a wide range of plants. Many trees like magnolia and holly prefer acid soil, as do forest understory shrubs like azaleas and rhododendrons, and low, creeping groundcovers like ferns, bugleweed, and sweet woodruff. Indeed, acid soil is such welcome news to these and many other plants that if your soil is neutral to slightly acid, growing a woodland-type garden in acid soil requires little effort on your part.

EXPANDING YOUR CHOICES

But not everyone wants a woodland in his or her yard. If you want to nurture colorful flowers and shrubs that aren't native to the woods, there's good news. The vast majority of favorite garden plants, from petunias to roses, grow best in soil that is only slightly acidic or "near neutral," meaning that it has a pH between 6.2 and 6.8. Fortunately, this is easily achieved by cultivating beds, working in ample compost to neutralize the pH, or by adding garden lime to over-acidic soil or adding garden sulphur to alkaline soil as directed on the package.

Made from crushed limestone, lime is a very simple mineral soil amendment. The preferred type for most gardens, dolomitic limestone, enriches the soil with the

OTHER BEDFELLOWS   Asarum, astilbe, azalea, bee balm, bluebeard, bugleweed, butterfly weed, caladium, calla Lily, camellia,

In the garden, as in nature, a woodland setting is a natural site for colorful acid- and shade-loving needled evergreens, broad-leaved evergreens like rhododendrons and azaleas, spring-flowering dogwood trees, and pieris shrubs.

plant nutrients calcium and magnesium while raising the soil pH. Unlike most fertilizers, lime usually persists in the soil for several years, until repeated rains wash it away. It is seldom necessary to lime a bed more than once every 3 years or so, but the only way to know for sure is to test your soil's pH annually, preferably in the fall.

You can add lime to your soil in any season. Most gardeners lime in either spring or fall, when they are digging new beds or renovating old ones. Because lime dissolves slowly, it must be thoroughly mixed into the soil. Lime that is simply dusted onto the soil's surface takes months to benefit plants' deep roots. This is fine for lawn grass, and it may be your only option when adjusting the pH for roses and other well-established plants.

Dense, heavy clay soils require more lime than their light-textured, sandy counterparts, so there is no set application rate. However, a good starting point is 24 kg per 100 m² (50 lb per 1,000 sq ft). If you check your soil's

pH before working in this amount and then recheck it 6 weeks later, you will have a good idea of how much change has resulted. If the soil is still very acidic, you can work in more lime the next time you dig the bed.

Although lime is nothing more than finely pulverized rock powder, wear gloves when handling it, and avoid breathing the dust. In its pure state, lime is sufficiently potent to dry your skin and irritate lung tissues. Some stores sell lime in a granular (pelleted) form that is easier to handle.

Garden sulphur, also known as wettable sulphur, is a fine powder consisting mostly of ground-up sulphur rock. It is used as a soil acidifier. Manure, peat moss, and acidic mulches like chopped oak leaves and pine needles will have a mildly acidifying effect on the soil. The effects of these acidifiers are short-lived, so if your soil is alkaline, you should check the pH each season and add amendments as recommended by the test results.

Carolina jessamine, clethra, climbing hydrangea, dead nettle, Dutchman's pipe, euphorbia, false cypress, ferns, garden phlox, geranium, holly, hollyhock, honeysuckle, magic lily, magnolia, mahonia, meadow rue, mountain laurel, river birch, serviceberry, silverbell, smokebush, snowbell, stewartia, sweet woodruff, trumpet vine, wisteria, witch hazel.

Plants for Alkaline Soil

SLIGHTLY ALKALINE SOIL IS THE PERFECT HOME FOR SOME PLANTS, but too much of a good thing can be detrimental to the health of many garden plants. One of the side effects of arid regions where rainfall is scant is alkaline soil with a high pH rating, but with attention and care, you can modify garden beds to lower the pH. Or you can choose plants that thrive in alkaline soil. Fortunately, here you'll find many low-maintenance, well-adapted performers that fill the bill.

If you need a groundcover for shade where ample water is available, consider adaptable burgundy-leaved bugleweed or lustrous green-leaved pachysandra. Trumpet vine and Japanese wisteria are alkaline-tolerant vines that will happily scramble over a rustic fence or arbor. Many shrubs are also adaptable. Doublefile viburnum, for example, is no less beautiful when grown in slightly alkaline soil than when it's rooted in slightly acid soil. Rather than amending your entire property, you can cut your workload considerably by grouping together foliage

Concrete driveways and sidewalks contribute lime to nearby beds. Lilacs, mugo pines, white-flowering candytuft, pink dianthus, hyacinth, and tulips are plants that can flourish in such alkaline soil.

and flowering plants that prefer alkaline soil, such as lilac, peony, gypsophila, pincushion flower, and sun rose.

Save the work of amending garden soil to lower the pH for those beds destined to host annuals or perennials that need neutral or slightly acidic conditions. Or, consider growing those plants in containers filled with their favorite soil mix.

ACIDIFYING ALKALINE SOIL

Lowering the pH of alkaline soil is time consuming, and it's impossible to permanently "fix" alkaline soil in one fell swoop. The most direct way to lower the pH of alkaline soil is to amend it with garden sulphur, which should be thoroughly mixed into the soil. Use caution, however, and apply only a small amount at a time. Soil sulphur is potent. About 0.5 kg per 10 m^2 (1 lb per 100 sq ft) will noticeably lower the pH, usually by 0.5 point on the pH scale, but you will need to wait 8 weeks before making another application. Even when it is thoroughly mixed in, using too much soil sulphur in one application will form pockets of strong acid in the soil that can burn plant roots, undoing all the good you are trying to do.

In combination with soil sulphur, work acidic soil amendments, such as peat moss, oak leaves, leaf mold, or rotted sawdust, into the soil. In addition to lowering the pH, these soil amendments will improve the soil's texture and help it to retain moisture, which is usually a pressing issue where alkaline soils reign.

To compound the problem of altering soil pH, the water, too, is often alkaline in areas where the soil has a high pH. As a result, the alkaline tendencies of the soil are reinforced each time you irrigate, using a garden hose and municipal water. You can help to offset the process by using fertilizers that are intended for acid-loving plants, in addition to making liberal use of organic matter and soil sulphur. Consider hooking up your house gutters to barrels and collecting rainwater, which is naturally soft, for use on special collections of acid-loving plants.

AMAZING ANNUALS

Annual flowering plants grow for only one season and are often surprisingly adaptable to soil pH, so they are ideal plants for gardens with

OTHER BEDFELLOWS
Bedding geranium, bergenia, Boston ivy, browallia, bugleweed, butter daisy, cockscomb, cotone-

Alkaline soil can support a wealth of beautiful flowering perennials. Adapted perennials include golden-flowered rudbeckia, purple coneflowers, and the airy blue flower spikes of Russian sage.

alkaline soil. Make the most of annuals by combining them according to time-honored garden design principles. Grow plants with a diversity of flower shapes and plant habits. Set rounded mounds of butter daisies alongside the upright flower plumes of celosia, for example. Add instant height to an annual bed by incorporating trellises for annual vines, such as scarlet runner bean, to climb. This is a design trick that adds the illusion of permanence to your garden design. And, underneath it all, grow evergreen groundcovers like licorice plant, or evergreen perennial groundcovers that can tolerate alkaline soil, such as bugleweed and pachysandra.

The beauty of annuals, for gardeners with alkaline soil, lies not only in their strong flowering performance but also in the fact that they bow out completely when their growing season is finished. This allows you to apply a fresh application of soil sulphur and to turn under old mulch to enrich the soil in beds with organic matter each fall when the bed is cleared of debris. Lay down a winter mulch of large bark chips, evergreen bough, pine straw, or some other mulch that won't blow away, to protect the soil from erosion, readying it for planting first thing in spring. Beds dedicated to annuals can become a movable feast, allowing you to experiment with new plants in new combinations each season.

THE CONTAINER ALTERNATIVE

Rather than fight the terrible twosome of constant dryness and alkaline soil that can be found in many areas, and even along lime-rich concrete foundations, driveways, and sidewalks, many gardeners color up their summer gardens with container gardens grown in neutral to slightly acid soil. Commercial potting soils are usually slightly acidic, and they can be amended, if necessary, with additional peat moss or organic material for growing hydrangeas, camellias, or other acid-loving plants.

Root's-eye View

Candytuft and dianthus are perfect companions for spring-flowering bulbs. You will need to mark the location of any bulbs that need to be divided in summer, just before they become dormant. Colored golf tees, hidden under groundcover foliage, work well for this purpose.

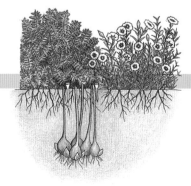

aster, doublefile viburnum, dusty miller, fuchsia, golden rain tree, gypsophila, honeysuckle, hyacinth bean, lacebark pine, lantana, larkspur, lavender, licorice plant, pachysandra, peony, pincushion flower, plectranthus, purple coneflower, redbud, scarlet runner bean, stock, sun rose, thyme, trumpet vine, wishbone flower, wisteria, yellowwood, yucca.

CARE-FREE ANNUALS

Annual plants complete their entire life cycle, from seed to flower and back to seed again, all in one season. Because their time is limited, annuals bloom with gusto, often for months on end. A number of perennials also are willing to grow as annuals, particularly semitropical plants, such as lantana, four-o'clock, and sweet potato vine. Many gardeners simplify this matter by referring to all plants that are easily grown for a single season as annuals.

Care-free annuals are the workhorses of the garden, providing reliable foliage and flower color from spring to fall, and throughout winter in mild climates. In mild climates, early-blooming, cool-season annuals such as pansies are perfect companions to spring-flowering bulbs and flowering shrubs. With the onset of summer, you can switch to heat-tolerant, warm-season annuals including marigolds, salvias, and zinnias.

The majority of bedding plants that fill stores in spring are annuals, so it is hard to imagine an easier way to kick off a colorful summer than to buy a few, prepare a suitable bed, and pop in these ready-to-grow plants. Many of the annuals sold as bedding plants are compact dwarf varieties, bred to need little maintenance and grow as well-behaved subjects in gardens, containers, and window boxes. They bloom for months and you can just toss them on the compost heap at season's end, and you're ready for next year.

Although annuals are, by definition, one-season wonders, they sometimes self-sow, making replanting unnecessary. The best of these are charmingly informal plants, such as forget-me-nots and poppies, that surprise us by cropping up in new places, and delight us with the bonus of free plants.

The more you try, the more of these care-free garden performers you'll fall in love with, and the more ways you'll find to use them. The annuals listed on the following pages will look good for an extended period of time without fuss or bother. Easy, fast, and inexpensive, they are ideal for busy gardeners.

A care-free swath of ageratums will contribute a sought-after shade of blue to any garden.

AGERATUM

Ageratum houstonianum

HARDINESS:
Tender

PREFERRED SOIL pH:
Near neutral

PREFERRED SOIL TYPE:
Well-drained, fertile

PREFERRED LIGHT:
Sun to partial shade

Ageratum in the Landscape

Known to old-time gardeners as floss-flower or pussy foot, ageratum is grown for its tiny, usually soft powder blue blossoms, which are packed into small, fluffy balls. While the clusters are small, new hybrid varieties are so packed with flowers that it's often difficult to see the leaves, making these low, spreading plants look like a carpet of blue flowers.

Willing to adapt to full sun or partial shade, dwarf ageratums are ideal plant partners for filling containers, edging beds, and planting in front of taller flowers. For a bold effect, try massing these fluffy bloomers in groupings of 10 or more, spacing the plants 15–20 cm (6–8 in) apart. Ageratums are easy to mix with annuals of any color, or you can tuck them between perennials to echo the shades of blue and purple flowers of campanulas and catmint. Or, use them to visually cool down the hot bright orange and yellow flowers of sulphur cosmos or yellow dahlias.

Expanding the Color Range

Back in the 1800s when ageratums first came into cultivation, flower colors were limited to blue. Blue ageratums remain garden treasures, but now there are white ageratums, such as the compact, 25 cm (10 in) tall 'White Ball', and innovative bicolors, such as the Capri series, which has medium blue flowers with contrasting white centers. Older, long-stemmed varieties are well worth seeking out if you grow cut flowers and are willing to grow the plants from seeds. 'Blue Horizon' and 'Blue Bouquet' produce a summer-long parade of blue flowers on 60 cm (2 ft) tall plants.

Growing Ageratum

It's easy to find ageratums in garden centers, discount stores, and nurseries as spring bedding plants. But you can easily start seeds indoors 8 weeks before the last frost. Use moistened, commercial sterile, soilless seed starting mix and lightly press the seeds, which need light to germinate, into the mix without covering them. Keep the soil moist and set the pots in a sunny window. When seedlings have two or three mature leaves, transplant them to individual pots and grow on. Set plants out after the last frost has passed, and keep the soil consistently moist for 3 weeks.

Ageratums thrive in hot weather. In locations where summers are very hot and humid, though, they prefer a little light shade. But watch out for too much shade, which can make these compact plants leggy. While prolonged droughts can wilt and weaken them, a deep drench of water will quickly revive them. Long-

Icy white-flowered 'Summer Snow', above, is a cooling influence on a hot garden.

stemmed varieties bloom longer if you promptly remove old flowers, but vigorous dwarf varieties flower non-stop with occasional pinching off of old blooms. These natives of Mexico and Central America truly resent a chill, and their leaves respond to frost by turning from green to black overnight. To get them through an early frost, cover them with blankets.

Ageratums are usually pest free but can fall prey to two types of tiny sucking insects. Barely visible spider mites feed on the backs of leaves, giving the foliage a pale, stippled appearance. You may even be able to see their fuzzy webs. Whiteflies look like white gnats and will fly up in a cloud when disturbed. Either pest can be dispatched by spraying the plant with a strong blast of water from a hose or by applying insecticidal soap, as directed, in the evening or on a cloudy day to prevent sun-scorched leaves.

FUNDAMENTAL FACTS

ATTRIBUTES	Blue, white, and bicolored flowers; for edgings, pots, cut flowers
SEASON OF INTEREST	Early summer through early fall
FAVORITES	'Capri' dwarf variety; taller 'Blue Horizon'
QUIRKS	Thrives in warm, humid weather
GOOD NEIGHBORS	Campanulas, catmint, dahlias, sulfur cosmos, salvias, zinnias
WHERE IT GROWS BEST	Moist, well-drained soil, where summer nights stay above 13°C (55°F)
POTENTIAL PROBLEMS	Spider mites, whiteflies
CRITTER RESISTANCE	Good
SOURCE	Bedding plants, seeds
DIMENSIONS	Dwarfs 15 cm (6 in) tall, 30 cm (12 in) wide; tall types 60 cm (2 ft) tall, 30 cm (1 ft) wide

BEGONIA
Begonia spp.

HARDINESS:
Tender

PREFERRED SOIL pH:
Near neutral

PREFERRED SOIL TYPE:
Well-drained, fertile

PREFERRED LIGHT:
Sun to partial shade

Continuously flowering wax begonias like 'Pink Powderpuff' are ideal edging plants.

Begonia in the Landscape

The beauty of begonias lies in their versatility. At 30 cm (1 ft) high or under, sun-loving, mound-shaped wax begonias are veterans of containers and favorites for edging shrub beds or mixing with other small annuals. These fibrous-rooted plants tolerate shade, drought, and humidity and spend the entire season smothered in a wealth of handsome little open-faced flowers. The waxy, rounded leaves are either deep emerald green or luscious bronze, but they are always half buried beneath snow white, pink, rose, or red blossoms with contrasting yellow centers.

Begonias like 'President Carnot', above, contribute nonstop foliage color to gardens.

Improving on Perfection

There are many different types of wax begonias sold in spring. If you prefer green leaves, look for the Wings mix with a range of flower colors and quite stunning wide, open-faced single flowers. For unique bronze foliage, try the dwarf Cocktail series, which remains 18–20 cm (7–8 in) tall. For many-petaled, spectacular flowers, look for 'Queen', which is also available in a range of attractive, vibrant colors.

Tuberous begonias brighten shady nooks with rose-shaped flowers in warm colors.

Growing Wax Begonias

Whatever you select, wax begonias appreciate fluffy soil enriched with compost or leaf mold, and they will flower continuously when fertilized throughout the growing season with a balanced formula, such as 20-20-20, applied every 3 weeks. Water when the soil dries and trim plants as needed to keep them neatly shaped. Of all begonias, wax begonias are the least susceptible to diseases and insects. If ragged holes appear in leaves, slugs are the likely culprits. Control these mollusks by putting out commercial traps or shallow saucers of beer, which lure and drown slugs.

You can easily increase your stock of wax begonias by rooting 8 cm (3 in) long stem cuttings in a pot of moist potting soil. To keep your favorite plants from freezing, dig them up in fall, pot, and overwinter indoors on a sunny windowsill.

Tuberous Begonia for Outdoors

While wax begonias are the queens of the bedding scene, the shade-loving tuberous begonias, with their large, roselike blossoms and deep green maple-shaped leaves, are head-turning accent plants for beds and containers. They come in many sizes and growth habits. The 30 cm (12 in) wide Nonstop hybrids produce masses of double and semidouble 5–8 cm (2–3 in) diameter blossoms in yellow, orange, red, burgundy, and pink virtually all summer. For breathtaking container plants, look for varieties with double blossoms in a solid color, or with petals edged in another color, such as 'Pacific Giant'. Giant Cascade Doubles yield a shower of 13 cm (5 in) wide blossoms in red, white, orange, pink, or yellow.

You can either buy potted plants or start your own from tubers, indoors in early spring, setting them just below the surface of moist, peat-moss-enriched soil. Set the pots in a sunny window and move them outdoors when the weather is warm. Keep tuberous begonias in partial shade and water them as soon as the soil is dry. Discourage disease by removing shriveled leaves and blossoms. Keep the foliage dry when watering to avoid sunburn and powdery mildew. Remove and dispose of infected leaves and move infected plants to a dry, airy location.

To overwinter tubers, allow the soil in the pots to dry in fall, then remove and store the dormant tubers in paper bags filled with dry peat moss, in a cool, dark place, until time to start them the following spring. Foliage and cane types, such as 'President Carnot', normally grown as house plants, can also be planted in the shade for the summer.

FUNDAMENTAL FACTS

ATTRIBUTES	Season-long flowers, neat plants; use for beds, baskets, and containers
SEASON OF INTEREST	Summer to fall
FAVORITES	Wax begonia 'Wings', 'Cocktail', and double 'Queen'; tuberous Nonstop hybrids, and Giant Cascade Doubles
QUIRKS	Wet leaves turn dry and brown in strong sun
GOOD NEIGHBORS	Impatiens, petunias, Shasta daisies, scabiosa
WHERE IT GROWS BEST	Partial shade with crumbly, fertile soil
POTENTIAL PROBLEMS	Powdery mildew, sunburn, slugs
SOURCE	Cuttings, seeds, tubers
DIMENSIONS	Wax 20–35 cm (8–14 in) tall and wide; tuberous 30 cm (1 ft) tall, 0.3–1 m (1–3 ft) wide

BORAGE

Borago officinalis

HARDINESS:
Frost tolerant

PREFERRED SOIL pH:
Near neutral

PREFERRED SOIL TYPE:
Fertile, well-drained

PREFERRED LIGHT:
Sun

The sky blue, nodding flowers of borage enliven gardens from spring to late summer.

Borage in the Landscape

There's an old New England saying that proclaims, "A garden without borage is like a heart without courage." At one time, this ornamental herb found its way into almost every piece of cultivated land because once you plant borage, it will self-seed and always stay with you. But then, with handsome, oval, edible leaves that taste like cucumber, crowned by a constant supply of sky blue or white, star-shaped blossoms, borage is one plant you'll want to keep around.

Standing 60 cm (2 ft) tall when in flower, borage adapts to many situations. Because its leaves are edible, borage is usually linked with herb gardens. The leaves are often tossed in salads, tasting best when they're young and tender. Starting in late spring, the blossoms provide a welcome splash of soft blue color that combines well with the purple-tinged leaves of lavender and purple-leaf common sage, and with the silver foliage of artemisia and dusty miller. Borage is equally appropriate in the herb garden and the perennial border, where it pops up in a different place every year but always looks great whether it appears beside the peonies or the iris.

Increasing the Bounty

Borage is easy to grow from seed. Chill the seeds in a refrigerator for a week before sowing directly in the garden in early spring. Even though established borage enthusiastically self-seeds, it is not invasive. If you have extra seedlings, or if borage happens to be where it isn't wanted, dig the seedlings when they're small and transplant them with care. Wait for a cloudy day, moisten the soil around a plant several hours in advance, dig a circle 15 cm (6 in) in diameter around the plant, and gently lift the seedling and surrounding soil. Transplant immediately, watering the seedling liberally when it's positioned in its new home. Shade the transplant for several days and continue to water regularly. In a week it should be safely settled in. On the West Coast, borage can be grown as a winter annual.

Growing Borage

Borage grows best in full sun, but it tolerates partial shade in the afternoon. It doesn't require fertile soil, but moisture-retentive soil is a definite asset. If direct-seeded in early spring, the plants send up flower stalks in early summer and continue to bloom for several months. If you don't want the plant to self-seed, clip off the flowers after they fade. Borage often wilts on hot days but will spring back to life when the sun sets.

Like many herbs, borage isn't bothered by diseases and is rarely pestered by insects, although slugs will occasionally chew holes in the foliage. If you see smooth-edged holes in the leaves, set out a commercial slug trap or a shallow saucer filled with beer at sundown to trap these nocturnal feeders. Attracted by the yeasty smell, the slugs will climb into the saucer and drown.

Borage, with edible leaves and plentiful flowers, is at home in both herb and flower beds.

FUNDAMENTAL FACTS

ATTRIBUTES	Edible leaves, blue star-shaped blossoms; for herb or flower garden
SEASON OF INTEREST	Early summer to frost
FAVORITES	Blue-flowered species; white-flowered 'Alba'
QUIRKS	Chill seeds for 1 week before planting
GOOD NEIGHBORS	Lavender, purple-leaf sage, peonies, iris
WHERE IT GROWS BEST	Fertile, humus-rich soil; full sun
POTENTIAL PROBLEMS	Slugs
CRITTER RESISTANCE	Good
SOURCE	Seeds
DIMENSIONS	60 cm (2 ft) tall, 60 cm (2 ft) wide

The starlike flowers of 'Blue Troll' browallia are set off by contrasting white centers, or eyes.

BROWALLIA

Browallia speciosa
B. americana

HARDINESS:
Tender

PREFERRED SOIL pH:
Neutral to slightly alkaline

PREFERRED SOIL TYPE:
Fertile, well-drained

PREFERRED LIGHT:
Partial shade

Browallia in the Landscape

When a plant performs well in a container, it wins general acclaim. But when that plant also bears quantities of purplish blue, 2.5 cm (1 in) wide, star-shaped blossoms, it becomes an instant hero. Browallias combine well with other shade-loving plants, and give contrast of form and color when grown beside tuberous begonias. The browallia palette also includes white-flowered plants, which are welcome to brighten the partly shaded garden niches preferred by this serene summer bloomer.

Although they make good bedding plants, browallias are often grown in pots. In partial shade, their deep green, 2.5 cm (1 in) long leaves form a tidy mound that spills over the edge of a window box, hanging basket, or whatever container you choose to plant them in. Browallia is a pretty sight even without blossoms, but add the profusion of flowers and you have something truly spectacular.

Selecting the Right Browallia

For prime performance, most browallias grow best in partial shade and with regular watering to prevent wilt. Those conditions please the deep indigo-flowering 'Heavenly Bells' and its white counterpart, 'Silver Bells'. If you occasionally miss a day when watering your containers, or if you have dry growing conditions in your garden, opt for the more drought-tolerant, compact-growing 'Amethyst Bells', which has purple blossoms accented by white centers.

Another browallia has recently stepped into the limelight. *B. americana* 'Cascade Sky Blue' is an interesting variation that produces quantities of 1.3 cm (1/2 in) pale violet-blue, star-shaped flowers on plants that form a compact 30–60 cm (1–2 ft) mound. 'Cascade Sky Blue' flowers from early spring until fall and tolerates either sun or shade.

Growing Browallia

The beauty of browallias is that they require so little fuss. But for best results, keep the soil they grow in moderately moist and fertilize regularly. It's easy to see when they are in need: Browallias quickly wilt when thirsty, and the leaves fade to a light green color when they need fertilizer. To keep plants green and in continuous bloom, provide containers with a weekly application of balanced fertilizer, such as a 20-20-20 formulation. Browallias are not prone to insect problems other than occasional bouts

Compact browallias light up hard-to-plant shady nooks with their profuse flowers.

of tiny, pear-shaped, sap-sucking aphids, which can be controlled with insecticidal soap.

Increasing the Bounty

You can buy browallias as bedding plants in spring or easily grow them from seed. Sow seeds indoors 10–12 weeks before the last frost. The seeds need light to germinate, so sprinkle them on the surface of a container filled with commercial seed-starting soil moistened lightly with a mister. Set the container on a sunny windowsill or under fluorescent lights, where the soil temperature will stay between 18° and 21°C (65° and 70°F), and keep the soil moist until the seeds sprout. Transplant seedlings into pots when they have two to three sets of mature leaves. Remove growing tips to encourage branching. Growing new plants from stem cuttings is not recommended.

FUNDAMENTAL FACTS

ATTRIBUTES	Blue or white, star-shaped blossoms on compact or cascading plants; for pots, boxes, baskets, beds
SEASON OF INTEREST	Summer to fall
FAVORITES	Blue-flowered 'Heavenly Bells'; white-flowered 'Silver Bells', drought-tolerant 'Amethyst Bells'
QUIRKS	Needs watering to avoid wilt in hot weather
GOOD NEIGHBORS	Tuberous begonias, flowering tobacco, petunias
WHERE IT GROWS BEST	Partial shade; moist soil
POTENTIAL PROBLEMS	Aphids
CRITTER RESISTANCE	Good
SOURCE	Bedding plants, seeds
DIMENSIONS	30–60 cm (1–2 ft) tall, 30–45 cm (1–1.5 ft) wide

BUTTER DAISY

Melampodium paludosum

HARDINESS:
Tender

PREFERRED SOIL pH:
Near neutral to slightly alkaline

PREFERRED SOIL TYPE:
Fertile, well-drained

PREFERRED LIGHT:
Sun

Butter Daisy in the Landscape

In some places you just crave sizzle and plenty of it. And that's the spot for butter daisies. Exceptionally easy to grow, with phenomenally prolific blossom output, butter daisies always seem to be dappled with 2.5 cm (1 in) wide sunshine-colored and sun-shaped flowers against a background of green triangular leaves. Sometimes called African zinnia or medallion flower, butter daisies are especially valued because they deliver their punch in small portions. Plants grow only 20–60 cm (8–24 in) tall with a similar spread, so their vivid hue works as an accent rather than monopolizing the scene.

Growing Butter Daisy

Butter daisies demand sun. Once that requirement is met, they're perfectly happy to branch out and blossom despite humidity, drought, and sweltering heat. In fact, they bask in hot weather and beg for more. They're self-cleaning, so your time won't be wasted with removing spent flowers. All these qualifications make butter

Butter daisies flower despite heat, humidity, and drought. No deadheading is ever required.

daisies ideal candidates for edging borders or hot driveways, filling sun-drenched hanging baskets, or growing in containers.

A Little Smaller, a Bit Bigger

Comparatively tall 'Medallion' grows to 38 cm (15 in) under normal conditions but will expand to 60 cm (2 ft) where the soil is rich, all the while covering its branching stems with a bounty of golden blooms. Or, if space is tight, take the opposite tack and opt for the dwarf 20 cm (8 in) tall 'Derby' to provide a bite-sized nugget of color. If you need flowers fast, 25 cm (10 in) tall 'Million Gold' rushes to the rescue with a profusion of flowers in less than 60 days after being started from seed.

Increasing the Bounty

The fastest way to grow butter daisies is from seeds sown indoors or directly in warm garden soil. For a head start, sow seed indoors 8 weeks before your last spring frost date. Cover the seeds lightly, and keep them moist and in a dark spot until they germinate. Then whisk them immediately into bright light and plant outdoors when the soil warms.

Butter daisies develop a long taproot that anchors the plants in the soil and gives them an edge against

drought. However, that same trait makes transplanting difficult when the plants gain maturity. Transplant butter daisies to their permanent home early and water them regularly until they become established. When they're comfortably situated, they'll withstand drought.

Growing Butter Daisy

Lime-loving butter daisies prefer a neutral to slightly alkaline, well-drained soil. When grown in beds, butter daisies often reseed, with seedlings appearing late in spring, after the soil is warm. Although they do endure drought, watering when the soil dries prevents stress. Stressed butter daisies can fall victim to sap-sucking whiteflies or aphids. To get rid of these pests, rinse them from the foliage with a strong stream of water from the hose and spray plants with insecticidal soap.

FUNDAMENTAL FACTS

ATTRIBUTES	Deep green heart-shaped leaves dappled with small golden daisies; for beds, hanging baskets, or containers
SEASON OF INTEREST	Early summer to fall
FAVORITES	'Medallion' for a broad spread; 'Derby' for miniature size; 'Million Gold' for quick flowers
QUIRKS	Transplant when young because of long taproot
GOOD NEIGHBORS	Ageratum, gomphrena, sunflower, tithonia, zinnia
WHERE IT GROWS BEST	Full sun in warm climates
POTENTIAL PROBLEMS	Whiteflies, aphids
CRITTER RESISTANCE	Good
SOURCE	Seeds
DIMENSIONS	20–38 cm (8–15 in) tall, to 60 cm (2 ft) wide

The compact, flower-covered mounds of butter daisies make admirable edging plants for sun-baked walks or driveways, or for growing in containers and baskets.

CALENDULA
Calendula officinalis

HARDINESS:
Frost tolerant

PREFERRED SOIL pH:
Neutral to slightly acidic

PREFERRED SOIL TYPE:
Fertile, well-drained

PREFERRED LIGHT:
Sun

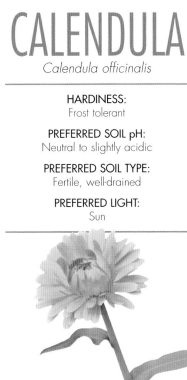

The ruffled petals of the calendula flower unfold from a central disk like petals of a daisy.

Calendula in the Landscape

Affectionately known as pot marigolds, calendulas radiate cheerful, bold, yellow or orange flowers above fresh green foliage. Taller varieties are at home in informal borders, whereas the shorter ones work well in containers and along the fronts of beds. In regions where summer is cool, calendulas bloom reliably from early summer to fall. Where winters are mild, pot marigolds will continue to flower and can be used as winter annuals.

Calendula flowers look like daisies, with a central disk surrounded by a ray of petals. There are numerous variations on this theme, including forms

Short varieties of calendula create a swath of pure gold when planted in a mass.

with single, semidouble, or fully double flowers in colors ranging from bright orange to lemon yellow to creamy parchment. Some varieties have a thin edging of sepia or a touch of pink in their petals. Ranging in height from 30 to 75 cm (12 to 30 in), the long-stemmed calendulas make great cut flowers.

In beds, weave calendulas among upright-growing blue-flowered plants, such as larkspur, bachelor's button, browallia, and borage, or mix them with the soft purple flowers of anise hyssop. Nasturtiums and other plants with yellow to orange flowers also combine well.

Calendula petals are edible, and their bright color is especially eye-catching when sprinkled over cream sauces, white rice, or potatoes. Calendula petals can be used as an inexpensive substitute for saffron coloring in some dishes, but the petals lack saffron's unique bitter, tangy taste.

New Colors and Sizes

Packets of calendula seeds may include a single color or a mixture of hues. The Kablouna series grows to 60 cm (24 in) tall. The flowers have prominent central disks and short,

shaggy petals that make the blossoms resemble strawflowers. Within the series, the 'Lemon Cream' variety is particularly attractive. The flowers have a bright yellow eye surrounded by white petals edged in yellow. The Prince series has double flowers with long stems, making them ideal for cutting. Where compact plants are needed, try the 30 cm (12 in) tall Bon Bon Mix or the 20 cm (8 in) tall 'Calypso', which is available in either orange or yellow.

Growing Calendula

You can grow calendulas from seed or start with bedding plants purchased at a garden center. Both prefer cool temperatures, so get an early start. Start seed indoors 4 weeks before your last frost. Sow the seeds on moist potting medium, covering with enough soil to provide darkness. Keep the soil moist and at room temperature until the seedlings have several sets of leaves. Set out seedlings or bedding plants at about the time the last frost passes. Calendulas benefit from a half-strength application of a balanced fertilizer, such as 10-10-10, well mixed into the soil prior to planting. Water as needed to keep the soil barely moist,

and surround plants with an 8 cm (3 in) thick layer of organic mulch, such as compost or leaf mold, to conserve soil moisture.

Snip off fading flowers regularly to encourage branching and flowering. Late in summer, when days are hot and nights cool, leaves may develop white powdery patches, a symptom of the fungal disease powdery mildew. Clip off disfigured leaves, or dispose of plants that are badly affected. While calendulas are virtually insect free, the leaves and flower buds can be munched, beginning in spring, by small green caterpillars called cabbage loopers, which double up like inch-worms as they move. Spray young loopers with the biological insecticide BT (*Bacillus thuringiensis*) as directed.

FUNDAMENTAL FACTS

ATTRIBUTES	Daisy-shaped flowers in bright shades of yellow or orange; use dwarf varieties in containers and window boxes; grow long-stemmed varieties in beds
SEASON OF INTEREST	Summer to fall
FAVORITES	'Lemon Cream' for color; 'Prince' series for cutting; compact Bon Bon Mix, 'Calypso' for containers
QUIRKS	May stop blooming in very hot weather
GOOD NEIGHBORS	Ageratum, borage, dusty miller, forget-me-not, bachelor's button, larkspur, nasturtium
WHERE IT GROWS BEST	Fertile, well-drained, sunny sites; cool climate
POTENTIAL PROBLEMS	Powdery mildew, cabbage loopers
CRITTER RESISTANCE	Good
SOURCE	Bedding plants, seeds
DIMENSIONS	20–75 cm (8–30 in) tall and in 30–45 cm (12–18 in) wide

CASTOR BEAN

Ricinus communis

HARDINESS:
Tender

PREFERRED SOIL pH:
Adaptable

PREFERRED SOIL TYPE:
Average, well-drained

PREFERRED LIGHT:
Sun

Bristly red blossoms and red-veined leaves distinguish the castor bean 'Carmencita'.

Castor Bean in the Landscape

Fast-growing castor bean plants are worth growing for their immense star-shaped burgundy or green leaves, which cast a spell of jungle magic over any garden. Castor bean's strange clusters of bristly red or pink flowers open in late summer and are followed by round pods covered with colorful spines, which contain bean-sized mottled seeds.

In a warm summer with plenty of rain, these dramatic plants can reach 3–3.7 m (10–12 ft) in height, with leaves up to 60 cm (2 ft) in diameter that may be bright green or bronze red, depending on the variety. If you need a fast-growing screen to block bad views or a giant self-supporting hedge, or you want to form a leafy background for a flower bed, no other annual or perennial will do the job like castor bean plants. And because the stems are spaced rather far apart, sufficient light reaches the insides of the plants to accommodate vines such as morning glories, which twine around the central stem for surprising special effects. Castor bean plants also work well as a leafy backdrop for larger-than-life flowering annuals such as love-lies-bleeding (amaranth), tall zinnias, or sunflowers.

Comely Castor Bean

You'll find that seed companies offer a few cultivars, but any gardener who grows castor beans will surely have a few seeds or volunteer seedlings to share. In the spring you can purchase bedding plants from garden centers. The 'Carmencita' variety has very large deep mahogany leaves and unusually large bright red flowers. 'Carmencita Pink' has pink flowers, while the flowers of Impala mix are carmine with maroon, followed by maroon seed pods.

Castor beans quickly reach human proportions, lending a look of maturity to new beds.

Growing Castor Bean

Start castor beans indoors 10 weeks before your last frost, taking care to wear gloves when handling the poisonous seeds. In areas with warm and long summers, you can plant the seeds directly outdoors. Soak the seeds for 24 hours in warm water before planting them 2.5 cm (1 in) deep in moist soil. Keep the soil moist and between 16° and 21°C (60° and 70°F). Sprouting, or germination, should begin within 15 days, and the seedlings can be planted out after the soil warms in late spring.

Castor beans do not require fertile soil, but the garden spot where you plant them should be loose and friable for at least 30 cm (12 in) deep so that the roots of seedlings can grow deeply. If their roots cannot penetrate the soil, a summer storm can blow these tall-growing beauties down. Space or thin seedlings to 1 m (3 ft) apart in the garden.

Because castor bean seeds are poisonous, a strong case can be made for not growing them in gardens visited by children. As an extra safety precaution, you can snip off the flowers before they set seed pods and dispose of them, since the seeds are the toxic part of the plants.

To their credit, pests of all kinds avoid castor beans, and also may ignore nearby plants. The seeds are widely believed to repel moles when dropped into mole tunnels.

FUNDAMENTAL FACTS

ATTRIBUTES	Large, fast-growing plants; use as screen, at back of border, with tall companion plants
SEASON OF INTEREST	Midsummer to frost
FAVORITES	'Carmencita' for burgundy leaves; 'Carmencita Pink' for pink flowers; 'Impala' for maroon seed pods
QUIRKS	All parts of the plant are toxic if ingested
GOOD NEIGHBORS	Amaranth, morning glory, sunflower, zinnia
WHERE IT GROWS BEST	Full sun, in warm, well-drained soil
POTENTIAL PROBLEMS	Wind can topple large plants
CRITTER RESISTANCE	Excellent
SOURCE	Bedding plants, seeds
DIMENSIONS	2.4 m (8 ft) tall, 1.2 m (4 ft) wide

When stems are pinched back in early summer, plants grow compact and flower heavily.

CHRYSANTHEMUM

Dendranthema x grandiflorum

Chrysanthemum in the Landscape

Chrysanthemums are the benchmark annuals for fall, whether grown in containers or beds. The "garden mums" sold in late summer bloom outdoors with enthusiasm and also make long-lasting cut flowers, staying fresh in a vase for 2 weeks or longer.

Many mums make fine garden perennials. These are usually different varieties from the mums that have been bred to provide instant fall color on leafy, well-branched plants of uniform size. Perennials include the many-colored Prophet series. 'Red Bravo', dark lavender 'Debonair', and numerous yellows including 'Jessica' are also popular. The longest-lasting bloomers will have the word "decorative" on the plant tag. This describes the flower form, a dahlia-type blossom packed with petals, in which the new petals emerging from the center of blossoms magically give week-old flowers a freshly opened appearance.

HARDINESS:
Tender

PREFERRED SOIL pH:
Near neutral

PREFERRED SOIL TYPE:
Well-drained, fertile

PREFERRED LIGHT:
Sun to partial shade

Flowers come in striking colors, such as the brilliant 'Crimson Yvonne Arnaud', above.

Preferred Perennials

If you live in Zones 7 and 8, try growing cold-hardy chrysanthemums as perennials. At 75 cm (30 in) tall, 'Single Apricot', also known as 'Hillside Sheffield Pink', requires little care and puts on a beautiful show each fall. For best results, order starter plants from mail-order catalogs and plant them in early summer so that they will be well rooted by winter.

Growing Chrysanthemum

When buying fall-blooming mums, select plants covered with buds. To reduce the frequency of watering, move mums into slightly larger pots. You can display mums in a shady spot, but shade sometimes causes the flowers to open unevenly. If you want to overwinter a potted mum, let it dry out and turn brown, but do not trim off the dead stems. Move the pot to a cool place and water to keep the soil barely moist. If the plant survives, small green shoots will appear at its base in early spring. Trim off the dead stems just before setting out the plant shortly after your last spring frost.

To keep growing plants compact and encourage maximum flowering, cut them back by half their height in

In addition to familiar pompons, mums come in elegant, spidery daisy shapes.

midsummer. For more mums, simply insert the cuttings into a pot of damp potting soil, set it in a shady place and keep the soil moist until the cuttings show new top growth, then transplant them into the garden. If plants begin to set buds before you want them to, delay flowering by pinching off buds up to the middle of August. If plants become crowded, divide and replant as you would any perennial (see the maintenance chapter).

Except for small sap-sucking thrips and aphids, and grasshoppers, mums have few pest problems. Knock thrips and aphids off with a spray of water or apply insecticidal soap as directed. Handpick grasshoppers, or tolerate their damage, because they are unstoppable in a populous year. Mums growing in hot, humid conditions can contract fungal ray blight, which causes flowers to turn brown and limp. Replace affected plants with healthy ones.

FUNDAMENTAL FACTS

ATTRIBUTES	Flowers in white, yellow, pink, red, and purple; use in containers or beds
SEASON OF INTEREST	Fall
FAVORITES	Multicolored Prophet series; 'Single Apricot' to grow as a perennial
QUIRKS	Blooms when days become short in the fall
GOOD NEIGHBORS	Asters, ornamental cabbage and kale, ornamental grasses, pansies
WHERE IT GROWS BEST	All climates and exposures
POTENTIAL PROBLEMS	Aphids, grasshoppers
CRITTER RESISTANCE	Good except for grasshoppers
SOURCE	Stem cuttings, division
DIMENSIONS	Potted mums less than 45 cm (18 in) tall, 38 cm (15 in) wide

COCKSCOMB

Celosia argentea

HARDINESS:
Tender

PREFERRED SOIL pH:
Adaptable

PREFERRED SOIL TYPE:
Average

PREFERRED LIGHT:
Sun

Cockscomb in the Landscape

Cockscomb are custom made for places with hot, sunny summers. This varied group of easy-to-grow annuals enriches the garden with vibrant colors and unusual flower forms. The most versatile types, called plume celosias, develop upright, fluffy flower spikes shaped like candle flames in yellow, red, pink, apricot, and orange. Cockscomb celosias have the same color range and broad pointed leaves of the plume types, but the flowers

Celosia 'Century Yellow' produces fluffy golden flamelike flowers.

The feathery flower plumes of cockscomb accent sunny flower beds.

resemble a rooster's comb. A taller, airier type, called wheat celosias, produces soft pink spikes that blend beautifully in the garden and make excellent cut flowers.

When designing annual flower beds, put each type of celosia to best use. Plume celosias bring an unusual color and texture to the garden, and yellow plumes in particular are fun to intersperse among flowers of various species to visually unify diversified plantings. Cockscomb celosias always attract attention, so grow them where their curious flowers are easily admired. Mass wheat celosias near the rear of sunny borders where they can work as a soft backdrop for other summer flowers.

Choice Cockscombs

Among plume types, the Castle series is invaluable for its lush, feathery, 38 cm (15 in) tall flower spikes. The spikes of the Century series are taller,

to 50 cm (20 in), and are favorites of gardeners who gather and dry the plumes for winter flower arrangements. The strongest color in cockscomb celosias is a rich red, and varieties that also show red tinting in their leaves such as 'Prestige Scarlet' contrast beautifully with any yellow, white, or blue bedfellows. Wheat celosias such as 'Pink Candle' and 'Purple Flamingo' grow 1–1.2 m (3–4 ft) tall and have narrow leaves and smaller, more lightweight flower spikes. Naturally upright wheat cockscombs never need staking and can tolerate drier soil conditions than the other types.

Growing Cockscomb

Cockscombs are widely available as spring bedding plants, or you can sow seeds. Start seeds indoors 8 weeks before your last frost. Sprinkle them over moist seed-starting medium and barely cover the seeds. Keep the soil moist and at room temperature until the seedlings have several sets of mature leaves. Transplant or sow seeds directly in the garden about 2 weeks

Pink 'Flamingo Feather', a wheat-type celosia, is a long-flowering garden cultivar.

FUNDAMENTAL FACTS	
ATTRIBUTES	Red, yellow, orange, or pink crested, plumed or spiked flowers; for beds
SEASON OF INTEREST	Midsummer to fall
FAVORITES	'Castle' or 'Century' for plumed type; 'Prestige Scarlet' for red flowers, reddish leaves; 'Pink Candle' wheat celosia
QUIRKS	Individual flower clusters last for weeks in garden
GOOD NEIGHBORS	All summer annuals, from ageratum to zinnias
WHERE IT GROWS BEST	Warm summer regions in fertile, sun-drenched soil
POTENTIAL PROBLEMS	Spider mites, prolonged drought
CRITTER RESISTANCE	Good
SOURCE	Seeds
DIMENSIONS	20–100 cm (8–40 in) tall, 30 cm (12 in) wide

after the last frost. Cockscombs germinate best in temperatures above 18°C (65°F). Transplant or thin seedlings to 30 cm (12 in) apart. The stems of young seedlings are often the same color as the flowers they will produce, which is an advantage when placing them in the garden.

Give young plants enough water to keep the soil consistently moist. Celosias wilt if the soil becomes too dry, but water will quickly revive them. Fertilize plants once with a balanced, granular, controlled-release fertilizer, or fertilize monthly with a water-soluble plant food. Remove fading flowers to promote the development of fresh blossoms. Should red spider mites, minute sap-sucking spider relatives, feed on leaf undersides, giving them a webbed, pale, stippled appearance, rinse them off with forceful, daily sprays of water from a hose or apply insecticidal soap.

Coleus with predominantly lime-colored leaves combine well with plants of all other colors.

COLEUS

Solenostemon hybrids

HARDINESS:
Tender

PREFERRED SOIL pH:
Adaptable

PREFERRED SOIL TYPE:
Loam

PREFERRED LIGHT:
Shade to partial shade

Coleus in the Landscape

If you want a dash of care-free color, plant coleus. The brightly variegated leaves are the real reason for growing coleus, and what a range of festive shades! Coleus leaves are speckled, splashed, banded, rimmed, and streaked with nearly every color and combination of colors imaginable including copper, deep maroon, pink, white, chartreuse, yellow, and orange. Leaf size and shape vary, too, from the tiny ruffled foliage of 'Duckfoot' to 20 cm (8 in) long leaves for big cultivars, such as 'Atlas'. Upright-growing dwarf coleus, such as 'India Frills', are perfect planted 30 cm (1 ft) apart as a 30 cm (12 in) tall colorful hedge.

Saber-leaved coleus are named for their unusually narrow, toothed leaves.

The larger, upright 60–90 cm (2–3 ft) tall versions, such as simmering pink-and-yellow-leaved 'Alabama Sunset', can fill in the middle or back of a shady border. Medium-sized coleus are often planted in perennial gardens to act as "accessories," providing a touch of color to echo the flower colors in companion perennials. Spreading plants such as 'Duckfoot' and the more common upright-growing coleus are custom-made for pots, and always make a big splash.

Not Just for Shade Anymore

Originally, coleus were only planted in warm shade, and the older varieties, such as 'Pineapple Queen', will scorch badly in full sun and show painfully slow growth. But many of the newer coleus varieties tolerate bright light, provided they receive enough water to prevent wilting. Still, in strong sun it's best to steer clear of coleus with pale yellow, white, or cream in the leaves and choose more sun-tolerant red-leaved varieties.

Increasing the Bounty

Coleus are easy to grow from cuttings. Simply snip a branch long enough to have three sets of leaves and place the lower, leafless 5 cm (2 in) of stem in a glass of water. Roots begin to sprout within 2 weeks. Pot the cutting as soon as roots develop, set the pot where it will be shaded, and water it generously for several weeks until new growth appears. Then you can move the young plant into a container or into the garden when the soil warms. Prized plants can be wintered over by rooting cuttings before the first frost in fall, potting and placing them on a sunny windowsill indoors.

It's easy to grow coleus from seed, but the choice of varieties is limited, and plants are generally less vigorous than named varieties grown from cuttings. Sow seed indoors 8 to 10 weeks before the last frost. Seeds need light to sprout, or germinate, so sprinkle them on the surface of moist, well-drained soil. Keep the soil moist and seeds will germinate in 1 to 2 weeks. Thin or transplant seedlings, preferably into individual cell-paks, when they have several sets of mature leaves.

Growing Coleus

Coleus are very tender and will be damaged by the slightest frost, so wait until the soil warms in spring to plant them outdoors. As summer heats up, coleus need plenty of water. Dry plants wilt readily, so you'll know when it's time to water. When growing coleus in containers, use a large

Red-spangled leaves denote 'Pineapplette'.

pot with plenty of room for roots. To encourage side branching, snip off the growing tips once or twice in early summer. Although coleus produce tiny blue flowers at the stem tips, many gardeners feel the flowers detract from the leaves and clip them off. The only pests to bother coleus are aphids and whiteflies, which are more prevalent indoors than out and are easily treated with insecticidal soap applied according to package directions.

FUNDAMENTAL FACTS

ATTRIBUTES	Multicolored leaves; for beds or containers
SEASON OF INTEREST	Early summer to fall
FAVORITES	Miniatures 'India Frills', 'Duckfoot'; medium Wizard mix, 'Brilliant Red'; 'Purple Emperor'
QUIRKS	Needs warm soil; plant outside in early summer
GOOD NEIGHBORS	Flowering tobacco, hosta, pansies
WHERE IT GROWS BEST	Shade or partial shade
POTENTIAL PROBLEMS	Aphids, whiteflies
CRITTER RESISTANCE	Good
SOURCE	Bedding plants, cuttings
DIMENSIONS	Dwarfs 30 cm (12 in) tall; others from 60–90 cm (2–3 ft) tall and wide

A care-free meadow is as easy as scattering a cosmos seed and sand mixture on soil.

Large flowers and lacy foliage are a bonus of drought-tolerant garden cosmos.

COSMOS
Cosmos spp.

HARDINESS:
Frost tolerant

PREFERRED SOIL pH:
Adaptable

PREFERRED SOIL TYPE:
Moderately fertile, well-drained

PREFERRED LIGHT:
Sun

Cosmos in the Landscape

When you want vivid garden color without a lot of fuss, look no further than cosmos. Native to Mexico, cosmos are a North American success story, well suited to lean soils and fluctuating weather. These plants have the airy look of a wildflower, standing 0.6–1.2 m (2–4 ft) tall and producing a bevy of white, pink, magenta, red, burgundy, bright yellow, or red-orange daisy-shaped flowers, each with a yellow center. Below the flowers, the leaves are lacy and finely cut, making them a perfect accent for blossoms that linger for weeks.

Even a small garden patch devoted to cosmos is a beautiful sight, especially when courted by butterflies. Intersperse tall varieties with other tall annuals or perennials in beds, or grow midsized cosmos in containers or in gaps in beds where you need a quick flower to fill in empty space. Some of the tall varieties may need staking, or you can grow them in close company with stiff upright flowers such as cleome or tall zinnias, whose stems will keep the cosmos propped up. Compact and dwarf varieties require almost no maintenance beyond clipping off the spent blossoms.

A Cosmos of a Different Color

The most popular cosmos is *Cosmos bipinnatus*, often called garden cosmos. This species adapts to cool weather and blooms in white, red, and many shades of pink. The 0.6 m (2 ft) tall Sonata multicolored mix is tremendously versatile. 'Candy Stripes' is taller with white flowers edged in crimson, while Seashells mix has unique rolled petals, also in a range of light pink to red shades. A different species of cosmos (*C. sulphureus*), often called sulphur cosmos, blooms in bright yellow, orange, red, and bicolors. The varieties 'Bright Lights', 'Cosmic Orange', and 'Lemon Twist' have a better appetite for hot weather than garden cosmos do.

Increasing the Bounty

To grow either type of cosmos as a wildflower, simply mix the contents of a packet of seeds with an equal amount of sand and broadcast them, scooping up handfuls of the mixture and tossing it with a broad, sweeping gesture onto cultivated, weed-free soil. Garden cosmos will germinate in cool soil, so you can sow seeds around the time of your last spring frost. Sulphur

cosmos is slightly more tender and should be started indoors about 6 weeks before the last frost date. If you are concerned about root damage, you can transplant the seedlings into individual cell-packs to minimize root damage at planting time.

Growing Cosmos

Cosmos benefit from soil that is loamy and deeply dug, but they need little, if any, fertilizer, even in poor soil. Dry conditions promote strong growth, and too much moisture can lead to root and stem rot. To prevent these and other diseases, it is wise to rotate cosmos by planting them in a different location every season.

If you find chewed flowers, hand-pick beetles in the morning when they are sluggish, or spray an insecticide labeled for cosmos containing the botanical insecticide pyrethrum.

FUNDAMENTAL FACTS	
ATTRIBUTES	Lacy foliage; white, pink, purple, yellow, or red daisylike flowers; for borders or pots
SEASON OF INTEREST	Early summer to fall
FAVORITES	Sonata mix, white and pink flowers; Seashells mix; fiery 'Bright Lights', 'Cosmic Orange' for orange and red flowers; yellow sulphur cosmos
QUIRKS	Grows poorly in damp, overly fertile soil
GOOD NEIGHBORS	Cleome, purple coneflower, gomphrena, salvia, zinnia
WHERE IT GROWS BEST	Sunny, modestly fertile, well-drained soil
POTENTIAL PROBLEMS	Stem or root rot in wet soil; beetles
CRITTER RESISTANCE	Good
SOURCE	Seeds
DIMENSIONS	0.6–1.2 m (2–4 ft) tall, 0.3 m (1 ft) wide

The silvery leaves of dusty miller provide a neutral background for colorful flowers.

DUSTY MILLER

Senecio cineraria

HARDINESS:
Frost tolerant

PREFERRED SOIL pH:
Adaptable

PREFERRED SOIL TYPE:
Any well-drained soil

PREFERRED LIGHT:
Sun

Dusty Miller in the Landscape

Not every plant was meant to be a star. Instead, some plants are used to make their showier neighbors look good, and playing the supporting role is the job at which dusty miller excels. The outstanding feature of this plant is its luminous silver, felt-textured leaves, which look as if they are covered with dust. In the sunshine, where dusty miller grows best, the silvery leaves shimmer and accent any plant that is growing around them, especially bedfellows with blue, pink, and yellow flowers, such as chrysanthemums, browallia, dianthus, and pansies. Because of its light-reflecting qualities, dusty miller works its magic wherever it is planted.

Dusty miller illuminates the garden without requiring exacting care. Standing only 30–45 cm (12–18 in) tall, the plants require no pruning and rarely need grooming except to remove aged, browning leaves. Dusty miller withstands drought without wilting and multiplies without encouragement.

Growing Dusty Miller

Except for occasional visits by pear-shaped, sap-sucking aphids, almost nothing bothers dusty miller. And you can easily dispatch these pests by spraying plants with insecticidal soap on an overcast day, so the leaves don't burn. Native to the Mediterranean, dusty miller laughs at sparse rainfall. As a veteran of window boxes and urns, it tolerates dry conditions without a problem.

However, persistent high humidity or torrential rain can cause the stems to rot or can wash the feltlike texture from the leaves, revealing the green beneath. Growing them in a well-drained, sandy soil is helpful in maintaining healthy plants in damp climates, and it's wise to position containers away from overhead drips. 'Cirrus' is a dwarf variety developed to resist rain damage. 'Silverdust' remains especially compact, rarely topping 30 cm (12 in) in height, making it a good choice for combining with other plants in containers and small beds.

Dusty miller can endure heavy frosts. On the West Coast it grows throughout the year and is often featured alongside pansies in winter gardens. In its first year, dusty miller is a handsome foliage plant, but in its second spring it will often send up flowers. The tiny yellow flowers aren't exciting and they obscure the handsome leaves, so they can be removed as soon as they appear.

Increasing the Bounty

Dusty miller is easily grown from seed. Sow seeds indoors in February

An edging of drought-tolerant dusty miller is ideal for lighting up paths and driveways.

FUNDAMENTAL FACTS

ATTRIBUTES	Felt-textured silver leaves that are rounded or lacy; for edging or pots
SEASON OF INTEREST	Spring to fall in cold-winter regions; all year in warm-winter climates
FAVORITES	'Cirrus' for rain tolerance; 'Silverdust' for compact growth habit
QUIRKS	Humid weather induces stem rot; heavy rain can remove silver leaf coating
GOOD NEIGHBORS	Browallia, campanula, geranium, pansy, poppy
WHERE IT GROWS BEST	Well-drained soil; full sun
POTENTIAL PROBLEMS	Aphids
CRITTER RESISTANCE	Good
SOURCE	Bedding plants, seeds
DIMENSIONS	30–45 cm (12–18 in) tall, and 30 cm (12 in) wide

in a moist, sandy, well-drained soil. Do not cover the seeds, because light is necessary for germination. Keep the containers in a location with temperatures between 18° and 21°C (65° and 70°F). Transplant the seedlings when their first set of mature, felted leaves appears, or set out bedding plants at the time of your last spring frost.

You can also take cuttings of dusty miller, severing 8 cm (3 in) long stems from the mother plant. The felt-like covering on the stems inhibits root formation, so gently scrape the felt off the lower part of the cutting with a sharp knife. Bury the scraped part of the stem in sandy potting soil, making sure to firm the soil around the stem. Moisten the soil around the cuttings when you first insert them, but don't water again until the soil is dry. They should make roots and be ready to transplant into the garden in 3 to 4 weeks.

FAN FLOWER

Scaevola aemula

HARDINESS:
Frost tolerant

PREFERRED SOIL pH:
Adaptable

PREFERRED SOIL TYPE:
Average

PREFERRED LIGHT:
Sun

Fan flower is named for the spreading flower petals of cultivars like 'Blue Fan'.

Fan Flower in the Landscape

The gardening world recognized a superstar the moment it discovered the Australian import known as fan flower. Also called by its botanic name scaevola, this spreading annual produces hundreds of small, mauve-blue blossoms shaped like old-fashioned, opened fans. 'New Wonder' boasts an even greater profusion of large, richly colored blue blossoms than the original species, making it ideal for pots, window boxes, hanging baskets, or the garden.

Fan flower is self-branching, drought tolerant, and wind resistant. It endures hot blasts of scorching weather. With shocking speed and no fuss, each plant spreads into a ravishing 0.6–1 m (2–3 ft) wide beauty.

When it comes to color, the blue blossoms of fan flower complement many other flower colors. In containers, fan flower mixes well with pink verbena, white annual zonal geraniums, marigolds, snapdragons, and most other summer bloomers.

Growing Fan Flower

Fan flowers are so new to the gardening scene that we've only just begun to explore their uses. But, because of their fortitude, fan flowers are top candidates for hanging baskets, where the soil dries out often and a plant must be steadfast to survive.

You can find hanging baskets already planted with fan flowers at many garden centers, or simply start your own. For fastest impact, set 3 small bedding plants 8 cm (3 in) apart in an 20 cm (8 in) diameter hanging basket or container filled with fertile, loamy potting soil. Firm the soil around each plant to eliminate air pockets. Water the newly planted container generously, and then put it in partial shade for a few

This flower-studded, spreading annual is as much at home in pots as it is in the garden.

days to allow it to adjust to its new home. After that brief transition period, shift the basket to its permanent location in full sun. During fair weather, most hanging baskets require daily watering and a weekly application of balanced, soluble fertilizer applied at half strength, according to package directions.

In beds, fan flowers are unfazed by wind, torrential rain, or occasional drought. Plant them as you would in a container, providing ample water during heat waves and a bit of extra fertilizer during the second half of summer to keep them blooming at their peak.

Increasing the Bounty

Begin each season by buying healthy plants that have been professionally propagated. You can grow a few new plants for home use in midsummer by rooting cuttings from a mature plant. Snip off 10 cm (4 in) long stem tips, strip leaves from the lower 5 cm (2 in) of stem, and insert the cutting by half its length into a mixture of damp sand and peat moss. Set the container in a shady spot and keep the

sand mix damp. The cuttings should root in about 3 weeks.

This tough plant is virtually never bothered by pests and diseases. If small, sap-sucking insects, such as aphids or whiteflies, attack tender stem tips, remove them with a forceful stream of water from the hose or apply insecticidal soap as directed.

FUNDAMENTAL FACTS

ATTRIBUTES	Spreading foliage studded with blue fan-shaped flowers; for pots or beds
SEASON OF INTEREST	From early summer to first fall freeze
FAVORITES	'New Wonder' for its bounty of blue flowers
QUIRKS	Grows best with ample water
GOOD NEIGHBORS	Annual zonal geraniums, phormium, verbena
WHERE IT GROWS BEST	Full sun; damp, well-drained soil
POTENTIAL PROBLEMS	Aphids, whiteflies (rare)
CRITTER RESISTANCE	Good
SOURCE	Cuttings
DIMENSIONS	0.3 m (1 ft) tall, 1 m (3 ft) wide

FLOWERING CABBAGE

Brassica oleracea var. acephala

HARDINESS:
Frost tolerant to about -7°C (20°F)

PREFERRED SOIL pH:
Adaptable

PREFERRED SOIL TYPE:
Average

PREFERRED LIGHT:
Sun

Flowering Cabbage and Kale in the Landscape

These unusual members of the cabbage clan have shed their identities as vegetables and moved into flower beds, pots, and window boxes where they are appreciated for their frilly-edged, colorful leaves. True, you can snip individual leaves from flowering cabbage or kale to use as garnishes or add color to salads, but these plants are not really grown for the table. Instead, use these cold-hardy, tough-leaved foliage plants to bring color to fall and winter flower beds or containers, which is a trick that they can carry off quite well on their own or in combination with color-coordinated chrysanthemums, asters, or pansies.

Flowering cabbages and kales are closely related and grown the same way, but there are differences in form. Flowering cabbages have broad leaves that form a flattened head, while the leaves of the kale types are heavily frilled. Leaves often start out green and then turn red, purple, pink, white, or a mixture of these shades, with the color concentrated on the

Veined and splotched outer leaves frame the pink flowering cabbage called 'Tokyo'.

inner leaves. The hues deepen as the plants mature and the weather becomes steadily cooler. By late fall, these plants are in their prime. The flowering kales in particular make wonderful accents in autumn window boxes and containers.

Colorful Cabbage Kings

Fast and reliable, the 'Color-Up' hybrid flowering cabbages grow into loose, 0.3 m (1 ft) wide heads with intensely hued red, pink, or white center leaves. For contrast in texture, mix them with the frilly leaves of 'White Peacock' or 'Red Peacock' flowering kale.

Growing Flowering Cabbage and Kale

You can buy plants at garden centers in the fall or start seeds indoors in summer, about 10 weeks before your first frost is expected. Plant seeds 1.3 cm (1/2 in) deep in moist seed-starting soil and keep the soil moist and at 18°C (65°F) until the seedlings are up and growing.

Summer insect pests are likely to chew the leaves, so wait until the weather is cool to move the plants outdoors. Because flowering cabbages and kales are attractive to the velvety

green caterpillars called cabbageworms, as well as to gray-green cabbage aphids, it's a good idea to keep plants in 10 cm (4 in) pots on a table or bench, away from garden soil. There you can keep a close eye on them and treat invasions promptly by rinsing pests off leaves with a firm spray of water from the hose or applying insecticidal soap as the package directs. Set plants out after frost has ruined tender summer annuals and pests have all but disappeared. After nights have chilled below 10°C (50°F), expect the plants to quickly gain size, change colors, and enjoy excellent and care-free health.

If winter temperatures suddenly take a downward plunge, flowering cabbage and kale can suffer badly. However, in years in which the plants can gradually become accustomed to cold, they often withstand temperatures that dip well below freezing, frequently surviving winters in Zone 6 and warmer areas. In the spring they

FUNDAMENTAL FACTS	
ATTRIBUTES	Cold-hardy annuals; pink, red, purple, white, or light green leaves; for cool-season beds or pots
SEASON OF INTEREST	Midfall to early spring
FAVORITES	'Color Up' for color; 'White Peacock' and 'Red Peacock' for frilly leaves
QUIRKS	Lengthening spring days trigger plants to flower
GOOD NEIGHBORS	Asters, chrysanthemums, pansies, snapdragons
WHERE IT GROWS BEST	Full sun, fertile soil, in cool weather
POTENTIAL PROBLEMS	Cabbageworms, aphids in late summer
CRITTER RESISTANCE	Good but deer may eat them
SOURCE	Bedding plants, seeds
DIMENSIONS	23–38 cm (9–15 in) tall and wide

will send up attractive spires of yellow flowers adding a dazzling finale to their long display.

Cool-season annuals, flowering cabbages color up fall, winter and spring flower beds.

Nicotiana alata hybrids come in a range of pastel shades.

FLOWERING TOBACCO

Nicotiana spp.

HARDINESS:
Varies with species

PREFERRED SOIL pH:
Adaptable

PREFERRED SOIL TYPE:
Average

PREFERRED LIGHT:
Sun to partial shade

Flowering Tobacco in the Landscape

Beautiful, fragrant flowering tobacco plants include old varieties that perfume summer evenings with the sweet scent of jasmine, hybrids that color sunny beds for weeks at a time in midsummer, and a few surprisingly hardy strains that grow as short-lived perennials in Zone 6 and warmer climates. All are tough and extremely heat tolerant, with upright flower stalks that preside over shorter flowering annuals such as petunias and marigolds. Flowering tobacco flowers best in full sun but plants can adapt to sites with a half day of shade.

Top-Grade Tobaccos

Flowering tobaccos sold as bedding plants in spring are hybrids developed for a colorful display, and they often lack fragrance. However, older varieties have a simple beauty and fragrance that should not be overlooked. 'Havana Apple Blossom', with its pure white flowers streaked on the reverse with a blush of pink, would be welcome in any garden. Container gardeners make great use of 'Lime Green', a prolific flowering tobacco that bears many short, trumpetlike, light green flowers. Not only does this variety offer unusually colored blooms, but its 0.6 m (2 ft) height makes it perfect as an upright element in container combinations.

If fragrance appeals to you, look no further than the 1 m (3 ft) tall jasmine tobacco, *Nicotiana alata*. Available with white flowers or in mixtures that include several shades of pink, these plants reseed readily in areas as cold as Zone 5, and roots often survive winters in Zone 8, sprouting in spring.

For a stately flowering tobacco, you can try the 1.2–1.5 m (4–5 ft) tall *N. sylvestris* in a partly shaded garden. An annual in most parts of Canada, this species, commonly known as Only the Lonely, has clusters of drooping white trumpets that perk up and send fragrance wafting through the air as the sun goes down.

Growing Flowering Tobacco

If local garden centers don't have bedding plants of the varieties you want, you can mail order seeds and start them indoors 6 weeks before the last frost. The seeds need light to germinate, so sprinkle them on the surface of moist potting soil. Put seed trays on a sunny windowsill or under grow lights and keep the soil evenly moist and at 21°C (70°F) until seeds sprout.

Seedlings can tolerate cool soil and can be planted outdoors as soon as the danger of frost has passed. Before planting, work a balanced, controlled-release fertilizer into the soil. Although adaptable, flowering tobacco grows best in slightly acid soil. After testing the soil, amend it as needed with either garden sulphur or garden lime according to the product package directions.

Pale-green flowered nicotianas successfully combine with other flowering plants.

FUNDAMENTAL FACTS

ATTRIBUTES	Colorful, often fragrant flowers in white, pink, green; for beds or pots
SEASON OF INTEREST	Summer
FAVORITES	*N. alata* and its cultivars, and *N. sylvestris*
QUIRKS	Older strains may close flowers during the day
GOOD NEIGHBORS	Petunias, marigolds, and other flowering annuals
WHERE IT GROWS BEST	Sun to partial shade in hot-summer areas
POTENTIAL PROBLEMS	Tobacco hornworms, aphids; fungal leaf disease in wet weather
CRITTER RESISTANCE	Good except for hornworms
SOURCE	Bedding plants, seeds
DIMENSIONS	0.3–1.5 m (1–5 ft) tall, 38 cm (15 in) wide

The plants form low-growing rosettes of broad fuzzy leaves, which send up tall stems of trumpet-shaped flowers. In midsummer, when the first flush of flowers begins to fade, trim the stalks back by half their height to encourage new flowering stems. Also make sure that plants receive a generous watering during hot, dry spells.

Check plants occasionally for leaf- and flower-chewing green caterpillars, called tobacco hornworms. Pick off and drown them in a bowl of soapy water, or spray plants with the biological insecticide BTK (*Bacillus thuringiensis* var. *kurstaki*). If tiny pear-shaped, sap-sucking aphids appear knock them off the plants with a strong spray of water from a hose.

In damp, cool weather, leaves can be disfigured by fungal gray mold, especially top leaves that catch and hold rain and dew, and lower leaves that touch wet soil. Trim off and dispose of disfigured leaves. Plants will recover in drier weather.

FORGET-ME-NOT

Myosotis spp.

HARDINESS:
Frost tolerant

PREFERRED SOIL pH:
Neutral

PREFERRED SOIL TYPE:
Moist, well-drained

PREFERRED LIGHT:
Sun to partial shade

Forget-me-nots form a carpet of blooms in spring and will self-sow where content.

Forget-Me-Not in the Landscape

Often willing to spread, or naturalize, in half-shaded flower beds and woodland gardens, forget-me-nots produce a profusion of pale blue blossoms that add a romantic note to spring. This plant supposedly gained its common name when a suitor picked a bouquet of its flowers along the banks of a swift-running river. He lost his footing and fell in, shouting "Forget me not" to his lady as the waters carried him away. Whether true or not, the story reveals the habitat that forget-me-nots love best. Often found by streambeds, forget-me-nots thrive anywhere that the soil remains damp and there is some protection from the heat of the sun.

In spring, the low, spreading plants are covered with dainty blossoms, which are usually blue with a yellow eye but can also be pink or white, depending on variety. These charmers are at home when tucked into rock gardens, used as groundcovers under the shade of tall trees and shrubs, such as roses or azaleas, or scattered in a wildflower garden. Forget-me-nots combine well with calendula and perennial candytuft and make a beautiful foundation for spring bulbs, such as daffodils or tulips.

Unforgettable Forget-Me-Not

The wild *Myosotis sylvatica* has small flowers and copious leaves, so it is better to choose one of the more floriferous named varieties. 'Victoria Blue' forms mound-shaped plants that are covered with gentian blue flowers, while 'Victoria Mixed' features a mixture of colors including blue, white, and rose. 'Rosylva' bears very bright pink flowers on 20 cm (8 in) tall plants, and 'Royal Blue Improved' is a little taller with indigo blue flowers. 'Blue Ball' is a very old variety, with rich blue blossoms on 20 cm (8 in) tall, rounded plants. When it is pleased with its growing conditions, this variety will self-seed and reappear year after year.

M. scorpioides 'Mermaid' is a water-loving forget-me-not that flowers in midsummer.

All in the Family

If you have gritty, gravelly, or very well-drained soil, you can try alpine forget-me-not (*M. alpestris*), an especially cold-tolerant perennial relative that comes from European woodlands. These are densely tufted plants that have very fine hairs covering their leaves and stems. In spring these lovely plants are frosted with lightly scented blue flowers.

Another good perennial type is *M. scorpioides*, known as true or water forget-me-not. This is an ideal choice for wet areas in the garden, such as around a pond, where waterlogged soil would drown most other plants. It blooms later than its relatives, in midsummer, but has the same small blue and pink flowers. The aptly name 'Mermaid' variety has bright blue blossoms and shiny leaves.

Growing Forget-Me-Nots

Forget-me-nots like moist, well-drained, fertile soil that never totally dries out. You can start seeds indoors in summer and set them out in early fall, or sow seeds where you want the plants to grow from spring through summer. Sow seeds over moist soil and cover the seeds with a 0.3 cm (1/8 in) layer of soil.

Forget-me-nots perform as biennials in most climates, blooming very little if at all their first year and covering themselves with flowers the following spring. If you allow time for seeds to ripen completely, forget-me-nots often reseed and appear year after year. Overcrowding doesn't bother forget-me-nots at all, but if too many seedlings appear where they're not wanted, simply pull them up in early summer. You should still see a number of volunteer seedlings emerge in early fall.

Forget-me-nots are usually pest free but tiny, sap-sucking aphids can sometimes attack new growth. Just knock them off with a forceful spray of water from the hose or apply insecticidal soap, as directed, on an overcast day or after the sun sets so that the young leaves don't get sunburned.

FUNDAMENTAL FACTS

ATTRIBUTES	Tiny blue blossoms in spring; for massing in small areas or edging, or as groundcover
SEASON OF INTEREST	Late spring to early summer
FAVORITES	'Victoria Blue' compact plants; 'Victoria Mixed' for blue, pink, white
QUIRKS	Grows best in moist soil; quickly dies back in hot weather
GOOD NEIGHBORS	Spring-flowering bulbs, calendula, candytuft, roses and other shrubs
WHERE IT GROWS BEST	Cool climates in filtered sun or partial shade
POTENTIAL PROBLEMS	Aphids
CRITTER RESISTANCE	Good
SOURCE	Bedding plants, seeds
DIMENSIONS	15–30 cm (6–12 in) tall, up to 30 cm (12 in) wide

True to their name, four-o'clocks open their fragrant tubular flowers in late afternoon.

FOUR-O'CLOCK

Mirabilis jalapa

HARDINESS:
Tender perennial

PREFERRED SOIL pH:
Adaptable

PREFERRED SOIL TYPE:
Average

PREFERRED LIGHT:
Sun to partial shade

Four-o'clocks in the Landscape

Although these care-free plants were popular garden staples until the 1950s, they fell out of style for several decades, perhaps because the flowers don't open until late afternoon and they close by the following morning. But today, many people don't get to enjoy their gardens until the workday is done, so the plant's late-day perfor-

mance is no longer seen as a drawback. It's great to come home to the colorful, tubular flowers of four-o'clocks, which emit a heady scent of sugar, lemon, and spice that varies from plant to plant.

The 0.6–1.2 m (2–4 ft) tall plants look festive grown in masses and more resemble leggy shrubs than annuals, making them suitable for use as a seasonal hedge. Even before the 5 cm (2 in) long blossoms emerge, the bright green leaves add a fresh accent to the landscape. The richly hued flowers combine well with magenta petunias or pink flowering tobacco, intensifying the colors.

A Carnival of Colors

Four-o'clock colors were once limited to yellow and magenta, and while four-o'clock flowers still tend to be mottled with those two colors, more choices are now available. An old variety that has been newly rediscovered is 'Broken Colors', which produces hundreds of 2.5–5 cm (1–2 in) long, trumpet-shaped flowers in colors including raspberry, orange, lemon

yellow, and white, with some of the flowers being striped or dotted with several colors. Specialty nurseries often stock a solid yellow variety simply called 'Jalapa Yellow'.

Growing Four-o'clock

Four-o'clocks are easy to grow from seed. In cold climates, start the seeds indoors 5 weeks before the last frost. Soak seeds in water overnight before sowing them on the surface of the soil. Keep the soil moist and at 21°C (70°F) until seedlings have several sets of adult leaves. Set seedlings out after danger of frost has passed, spacing them about 35 cm (14 in) apart in a sunny site with fertile, well-drained soil. Four-o'clocks will bloom the first season.

Four-o'clocks are perennials, and will form tuberous roots. You can dig the tubers up in the fall after the first frost, the same way you would dig dahlias, and store the tubers in a dark, dry place that remains above 10°C (50°F) over winter. Plant the tubers outdoors in spring as soon as the ground warms. Saving tubers is a way to keep a favorite color year after year. In time, the tuber becomes very large

Flowers can be magenta, yellow, raspberry, orange, lemon, yellow, or white.

FUNDAMENTAL FACTS	
ATTRIBUTES	Multicolored, fragrant flowers open in late afternoon; for beds
SEASON OF INTEREST	Summer to fall
FAVORITES	'Jalapa Yellow' for yellow flowers; 'Broken Colors' for confetti colors
QUIRKS	Well-grown four-o'clocks are shrubby
GOOD NEIGHBORS	Petunias; other night-blooming annuals, such as flowering tobacco
WHERE IT GROWS BEST	Full sun to partial shade
POTENTIAL PROBLEMS	Japanese beetles
CRITTER RESISTANCE	Good
SOURCE	Seeds, tuberous roots
DIMENSIONS	1 m (3 ft) tall, 75 cm (30 in) wide

and can then be divided just before planting. Pot the tuber and bring it into a warm place to sprout new shoots. When growth begins, unpot and cut into smaller pieces, each with new shoots. Treat the cut surfaces with powdered sulphur and pot individually.

Because four-o'clocks have fleshy stems, they will wilt quickly if they're growing in dry soil. Water as needed during droughts to prevent wilting. Small and spindly plants may need fertilizer, which is easily provided by a monthly application of a balanced, soluble, all-purpose plant food, as directed on the package.

Pests are few but do include the metallic green Japanese beetle, which chews holes in blossoms for a few weeks in summer. Plants recover quickly when the beetles' feeding frenzy ends. Handpick beetles early in the morning, when they are sluggish, and drop them into a bowl of soapy water, or spray the plants with insecticidal soap, according to package directions.

FUCHSIA

Fuchsia spp.

HARDINESS:
Tender

PREFERRED SOIL pH:
Neutral to slightly alkaline

PREFERRED SOIL TYPE:
Fertile, well-drained

PREFERRED LIGHT:
Partial shade

'Royal Velvet' is robed in purple and fuchsia flower petals.

Fuchsia in the Landscape

Once called lady's eardrops because the pendant blossoms resemble earrings, fuchsias have developed an undeserved reputation as a fussy exotic. Yet fuchsias are easy to grow, whether they are compact specimens in hanging baskets or 60 cm (2 ft) tall upright plants in pots or beds.

Fuchsia flowers look something like ballerina tutus. They come in double or single forms. Doubles, such as red-and-white 'Yuletide' and pink 'Flirtation Waltz', look as if they are harboring layers of crinolines. The flower color range includes fuchsia, of course, along with white, pink, purple, and salmon, with two colors commonly represented in a flower. Some are famed for their foliage, especially *F. magellanica* 'Aurea', which has narrow golden leaves on red stems and matching red blossoms. Another is 'Little Jewel', which has leaves variegated with white, green, and blush pink, and purple-and-red blossoms.

In mild-winter climates, such as southern Vancouver Island, fuchsias can be grown outdoors year-round. But elsewhere fuchsias are best handled outdoors as container-grown annuals, which can be overwintered indoors or grown as houseplants.

Growing Fuchsia

In the right environment, fuchsias practically take care of themselves. Filtered light or shade is essential, especially in hot-summer climates. The plants wilt easily in hot and humid weather, making your first concern keeping the soil moist, particularly if the plants are growing in hanging baskets. Plants don't like to have their roots cramped, so make sure the container is large enough to allow for growth. Fuchsias grow best in sandy soil made fluffy by the liberal addition of compost or peat moss with a little garden lime mixed in to neutralize the acidity. For maximum flowering, fertilize plants every 2 to 3 weeks during the peak of flowering in summer with a soluble, balanced formula mixed to half strength.

During a long bout of damp, rainy weather, fungal leaf diseases like powdery mildew or botrytis occasionally trouble fuchsias. At the first sign of powdery spots that cannot be rubbed off, or dark leaf spots, move plants to a place with good air circulation and pick off and dispose of affected leaves. Plants that have not been watered enough can fall prey to the sap-sucking insects aphids and whiteflies. These pests are easily controlled by spraying the plant with a strong stream of water from the hose or applying insecticidal soap according to package directions.

Should plants become spindly, cut the branches to within 15 cm (6 in) of the base of the plant. They will sprout immediately and resume flowering. If you plan to keep your fuchsia from year to year, prune the plant back by two-thirds in the fall and bring it indoors to winter in a warm east- or west-facing window.

Increasing the Bounty

You can purchase handsome fuchsias in full flower from garden centers, or mail order small, starter plants. You can also start your own plants by taking stem cuttings from mature plants when new growth begins in early spring. Take 10 cm (4 in) stem cuttings, remove the bottom set of leaves, and "plant" the cuttings up to the first

Many fuchsia varieties feature bicolored blossoms, such as this dainty 'Lady Thumb'.

set of leaves in a pot of damp sand. Set the pot in a warm, sunny window and keep the sand moist until the cuttings root in 2 to 3 weeks. Then you can set them into a container of potting soil.

Upright-growing fuchsias are a colorful way to fill gaps in summer flower beds.

FUNDAMENTAL FACTS

ATTRIBUTES	Pink, purple, salmon, and fuchsia flowers, green or variegated foliage; for baskets, pots
SEASON OF INTEREST	Summer to fall; can be grown as a houseplant
FAVORITES	'Yuletide', 'Flirtation Waltz' for double flowers; 'Aurea', 'Little Jewel' for interesting foliage
QUIRKS	Needs frequent watering to prevent wilt; does not thrive in hot weather
GOOD NEIGHBORS	Licorice plant, coleus, pansy, plectranthus
WHERE IT GROWS BEST	Cool-summer locations; needs shade in hot areas
POTENTIAL PROBLEMS	Powdery mildew, botrytis, aphids, whiteflies
CRITTER RESISTANCE	Good
SOURCE	Bedding plants, cuttings
DIMENSIONS	60 cm (2 ft) tall, 30–35 cm (12–14 in) wide; width varies by variety

BEDDING GERANIUMS

Pelargonium spp.

HARDINESS:
Frost tolerant

PREFERRED SOIL pH:
Neutral to slightly alkaline

PREFERRED SOIL TYPE:
Well-drained loam

PREFERRED LIGHT:
Sun to partial shade

Thriving on neglect,
geraniums flower unceasingly in summer.

Bedding Geranium in the Landscape

A flowering plant that flourishes in window boxes and containers on every Main Street in the country has to be easy to please. Plants that are traditionally left on cemetery plots from Victoria Day through the end of summer to fend for themselves are bound to be low maintenance. That's the destiny of bedding geraniums. Not only do we love and leave them to care for themselves, we also call them by the wrong name.

The annual bedding geranium isn't a true geranium. Its proper botanical name is *Pelargonium*. Bedding geraniums, also called zonal geraniums, are actually tender perennials that hail from South Africa, where they thrive in lean soil and without reliable rainfall. This undaunted bloomer cut its teeth under those rigorous, survive-or-die conditions, and that explains why geraniums are often popped into tough places and nonetheless produce quantities of lollipop-like flower clusters crowning scalloped, velvety, deep green or variegated leaves.

In cool weather and in partial shade, geranium leaves are often marked with a reddish horseshoe-shaped band or zone, a trait that has won the plant its nickname of zonal geranium. In some varieties the leaves are almost as ornamental as the flowers. 'Flowers of Spring' has leaves variegated with silver, while those of 'Crystal Palace Gem' are golden. There are even geraniums with leaves accented by bands of several colors, such as old-fashioned 'Skies of Italy', which was popular in Victorian times. Such specialty geraniums can usually be found at mail-order nurseries.

These showy varieties, which are propagated exclusively by cuttings, are most appropriate as container plants for sunny indoor windowsills, where they bloom off and on year-round. For outdoor beds, seed-sown bedding geraniums, such as 'Elite' or 'Orbit', which branch freely and produce a summer-long display of self-cleaning flowers that need no grooming, are simply unbeatable. Flower colors include white, pink, red, magenta, lavender, salmon, and orange. And if you want especially dramatic geraniums to showcase in containers or window boxes, there are double- and semidouble-flowered varieties that produce breathtakingly large blossoms. The best of these are grown from cuttings rather than from seed, and are sold in roomy pots at garden centers in the spring.

Ivy Geranium

Although the beautiful upright-growing zonal geraniums are by far the most familiar members of the family, there are other care-free annual geraniums worth considering. Ivy geraniums (*P. peltatum*), which are sold as bedding plants, are a boon to any window box or hanging basket where nights remain cool through the summer. These enthusiastic growers will tumble and cascade out of their containers, concealing them behind a curtain of long, trailing stems. Ivy geraniums can also be used as a trouble-free groundcover to camouflage steep hillsides with a generous crop of blossoms, where summers are cool.

As you might imagine from the plant's name, ivy geraniums have something in common with ivy. Both have vinelike, spreading stems and thick, shiny, lobed, slightly curly leaves. While the geranium can't cling to surfaces as true ivy can, it has the bonus of profuse flower clusters

Ivy geraniums, noted for trailing habit, make a strong groundcover when massed.

Semidouble flowers smother 'Catford Belle' geranium with a haze of pink and burgundy.

Crimson blossoms of 'Flowers of Spring', glow against silver-edged, lobed leaves.

bearing single star-shaped blooms in white, pink, red, lavender, burgundy, or salmon flowers. The petals are often veined in a contrasting color near the center, adding a little drama. 'Summer Showers' is a particularly profuse-blooming strain. Give ivy geraniums full or partial sun, especially in hot-summer climates, water them sparingly, and they'll be perfectly happy to bloom with abandon.

Scented-Leaf Geranium

If you like to "garden" with your nose, you will quickly fall in love with the lemon, mint, apple, spice, and even chocolate scents given off by the leaves of some very special *Pelargoniums* called scented-leaf geraniums. The leaves not only smell delicious but are edible and can be used as garnishes or flavorings in salads, jellies, or in baked goods.

Also native to South Africa, these geraniums have foliage and growth habits as varied as their fragrances. Some, such as 'Nutmeg', have leaves no bigger than a thumbnail and spread by runners along the ground. 'Lemon' is a small plant with tiny

leaves and a stiffly upright growth habit. Others, such as 'Peppermint', stand 1 m (3 ft) tall and have leaves the size of a man's hand.

Most scented-leaf geraniums flower primarily in spring with white, pink, lavender, or red blossoms. But a few, such as the rose-scented 'Little Gem' and piquant 'Old Spice', bloom throughout the summer. Even when the plants are not in flower, the leaves can add pretty texture and color to the garden. One variety may have deeply cut leaves rimmed with ivory, while another has heart-shaped foliage covered with a soft hairs like fur.

Scented-leaf geraniums are ideal for containers or as accents in the garden. To overwinter pot-grown plants, you can move them at season's end to a cool place where temperatures will not drop below about -4°C (25°F). In summer, be sure to place them where you can enjoy their fragrance, such as beside a bench or along a path. The leaves need only a light stroking for the scent to be released. Full sun is best for plants in the North. Where summers are hot, grow scented-leaf geraniums in partial shade.

Increasing the Bounty

Ready-to-plant bedding geraniums grown from seed are inexpensive and easily available at garden centers and supermarkets, but if you have a favorite plant and want to increase it, you can easily take cuttings. Snip off a stem just below 3 sets of leaves, remove all but the top 2 leaves, and dip the cut end of the stem into commercial rooting hormone. Insert the bottom inch of the stem in a pot of moistened potting soil, firming the soil around the stem. Water lightly and keep the pot in partial shade, watering the soil only when it dries out. In 4 to 6 weeks, the cutting should have roots and be ready to transplant into a container or in the garden when the soil is warm.

Growing Geranium

Except in areas with very hot summers, bedding geraniums flower best with at least 6 hours of full sun each

FUNDAMENTAL FACTS

ATTRIBUTES	Profuse, large flowers in white, pink, red; for beds, pots, baskets
SEASON OF INTEREST	Early summer to fall
FAVORITES	Seed-sown hybrids, such as 'Elite' or 'Orbit'; 'Summer Showers' ivy geranium; all scented-leaf geraniums
QUIRKS	Allow soil to dry between waterings to avoid rot
GOOD NEIGHBORS	Browallia, dusty miller, lobelia, petunia, verbena
WHERE IT GROWS BEST	Sunny site, well-drained soil, windowsill, outdoors
POTENTIAL PROBLEMS	Geranium budworm, blossom blight
CRITTER RESISTANCE	Good
SOURCE	Bedding plants, seeds
DIMENSIONS	0.3–1 m (1–3 ft) tall, 0.3–1 m (1–3 ft) wide

day. All geraniums benefit from well-drained soil enriched with compost or other organic matter, but they do not need large amounts of fertilizer. Apply it only periodically, to get them off to a good start and to support spurts of new growth. And because geraniums have a special fondness for soil that becomes almost dry between waterings, you can easily satisfy them by drenching them with a balanced, water-soluble fertilizer every 3 to 4 weeks. The secret to keeping bedding geraniums healthy and care-free lies in watering them before the soil becomes bone dry, and feeding when the plant leaves start to yellow.

Pest problems with geraniums are rare, but the geranium budworm occasionally causes damage where winter temperatures seldom fall below -7°C (20°F). The larvae of a moth, budworms bore inside the buds and ruin the blossoms. Use the biological insecticide BT (*Bacillus thuringiensis*), a caterpillar stomach poison, applied as directed to control this pest. Blossom blight is caused by a fungus and is quite common where summers are humid. Spray with a copper-based fungicide.

GLOBE AMARANTH

Gomphrena spp.

HARDINESS:
Tender

PREFERRED SOIL pH:
Slightly alkaline to neutral soil

PREFERRED SOIL TYPE:
Well-drained loam

PREFERRED LIGHT:
Sun to filtered shade

Gomphrena in the Landscape

The papery little pompon flowers of gomphrenas color the garden for weeks in late summer. Tolerant of drought as well as heat and humidity, care-free gomphrenas form 60 cm (2 ft) tall, angular plants clothed in light green, fuzzy, oval leaves. The flowers sit atop the stem tips and resemble stiff clover blossoms in white, pink, purple, or orange. Use

The flowers mimic papery clover blossoms.

these tough, heat-tolerant annuals to replace cool-season annuals that stop blooming in early summer and to bring welcome relief to gardens dominated by daisy-shaped flowers. You can mass gomphrenas, mingle them with other annuals and perennials, or relegate them to a cutting garden to provide fresh and dried flowers.

To enjoy gomphrena flowers all year, cut the flowers just as the blossoms fully open, strip off the leaves, tie the stems in small bundles, and hang the bundles upside down in a cool, well-ventilated place. In only a few days they will be fully dry and ready for dried arrangements.

Everlastings in Many Hues

Variety names including 'Rose Pink', 'White', and 'Lavender Lady' describe the varied flower colors. Dramatic 'Bicolor Rose' adds another dimension with its soft lilac-rose flowers accented by white centers. A popular low-maintenance dwarf form, the 25 cm (10 in) tall 'Gnome', makes a fine edging flower or can be used to brighten a hanging basket or pot.

Gomphrena haageana is a tropical perennial form of gomphrena usually grown as an annual, with flowers in shades of burnished orange. These 60 cm (2 ft) tall plants include the bright orange 'Aurea' variety and 'Strawberry Fields', which has quantities of flowers in a rich shade of red-orange.

Growing Gomphrena

Bedding plants of gomphrenas are available in late spring, or you can start seeds indoors 6 to 8 weeks before the last frost. Look for seed packages labeled "rubbed seed," which means that the cottony chaff that clings to these seeds has been removed. Barely cover the seeds with soil. Keep the soil moist and above

Heat- and drought-tolerant globe amaranths offer profuse flowers for beds in the dog days of summer.

21°C (70°F) until young plants have several sets of adult leaves. These plants truly resent chills, so wait until the weather is warm and settled to set plants in the garden, spacing them 30 cm (1 ft) apart. Because gomphrenas are so heat and drought tolerant, they are excellent candidates for pots.

Plant gomphrenas in full sun, in any well-drained soil. They thrive on warmth, but where summers are hot and dry, it is worthwhile to mulch these beauties with an 8 cm (3 in) thick layer of organic mulch, such as shredded bark, to conserve soil moisture. Do not be alarmed if the plants seem slow to flower. Once they produce blooms, they will hold them in pristine condition for weeks. Cutting plants back to half their height before they set buds will produce bushier plants with more flowers.

Little pear-shaped sap-sucking aphids may gather on stem tips to suck juices or minute red spider mites may colonize the backs of leaves in the heat of summer, giving the leaves a bleached appearance. If so, knock them off with a daily spray of water from a hose or spray insecticidal soap.

In unusually rainy weather, leaf-spotting fungal diseases can develop, disfiguring leaves with powdery or sooty deposits. But planting in a spot with well-drained soil and brisk air circulation prevents these problems.

FUNDAMENTAL FACTS

ATTRIBUTES	Long-lasting, heat-tolerant white, pink, purple, and orange, cloverlike blossoms in summer; grow in beds or in containers; cut for fresh or dried flower arrangements
SEASON OF INTEREST	Midsummer to frost
FAVORITES	'Bicolor Rose' with white centers surrounded by a haze of lilac-rose; 'Strawberry Fields' for orange flowers
QUIRKS	Plants are slow to flower
GOOD NEIGHBORS	All summer-flowering annuals and perennials including black-eyed Susan, cosmos, marigold, zinnias
WHERE IT GROWS BEST	Fertile, well-drained soil in full sun and warm summer climates
POTENTIAL PROBLEMS	Aphids, red spider mites; leaf-spotting fungal diseases
CRITTER RESISTANCE	Excellent
SOURCE	Bedding plants, seeds
DIMENSIONS	25–60 cm (10–24 in) tall, and are 30 cm (12 in) wide

Burgundy leaves and feathery flowers distinguish *Pennisetum setaceum* 'Rubrum'.

GRASSES

Ornamental, various spp.

HARDINESS:
Frost tolerant

PREFERRED SOIL pH:
Near neutral

PREFERRED SOIL TYPE:
Average, well-drained

PREFERRED LIGHT:
Sun

Annual Grasses in the Landscape

With graceful, bladelike leaves crowned by flower heads whose silhouettes range from fluffy plumes to dangling jewels, annual ornamental grasses offer an easy way to add unique seasonal texture to the garden. These talented performers sing and dance when stems and leaves rustle in the slightest breeze, creating graceful movement and soothing sounds.

You can plant annual ornamental grasses in hedgelike rows to divide areas of your landscape, mass them in informal drifts alongside perennial flowers to fill gaps in beds, line them up along paths, or use them as accents to add height to container plantings. They are also ideal as a seasonal screen, to provide a "rest" for the eye in a busy landscape of flowers, and they can even work as an attractive "tenant" in spots where your landscape plans are still unsettled.

If your primary reason for growing these plants is to use the flower heads in fresh or dried arrangements, any sunny spot in a cutting garden or vegetable plot will do. In addition, you might consider using tall, upright ornamental grasses that are really decorative strains of wheat or corn as surprising textural accents in a summer flower garden.

Selecting Annual Grasses

If you want to grow annual ornamental grasses with the demeanor of flowers, the first candidates to consider are quaking grass (*Briza maxima*) and hare's tail grass (*Lagurus ovatus*). Both have a penchant for cool weather. Planted in spring, they quickly grow from green slivers into tight bunches of leaves topped with showy flower heads. Left in the garden into summer, they will turn a tawny brown color that becomes more beautiful when set in motion by the wind.

Quaking grass produces thin stalks up to 60 cm (2 ft) tall. Its flattened seed-containing cones dangle at the ends of the stems, resembling little rattles that flutter and shimmer in every breeze. To dry cut stems, simply place them in an empty vase, where they'll last indefinitely.

With a mature height of only 45 cm (18 in), hare's tail grass is compact enough to use as an edging in difficult spots, such as along a concrete driveway. This grass earns its name from the fluffy 5 cm (2 in) long seed heads that have the cottony texture of rabbits' tails. When cut and dried just as they lighten to buff brown, the stems will last for years.

The shiny, round, hard seeds give Job's tears (*Coix lacryma-jobi*) its common and botanical names. In late summer, arching sprays of flowers produce these seeds, green at first, then grayish-purple. They can be dried for winter use.

Half-Hardy Perennials

If you live in a cold climate where many perennial ornamental grasses are not winter hardy, you can try raising the few perennial species that grow fast enough from a spring sowing to be treated as annuals. At 1.2 m (4 ft) tall, fountain grass (*Pennisetum setaceum*) has arching leaves and produces long beige plumes lightly blushed with lavender. It's a classic companion for butterfly bush, whose purple flowers emerge in summer and last into fall.

Slightly shorter, with deep red blades and rose-tinted plumes, purple fountain grass (*P. setaceum* 'Rubrum') makes a perfect upright specimen for a large container. Pair it with mounding and trailing plants, such as trailing petunias and ornamental sweet potato vine. Feathertop (*P. villosum*) has a more elegant look than the other fountain grasses. Its creamy white, feathery plumes dance atop 60 cm (2 ft) tall plants. Unfortunately, the flower heads

(continued on next page)

The delicate, flattened subheads of quaking grass flutter in the slightest breeze.

(continued from previous page)

shatter when dry and cannot be used in arrangements.

All of the fountain grasses are perennials, but because they are tender, they are best handled as annuals. In mild areas, you can try growing them in containers and overwintering them by trimming the foliage in fall and storing the pots in a cool basement or garage.

Gracious Grains

Ornamental varieties of wheat make outstanding plants for an informal

garden. They have a mature height of 1 m (3 ft) or more, and produce long-stemmed seed heads with unusually long awns, or "whiskers." 'Black Tip' (*Triticum durum*) is a widely available wheat with dark black awns, while the light-colored 'Silver Tip' (*Triticale durum*) is a wheat-rye hybrid.

There also are special varieties of corn (*Zea mays*) grown for their colorful foliage. Varieties of so-called striped corn include 'Japonica' and 'Harlequin', both with cream, pink, and green striping on the leaves. Although the plants, which grow to 2 m (6 ft) tall, do produce ears, the fruits are not edible. This corn is strictly ornamental, so enjoy the colorful striped foliage in the summer garden, and then bundle stalks into shocks for fall decorating.

Growing Annual Grasses

There are two good reasons to start seeds of true ornamental grasses indoors about 8 weeks before your last spring frost. The seeds germinate

best at 21°C (70°F) but grow best under cooler conditions, with temperatures between 10° and 16°C (50° and 60°F). So they are well pleased with an early start indoors followed by transplanting to cooler outdoor temperatures. Plant seeds 0.3 cm (1/8 in) deep in individual containers or flats, and transplant outdoors when the seedlings are 5 cm (2 in) tall with several leaf blades.

Ornamental wheat varieties can be sown in early spring, as soon as the soil can be worked. Plant seeds about 8 cm (3 in) apart. Deer adore winter wheat, cover young plants securely with bird netting, tuck bars of strongly scented soap around plantings to deter them, or purchase a deer repellent. Luckily, few other pests bother either true ornamental grasses or ornamental wheat. Striped corn is a warm-weather crop. Wait until the last frost has passed to plant seeds 25 cm (10 in) apart outdoors.

All the grasses mentioned prefer full sun and fertile, well-drained soil. Prior to planting, work a balanced,

Arching leaves of *Pennisetum villosum* have a softening effect on the landscape.

all-purpose fertilizer, such as 10-10-10 formula into the soil at the rate recommended on the package label.

FUNDAMENTAL FACTS

ATTRIBUTES	Grassy texture, seed heads; use in beds, as specimens, pots, for fresh or dried arrangements
SEASON OF INTEREST	Late spring through fall
FAVORITES	Hare's tail grass, quaking grass, 'Black Tip' wheat
QUIRKS	Seedlings may be mistaken for crabgrass
GOOD NEIGHBORS	Black-eyed Susan, goldenrod, Joe Pye weed
WHERE IT GROWS BEST	Sunny spots with fertile, well-drained soil
POTENTIAL PROBLEMS	Not winter hardy, grow as annuals
CRITTER RESISTANCE	Good except for deer
SOURCE	Seeds
DIMENSIONS	45 cm–1.8 m (18 in–6 ft) tall, up to 30 cm (12 in) wide

Hare's tail grass is a fast-growing annual grass named for its fluffy flower heads, which are shaped like rabbits' tails. This showy grass is at home in a flower border or pot.

Impatiens offer over 20 lively flower colors, such as red and lilac, for brightening shade.

New Guinea hybrids like 'Tonga' have larger flowers and tolerate sun.

Lilac impatiens and other light colors shine in even the darkest garden corner.

IMPATIENS

Impatiens spp.

HARDINESS:
Tender

PREFERRED SOIL pH:
Adaptable

PREFERRED SOIL TYPE:
Average, well-drained

PREFERRED LIGHT:
Filtered shade

Impatiens in the Landscape

Impatiens seem to glow in low-light situations, brightening such spaces with panache and profuse flowers. Also known as busy Lizzie, sultana, or patience plant, impatiens bloom with unabashed energy. Flower colors number beyond 20 and include white, pink, lavender, salmon, and cherry. There are also varieties with contrasting edges, bull's-eye blotches, festive streaks, or swirls of more than one color enhancing their open-faced petals. Double-flowered impatiens, such as Rosette mix and 'Rose Parade', boast petal-packed flowers.

Pastel impatiens in particular light up shade like no other flowers. Where shallow-rooted trees are close by, build up a shallow bed of organically rich soil for planting impatiens so they won't compete for moisture. Mass them for a sea of color or mix them with shade-loving perennials such as ajuga, hosta, and astilbe.

Beyond Busy Lizzies

Although the bedding-plant type of impatiens is by far the most popular, other impatiens also have a following. In Victorian times, balsam, or touch-me-not (*Impatiens balsamina*), were all the rage for their vertical, pointed-leaved spikes with a treasure trove of snapdragon-like blossoms and seed-pods that pop open, flinging their seeds when touched. Self-seeding balsam is a care-free annual for naturalizing in moist shade. Far larger and showier are New Guinea hybrids, with flowers of white, pink, red, blue, purple, and orange amid shiny dark green leaves that often have golden variegation. New Guinea hybrid impatiens tolerate more sun than regular impatiens, and deer detest them.

Increasing the Bounty

Bedding plants sold in spring often show a blossom or two, making it easy to choose the desired colors. But it's easy to grow your own seedlings. Nine weeks before the last frost date, scatter the fine seeds on top of moist seed-starting soil. Press seeds into the soil so that they remain exposed to light. Keep the soil moist and at 24°C (75°F) until seedlings have several sets of mature leaves. Impatiens will stop growing in cold soil, so wait until 2 weeks after your last frost to move them into the garden.

Growing Impatiens

Impatiens need fertile, moisture-retaining soil, and container-grown plants in particular benefit from regular fertilizing. To encourage nonstop flowering, fertilize containers every 2 to 3 weeks with any balanced plant food. In beds, a single application of a controlled-release fertilizer after planting is usually sufficient. To propagate more of your favorites, simply root 10 cm (4 in) long stem cuttings in water and plant them when they have roots.

While usually trouble free, aphids or whiteflies sometimes attack impatiens. Either pest can be combated by squirting the plants with a strong stream of water from the hose.

FUNDAMENTAL FACTS

ATTRIBUTES	Compact, mounded plants; white, pink, purple, or red flowers; for shady beds or pots
SEASON OF INTEREST	Summer, early fall
FAVORITES	All varieties are good, so select by color; New Guinea hybrids are sun tolerant, deer resistant
QUIRKS	Needs moist soil; touch-me-not flings its seeds
GOOD NEIGHBORS	Ajuga, ferns, foxglove, lady's mantle
WHERE IT GROWS BEST	Shade, filtered or partial sun
POTENTIAL PROBLEMS	Aphids, whiteflies
CRITTER RESISTANCE	Good, New Guinea impatiens are excellent
SOURCE	Bedding plants, seeds, cuttings
DIMENSIONS	30–60 cm (1–2 ft) high, 60 cm (2 ft) wide

The tiny florets of lantana change colors as they age, resulting in confetti hues.

LANTANA
Lantana camara and hybrids

HARDINESS:
Tolerates light frost

PREFERRED SOIL pH:
Adaptable

PREFERRED SOIL TYPE:
Average, well-drained

PREFERRED LIGHT:
Full sun to partial shade

Lantana in the Landscape

Any flower that is planted in turnpike median strips in the southern United States has to be able to take scorching heat. Lantanas are such plants. They gladly grow in the toughest situations and actually branch out and produce more blossoms the hotter it gets. They rarely need supplemental watering, and they are so fond of roughing it that frequent doses of fertilizer actually inhibit their output of blossoms.

You can find lantanas in confetti combinations of colors, pure white, or soft yellow. The brightly colored, nectar-rich flowers draw butterflies in droves. It's difficult to find named varieties except for very well known strains, such as 'Samantha', the darling of container combinations because of its clear yellow flowers and foliage gently marbled with gold. Another well-known variety, 'Greg Grant', has variegated leaves, which accent its pink-and-yellow blossoms.

Heat-tolerant annuals make fine companions for lantana, including regular and spreading zinnias, sulphur cosmos, and four-o'clocks. If you find a lantana with subtle shades of blue in its palette, team it up with blue ageratum for a combination that will visually cool the hottest days.

Growing Lantana

Most lantanas are grown from rooted cuttings, so they are sold in slightly larger pots than other bedding plants. Often you will find unnamed plants at garden centers in late spring or early summer, showing tempting samples of the colors they will strut in your garden. Each flower cluster contains a dozen or more tiny tubular blossoms, in a rainbow of yellow, orange, blue, and pink. Watch them carefully in the garden, and you will notice that the colors of the individual florets change as they age. Butterflies notice this, too, and quickly learn to approach the newest florets in search of a sip of the sweet nectar.

All parts of lantana are poisonous, and the dark berries that form after each flush of flowers fades may appear tempting to children and pets. Clip-ping and disposing of the berries will give you peace of mind while encouraging the plants to develop new flowering branches.

Increasing the Bounty

Because of lantana's tremendous tolerance of high heat and humidity, it makes an ideal replacement for pansies and other cool-season flowers that grow lanky and stop flowering in early summer. If you want to increase your supply, it's a simple process to root 10 cm (4 in) long stem cuttings outdoors in a shady spot. After taking the cuttings, remove all but the top 2 sets of leaves. Insert the lower 5 cm (2 in) of bare stem into a container of moistened potting soil. Set the container in a shady spot and keep the soil moist until roots form in a few weeks. Then the new plants will be ready to transplant into a container or the garden.

A Virtually Trouble-Free Plant

Lantanas have almost no problems outdoors. The foliage has a musky scent that is only noticeable when you rub the leaves, but that aroma deters pests. Indoors, lantanas are sometimes bothered by sap-sucking whiteflies and mealybugs, but these are easily dispatched by applying insecticidal soap according to package directions.

FUNDAMENTAL FACTS

ATTRIBUTES	Heat tolerant; flowers attract butterflies; for beds, pots, ground covers
SEASON OF INTEREST	Summer, early fall
FAVORITES	'Greg Grant', 'Samantha' for variegated leaves; unnamed types for multicolored flowers
QUIRKS	All plant parts are toxic if eaten; dispose of berries; flowers attract butterflies
GOOD NEIGHBORS	Zinnia, ageratum, sulphur cosmos, four-o'clock
WHERE IT GROWS BEST	Hot, humid locations; well-drained soil
POTENTIAL PROBLEMS	Mealybugs and whiteflies
CRITTER RESISTANCE	Excellent
SOURCE	Bedding plants, cuttings
DIMENSIONS	0.6–1 m (2–3 ft) tall, 0.6–1 m (2–3 ft) wide

Varieties with subtle blue flowers visually cool the garden even on the hottest summer days.

LARKSPUR

Consolida ajacis

HARDINESS:
Freeze tolerant

PREFERRED SOIL pH:
Neutral to slightly alkaline

PREFERRED SOIL TYPE:
Fertile, well-drained

PREFERRED LIGHT:
Sun

Larkspur in the Landscape

Larkspur was once a mainstay of the garden, just as popular as roses, lilies,

Spires of simple, spurred blue flowers contribute to the nostalgic appeal of larkspur.

An informal row of larkspur appears brilliant blue when set against a dark background.

and hollyhocks. Apt to be found in every garden, the airy flowers of larkspurs were also apt to be seen in every garden bouquet. In recent years, delphiniums, their close relatives, have stolen larkspurs' place of honor in garden beds. Although it's true that perennial delphiniums have larger spires composed of fancier flowers, they can't beat larkspurs for care-free cultivation. There's also no comparison when it comes to nostalgic appeal. Something about the 1 m (3 ft) spires bristling with snow white, tissue pink, powder blue, or navy blue florets tugs at our hearts.

Comfortable in herb gardens as well as flower beds, larkspurs are especially eye-catching when planted where their blue flowers can echo the color of a nearby pond or patch of sky. But larkspurs look best in a small grouping of mixed colors. The Giant Imperial series, with a color range that includes carmine, deep blue, rose, powder blue, lilac, pink, salmon, and white, is the standard for cut-flower purposes. The 'Messenger' series blooms 2 weeks earlier.

Growing Larkspur

Unlike the upright-growing, high-maintenance delphiniums, larkspurs are informal, open-limbed plants that are likely to self-sow and sprout in just the right place without effort on your part. But, given a choice, they'd like to have fertile, fluffy, well-drained soil with plenty of lime and regular, reliable moisture. To insure that the spires aren't buffeted by wind, stake them as they begin to shoot up.

Increasing the Bounty

If larkspurs have any failure, it is that the flowers don't linger long. Because hot weather is not to their liking, sow larkspurs in the garden in early spring when the ground thaws, or in autumn for flowering the following spring. In cold regions, sow in September; on the West Coast, you can safely sow until the end of November. The seeds can take up to 20 days to sprout, and germination from fall sowing is often erratic. The goal is to get larkspurs to sprout as early as possible. The seedlings tolerate extreme cold, but mature plants subjected to nighttime

temperatures above 13°C (55°F) for any length of time fail to flower well.

Larkspurs don't like to be transplanted. It's more effective to sow the seeds directly in the ground than attempt to transplant seedlings. Larkspur seeds require darkness to germinate, so sprinkle them over good garden soil and cover them with a thin layer of finely sifted soil. Sprinkle to moisten the seedbed, keeping it moist until they sprout.

Although pests aren't usually a problem, larkspurs sometimes succumb to fungal diseases, such as powdery mildew, crown rot, and root rot. Increasing air circulation by thinning plants is an effective preventative for mildew, while rotating, or sowing seeds in different locations every year, and incorporating compost into the soil to improve drainage will keep rot from occurring. The seeds and leaves of larkspurs are poisonous if eaten, so place the plants in an area away from children and pets.

FUNDAMENTAL FACTS

ATTRIBUTES	Pastels flower spires; for flower or herb gardens, fresh cut or dried flowers
SEASON OF INTEREST	Spring to summer, depending on climate
FAVORITES	'Giant Imperial' for many colors, tall spires; 'Messenger' for early flowers
QUIRKS	Toxic plants and seeds; poor transplant survival
GOOD NEIGHBORS	Alliums, poppies, monkshood, peonies, yarrow
WHERE IT GROWS BEST	Moist, fertile, alkaline soil; cool weather
POTENTIAL PROBLEMS	Powdery mildew, crown rot, root rot
CRITTER RESISTANCE	Good
SOURCE	Seeds
DIMENSIONS	1–1.2 m (3–4 ft) tall, 30 cm (1 ft) wide

Although short-lived, the lush, cup-shaped flowers are produced all summer long.

LAVATERA
Lavatera trimestris

HARDINESS:
Frost tolerant

PREFERRED SOIL pH:
Near neutral

PREFERRED SOIL TYPE:
Average, well-drained

PREFERRED LIGHT:
Sun

Lavatera in the Landscape

When summer begins to heat up, lavatera starts to glow with luminous pink or white, cup-shaped blossoms that continue day after day for the duration of the season. Closely related to hibiscus, lavatera has flowers with a similar shape and the same impact, but lavatera packs its punch into compact, 30–90 cm (1–3 ft) tall plants, each with a 75 cm (30 in) spread, causing these annuals to look more like a stalwart perennial or minishrub. Individual blossoms are short-lived, but lavateras make up for that by generating new blossoms all summer.

Grown in groups of 3 or more plants, lavateras will form a lush mound or uniform hedgelike edging for a sunny flower bed or walkway. The most challenging part of growing care-free lavateras is remembering to sow the seeds, because this is one flower that transplants so poorly that it is seldom sold in 6-packs. You should sow seeds where you want the plants to spend the rest of the summer.

Selecting Seeds

There are a number of very beautiful varieties of lavateras. High on the list is 'Silver Cup', with its bright, shiny rose pink flowers that often span 10 cm (4 in) across. 'Mont Blanc' bears equally large, white flowers on 60 cm (2 ft) tall plants. 'Ruby Regis' sports flowers 9 cm (3-1/2 in) in diameter, with vibrant cerise pink petals like glowing satin. 'Dwarf White Cherub' is a newer variety bearing snow white flowers that almost cover the 30–35 cm (12–14 in) plants. 'Parade Mix' offers similar flowers but with the widest range of colors, from deep rose to nearly white.

Growing Lavatera

Success is easy with lavateras if their few needs are met. Sow the seeds on loose, friable soil. Incorporate compost, bagged humus, or another form of organic matter before attempting to grow lavateras in heavy clay soil. Sandy or loamy, well-drained soils need little more than a half-strength application of a balanced fertilizer, such as a 10-10-10 formulation, at the time of sowing. Sow seeds in a sunny site about 2 weeks before your last frost is expected, and barely cover the seeds with soil. Thin seedlings to 50 cm (20 in) apart when they are 5 cm (2 in) tall. Seeds also may be started indoors in individual peat pots containing moist soil. Barely cover the seeds with soil, keep the soil moist, and transplant outdoors when the seedlings are only 3 to 4 weeks old, planting them in their peat pots.

Once lavatera plants are up and growing, they require little. Clip off faded blossoms once a week. In midsummer, apply a soluble, all-purpose fertilizer according to package directions to keep plants blooming steadily until fall. Water deeply if they wilt during a drought.

Prolonged wet, humid weather can create conditions conducive to hollyhock rust, evidenced by cinnamon-colored fungal deposits on leaves. Remove any disfigured leaves, and pull out severely affected plants.

FUNDAMENTAL FACTS

ATTRIBUTES	Trumpet-shaped, satiny, white or pink flowers; for beds, hedges, or masses
SEASON OF INTEREST	Summer through fall
FAVORITES	Pink 'Silver Cup'; white 'Mont Blanc'; deep pink 'Ruby Regis'
QUIRKS	Poor survival rate for transplants
GOOD NEIGHBORS	Meadow sage, ornamental grasses, yellow- or white-flowered annuals
WHERE IT GROWS BEST	Full sun; well-drained soil
POTENTIAL PROBLEMS	Rare; hollyhock rust in extremely damp situations; Japanese beetles
CRITTER RESISTANCE	Good
SOURCE	Seeds
DIMENSIONS	45–90 cm (18–36 in) tall, up to 75 cm (30 in) wide

Leaf-chewing Japanese beetles can also be a problem. Pick and dispose of them early in the morning when they are sluggish, or use insecticidal soap, and apply according to package directions. You may need to spray again if they reappear.

In groups of three or more, lavatera forms a lush, hedgelike edging for a bed or walkway.

LICORICE PLANT

Helichrysum petiolare

HARDINESS:
Tender

PREFERRED SOIL pH:
Neutral to slightly alkaline

PREFERRED SOIL TYPE:
Well-drained, fertile

PREFERRED LIGHT:
Sun to partial shade

Licorice plants are grown for their fuzzy foliage. Flowers are few and insignificant.

Licorice Plant in the Landscape

Licorice plant produces furry stems to 60 cm (2 ft) long, sometimes longer. Because of their subdued leaf colors and spreading habit, care-free licorice plants fill many job descriptions. They're ideal for edging flower beds, and as additions to window boxes, containers, and hanging baskets. When grown with other plants, they interweave nicely, and they look stunning beside blue-flowered plants, such as brachychome or browallia.

Why this plant was nicknamed the licorice plant is a mystery, because it neither smells nor looks like licorice. Fancy foliage is the main attraction, as it rarely flowers. But who needs flowers when the plant has soft, felt-textured leaves that beg to be touched? In the species, the green leaves bear a silver sheen that reflects light, making them glow. 'Limelight' is a chartreuse version, with pale green fuzzy leaves.

Growing Licorice Plant

Licorice plants grow best when shaded from the noonday sun. For best results, water the plants regularly, especially when their roots are confined in a container. If plants go into a serious wilt, the leaves often brown and shrivel. But even if a plant appears to have perished, don't give it up entirely; it will make new growth again if you continue to care for it. Water as needed to keep the soil moist, and take a few minutes now and then to pick off brown leaves. They do not fall away on their own.

Eager eaters, licorice plants should be fertilized every 2 to 3 weeks with a balanced fertilizer. And because they don't like cramped containers, repot when the roots fill the pot, graduating the plant to a container that is no more than two sizes larger than the pot it had previously occupied.

When sited well, licorice plants can grow into a seasonal groundcover.

Thanks to its thick leaves, which insects find difficult to chew, licorice plant is not prone to pest problems. If it is neglected, aphids or mealybugs could settle in, but those problems are rare. To prevent them, keep plants stress free by watering regularly.

Increasing the Bounty

It isn't easy to propagate the licorice plant, but, if you want to try, take 8 cm (3 in) long stem cuttings in spring. To encourage root initiation, remove the lowest set of leaves from the stem and carefully scrape the fuzzy coating from the lower portion of the stem. Insert the lower portion of the cutting into light, fluffy soil, and keep it barely moist while it is rooting. Do not enclose cuttings in a plastic bag, which can lead to rot. After the cuttings root in 6 to 8 weeks, they can be planted in containers.

FUNDAMENTAL FACTS

ATTRIBUTES	Felted leaves in silver or green; dense spreading habit; for pots, baskets, window boxes, bedding
SEASON OF INTEREST	Early summer to fall; all year in frost-free regions
FAVORITES	*Helichrysum petiolare* for silver leaves; 'Limelight' for chartreuse foliage
QUIRKS	Keep soil moist to prevent wilting
GOOD NEIGHBORS	Brachychome, browallia, larkspur, torenia
WHERE IT GROWS BEST	Partial shade; moist, organic soil
POTENTIAL PROBLEMS	Humid air can induce rot
CRITTER RESISTANCE	Good
SOURCE	Bedding plants; difficult but possible to root from cuttings
DIMENSIONS	25 cm (10 in) tall, 0.6–1 m (2–3 ft) wide

LOBELIA

Lobelia erinus

HARDINESS:
Frost tolerant

PREFERRED SOIL pH:
Adaptable

PREFERRED SOIL TYPE:
Average

PREFERRED LIGHT:
Sun or partial shade

'Crystal Palace' lobelia displays a brilliant, summer-long pageant of lilac blossoms.

Lobelia in the Landscape

Here is the perfect plant for the edge of anything. Edging a garden bed, filling a window box, or spilling out of containers or hanging baskets. If you enjoy teaming up different annual combinations in containers, lobelia will quickly become an essential source for that hard-to-find shade of true blue, as well as contributing purple, violet, and white to the scene. The tiny, 2 cm (3/4 in) flowers are prolific, and plants always have new flowers to offer throughout the season with no fuss whatsoever.

These annual edging lobelias grow best when summer nights remain between 10° and 21°C (50°F and 70°F), but they are such prompt and continuous bloomers that gardeners in warm climates can enjoy them as lovely, but fleeting flowers from spring to early summer when nights turn from cool to warm. Petunias have similar weather preferences, so the two make an unbeatable combination in beds or containers. Yellow dwarf marigolds are also excellent companions, and lobelia is a great way to hem a patchwork of multicolored snapdragons or compact zinnias. Weave lobelia among silver-leaved dusty miller for a neat, trouble-free edging in foundation beds.

Specialized Varieties

Lobelias grow to 15 cm (6 in) tall, but varieties vary in growth habit. Some form rounded mounds, while others are more intent on spreading, making them suitable for cascading over the edges of containers. If you want to use lobelia to edge a bed, choose a mounding variety, such as violet-blue 'Blue Moon' or white 'Paper Moon'. 'Midnight Blue' has bronzy foliage that contrasts vividly when paired with silvery dusty miller or any plant with white or pale yellow flowers. Choose a cascading variety, such as the Fountain series for containers, baskets, or for planting at the top of a stone wall.

Growing Lobelia

Lobelias need an 8- to 10-week start from seeds before they reach transplanting size, so in this case, bedding plants are a good buy. Keep the soil in their containers moist until you plant them. Set the bedding plants in the garden after your last spring frost date, spacing them 15 cm (6 in) apart. Lobelias grow best in a cool spot with partial shade in areas where days are often above 26°C (80°F). Before planting lobelias in beds, mix a balanced, organic, or controlled-release fertilizer into the soil. Fertilize pot-grown lobelias every 2 weeks during the growing season, using an all-purpose plant food.

In midsummer, you can rejuvenate lobelia by cutting the plants back by half their height, reapplying fertilizer, and watering them well. This is worth a try in all climates, but it may not succeed in hot, humid areas, where lobelias often wither away in July. However, this is an honorable end after their many weeks of valiantly producing intense, nonstop color.

Lobelias are easy to propagate by rooting 10 cm (4 in) long stem cuttings taken at any time. Remove leaves from the lower 5 cm (2 in) of stem and insert the cuttings halfway into moistened potting soil. Set the containers in a shady spot and keep the soil moist until new growth signifies that they are rooted. Plants can be cut back and wintered over indoors on a sunny windowsill, where they'll keep on blooming and be ready to go out to the garden the next spring.

FUNDAMENTAL FACTS

ATTRIBUTES	Intense true blue, violet-blue, or white flowers on cascading or mounding plants; for edging, window boxes, and containers
SEASON OF INTEREST	Spring to fall
FAVORITES	For edging, blue 'Blue Moon' or white 'Paper Moon'; 'Midnight Blue' has bronzy red foliage; the Fountain series for its cascading habit
QUIRKS	Plants stop blooming and may die in hot weather
GOOD NEIGHBORS	Yellow dwarf marigold, dusty miller, petunia, snapdragon, zinnia
WHERE IT GROWS BEST	Cool summer climates, and a site in full sun
POTENTIAL PROBLEMS	Excessive warmth can wither plants
CRITTER RESISTANCE	Good
SOURCE	Seeds, cuttings
DIMENSIONS	15 cm (6 in) high, 15–30 cm (6–12 in) wide, depending on variety

Free-flowering lobelia creates a colorful edging for lawns, beds, and walkways.

Love-in-a-mist is named for its flowers, which seemingly float above misty, feathery leaves.

The 'Persian Jewels' variety brings a new color range to an old garden favorite.

Compact plants soften the front of beds.

LOVE-IN-A-MIST

Nigella damascena

HARDINESS:
Tender

PREFERRED SOIL pH:
Adaptable

PREFERRED SOIL TYPE:
Fertile, well-drained

PREFERRED LIGHT:
Full sun

Love-in-a-Mist in the Landscape

Love-in-a-mist, also called nigella, is a hard working garden performer. It was popular in Victorian times, and it deserves more attention in modern gardens. Beyond being low maintenance, love-in-a-mist produces some of the most complex and beautiful blossoms in the floral kingdom.

Arising from an airy cloud of lacy, fernlike foliage are white, blue, or pink flowers. But the color isn't their most remarkable quality; it's the configuration that's unique. The pointed petals are laid out like those of a bachelor's button, and each 2.5 cm (1 in) flower has a green many-pointed topknot like a jester's hat that accents the center. Below the petals is an Elizabethan-collar of green sepals.

But that's not all. Blossoms you do not cut for summer bouquets will mature into inflated seedpods that resemble little spiny, puffed-up blowfish. They practically dry themselves for use in dried arrangements.

For all its small delights, love-in-a-mist isn't a star-quality individual. It makes a statement only in a mass of 5 or more plants, which will become a patch of color that demands visiting while at its peak. Keep in mind that love-in-a-mist comes and goes rapidly. It can germinate, blossom, and go to seed in only 8 weeks. Several successive sowings will be necessary for a lasting display, making love-in-a-mist a perfect partner for similarly short-lived annual poppies.

It Just Gets Better

The plain old love-in-a-mist is pretty exciting, but newer varieties are even better. Much-treasured 'Miss Jekyll' has semidouble flowers that sparkle in brilliant sky blue shades, as well as pearly white flowers, standing on relatively compact, 60 cm (2 ft) stems. The 'Persian Jewels' strain increases the color range to include rose, lavender, pink, purple, and carmine.

Increasing the Bounty

Love-in-a-mist prefers to be sown directly in the garden where you want it to grow. Scatter the seeds in a sunny spot. Prepare the soil by digging in a generous amount of peat moss, compost, or humus to give the soil a fluffy texture. Water lightly and frequently until the seedlings appear, gradually thinning them to 20 cm (8 in) apart. Quite often, an established planting of these trouble-free plants will self seed, scattering seeds that germinate and grow the following summer. Thin these volunteers to 15–20 cm (6–8 in) apart and enjoy the show.

To dry flowers for everlasting arrangements, wait until the seedpods are brittle, then cut the flower stems as long as possible. Bind several stems together with a rubber band and hang the bunches upside down in a dry, dark, well-ventilated room. Dried pods last for years.

FUNDAMENTAL FACTS

ATTRIBUTES	Uniquely shaped blue, white, pink, or lavender blossoms; lacy foliage. Use for beds; cut flowers for bouquets; dried seedpods for dried-flower arrangements
SEASON OF INTEREST	Summer to fall
FAVORITES	Blue-flowered 'Miss Jekyll' for compact stature; 'Persian Jewels' for dynamic, mixed colors
QUIRKS	Short-lived annual; sow successively for longer flowering
GOOD NEIGHBORS	Calendula, phlox, annual poppies, sweet alyssum
WHERE IT GROWS BEST	Rich, fertile soil; full sun
POTENTIAL PROBLEMS	Hot weather may delay flowering
CRITTER RESISTANCE	Good
SOURCE	Sow seeds; self-sows
DIMENSIONS	0.6–1 m (2–3 ft) tall, 30 cm (1 ft) or more wide

LOVE-LIES-BLEEDING

Amaranthus spp.

HARDINESS:
Tender

PREFERRED SOIL pH:
Slightly acidic

PREFERRED SOIL TYPE:
Average

PREFERRED LIGHT:
Sun to partial shade

Love-Lies-Bleeding in the Landscape

With one of the most vivid names in the plant world, love-lies-bleeding (*Amaranthus caudatus*) boasts tiny blood red flowers that dangle from arching, 60 cm (2 ft) long ropelike stems that droop from plants that are 1.2 m (4 ft) tall or taller. No doubt about it, this plant is no shrinking violet. The flower color is astonishing, the cascading tassels of flowers are difficult to ignore, and the plant's dimen-

A. caudatus 'Viridis' has vivid yellow-green tassels, as striking as the usual red flowers.

When planted in a mass, love-lies-bleeding creates a towering, flowering summer hedge.

sions are practically larger than life.

If you want to downplay the drama, tuck the plant into the back of the border behind shorter summer flowering plants, such as lavatera, gomphrena, marigolds, or celosia. For a braver approach, plant it beside a gate, porch, or front door. Love-lies-bleeding is equally striking in a container, as long as the scale is large.

Although love-lies-bleeding is a giant among annuals, its needs are few. It thrives on summer heat and asks little of your time. Once planted, it takes poor soil and dry conditions in stride. The blossoms make wonderful cut flowers, or you can dry them for use in winter arrangements.

The Many Shades of Drama

If the typical red flowers and towering stature of love-lies-bleeding aren't your heart's desire, try a different amaranth. The variety known as 'Green Thumb' bears vivid green upright flower spikes on a demure plant that stands 30–60 cm (1–2 ft) tall. 'Pygmy Torch' is its garnet-

flowered dwarf counterpart.

If you feel that big is beautiful but want toned-down flowers, try the 1.5–1.8 m (5–6 ft) tall *A. cruentus* 'Hot Biscuits', which is topped by huge, buff brown, upright plumes. A midsized compromise is *A. giganticus*, called the elephant head amaranth because of its immense, upright, blood red plumes.

Flowers aren't amaranthus' only assets. The closely related plant called summer poinsettia (*A. tricolor*) stands 1.2–1.5 m (4–5 ft) tall and features a flowing crown of brilliantly colored foliage. The uppermost leaves of 'Aurora' are sunshine yellow, while those of 'Illumination' are crimson.

Growing Love-Lies-Bleeding

Love-lies-bleeding and the other amaranths will grow in any soil, including heavy clay. Plants grown in full sun are stiffly upright, but you may need to stake those in partial shade. Love-lies-bleeding prefers warm temperatures, so there's nothing to be gained from sowing seeds early. Sow seeds indoors 6 weeks before your last frost date.

Barely cover the seeds with soil and keep the soil barely moist and at room temperature till seedlings have several sets of leaves. Transplant them into the garden when the weather is warm and settled. You may also seed directly into the garden in well-drained soil and full sun. Space plants 45 cm (18 in) apart, and mulch between them to discourage weeds. There is no need to fertilize, and these drought-tolerant plants seldom need watering.

The only significant insect foes of amaranths are tiny pear-shaped, sap-sucking aphids, which can be dispatched with a forceful spray of water or insecticidal soap. Deer, however, enjoy eating love-lies-bleeding. Discourage them by tying a bar of deodorant formula bath soap to a stake and tucking it among the plants. The only potential for disease is root rot, but planting in well-drained to dry soil will prevent rot.

FUNDAMENTAL FACTS

ATTRIBUTES	Red, garnet, or green flower tassels; tolerates heat; for beds or pots
SEASON OF INTEREST	Early summer to fall
FAVORITES	Red-flowered *A. caudatus*; dwarf green 'Green Thumb'; dwarf red 'Pygmy Torch'; *A. cruentus* 'Hot Biscuits' for buff brown flowers; *A. tricolor* for yellow or red leaves
QUIRKS	Plants need warm soil
GOOD NEIGHBORS	Celosia, gomphrena, lavatera, marigolds, flowering tobacco
WHERE IT GROWS BEST	Well-drained soil in warm summer climates
POTENTIAL PROBLEMS	Aphids, deer
CRITTER RESISTANCE	Good except for deer
SOURCE	Seeds
DIMENSIONS	0.6–1.8 m (2–6 ft) tall, 0.6–0.9 m (2–3 ft) wide

French marigolds, with their dainty blooms and stature, are ideal for containers.

MARIGOLD

Tagetes spp.

HARDINESS:
Tender

PREFERRED SOIL pH:
Adaptable

PREFERRED SOIL TYPE:
Moderately fertile

PREFERRED LIGHT:
Sun

Marigold in the Landscape

Marigolds have been treasured in gardens for centuries; even the Aztecs grew these golden bloomers. Famous for their profuse floral performance, marigolds begin blooming a few weeks after sowing and continue to produce fiery-colored blossoms throughout the summer, no matter what the weather happens to hand out. Few flowers are as easy to cultivate as marigolds, which explains why they are often a child's first experiment in gardening.

Marigolds fill several positions in the garden. Because the lacy-leaved stems remain both compact and dense, shorter varieties of marigolds are often used as a colorful edging, forming a ribbon of gold, yellow, or mahogany at the front of a sunny border. When used as bedding plants, marigolds of different colors can be arranged in blocks side by side to form a patchwork. They're equally useful planted in a container or window box to add a splash of color, or scattered through the vegetable garden, where their pungent scent is used traditionally to repel insect pests both above and below ground.

A Marigold for Every Garden

If your garden lacks pizzazz, just plant a grouping of several hybrid American marigolds (*Tagetes erecta*) to liven up the scene. Sometimes called African marigolds, American hybrids stand 1 m (3 ft) tall and produce a bumper crop of rounded, ruffled, powder-puff shaped yellow to orange blossoms up to 10 cm (4 in) wide. The Inca series make good cutting flowers. If you want the unusual, try a white-flowered one, such as 'Snowdrift'.

Stately American marigolds like full sun and rich, fertile soil, and should be watered to prevent wilting when rain doesn't furnish adequate water weekly. Because of their height, American marigolds sometimes need staking to support their tall stems when they are heavily laden with their large flowers.

French marigolds (*T. patula*), which are native to Mexico, are more dainty, shorter, 25–45 cm (10–18 in) tall plants with a broader range of colors including yellow, orange, and brick red in single, double, and semidouble forms. Good varieties include 'Janie' and 'Sophia'. French marigolds thrive in full sun and lean soil, and are used to repel rootknot nematodes, a serious soil-borne pest that attacks many species of ornamental and edible plants in warm-winter climates.

For a window box combination or a garden edging, you might prefer the subtler flowers of old-fashioned signet marigolds. Signet types, such as 'Lemon Gem' and 'Golden Gem', stand only 30–38 cm (12–15 in) tall and have lacy foliage and a profusion of button-sized, five-petaled blossoms. As a bonus, the flowers of signet marigolds are edible.

Increasing the Bounty

You can buy marigolds as bedding plants or easily grow them from seed. Scatter seeds on garden soil 15–20 cm (6–8 in) apart after the danger of frost has passed, cover them with 0.6 cm (1/4 in) of soil, and water gently with a watering can fitted with a sprinkling head. The seeds will sprout within a week. Two or 3 weeks later, you'll see plants produce the first of many marigold flowers to come. Occasionally spidermites or grasshoppers may munch plants in late summer. Dispatch mites with a strong stream of water. Tolerate damage from grasshoppers, which are usually too numerous to control.

FUNDAMENTAL FACTS	
ATTRIBUTES	Quick and easy to grow; for beds, edging, pots, and window boxes
SEASON OF INTEREST	Early summer to fall
FAVORITES	'Inca', 'Snowdrift', 'First Lady' American marigolds; 'Janie', 'Sophia' French marigolds; 'Lemon Gem', 'Golden Gem' signet marigold
QUIRKS	Temporarily stops flowering during hot spells
GOOD NEIGHBORS	Campanula, lobelia, euphorbia, flowering tobacco
WHERE IT GROWS BEST	Sunny locations with ample rainfall
POTENTIAL PROBLEMS	Grasshoppers (occasionally), spidermites
CRITTER RESISTANCE	Good
SOURCE	Seeds
DIMENSIONS	0.3–1 m (1–3 ft) tall, 0.3–0.6 m (1–2 ft) wide

Marigolds come in a warm range of colors including yellow, gold, rust, and bicolored flowers. These cheerful companion plants brighten gardens and are thought to repel insect pests.

Nasturtiums may have single or double flowers and are best sown directly into the soil.

NASTURTIUMS

Tropaeolum spp.

HARDINESS:
Tender

PREFERRED SOIL pH:
Near neutral

PREFERRED SOIL TYPE:
Well-drained, fertile

PREFERRED LIGHT:
Sun to partial shade

Nasturtium in the Landscape

Easy to grow and easy to please, nasturtiums thrive in modest garden conditions. With no better than average soil underfoot, they'll produce abundant round, lotuslike leaves of medium green or green streaked with white. Leaves are smothered by a generous quantity of 5 cm (2 in) wide trumpet-shaped, spurred flowers in orange, yellow, salmon, maroon, scarlet, or creamy white, often with streaks and blotches of contrasting shades. Nasturtium stems and leaves retain water well, making them care-free plants for containers or garden plants in low-rainfall regions. They thrive and flower best in full sun.

Some varieties show enthusiasm for climbing if you coax the young stems soon after they sprout. If you want them to go up, provide a wire fence or a slender trellis within 5 cm (2 in) of the plants' stems. They are equally brilliant dangling from a window box, tumbling over the edges of a container, or spreading around the garden in lush mounds. They're great for the front of a border, forming a thick carpet of flowers and handsome leaves. The luminous yellow blossoms of the variety 'Moonlight' pop out of the dark, brightening an evening garden. 'Jewel of Africa' has a pretty speckling of cream on its green leaves and flowers in shades of cream, yellow, peach, and red.

Edible Flowers

Besides looking great, nasturtiums have culinary uses. Long before they were valued in the flower garden, nasturtiums were grown in vegetable gardens as a salad ingredient. Young leaves impart a peppery flavor, flowers have a delicate taste, and the mild green flower buds can be used raw or pickled like capers.

Growing Nasturtium

Nasturtiums are bothered by few pests. If tiny, pear-shaped insect aphids gather on buds and stem tips, rinse them off with a strong stream of water. Happily, these plants require watering only in a severe drought, and flower best without fertilizer. They do benefit from removing leaves that turn brown and cling to the stems. Keep abreast of trimming spent flowers and leaves, and the plant will remain tidy and perform well throughout the entire summer.

When growing nasturtiums in a hanging container or window box, rejuvenate your plants halfway through the summer by snipping off the dangling stems, leaving 15 cm (6 in) of stem at the base of each plant. Within a week, new flowering shoots will sprout from the base, making the plant look dense and like a new planting.

Increasing the Bounty

Nasturtium plants are readily available at garden centers, but they are one of the easiest plants to start from seed. Because they don't transplant well, sow the seeds directly in the ground where you want the plants to grow after the danger of frost has passed. Nick, or scarify, the seed coats before planting to make it easier for seeds to absorb moisture. Space seeds 23–30 cm (9–12 in) apart, barely covering the seeds with soil, and firm the soil around the seeds by pressing it lightly with the head of a hoe. Water the seed bed with a watering can fitted with a sprinkler head. Seeds should germinate within 1 to 2 weeks.

FUNDAMENTAL FACTS

ATTRIBUTES	Flowers in warm colors, variegated leaves on some varieties, light fragrance; edible plants; for beds, pots, baskets
SEASON OF INTEREST	Early summer to late fall
FAVORITES	'Glorious Gleam', 'Moonlight'; 'Alaska' has variegated leaves
QUIRKS	Nick seeds before sowing; do not fertilize
GOOD NEIGHBORS	Annual geraniums, iris, morning glories
WHERE IT GROWS BEST	Sunny, dry location
POTENTIAL PROBLEMS	Aphids, otherwise good
CRITTER RESISTANCE	Good
SOURCE	Seeds, bedding plants
DIMENSIONS	30 cm–1.8 m (12 in–6 ft) tall, 30–75 cm (12–30 in) wide

PANSY

Viola spp.

HARDINESS:
Frost tolerant

PREFERRED SOIL pH:
Neutral

PREFERRED SOIL TYPE:
Average

PREFERRED LIGHT:
Sun to partial shade

Pansies may be one color or two-toned.

Pansies supply nearly every known color.

Pansies in the Landscape

Pert, saucy, and perfect for a quick spark of color in spring and fall, pansies (*Viola* × *wittrockiana*) are the modern hybrids of violets. Famed for their intricate markings and long flowering time, pansies bloom in a wide color range, from white to wine. In addition to beloved older strains with blotched flowers that look like faces, there are modern varieties that may have no blotch at all or be "mini-pansies" (*V. tricolor*), which are small-flowered hybrids of Johnny-jump-ups.

Flower breeders have improved the winter hardiness of pansies, so much so that hardy varieties, such as the Sky and Delta series can be planted in fall in Zone 6. In all areas pansies can go into beds, containers, or window boxes even before the last frost in spring. Use pansies as constants in the spring garden to unify colors that come and go on spring-flowering bulbs and shrubs. Yellow or white pansies are invaluable for this purpose, and mixing in blues provides a beautiful contrast.

Almost Limitless Choice

Pansies have been bred primarily for color, making it easy to paint your landscape with them. Generally, varieties with large, 8 cm (3 in) flowers, such as the Majestic Giant series, set fewer blooms than smaller-flowered varieties, such as the Crystal Bowl series. Vigorous minipansies, often called violas, produce hundreds of 2.5 cm (1 in) diameter flowers on mounding plants, and bloom better in cold weather than do fancier hybrids. The Sorbet series is an example of this impressive new type of pansy.

Growing Pansies

Bedding plant pansies are inexpensive and come in great variety at garden

In some parts of the country, pansies deliver 8 months of color from fall to early summer.

centers, usually with a bloom or two showing the flower colors. Look for compact young plants that have not begun to flop. Space larger-flowered types 20 cm (8 in) apart, but allow 25 cm (10 in) for bushy mini pansies. Before planting, work a balanced organic or timed-release fertilizer into the soil at the rate recommended on the label. Set out pansies as early as possible in the fall so they will be well rooted when soil temperatures fall below 7°C (45°F). In spring, begin setting out pansies up to a month before your last frost is expected.

Should your plants grow lean and leggy, they probably need more fertilizer or more sun. Pinching off old flowers helps promote bloom. However, in warm climates, pale, scrawny-looking pansies may fall victim to minute, wormlike soil organisms called rootknot nematodes, for which there is no cure. Check for hard, swollen nodules on roots to confirm this problem and dispose of infested plants. Leaves and flowers that are chewed and marked with slimy trails are the handiwork of slugs and snails. Set saucers of beer on the ground to lure and drown these pests. Pansies

stop flowering and die out in hot weather, and it's best to replace them with heat-tolerant flowering annuals.

FUNDAMENTAL FACTS

ATTRIBUTES	Long-blooming, colorful flowers on compact plants; for pots, boxes, or edging in spring and fall
SEASON OF INTEREST	Spring to summer; winter in Zones 8 and 9
FAVORITES	'Crystal Bowl' for wide color range; 'Majestic Giants' for large flowers with interesting markings; 'Sorbet' and other minipansies for winter bloom in warm climates
QUIRKS	Blooming stops when summer nights rise above 16°C (60°F)
GOOD NEIGHBORS	Sweet alyssum, larkspur, ornamental cabbage, snapdragon, bulbs
WHERE IT GROWS BEST	Fertile, well-drained soil
POTENTIAL PROBLEMS	Nematodes in warm climates; slugs, snails
CRITTER RESISTANCE	Good
SOURCE	Bedding plants, seeds
DIMENSIONS	15–20 cm (6–8 in) tall, 15–30 cm (6–12 in) wide

PERILLA

Perilla frutescans var. *crispa*

HARDINESS:
Tender

PREFERRED SOIL pH:
Adaptable

PREFERRED SOIL TYPE:
Adaptable

PREFERRED LIGHT:
Sun to partial shade

Perilla in the Landscape

This care-free member of the mint family has many virtues. Closely related to the purple-leaved herb opal basil, perilla has bronze leaves that are similarly crinkled, scented, and hemmed with serrated edges. It's absolutely beautiful when sunlight causes its leaves to shimmer with a metallic sheen. In times past the edible leaves were used for tenderizing meat, which might account for the British nickname for perilla: beefsteak plant. In Asia the leaves are still used as a seasoning in cuisine.

Once you plant perilla, seedlings will be sprouting in future seasons. In this case, that's good news because perilla is a lovely addition to any garden. Humans are not the only ones to appreciate perilla. Birds dine on the seeds that follow quickly in the wake of pink flower spires in midseason. Birds merely make a dent. To control the bounty, weed out excess seedlings with a flick of the wrist, or prune off flower spikes before they go to seed.

Use perilla as a colorful accent within eyeshot of castor bean plant, bronze phormium, bronze-and-pink coleus, or heuchera. Like those plants, perilla tolerates full sun or partial shade and just about any soil that happens to be underfoot. Standing bolt upright, perilla forms a slender 0.6–1 m (2–3 ft) tall plant. 'Purple Hedge' is a popular variety of this plant, which is most often sold as a species. For a fuller effect, several perillas should be nestled closely together.

Growing Perilla

Few plants are as easy to please as perilla. It needs only sun or partial shade and will thrive in any type of soil. Additional watering is seldom necessary; only plants growing in hot, sunny places will wilt. The best show is accomplished by grouping several perilla plants closely side by side with only 10–15 cm (4–6 in) between neighbors.

Perilla isn't bothered by disease and rarely by insects. Flea beetles and slugs occasionally chew holes in leaves, and sap-sucking, pear-shaped aphids can cluster at the tips of buds and juicy leaves. Set out saucers of beer at sundown to trap and drown nocturnal slugs. Knock flea beetles and aphids off plants with a strong spray of water or spray with insecticidal soap, according to label directions. Remove plant debris from the garden to eliminate places where pests can hide and overwinter.

Increasing the Bounty

Perilla is easily grown from seed, or you can propagate existing plants by rooting 10 cm (4 in) long cuttings taken from the growing tips of the plants before they begin to flower. To properly sow seeds, refrigerate them for 1 week. Then sow them indoors 6 to 8 weeks before your last spring frost, or directly in the garden bed when spring is in full swing and the soil is warm. Scatter the small seeds on the surface of a pot of moistened seed-starting soil or outdoors over finely raked garden soil. Perilla seeds require light to germinate, so the seeds should be left uncovered. Mist the soil immediately after sowing and keep the soil moist until germination occurs, in 1 to 2 weeks. To encourage branching, pinch off the tip of the main stem when the second set of mature leaves develops. Seedlings can be thinned or transplanted when they have several sets of mature leaves.

FUNDAMENTAL FACTS

ATTRIBUTES	Bronze leaves; pink flowers; for beds, pots
SEASON OF INTEREST	Summer to fall
FAVORITES	'Purple Hedge'; seeds sold by species name
QUIRKS	Reseeds prolifically
GOOD NEIGHBORS	Castor bean, coleus, heuchera, phormiums
WHERE IT GROWS BEST	In any climate, any soil, full sun or partial shade
POTENTIAL PROBLEMS	Flea beetles, aphids, slugs
CRITTER RESISTANCE	Good
SOURCE	Bedding plants, seeds, or cuttings
DIMENSIONS	0.6–1 m (2–3 ft) tall, 20–30 cm (8–12 in) wide

Perilla is grown for its fragrant, frilly leaves.

Purple perilla leaves are handsomely set off by companions with lime-green leaves.

PERIWINKLE

Catharanthus roseus

High temperatures won't wilt periwinkle, which stands stiffly upright in midsummer.

HARDINESS:
Tender

PREFERRED SOIL pH:
Neutral

PREFERRED SOIL TYPE:
Average

PREFERRED LIGHT:
Sun to partial shade

Periwinkle in the Landscape

In the heat of July and August when many garden plants are taking a siesta, periwinkle is at its best, soaking up the most blistering weather of the season. This easy-care performer loves high temperatures and thrives equally in the dry heat of a prairie summer or the sticky atmosphere of the southeastern areas.

Often called annual vinca, this flower also goes by the name of Madagascar periwinkle. Shiny dark green leaves frame flat, 5 cm (2 in) wide flowers that often show a contrasting white or red central eye. The highly uniform plants grow 30–38 cm (12–15 in) high and wide, making them ideal for edging and mass planting. Depending on variety, flower colors may be neon pink, soft lilac, or white with pale yellow centers, and virtually any shade in between. The flowers are not only colorful but also self-cleaning, which means that they drop from the plant as they fade.

Choosing a Periwinkle

Because vinca is such an excellent annual for the hottest part of the season, it's not surprising that soft pink and lilac-colored plants are valued for their icy cool hues. Popular series including Cooler and Pacifica offer these shades along with much brighter ones. If you want to attract plenty of attention from a distance, choose deep pink 'Stardust Orchid', which is marked with a star-shaped white eye, or the dark, rose-pink variety 'Pacifica Punch'.

Some periwinkles are bred to be more compact than others, but the height a variety attains depends more on the length of the growing season than its genes. In the North, periwinkle rarely grows taller than 20 cm (8 in), but in warmer climates gardeners can expect it to grow to 45 cm (18 in) tall or even taller. Plants may reseed, too, although seedlings

White-flowered periwinkle glows in the low light of partial shade and evening gardens.

Periwinkle's starlike flowers, often marked with an eye, twinkle above glossy, ribbed leaves.

do not appear until late spring, after the soil has warmed.

Growing Periwinkle

Periwinkle is not difficult to start from seed, but you will save time and trouble by buying bedding plants. Wait until the soil is warm to set out seedlings, or use them as early summer replacements for cool-season annuals. Amend poor soil with a balanced organic or controlled-release fertilizer at the rate recommended on the label, but do not overfertilize this flower. In fact, it is more important to provide a well-drained spot and soil that is warm enough to promote fast growth. Plants grown in cold, clammy soil may develop problems with root rot, which causes them to suddenly collapse and die. In cool climates, it's best to grow periwinkles in dark-colored, sun-absorbing pots until summer weather becomes suitably warm, then set them in the ground.

Periwinkles need no grooming or trimming, though they often benefit from a booster feeding of a balanced fertilizer, such as 10-10-10 sprinkled over the root zones of the plants in midsummer. Also, do not plant periwinkle in the same place more than once every 4 years. The roots host a potentially deadly fungus, which can become a serious problem if the growing site is not rotated properly.

FUNDAMENTAL FACTS

ATTRIBUTES	Compact plants; blue, pink, red, purple, white flowers; for beds or pots
SEASON OF INTEREST	Summer to fall
FAVORITES	Cooler and Pacifica for a range of colors
QUIRKS	Grows poorly in cool, damp conditions
GOOD NEIGHBORS	Ageratum, buddleia, marigold, salvia, zinnia
WHERE IT GROWS BEST	Full sun in warm, well-drained soil
POTENTIAL PROBLEMS	Root rot in cold, wet soil
CRITTER RESISTANCE	Excellent
SOURCE	Bedding plants
DIMENSIONS	15–20 cm (6–18 in) tall, 20–30 cm (8–12 in) wide

PETUNIA

Petunia hybrids

HARDINESS:
Frost tolerant

PREFERRED SOIL pH:
Adaptable

PREFERRED SOIL TYPE:
Moist, well-drained

PREFERRED LIGHT:
Sun

Petunia in the Landscape

Pretty petunias seem to be everywhere in summer, spilling over the sides of window boxes, containers, and hanging baskets, and brightening garden beds with their rainbow colors and trumpet-shaped flowers. In fact, few flowers come in the color range that petunias boast. Petunia blossoms can be pink, scarlet, red, white, blue, purple, or yellow. Some are subtly pastel, others are brazenly bright. They can be striped, streaked, or enhanced by a contrasting central white "star" in the throat. Some varieties have double flowers with a fluff of petals in the center, while traditional types are single-flowered. Evening fragrance is

Vivid petunias are ideal for a planting that needs to be visible from a distance.

Petunias sport rainbow hues. Petite plants in the Fantasy series make a lacy edging.

often another virtue. Petunias are such strong summer bloomers that they're sometimes thought overused in the garden, but why resist a flower that grows so easily and always delivers?

Keeping Up With the Flowers

Petunias are such steadfast performers that the biggest challenge is keeping abreast of the comings and goings of their flowers. Petunias don't drop their flowers after they fade; instead you need to keep them tidy. At least once a week, more often if possible, clip off the dead blooms to keep them looking neat and to encourage new flowers. Petunias often will bloom themselves ragged by midsummer, but you can easily help them make a comeback by clipping old stems back to 15 cm (6 in) in length, and then applying a soluble high-phosphorus "bloom-booster" formula fertilizer.

The Best Petunias

There are so many petunias on the market, it's difficult to choose the best. Supertunias™ and the Surfinia series are such vigorous performers that they blossom continually through the summer. Supertunias are reputed to grow 2.5 cm (1 in) a day to cover

ground quickly and give a nearly instant show. Especially heat- and drought-tolerant varieties with a broad range of colors include 'Madness', 'Primetime', and 'Celebrity'. If you want yellow flowers, try 'Prism Sunshine'. If you find the flowers of the doubles intriguing, go for the Cascade series. For vivid pink and purple petunia blooms galore, the Wave series are hard to beat. Petite 'Fantasy' petunias make lacy-looking, compact edging plants.

Increasing the Bounty

In spring and early summer, petunias are readily and inexpensively available as bedding plants at garden centers, discount stores, and supermarkets. And some of the most vigorous petunias are propagated from cuttings and only sold as bedding plants. But if you like to start seeds, sow petunia seeds indoors 8 to 10 weeks before your last frost date. Sprinkle the super-fine,

powderlike seeds over the top of moistened commercial seed-starting soil, and don't cover them. Keep the soil moist and place the container in a sunny, warm place at 21°–26°C (70°–80°F) for 2 weeks. After sprouting, grow seedlings in a sunny, 16°C (60°F) place (preferably a greenhouse or under grow lights). In 4 to 6 weeks you can transplant the seedlings into pots and continue to grow them in a sunny place until planting outdoors after danger of frost is past. Petunias are generally trouble free. If smooth-edged holes appear in leaves and flowers suspect slugs. Place shallow saucers of beer (slugs crawl in and drown) among plants in the evening to dispense with these night-feeding pests. Petunias are sometimes affected by incurable viruses. If leaves begin to wilt or brown on well-watered plants, destroy and replace affected plants.

FUNDAMENTAL FACTS

ATTRIBUTES	Trailing plants covered with colorful flowers from June until frost; for beds, pots, or baskets
SEASON OF INTEREST	Early summer to fall
FAVORITES	Ground-hugging 'Purple Wave', trailing 'Misty Lilac Wave'; 'Madness' or 'Primetime', double-flowered 'Cascade'
QUIRKS	Retains spent flowers: trim to promote flowering
GOOD NEIGHBORS	Verbena, fan flower, roses, zonal geraniums
WHERE IT GROWS BEST	Full sun, moist soil
POTENTIAL PROBLEMS	Viruses
CRITTER RESISTANCE	Good
SOURCE	Seeds, bedding plants
DIMENSIONS	15–20 cm (6–8 in) tall; stems cascade 0.3–1 m (1–3 ft), depending on variety

PLECTRANTHUS

Plectranthus spp.

HARDINESS:
Tender

PREFERRED SOIL pH:
Near neutral

PREFERRED SOIL TYPE:
Well-drained, fertile

PREFERRED LIGHT:
Sun to partial shade

Variegated plectranthus stand out in pots.

Plectranthus in the Landscape

There's always room in the garden for plants that feature textured, variegated, or otherwise intriguing foliage, and this is just what you get with the garden newcomer plectranthus. Related to coleus, another care-free annual, plectranthus, like coleus, is valued more for its beautiful, architecturally refined foliage rather than the slender spires of white blossoms that appear late in the season. But unlike the brazenly colored leaves of coleus, plectranthus leaves are discreetly handsome combinations of silver, green, and creamy white. Best of all, plectranthus can tolerate all sorts of abuse including strong wind, drought, and even salt spray. The plants bask in full sun as well as luxuriating in

Lime-hued plectranthus set off blue flowers.

partial shade. Often used in containers and featured in hanging baskets, plectranthus can go solo or fit into colorful plant combinations.

Meet the Candidates

There are lots of plectranthus species and varieties to choose from. Because of its velvety textured, shimmering silver leaves, *P. argentatus* is currently one of the garden's biggest celebrities. *P. argentatus* prefers moist soil and partial shade, although it endures occasional drought and full sun. It's a husky plant, reaching 1 m (3 ft) in height with an equal girth and is fully capable of becoming the centerpiece of a container. Also upright, but forming a more compact, leafy plant, *P. forsteri* has felted, pale-green leaves that emit a pleasant nutty scent when bruised. The species is beautiful, but its varieties are even more intriguing. *P. forsteri* 'Marginatus' has a snowy white scalloped margin accenting

each leaf, while 'Athens Gem' is mottled in different shades of chartreuse, ranging from apple green to olive. Both work wonderfully in tandem with other plants, especially blue-flowering ones, such as larkspur, campanula, phlox, and verbena.

Although *P. madagascariensis* 'Marginatus' doesn't begin its career as a trailer, it assumes that stance as soon as the branches stretch to 1 m (3 ft) or longer. Each two-tone green leaf is scalloped and edged in glistening white. Also prone to sprawling, *P. amboinicus* 'Green Heart' and 'Marginatus' have leaves in shades of green and white. Used in Spanish cooking, *P. amboinicus* and its varieties, sometimes called Greek oregano or Spanish thyme, also earn their keep in the kitchen. The leaves can substitute for thyme or mint, depending upon your taste.

Because of their thick, aromatic leaves, plectranthus are virtually impervious to insects. Similarly, they rarely succumb to diseases, but growing in soggy soil can lead to fatal root rot. Plant in well-drained soil, and allow the soil to dry between waterings to prevent this.

Shades of lime and grass green make this plectranthus a subtly interesting plant.

Increasing the Bounty

Plants are typically grown from cuttings and sold in garden centers as starter plants or as larger plants in hanging baskets. Enjoy the plants outdoors during the summer, and either overwinter them in containers as houseplants, or take cuttings to make plants for next year's garden.

Like their coleus kin, plectranthus cuttings are easy to root in a glass of water. Take cuttings of stems with 3 sets of leaves and remove the lower 4 leaves. Then submerge the bottom 5 cm (2 in) of the stems in a container of water. When they have a few strong roots, pot up the rooted cuttings in a mixture of peat moss and potting soil, and water the newly potted plants generously for the first couple of weeks while they become established and begin new growth. Pinch off tips of the growing plants frequently to encourage branching.

Red-flowered corn poppies are care-free and prolific, filling the garden with color.

POPPY

Papaver and other spp.

HARDINESS:
Frost tolerant

PREFERRED SOIL pH:
Adaptable

PREFERRED SOIL TYPE:
Average

PREFERRED LIGHT:
Sun

Poppy in the Landscape

Poppies are among the easiest flowering plants to grow. They can be grown from seed sown directly in the garden and often reseed each year. You can let the lantern-shaped seed pods mature and dry on the plants, harvest them and shake the seeds into an envelope for replanting, then use the handsome pods in dried flower arrangements.

The Poppy Palette

The red poppies that often grow along roads, called corn poppies (*Papaver rhoeas*), are frost-tolerant annuals that can be sown in fall or early spring. Varieties in other colors, called Shirley poppies, include 'Mother of Pearl', a mix of mauve, blue-gray, and dusty pink. 'Angels' Choir' is a double-flowered mix in shades of soft pink and white, with 8 cm (3 in) diameter flowers borne on 60 cm (2 ft) stems.

California poppies (*Eschscholzia californica*) are less tolerant of cold but will flower heavily in hot weather. The species blooms in rich orange, but new varieties have expanded the color range. The Thai Silk series and Gloriosa Double Mix include yellow, red, and apricot, all with semidouble petals. 'White Linen' blooms in a creamy white that can be used in complicated color combinations.

Growing Poppy

In Zones 7 to 9, corn poppies and California poppies are best sown in

Shirley poppies extend the color range with papery flowers in pink, mauve, and white.

California poppies are valued for their brilliant orange flowers and heat tolerance.

FUNDAMENTAL FACTS

ATTRIBUTES	Crepe-paper textured blossoms in soft colors; for beds, meadows, or wildflower gardens
SEASON OF INTEREST	Spring and summer
FAVORITES	'Mother of Pearl' and 'Angels' Choir' Shirley poppies; 'Thai Silk', 'Gloriosa Double Mix', and 'White Linen' California poppies
QUIRKS	Seedlings seldom survive transplanting
GOOD NEIGHBORS	Bachelor's button, foxglove, hollyhock, larkspur, peony
WHERE IT GROWS BEST	Sun, well-drained soil
POTENTIAL PROBLEMS	Plants grow and bloom poorly in dry, infertile soil; may rot in wet soil
CRITTER RESISTANCE	Excellent
SOURCE	Seeds
DIMENSIONS	45 cm–1.2 m (18 in–4 ft) tall, 30 cm (12 in) wide

fall, atop finely cultivated soil. Seeds germinate sporadically all winter, and the tiny plants grow quickly as days lengthen in spring. In colder regions, sow seeds in early spring, while the soil is still cold. Once growth begins, thin plants to at least 25 cm (10 in) apart and dispose of thinnings.

Despite their wildflower reputation, poppies bloom best when grown in soil of average fertility. After thinning, apply a balanced granular fertilizer at half strength.

California poppies are ideal for dry climates but will bloom best if given water when the soil is dry, particularly when the plants are about ready to flower. Poppies are virtually pest and disease free but plants may succumb to fungal root rot when grown in soggy soil.

PORTULACA

Portulaca grandiflora

HARDINESS:
Frost tolerant

PREFERRED SOIL pH:
Adaptable

PREFERRED SOIL TYPE:
Average

PREFERRED LIGHT:
Sun

Portulaca in the Landscape

Portulaca is a flowering annual that thrives where others shrivel, perking up seemingly hopeless sites with a summer-long supply of 5 cm (2 in) diameter, delicate-looking double blossoms atop fresh, succulent foliage. They bloom in colors ranging from deep magenta and many shades of orange and yellow to white, salmon, and a peppermint pink color that's patterned with frosty white.

In fact, recent improvements in portulaca are so dramatic that portulaca's status has been raised from a fill-in plant for problem spots to a featured flower in beds, containers, and even hanging baskets. Portulaca spreads out to form soft mounds of

Showy portulaca flowers have a soft, silky sheen that enhances their brilliant colors.

Portulacas spread to cover large areas with color and will flower despite sun and heat.

delicate, succulent foliage. It is ideal for planting in broad bands along a sun-baked walkway, for spilling over warm stones atop a wall, edging a bed filled with taller flowers, or for bedding alongside roses or other bare-stemmed shrubs.

Growing care-free portulaca does require a few special considerations. The flowers open wide in bright, sunny weather and close during rainy weather, and at night. While open, flowers attract honeybees, so avoid stationing a planting right next to a doorway or other high-traffic area. Portulaca often reseeds, and even hybrids produce offspring well worth keeping. Best of all, portulaca is a champion at withstanding drought, capable of going without water longer than almost any other garden flower.

Modern Wonders

The Sundial series has earned a well-deserved reputation for beauty and dependability. Its color range is outstanding, too, particularly if you like

soft sherbet shades like 'Peach' and 'Mango'. Sundial portulacas grow 15 cm (6 in) tall and spread 35 cm (14 in) wide, which makes quite a sight when they're allowed to cascade over the top of a wall or large container. The Margarita series is similar in its mix of colors, but the plants form more compact mounds only 25–30 cm (10–12 in) wide. This makes Margarita portulacas perfect for use as an edging or a blooming ground cover in sunny spots.

Growing Portulaca

Inexpensive bedding plants of portulaca are easy to find in garden centers in spring, or you can start seeds indoors 4–6 weeks before your last frost. Seeds have a wide tolerance for germination temperatures, so you can even sow them outdoors in beds or containers in late spring. Sow the tiny seeds on top of the soil, barely pressing them in, because they need light to germinate. There is no great hurry to get seedlings started because they

grow best in warm or even hot weather. And although established plants tolerate drought very well, it's important to provide enough moisture to young plants to support strong, steady growth. Ideally, you should allow the soil to become barely dry between waterings.

Portulacas are not heavy feeders, but they will stay in bloom longer if you drench them with a soluble all-purpose fertilizer, applied according to package directions, monthly during the summer. Should the plants eventually become thin and leggy looking, you can shear them back by about half their size to force out fresh new flowering stems.

True to their care-free character, portulacas are ordinarily impervious to insect attack and diseases, only succumbing to root rot in soggy soil. If this happens set healthy plants in a new location with well-drained soil.

FUNDAMENTAL FACTS

ATTRIBUTES	Flowers in many colors for hot, dry spots; as ground cover and edging, in pots and baskets
SEASON OF INTEREST	Summer
FAVORITES	Sundial series for spreading habit; Margarita series for compact plants
QUIRKS	Flowers close in the evening and during rainy weather
GOOD NEIGHBORS	Gladiolus, larkspur, petunia, scabiosa
WHERE IT GROWS BEST	Hot, sunny site; well-drained soil
POTENTIAL PROBLEMS	Root rot in soggy soil
CRITTER RESISTANCE	Excellent
SOURCE	Bedding plants, seeds
DIMENSIONS	15 cm (6 in) tall, 25–40 cm (10–16 in) wide

The blue flowers of mealycup sage are a cool counterpart to the usual red shades.

SALVIA
Salvia spp.

HARDINESS:
Tender

PREFERRED SOIL pH:
Near neutral

PREFERRED SOIL TYPE:
Fertile

PREFERRED LIGHT:
Sun or partial shade

Salvia in the Landscape

Salvias feature an abundance of small tubular flowers in warm colors. They are clustered along upright flower spikes held above the foliage. Reliable garden salvias (*Salvia splendens*), sometimes called St. John's fire or scarlet sage, grow best in full sun but adapt to a half day of shade, and are easy to grow in both containers and beds.

Because of their naturally neat shape, salvias make a handsome border for a driveway or walkway, and they are ideal for growing near buildings that cast shade for part of the day. Red-flowered salvias mix beautifully with white petunias, or you can pair them with blue ageratum. For a festive look, mix purple or salmon-flowered salvias with marigolds and cockscomb. Salvias also make fine upright flowers for container bouquets composed of several different annuals.

Beyond Red

Red has long been a popular color in annual salvias. 'Flare' produces scarlet 45 cm (18 in) tall spikes on top of handsome green foliage through the hottest summer weather. You will probably find several other choices in red when shopping for bedding plants in the spring. For a broader color range, try the Hotline hybrids, which feature purple-flowered 'Blue Streak' as well as burgundy, salmon, scarlet, and bright white flowers.

All in the Family

Mealycup sage or blue sage (*S. farinacea*) is a half-hardy plant that is usually grown as an annual. A valuable source of hard-to-find blue flowers on an upright plant, mealycup sage is ideal for mixing with zonal geraniums, yellow marigolds, and numerous other summer-garden annuals.

Another care-free relative is coral sage (*S. coccinea*), which is a drought-tolerant salvia that blooms nonstop all summer, producing red, white, or coral flower spikes that are of tremendous interest to hummingbirds and honeybees.

A salvia grown more for its foliage than its flowers is silver sage (*S. argentea*). With big, broad, lobed leaves covered in woolly silver hairs, this salvia brightens up the garden and adds a feltlike texture that you'll want to touch. Its cream to purple upright flowers are a bonus.

Growing Salvia

You can start salvia seeds indoors 8 weeks before your last frost, but because potted salvia seedlings are very sensitive to the accumulation of minerals often found in tap water, it is easier to buy them as bedding plants. Look for young plants that have not yet begun to bloom. Young salvias grow and flower better than plants forced to grow too long in cramped nursery containers.

It is safe to plant salvias in the garden after the danger of frost has passed. When planting, mix organic fertilizer, such as composted manure, or a controlled-release fertilizer, into the soil before setting out plants. Set seedlings 30 cm (1 ft) apart, and mulch between plants with

'Lady in Red' is a variety of coral sage that is dressed all season in striking scarlet.

FUNDAMENTAL FACTS

ATTRIBUTES	White, pink, salmon, purple, or red flower spikes on naturally neat plants; for edging, pots, or beds
SEASON OF INTEREST	Late spring to fall
FAVORITES	*Salvia splendens; S. farinacea* for blue flowers; *S. coccinea* for drought tolerance
QUIRKS	Mature plants need abundant water
GOOD NEIGHBORS	Blue ageratum, cockscomb, marigold, petunia
WHERE IT GROWS BEST	Rich, moist soil; partial afternoon shade
POTENTIAL PROBLEMS	Japanese beetle, whitefly, red spider mite
CRITTER RESISTANCE	Moderate
SOURCE	Bedding plants, seeds
DIMENSIONS	60 cm (2 ft) tall, 30 cm (12 in) wide

a 5 cm (2 in) thick layer of moisture-retaining shredded bark, compost, or other organic material. Water as needed to keep the soil slightly moist at all times. Snip off fading flower spikes to encourage production of new ones. After each grooming, fertilize plants with an all-purpose liquid plant food at half strength to ensure summer-long performance.

While salvias are relatively care-free, they can be chewed by iridescent daytime-feeding Japanese beetles, and minute sap-sucking whiteflies or red spider mites can cause leaves to appear yellowish and limp. Pick and dispose of Japanese beetles early in the morning, when they are sluggish. Spraying the undersides of leaves with water will dislodge whiteflies and red spider mites, which prefer feeding in dry conditions, or control these pests with insecticidal soap applied according to the package label directions.

SNAPDRAGON

Antirrhinum majus hybrids

HARDINESS:
Frost tolerant

PREFERRED SOIL pH:
Neutral to slightly alkaline

PREFERRED SOIL TYPE:
Well-drained, loam

PREFERRED LIGHT:
Sun to partial shade

On close inspection, it's easy to see the "dragon" head, with an open mouth formed by pouch-like, "lips."

Snaps offer a broad color range, from deep jewel tones to soft pastels, like lemon.

Snapdragon in the Landscape

Snapdragons are whimsical plants with lots of care-free appeal. Wands of flowers appear persistently throughout the summer, keeping bees busy, filling bouquets, and enchanting children, who like to make the "dragon" mouths of the trumpet-shaped flowers snap. Snapdragons have an alluring perfume, and if you pick the spike when only the lower blossoms are open, they last for a week in a vase of water. There's no need to gather other blossoms; a bunch of snapdragons makes a complete bouquet. You can harvest the flowers freely, as cutting keeps the plants performing throughout the summer.

The flowers come in a variety of shades, from subtle pastels to strident, fiery hues. Snapdragons are veterans of the cut-flower garden. But, because of their care-free temperament, tidy growth habit, and prolonged flower performance, they are finding their way into container plantings and perennial beds as colorful accents to prolong the flowering season. Standing 0.3–1 m (1–3 ft) tall, depending on the cultivar, their slender flower spikes make them team players that are easy to tuck between other plants for all-season color. The only care needed is removing spent flowers, or deadheading, to keep the plant producing yet more spires.

Snapdragons with compact dimensions are perfect temporary space fillers for new perennial beds of fledgling plants. They take up little space but blossom freely until the perennials mature and bloom, usually in their second season. The compact habit of dwarf series such as Floral Carpet makes them ideal edging plants or bedding plants to place beneath taller, bare-stemmed perennials and roses. Varieties like 'Little Darling' have open azalea-type flowers.

Increasing the Bounty

Snapdragons are readily available where bedding plants are sold, and buying bedding plants is the simplest way to infuse your garden with a few spires of sizzling color. For the broadest range of colors and two-toned flowers, called bicolors, buy seeds. Sow them indoors 8–12 weeks before the last frost. The seeds need light to germinate, so sprinkle them over moistened, commercial seed-starting soil, and do not cover them. They also prefer chilly temperatures, so cover the seed container with plastic wrap to keep the soil moist and set it in the refrigerator for 2 weeks before bringing it out and onto a warm windowsill. The seeds will begin to sprout in 7–10 days. Move seedlings into larger pots when they have 2 or 3 sets of leaves and grow them to sturdy size on a windowsill before planting out.

Spires Through All Seasons

There's no reason to wait with snapdragons. Transplant seedlings outside early in spring; or in warm-winter regions set them out in fall for a splash of color all winter, spacing them 20 cm (8 in) apart. If they've been acclimated to cold evenings, they will endure a few degrees of frost and perform most prolifically before hot weather sets in. During hot weather, snapdragons often stop blooming, but will resume as soon as the heat wave goes by. In summer apply an 8 cm (3 in) thick layer of organic mulch, such as compost, shredded bark, or shredded leaves, to the soil to prolong flowering by keeping it cool and moist.

Snapdragons require watering only to prevent wilting in a drought. Although rarely troubled by disease, they can fall prey to rust, a fungal disease that disfigures leaves with rust-colored spots. To prevent rust, water at ground level to avoid wetting leaves, or grow resistant varieties. 'Rocket' snapdragons show good rust resistance and make tall, straight spires for cutting. If aphids, small, pear-shaped sucking insects, infest growing tips, simply dislodge them with a strong spray of water from a hose, or apply insecticidal soap applied per label.

FUNDAMENTAL FACTS

ATTRIBUTES	Compact, colorful, fragrant flowers; for beds, pots, and cutting
SEASON OF INTEREST	Early summer and fall; winter in mild climates
FAVORITES	'Rocket' for cutting; Floral Carpet and 'Little Darling' for edging
QUIRKS	Remove spent flowers to encourage flowering
GOOD NEIGHBORS	Ornamental grasses, irises, roses
WHERE IT GROWS BEST	Cool weather; sun
POTENTIAL PROBLEMS	Fungal rust disease, and aphids
CRITTER RESISTANCE	Good
SOURCE	Bedding plants, seeds
DIMENSIONS	25–90 cm (10–36 in) tall, 25–35 cm (10–14 in) wide

Crowned with huge pink flower heads, 'Royal Queen' reigns over the summer garden.

SPIDER FLOWER

Cleome hassleriana

HARDINESS:
Frost tolerant

PREFERRED SOIL pH:
Adaptable

PREFERRED SOIL TYPE:
Average

PREFERRED LIGHT:
Sun to partial shade

Cleome in the Landscape

An old-fashioned flowering plant once grown in every country garden, cleomes get their common name of spider flower from their loose blossom clusters of individual flowers studded with 8 cm (3 in) long waving stamens. The flowers can be pink, white, or rosy purple. In a good growing season, cleomes quickly reach a height of 1.2–1.5 m (4–5 ft), with the long, slender stems below the flowers clothed in palm-shaped leaflets. The stems have a slightly prickly texture, and the blooms emit a pungent, but not unpleasant, smell.

Most often grown as back-of-the-border plants in summer flower beds, cleomes also look heavenly jostled cheek to jowl with other annuals planted in large containers. Another way to do majestic cleomes justice is to plant them in groups of 5 or more plants, so that the profusely flowered stems cut a wide swath in a flower bed. Growing cleomes behind a short hedge that hides the stems and allows the feathery flowers to billow above the greenery composes an especially effective planting.

As the flowers fade, long, beanlike seedpods form along the lower stem, eventually shedding hundreds of seeds. In mild climates cleomes reseed so reliably that they reappear year after year in early summer. Tolerant of heat and drought, cleomes often flower nonstop until the plants are felled by hard freezes in the fall.

Spiders in Different Colors

Sometimes you can't improve on a good thing. The same cleomes that our grandmothers grew remain steadfastly popular. The variety 'Cherry Queen' has flowers of bright rose, 'Helen Campbell' is pure white, 'Pink Queen' is a vibrant pink, and 'Violet Queen' has violet blossoms. If you have sufficient space, a breathtaking scene can be composed by planting cleomes in single-color drifts, with dark-flowered 'Violet Queen' in the rear, fronted by the rose, then lighter pink, with the white variety in front. The result is a lovely study in perspective that makes the bed look twice as deep as it really is.

'Helen Campbell' is an old-fashioned favorite with large globes of white blooms.

FUNDAMENTAL FACTS

ATTRIBUTES	Tall stems topped by feathery white, pink, or purple flowers; for beds, large pots
SEASON OF INTEREST	Midsummer to fall
FAVORITES	Purple 'Violet Queen'; white 'Helen Campbell'
QUIRKS	Stems are prickly
GOOD NEIGHBORS	Evergreen shrubs, white- or pink-flowered annuals
WHERE IT GROWS BEST	Sun or partial shade; warm-summer areas
POTENTIAL PROBLEMS	Decreased flowering and foliage in late summer; cut back to remedy
CRITTER RESISTANCE	Excellent
SOURCE	Seeds, plants
DIMENSIONS	1.2–1.5 m (4–5 ft) tall, 45 cm (18 in) wide

Growing Cleome

Purchase bedding plants in spring, start seeds indoors 4 weeks before your last frost, or sow seeds directly in the garden around your last frost date. The seeds need light to germinate, so barely cover with soil, and keep the soil barely moist and at normal room temperature (or sow outdoors in warm soil) until the seedlings have several leaves. Transplant or thin seedlings to 30 cm (12 in) apart.

Cleomes are self-supporting, so staking is rarely necessary. They only need watering during extended droughts. As cleomes gain height, the lowest sections of the stems often become thin and leggy, and the bloom display may weaken. To help plants make a comeback, prune back half of the stems by half their length to prompt the emergence of new blooming branches. The prickly stems clad with sporadic thorns discourage pests and disease, but also make it wise to wear gloves when pruning cleomes.

STATICE

Limonium and other spp.

HARDINESS:
Frost tolerant

PREFERRED SOIL pH:
Adaptable

PREFERRED SOIL TYPE:
Well-drained

PREFERRED LIGHT:
Sun

Statice in the Landscape

Statice, or sea lavender, is a lovely sight at the front of a flower bed or growing in a container with other long-flowering annuals such as cosmos, gomphrena, or zinnias. The stiff, sparsely leaved stems are topped by white, pink, blue, purple, yellow, apricot, or burgundy flowerlike, papery bracts. Within each bract hide tiny true flowers. The showy flowerlike bracts are destined to be cut and harvested often, so you may want to grow some statice in a special cutting garden where you don't mind stripping their beauty on a regular basis.

To take advantage of their long-lasting beauty, use statice flowers in fresh floral arrangements. But if you grow only one flower to hang in clusters to dry in summer and then bring out to redeem a dreary winter day, it should be statice. Stems cut when the bracts are just opened and fully colored, and hung upside down will dry in a few days in any warm room.

Beyond the Blues

The strongest color in statice has traditionally been blue, a flower color that is always in demand. For a vigorous plant with classic blue flowers,

'Forever Gold' has vivid yellow flowers.

look for 'Azure', prized for its pure color. If you like variety, newer types show varying shades of blue, cream, yellow, or red. 'Forever Moonlight' bears large creamy yellow to clear yellow flowers on strong, square stems. 'Pastel Shades' is a tempting, 35 cm (14 in) tall mixture with several soft colors including fawn, mauve, and apricot. Bolder hues are the strong suit of the Fortress and Soiree series, which produce 45 cm (18 in) long stems, which are suitable for cutting and are well clothed with beautiful flower bracts.

Russian statice (*Psylliostachys suworowii*) has an entirely different look from the sea lavender statice. These spectacular plants have 45 cm (18 in) long stems covered with tiny star-shaped pink flowers.

Growing Statice

Bedding plants of statice are a rare find at garden centers, so plan to start seeds indoors 8 weeks before your last spring frost. Sow seeds in a container of moistened seed-starting soil and cover with an 0.3 cm (1/8 in) layer of soil. Place the container in a sunny window and keep the medium constantly moist until the seedlings have several sets of mature leaves. Begin setting the seedlings outdoors to accustom them to the weather, called hardening off, while the weather is cool. Chilling the seedlings outdoors through 2°–10°C (35°–50°F) spring nights actually aids their growth. This is especially important where hot weather arrives soon after winter.

Drainage is all-important. Sandy soil enriched with organic matter is ideal, but heavy clay must be substantially lightened with compost or other organic matter to make it acceptable. Raised beds or pots may be the easiest answer for gardeners with dense clay soil. The plants will bloom best if drenched with a soluble all-purpose plant food, applied as directed, once a month during the growing season.

Statice has very few pest problems, but when the roots are exposed to wet soil for prolonged periods, the plants may contract root rot, causing them to collapse unexpectedly and wither.

FUNDAMENTAL FACTS

ATTRIBUTES	Colorful flowers for beds or cutting gardens
SEASON OF INTEREST	Early summer
FAVORITES	'Azure' for blue flowers; 'Forever Moonlight' for yellow; 'Pastel Shades' and Soiree and Fortress series for mixed colors; Russian statice for pink
QUIRKS	Seedlings benefit from chilling in spring
GOOD NEIGHBORS	Cosmos, gomphrena, zinnia
WHERE IT GROWS BEST	Sun with excellent drainage
POTENTIAL PROBLEMS	Root rot due to wet soil
CRITTER RESISTANCE	Good
SOURCE	Seeds
DIMENSIONS	30–35 cm (12–14 in) tall, 38 cm (15 in) wide

A planting of statice in mixed shades provides long-lasting color in the summer garden.

STOCK

Matthiola incana

HARDINESS:
Tender

PREFERRED SOIL pH:
Neutral to slightly alkaline

PREFERRED SOIL TYPE:
Fertile, well-drained

PREFERRED LIGHT:
Sun to partial shade

'Giant Excelsior' stocks send up tall columns, each with one large flower spike.

Stock in the Landscape

Stocks are quick starters. They sprout in a week and rush to blossom, usually within 10 weeks of sowing, providing glorious color and fragrance before other plants set their first flower buds. When spring temperatures hover around 10°C (50°F) at night and remain below 18°C (65°F) during the day, stocks grow steadily, sending up 45–75 cm (18–30 in) tall flower spires. Each is thick with rosette-shaped single or double blossoms in white, lilac, purple, peach, pink, red, or yellow. Double stocks also boast a spicy scent.

Spring-sown plants won't last in hot weather, and fall-sown plants are felled by freezing temperatures. So plant stocks where you need a dash of color before later-blooming perennials perform, or combine them with other early bloomers, such as pansies and primroses. Stocks can also be grown in a greenhouse and be used as cut-flower annuals for filling vases throughout the winter.

Investing in Stock

You can buy seedlings, but stocks are easily grown from seeds. Sow indoors 6 weeks before your last frost, or before the onset of cool fall weather. The seeds need light to germinate, so sprinkle them on the surface of moistened commercial seed-starting soil. Put the container on a well-lighted windowsill or under fluorescent lights. Keep the soil moist and between 10° and 16°C (50° and 60°F) for 1–2 weeks to ensure germination.

A certain percentage of stocks grown from seed have single flowers, but you can pull them out and discard them after sprouting. The leaves of single stocks are a darker green than those of doubles. Transplant light green seedlings into 5 cm (2 in) pots

Stock blossoms plentifully in warm shades, such as purple, mauve, and pink.

when their second pair of mature leaves develops, and transplant to the garden when conditions are favorable. You can also sow seeds outdoors, when the weather is cool, in moist, fertile, neutral to slightly alkaline soil in sun or partial shade.

For fragrant, early blossoms in a range of colors, grow Trisomic Giant Imperial Mix. Heat-tolerant 'Brilliant' is for areas where spring is quickly followed by hot summer temperatures. If cool weather lasts in your area, go for 'Excelsior', also known as 'Giant Excelsior', which has carmine red, white, midblue, or pink blooms.

Growing Stock

The biggest problem for stocks is heat, which causes plants to become dwarfed and reduces flowering. To prevent it, plant early. As a precaution against bacterial rot, a disease that fells seedlings, soak the seeds in hot water 55°C (130°F) for 10 minutes before sowing. In damp, humid conditions, a fungal disease called powdery mildew can disfigure leaves. Control it by clipping and disposing affected leaves, and prevent it by spacing plants far enough apart for good air circulation. Sap-sucking insects, such as aphids and flea beetles may feed on leaves. Knock them off with a strong spray of water from a hose, or apply insecticidal soap according to label directions.

FUNDAMENTAL FACTS

ATTRIBUTES	Gray-green leaves; white, lilac, pink, red, or yellow spires of rosebud-like, fragrant flowers
SEASON OF INTEREST	Spring to early summer; fall; frost-free winters
FAVORITES	Trisomic Giant Imperial Mix; 'Giant Excelsior' for tall spires; 'Brilliant' for heat tolerance
QUIRKS	Needs cool nights to flower well
GOOD NEIGHBORS	Iris, poppy, primrose, pansy, rose
WHERE IT GROWS BEST	Cool climate; fertile, neutral to slightly alkaline soil; sun or partial shade
POTENTIAL PROBLEMS	Rot, powdery mildew; aphids, flea beetles
CRITTER RESISTANCE	Good
SOURCE	Bedding plants, seeds
DIMENSIONS	0.6–1 m (2–3 ft) tall, 0.3 m (1 ft) wide

SWAN RIVER DAISY

Brachycome iberidifolia

HARDINESS:
Tender

PREFERRED SOIL pH:
Adaptable

PREFERRED SOIL TYPE:
Loam

PREFERRED LIGHT:
Sun to partial shade

Brachycome in the Landscape

Brachycome, or Swan River daisy, is a care-free annual that forms a cloud of soft color. Dozens of beautiful, dainty, 2.5 cm (1 in) flowers appear all at one time, most often in a light violet hue, each with a canary yellow center rimmed in white. The cheerful little pinwheels form at the ends of the stalks and are held above pale green, feathery foliage, which creates a delicate interplay of texture and shape in the garden.

The cool flower color makes brachycome a pretty companion to any plant with pink, purple, violet, white, or yellow flowers. The plant is a handsome complement to verbena and coreopsis and forms an interesting contrast with the broad leaves of sweet potato vine. Its tidy, mounding growth habit is welcome toward the front of the border or as an edging. Brachycome is also a good choice for filling in around tall, leggy plants and carpeting bare spots. In a container or window box, brachycome sends its short, sprawling stems cascading downward over the rim, showering

The dainty pinwheels of brachycome flowers rise above mounds of feathery foliage.

flowers that are 15–20 cm (6–8 in) in diameter over the sides.

Growing Brachycome

This flexible plant tolerates either sun or partial shade but demands excellent drainage. It hates to be waterlogged, making brachycome ideal for rocky, sandy soil, where water can pass through quickly. And if you have a windy location—perhaps on an exposed porch or balcony or beside an open field, a lake, or the ocean—brachycome will hold up well where many other plants would perish. It is often used to tuck into crevices in stone walls or fill cracks between flagstones in walkways.

This little daisy thrives in containers, but only if the pot is equipped with fast-draining soil and a generous drainage hole. Rainy or humid weather can wreak havoc with this native of Australia, which is adapted to sparse rainfall and dry air. It does not fare well in hot, humid summers, but it performs admirably in cooler or drier climates.

Making a Good Plant Better

Although brachycome has stepped into stardom only recently, new varieties are appearing every year. 'Ultra'™ and 'Bravo' are particularly floriferous, tidy, compact versions. As an expansion of the color range, 'Bravo' is also available with white petals that bear the ever-present yellow center. 'Strawberry Mousse' adds pink to the brachycome spectrum and has broader leaves than other varieties. 'Lemon Mist' does not form the tight mound of closely held flowers that the violet-flowered brachycome boasts, but is clad in a generous quantity of dainty yellow blossoms.

Increasing the Bounty

For best results, purchase bedding plants in spring. You can also sow seeds indoors 6 weeks before the last frost, but take note that seed-sown plants need a lot of time to mature enough to bloom. Seeds require light to germinate, so sprinkle seeds on the surface of a moistened commercial seed-starting medium. Moisten the seeds with a mister immediately after sowing, and then mist them lightly each day until they have germinated.

Set the container on a sunny windowsill or under fluorescent lights at warm room temperatures. To encourage branching, cut off the growing tips of the seedlings when they are 13 cm (5 in) tall, transplant them into small pots, 5 cm (2 in) in diameter, and grow them on a sunny windowsill where there is low humidity.

The seedlings can be planted outdoors when evening temperatures remain above 10°C (50°F) in a sunny, well-drained location.

A Trouble-Free Plant

Brachycome is not a plant that's prone to problems, if you provide the dry, well-drained conditions that it prefers. However, the plants quickly rot when the atmosphere is very humid, or the soil is soggy.

Small, pear-shaped, sap-sucking insects called aphids can occasionally be a problem. To control aphids, knock them off plants with a strong stream of water from a hose or apply insecticidal soap according to the package directions. Apply insecticidal soap on an overcast day or late in the afternoon to avoid sunburning the foliage, which causes leaves to develop brown, crisp spots and edges.

FUNDAMENTAL FACTS

ATTRIBUTES	Tidy mound of airy foliage and violet, white, pink, or yellow daisy flowers; for beds, edging, rock garden. pots
SEASON OF INTEREST	Summer to fall
FAVORITES	Blue 'Ultra', blue or white 'Bravo', pink 'Strawberry Mousse', yellow 'Lemon Mist'
QUIRKS	Dislikes humid, moist growing conditions
GOOD NEIGHBORS	Verbena, coreopsis, portulaca, sweet potato vine
WHERE IT GROWS BEST	Partial shade with sandy, well-drained soil and good air circulation
POTENTIAL PROBLEMS	May rot in warm, humid conditions; aphids
CRITTER RESISTANCE	Good
SOURCE	Bedding plants, seeds
DIMENSIONS	30 cm (1 ft) tall, 30 cm (1 ft) wide

White-flowered varieties, such as 'Carpet of Snow', cover beds in a blizzard of blooms.

SWEET ALYSSUM

Lobularia maritima

HARDINESS:
Frost tolerant

PREFERRED SOIL pH:
Adaptable

PREFERRED SOIL TYPE:
Average

PREFERRED LIGHT:
Sun

Sweet Alyssum in the Landscape

A dainty, undemanding little plant like sweet alyssum is just what every gardener needs to edge a bed, line a walkway, fill a bare spot, or serve as an accent. Whether you want to add a dash of color around the edge of a container or carpet a broad swath of the garden with a reliable, durable bloomer, sweet alyssum is at your service. Smothered by so many honey-scented flowers throughout the summer that you can't see its needlelike leaves, this short, dense, mounding plant adds lacy texture to hanging baskets, fills the crevices of rock walls, or creates a colorful hem for paths. It also works as a magnet for nectar-seeking butterflies. In Zone 9, sweet alyssum can also be sown in autumn for winter performance.

Sweet alyssum's dimensions are discreet. Each plant stands less than 15 cm (6 in) tall with a 30 cm (1 ft) spread. Despite this small stature, few sights compare with the ground-hugging sea of blossoms in white, pink, rose, and lavender that result if you plant Easter Basket mix, a hybrid that stays compact even in the heat of summer. If you plant the pearly 'Wonderland White', your garden will look as though it's been blanketed by a blizzard in July. Combine this small wonder with petunias, herbs, lady's mantle, or annual geraniums, and you can't fail to make a garden statement.

Growing Sweet Alyssum

Bedding plants are available at garden centers in spring, but sweet alyssum is very easily grown from seeds sown in the garden. Two weeks before the last spring frost simply scatter the seeds thinly on the ground, rake lightly to cover them, and water the soil gently. Seeds germinate quickly and should be thinned to 12 cm (5 in) apart. In only 6 weeks you'll begin to see flowers. It's a good idea to keep a container of white-flowered sweet alyssum seedlings on standby. If you need fillers for containers or beds, simply cut out a brownie-sized chunk of alyssum and drop it into place.

Sweet But Tough

Veterans of the toughest assignments in the flower garden, sweet alyssum doesn't give up easily. If granted its wishes, it would have full sun, water when the soil is dry, cool summer temperatures, and fertile, well-drained soil. However, this plant tolerates conditions that are considerably less than ideal without complaining. Over-watering is its primary stumbling block, as soggy soil can lead to fatal root rot, so water plants only when the soil becomes dry.

Where summers are long, older varieties in particular benefit from shearing back in midsummer to prolong flowering. Use shears or a string

Sweet alyssum forms numerous rounded flower clusters that obscure the leaves.

trimmer to clip the plants back to half their height. Drench them with a balanced, water-soluble fertilizer and look forward to strong growth and flowering as cool nights approach.

Sweet alyssum, while virtually trouble free, is prone to minute spiderlike pests called spider mites, which most often attack during the hot, dry weather of late summer. You will know they've arrived when the leaves have a pale, stippled appearance, caused by the pests' feeding. You will also see fine webs on the leaf undersides. Apply a forceful spray of water from a hose every other day until the infestation subsides.

In late summer when days are warm and humid and nights are cool, powdery mildew, a fungal disease, can settle in, coating leaves with a white powder that won't rub off and weakening the plants. Cutting the plants back and allowing healthy foliage to appear is an easy and effective control.

FUNDAMENTAL FACTS

ATTRIBUTES	Low mounds of foliage; fragrant, dainty flowers in white, pink, rose, or lavender; use in beds, in pots, and as edgings
SEASON OF INTEREST	Late spring to fall
FAVORITES	Easter Basket mix and 'Wonderland White'
QUIRKS	Cutting back in midsummer promotes flowering
GOOD NEIGHBORS	Geraniums, herbs, lady's mantle, petunias
WHERE IT GROWS BEST	Sun, cool temperatures, fertile soil
POTENTIAL PROBLEMS	Spider mites; powdery mildew
CRITTER RESISTANCE	Good
SOURCE	Bedding plants, seeds
DIMENSIONS	10–15 cm (4–6 in) tall, 25–30 cm (10–12 in) wide

SWEET POTATO VINE

Ipomoea batatas

HARDINESS:
Tender

PREFERRED SOIL pH:
Adaptable

PREFERRED SOIL TYPE:
Moist loam

PREFERRED LIGHT:
Sun to partial shade

Sweet Potato Vine in the Landscape

Ornamental sweet potato vine is the same species as the root vegetable that we put on the table, but these ornamental versions are valued for their large, fancy leaves that may be deep burgundy, bright chartreuse, or variegated with pink, white, and green. The first variety to capture the gardener's eye was 'Blackie', with its maple-leaf shaped, deep purple leaves. Perfect for sending plentiful stems spilling over the edge of containers or adding a splash of burgundy to beds, 'Blackie' was an overnight sensation. Invariably handsome and care-free, the plant has only one drawback: It lacks flowers. But who cares when it has such other attributes?

Then along came 'Margarita', a variety with abundant, silky, heart-shaped, chartreuse leaves on thick, wandering stems. 'Margarita' makes a fast-growing groundcover, carpeting the soil with its plush, golden leaves.

Sweet potato vine is grown for its outsized leaves, which may be dazzling chartreuse.

A third variety, named 'Tricolor', has smaller, heart-shaped leaves variegated with rose pink, white, and green. Its growth tends to be less robust than that of the other two, making it more appropriate for containers, where it can be easily tended.

Growing Sweet Potato Vine

Few annuals fill as many job descriptions as the sweet potato vine. While all varieties can handle full sun, the leaves of 'Blackie' blanch to a wine color when light levels are low. 'Margarita' grows equally well in sun or light shade, but in full sun the leaves attain striking red edges. As shade increases, the leaves of 'Margarita' glow with more of a golden hue, and often become larger, reaching 10–12 cm (4–5 in) in width. Sweet potato vines thrive in hot summer weather but wilt when rain is scarce. Weekly watering is usually sufficient in beds, but sweet potato vines in containers usually need water daily to prevent wilt. Avoid leaf spotting from sunburn by watering early or late in the day, when the sun doesn't shine directly on the leaves.

As care-free as sweet potato vines are, their juicy, big leaves do attract slugs, especially in damp, shady environments. If you see numerous clean-edged holes in the leaves, set out slug traps in the evening. Use either commercial traps or shallow saucers of beer. The yeasty smell attracts slugs, which crawl in and drown. Entire leaves that disappear overnight are usually the work of foraging deer. Tucking a bar of deodorant bath soap into plantings is a good deterrent.

Increasing the Bounty

Cuttings 10 cm (4 in) long taken from stem tips of any sweet potato vine will root in a week in a glass of water. As soon as roots appear, plant the cuttings in a pot of loose, fertile potting soil, set it in a shady place, and water it daily. You can transplant the young plants to the garden or a container outdoors 2 weeks later, in warm weather. Sweet potato vines prefer warm soil and are quickly killed in frosty conditions.

Because sweet potato vines do produce tubers, you can dig those

FUNDAMENTAL FACTS

ATTRIBUTES	Trailing stems with large, lime, purple, or variegated pink, green, and white leaves; for pots, baskets, groundcover
SEASON OF INTEREST	Summer
FAVORITES	'Blackie' for burgundy leaves; 'Margarita' for lime leaves; 'Tricolor' for leaves variegated in pink, white, and green
QUIRKS	Craves warm weather, warm soil
GOOD NEIGHBORS	Coleus, grasses, licorice plant, verbena
WHERE IT GROWS BEST	Sun or partial shade
POTENTIAL PROBLEMS	Grows poorly in dry soil
CRITTER RESISTANCE	Good except for slugs, deer
SOURCE	Bedding plants, cuttings, tubers
DIMENSIONS	Vines trail 45–90 cm (18–36 in) in length

swollen roots in fall, before soil temperatures drop below 13°C (55°F), and store them over the winter in a paper bag in a cool, dark location. To start growth in spring, replant the tubers, laying them on their sides 5 cm (2 in) below the soil surface, after the soil warms in late spring.

'Blackie' gives a good contrast of leaf color and blends well with other flowers.

TITHONIA

Tithonia rotundifolia

HARDINESS:
Tender

PREFERRED SOIL pH:
Slightly alkaline to neutral soil

PREFERRED SOIL TYPE:
Well-drained loam

PREFERRED LIGHT:
Sun to filtered shade

Tithonia in the Landscape

If you want to make a bold statement in the garden, tithonia, or Mexican sunflower, is the plant for the job. The 8 cm (3 in) diameter, scarlet-orange or yellow blossoms have brazen appeal, and at 1.2–1.8 m (4–6 ft) tall, with large leaves, most tithonias traditionally reside in big spaces. In a small yard, the 1.8 m (6 ft) tall, vibrant orange-flowered 'Torch' may appear too big for its britches and "muscle out" its bedfellows. But the relatively tame, 1.2 m (4 ft) versions, such as the golden apricot-flowered 'Aztec Sun' and deep orange 'Goldfinger', can be grown in the company of mid-sized plants. The even newer 'Fiesta Del Sol', which reaches a demure 70–75 cm (28–30 in) in height, can star as a solo act in a pot.

Wherever you plant them, tithonias put a spark into the scene in mid to late summer. Related to both sunflowers and zinnias, tithonias have a dense, bushy habit, with deep green, heart-shaped leaves. Several planted side by side can form a nearly instant hedge for the growing season, and the flowers combine well with ornamental grasses and Russian sage. The riveting, sometimes shockingly bright

'Goldfinger' is a mid-sized plant with deep golden orange blooms.

blossoms make good cut flowers. To maximize vase life, seal the tips of their hollow stems by plunging them into boiling water after cutting, or singe the cut ends with a flame before placing the stems into a vase of water.

Care-Free Pizzazz

Adapted to dry regions with poor soil, tithonias are plants that don't require fussing. In fact, if the soil is too fertile, they will grow leaves at the expense of flowers. As their common name implies, Mexican sunflowers are sun worshipers. In keeping with their tough-as-nails personality, they tolerate drought bravely. However, it's a wise idea to irrigate as needed to provide 2.5 cm (1 in) of water weekly during summer dry spells.

There's one problem inherent in the fact that they are tall and leafy. Tithonias can be toppled in brisk winds. To prevent disaster before it strikes, stake the plant when it nears its full height.

Increasing the Bounty

Tithonias are easy to start from seed and the seedlings sprout and grow rapidly. To get a head start on the season, sow seeds indoors 4 weeks before frost-free weather on moistened commercial seed-starting soil, and lightly press them into the soil.

Keep the soil moist and set pots in a well-lighted place, providing them with warm room temperatures to quicken germination. To keep the roots from becoming crowded, transplant seedlings into 5 cm (2 in) pots as soon as the first true leaves develop, and grow on in a sunny place at 16°C (60°F). After the danger of frost has passed, you can transplant seedlings into the garden, or sow seeds directly into sunny, well-drained beds, leaving at least 30 cm (1 ft) between the seeds.

Tithonias are not prone to diseases or insect infestations, although leaf-chewing Japanese beetles occasionally become a problem in the East. Hand-pick and dispose of beetles in the morning, or apply insecticidal soap following the package directions and spraying early in the day to prevent leaf scorch.

FUNDAMENTAL FACTS

ATTRIBUTES	Statuesque plants with orange or yellow daisy-shaped flowers; for beds, hedges, cutting
SEASON OF INTEREST	Midsummer to frost
FAVORITES	'Fiesta Del Sol' for orange flowers, short height; 'Goldfinger', 'Torch' for orange flowers, tall height; 'Aztec Sun' for apricot flowers
QUIRKS	Tall varieties need staking
GOOD NEIGHBORS	Ornamental grass, Joe Pye weed, Russian sage, shrub roses
WHERE IT GROWS BEST	Warm summers, average soil, sun
POTENTIAL PROBLEMS	Japanese beetles
CRITTER RESISTANCE	Good
SOURCE	Seeds
DIMENSIONS	0.7–1.8 m (28 in–6 ft) tall, 1 m (3 ft) wide

With their fiery orange blossoms, tithonia will set the garden ablaze in summer.

VERBENA

Verbena spp.

HARDINESS:
Frost tolerant

PREFERRED SOIL pH:
Neutral

PREFERRED SOIL TYPE:
Well-drained loam

PREFERRED LIGHT:
Sun

'Silver Anne' sports fragrant pink flowers.

Purple-top verbena has a stiff, upright habit, with lavender flowers held high on wiry stems.

FUNDAMENTAL FACTS

ATTRIBUTES	Handsome, sprawling plants tipped with dense flower clusters in many colors; for beds, pots, hanging baskets
SEASON OF INTEREST	Early summer to late fall
FAVORITES	'Silver Anne' for scent; moss verbena 'Imagination' for pots; *V. bonariensis* for cutting; *V. peruviana* as ground cover
QUIRKS	Pinch back stem tips early to encourage branching
GOOD NEIGHBORS	Geraniums, herbs, petunias, roses
WHERE IT GROWS BEST	Sunny, dry locations
POTENTIAL PROBLEMS	Aphids; powdery mildew
CRITTER RESISTANCE	Excellent
SOURCE	Bedding plants, cuttings
DIMENSIONS	20 cm–1.2 m (8 in–4 ft) tall, spreading 0.6 m (2 ft) in diameter

Verbena in the Landscape

If it has any faults at all, verbena could only be accused of working too hard and producing an overwhelming crop of colorful flowers. Verbena blooms throughout the summer in full sun despite dry, parched soil and inconsistent watering, and can play several roles. As a mainstay in containers, it sends out numerous stems swooping over the sides of pots, which brings texture to the display. When used as bedding plants, verbenas elegantly grow together to fill a garden with color or cover the ground below tall, bare-stemmed, "leggy" plants. They can also be persuaded to interweave with foliage or flowering plants, with no maintenance needed.

Verbenas are available with white, pink, blue, purple, red, and two-toned flowers. The flower heads form at the ends of the stems, with numerous tiny, brightly colored flowers clustered into a tight mound that resembles a clump of snowflakes. At night, varieties like 'Silver Anne' send their sweet perfume roaming. Through the day, butterflies and hummingbirds court the nectar-rich flowers.

Except for occasional visits from aphids, which can be rinsed off or controlled with insecticidal soap, few pests bother care-free verbenas. Even deer shy away, and verbenas laugh in the face of drought. For maximum performance, spent flowers should be removed by clipping back older stems, which also encourages the emergence of new branches. But even when left to their own devices, verbenas just keep performing.

A Flower of Many Faces

The most popular verbenas by far are the annual verbena hybrids that form loose mounds of slightly felted, deep green leaves and 8 cm (3 in) wide flower clusters. But they're not the only game in town. Consider moss verbena (*V. tenuisecta*), with its thin, lacy leaves on trailing stems, making it perfect as a vertical accent in containers. 'Imagination', with its violet-blue flowers, is a particularly impressive variety. Purple-top verbena (*V. bonariensis*) has an entirely different posture. It stands bolt upright, balancing its clusters of purple blooms on stiff, sparsely clad stems, up to 1–1.2 m (3–4 ft) in height, making it ideal for interweaving with perennials and cutting for bouquets. For a good creeper at the front of a bed or a temporary ground cover, try Peruvian verbena (*V. peruviana*), a low-growing type with scarlet flowers. These accommodating species can also be grown as perennials in the West.

Increasing the Bounty

Verbenas are difficult to start from seed, so you're better off buying them as bedding plants, but they are easy to root from cuttings. In fact, if you pin a stem to the soil with a hairpin or bent piece of wire, it will make roots at the point of contact within a couple of weeks. You can then sever the rooted stem from the mother plant and plant it separately.

WISHBONE FLOWER

Torenia fournieri; T. flava

HARDINESS:
Tender

PREFERRED SOIL pH:
Neutral to slightly alkaline

PREFERRED SOIL TYPE:
Moist, well-drained

PREFERRED LIGHT:
Sun to partial shade

Torenia in the Landscape

When you need a little whimsy, the pertly colored, trumpet-shaped blossoms of torenia are guaranteed to add cheer to your garden. Also known as wishbone flower, torenias have a delightfully clownish quality, with 2.5 cm (1 in) wide, two-toned flowers covering compact 20–30 cm (8–12 in) tall plants, whether they are grown in sun or partial shade. Torenias withstand summer heat in champion style and ask only for moist soil to stay in bloom through summer continuously until frost.

Native to Indochina, torenias bear bicolored flowers reminiscent of

Like pansies, "faces" of torenia flowers bring a cheerful look to shady spots.

The Duchess series added pink, plum, and lavender to the usual blue flowers.

pansies, traditionally sporting a light blue hooded upper "lip" and a blotched royal purple lower "jaw." As if that weren't enough, a prominent yellow "throat" enhances each flower.

In addition to the blue motif, other colors have been added to torenia's bag of tricks. The heat-tolerant 'Happy Faces' series and the dwarf Duchess series includes flowers in plum, blush pink, white, and lavender . A selection of another species, *T. flava* (formerly *T. baillonii*), sold as 'Suzie Wong', is similar, but has a more mounding growth habit and an abundance of striking yellow-orange blossoms with purplish, nearly black throats.

Because they pack so much pizzazz, torenias work wonders in small spaces and bring a great change of pace to sites in partial shade. You can also use them in combinations in window boxes and other containers or as an edging in the garden.

Growing Torenia

Not everything this fancy is equally easy to please. Torenias will grow in full sun in cool-summer areas, but where summers are hot they require at least a half day of shade. Fertile, well-drained soil that holds moisture well is ideal. Apply an 8 cm (3 in) thick layer of organic mulch to reduce evaporation from the soil, and water as needed to prevent wilting. To promote abundant flowering, apply a balanced, soluble fertilizer every 2 or 3 waterings during the summer and pinch off seedpods.

Increasing the Bounty

As torenia's popularity has grown, so has its availability as a bedding plant. Look for healthy bedding plants at garden centers in the spring, and keep them constantly moist until you plant them. To sow the small seeds, it's best to sow them indoors about 10 weeks before your last spring frost. The seeds need light to germinate, so sprinkle them over moistened seed-starting soil and place on a sunny windowsill or under fluorescent lights and keep the soil at 21°C (70°F). After seedlings sprout, grow

them at 16°–18°C (60°–65°F). Transplant them into 5 cm (2 in) diameter pots when they have 3 sets of mature leaves. Move seedlings outdoors when the weather is warm and there is no danger of frost. In mild regions, sow seeds directly on moist, fine-textured garden soil and keep it barely moist until the seeds germinate and have several sets of mature leaves.

Torenias are not prone to pests but occasionally do fall victim to sap-sucking pests, usually tiny, pear-shaped aphids and spider mites, which can be recognized by leaves marred with pale, stippled spots. Simply rinse off the leaves, especially the undersides, with a firm spray of water several times a week until they are gone. Control tiny whiteflies with insecticidal soap per label directions.

FUNDAMENTAL FACTS

ATTRIBUTES	Pansy-shaped purple, plum, lavender, pink, white, or yellow flowers on compact plant; for beds, edging, pots
SEASON OF INTEREST	Spring and summer; winter in frost-free regions
FAVORITES	Duchess series for dwarf form; Happy Faces series for color range; 'Suzie Wong' for yellow-orange flowers
QUIRKS	Needs shelter from hot afternoon sun
GOOD NEIGHBORS	Campanula, Russian sage, dusty miller, snapdragon
WHERE IT GROWS BEST	Moist, fertile soil in sun or partial shade
POTENTIAL PROBLEMS	Whiteflies, aphids, spider mites
CRITTER RESISTANCE	Good
SOURCE	Bedding plants, seeds
DIMENSIONS	15–30 cm (6–12 in) tall, 30 cm (12 in) wide

Tall-stemmed zinnias are great for back of the border or to cut for fresh arrangements.

ZINNIA

Zinnia elegans hybrids;
Z. angustifolia

HARDINESS:
Tender

PREFERRED SOIL pH:
Slightly acidic to neutral

PREFERRED SOIL TYPE:
Well-drained loam

PREFERRED LIGHT:
Sun

Zinnia in the Landscape

Impatient gardeners love the instant gratification zinnias provide. These care-free annuals are a cinch to grow from seed and blossom weeks after sprouting. Adaptable and prolific, zinnias range in height from 0.3 m (1 ft) dwarfs, such as Peter Pan and Thumbelina mixes, to 1 m (3 ft) tall head turners, such as Candy Stripe and Ruffles. All of these seed mixes boast a broad range of shades including every color except blue. While the first zinnias on the market had single flowers, pompon, dahlia-flowered, ruffled, and quill-petal types are now gaining supremacy.

Zinnias make the strongest splash if you mix their festive colors together in masses. For the middle of the garden, select a taller type, such as 'Oklahoma', a bright beauty with good disease tolerance. Use dwarf zinnias, such as 'Dreamland', to edge a bed in a ribbon of blooms. All zinnias naturally develop numerous flowering stems, so no pruning is required. They also don't need staking.

A Fiesta of Cut Flowers

Zinnias are one of the easiest and most plentiful cut flowers to grow for fresh arrangements. Given fresh water every couple of days, zinnias will stay in prime condition in a vase for more than a week. Spend a few minutes collecting a fistful of zinnias, stripping the lower leaves as you go, and you have an instant bouquet. 'Ruffles', with its large, 8 cm (3 in) wide double blossoms, and the stiff-stemmed 'Blue Point', are popular for cut flowers, as is the aptly named 'Cut and Come Again' mix.

Growing Zinnia

Zinnia seeds germinate quickly and easily in warm soil, so wait until summer is in full swing to sow seeds or transplant seedlings. Although zinnias withstand drought with a stiff upper lip, they perform best if given supplemental water early in the season if rain doesn't fall regularly. Later on, dry weather will prevent fungal diseases like leaf spotting and powdery mildew, which often causes white powdery patches to form on leaves in humid weather. To prevent it, keep leaves dry by watering at soil level, avoid watering in the evening, space plants 30–35 cm (12–14 in) apart to allow air circulation, and choose disease-resistant types, such as 'Oklahoma' and 'Profusion', and the straight species *Zinnia angustifolia*.

Lesser-Known Care-Free Zinnias

Although *Z. elegans* is great for eye-catching color and cut flowers, the more petite *Z. angustifolia*, also called narrow-leaf or spreading zinnia, is a hardworking annual for the garden. Naturally disease resistant, it's ideal for adding to borders in midsummer, when perennials sometimes stop blooming. It stands 30 cm (12 in) tall, with small flowers in white, yellow, and copper. New interspecies hybrids, such as the Profusion series combine the flower size and colors of regular zinnias with the care-free culture of narrow-leaf zinnia.

FUNDAMENTAL FACTS

ATTRIBUTES	Profuse flowers in many colors and shapes; for beds, pots, cutting
SEASON OF INTEREST	Midsummer to fall
FAVORITES	'Ruffles', 'Blue Point', and 'Cut and Come Again' for cutting; dwarf 'Dreamland'; 'Oklahoma', 'Profusion', and *Z. angustifolia* for disease resistance
QUIRKS	Grows best in hot, dry weather in midsummer
GOOD NEIGHBORS	Gomphrena, lady's mantle, lavender, verbena
WHERE IT GROWS BEST	Well-drained soil that is not high in nitrogen
POTENTIAL PROBLEMS	Foliar fungal diseases in hot, humid climates
CRITTER RESISTANCE	Good
SOURCE	Seeds, bedding plants
DIMENSIONS	30–90 cm (12–36 in) tall, 30 cm (12 in) wide

Zinnias sprout quickly and supply care-free color to the garden till felled by frost.

CHAPTER EIGHT

CARE-FREE PERENNIALS

Perennials are the workhorses of the garden. These herbaceous plants that live for three or more years bridge the gap between the permanence of woody plants and the transience of annuals. They easily fit gardens of any proportion and don't have to be replanted every spring. Although most perennials produce flowers, often their foliage is so lovely that the leaves alone are reason enough to grow them. The sheer diversity of perennials makes it easy to build a satisfying garden using little else. Plant them abundantly in a border or combine them with woody plants, annuals, vines, and bulbs for a garden with a many-sided personality.

Your climate can determine the number and type of perennials you can grow, but resourceful gardeners know ways to stretch the limits. Coax slightly tender plants into overwintering in cold climates by planting them in protected spots that capture the sun's warmth and provide shelter from wind. In warm regions, accommodate plants that dislike heat and humidity by siting them where they'll have midday shade, and by providing them with generous spacing for air circulation. Some perennials have a compact habit that suits them to container use. The only special care they require is storing the containers in a place during the winter that remains around 4°C (40°F) so that the plants have the dormancy they require without suffering frost damage.

Plant a variety of perennials for different bloom times and focus on long bloomers to maximize your floral show. In most parts of North America, perennials go dormant in winter, providing the ideal opportunity to divide and transplant. Division every few years reinvigorates old plants and produces more plants to expand your garden or share with friends.

Use the information in this section to identify candidates for your conditions, taking into consideration sun, shade, soil type, and your hardiness Zone. You'll soon have a list of care-free perennials custom-made for your garden.

Showy but never a show-off, anise hyssop mixes handsomely with flowers of every color.

ANISE HYSSOP

Agastache foeniculum

HARDINESS:
Zone 6

PREFERRED SOIL pH:
Neutral

PREFERRED SOIL TYPE:
Well-drained, moderately fertile

PREFERRED LIGHT:
Sun to filtered shade

Anise Hyssop in the Landscape

Anise hyssop is a trouble-free addition to an informal garden, taking its place equally among herbs or perennials. This stalwart, pretty, purple-flowered plant is a must for mid- to late-summer color. Placement is important: Anise hyssop wants bright sun, good drainage, and room to reseed. Once those conditions have been met, there is nothing more for you to do but enjoy the show of flowers.

Start cautiously, with just a few plants, set 30–60 cm (1–2 ft) apart in the middle or back of a flower bed. The plants may emerge as handsome rosettes of leaves in spring, but they quickly add height and girth, eventually growing 1 m (3 ft) tall and 0.6 m (2 ft) wide. While waiting for the flowers to develop, you can enjoy the edible dark green heart-shaped leaves that smell and taste like licorice.

The fuzzy flower spikes appear in midsummer, with colorful blue, pink, or soft yellow blossoms that last for weeks. The individual spikes are only 5–8 cm (2–3 in) long, but when plants are massed, the effect is showy. While anise hyssop blooms mingle well with most neighbors, they are particularly good companions for the lavender-blue flowers of Russian sage and the yellow ones of yarrow.

Because of its handsome appearance and ease of cultivation, anise hyssop has attracted the attention of enterprising nurseries. Among the new varieties that offer a range of colors are the dark blue 'Blue Fortune', coral 'Firebird', burnt lemon 'Apricot Sunset', raspberry 'Tutti-frutti', and white 'Snow Spike'. At season's end, unless you have intervened and clipped the blossoms for long-lasting bouquets, they'll shed plenty of seeds for expanding next year's display.

Further Delights

Honeybees, hummingbirds, and butterflies flock to the flowers of anise hyssop, adding allure and movement to the garden, and honey made from the flowers is prized by beekeepers. The tangy leaves, with a mint-licorice taste, make a nice garnish for cold summer soups, iced tea, or frozen drinks. When dried, they can be brewed to make a tasty tea sweetened with honey. And the flowers, picked in full bloom, have a soft anise-mint flavor that enhances fruit salads.

Growing Anise Hyssop

Although thriving in average soil in full sun or part-day shade, anise hyssop does demand a well-drained site. Soggy soil conditions can induce disastrous root rot. You can begin with nursery grown plants in spring, or start seeds indoors 6–8 weeks before your last spring frost. Plants always flower the first year they are planted, and are winter hardy to Zone 6. In colder climates, protect the roots from winter damage by covering them with an

Anise hyssop sends up spikes of fuzzy purple flowers atop mintlike leaves that smell like licorice.

8 cm (3 in) deep layer of loose organic mulch, such as straw or dried, chopped leaves, in early winter.

Should too many volunteer seedlings appear in spring, you can simply pull and discard them, or gently dig them up and transplant them where you want them to grow. In late summer, when warm, humid days are followed by cool nights, anise hyssop occasionally contracts powdery mildew, a fungal disease that disfigures leaves with powdery gray or white blotches. Control a light case by removing and disposing of affected leaves, or simply tolerate the presence of leaves that are only slightly blemished, but do not eat them. Cut back any severely affected plants to within 15 cm (6 in) of the soil and allow healthy new growth to appear in a few weeks.

FUNDAMENTAL FACTS	
ATTRIBUTES	Blue, coral, yellow, purple, white flower spikes; for beds, cutting
SEASON OF INTEREST	Summer
FAVORITES	'Blue Fortune', 'Firebird', 'Tuttifrutti', 'Apricot Sunset', 'Snow Spike'
QUIRKS	Plants can reach their mature size and flower in a single season
GOOD NEIGHBORS	Blanket flower, Russian sage, salvia, yarrow, tithonia, herbs
WHERE IT GROWS BEST	Sun to part shade in average soil
POTENTIAL PROBLEMS	Root rot in wet soil; powdery mildew
RENEWING PLANTS	Lives several years; divide every 2 years
CRITTER RESISTANCE	Good
SOURCE	Starter plants, seeds, division
DIMENSIONS	0.6–1.2 m (2–4 ft) tall, 0.3–0.6 m (1–2 ft) wide

ARTEMISIA
Artemisia spp.

HARDINESS:
Zones as indicated

PREFERRED SOIL pH:
Neutral

PREFERRED SOIL TYPE:
Average, well-drained

PREFERRED LIGHT:
Sun

Artemisia in the Landscape

Grown for its frosty-looking foliage, artemisia is especially radiant in the soft light of early morning and again at dusk. Its silver leaves even shine, reflecting light well into the evening on moonlit nights. These outstanding foliage plants come in a range of sizes, from 15 cm (6 in) to 1 m (3 ft) tall, and can hug the ground or grow into shimmering, shrub-sized specimens. Beautiful all summer, artemisias thrive with little care provided they get plenty of sun and fresh air to keep their felt-textured leaves dry.

All artemisia leaves are silvery. Those of *A. stelleriana* are deeply cut in rounded lobes.

A tremendous texture plant, artemisia makes a fine partner for perennials with dark, smooth foliage, such as peonies and bearded iris, and they are natural allies for fall-blooming asters. The gray leaves of artemisia are valuable for their calming effect when placed near flowers with bold "hot" colors, such as orange Asiatic lilies, wine-colored cockscomb, and yellow black-eyed Susans. They also make the red of crocosmia or annual geranium flowers seem more intense.

Artistry with Artemisia

Versatile and well-behaved, 'Silver Brocade' (Z4) is a variety that grows 0.3 m (1 ft) tall and wide, and its deeply cut leaves look much like those of annual dusty miller. Larger 'Powis Castle' (Z5) grows to 0.6 m (2 ft) and stands up well to humid summer heat provided it is kept trimmed to maximize air circulation around the plant.

Both are welcome additions to either gardens or containers, and the cut stems make useful fillers for indoor arrangements. For tight spots, edgings, or luminous highlights in rock gardens, heat- and cold-tolerant 'Silver Mound' (Z4) has a low-lying profile and finely cut, lacy leaves.

A famous edible artemisia is *A. dracunculus*, commonly called French tarragon (Z4). It is grown for its aromatic, green, willowlike leaves. French tarragon makes rapid growth in summer herb gardens, reaching 1 m (3 ft) in height. It is far superior to the similar Russian tarragon.

Growing Artemisia

Spring is the best time to set out container-grown specimens, planting them 30–60 cm (1–2 ft) apart, depending on the width of their spread, when mature. If your soil is not well drained, enrich planting holes with sand and compost before setting in the plants. Add half the package recommendation of a balanced organic or controlled-release fertilizer, such as a 10-10-10. Water every few days for 2 to 3 weeks until the new plants begin to grow. About once a month through summer, trim back the growing tips of the leaves to keep plants compact and to encourage the development of new stems. Pests seldom bother aromatic artemisias, which are naturally repellent.

Increasing the Bounty

Most artemisias root from stem cuttings taken in late summer, but it is far simpler to divide clumps in early spring. Dig a clump and pull its roots apart into 2 or 3 equal sections. Or dig just a bit from the outer edge of the clump, and replant immediately.

FUNDAMENTAL FACTS

ATTRIBUTES	Silvery, fine-textured foliage; for beds, edging, pots
SEASON OF INTEREST	Spring through fall
FAVORITES	'Silver Brocade', 'Powis Castle', compact 'Silver Mound'
QUIRKS	Usually grown for foliage; you may trim and discard flowers
GOOD NEIGHBORS	Aster, iris, peony, rudbeckia, evergreen shrubs
WHERE IT GROWS BEST	Sun to part shade in average soil
POTENTIAL PROBLEMS	Unlike named cultivars, some species are too invasive for the garden
RENEWING PLANTS	Lives many years; divide every few years
CRITTER RESISTANCE	Excellent
SOURCE	Division in spring; cuttings in summer
DIMENSIONS	Up to 1 m (3 ft) tall, 0.3–0.6 m (1–2 ft) or more wide

The compact shape of artemisias make them perfect specimens for growing as an edging or low hedge. They really stand out against a background of solid green plants.

ASARUM

Asarum canadense;
A. europaeum

HARDINESS:
Zones as indicated

PREFERRED SOIL pH:
Slightly acidic to neutral

PREFERRED SOIL TYPE:
Moist, fertile

PREFERRED LIGHT:
Partial to full shade

Asarum in the Landscape

Low-maintenance and also low to the ground, asarum is made for the shade. Any place protected from sun will suit this cold-tolerant perennial, which is often called wild ginger. When crushed, the leaves will release the scent of ginger, although they are not considered edible. The plant is so named because its root was once used as a substitute for that exotic spice.

If you need a groundcover plant that's always trim, tidy, and impeccably well-groomed, look no further than *Asarum canadense* (Z3), a native of the North American woodlands. Grown for its 13 cm (5 in) tall, downy green, heart-shaped leaves, this species forms a carpet that bears up well when summer weather becomes torridly hot. Its European counterpart, *A. europaeum* (Z4), is similar in shape and size, but its leaves are brighter green with a glossy, waxy shine and subtle veining. It is somewhat less tolerant of heat and drought than its native cousin but remains reliably evergreen through winter.

Both wild gingers bloom in early spring as the leaves unfold, but the flowers are easy to miss. Appearing

The glossy, ground-hugging leaves of asarum distinguishes this tough groundcover.

close to the ground, the small, brownish purple, urn-shaped flowers are inconspicuous except for their gently refreshing scent. You'll have to lift the leaves to see, and smell, them.

Care-Free Plants for Shade

Asarums are tough and care-free, and although they spread over time, they are not invasive. New foliage sprouts from wiry underground stems called rhizomes. Wild gingers thrive in shade even where the soil is not deep or rich. They prosper under trees and shrubs, on the northern side of buildings or walls, and in other hard-to-plant spots where sun seldom shines.

Ideal landscape partners for these rich, glossy leaved groundcovers include other light-shunning perennials, such as epimedium, hosta, Solomon's seal, and trillium, as well as trees and shrubs of all sorts. Wild ginger's broad, smooth leaves are particularly attractive when they are played against the feathery foliage of ferns, astilbe, and meadow rue.

Planting and Caring for Asarum

Buy potted nursery-grown plants of wild ginger in early spring. Dig a 5 cm (2 in) deep layer of compost into a shady site and set the plants in at the same depth they grew in their containers, spacing them 15 cm (6 in) apart for good ground coverage in time. Growth will be slow for the first year, or maybe two, but eventually asarum forms handsome mats that creep outward while staying low. It looks better and better each season and lasts for many years.

To encourage strong spring growth, spread 2.5 cm (1 in) of compost over the bed every fall. If any of the evergreen leaves show brown edges or other damage from the winter, simply clip back the stem to ground level, and the plant will quickly send up fresh new foliage.

Like many other woodland perennials, asarums defend themselves during drought by going dormant. To keep the plants in leaf through dry spells, water weekly and mulch with

a 5 cm (2 in) thick layer of fine bark chips or compost to safeguard soil moisture. At the same time, beware of slugs and snails, which can make a home in damp mulch. Handpick them in the evening, set out saucers of stale beer to trap them, or deter them with a barrier of coarse sand or crushed eggshells around plants.

Increasing the Bounty

Wild ginger grows slowly and rarely needs dividing, but you can dig out rooted sections of the plant about 10 cm (4 in) in diameter and transplant them to a new place in early spring if you want to introduce it to a new area. Fill the hole left behind with loamy soil, and neighboring asarum plants will soon fill the gap.

FUNDAMENTAL FACTS

ATTRIBUTES	Handsome mat-forming plants that spread slowly; for groundcover, beds
SEASON OF INTEREST	Spring through fall
FAVORITES	*A. canadense* as woodland groundcover; *A. europaeum* as specimen
QUIRKS	Drought can cause plants to become temporarily dormant
GOOD NEIGHBORS	Cohosh, epimedium, astilbe, hosta, Solomon's seal, trillium, ferns, trees
WHERE IT GROWS BEST	Partial to full shade in moist soil enriched with humus
POTENTIAL PROBLEMS	Slugs and snails
RENEWING PLANTS	Lives many years; top-dress with 2.5 cm (1 in) of compost in the fall
CRITTER RESISTANCE	Good
SOURCE	Division
DIMENSIONS	13 cm (5 in) tall, spreads to broad mats several meters (feet) wide

'Rosa Sieger' has extra-large pink flowers.

ASTER

Aster spp.

HARDINESS:
Zone 4 unless otherwise indicated

PREFERRED SOIL pH:
Neutral

PREFERRED SOIL TYPE:
Average, well-drained

PREFERRED LIGHT:
Sun to partial shade

Aster in the Landscape

Just when you think there's nothing to look forward to in the garden in fall except the sunset colors of tree leaves, asters burst on the scene with cool blue and silvery pink flowers. While a few species do bloom willingly earlier in the summer, the easiest asters to grow save their fireworks for autumn. The starry blue or pink blossoms with yellow centers are so numerous that they often hide the leaves entirely. And a few stems won't be missed if you bring them indoors to admire in a vase of water.

Asters often bloom in tandem with chrysanthemums, but this partnership works best with compact aster varieties that match the mums in terms of plant form and stature. Taller asters usually require staking, and are thus beloved fence plants suited to tying to posts or open rails. Goldenrod and sneezeweed are always welcome company for fall-blooming asters, as are the last of the marigolds and rudbeckias that manage one final autumn flush of flowering.

Sorting Through the Masses

Most of the asters sold by nurseries are descendants of two North American native species: New England aster (*A. novae-angliae*) and New York aster (*A. novi-belgii* [Z3]), including hundreds of named cultivars. If ease of culture is your goal, begin with a naturally compact cultivar, such as 'Purple Dome', which grows to only 45 cm (18 in) tall and needs no pinching or staking. Where you want more height, consider 'Hella Lacy', a 1 m (40 in) tall purple bloomer with excellent cold hardiness and good resistance to fungal leaf disease.

Indeed, disease can be a worry with many asters when they grow in warm, humid climates. If you notice fuzzy or moldy-looking spots on the foliage, trim off affected leaves and prune back or space plants widely to increase air circulation. Or consider growing a disease-resistant aster, such as the shade-tolerant white wood aster (*A. divaricatus*), which has starry white flowers and is happy under larger shrubs or in the dry shade of trees. Another disease fighter is *A.* × *frikartii*, which flowers prolifically with big blooms and is very vigorous.

Growing Aster

Set out purchased plants in spring, in soil that is of average fertility. A scant ration of fertilizer can help get new plants going, but avoid feeding asters after summer begins. These tough flowers prefer to fend for themselves, and too much fertilizer can make them grow big, but weak-stemmed and short on flowers.

Pinch back tall varieties at least once, in early summer, to encourage branching. Stake or tie up the stems when they have grown more than 0.6 m (2 ft) tall.

Increasing the Bounty

After only two to three seasons, asters grow into large, crowded clumps. To relieve crowding, either pinch out one-third of the new stems soon after they appear in early spring, or dig up and divide the clump if you want to expand your collection. Small divisions can be dug from the outer edges of a clump well into early summer. If transplanted promptly and given plenty of water, the new divisions will bloom heavily in fall the same season.

A. novi-belgii 'Albanian' blooms with double white stars held in branched sprays.

FUNDAMENTAL FACTS

ATTRIBUTES	Starry lavender, purple, pink, or white flowers in profusion in the fall
SEASON OF INTEREST	Late summer to fall
FAVORITES	'Purple Dome' for compact habit; *A. divaricatus* for dry shade
QUIRKS	Plants more than 0.6 m (2 ft) tall require support
GOOD NEIGHBORS	Chrysanthemum, goldenrod, rudbeckia, marigold, sneezeweed
WHERE IT GROWS BEST	Sun to part shade in average soil and a wide range of climates
POTENTIAL PROBLEMS	Fungal leaf diseases
RENEWING PLANTS	Lives several years; dig and divide every 3–4 years
CRITTER RESISTANCE	Good
SOURCE	Division
DIMENSIONS	0.3–1.5 m (1–5 ft) tall, 0.3–1 m (1–3 ft) wide

A. × *frikartii* is a reliable, disease-resistant bloomer with fragrant purple flowers.

A. chinensis var. pumila is unusual for its rounded, fuzzy spikes of purplish flowers.

ASTILBE
Astilbe spp.

HARDINESS:
Zone 3

PREFERRED SOIL pH:
Slightly acidic

PREFERRED SOIL TYPE:
Moist, fertile, organic

PREFERRED LIGHT:
Partial shade

Astilbe in the Landscape

Plush plumes of color wave above the fernlike foliage of these splendid and extremely cold-hardy perennials. Astilbes are truly majestic when topped by a profusion of white, pink, salmon, lilac, or red feathery blossoms that linger for weeks in summer.

Astilbes are not strictly for shade, although they are often grown there. Where summers are not oppressively hot, you can grow this plant in full sun. Astilbes are ideal for brightening patches under tall trees or walls and fences. A swath of astilbes turns a damp, hard-to-plant area into a showpiece. In shady settings, plant astilbes with hostas. Given a little more sun, astilbes make pretty companions for bee balm, lady's mantle, and irises. Astilbes look gorgeous in containers with ornamental sweet potato vines, dahlias, and licorice plants.

A Carnival of Color

Astilbes offer a broad range of flower colors, and bloom times vary, so you can combine them for an extended period of color. 'Sprite' is a charming pink-flowered miniature, perfect for edging or pots, and hardy enough to overwinter in outdoor pots. The widely available *Astilbe* × *arendsii* cultivars bloom in June and July and range from the deep red-flowered 'Fanal' and dark pink 'Gloria Purpurea' to purple 'Hyacinth' and frothy white 'Bridal Veil'. *A. chinensis* cultivars, such as mauve-flowered 'Finale' and rich rose 'Serenade', usually bloom in August, as do the tall and stately 'Superba' and other *A. tacquetii* cultivars. Very late-blooming *A. chinensis* 'Purple Candles' begins in August and continues into September.

Growing Astilbe

Astilbes are no-nonsense, trouble-free plants that will survive for years. The optimal growing site has consistently moist, fertile soil. Dig in a 5–8 cm (2–3 in) thick layer of organic matter at planting time, and cover the soil around plants with a 5 cm (2 in) layer of moisture-retaining compost or leaf mold. To increase flowering in subsequent years, fertilize in spring with an organic or controlled-release fertilizer. After 3 to 5 years the plants may become crowded. Rejuvenate by lifting the plants and using a knife or

The 'Deutschland' variety is famous for its large feathery fronds of white flowers.

The pink blooms of 'Bressingham Beauty' clothe tall, stiff stems that won't droop.

sharp shovel to divide the woody bases before replanting.

Astilbes wilt and brown quickly if not watered during drought. They can go dormant and may eventually perish. The first symptom of dissatisfaction is leaf tip browning, but new growth will sprout if supplemental water is forthcoming. When you water, soak the soil deeply, allowing it to dry between waterings. Other than root rot, which occurs when the soil is constantly soggy, astilbes resist disease. Although the plants are virtually pest free, raggedly chewed leaves can reveal the work of night-feeding slugs and snails. Set saucers of beer on the soil to lure and drown these pests. In the eastern part of the country, Japanese beetles may chew leaves of plants growing in full sun. Spray with insecticidal soap. To avoid future problems with sun-loving beetles, plant in partial shade.

FUNDAMENTAL FACTS

ATTRIBUTES	White, pink, purple, or red plumelike flowers; ferny foliage; for beds
SEASON OF INTEREST	Summer
FAVORITES	Red 'Fanal', purple 'Hyacinth', pink 'Sprite', white 'Bridal Veil'
QUIRKS	Needs consistently moist soil
GOOD NEIGHBORS	Bee balm, ferns, hostas, iris, lady's mantle
WHERE IT GROWS BEST	In light shade and moist soil
POTENTIAL PROBLEMS	Slugs and snails, Japanese beetles
RENEWING PLANTS	Lives many years; dig and divide every 3–4 years, in spring or fall
CRITTER RESISTANCE	Good
SOURCE	Nursery plants, division
DIMENSIONS	0.3–1.2 m (1–4 ft) tall, 0.6–1.2 m (2–4 ft) wide

BALLOON FLOWER

Platycodon grandiflorus

HARDINESS:
Zone 3

PREFERRED SOIL pH:
Near neutral

PREFERRED SOIL TYPE:
Average, moist, well-drained

PREFERRED LIGHT:
Sun to partial shade

Balloon Flower in the Landscape

A unique perennial for the summer garden, balloon flower is dependable and persistent, flowering year after year with minimal care. The plant's common name accurately describes its flower buds, which swell up like inflated balloons before popping open to reveal 5-pointed, star-shaped blossoms in blue, pink, or white.

Late to emerge in spring, balloon flower can be interplanted successfully with many spring-flowering bulbs and hardy annuals, such as pansies. Its bloom time often coincides with that of lilies, which make excellent companions. In fall, its foliage briefly turns an attractive shade of yellow that can be a good foil to late bloomers, such as asters or chrysanthemums. In a large bed, place balloon flower near the front, where its curious flowers can be appreciated.

A Bouquet of Balloons

Balloon flower is a fine source of rich indigo blue color for the early-summer garden. Blue varieties include 'Fuji', which can be grown from seed

The balloon flower's bud swells up, then bursts open into a starlike flowering.

or from nursery grown plants, and 'Mariesii', which is grown only from cuttings and sold as nursery plants. 'Fuji' is also available in pink or white. The blooms of pink balloon flowers tend to be pale, aging to nearly white.

Compact forms have the same basic appearance as taller ones but are more suitable for edging or growing in containers, and their extreme hardiness helps them overwinter in pots. Indigo-flowered 'Sentimental Blue' reaches only 20–25 cm (8–10 in). Double-flowered selections offer a significantly different look, producing blooms that, individually, resemble those of delphiniums. However, the weight of the double flowers makes staking these plants essential.

Growing Balloon Flower

Easy to grow, balloon flower prefers moist, well-drained soil. It requires nearly full sun in cool summers to look its best. In hot-summer regions, balloon flower can handle up to a half day of shade, and looks the better for it. Full-sized balloon flower plants can fall over once they become heavy with blossoms, so plan ahead and stake them early. Linking wire stakes work for small plants; use wire peony grids for big clumps.

Balloon flower rarely needs division, so you can leave a plant in the garden, undisturbed, for many years. Its heavy gnarled roots resent disturbance, so the preferred way to propagate from old plants is to use a sharp knife to dig down and nick new shoots off along with a piece of the root in spring, when the new stems are about 10 cm (4 in) long. Transplant them into pots, and they should be well rooted and ready for the garden in about 6 weeks.

Few pests or diseases bother balloon flowers. If slugs and snails do feed on the leaves, hand collect them or set out saucers of beer as bait, to attract and drown them.

FUNDAMENTAL FACTS

ATTRIBUTES	Large blue, pink, or white flowers with a unique shape in bud
SEASON OF INTEREST	Early to midsummer
FAVORITES	'Fuji', 'Mariesii'
QUIRKS	Lax stems require support when heavy with flowers
GOOD NEIGHBORS	Columbine, daylily, iris, lady's mantle, pansy
WHERE IT GROWS BEST	Average soil; sun in cool regions, afternoon shade in warm regions
POTENTIAL PROBLEMS	Occasionally slugs and snails
RENEWING PLANTS	Lives many years, division seldom necessary
CRITTER RESISTANCE	Excellent
SOURCE	Young stem cuttings taken from the root in spring and planted
DIMENSIONS	20–50 cm (8–20 in) tall, less than 35 cm (14 in) wide

The blossom color of balloon flower ranges from a vivid indigo blue to a pale pink that fades to nearly white, as seen in the 'Fuji Pink' variety at right.

BEE BALM

Monarda didyma

HARDINESS:
Zone 4

PREFERRED SOIL pH:
Slightly acidic

PREFERRED SOIL TYPE:
Moist

PREFERRED LIGHT:
Partial shade

Rangy stems and shaggy blooms give bee balm a casual charm ideal for country gardens.

Bee Balm in the Landscape

If you have a damp spot in the yard, fill it with bee balm. Then, in early summer, feast your eyes on the amazing display of flowers produced by the showiest member of the mint family. This plant features shaggy blooms composed of many narrow, tubular flowers arrayed in 5–8 cm (2–3 in) wide topknots held on long stems. Colors include pink, lilac, and riveting reds that hummingbirds adore. The green leaves, sometimes tinged with red, give off a minty fragrance when crushed.

Bee balm thrives in moist soil, so it's a natural companion for astilbes. In hot-summer areas, it needs partial shade and can be paired with impatiens, coleus, or wishbone flower. In colder climates bee balm will grow in partial shade or sun provided the plants are well mulched in winter. In dry regions, they'll appreciate regular watering; consider planting them near an outdoor water faucet where they can benefit from spillage. Its slightly gangly posture and ragged-looking blossoms make bee balm ideal for naturalistic settings. Keep the plants far from high-traffic paths, however, because they attract bees in droves.

Better Bee Balms

Powdery mildew, a disfiguring fungal leaf disease, has long been a weakness of bee balm, but many cultivars offer good resistance to the white leaf spots that slowly destroy bee balm leaves and weaken the plants. At the first sign of trouble trim off and dispose of affected leaves. If the plant is badly infested, trim it to within a few inches of the ground and it will produce healthy new foliage.

To ward off mildew problems, buy resistant varieties. Good choices include 'Marshall's Delight', a vigorous producer of 5 cm (2 in) wide purplish pink blossoms on stiff 1 m (3 ft) stems, and 'Raspberry Wine', with purplish red flowers on 1.2 m (4 ft) stems. Among red bee balms, 'Jacob Kline' and 'Gardenview Scarlet' defend themselves well from mildew. These cultivars must be purchased and propagated by division or cuttings rather than being grown from seed.

Growing Bee Balm

Set out purchased plants in spring, in moisture-retentive soil, preferably in a spot convenient to water. Enrich the soil with compost or other organic matter but fertilize lightly, if at all. Apply an 8 cm (3 in) thick layer of organic mulch to conserve soil moisture. In the second year, pinch out a few stems in the middle of the clump to improve air circulation, which in turn discourages mildew.

Bee balm spreads by sending out shallow horizontal roots called

'Croftway Pink' produces salmon flowers.

stolons, which develop underground buds that grow into new plants. Bee balm can sometimes spread quickly, but you can usually restrain it and keep colonies healthy by thinning out old crowns so that the younger ones can flourish. Dig and divide established clumps every 2–3 years in early spring, refreshing the soil with compost or peat moss in the process.

FUNDAMENTAL FACTS

ATTRIBUTES	Shaggy pink, purple, or red flowers; attracts hummingbirds; for beds
SEASON OF INTEREST	Early to midsummer
FAVORITES	'Gardenview Scarlet', 'Marshall's Delight', 'Raspberry Wine'
QUIRKS	Wilts quickly when soil becomes dry
GOOD NEIGHBORS	Astilbe, columbine, cranesbill geranium, dusty miller, impatiens
WHERE IT GROWS BEST	Partial shade, moist soil
POTENTIAL PROBLEMS	Powdery mildew; prevent by growing resistant varieties and thinning plants
RENEWING PLANTS	Plants live for 3 years; colonies persist longer; divide every 2–3 years
CRITTER RESISTANCE	Good
SOURCE	Division, cuttings, seeds
DIMENSIONS	0.6–1.2 m (2–4 ft) tall, colonies grow 0.6 m (2 ft) or more wide

Bees love bee balm. Plant it toward the middle of the garden, away from high-traffic areas.

Flower tresses rise over the leaves in spring.

BERGENIA

Bergenia cordifolia

HARDINESS:
Zone 3

PREFERRED SOIL pH:
Neutral to slightly alkaline

PREFERRED SOIL TYPE:
Organically rich, well-drained

PREFERRED LIGHT:
Partial shade

Bergenia in the Landscape

When you need a fast and easy plant to cover a piece a shady ground, bergenia is the rock-solid perennial for the job. Sporting oval, slightly ruffled, glossy green leaves, some up to 30 cm (1 ft) long, bergenia asserts itself dramatically. The key to a standout performance is moderation: not too much moisture, average soil, and protection from midday sun.

As a foliage plant, bergenia is without peer. The densely packed clumps make a strong statement in shady gardens, carpeting the ground with bold leaves. Equally qualified for edging a pond or holding the soil of a hard-to-mow slope, bergenia also looks handsome fronting a stone wall or spilling over a path. Mix it with columbine, ferns, or other "feathery" plants that contrast with bergenia's fleshy foliage. Because the mounds of leaves look attractive on all sides, bergenia is a good candidate for a container planting, as long as the pot is at least 60 cm (24 in) wide and deep, and its cold-hardiness assures its survival in containers overwintered outdoors.

Fancy Flowers and Foliage

In all but the hottest climates, tresses of tiny flowers carried on short reddish stems crown the foliage in spring and last for a few weeks. It is here that plant breeders have nurtured some variation on the standard pink flowers. 'Evening Glow' has crimson blooms, 'Perfecta' has rosy red ones, and 'Silver Light' has white flowers with reddish pink in the center. If you clip off blooms as they begin to fade, you may get a repeat performance of flowering later in the season.

Bergenia changes personality in late summer or early fall. As cold weather approaches, the leaves convert from green to bronze, purple, or russet. Even more dramatic, 'Evening Glow' is transformed into a maroon carpet in winter. In mild climates, the colorful leaves persist over the winter months, an attribute that is especially appreciated in regions where the ground is bare of snow.

Growing Bergenia

Location is the key to success with bergenias. Protect them from strong summer sun. If you have problematic, alkaline soil, this plant's for you. If, on the other hand, you admire bergenia and your soil is a bit acid, simply add compost to neutralize the soil, and to help it retain moisture and drain well. Or add garden lime according to package directions to raise the pH of the soil to neutral or a bit on the alkaline side. The dry soil that is typical of late summer in many places can cause leaf edges to brown, but you can avoid this problem by mulching between plants and watering if needed until it rains again. Each spring, fertilize plants with an organic mulch of compost, or sprinkle balanced-formula controlled-release fertilizer to provide a light buffet of nutrients over a 3-month period.

Be on the lookout for the occasional slug or snail, as these pests relish bergenia's lush leaves. To discourage them, thin the plants when they become crowded, and don't overwater. Remove slug-hiding spots like stones or logs on the soil's surface. If slugs appear, set out saucers of beer to lure and drown the pests, or sprinkle sharp diatomaceous earth on soil to deter the soft-bodied pests.

FUNDAMENTAL FACTS

ATTRIBUTES	Clumping plants; glossy evergreen leaves; red, pink, or white flowers
SEASON OF INTEREST	Spring for flowers; nearly year-round for foliage
FAVORITES	Crimson 'Evening Glow'; red 'Perfecta'; white 'Silver Light'
QUIRKS	Leaf edges brown in hot sun or dry soil
GOOD NEIGHBORS	Columbines, perennial geraniums, hostas, lungwort, ferns
WHERE IT GROWS BEST	Partial shade in average, cool soil
POTENTIAL PROBLEMS	Slugs and snails
RENEWING PLANTS	Lives several years; divide in early spring and replant immediately
CRITTER RESISTANCE	Good
SOURCE	Division
DIMENSIONS	0.3–0.6 m (1–2 ft) tall, 0.3–0.6 m (1–2 ft) wide

A groundcover for all seasons, bergenia sports colorful flowers in spring and lush foliage that remains beautiful year-round, turning from green to bronze during mild winters.

BLANKET FLOWER

Gaillardia x grandiflora

HARDINESS:
Zone 3

PREFERRED SOIL pH:
Adaptable

PREFERRED SOIL TYPE:
Fertile, well-drained

PREFERRED LIGHT:
Sun

Blanket flower brings the sun of big sky country to the garden, in vibrant yellow and red.

Blanket Flower in the Landscape

Heat-tolerant, drought-resistant blanket flower billows across the ground in a blaze of glorious shades of red, mahogany, and yellow. All hues are represented in each daisylike flower. The effect is arresting, which explains why this native of the Great Plains is a much loved flowering garden plant.

'Dazzler' blazes with yellow-tipped petals.

When given a place in the garden, particularly a dry spot where irrigation is inconvenient, blanket flowers grow into lush, bushy plants bearing such a profusion of bright blossoms that they are easily seen from a distance. Tremendously tolerant of sultry weather, blanket flowers seem to gain strength from each heat wave that passes, and humidity doesn't slow them down at all.

Bold New Colors

The unaltered color combo of red, red-orange, and yellow found in wild blanket flowers is guaranteed to anchor beds devoted to hot colors, but you can try a couple of color variations. 'Burgundy' bears wine red flowers without yellow tips, which are as lovely in fresh arrangements as in the garden. 'Dazzler' takes the opposite approach, featuring clear contrast between dark maroon centers and a tip of deep yellow on each petal. These plants, often sold simply as gaillardia, grow to nearly 1 m (3 ft) tall and benefit from staking to keep the flowers holding their heads high.

Feisty little 'Goblin' is very dwarf at only 0.3 m (1 ft) tall. It's a real eye-catcher in containers or tucked into a hot, sunny garden corner.

Growing Gaillardia

There's no need to buy more than one bedding plant of blanket flower, as the plant reseeds. Two- and 3-year-old plants, which have survived at least one winter, are usually the most robust bloomers, but longevity isn't one of this plant's virtues. Plants that have passed their third growing season tend to collapse or fail to appear for no apparent reason. But fear not, more seedlings are always there to pick up the torch.

You can buy bedding plants, or start plants from seeds. Start seeds indoors 8 weeks before the last spring frost. The seeds need light to germinate, so sprinkle them over moistened seed-starting soil, and keep the soil moist and at room temperature until the seedlings produce mature leaves. Set them out as soon as they have a set of mature leaves, even if the weather is still chilly. Spring-sown plants

bloom half-heartedly their first year and much more the second. If you cut plants back by one-half after the first flush of flowering, they will produce more flowers later in the season. Volunteer seedlings can be dug and moved in fall or early spring. When lifting seedlings, keep as much soil as possible packed around their roots to minimize transplanting trauma.

Problems don't usually plague blanket flowers, but they occasionally fall victim to the fungal leaf disease powdery mildew, or to viral wilt, especially if grown in moist soil. Remove and dispose of leaves with powdery gray or white deposits, and dispose of any plants that wilt and do not recover when watered. Small sap-sucking aphids and thrips occasionally visit. Control them with insecticidal soap, used per label directions and applied early in the day.

FUNDAMENTAL FACTS

ATTRIBUTES	Summer-long red or red-and-yellow flowers; for beds
SEASON OF INTEREST	Summer
FAVORITES	Dwarf 'Goblin'; red-flowered 'Burgundy'; yellow-tipped 'Dazzler'
QUIRKS	Short-lived but reseeds
GOOD NEIGHBORS	Black-eyed Susan, butterfly weed, coreopsis, rudbeckia, yarrow
WHERE IT GROWS BEST	Sun, dry soil.
POTENTIAL PROBLEMS	Rarely: root rot, powdery mildew, viral wilt; aphids, thrips
RENEWING PLANTS	Plants live 2–3 years; colonies reseed; or plant seedling replacements
CRITTER RESISTANCE	Good
SOURCE	Bedding plants, seeds
DIMENSIONS	0.3–1 m (1–3 ft) tall, 0.3–0.6 m (1–2 ft) wide

Little hot pink hearts dangle from arching stems above divided leaves on *D. spectabilis*.

The shape of its flowers inspired its name.

The fringed bleeding heart has smaller flowers and lacier foliage.

BLEEDING HEART

Dicentra spp.

HARDINESS:
Zone 3 unless otherwise indicated

PREFERRED SOIL pH:
Neutral to slightly acidic

PREFERRED SOIL TYPE:
Fertile, moist but well-drained

PREFERRED LIGHT:
Full to partial shade; more sun in cool, moist climates

Bleeding Heart in the Landscape

Clearly a perennial designed for romance, bleeding heart casts a spell with its graceful, arching sprays of dangling heart-shaped blossoms and blue-green, fernlike leaves. Whether planted on the shady north side of a building or under trees along a woodland walk, bleeding heart catches your eye with its 2.5 cm (1 in) long blossoms that look like little hearts torn apart and shedding drops of blood. The flowers dangle gracefully from many arching flower stems.

One meter (3 ft) tall and equally wide, bleeding heart thrives in the shade of leafy trees. It emerges when the gentle spring sun warms the soil, then lasts into summer, protected by the leafy canopy overhead. The flowers are delightful additions to bouquets. Cut the stems when half of the flowers are open, in early morning, and plunge the stems into cold water for several hours before arranging.

Whether in a bouquet or in your garden, savor most bleeding hearts while they last. In midsummer, as the last blossoms fade, the foliage of the species *Dicentra spectabilis* may yellow and the plant go into dormancy. This happens when the plant gets either too much sun or too little water. Either move it or interplant bleeding hearts with ferns or hostas to fill the vacancy during the second half of summer.

An Ever-Blooming Heart

To extend the show, try the fringed bleeding heart, *D. eximia* (Z4). Although smaller and less showy than *D. spectabilis*, this North American native keeps its handsome foliage all summer and sends up flowers from late spring into fall. Just pinch out the old flower stems to encourage more blooms.

Fringed bleeding heart has been crossed with several other species, and hybrid plants in varying shades of pink, such as 'Luxuriant' and 'King of Hearts', as well as the pure white 'Snowdrift' and 'Purity' varieties are available. They have such a long-running act that hardy fringed bleeding hearts are perfect for containers, provided they receive shade and moisture. Similarly, they can line woodland paths or grace spots with dappled shade in perennial borders.

FUNDAMENTAL FACTS

ATTRIBUTES	Graceful, heart-shaped, pink or white flowers; blue-green, ferny foliage
SEASON OF INTEREST	Midspring to summer
FAVORITES	*D. spectabilis*; ever-blooming *D. eximia* 'Luxuriant', 'Snowdrift'
QUIRKS	White-flowered types are slightly less vigorous than the pinks
GOOD NEIGHBORS	Ajuga, ferns, hostas, Solomon's seal, trillium
WHERE IT GROWS BEST	Full to partial shade in rich, moist soil
POTENTIAL PROBLEMS	Fungal leaf diseases can occur in damp sites with poor air circulation
RENEWING PLANTS	Plants live many years; divide overgrown clumps
CRITTER RESISTANCE	Excellent
SOURCE	Division; seeds of pure species
DIMENSIONS	0.6–1 m (2–3 ft) high, 0.6–1 m (2–3 ft) wide

Growing Bleeding Heart

Loosen the soil and dig in plenty of organic matter when planting. Set out potted plants in early spring, or plant dormant roots as soon as the soil can be worked in late winter. Keep the soil moist until the young plants are established. An organic mulch will cool the roots and retain moisture, but to prevent root rot, keep the mulch away from the plant crowns, or growing points where leaves emerge. When plants go dormant, trim away faded foliage and mark the site so you don't accidentally dig into the roots while they're at rest. Established plants are best left undisturbed. Mulch with 2.5 cm (1 in) of compost in spring, and you'll enjoy years of care-free flowers.

BLUESTAR

Amsonia tabernaemontana;
A. hubrectii

HARDINESS:
Zone 4 unless otherwise indicated

PREFERRED SOIL pH:
Neutral

PREFERRED SOIL TYPE:
Average, well-drained

PREFERRED LIGHT:
Sun to partial shade

Bluestar in the Landscape

Like other plants with blue flowers, bluestar is always welcome in the garden because of its ability to flatter everything in its presence. Hardy and dependable, bluestar is a cinch to grow. A wildflower that thrives in meadows and on roadsides, bluestar is accustomed to neglect in the field, making it a care-free natural for any low-maintenance garden.

Bluestar's airy flower clusters are composed of dozens of tiny porcelain-blue stars that appear from spring to well into summer. This is a perennial that looks shrubby because of its narrow leaves, woody stems, and stocky posture. To make the blue flowers stand out to best effect, put bluestar in the company of other early-summer favorites, such as yellow coreopsis or pastel-hued col-umbine and foxglove. You can also use bluestar to create a cooling patch of blue that works as a garden accent in front of shrubs or evergreens.

Autumn Surprise

Many early-season bloomers fade away when fall rolls around, but not bluestar. The elegant foliage turns golden yellow, creating a lovely accent late in the year. This part of bluestar's life cycle gives you a little extra mellow color to combine with

The flowers open into tiny, china blue stars.

fall-blooming asters, crysanthemums, butterfly weed, or rudbeckias, all of which stand at approximately the same height as bluestar and benefit from the background color.

Other Blues

In the North the name bluestar goes to *Amsonia tabernaemontana*, also known as willow amsonia, for its willowlike leaves. In warmer climates that name is applied to another species. Some-times called Arkansas bluestar, *A. hubrectii* (Z5) is a taller, wispier plant with almost needlelike foliage. Like its hardier cousin, Arkansas bluestar is easy to grow in any sunny, well-drained spot. Arkansas bluestar reaches 1–1.2 m (3–4 ft) at maturity. The profuse flowers in late spring are pale periwinkle to steel blue, and the dazzling fall foliage is a glowing gold.

Planting Bluestar

This native wildflower luxuriates in moist but well-drained soil, but it can endure dry conditions later in the summer when drought is most likely to hit and the flowering period is behind it. Don't bother to lavish this tough perennial with rich compost or copious fertilizer, because too many nutrients can lead to soft, floppy growth and fewer flowers. Full sun is best in cool-summer climates, but partial or afternoon shade is preferred where summers are hot and dry.

If the plants become leggy in mid-summer, trim them back by about one-third to enhance the appearance of the golden fall foliage. Pruned plants will rebound and fill out, although they won't flower again until the following year.

Bluestar is a modest spreader that is always willing to give up small divisions dug from the outer edges of the clump in early spring. When transplanting divisions, allow 0.6–1 m (2–3 ft) of space between new plants to allow enough room for them to spread as they mature.

A. tabernaemontana forms a feathery plant that lends an informal look to the garden.

FUNDAMENTAL FACTS

ATTRIBUTES	True-blue flowers in early summer, golden fall foliage; for beds
SEASON OF INTEREST	Early summer and fall
FAVORITES	*A. tabernaemontana* for Zone 4; *A. hubrectii*, Zone 5
QUIRKS	Needs good soil drainage, little or no fertilizer
GOOD NEIGHBORS	Fall asters, butter daisy, butterfly weed, coreopsis, rudbeckia
WHERE IT GROWS BEST	Sun, well-drained soil
POTENTIAL PROBLEMS	Pest and disease problems are rare
RENEWING PLANTS	Lives many years; divide in early spring
CRITTER RESISTANCE	Good
SOURCE	Division, seeds
DIMENSIONS	0.6–1.2 m (2–4 ft) high, 0.6–1.2 m (2–4 ft) wide

The tiny bugleweed plant produces profuse flower spikes towering three times its height.

BUGLEWEED

Ajuga reptans

HARDINESS:
Zone 3

PREFERRED SOIL pH:
Neutral to slightly acidic or alkaline

PREFERRED SOIL TYPE:
Moist, fertile, well-drained

PREFERRED LIGHT:
Partial shade

Bugleweed in the Landscape

When you need something to cover the ground quickly, try bugleweed, which will form a thick, tidy carpet in the most challenging places. Also called ajuga, the plant produces a flat little soil-hugging rosette of nearly evergreen oval leaves, adorned in spring by 15 cm (6 in) spires densely packed with small blue bugle-shaped blossoms. Standing only 5 cm (2 in) tall when not in flower, bugleweed has the heart of a mountain goat and is fully capable of scaling slopes and hopscotching between paved areas or stepping-stones. For knock-'em-dead impact in spring, underplant rose-colored azaleas with blue-flowering bugleweed, or try these very hardy plants in containers.

Bugleweed blossoms last only a few weeks but form a haze of faintly fragrant flowers that attract honeybees. Most strains bloom purplish blue, though 'Alba' blooms white and 'Pink Surprise' and 'Pink Elf' produce pink blossoms. Leaf colors also vary widely, and include the rich shiny green of the most vigorous spreaders, the deep burgundy of 'Atropupurea', the silver frosting of 'Silver Carpet', and the mix of rose, white, and green found in 'Burgundy Glow'.

Keep Bugleweed Moving

Colonies march speedily on, with plants multiplying by forming a ring of a dozen or so new plants each summer, all connected to the parent by stemlike structures, or stolons. To keep beds full and fresh, dig out the new plants and reset them at 8 cm (3 in) intervals where needed to fill in gaps or expand the planting. Use a garden trowel to sever the little plantlets and lift them, because they will have a sturdy tuft of fibrous roots attached. For the best show of spring flowers, transplant in fall and keep the plants very well watered until they are established. In addition, bugleweed self-sows when happy, so you often find volunteers in the lawn that can also be rescued for garden or container use.

Growing Bugleweed

To start a new planting, dig the soil well and add a generous amount of organic matter to improve drainage, along with a little balanced fertilizer for strong growth. Preferring shade but tolerant of sun, bugleweed competes well with tree or shrub roots as long as you water generously while the bugleweed is becoming established its first season in the ground. For neatness, cut off flower spikes after the blooms fade. You can easily do this by setting your mower blade high and running over the bed.

Sap-sucking insect aphids may cluster on leaves, but they can be rinsed off with water from a hose, or controlled with insecticidal soap, applied per label directions. A serious problem entails plants suddenly collapsing from fatal fungal root rot. The soil-borne fungi flourish in warm, damp weather. There is no cure other than starting over in a new place.

FUNDAMENTAL FACTS

ATTRIBUTES	Blue, pink, or white flowers; colorful foliage; for groundcover, pots
SEASON OF INTEREST	Spring to early winter
FAVORITES	'Burgundy Glow' for variegated leaves; pink-flowered 'Pink Surprise'
QUIRKS	Spreads fast; benefits from division
GOOD NEIGHBORS	Shrubs and trees, especially azaleas and rhododendrons
WHERE IT GROWS BEST	Fertile, well-drained soil in partial shade
POTENTIAL PROBLEMS	Aphids, root rot; can be invasive if neglected
RENEWING PLANTS	Benefits from division every 2–3 years in the fall
CRITTER RESISTANCE	Excellent
SOURCE	Division
DIMENSIONS	Plant 5 cm (2 in) tall, 8 cm (3 in) wide; flowers 15 cm (6 in) tall

Bugleweed needs plenty of room to roam, because it will quickly colonize a site.

BUTTERFLY WEED

Asclepias tuberosa, A. incarnata

HARDINESS:
Zone 4

PREFERRED SOIL pH:
Slightly acidic

PREFERRED SOIL TYPE:
Average to moist

PREFERRED LIGHT:
Sun

The orange flowers are a butterfly magnet.

Butterfly Weed in the Landscape

If your yard includes an area that's hot and dry, light it up with butterfly weed, *A. tuberosa*. This durable native plant is a little slow to get started, but once established it will thrive on neglect. It's a handsome, compact plant that blazes gloriously for many weeks in midsummer when it displays a crown of waxy, bright orange flowers.

Easily seen from afar but also interesting up close, butterfly weed's dense flower clusters comprise many small flowers, each with a yellow center and back-flung petals. Despite wilting heat, the flowers stand firm on 0.6 m (2 ft) tall rigid stems framed by leathery drought-resistant foliage. In late summer you will have to choose between coaxing the plant to produce a second flush of bloom by cutting off the old flowers or letting them ripen into ornamental seedpods.

Use masses of butterfly weed in sunny wildflower borders and on sunny slopes that are too rugged for other plants to thrive. In warm-summer climates, butterfly weed does fine in full sun, but it can also be grown in partial shade.

Other Shades of Butterfly Weed

In the wild, butterfly weed flowers are always bright tangerine, though variations that shift toward yellow or red hues are not uncommon. For a white-flowered version, try *Asclepias incarnata* 'Ice Ballet', which stands substantially taller, at 1 m (40 in). Other cultivated selections of *A. incarnata* have pink flowers, and are often called swamp milkweed. As the name suggests, this species does best in a moist soil. Unfortunately, aphids love this species more than the orange butterfly weed, making it somewhat less care-free.

A Bevy of Butterflies

Monarch caterpillars and several other species feed on butterfly weed foliage. You can pick the caterpillars off, but try to relocate them to plants that are out of sight so that the caterpillars can mature into majestic orange-and-black butterflies. If you intend to let some plants serve as butterfly nurseries, locate them behind other flowers where the tattered foliage will not show in summer. Many other butterfly species also visit the plant to sip the blossoms' sweet nectar.

Growing Butterfly Weed

To get butterfly weed off to a strong start, set out container-grown plants in spring. Refrain from digging plants when they are actively growing, because the risk of breaking the brittle taproot and losing the plant is high.

A kinder way to propagate plants is to take 10 cm (4 in) stem cuttings in spring, strip off leaves from the lower half of the stem, and insert them half their length into a mixture of damp sand and peat moss. Keep the soil around cuttings moist and shade them until they are well rooted; then plant them in the garden.

Give new plants occasional water if a serious drought strikes the first summer after planting, and keep weeds pulled away from the growing points, or crowns. By their third summer, the plants should have thick tuberous roots and be able to fend for themselves in any type of weather.

Except for butterfly larvae (caterpillars), which eat leaves, pests are few. Bright yellow aphids sometimes appear in large numbers on new growth. You can simply rinse them off with water from a hose, pick off and dispose of infested leaves, or apply insecticidal soap per label directions.

FUNDAMENTAL FACTS

ATTRIBUTES	Masses of orange flowers on compact, drought-tolerant plants; for beds
SEASON OF INTEREST	Summer
FAVORITES	The species, *Asclepias tuberosa*
QUIRKS	Late to emerge in spring and difficult to transplant
GOOD NEIGHBORS	Aster, ornamental grasses, rudbeckia, sneezeweed, stonecrop
WHERE IT GROWS BEST	Sun and average soil
POTENTIAL PROBLEMS	Butterfly larvae, occasional aphids
RENEWING PLANTS	Plants live for decades; seldom needs dividing
CRITTER RESISTANCE	Good
SOURCE	Seeds, rooted cuttings
DIMENSIONS	To 75 cm (30 in) tall, 45 cm (18 in) wide

Butterfly weeds are great for a sunny spot. They thrive in heat, and the flowers radiate fire.

CAMPANULA

Campanula spp.

HARDINESS:
Zone 3 unless otherwise indicated

PREFERRED SOIL pH:
Near neutral

PREFERRED SOIL TYPE:
Fertile, well-drained

PREFERRED LIGHT:
Sun to partial shade

'Boule de Neige' is a peachleaf bellflower with roselike double blooms of snow white.

Campanula stems support plentiful, bell-shaped flowers in purple, white, or pink.

Campanula in the Landscape

Beloved for blue, violet, pink, white, and purple bell-shaped blossoms, the campanulas in their many forms and sizes are all perennial summer charmers. Also called bellflowers, campanulas are easy to grow as long as your climate, or planting site offers cool nights to offset the warm days of summer. Campanulas are among the most care-free and finest flowers for perennial borders and rock gardens. Upright types team up beautifully with iris, foxglove, peonies, and perennial geraniums in mixed borders, and those that hug the ground are invaluable for the rich hues their flowers bring to rock garden areas.

A Medley of Bells

Carpathian bellflower (*Campanula carpatica* [Z4]) does exactly what a good rock garden flower should do. It produces large, 5 cm (2 in) wide blue or white blossoms on petite, low-growing plants. The cultivars 'Blue Clips' and 'White Clips' mix well with yellow-flowered sedums, sun rose, and many other small rock garden plants in sunny, well-drained spots.

A more upright campanula that seldom fails is milky bellflower (*C. lactiflora*), which grows to 1.2 m (4 ft) tall and produces softly rounded spikes of lilac flower clusters in midsummer. If old flower clusters are trimmed off, the bushy plants will stay in bloom for several weeks. Milky bellflower often reseeds itself here and there in the garden, but it is far from invasive.

There are many other upright campanulas to try, all of which need well-drained soil of average fertility. Peachleaf bellflower (*C. persicifolia*) produces very large, upward-facing blossoms on 0.6 m (2 ft) tall stems. While all campanulas are relatively free of pests, the campanulas described above grow best where summer nights are cool. In the high heat and humidity of summer, they can be subject to crown rot, a fatal, incurable fungal disease.

Less picky about weather is a very different species that grows as a blooming summer groundcover. Commonly called Serbian or Dalmatian bellflower, *C. poscharskyana* produces underground runners that quickly establish a low clump, only a few inches high but several feet wide. In sun or shade, this lavender-flowering campanula spreads vigorously, so site it with care. Another heat-resistant species is the clustered bellflower (*C. glomerata*). It is an upright plant that grows from 0.3 to 1 m (1 to 3 ft) tall.

Growing Campanula

Campanulas respond dramatically to fertile, well-drained soil, so dig in a 5 cm (2 in) blanket of good compost before setting out new plants in

Although usually purple, campanulas also come in pastel pink-flowered forms.

FUNDAMENTAL FACTS

ATTRIBUTES	Bell-shaped blue, violet, pink, or white flowers; for rock gardens, beds
SEASON OF INTEREST	Late spring through summer
FAVORITES	Tall *C. persicifolia*; short *C. carpatica*; heat-resistant *C. glomerata*
QUIRKS	Some grow poorly where summer nights are hot
GOOD NEIGHBORS	Cohosh, foxglove, peony, stonecrop, sun rose
WHERE IT GROWS BEST	Sun to partial shade in loamy soil
POTENTIAL PROBLEMS	Plants become overcrowded after growing for a year or two
RENEWING PLANTS	Plants live for decades; divide every 3–4 years in spring or fall
CRITTER RESISTANCE	Good
SOURCE	Division
DIMENSIONS	15 cm–1.2 m (6 in–4 ft) tall, 0.3–1 m (1–3 ft) wide

early spring. Space them 30–45 cm (12–18 in) apart, and keep the plants weeded to eliminate competition. After they have bloomed, cut the plants back by half their height to neaten the clump and stimulate a new flush of flowers. In the fall, mulch plants with a 2.5 cm (1 in) thick layer of compost to protect them over winter.

Divide plants every third year in spring as new growth begins, or when clumps are crowded and flowering diminishes. Lift a clump, cut away healthy young crowns, and reset them in freshly dug soil, spacing them one-and-a-half times their height to allow room for them to spread as they mature. Keep the soil moderately moist for several weeks after transplanting so that the young plants do not dry out as they establish.

Aptly named, candytuft forms little tufted cones of blooms as fluffy as cotton candy.

CANDYTUFT

Iberis sempervirens

HARDINESS:
Zone 3

PREFERRED SOIL pH:
Neutral

PREFERRED SOIL TYPE:
Well-drained

PREFERRED LIGHT:
Sun to partial shade

Candytuft in the Landscape

Like late-season snow, candytuft flowers bring drifts of fluffy white to the spring scene. The blooms waver above loose mounds of fleshy stems studded with slender, glossy green, 2.5 cm (1 in) long leaves that form an attractive groundcover even after the flowers have faded. In warmer climates, candytuft foliage can persist year-round, but the flowers usually disappear for the rest of the season when summer nights turn sultry.

Never growing more than 30 cm (12 in) tall, candytuft mixes beautifully with woodland phlox (*Phlox divaricata*) and makes a lacy skirt at the base of upright bloomers, such as red tulips and blue iris, or around azaleas and other spring-flowering shrubs. Alone or combined with its many possible companions, candytuft is ideal for edging the front of perennial beds, flanking sidewalks, or tucking into the crevices of stone walls.

Some dwarf varieties, such as 'Snow White', are beautiful when allowed to tumble over the edge of a brick wall or stone planter. They are also handy for filling little bare spots in rock gardens. Choose larger varieties, such as the 25 cm (10 in) tall 'Alexander's White' for edging beds, where the dense foliage does a better job of discouraging weeds. For gardeners who can't get enough of candytuft flowers, there is 'Autumn White', a reblooming variety that will stage a second coming in the fall.

Smart Shearing

A rigorous shearing back after the plants finish blooming in late spring will encourage compact new growth and possibly a second flush of flowering. For large colonies, use manual or electric hedge trimmers to make quick work of cutting the plants back by half their size. Lightly rake out the trimmings, and then add a balanced organic or controlled-release fertilizer according to package directions to the soil in the bed to encourage plants to produce a bumper crop of flowers the following season.

Planting Candytuft

Candytuft needs full sun but will survive in early morning or late afternoon shade. It thrives in soil that has good drainage and a nearly neutral pH value. The plants will fill in faster if you amend sandy or clay soil with compost before planting; compost has the added benefit of neutralizing the pH of the soil.

Some varieties can be grown from seed, but it's simpler to buy plants and set them out 15 cm (6 in) apart in early spring. Fall planting is practical in warm-winter regions. Weed as needed during the first growing season to help candytuft claim its space, and from then on, it's care-free.

Animal and insect pests seldom visit candytuft, and it is remarkably

disease resistant. When days are warm and nights are cool and damp, you may occasionally find leaves that show the grayish white deposits of fungal powdery mildew. Simply pick off the affected leaves and dispose of them.

Because of its talent for accenting other spring bloomers, keep a few plants in little pots to use for filling gaps between bulbs or tucking into containers. In late spring or early fall, use a sharp knife to sever any stems that have developed roots where they touch the ground. Scoop up the rooted cuttings with a garden trowel and pot them up, keeping them moist and shaded for a few weeks. If you plan to overwinter potted plants, store them in a location where temperatures will remain around freezing to prevent root damage.

When planted in a mass, candytuft makes a handsome, snowy flowering groundcover.

CATMINT

Nepeta x faassenii

HARDINESS:
Zone 4

PREFERRED SOIL pH:
Neutral

PREFERRED SOIL TYPE:
Average, well-drained

PREFERRED LIGHT:
Sun to partial shade

'Six Hills Giant' is famous not only for its tall stature but also its deep violet blooms.

Catmint in the Landscape

If you want a care-free perennial plant loaded with white or blue-hued flowers, opt for catmint. In summer, its profuse wands of small, trumpet-shaped, flowers cover the compact 0.3–1 m (1–3 ft) tall plants, contrasting nicely with the silver gray foliage. Catmint should not be confused with catnip (*Nepeta cataria*), which, unlike catmint, is fascinating to felines but makes a comparatively unexciting garden plant for humans.

Catmint works well anywhere you want strong color in early summer, whether in an herb garden, along a path, or at the feet of rose bushes. After the prolific blooms pass, the dense, velvety, lightly fragrant foliage persists the rest of the season. If you want catmint to rebloom, cut it back by a third right after the first round of flowers fades. For a while, you'll have a small shrubby-looking plant. By late summer or early fall, that little bush will stage a flowery encore.

Cats of a Different Color

Plant breeders have expanded catmint's color range and created plants of varying statures to give gardeners more flexibility with this handsome, durable plant. 'Dropmore', at only 0.3 m (1 ft) tall, has deep lavender flowers that are larger than those of other varieties. 'Snowflake' is similar in stature but has white flowers, while the blossoms of the 1 m (3 ft) tall 'Dawn to Dusk' are light pink. Perhaps the best-known catmint is 1 m (3 ft) tall 'Six Hills Giant', a lush beauty with violet-blue flowers, splendid for use as a low-maintenance, seasonal hedge. Standing equally tall, despite its name, 'Walker's Low' has the benefit of forming a nice round orb that doesn't part in the center under the weight of its own flowers, making it ideal for use as a hedge.

Planting Catmint

Once established, catmint is a tough plant well adapted to poor, gritty soil. However, it grows best in soil of average fertility in full sun or with a little afternoon shade in hot-summer areas. Mulch and fertilizer are unnecessary. In fact, fertilizer can cause catmint to stretch, growing unattractively long and lanky. Although catmint is in the mint family and will grow in average-to-moist soil, it's not a water guzzler like its relatives. Instead, once established, it is admirably drought tolerant, and too much water can also cause stretching and flopping. It's virtually pest and disease free.

Start with small nursery plants. Dig a hole as deep and twice as wide as the root ball and gently pull the roots loose so they can grow freely. Set the plant into the hole and fill with crumbly soil. After planting, water well to eliminate air pockets, and water every few days until you see new growth. From then on, water only if the plants begin to wilt in the heat. Established plantings survive for years. Divide clumps only when the central portions of plant clumps begin to stop flowering and die, or if you want to increase your stock.

With its soft purplish blooms and silvery foliage, catmint blends beautifully in any scheme.

FUNDAMENTAL FACTS

ATTRIBUTES	Profuse flowers on compact plants; for edging, beds, hedges
SEASON OF INTEREST	Late spring through summer
FAVORITES	'Dropmore', 'Snowflake', 'Six Hills Giant', 'Dawn to Dusk', 'Walker's Low'
QUIRKS	Grows poorly in wet soil and when overfertilized
GOOD NEIGHBORS	Herbs, roses, yarrow, verbena
WHERE IT GROWS BEST	Sun, average soil
POTENTIAL PROBLEMS	Virtually pest and disease free; grows poorly in hot, humid weather
RENEWING PLANTS	Plants live many years; divide every 3 years or when clumps start to die
CRITTER RESISTANCE	Good
SOURCE	Division
DIMENSIONS	0.3–1 m (1–3 ft) high, 0.3–1 m (1–3 ft) wide

Mountain bluet produces airy, fringed flowers in bright blue tinged with violet.

C. montana 'Alba' is a white-flowered form with the same violet center as the species.

Cornflowers contribute color to the garden; the ferny leaves fill garden gaps beautifully.

CENTAUREA

Centaurea spp.

HARDINESS:
Zones as indicated

PREFERRED SOIL pH:
Near neutral

PREFERRED SOIL TYPE:
Average

PREFERRED LIGHT:
Sun to partial shade

Centaurea in the Landscape

They may have humble origins as European wildflowers, but centaureas do deserve a place in any flower or cutting garden. The bushy, somewhat spreading plants produce thistlelike blossoms for weeks in midsummer, often continuing into fall if flowers are cut regularly. The best ones for the garden produce rosy purple or deep blue flowers that pair beautifully with yellow-flowering perennials, such as coreopsis, rudbeckia, and yarrow.

Centaurea's other common name, knapweed, gives a clue to the one risk involved in growing it. Popular centaureas reseed with enthusiasm if the old flowers are not snipped off before they go to seed. This is a welcome task, however, because the flowers are such pretty additions to bouquets.

A Centaurea Sampler

You may never tire of Persian cornflower (*Centaurea dealbata* [Z4]), whose fringed blossoms rise on 0.6 m (2 ft) stems above woolly, gray-green foliage. Cut them soon after the buds open, and they'll keep in a vase for a week or more. The cultivar 'Steenbergii' features a soft white center in each blossom, which gives it a delicate look. 'John Coutts' (Z5) has a light fragrance in addition to 5–8 cm (2–3 in) wide rose pink flowers atop 45 cm (18 in) tall stems. Except for regular flower cutting or deadheading, no special care is needed to keep this centaurea in flower all summer. In nurseries or catalogs, 'John Coutts' is sometimes listed as *C. hypoleuca*.

A blue-flowering centaurea, mountain bluet (*C. montana* [Z3]) is an energetic spreader in cool gardens and should be considered invasive. However, hot summers suppress its growth, so it is definitely worthy of garden space in warmer regions.

Growing Centaurea

Early in spring, centaureas may be purchased in containers from garden centers or as bare-root specimens from mail-order catalogs. Plant them in well-worked garden soil about 2 weeks before your last frost date. Set them 60 cm (24 in) apart and spread an 8 cm (3 in) thick layer of organic mulch around each plant to suppress weeds. Once flowering begins, gather cut blossoms for bouquets every few days or deadhead plants weekly to keep the new flower buds coming.

Centaureas grow so vigorously that their crowns become crowded in two or three seasons. In early fall or early spring, dig up plants, cut away and dispose of the old crowns, and reset divisions at the same depth at which they previously grew.

Mountain bluet spreads by underground roots, which hide beneath the foliage in summer, then emerge in the spring. To control its spread in cool-climate gardens, pull out about half of the outer stems in late summer. In warm regions, dig and divide plants every other year in the fall to help them maintain their natural vigor.

These virtually pest-free plants are drought resistant, but it's best to site them in well-drained soil, because wet soil in winter leads to root rot.

FUNDAMENTAL FACTS

ATTRIBUTES	Long-flowering, fringed blue or rose pink flowers; for beds, cutting
SEASON OF INTEREST	Summer through fall
FAVORITES	C. dealbata 'Steenbergii', 'John Coutts' for pink blossoms; C. montana for blue flowers
QUIRKS	Cutting blossoms boosts flower production
GOOD NEIGHBORS	Artemisia, coreopsis, ornamental grasses, rudbeckia, yarrow
WHERE IT GROWS BEST	Sun
POTENTIAL PROBLEMS	Some species can be invasive in cool climates; wet soil in winter can lead to root rot
RENEWING PLANTS	Lives many years; dig and divide clumps
CRITTER RESISTANCE	Excellent
SOURCE	Bedding plants, division
DIMENSIONS	45–70 cm (18–28 in) tall and plants are equally wide

Cohosh is a reliable source of late-season flowers. The white "candles" persist into autumn.

C. racemosa blooms early and grows tall, with spikes that can reach 2 m (7 ft).

COHOSH
Cimicifuga spp.

HARDINESS
Zones as indicated

PREFERRED SOIL pH:
Neutral

PREFERRED SOIL TYPE
Rich, moist

PREFERRED LIGHT
Full to partial shade

Cohosh in the Landscape

Cohosh is a plant with several common names, including bugbane and snakeroot, which reflect ancient uses of the root as an insect repellent and snakebite antidote. But nothing describes the plant's ornamental virtues like another of its names: fairy candles, which refers to its tall, graceful wands of creamy white flowers, visible even in twilight.

A true shade lover even in areas with cool summers, cohosh forms bunches of feathery foliage reminiscent of parsley, standing about 0.6–1.2 m (2–4 ft) tall. From midsummer through fall, it sends up tall, fragrant, bottlebrush-shaped flower spikes. A mature cohosh in full bloom can tower 1.5–2 m (5–7 ft). Station this plant at the entrance of a woodland garden or use it to flank a shaded gateway. It is especially handsome in tandem with astilbe and Japanese anemone. If you crave high drama, put cohosh in a spot where the flowers will be backlit by the setting sun, making the "candles" blaze.

Cohosh Choices

At only 1 m (3 ft) tall, *Cimicifuga simplex* 'White Pearl' (Z4) is relatively compact. It has handsome green leaves and fragrant fall flowers on arching stems. 'Pritchard's Giant', which reaches 1.5 m (5 ft), has sweet-scented white flowers in late summer. Several cultivars, such as 'Brunette' and 'Hillside Black Beauty', start with burgundy leaves that fade to green as the season progresses. These need a few hours of sun each day to maintain the maroon pigment, which also appears in the flowers, giving them a pink cast. *C. racemosa* (Z3) is one of the tallest species and blooms ahead of other species, in summer. Its flowers have a musky scent that some people find unpleasant.

Growing Cohosh

Although cohosh grows wild in areas with moist soil, it will thrive in average garden conditions in cool regions once established. However, the plant can be a challenge in hot-summer areas, where the burgundy-leaved cultivars can be especially problematic when exposed to the few hours of sun they need to maintain their coloring. It's generally best to grow these plants where they'll receive afternoon shade.

It's advisable to amend soil with abundant organic matter before planting. This hardy perennial forms large, impressive clumps over the years, which need division only about once a decade. To increase your collection, dig and divide cohosh early in spring. The first year after dividing, however, flowers may be sparse.

True to its name of bugbane, these plants are rarely bothered by pests. Red-orange spots on leaves may indicate a disfiguring fungal disease called rust. If this occurs, clip and destroy affected foliage and thin surrounding plants to improve air circulation.

FUNDAMENTAL FACTS	
ATTRIBUTES	Fragrant spikes of white flowers in summer; neat clumps of lacy foliage
SEASON OF INTEREST	Spring through fall for foliage; summer to fall for flowers
FAVORITES	C. simplex 'White Pearl'; C. racemosa 'Brunette'; C. ramosa, the species
QUIRKS	C. racemosa flowers have a scent that is more musky than fragrant
GOOD NEIGHBORS	Astilbe, Japanese anemone, ferns, hydrangeas
WHERE IT GROWS BEST	Moist soil in shade
POTENTIAL PROBLEMS	Rust
RENEWING PLANTS	Plants live for decades; rarely needed; if so, divide in early spring
CRITTER RESISTANCE	Excellent
SOURCE	Bedding plants, division
DIMENSIONS	In flower, 1–2.1 m (3–7 ft) tall and 1 m (3 ft) wide

A. canadensis is a North American native that reseeds readily to form plant colonies.

COLUMBINE
Aquilegia spp. and hybrids

HARDINESS:
Zone 3

PREFERRED SOIL pH:
Adaptable

PREFERRED SOIL TYPE:
Rich, moist, well-drained

PREFERRED LIGHT:
Partial shade to sun

Columbine in the Landscape

Affectionately known as granny's bonnets in bygone days, columbines provide brightly colored, graceful flowers and elegant foliage reminiscent of maidenhair fern for very little effort. The unique flowers are composed of spurred, back-swooping outer petals surrounding cupped inner petals, often in two colors, such as red and white or two tones of yellow. Blossoms are borne on slender, arching stems, so that they dance in the slightest breeze. Although columbines make fine cut flowers, it is difficult to take the fragile looking flowers from the garden without feeling like a thief.

A Columbine in Every Spot

Different columbines suit different garden styles. In a shady woodland garden, look to the North American native *Aquilegia canadensis*, which has

Columbine flowers are instantly recognized by their graceful, back-swooping spurs.

red-and-yellow flowers. For naturalizing in low-maintenance gardens that receive some shade, the time-tested *A. vulgaris* Barlow series is tough and adaptable, with spurless double flowers in pink, white, and lime green.

For more formal situations, choose hybrids such as the 1 m (3 ft) tall McKana Giants, which feature a wide range of beautiful bicolored flowers that are perfect for mixing with peonies, lady's mantle, golden yarrow, and foxglove. More compact at 50 cm (20 in), yet with very large flowers, are the Music and Songbird series. Both are easy to grow and offer the full range of columbine colors.

Short but Sweet

Columbines bloom like gangbusters for 2–3 years and then start to lose energy or perish altogether by their fourth season. *A. canadensis* and *A. vulgaris* Barlow series shed numerous seeds after flowering, offering up an annual supply of new seedlings to perpetuate the colony. But when the big, handsome hybrids generate offspring, their progeny won't necessarily have the beautiful blooms or vigor of their parents. Rather than letting hybrids reseed, cut off old flowers and replace the plants every 3 years.

Planting Columbine

Plant columbines in spring or fall in organically rich, well-drained soil. Columbines are a cinch to grow from seed. In late winter or midsummer, chill seeds in the refrigerator for 2 weeks, plant by pressing them into the surface of damp soilless mix, and germinate at 21°C (70°F). Move homegrown or purchased seedlings outside as soon as the last frost passes, or when soil cools in early fall.

After setting out the plants, mulch between them with a 2.5 cm (1 in)

layer of compost or leaf mold spread around the bases of the plants. This is essential if you're expecting a long, hot summer, and is also advisable at season's end to help the shallow-rooted plants get through the winter without being heaved out of the ground by freeze-and-thaw cycles.

Trouble in Paradise

Generally trouble free, columbines are sometimes visited by leaf miners. These are actually fly larvae. They tunnel between the two surfaces of a leaf, and make pale, winding trails as they tunnel. Gardeners resent this more than the columbines do, so it's sufficient to simply pinch off and discard affected leaves when you notice them. If you see any small, pear-shaped, sap-sucking insects called aphids, knock them off plants with a strong stream of water from a garden hose.

FUNDAMENTAL FACTS

ATTRIBUTES	Colorful, often two-toned flowers on graceful plants; for borders
SEASON OF INTEREST	From late spring through early summer
FAVORITES	A. canadensis; A. vulgaris Barlow series; Songbird, Music series
QUIRKS	Mulch roots for summer cooling, winter insulating
GOOD NEIGHBORS	Bluestar, monkshood, perennial geraniums, spring-flowering bulbs
WHERE IT GROWS BEST	Partial shade in fertile, moist soil
POTENTIAL PROBLEMS	Leaf miners, aphids
RENEWING PLANTS	Short-lived; replace with seedlings every 3 years
CRITTER RESISTANCE	Good
SOURCE	Bedding plants, seeds
DIMENSIONS	45–90 cm (18–36 in) tall, 30–60 cm (12–24 in) wide

COREOPSIS

Coreopsis spp.

HARDINESS:
Zone 4 unless otherwise indicated

PREFERRED SOIL pH:
Neutral to slightly acid

PREFERRED SOIL TYPE:
Average

PREFERRED LIGHT:
Sun

This American native wildflower is tame enough to live in any sunny garden.

Coreopsis in the Landscape

Sunny yellow blossoms are the hallmark of native North American coreopsis. This is a varied group of plants ranging from the 1.2 m (4 ft) tall lanceleaf coreopsis (*Coreopsis lanceolata*), which should be a resident in every wildflower meadow, to several com-pact modern counterparts that stand less than 45 cm (18 in) tall. All are among the most dependable summer-flowering perennials you can grow.

The yellow flowers combine beautifully with soft blues and pinks, but you may need to experiment to find companions that share the same bloom time. On the West Coast coreopsis remains green through winter and may bloom in late spring, along with fall-sown larkspur, Shirley poppies, and roses. Where winters are colder and coreopsis holds its new growth until spring, mix them with mid- to late-season bloomers such as campanula or pastel-flowered yarrow, or set them against a background of Russian sage.

Compact Coreopsis

Some coreopsis cultivars come in neat garden-sized packages. *C. verticillata* 'Moonbeam' (Z3) stands 45 cm (18 in) tall. Its airy, threadlike foliage is topped by petite, 2.5 cm (1 in) wide, pale yellow, daisy-shaped flowers. *C. grandiflora* 'Early Sunrise' has yellow semidouble blossoms held on stiff, 40 cm (16 in) tall stems. Shorter still is *C. auriculata* 'Nana', with 2.5–5 cm (1–2 in) yellow-orange flowers topping 30 cm (12 in) tall plants.

C. rosea adds pale rose flowers to the spectrum. At 38 cm (15 in) tall, *C. rosea* requires supplemental watering in hot, dry weather. If grown in favorable conditions, it makes a handsome groundcover.

Growing Coreopsis

Coreopsis will survive in poor, dry soil, but it produces more flowers if given regular water and a little organic or controlled-release fertilizer each spring. However, once it's well established, coreopsis won't perish in a drought. If you garden in an area with wet winters, be sure to plant it

Coreopsis is a drought-tolerant, sun-loving plant with a neat habit and bright flowers.

C. rosea adds a rosy pink color choice.

in well-drained soil to prevent root rot. Deadheading, or removing spent flowers, keeps the plants neat and encourages reblooming. Insects rarely visit, but the occasional aphid can be knocked off with a spray of water from a hose. Remove weeds and garden debris to discourage nesting places for insect pests.

If you encourage coreopsis to grow into small colonies, they will practically take care of themselves. To increase your supply or rejuvenate old clumps, divide plants in late summer

FUNDAMENTAL FACTS

ATTRIBUTES	Yellow or pink flowers; mounds of ferny foliage; for beds, pots
SEASON OF INTEREST	Summer to fall
FAVORITES	'Early Sunrise', 'Moonbeam', *rosea*
QUIRKS	Grows best when clumps become crowded
GOOD NEIGHBORS	Campanula, larkspur, Russian sage, rudbeckia, Shirley poppies
WHERE IT GROWS BEST	Full sun, average soil
POTENTIAL PROBLEMS	Root rot can develop in wet winter soil
RENEWING PLANTS	Lives many years; divide clumps as desired
CRITTER RESISTANCE	Good
SOURCE	Division
DIMENSIONS	0.3–1 m (1–3 ft) tall and wide

using a stout knife. Locate a tuft of foliage growing outside the mother plant, cut a circle around it to take out a few roots with the surrounding soil, and lift it out of the ground with the knife blade. Replant right away so that it will be well rooted by spring.

DAYLILY

Hemerocallis spp.

HARDINESS:
Zone 3

PREFERRED SOIL pH:
Neutral

PREFERRED SOIL TYPE:
Average

PREFERRED LIGHT:
Sun to partial shade

Daylily in the Landscape

Few plants are as dependable as day-lilies. Their trumpet-shaped flowers come in a rainbow of colors, from rich magenta to chiffon yellow, often enhanced by stripes, streaks, or bands at the throat. Daylilies merge harmoniously with many foliage and flowering plants, or they can be massed for a swath of summer color, a good tactic for planting on slopes. The new dwarf, continuous-blooming types, such as 'Stella de Oro', 'Happy Returns', and 'Fairy Tale Pink', which top out at a mere 0.6 m (2 ft), are ideal for the front of the border and for containers.

All daylilies have long, arching, grasslike leaves that look good before, during, and after blooming. Pests or

'Betty Woods' has double flowers in clear yellow, with a green flush at the throat.

Daylily flowers open and fade in a single day, but plants produce new flowers daily for a month or more.

diseases aren't usually a problem, and drought or neglect rarely causes daylilies to flag. The flowers, as their name indicates, usually last only a day, but you can count on most plants to put on a display for a month. By combining varieties that bloom in early or late in the season, you can lengthen the show by a few weeks. Some continuous bloomers can be counted on to flower into fall.

Increasing the Bounty

Daylilies are famous "pass-along" plants that are shared freely between gardeners because they're so easy to divide. Just make sure that each piece you remove from the parent clump has roots and at least one fan of foliage. For best results, trim the leaves to 15 cm (6 in) above the ground before dividing to make it easier to see where to separate it.

Growing Daylily

The best time to plant daylilies is in spring or fall. A site in full sun is best, but daylilies will tolerate partial or afternoon shade and actually prefer it in hot-summer areas. Plant them in well-drained, moderately fertile, weed-free soil. In good soil, fertilizer is not needed, and a diet too rich in nitrogen can lead to sparse flowers and floppy leaves. After planting, daylilies are virtually maintenance free. The leaves of some cultivars may yellow after flowering, but you can easily remove them; if there are many, you can shear plants to within 15 cm (6 in) of the soil to produce new growth. Dividing is necessary only when the central portions of clumps become crowded. During freezing winters, an 8 cm (3 in) thick mulch of straw, dry leaves, or salt hay applied after the first hard freeze will protect daylilies from the bitterest weather.

Sap-sucking pests, such as spider mites and thrips, may disfigure leaves and flowers, creating pale, stippled areas. Control light infestations by rinsing plants with a firm spray of water from a hose, or apply insecticidal soap according to the package label. In warm, wet weather, leaves

FUNDAMENTAL FACTS	
ATTRIBUTES	Trumpet-shaped flowers in many colors; grasslike foliage; for beds, pots
SEASON OF INTEREST	Summer
FAVORITES	'Stella de Oro', 'Happy Returns', 'Fairy Tale Pink' for repeat bloom
QUIRKS	Flowers last one day, but new ones open daily
GOOD NEIGHBORS	Artemisia, herbs, roses
WHERE IT GROWS BEST	Sun, well-drained soil
POTENTIAL PROBLEMS	Spider mites, thrips; fungal leaf spot
RENEWING PLANTS	Plants live many years; divide crowded clumps
CRITTER RESISTANCE	Good
SOURCE	Nursery plants, division
DIMENSIONS	0.6–1.8 m (2–6 ft) tall for standards; 0.3–0.6 m (1–2 ft) tall for dwarfs; 0.6 m (2 ft) wide

may develop black spots caused by a fungus. This fungal leaf spot is a cosmetic nuisance rather than a threat to the plant's health, so simply remove and dispose of infected leaves.

Daylilies look magnificent in masses, creating a swath of color in beds or on slopes.

The soft pink flowers of 'Roseum' intensify the silvery markings on the mintlike foliage.

DEAD NETTLE

Lamium maculatum

HARDINESS:
Zone 3

PREFERRED SOIL pH:
Neutral to slightly acid

PREFERRED SOIL TYPE:
Average

PREFERRED LIGHT:
Partial to full shade

Dead Nettle in the Landscape

If you want to brighten a shady spot with delicate light-reflecting foliage plants that also produce spring flowers, dead nettle is the happy wanderer for the job. The mint green leaves of this groundcover are streaked with white or silver and are nearly evergreen, disappearing only when snow blankets the garden. Although famed for its foliage, dead nettle throws flowers into the deal as well, with small clusters appearing in late spring or early summer. The white flowers of silver-leaved cultivars, notably 'White Nancy', are spectacular against the variegated leaves. 'Beacon Silver', 'Pink Pewter', and 'Chequers' have pink flowers, which furnish a striking contrast to the foliage. If you like yellow blossoms, try *Lamium galeobdolon* 'Herman's Pride' or 'Silver Spangled'. Both tolerate dry soil and are very hardy.

Springing into action when most spring bulbs are beginning to flag, dead nettle carpets an area as quickly as bulbs vacate it. It can't always hide fading bulb foliage from view—dead nettle stands only 30 cm (12 in) high—but it diverts attention with its sparkling demeanor. Bright clumps of dead nettle foliage also work well as a living mulch among more imposing shade plants, such as hostas. A fast spreader, dead nettle will eagerly move into any available open space.

Dead nettle isn't always polite about conquering turf. Should the plant move into areas where it isn't wanted, simply stop its progress by digging out any invaders. It's easier to correct the march while the plants are young and roots are shallow, so make adjustments in early summer.

Keeping Dead Nettle Tidy

By the middle of the summer, you might want to tidy up the scene if the leaves become tattered. To make the foliage fill in, cut plants back by snipping off about half of the foliage. The plants will respond by producing a thick covering of foliage for the rest of the summer, creating a weed-excluding mat.

Growing Dead Nettle

Aside from a preference for partial shade, dead nettle is an easygoing plant that wants little more than well-drained soil. In cool-summer climates dead nettle will endure full sun gracefully as long as you keep the soil moist. Transplanting is usually best done in the spring so that the plant will have an entire season to recover, but dead nettle really doesn't mind being moved at any time during the growing season. Have a weed-free spot ready. For a dense carpet, space plants about 25 cm (10 in) apart. Plant them as deep as they grew previously, whether in a nursery pot or in the garden before dividing. Water the transplants well and mulch around them to keep the ground damp until they are established. If you're growing dead nettle under the shelter of high trees, the fallen leaves may be sufficient for the job. Dead nettle is relatively pest free, but do watch out for slugs in moist soil. If you should notice ragged holes in the leaves, handpick and dispose of slugs at twilight, or set shallow saucers of beer on the soil to lure and drown them.

The tubular, hooded flowers appear in late spring and can last through summer.

FUNDAMENTAL FACTS

ATTRIBUTES	Variegated leaves; white or pink flowers; for groundcover
SEASON OF INTEREST	Spring through summer; evergreen in mild-winter climates
FAVORITES	White-flowered 'White Nancy'; pink 'Beacon Silver', 'Chequers'; yellow 'Herman's Pride'
QUIRKS	Spreads quickly in moist soil
GOOD NEIGHBORS	Spring-flowering bulbs, shade-loving perennials
WHERE IT GROWS BEST	Under the shelter of tall trees in partial shade
POTENTIAL PROBLEMS	Some species are invasive; wet winter soil causes root rot
RENEWING PLANTS	Colonies persist for many years; divide crowded clumps
CRITTER RESISTANCE	Good except for slugs when plants are grown in damp soil
SOURCE	Bedding plants, division
DIMENSIONS	30 cm (12 in) tall and equally wide

With luminous variegation, 'Beacon Silver' is an ideal groundcover for the shade.

'Brilliant' is a maiden pink that has rose-colored flowers with darker centers.

DIANTHUS
Dianthus spp.

HARDINESS:
Zones as indicated

PREFERRED SOIL pH:
Neutral to slightly alkaline

PREFERRED SOIL TYPE:
Well-drained

PREFERRED LIGHT:
Sun

Dianthus in the Landscape
It's easy to fall in love with dianthus. You may be charmed by the fragrance, silvery foliage, or simplicity of the blossoms. Fortunately, the plants that boast these features are easy to grow.

'Dewdrop' is a petite plant with gray-green foliage that is ideal for a rock garden.

Dianthus need good soil drainage, which makes these low-growing plants a natural for rock gardens and crevices in stone walls. They look superb edging the front of a border or spilling over a concrete curb in the company of candytuft or thyme. Pink-flowered types are usually easy to mix with other spring-blooming perennials. Once the bloom period passes in late spring, you have a groundcover of fine-textured, gray-green foliage that blends with all plants.

Cottage, Cheddar, and Maiden Pinks
Often called pinks because the zigzag petal edges appear to have been cut with pinking shears, dianthus include dozens of named cultivars of confusing lineage. These cultivars are now sorted into groups rather than by species. The cheddar pink types offer spicy fragrance and tight blue-gray foliage that often persists year-round. Cultivars such as 'Bath's Pink' (Z5) and the more cold-tolerant 'Mountain Mist' (Z4) bloom light pink in spring and make a fine edging or ground cover.

Cottage pinks also have a spicy fragrance, and though their foliage is not as fine and grasslike as that of the cheddars, their bloom time is longer. Deadheading, or removing spent blooms, will extend flowering even longer. 'Essex Witch' (Z5) produces rose pink flowers, and there are many others with flowers of varying shades, some with double flowers. Cottage pinks grow 30 cm (12 in) tall.

Petite maiden pinks offer no fragrance, but they bloom for a long period if trimmed often. Cultivars, such as the rose red 'Zing Rose' or deep pink 'Brilliant', are dependable from Zone 3 but often need replacing after 2 years or so in hot and humid regions, even when deadheaded regularly.

Growing Dianthus
Provide dianthus with sun and well-drained, slightly alkaline soil. Work in a modest amount of organic matter at planting time, and in acid soil, add garden lime according to package directions to raise the pH to nearly neutral. You can also mulch around plants with limestone pebbles, which will continuously contribute lime to the soil. Discourage fungal leaf diseases and root rot by planting where air circulation and soil drainage are good. Withhold nitrogen fertilizers or your plants will produce leaves at the expense of flowers. Pests are few, but

Sweet William is a fragrant dianthus that has both solid and bicolored blossoms.

occasional sap-sucking insects, such as aphids or spider mites, which are spider relatives, can be dislodged with a strong spray of water or treated with insecticidal soap per label directions.

Rejuvenate clumps every 2–3 years, a necessary step to relieve crowding, which in turn invites fungal diseases. In late summer or early spring, use a sharp knife and a trowel to cut out and lift the oldest crowns from the center of the clump. Throw the old plants away. Fill the holes left behind with a mixture of compost and sand, and the surrounding plants will spread out to quickly fill the gap. You can also increase your supply by cutting small divisions from a clump and replanting them within a few days, where you want them to grow.

FUNDAMENTAL FACTS

ATTRIBUTES	Fragrant flowers and low, grasslike, gray-green foliage; for beds, edging
SEASON OF INTEREST	Flowers in spring; evergreen foliage in mild-winter climates
FAVORITES	'Bath's Pink', 'Mountain Mist', 'Essex Witch', 'Zing Rose', 'Brilliant'
QUIRKS	Wet soil in winter leads to fatal root rot
GOOD NEIGHBORS	Candytuft, iris, salvia, thyme, veronica
WHERE IT GROWS BEST	Sun and well-drained, neutral soil
POTENTIAL PROBLEMS	Root rot and fungal diseases in high humidity or poorly drained soil
RENEWING PLANTS	Lives for years if crowded clumps are thinned or divided every few years
CRITTER RESISTANCE	Excellent
SOURCE	Bedding plants; division: late summer or spring
DIMENSIONS	15–60 cm (6–24 in) tall, 20–40 cm (8–16 in) wide

Delicate spurred flowers, often in shades of yellow, appear in early spring.

The white-spurred flowers of 'Rose Queen' accent the bronze tinge on the leaves.

Low-growing epimedium is ideal as an informal edging in shady locations.

EPIMEDIUM

Epimedium spp.

HARDINESS:
Zone 4

PREFERRED SOIL pH:
Near neutral

PREFERRED SOIL TYPE:
Fertile, moist

PREFERRED LIGHT:
Full to partial shade

Epimedium in the Landscape

Imagine a group of plants that tolerate shade and drought, thrive on neglect, flower profusely in many colors, are untroubled by pests and disease, and are often evergreen. Wishful thinking? Not at all. It's the genus *Epimedium*.

Also called barrenwort, epimediums flower early in spring, before the leaves appear. The heart-shaped leaves are often tinged red for a few weeks, then fade to medium green. When cold weather comes, the leaves are again blushed with red and often persist through winter in mild climates.

Epimediums spread slowly by rhizomes, or fleshy roots, to form a groundcover carpet 20 cm (8 in) tall. Try combining them with other plants that have reddish foliage, such as red-leaved Japanese maples, bronze-leaved heucheras, or red-flowered astilbes with reddish stems.

A Gallery of Charmers

For colorful, red-tinged foliage and showy pink-and-white flowers, go for *E. alpinum* 'Rubrum'. Evergreen where winters are mild, it is deciduous in colder climes. Another good choice is *E. grandiflorum* 'Rose Queen', which has bronze foliage. Of the evergreen epimediums, the best for winter foliage retention in cold climates is *E. × perralchicum* 'Fröhnleiten'. Its substantial leaves display dramatic red leaf margins in spring, turning green in summer and bronze in winter. In spring, 'Fröhnleiten' holds its medium yellow flowers well above emerging foliage. Other species are available with white, mauve, red, or purple flowers. For the best effect, choose plants with one bloom color and let them form a colony.

Growing Epimedium

Grow epimediums in full to partial shade. They appreciate friable soil and even moisture, but in cool areas they are very drought tolerant once established. Although they contend with poor soil and tree-root competition, amend sandy or clay soils generously with organic matter before setting out purchased plants. Plant them 25 cm (10 in) apart and water regularly the first season. Apply an 8 cm (3 in) thick layer of organic mulch to retain soil moisture, pull out any weeds, and be patient. Epimediums often do not show vigorous growth until their second season. Thereafter, new stems

will routinely knit themselves into a lush groundcover in early summer.

For the best floral display, cut back old foliage in late winter before flower stalks emerge. In cool climates, protect evergreen epimediums from the winter wind to help them hold their leaves. At winter's end, pick off tattered leaves to help make way for the new crop.

These tough plants are nearly impervious to disease, insects, and four-footed pests such as deer. And they need division infrequently because of their slow growth. To divide an overgrown clump, dig the rhizomes carefully, ideally in late winter before flowering begins. Cut them apart cleanly and replant immediately, discarding any sections that are damaged or shriveled.

FUNDAMENTAL FACTS

ATTRIBUTES	Reddish leaves; white, yellow, pink, or purple flowers; for groundcover
SEASON OF INTEREST	Nearly year-round for foliage in mild climates; spring for flowers
FAVORITES	*E. alpinum* 'Rubrum', *E. × perralchicum* 'Fröhnleiten'
QUIRKS	Flowers usually emerge before leaves
GOOD NEIGHBORS	Astilbe, fern, hosta, Japanese maple, other deciduous trees
WHERE IT GROWS BEST	Full afternoon shade; fertile, moist soil
POTENTIAL PROBLEMS	None
RENEWING PLANTS	Lives many years; divide crowded clumps in late winter
CRITTER RESISTANCE	Excellent
SOURCE	Bedding plants, division
DIMENSIONS	15–25 cm (6–10 in) tall and up to 45 cm (18 in) wide

Cushion spurge forms domes of foliage smothered by yellow flower bracts in spring.

'Chameleon' features chartreuse flower bracts against dark purple leaves.

Euphorbias are drought-tolerant, long-blooming perennials for sunny gardens.

EUPHORBIA

Euphorbia spp.

HARDINESS:
Zones as indicated

PREFERRED SOIL pH:
Neutral to slightly acid

PREFERRED SOIL TYPE:
Average to poor, well-drained

PREFERRED LIGHT:
Sun to partial shade

Euphorbia in the Landscape

Producing long-lasting flowerlike bracts above handsome foliage, euphorbias are dependable, virtually trouble-free plants for any sunny garden. Also known as spurge, euphorbias grow into mounds of green, bronze, or golden leaves ranging in height from 0.3–1.8 m (1–6 ft). While it's a lovely foliage plant, it is ravishing when outfitted with colorful buttonlike springtime bracts, which are actually modified leaves at the base of the inconspicuous flowers. Besides being well-behaved garden subjects that combine easily with other peren-

nials, euphorbias adapt to poor soil, tolerate drought, and appear impervious to pests and diseases.

Although care-free, euphorbias do require careful handling. The same milky sap that deters pests can cause allergic skin reactions in some people. Wear gloves when handling the plants, and use a flame to promptly sear and seal the ends of stems gathered for cut-flower arrangements.

Colorful Effects with Euphorbias

Euphorbias feature fascinating variations in color and texture. Cushion spurge (*Euphorbia polychroma* [Z4]) covers itself with bright chartreuse flower bracts in spring, and its soft green foliage turns red in fall. A stone wall or weathered wooden fence as a background sets it off perfectly. It grows about 30 cm (12 in) tall.

Equally well-behaved is the slightly taller *E. dulcis* 'Chameleon' (Z8), which has purple foliage topped by 45 cm (18 in) spikes of chartreuse flower bracts in early summer. The airy sprays of white bracts produced by *E. corollata* (Z5), or flowering spurge, resemble baby's breath, but these plants are easier to grow in poor, heavy soil and are slow to spread. A good choice for the center of a border is *E. griffithii* (Z4), with narrow leaves tinged red when young, and orange-red bracts in early summer. 'Dixter' has copper-tinted foliage and darker flower heads.

Growing Euphorbia

You can grow cushion spurge from seed, but seedlings need 3 years to develop into mature clumps. It is faster to begin with purchased plants. Set them out in early spring and give them sun in cool-summer regions and partial shade in warm climates. As long as the site is well drained, the soil need not be extremely fertile.

Starter plants have sparse roots and benefit from supplemental watering to keep soil barely moist for 2 months or so after planting.

In subsequent seasons, fertilize plants each spring with an organic or controlled-release fertilizer applied according to label directions. If plants look messy after flowering, trim them back by half their size, and they will produce compact new growth.

Increasing the Bounty

Euphorbias can be left alone for decades, but you can dig and divide cushion spurge as often as every 3 years to propagate it. When dividing, dig clumps as soon as the first shoots poke through the soil in early spring. Cut the roots into thirds or fourths with a sharp knife and promptly replant them.

FUNDAMENTAL FACTS

ATTRIBUTES	Chartreuse flower bracts on mounded plants; red fall foliage; for beds
SEASON OF INTEREST	Spring through fall
FAVORITES	Cushion spurge; *E. dulcis* 'Chameleon'; flowering spurge, *E. griffithii*
QUIRKS	Milky sap can irritate skin on contact
GOOD NEIGHBORS	Campanula, coreopsis, iris, larkspur, marigolds, peony, yarrow
WHERE IT GROWS BEST	Sun to partial shade; average to infertile, well-drained soil
POTENTIAL PROBLEMS	Foliage can be damaged if grown in full sun in hot climates
RENEWING PLANTS	Lives years; divide clumps in early spring
CRITTER RESISTANCE	Excellent
SOURCE	Bedding plants, division
DIMENSIONS	0.3–1.8 m (1–6 ft) tall and wide

Few plant families are as elegant as ferns, which bring soft texture to shady spots.

FERNS
Numerous species

HARDINESS:
Zones as indicated

PREFERRED SOIL pH:
Slightly acid to slightly alkaline

PREFERRED SOIL TYPE
Moist, organic

PREFERRED LIGHT:
Full to partial shade

Ferns in the Landscape

Ferns lend a graceful air to gardens that no other group of plants can match. From the lacy fronds of the maidenhair fern to the bold glossy leaves of holly ferns, these plants provide form, color, and texture for shaded nooks and woodlands.

Don't be fooled by ferns' delicate appearance. They are among the oldest plants on earth, and when grown in suitable sites, they are tough, durable, and vigorous. They are perfect for filling low-light pockets in foundation plantings, bedding beneath dense shrubs, or covering ground shaded by buildings or a thick canopy of trees.

Sorting Through Ferns

The greatest challenge in growing ferns is choosing from the bounty of beautiful specimens. Local nurseries are often the best source of species known to grow well in your area, and it's a sound strategy to try several types in different places in your landscape to see which flourish. Mix ferns with spring-flowering bulbs, flowering annuals such as impatiens, and shade-loving perennials such as hellebore, hosta, woodland phlox, and Solomon's seal.

Ferns may be evergreen, semievergreen, or deciduous, depending on the species and the climate of your garden. Reliable evergreen ferns are rare except in mild-winter climates, but promising species are always worth trying. Ferns that go dormant in winter make up for their temporary absence by the show they stage beginning in spring, when the curled new fronds, called fiddleheads, emerge and slowly unfurl. As an added bonus, the texture of deciduous ferns tends to be delicate, making them irresistible garden subjects. Whether evergreen or deciduous, you can cut back winter-tattered fronds in early spring to make way for the fresh new growth.

The Forms of Ferns

Ferns can be classified into two groups based on their growth habit. Running ferns grow from creeping stolons that push outward through the soil, producing new fronds as they creep. Often, new fronds will appear in rows along a stolon. Clumping ferns produce new fronds in clusters that spring up close to the mother plant. Species with creeping stolons grow faster and are more prolific spreaders, whereas clumping species tend to stay in place.

Choice Deciduous Ferns

Maidenhair fern, or *Adiantum pedatum*, features erect to arching 45 cm (18 in) fronds. The fiddleheads emerge in spring looking like pink, clenched fists with ebony stems and quickly expand to produce clumps of overlapping fronds that dance in the breeze. Hardy from Zone 4, maidenhair fern prefers near neutral, moist soil and needs little if any fertilizer. After a few years, the plants form wide, loose clumps that can be easily divided.

Hardy from Zone 5, Japanese painted fern, or *Athyrium nipponicum* 'Pictum', is a showstopper with pinkish stems and arching, triangular, gray-green fronds accented in silver and dark red. The fiddleheads emerge early in spring and quickly unfurl into lacy, 45 cm (18 in) long, spear-shaped fronds. Plants grow best with good light, so place them in partial rather than deep shade. Mulch with a thin topping of rotted manure or compost in early spring, and mist the young plants lightly in early evening during summer dry spells.

Adding height and motion to the garden, the beech ferns, such as *Phegopteris decursive-pinnata* (formerly *Thelypteris decursive-pinnata*) have bold 60 cm (2 ft) tall antlerlike fronds.

(continued on next page)

Japanese painted ferns display triangular fronds marked with silver and dark red.

Fern fronds unfurl from curious fiddleheads, which are usually covered in tawny down.

(continued from previous page)

Hardy from Zone 8, beech ferns produce bright green fronds from runners, so they eventually grow into a lush mass. This species likes moist, slightly acidic soil and benefits from light fertilization in early summer. In autumn, plants turn a tawny yellow before drying to chocolate brown.

Elegant Evergreen Ferns

Autumn fern, or *Dryopteris erythrosora*, is one of the most popular ferns. In spring its glossy fronds unfurl deep rust red, then turn green. From fall through winter, they take on a burnished sheen. Don't worry if a harsh winter ruins the fronds, because they

Lady fern (inset) is very lacy, with delicately cut, lance-shaped pale green fronds. *Polystichum aculeatum* (above), a holly fern, has glossy, dark green fronds.

recover quickly in spring. Hardy from Zone 6, autumn ferns stand 45 cm (18 in) tall, prefer neutral to slightly acid soil, and benefit from a half-strength application of balanced fertilizer or a shallow mulch of compost early in the season. Along with autumn fern, the *Dryopteris* genus includes many other species, collectively called wood ferns, that make excellent garden plants. Most of them are semi-evergreen, and all are easy to grow.

Often called holly or Christmas ferns, various *Polystichum* species are the hardiest evergreen ferns. There are several North American natives, in addition to lovely forms from Asia and Europe. These ferns can grow on cold northern slopes, especially when they are kept moist and well fed. The foliage is typically dark and leathery, with plants growing in small clumps.

Growing Ferns

Ferns repay you with years of beauty for little fuss. Give them partial to full shade with humus-rich, evenly moist

The popular maidenhair fern has finely cut green leaves on softly arching black stems.

soil, and they will grow without need for spraying, staking, or dividing.

Set out young potted plants from spring to early summer, paying close attention to planting depth. Set clump types with the vase of foliage and the crowns of new fronds level with or slightly above the soil surface. Do not bury the crowns, or growing points. For running ferns, set the crowns about 2.5 cm (1 in) below the surface, with the roots and runners spread out within the hole. After planting, firm the soil and water well. Many ferns, especially the clumping species, are slow to establish and may need a little coddling for a full growing season in the form of attentive watering to keep the soil moist.

Mulch ferns with chopped leaves year-round to keep the crowns from drying out and enrich the soil with organic matter. A spring top-dressing with 2.5 cm (1 in) of compost may provide all the nutrients ferns need. However, established ferns that lack vigor often grow noticeably better when fertilized with an organic fertilizer that is high in nitrogen, such as fish emulsion mixed at half strength. Or, you can use a half-strength application of a controlled-release fertilizer distributed evenly on the soil between the plants. Avoid using full-strength

chemical fertilizer; fern roots are easily damaged by fertilizer burn, which causes leaves to brown and curl.

While insects or diseases rarely bother ferns, the tender fiddleheads can attract deer in spring. Tuck a bar of deodorant bath soap among the plants or purchase a commercial deer repellent and apply as directed.

Increasing the Bounty

These ancient plants reproduce by dustlike spores that drop onto moist soil and go through stages of development, eventually producing small ferns. In the home garden, the best way to propagate ferns is to dig and divide them in early spring. After dividing, be sure to provide supplemental water to keep the soil evenly moist until the plants are established.

FUNDAMENTAL FACTS

ATTRIBUTES	Elegant, fine-textured foliage in varied shapes; for groundcover, beds
SEASON OF INTEREST	Early spring to fall for deciduous species; year-round for evergreens
FAVORITES	Autumn fern, holly fern, Japanese painted fern, maidenhair fern
QUIRKS	New plantings are slow to become established
GOOD NEIGHBORS	Bulbs, hosta, woodland phlox, Solomon's seal, hellebore, pulmonaria
WHERE IT GROWS BEST	Full to partial shade in fertile, organic, moist soil
POTENTIAL PROBLEMS	Can be damaged by drought or fertilizer
RENEWING PLANTS	Lives many years; dig and divide crowded clumps in early spring
CRITTER RESISTANCE	Good except for deer browsing fiddleheads in spring
SOURCE	Bedding plants, division
DIMENSIONS	0.3–1 m (1–3 ft) tall and equally wide

Ideal for shade, *D. purpurea* produces spikes packed with pink, bell-shaped flowers.

FOXGLOVE
Digitalis spp.

HARDINESS:
Zone 4

PREFERRED SOIL pH:
Near neutral

PREFERRED SOIL TYPE:
Average, well-drained

PREFERRED LIGHT:
Partial shade

Foxglove in the Landscape

Foxgloves dramatize the shade with masses of bell-shaped flowers aligned on 1–1.5 m (3–5 ft) spires. These flowers open gradually from bottom to top, which makes for a long show, and plants can sometimes be coaxed to bloom again if spent spikes are cut back. These are perfect plants for the edge of a woodland or a shaded entryway. Note that all parts of foxglove, which is the source of digitalis, a prescription heart medication, are toxic if eaten. Avoid siting them where children or pets may be tempted.

Foxgloves Forever

The common garden foxglove, *Digitalis purpurea*, is technically considered a biennial: It grows from seed one year, then blooms, sets seeds, and dies the next. Many foxgloves, however, prosper for up to 4 years, often self-sowing. The downy oval leaves form a rosette on young plants that spreads until, in the second spring, a flower spike appears. Varieties abound in a range of colors and sizes. 'Alba' has pure white blossoms with dark speckles at the throats. Excelsior hybrids offer a range of colors including pink and yellow. Fast-growing, 60 cm (24 in) tall 'Foxy' usually blooms the first year it's planted from seed.

A longer-lived perennial foxglove, *D. grandiflora*, has glossy foliage and buttery flowers with reddish speckles in the throat. It is hardy to Zone 3 and grows to about 60 cm (2 ft) tall. A new dwarf, named 'Carillon', is only 30 cm (12 in) tall and wide.

Growing Foxglove

To be successful, you need only set out purchased plants, protect them from extreme cold with mulch, and wait for them to bloom the next year. To keep common foxglove coming back, learn to recognize the seedlings and move them while they're small.

Self-sown seedlings have the best chance of settling into the garden. In midsummer, you can also collect and

D. grandiflora is a perennial foxglove with butter yellow flowers speckled in red-brown.

start seeds in a shady bed or in pots filled with sterile commercial seed-starting mix. Fresh seeds gathered from plants sprout in 10 days, but dried seeds from commercial seed packets can take several weeks. Barely press the seeds into the moistened mix, since they need light to germinate. After seedlings have 4–6 leaves, transplant them to the garden. Mulch lightly to protect them in winter.

Perennials should be divided every 3–4 years. Divide them in spring in cold climates and in late summer in warm areas, being sure to keep the soil moist until plants are established.

Though rarely bothered by insects, slugs and snails may visit. If you see ragged holes in leaves and flowers, set out shallow saucers of beer to attract and drown them, or handpick and dispose of the pests at twilight.

FUNDAMENTAL FACTS

ATTRIBUTES	Bell-shaped flowers in various colors on tall spikes; for beds
SEASON OF INTEREST	Late spring through summer
FAVORITES	Biennial 'Foxy', Excelsior hybrids; perennial *D. grandiflora*, 'Carillon'
QUIRKS	All parts of foxglove plants are toxic if eaten
GOOD NEIGHBORS	Columbine, ferns, hydrangea, roses, deciduous trees
WHERE IT GROWS BEST	Partial shade in moist, fertile, organic soil
POTENTIAL PROBLEMS	Root rot due to cold, wet winter weather
RENEWING PLANTS	Biennials live 2–3 years, start seeds; perennials live 2–4 years, divide
CRITTER RESISTANCE	Excellent, except slugs and snails
SOURCE	Seeds, division
DIMENSIONS	0.6–1.5 m (2–5 ft) tall, 0.3 m (1 ft) wide; dwarf, 0.3 m (1 ft) tall, wide

'Johnson's Blue' blooms sporadically from late spring into fall with clear blue flowers.

The flowers of *G. sanguineum* 'Album' shine starlike over foliage that turns reddish in fall.

GERANIUM
Geranium spp.

HARDINESS:
Zone 4

PREFERRED SOIL pH:
Neutral to slightly acid

PREFERRED SOIL TYPE:
Average

PREFERRED LIGHT:
Sun to partial shade

Geranium in the Landscape

Although the name geranium is usually used to describe the bright-flowered summer bedding annuals, perennial geraniums are the true geraniums from a botanical point of view. Also commonly called cranesbill or hardy geraniums, these plants produce masses of flowers with fluttery, thin petals in luminous color shades of rose, white, blue, lavender, purple, and carmine, and some flowers are punctuated with darker centers and veins. Each charming flower is about 2.5 cm (1 in) in diameter, and the blooms are held loosely on stems that range from several centimeters (a few inches) to 0.6 m (2 ft) long, depending on the species. The ferny, divided foliage is deep green through spring and summer, often with chocolate markings, and changes to shades of fiery red and orange in fall.

Geraniums play plenty of garden roles beyond being accents in the perennial border, where they provide soft color for many weeks Some geraniums can be used as groundcovers, and others are sufficiently wild to hold their own in a woodland setting.

Geraniums for Every Purpose

Geraniums are a large and diverse group, with plants adapted to practically any garden purpose or spot. Because they vary so drastically in their preferences for light and root space, the best way to select a geranium is to match its needs to your situation. Here are some matchups that are bound to work.

In Flower Borders

Hardy and reliable, *Geranium* × *oxonianum* 'Claridge Druce' is an easily grown, spreading, pink-flowering plant, that is 45 cm (18 in) tall and can grow twice as wide. It blooms prolifically all summer and has handsome gray-green leaves.

A closely related hybrid, 'Johnson's Blue', adds another shade to the geranium rainbow with purple-veined sky blue blossoms in early summer on plants that are 38–45 cm (15–18 in) tall and equally wide. Another rich addition to the perennial border with an almost vining habit is 'Ann Folkard', which grows 50 cm (20 in) tall and 60 cm (24 in) wide, bearing rich purple flowers for 4 months or more. Although 'Ann Folkard' is a great mixer in a flower border, its spreading habit makes it suitable as a groundcover, too. Let it weave through other plants for a charming effect.

Geraniums for Groundcovers

Cultivars of *G. macrorrhizum*, sometimes called bigroot geranium, are equipped with thick roots that help them spread into a tight mat of foliage 30 cm (12 in) tall and 60 cm (24 in) wide. Like other bigroot geraniums, magenta-flowered 'Bevan's Variety' tolerates dry shade, so it works as groundcover beneath trees. Where shade is limited to only part of the day, *G. endressii* 'Wargrave Pink' also spreads into a mass 60 cm (24 in) or more in width with the help of shallow, wandering rhizomes. It flowers grandly, bristling with porcelain pink blossoms in late spring and early summer.

The species known as bloody cranesbill, *G. sanguineum*, includes numerous cultivars that are hardy enough to withstand both cold winters and humid summers. Varieties

Many geranium flowers are faintly veined in a color that is darker than the petals.

Geraniums with thick, ground-hugging growth are ideal for use as groundcovers.

vary in color and compactness, but all can be used as groundcover when grown in close quarters. Most cultivars have deep mauve-pink flowers, but if you want a lighter hue, consider long-blooming 'Striatum', which has light pink petals streaked with reddish veins, or the white 'Album'.

In Woodland Gardens

Wood geranium, or *G. maculatum*, is native to North America's eastern forests and makes a lovely companion to ferns, with its pale rose to lavender flowers brightening the shade. Not only shade-loving but drought-tolerant as well, *G. maculatum* blooms in late spring on 30–45 cm (12–18 in) plants of the same width. Its flowering time is limited to spring, however, and the plants often become dormant by midsummer.

In Rock Gardens

In high-rainfall areas, grow geraniums that require excellent drainage in the fast-draining environs of a rock garden. Though these plants can't tolerate having wet roots, they handle abundant sun without complaint. Crevice-loving *G. × cantabrigiense* 'Biokovo' grows up to 30 cm (12 in) wide and tall, gleaming with masses of white flowers tinged delicately with pink.

For a more colorful pink flower with contrasting dark centers, *G. cinereum* 'Ballerina' makes a charming rock garden plant.

Growing Geranium

In spring, set bare-root or container-grown plants 30 cm (12 in) or more apart in good garden soil, amended if necessary with compost or peat moss to improve its drainage and texture. Make groups of at least 3 or more plants and water well after planting. If taller types become leggy in midsummer, cut them back by half their size, promoting a new crop of leaves and a second set of flowers for late summer and early fall.

Geraniums are virtually disease and insect free except for slugs, which occasionally chew holes in the leaves, especially in shady sites. Handpick and dispose of them at twilight, or set out saucers of beer to lure and drown them. Leaves of hardy geraniums can become mottled with random red spots in summer, but this is a natural coloring and does not hurt the plants.

Increasing the Bounty

Geranium clumps are easily divided when they become crowded. Pick an overcast day in spring or fall to do the job. If you're dividing in fall, cut the foliage back by about one-third to make it easier to see where to cut the roots apart. Dig up the clump and separate the somewhat stiff main roots. Reset the divisions into the garden, spacing them at least 30 cm (12 in) apart and taking care not to bury the growing points, or crowns.

G. sanguineum 'Shepherd's Warning' is a good choice for tucking in stone walls.

FUNDAMENTAL FACTS

ATTRIBUTES	Flowers in many colors on spreading plants; for beds, groundcover
SEASON OF INTEREST	Spring through fall
FAVORITES	'Johnson's Blue', 'Wargrave Pink' in sun; 'Bevan's Variety' in shade
QUIRKS	Use different species for sun, shade, dry shade
GOOD NEIGHBORS	Campanula, daylily, dianthus, hydrangea, iris, lily, lobelia, peony
WHERE IT GROWS BEST	Sun to partial shade in cool-summer climates
POTENTIAL PROBLEMS	Excessive summer heat and drought may temporarily shorten flowering
RENEWING PLANTS	Lives many years; divide crowded clumps every 3–4 years
CRITTER RESISTANCE	Good except for slugs in damp areas
SOURCE	Bedding plants, division
DIMENSIONS	15–60 cm (6–24 in) tall and equally wide

G. psilostemon produces cuplike blooms in brilliant magenta, with piercing black eyes.

A. *dioicus* produces plumes of spidery flowers that turn from greenish white to cream.

GOATSBEARD

Aruncus spp.

HARDINESS:
Zone 3 unless otherwise indicated

PREFERRED SOIL pH:
Near neutral

PREFERRED SOIL TYPE:
Average

PREFERRED LIGHT:
Sun to shade

Goatsbeard in the Landscape

Goatsbeard is great for growing in masses as a backdrop for smaller plants. A care-free shade lover where summers are hot, goatsbeard accepts more sun in cool climates. Although the giant goatsbeard grows more than 1.5 m (5 ft) tall, compact varieties are available for smaller gardens. Male and female flowers are on separate plants. The males have fuller sprays of feathery flowers, making them better subjects for gardens.

Goatsbeard flowers resemble those of astilbes. They start off a greenish white and then turn to creamy white, sending forth a faint scent as they mature in summer. The restful flower color and grass green oval leaves blend well with virtually all other plants, easing the transition nicely from one color scheme to another.

A garden giant, A. *dioicus* is best at the back of the border or as a bold specimen.

From Prodigious to Petite

The king of goatsbeards, *Aruncus dioicus*, is perhaps the most statuesque of all shade-loving hardy perennials. It can be gangly when young, but give it a few years to put on girth and it becomes a truly magnificent plant, resembling a huge astilbe. It forms a dense, well-shaped mound of foliage, eventually attaining a height of 1.8 m (6 ft) when in flower, with an ample 1.5 m (5 ft) width. Use it at the rear of a border, mass it in naturalized areas, or display it as a specimen.

A. dioicus 'Kneiffii' is a smaller cultivar sized for any garden at 1 m (3 ft). While the flowers are like those of the species, the green leaves are deeply divided into threads, much like cutleaf Japanese maple foliage.

At the other end of the size scale is a truly dwarf plant called Korean goatsbeard, or *A. aethusifolius* (Z4). This beautiful little goatsbeard grows only 30 cm (12 in) tall, with a lush show of deeply divided, ferny leaves that become brushed with bronze in the fall. Studded with open bottlebrush-shaped sprays of creamy flowers in summer, dwarf goatsbeard is excellent for small gardens, the top of a retaining wall, or containers.

Growing Goatsbeard

In regions with cool summers, goatsbeard can adapt to either sun or shade, but where summers are hot and humid, it needs a shady shelter from the afternoon summer sun. Goatsbeard likes moist soil, but established plants grown in the shade can tolerate dry conditions and root competition from trees. For best results, amend garden soil with generous quantities of aged manure, compost, or leaf mold before planting, and mulch annually with the same materials to help retain soil moisture.

When finding a home for giant goatsbeard, select a spot with care, because after a few years it develops a massive root system that requires a monumental effort to dig up. Its wandering roots are undoubtedly the reason it is quite drought tolerant once established. To divide goatsbeard, dig the plants in early spring or fall and divide them by sawing the rhizomes apart, making sure each piece has at least one prominent, fleshy, up-facing growing tip. Goatsbeard can withstand a lot of rough handling, but take care not to snap off too many of the growing tips when replanting. Set the divisions at the same depth the parent plant grew and water them thoroughly after replanting. Aruncus are hardy and blessedly free of problems from pests and diseases.

FUNDAMENTAL FACTS

ATTRIBUTES	White plumes of flowers, graceful foliage; for back of border, as specimen
SEASON OF INTEREST	Spring through fall
FAVORITES	Giant A. *dioicus*; cut-leaf A. *dioicus* 'Kneiffii'; dwarf A. *aethusifolius*
QUIRKS	Male plants have showier flowers than female plants
GOOD NEIGHBORS	Astilbe, cohosh, hellebore, hydrangea, ferns, Japanese anemone
WHERE IT GROWS BEST	Shade, moist soil, cool-summer climates
POTENTIAL PROBLEMS	A. *dioicus* is difficult to move once established
RENEWING PLANTS	Lives many years; divide crowded clumps only when necessary
CRITTER RESISTANCE	Excellent
SOURCE	Bedding plants, division
DIMENSIONS	1–1.5 m (3–5 ft) tall and wide; dwarf, 30 cm (12 in) tall and wide

GOLDENROD

Solidago spp.

HARDINESS:
Zone 4

PREFERRED SOIL pH:
Neutral to slightly acid

PREFERRED SOIL TYPE:
Poor to average, well-drained

PREFERRED LIGHT:
Sun

'Peter Pan', derived from a North American native, has especially elegant gold clusters.

Goldenrod in the Landscape

In true Cinderella fashion, goldenrod has gone from being considered a weed to earning its place as a valued garden flower. It has received a make-over by plant breeders determined to transform the wild thing into a dense, brightly colored flowering perennial with garden-worthy manners. In sun and well-drained soil, goldenrods are extremely easy to grow, settling in and becoming luxuriant sentinels of fall, showering your garden with beautiful golden flower plumes.

Together with other autumn favorites, such as asters, chrysanthemums, and Russian sage, goldenrods bring the season to an end in glowing color. A classic combination is goldenrod and a rich purple-flowered aster, such as 'Purple Dome'. The fleecy yellow goldenrod plumes dramatically accent the yellow button at the center of each aster blossom. Be generous when you plant goldenrod. Because of its lean stature, it is best planted in groupings of 3 or more plants.

If you've avoided goldenrods to keep from sneezing, you need not hold them at arm's length any longer. The truth is that goldenrod pollen is not the culprit that triggers allergic reactions; rather, pollen allergies are aggravated by ragweed (*Ambrosia* spp.), which is an entirely different family of annual and perennial weeds that flower at the same time as goldenrod.

Garden Worthy Goldenrods

Solidago rugosa 'Fireworks' has a compact clumping habit suited to a perennial border or to placement in front of shrubs. *S. sphacelata* 'Golden Fleece' is a petite, 30 cm (12 in) tall version that carries its cheery golden sprays in tidy pyramids. Tuck it among other plants, employ masses of it as ground-cover, or feature it as part of a container planting.

Growing Goldenrod

Like their weedy ancestors, garden goldenrods are not fussy. They thrive in soil with poor to average fertility, and require little water and no fertilizer. In fact, goldenrods grown in overly rich soil are likely to flop over and flower poorly. To promote flowering, however, sun exposure is a must.

Plant goldenrods in spring so that you can enjoy the show the following fall. Dig a hole roomy enough for the plant's roots and untangle the root ball with your fingers before setting it in the hole so that the roots can grow into the surrounding soil. Set plants at least 30 cm (12 in) apart. The planting may look puny at first, but it will fill the gaps as it matures.

While remarkably insect free, goldenrod leaves may contract powdery whitish patches of a disfiguring fungal disease called powdery mildew in late summer, when days are hot and nights are cool and damp. Trim off and dispose of affected foliage and thin surrounding plants to promote better circulation, which will in turn discourage the disease.

The bright golden flowers mix well in the garden with both hot pinks and cool blues.

FUNDAMENTAL FACTS

ATTRIBUTES	Late-season golden flowers on shrubby plants; for beds, pots
SEASON OF INTEREST	Late summer and fall
FAVORITES	'Fireworks', 'Golden Fleece'
QUIRKS	Plant these rapidly expanding perennials 30 cm (1 ft) apart
GOOD NEIGHBORS	Aster, chrysanthemum, Joe Pye weed, Russian sage, viburnum
WHERE IT GROWS BEST	Sun; well-drained, poor to average soil
POTENTIAL PROBLEMS	Grows poorly in damp soil; powdery mildew in cool, damp weather
RENEWING PLANTS	For best effect, divide clumps every 3 years in spring
CRITTER RESISTANCE	Good
SOURCE	Division
DIMENSIONS	0.3–1.2 m (1–4 ft) tall, 0.3–1 m (1–3 ft) wide

'Fireworks' shoots up arching sprays of golden flowers to illuminate the late-summer garden.

The aptly named fountain grass sends out flowing sprays of foliage and fuzzy flowers.

ORNAMENTAL GRASSES

Various species

Miscanthus sinensis is topped by feathery flowers that turn purplish bronze in fall.

HARDINESS:
Zones as indicated

PREFERRED SOIL pH:
Near neutral

PREFERRED SOIL TYPE:
Average

PREFERRED LIGHT:
Sun to partial shade

Perennial Grasses in the Landscape

Essential components of contemporary landscape design, perennial grasses have become very popular, and for good reason. They are the ultimate care-free plants, enriching the landscape year-round and usually requiring only to be cut back each spring to allow for lush new growth. There are numerous species of ornamental grasses, with a variety of sizes, colors, and textures appropriate for many garden situations. These plants are as comfortable in a garden that is devoted to grasses as they are standing alone as specimens or rubbing shoulders with shrubs or other perennials.

Good Bedfellows

When choosing companions for grasses, select plants of similar stature and compatible needs. Tall, summer-flowering perennials, such as Joe Pye weed and black-eyed Susan, make good partners for grasses that grow to 1.2 m (4 ft) or more in height. Midsized grasses can be paired with garden phlox, daylilies, stonecrop, or purple coneflower, while smaller grasses can be grown with flowering annuals, blanket flower, and yarrow. There are also shade-tolerant grasses that look great flanked by hostas, astilbes, hellebores, and asarum.

Tall and Midsized Grasses for Sun

Eulalia grass (*Miscanthus sinensis*) is the most widely grown ornamental grass. With graceful leaves and showy flowers that often feature curling tendrils, it is the definition of elegance. It is well adapted from Zone 5, and a few varieties, such as 'Purpurascens', are hardy to Zone 4. All flourish in average garden soil and grow to about 1.8 m (6 ft) tall. Foliage and flower colors vary. The green leaves of 'Purpurascens' turn rosy red with the onset of fall. 'Silver Feather' has green leaves topped by shimmering, nearly white, fan-shaped flower plumes.

Feather reed grass (*Calamagrostis* × *acutiflora* 'Karl Foerster') produces soldier-straight flowers above clean green foliage in late spring. Best grown in moist, heavy soils, this grass makes a fine 1.5–1.8 m (5–6 ft) background screen for annuals and perennials from Zone 4.

Another tall and upright grass is switch grass (*Panicum virgatum*), a North American native. The cultivar 'Heavy Metal' is popular for its striking blue leaf coloration, while the blades of 'Haense Herms' have a reddish cast. Easily grown in Zone 4, switch grass tolerates lean soil and salt spray and reaches a height of 1.2 m (4 ft).

Of the midsized grasses, fountain grass (*Pennisetum alopecuroides*) is especially popular. It forms a neat mound, 1 m (3 ft) tall and wide, and produces dense, tawny, bottlebrush-shaped flowers. Fountain grass takes on an attractive blond color for fall and winter. Some selections, such as the compact 'Hameln', are hardy from Zone 5. But the purple-leaved 'Rubrum' is often treated as an annual or grown in pots and wintered indoors because it is not reliably hardy, even in British Columbia.

Little Blues and Japanese Red

More diminutive and prized for its unusual colored foliage, blue oat grass (*Helictotrichon sempervirens*) forms a 30–60 cm (1–2 ft) tall tuft of spiky, metallic blue leaves. This drought-tolerant grass is a favorite for low-maintenance plantings. Blue fescue (*Festuca glauca*) looks like a miniature

Blue fescue forms dense, petite tufts of threadlike leaves in a striking silvery-blue.

blue oat grass and flourishes under the same conditions. The most common cultivar is 'Elijah Blue', which stands a mere 15–20 cm (6–8 in) tall and is a good choice for edgings or rock gardens, particularly in cold climates. Blue oat grass is hardy to Zone 4, but blue fescue will survive in Zone 3.

Japanese blood grass (*Imperata cylindrica* 'Red Baron') gets its name from the brilliant red that tips the young chartreuse leaves and then expands to flush the whole stem ruby by fall. Never more than 30 cm (12 in) tall, Japanese blood grass produces no flowers and spreads moderately, which can be controlled by division. It is hardy to Zone 5.

Shade-Tolerant Grasses

There is also a plentiful variety of grasses and grasslike plants that grow in shade. The sedges (*Carex* spp.) are the most shade tolerant, needing only indirect light. *C. siderosticha* 'Variegata' produces thick, arching mounds of white-rimmed, lance-shaped leaves. Its 30 cm (12 in) height and slowly spreading habit make it a natural choice for edging or groundcover use.

Northern sea oats has bladelike leaves and can grow to 1.5 m (5 ft) tall, even in shade.

Sedge selections are numerous, are generally hardy to Zone 4, and include many shades of green.

Golden hakone grass (*Hakonechloa macra* 'Aureola') has golden bamboo-like leaves that form a lax, 30 cm (12 in) tall mop-head shape. It is particular about growing conditions, disliking dry or poorly drained soil. This grass looks best when it receives a couple of hours of morning sun and enough room for its leaves to drape naturally. It is hardy to Zone 5, but gardeners in colder climates can grow it in pots and keep it through winter in an unheated garage.

Northern sea oats (*Chasmanthium latifolium*) is a North American native that makes a soft screen or backdrop for flowers. Growing to 1.5 m (5 ft), it has slender stalks with fresh green bladelike leaves and flattened flower heads that dangle gracefully from the stems. Hardy to Zone 5, it turns yellowish tan in autumn.

Growing Perennial Grasses

Because grasses are among the most numerous and widespread plants on earth, they have a wide range of needs. However, the majority of ornamental perennial grasses require 6 hours or more of sun per day and fertile, moist, but well-drained soil.

Early spring is the best time to plant new grasses. Get them situated early in the season so that they can develop reliable roots before their vigorous growth begins in summer. Most grasses appreciate a loose, crumbly soil, so amend the site with organic matter before planting and then mulch. Fertilization is rarely necessary. When established, most grasses are quite drought tolerant.

Both the leaves and flowers dry in winter to soft shades of russet, tan, or tawny blond. To enjoy the plants'

winter glory, let the foliage remain in place until early in spring. Shear off the tattered tops before new green growth appears, leaving only 10–20 cm (4–8 in) stubs visible. This is easily done with hedge clippers or a gas- or electric-powered weed trimmer. If you accidentally wait too long, no problem; cut the grass back to a point just above the top of the new growth, and the old foliage will be shed or overgrown quickly.

Rarely visited by insect pests, grasses are usually trouble free. However, they can occasionally be plagued with rust, a fungal disease that causes raised reddish spots to appear on the leaves in damp weather. To discourage fungal infections, allow room for air to circulate between plants when you set them out, and treat rust with a commercial sulphur fungicide according to package directions.

Most ornamental grasses will live for many years, with the clumps gradually increasing in size. To contain their size, or to propagate, simply dig the clumps up in the spring and divide them into smaller, manageable clumps and replant them where you want them, setting them at the same depth as the parent plant.

Grasses mix easily in flower gardens (above). *Carex siderosticha* 'Variegata' (right) has white-edged leaves.

FUNDAMENTAL FACTS

ATTRIBUTES	Dramatic foliage and flower plumes; for beds, specimen plants, or pots
SEASON OF INTEREST	Year-round
FAVORITES	Eulalia grasses, fountain grasses in sun; golden hakone grass in shade
QUIRKS	Most require shearing in early spring
GOOD NEIGHBORS	Black-eyed Susan, blanket flower, garden phlox, rudbeckia, sedum, yarrow
WHERE IT GROWS BEST	Varies by type; most grow best in full sun and well-drained soil
POTENTIAL PROBLEMS	Rust, a disfiguring fungal leaf disease, can occur during humid summers
RENEWING PLANTS	Lives many years; divide as needed to control the size of clumps
CRITTER RESISTANCE	Excellent
SOURCE	Bedding plants, division
DIMENSIONS	0.3–1.8 m (1–6 ft) tall, 0.3–1.2 m (1–4 ft) wide

Billowing delicate flowers work well as a filler in the garden and in flower arrangements.

GYPSOPHILA

Gypsophila spp.

HARDINESS:
Zone 4

PREFERRED SOIL pH:
Near neutral

PREFERRED SOIL TYPE:
Well-drained

PREFERRED LIGHT:
Sun

Gypsophila in the Landscape

If you've ever gotten a bouquet from a florist, you will probably recognize *Gypsophila paniculata*, also called baby's breath. This indispensable floral filler produces clouds of tiny blossoms, lending airiness to both the garden and the vase. The tiny white or pink flowers counterbalance plant neighbors with dark or very bright flowers or bold foliage. Baby's breath is a classic partner for roses, and pink-flowered types complement plants with burgundy leaves especially well.

Although baby's breath looks like a cloud from a distance, up close you'll notice that the blossoms come in single and double forms. The flowers are held on fragile, wiry, multibranched stems clothed at the base with narrow gray-green to blue-green leaves.

A Baby's Breath for Every Need

G. paniculata 'Bristol Fairy' is a widely available double white-flowered form that grows 1 m (3 ft) high. Slightly smaller is its rosy counterpart, 'Pink Fairy'. Growing to 1.2 m (4 ft) or more, 'Perfecta' is an exceptionally vigorous double-flowered white baby's breath with larger flowers than other selections. On the flip side, 'Viette's Dwarf' is only 38 cm (15 in) tall, with flowers that open pink and then turn white.

Although its flowers are similar to those of *G. paniculata*, *G. repens* spreads into 60 cm (2 ft) wide mats. At only 15 cm (6 in) tall, it is beautiful when grown so that it drapes over a wall or softens the edge of a border. There are also easy-to-grow annuals, such as 'Early Summer Lace'.

Growing Baby's Breath

Excellent drainage is required for all baby's breath, especially perennials grown in cold areas. Work sand and compost into the soil before setting out plants or dormant roots in early spring, and add garden lime according to package directions to adjust soil to a neutral or slightly alkaline pH. Rake the prepared soil into a small mound when setting the plant into the hole to create superior drainage and protect against deadly crown rot. Site baby's breath where you want it to grow permanently, as it develops deep-growing, thick roots that are difficult to dig up. If you must move a plant, do so in early spring, being careful not to break the roots.

The easiest way to grow the annual types is to sow seeds directly onto a sunny patch of garden soil after all danger of frost is past. Barely cover the seeds with soil and keep it moist until plants are growing vigorously. Start seeds every other week from spring through early summer to enjoy the flowers all summer long.

Stake baby's breath early in the season, using stakes and twine. In midsummer, shear plants lightly to remove spent flowers and encourage

G. repens 'Rosea' is a spreading plant with pink buds and long-lasting flowers.

Baby's breath turns into a pastel cloud that enhances dark or bright plant neighbors.

a second flush of bloom. Although insects or four-footed pests rarely visit baby's breath, in humid climates plants may die back in late summer from fungal leaf diseases. Trim off affected foliage to encourage healthy new growth; the plants will return in excellent health the following spring.

FUNDAMENTAL FACTS

ATTRIBUTES	Airy clusters of tiny white or pink blossoms; for cutting, beds
SEASON OF INTEREST	Midsummer
FAVORITES	Tall white 'Perfecta'; rose-flowered 'Pink Fairy'; spreading *G. repens*
QUIRKS	Tall types must be staked while small to keep them upright as they mature
GOOD NEIGHBORS	Oriental poppy, roses, and plants with dark or bold foliage
WHERE IT GROWS BEST	In sun and well-drained soil that is neutral to slightly alkaline
POTENTIAL PROBLEMS	Crown rot in poorly drained soil; fungal leaf diseases in humid heat
RENEWING PLANTS	If sited well, plants can live many years; unlikely to need rejuvenation
CRITTER RESISTANCE	Good
SOURCE	Division, seeds
DIMENSIONS	15 cm–1.2 m (6 in–4 ft) tall, 30–60 cm (12–24 in) wide

HELLEBORE

Helleborus spp.

HARDINESS:
Zone 4

PREFERRED SOIL pH:
Near neutral

PREFERRED SOIL TYPE:
Average

PREFERRED LIGHT:
Partial to full shade

Hellebore in the Landscape

Hellebores are tough perennials that bloom in winter, when most of their fellows are dormant. The lovely 5-petaled blossoms poke through patches of melting snow in late winter and can last for 3 months.

Helleborus foetidus has dark, glossy green leaves and pale green bell-shaped flowers that develop a rosy purple rim as they age. It is not fussy about soil, but because its flowers have a rancid scent, plant this species, also called stinking hellebore, where it can be seen but not smelled.

The flowers of two other hellebores resemble single rose blossoms, hence their common names of Christmas rose (*H. niger*) and Lenten rose (*H. orientalis*). Christmas rose flowers open creamy white and age to pink. Those of Lenten rose are more variable because the plant easily hybridizes and reseeds. It blooms in shades of rose, pink, lavender, burgundy, and lettuce green, with petals that are often speckled with a darker color.

Because of this varied flower color, plants look best in casual drifts. Let them flow beneath bare winter trees or shrubs, preferably in a place near a path or entryway that's easily seen in winter. You also can mix hellebores

Lenten rose, so named because it blooms in spring, is also famous for its nodding, speckled flowers

into flower beds close to the house or use their evergreen foliage and height in a bulb garden that includes early-blooming crocus and grape hyacinth. Because the blossoms nod downward, growing plants atop walls, on ledges, or in raised beds makes them easier to admire. But keep them away from young children and pets, as all parts of the plants are toxic if eaten.

Laughing at the Cold

Hellebores grow from thick creeping rhizomes, remain evergreen in all but the most brutal winters, and return reliably every year. The 60 cm (2 ft) high stems are erect and succulent, and the leaves and petals are almost waxy in texture, a quality that protects them from frost damage.

Growing Hellebore

Choose a spot that receives some winter sun and then becomes shady when trees leaf out and temperatures rise. Dig in compost, leaf mold, or other organic matter before setting out purchased plants in spring or fall, spacing them 30 cm (12 in) apart. Each spring thereafter, apply a 5 cm (2.5 in) layer of rotted manure or compost at the base of plants. Hellebores often need at least 2 years to settle in and start blooming prolifically, so be patient. Once established they are quite tough, tolerating drought and even alkaline soil.

Increasing the Bounty

Hellebores are not easily grown from seed, and it takes up to 3 years for a seedling to reach blooming size. If you already have plants, let them shed ripe seeds that will fall to the ground, sprout erratically, and eventually fill in holes in the colony. When small, seedlings can be lifted and replanted where you want them to grow. Once you've planted hellebores, there's no need to disturb them again. Digging them always sets them back, and a full year may pass before the plants regain good blooming energy. However, if you must move or divide plants, do so in spring, immediately after flowering. These plants are remarkably resistant to pest and disease problems.

FUNDAMENTAL FACTS

ATTRIBUTES	Long-lasting white, pink, purple, or green flowers in late winter; for beds
SEASON OF INTEREST	Evergreen foliage; flowers in winter and spring
FAVORITES	Christmas rose, Lenten rose, stinking hellebore
QUIRKS	All plant parts are poisonous; mature plants transplant poorly
GOOD NEIGHBORS	Crocus, tulips, grape hyacinth, deciduous trees, red-osier dogwood
WHERE IT GROWS BEST	In the light shade of deciduous trees
POTENTIAL PROBLEMS	Persistently dry soil can be fatal
RENEWING PLANTS	Colonies live for years; unlikely to need rejuvenation; trim tattered leaves
CRITTER RESISTANCE	Excellent
SOURCE	Bedding plants, seed
DIMENSIONS	30–60 cm (1–2 ft) tall and equally wide

Massed plantings of Lenten roses show their varied flower colors to best advantage.

HENS AND CHICKS

Sempervivum spp.

HARDINESS:
Zone 4

PREFERRED SOIL pH:
Neutral to slightly acid

PREFERRED SOIL TYPE:
Average

PREFERRED LIGHT:
Sun to partial shade

Sempervivum 'Rosie' features lime-green leaf rosettes tipped in rose, a striking combination.

Hens and Chicks in the Landscape

It's hard to resist the succulent, fleshy rosettes of hens and chicks, properly known as sempervivums, which manage to be tough and cute at the same time. Their long lives and dependability are reflected in their botanical name, which translates as "live forever." They are called hens and chicks because the round offshoots on short stems crowd around the mother plant like chicks around a hen.

These sun-resistant plants form wonderful patches of texture and

Spiderweb houseleeks look as if they've been trapped inside a downy spiderweb.

foliage color in rocky or dry, parched places. They can take a beating, with very little water or even soil, for they originated in the rugged mountains of Europe and the Middle East. They do well on slopes, in rock gardens, and in other sites that offer excellent drainage. With a little encouragement, the clumps will carpet wide swaths, filling every nook and cranny with their many "chicks."

Hens and chicks are also suitable for low, broad containers where they can be viewed from above. Where winters are too cold to grow sempervivums outdoors, containers can be kept through the coldest months in a cool garage or enclosed porch.

Sempervivum foliage is usually light or dark green, but may also be brownish or reddish, either at the fleshy leaf tips or throughout the whole plant. The star-shaped flowers are usually pink or white. Oddly, most types look much better when they are not flowering because the flowers, which shoot upward on spindly stems, detract from the neat, ground-hugging habit of the plants.

Sempervivum Variations

Commonly called houseleek, *Sempervivum tectorum* is a popular, easy-to-grow species, with big green or bronzy pointed rosettes that need almost no care and increase quickly. This and several other old favorites are often shared among gardeners because of their prolific habits and willingness to be transplanted. Of special interest are spiderweb houseleeks, *S. arachnoideum*, with white hairs covering the reddish rosettes in a "spiderweb." The species *S. octopodes* has long, chick-bearing stems, creating an unusual effect.

Rose red blooms complement the slight reddish tinge on houseleek foliage.

Growing Hens and Chicks

Set plants in a site with full sun and sandy, well-drained soil. In heavy clay soils, plant them on slopes to maximize drainage. The only time hens and chicks need extra moisture is when new plants are set out. Keep them barely moist for a few weeks, then they can fend for themselves.

After a rosette matures and flowers, it dies, so simply remove it and fill the space with a younger offset. When removing a chick from its mother, take at least a 2.5 cm (1 in) long stem along with it. Bury the stem stub under 2.5 cm (1 in) of gritty soil, and use pebbles to hold it in place until the chick develops roots and can hold its own. While virtually pest and disease free, hens and chicks can succumb to root rot if they are exposed to waterlogged soil, particularly in hot, humid climates.

FUNDAMENTAL FACTS

ATTRIBUTES	Low-growing green or bronze foliage rosettes; for edging, pots, beds
SEASON OF INTEREST	Evergreen foliage has year-round appeal
FAVORITES	*S. tectorum*, *S. arachnoideum*, *S. octopodes*
QUIRKS	Leaves resist fire; one species was once grown on roofs to retard fire
GOOD NEIGHBORS	Mugo pine, sedums, sun rose
WHERE IT GROWS BEST	In sun to partial shade and gritty soil
POTENTIAL PROBLEMS	Excessive moisture and shade can cause rot
RENEWING PLANTS	Lives years; remove damaged plants and flowering stems as needed
CRITTER RESISTANCE	Good
SOURCE	Plant offsets
DIMENSIONS	Less than 10 cm (4 in) tall; clumps spread to 30 cm (12 in) wide

The lobed leaves of 'Pewter Moon' are marbled in gray and topped with pink blooms.

HEUCHERA

Heuchera spp.

HARDINESS:
Zone 4

PREFERRED SOIL pH:
Near neutral

PREFERRED SOIL TYPE:
Moist, fertile, well-drained

PREFERRED LIGHT:
Partial shade

Heuchera in the Landscape

The most difficult thing about these versatile garden standouts may be pronouncing their name: HEW-ker-a. Although their ancestors are humble native plants from both eastern and western regions of North America, modern garden heucheras are anything but plain. Showy hybrids often have deep red-bronze evergreen leaves marked with purple, such as the award-winning 'Palace Purple', or silver, such as 'Persian Carpet'. Others, which are suitable for sunnier spots, have green leaves marbled with white and sometimes blushed with pink.

All heucheras produce airy flower spikes studded with tiny bell-shaped flowers in early summer. The flowers are pale and spindly on most dark-leaved cultivars, so many gardeners simply snip them off. But keep the snippers sheathed if you choose varieties bred to live up to their common name of coral bells. These heucheras, including 'Mt. St. Helens' and 'Raspberry Regal', are crowned with wiry, 50 cm (20 in) flower stems heavily laden with abundant salmon to deep red miniature bells that persist for weeks. After the flowers fade, snip out old stems to encourage an encore.

Growing Heuchera

To prod heucheras to really strut their stuff, give them exactly the right amount of light. Dark-leaved varieties scorch quickly when forced to bake in hot sun, so they are best grown in beds that get no more than 4 hours of direct sun. In shade gardens, where white-variegated plants are often prominent, dark-leaved heucheras provide incomparable contrast.

Heucheras that have green leaves can tolerate more sun, but they still may suffer, so monitor their welfare and move them to a shadier spot if leaf edges appear curled and dry at the end of a hot summer day.

Light-textured, quick-draining soil enriched with compost is ideal for heuchera. In soggy soil, these cliff-dwelling natives can succumb to root rot. Set container-grown plants at the same depth at which they were growing in their pots. Fill the hole around the root ball, firm the soil with your hands, and water well. Never allow heucheras to dry out completely or growth will come to a screeching halt.

Heucheras have shallow roots, a trait that can make them heave out of the ground as it freezes and thaws in cold-winter areas. To prevent this, cover them with a fluffy mulch of evergreen boughs after the soil freezes hard. In climates where the soil does not stay frozen all winter, check plants several times and gently push them down if they seem to be popping out of their places.

Dig and divide heucheras every 3 years in late winter or early spring. Dig up the clump and use a sharp knife to cut it into 4 sections. Pick away dead material with your fingers, and then immediately replant the divisions where you want them to grow. Heucheras are for the most part pest and disease free.

Heucheras are related to strawberries and can fall prey to strawberry root weevils. The adults chew holes in the leaves, and the larvae eat the roots. Apply beneficial nematodes to the soil

Made to brighten shade, 'Persian Carpet' has silver-flushed leaves on reddish stems.

according to package direction in midspring to control the larvae, which can reduce healthy plants to tumbleweeds. Hungry deer may also nibble the plants. If you find that leaves have been neatly nipped off, tuck a bar of deodorant bath soap into the planting to repel deer or purchase a commercial repellent.

'Palace Purple' is a garden favorite thanks to its maplelike leaves in a rich plum color.

FUNDAMENTAL FACTS

ATTRIBUTES	Purple, silver, or marbled foliage; salmon to red flowers; for beds, pots
SEASON OF INTEREST	Spring to fall
FAVORITES	'Palace Purple', 'Persian Carpet', 'Mt. St. Helens', 'Raspberry Regal'
QUIRKS	Grows poorly in hot sun or dry soil
GOOD NEIGHBORS	Euphorbia, hosta, lamb's ears, meadow rue
WHERE IT GROWS BEST	In partial shade and moist, well-drained soil
POTENTIAL PROBLEMS	Shallow roots can be heaved up in winter
RENEWING PLANTS	Lives to 5 years; divide every 3 years, before plants become woody
CRITTER RESISTANCE	Deer, strawberry root weevil
SOURCE	Bedding plants, division
DIMENSIONS	0.3–1 m (1–3 ft) tall, 30–60 cm (1–2 ft) wide

Hollyhocks bloom in every color but blue, creating a high-flying rainbow in the garden.

With typical crinkled petals, the flowers of *A. rosea* 'Nigra' look like crushed velvet.

HOLLYHOCK

Alcea spp.

HARDINESS:
Zone 3

PREFERRED SOIL pH:
Neutral to slightly acid

PREFERRED SOIL TYPE:
Fertile, well-drained

PREFERRED LIGHT:
Sun

Hollyhock in the Landscape

Hollyhocks are legendary among perennials, famed for their 1.5 m (5 ft) height, 10 cm (4 in) wide flowers, and broad color range. But the main reason hollyhocks have endured is their easy-to-please nature. These are survivors that return season after season for enthusiastic encores.

Place hollyhocks anywhere you need a strong vertical statement. With their tall upright stance, impressively sized rounded leaves and dramatic flower spikes, hollyhocks are unsurpassed as backgrounds in a flower border, for enhancing a wall or fence, or for sidling up to an arbor or gate.

A Rainbow of Hollyhocks

The flowers open from bottom to top, and it's always suspenseful to see what colors appear. Most hollyhocks are available as mixes, such as 'Old Barnyard Mix' and 'Country Romance'. Double hollyhocks are often sold in single colors, making it easy to capitalize on their more formal demeanor.

Growing Hollyhock

Set out seedlings in spring or early fall, in soil fortified with compost or rotted manure and in sun. Set plants 60 cm (2 ft) apart and group them in trios. Water during dry weather to prevent wilting and fertilize twice during the growing season with a balanced fertilizer applied per package directions. In late spring, stake flower spikes to 1.8 m (6 ft) poles to keep them from blowing over in wind, a crucial step when growing the big double-flowered varieties.

Cut off the spires after the flowers are spent. Sometimes plants rebloom on new, shorter spikes. Leave some old flowers at the bottom to ripen a new batch of seeds. Gather and plant the seeds after they turn black in fall, or store them in an envelope and plant them outdoors in spring.

Where summers are long and hot, you may get best results growing certain varieties as biennials, which are sown in fall for flowering the next spring and are not expected to return thereafter. However, given a chance, hollyhocks will persist as a perennial.

A fungal disease called rust, which leaves orange powdery deposits on leaves, can be a problem. Fig hollyhock (*Alcea ficifolia*) shows good resistance. If problems arise with other varieties, remove and dispose of affected leaves. If minute, sap-sucking spider mites make webs on leaf undersides, spray the foliage with a stream of water, or treat them with insecticidal soap per label directions.

Japanese beetles may chew leaves and flowers. Handpick and dispose of them in the morning when the beetles are sluggish or apply a botanical insecticide as directed. The beetles feed most in sun, so try growing hollyhocks in partial shade. If deer nibble plants, tuck a bar of deodorant soap into clumps to repel them or use commercial repellent as directed.

FUNDAMENTAL FACTS

ATTRIBUTES	Tall flower spikes in a range of colors; for back of border, as specimens
SEASON OF INTEREST	Late spring to mid-summer
FAVORITES	'Old Barnyard Mix', 'Country Romance Mix'
QUIRKS	Plants are generally short-lived but easy to grow from seed
GOOD NEIGHBORS	Catmint, cleome, coreopsis, daylily, ornamental grasses, yarrow, zinnia
WHERE IT GROWS BEST	Sun, fertile soil in a wide range of climates
POTENTIAL PROBLEMS	Spider mites, Japanese beetles; fungal leaf disease rust
RENEWING PLANTS	Usually lasts 3–5 years; start new seeds to replace older plants
CRITTER RESISTANCE	Good except for deer
SOURCE	Seeds
DIMENSIONS	Flower spikes to 1.5 m (5 ft) tall, plants to 60 cm (2 ft) wide

The ribbed, heart-shaped leaves of heavy-blooming 'Halcyon' are frosted silver blue.

HOSTA

Hosta spp.

HARDINESS:
Zone 4

PREFERRED SOIL pH:
Neutral

PREFERRED SOIL TYPE:
Adaptable

PREFERRED LIGHT:
Full to partial shade

Hosta in the Landscape

There are many good reasons for the enduring popularity of hostas among shade gardeners. They grow easily, forming lavish mounds of handsome foliage. And they remain attractive throughout the growing season. Hostas make a strong statement in a border or woodland garden, as a groundcover beneath trees, or as an edging along a walk or driveway.

Hostas don't unfurl their leaves until late in spring, making them ideal for interplanting with spring bulbs. They quickly and effectively hide the unsightly spent leaves of daffodils and crocus as they emerge in spring. But hostas aren't just foliage plants. At some point in the season, the timing depends on the variety, hostas send up

'Krossa Regal' is famed for its long-stemmed blue-gray leaves that form a vaselike clump.

long, slender flower stalks lined with white or lavender flowers, often fragrant, that linger for several weeks.

Beyond Plain Vanilla

If you like plain green leaves, there are a number of hostas that fit the bill, ranging from pale lime to deep forest. But there are alternatives, including hostas with solid blue leaves, such as 'Krossa Regal', or golden ones, such as 'August Moon'. The leaves may also be variegated: marked with edging, marbling, or center splotches in white or yellow that is luminous in shade. Some hostas have softly ribbed leaves, while others, such as 'Frances Williams', are puckered or quilted. These versatile plants come in large and small, varying from the demure, 15 cm (6 in) high 'Little Aurora' to the immense, 75 cm (30 in) tall and wide 'Sum and Substance'.

Growing Hosta

The secret to growing spectacular, low-maintenance hostas is good soil. In early spring, or in fall in mild areas, plant in organically rich, well-drained soil. They'll be fine without further fuss as long as they're neither overwatered nor allowed to dry in a drought. They thrive in good but indirect light. For sunnier spots, select a more light-tolerant hosta, such as 'Sun Power'.

Shady spots that welcome hostas are often damp as well. This saves you the trouble of regular watering, but it also means that slugs and snails may be lurking. These pests can deface the leaves with holes, although new foliage quickly fills the gaps. To keep these marauders at bay, water only in the morning so that the plants are not moist overnight to tempt these nighttime feeders. Don't fertilize, which encourages succulent, vulnerable growth. Set out slug traps, such as saucers of beer; use copper barriers, which give the pests an electric shock upon contact; or sprinkle the area with diatomaceous earth, which forms a sharp barrier that cuts slugs' skin. Varieties with thick, quilted leaves, such as 'Frances Williams' are less appealing to slugs.

Deer may also dine on hostas. To dissuade them, tuck a bar of deodorant soap among your hostas, or spray plants with a commercial deer deterrent as directed on the label.

FUNDAMENTAL FACTS

ATTRIBUTES	Big leaves; white or lilac flowers; for beds, edging, groundcover
SEASON OF INTEREST	Spring through fall
FAVORITES	'Krossa Regal', 'Frances Williams', 'Little Aurora'; 'Sun Power' for sun
QUIRKS	Needs ample water to prevent scorching, especially if grown in sun
GOOD NEIGHBORS	Astilbe, epimedium, monkshood, primrose
WHERE IT GROWS BEST	Partial shade in fertile, moist soil
POTENTIAL PROBLEMS	Slugs and snails
RENEWING PLANTS	Plants live many years; divide overcrowded clumps in spring or fall
CRITTER RESISTANCE	Good except for deer
SOURCE	Bedding plants, division
DIMENSIONS	35–90 cm (14–36 in) high, wide; dwarf, to 30 cm (1 ft) tall, wide

Hostas of all foliage colors produce stalks of trumpet-shaped flowers in white or lavender.

IRIS

Iris spp.

HARDINESS:
Zone 3 unless otherwise indicated

PREFERRED SOIL pH:
Slightly alkaline to neutral

PREFERRED SOIL TYPE:
Well-drained loam

PREFERRED LIGHT:
Sun to filtered shade

Iris in the Landscape

Irises are care-free survivors par excellence. You can find them lingering in abandoned gardens long after other plants have disappeared. Named for the ancient Greek goddess of the rainbow, irises are available in every color and combination of colors except true red. In early summer, they send up their famous fleur-de-lis blossoms. Each lingers for several days, then another opens to continue the show for 3–4 weeks. Out of flower, the fans of green or variegated leaves enhance beds. No pruning is necessary, and they're nonaggressive companions.

The deep-blue flowers of Siberian iris dance like butterflies atop the foliage fans.

'Beverly Sills' is a tall bearded iris with pale pink petals surrounding a salmon center and "beards."

Tall Bearded Irises

The best known irises are the tall bearded types, named for the fuzzy, caterpillar-like "beard" at the center of each outer petal, or "fall." Traditional tall bearded irises send their flower spikes up 1 m (3 ft) or more. But beardeds now come in several variations, including miniature dwarfs, at 20 cm (8 in); medians up to 68 cm (27 in); and large-flowered "tetraploid" varieties. However, old hybrids tend to be tougher and are often more fragrant. The wonderful bubble gum scent is something you'll never forget.

An important innovation is the development of reblooming irises. White-blooming 'Immortality' and yellow-flowering, dwarf 'Baby Blessed' are superior examples.

Bearded irises are prone to two main problems, iris borers and soft rot. To control borers, which tunnel in leaves and rhizomes, remove and dispose of infested tissue. Soft rot is a bacterial disease that gains entry when rhizomes are damaged by cultivation or borers. They become soft and evil-smelling. Dig plants, select healthy rhizomes and replant in a different place.

Siberian Irises

Elegant Siberians (Z4) have flowers held on slender spikes above grasslike leaves. Colors include purple, blue, wine, pink, and yellow. There are also reblooming varieties. Although tolerant of shade, Siberians thrive where they have sun, abundant moisture, and good drainage. Best of all, they are not prone to borers or leaf spots.

Species Irises

There are several durable and adaptable species. These include Louisiana irises (Z6), with showy 15 cm (6 in) flowers; miniature reticulata irises (Z5) that sprout from bulbs early in spring, even in snow; and 1.8 m (6 ft) tall, water-loving flag iris (*Iris pseudacorus* [Z4]).

Planting and Dividing Iris

Most irises grow from rhizomes that wander horizontally just below the soil's surface. Divide plants a month or so after blooming. Unearth the rhizomes and cut off 5–8 cm (2–3 in) long segments with a fan of leaves and some roots attached. Dry rhizomes in an airy, shaded place for several days.

FUNDAMENTAL FACTS

ATTRIBUTES	Colorful flowers; green or variegated fan-shaped foliage; for beds, ground-cover, water gardens
SEASON OF INTEREST	Early summer to fall
FAVORITES	Reblooming 'Immortality'; dwarf 'Baby Blessed'; Siberian iris for shade; flag iris for wet soil
QUIRKS	Irises grow poorly in hot, humid environments
GOOD NEIGHBORS	Lamb's ears, peonies, roses, clematis
WHERE IT GROWS BEST	Moist, well-drained soil; wet soil for flag iris; sun, filtered shade
POTENTIAL PROBLEMS	Iris borer; soft rot; fungal leaf diseases
RENEWING PLANTS	Lives years; divide clumps 3–5 years
CRITTER RESISTANCE	Excellent
SOURCE	Bedding plants, division
DIMENSIONS	20 cm–1.8 m (8 in–6 ft) tall, 10–20 cm (4–8 in) wide

Replant them just below the soil surface. However, in damp locations leave the rhizomes slightly exposed. Siberian iris rhizomes should be soaked overnight if you can't transplant them immediately.

Yellowflag iris love water and will thrive around or even in a pond, pool, or creek.

So-called dwarf Japanese anemone average 60 cm (2 ft) tall and are packed with blooms.

JAPANESE ANEMONE

Anemone spp.

HARDINESS:
Zone 4

PREFERRED SOIL pH:
Near neutral

PREFERRED SOIL TYPE:
Fertile, moist soil

PREFERRED LIGHT:
Partial shade

Japanese Anemone in the Landscape

Among the last perennials to bloom, Japanese anemones finish the season with style. The 5 cm (2 in) wide, open-faced, soft pink to white flowers are held high above divided green leaves and appear well into fall. Combine them with hostas and the compact, golden-leaved 'Gold Mound' spiraea. Or grow them in masses where they can spread without bothering their neighbors.

The Tall, the Short, and the Hardy

Most Japanese anemones offered for sale are *Anemone* × *hybrida*. Among the taller cultivars are the single-flowered 'Honorine Jobert' and semidouble 'Whirlwind', both with white blooms that reach 1.2 m (4 ft) tall. 'Königin Charlotte' is another tall type, with semidouble rose pink flowers.

Dwarf Japanese anemones (*A. hupehensis* var. *japonica*) stand only 0.6–1 m (2–3 ft), making them suitable for the front or middle of the border. These include 'September Charm', which has silvery pink single flowers, and 'Bressingham Glow', with vivid rose semidouble blossoms. The most reliable Japanese anemone for Zone 4 gardens is *A. tomentosa* 'Robustissima'. True to its name, this is a hardy, pink-flowered cultivar that thrives in cold-winter areas where other Japanese anemones struggle or die.

Planting and Caring for Japanese Anemone

To give Japanese anemones a good start, turn the soil and amend it generously with aged manure or compost before setting out plants in spring. Water them to keep the soil slightly moist, and mulch with chopped leaves or another organic mulch. Be patient, as plants often take a year or two to show vigorous growth. In Zones 4 and 5 add a 10 cm (4 in) thick mulch of shredded leaves after the first hard freeze in late fall to help ensure the plants' winter survival.

The more sun Japanese anemones get, the faster they spread. Shade slows this tendency but also diminishes flower production. Experiment with sun exposure in your garden to find the right balance of vigor, strong flowering, and restrained spread.

Plants might require division as often as every 3 years if grown in sun, or as seldom as once a decade if grown in shade. To separate crowded clumps or increase your plantings, dig and cut apart the growing points, or crowns, in early spring, making sure each division has healthy roots and a growing point. Replant at the same depth at which the parent plants grew.

Few pests or diseases plague Japanese anemones, but the exceptions are formidable: deer and Japanese beetles. Tuck bars of deodorant soap among plants to repel deer, or apply commercial repellents per label directions. Japanese beetles are more attracted to plants growing in sun than shade, so site plants in shade to discourage this pest. You can also pick and dispose of the beetles in the morning when they are sluggish, or in spring apply the biological insecticide beneficial nematodes to the soil according to package directions to control their larvae.

With pure white blooms, 'Honorine Jobert' has been a fall favorite since the 1800s.

FUNDAMENTAL FACTS

ATTRIBUTES	White or pink flowers; divided green foliage; for beds
SEASON OF INTEREST	Late summer to autumn
FAVORITES	'Honorine Jobert', 'September Charm', *A. tomentosa* 'Robustissima'
QUIRKS	Spreads quickly when grown in full sun
GOOD NEIGHBORS	Astilbe, cohosh, hosta, hydrangea, spiraea
WHERE IT GROWS BEST	Fertile, moist soil in partial shade
POTENTIAL PROBLEMS	Poor flowering when grown in deep shade
RENEWING PLANTS	Lives many years; divide clumps in spring and replant immediately
CRITTER RESISTANCE	Good except for deer and Japanese beetles
SOURCE	Bedding plants, division
DIMENSIONS	0.6–1.2 m (2–4 ft) tall, 0.3–1 m (1–3 ft) wide

A true garden giant, Joe Pye weed grows head high without the need for staking.

JOE PYE WEED

Eupatorium purpureum

HARDINESS:
Zone 3

PREFERRED SOIL pH:
Near neutral

PREFERRED SOIL TYPE:
Average, moist

PREFERRED LIGHT:
Sun to partial shade

Joe Pye Weed in the Landscape

When you want a statuesque plant to fill the back of the border or line a fence, Joe Pye weed is a prime candidate. Improved varieties of this North American native from damp meadows are an asset to any sunny garden.

The flower clusters are big enough to balance the tall stems visually but won't topple them, thanks to strong stalks that don't need staking. Because

Joe Pye weed attracts little attention through the first half of summer, it is a good plant to set behind daylilies, rudbeckias, ornamental grasses, or other perennials. Or you can use it as a backdrop for zinnias and other tall annual flowers.

'Gateway' grows a bit shorter than the native species, and has a vanilla scent.

Gentle Giants

Standing up to 2 m (7 ft) tall, with long, pointed leaves growing in whorls around thick stems, the widely available 'Atropurpureum' is nothing less than colossal. Its clusters of dusty pink flowers burst into bloom in mid to late summer and last for weeks. If you prefer shorter plants, cut the stems back by a third in late spring. They will rebound and flower but stand at least 30 cm (1 ft) shorter than untrimmed plants. Another option for shorter plants is to grow 'Gateway', a dark pink-flowered version that tops out at 1.2–1.8 m (4–6 ft). Another popular cultivar, 'Bartered Bride', features attractive white flowers.

Butterfly Haven

Joe Pye weed's fragrant flowers entice man and insect alike. The large clusters of tiny nectar-rich flowers make a good landing pad and sipping station for butterflies. On a warm, drowsy summer day, a single plant may be covered with dozens of swallowtails.

Growing Joe Pye Weed

Don't fret if Joe Pye weed is slow to emerge in spring. This hardy perennial is rarely winter-killed and makes up for lost time when it does emerge. However, this is a shallow-rooted plant that needs to be grown where it won't be disturbed, in a sunny spot with moist soil. Joe Pye weed wilts in dry weather but is unequaled for tolerating standing water. This energetic grower is also a big feeder. Spread a 5 cm (2 in) thick layer of composted manure over the dormant plants every spring to keep them at their peak of perfection.

Watch for fungal diseases typical of overly moist sites: powdery mildew and fungal leaf spot. Thinning stems to promote better air circulation is a good preventative. If you do see white powdery or dark sooty spots on leaves, remove and dispose of the affected foliage. The symptoms will naturally diminish in drier weather.

While insects don't inflict life-threatening damage, grasshoppers and flea beetles sometimes chew the leaves in late summer. The possibility of unsightly late-season foliage is a good reason to keep Joe Pye weed at the back of the border, where its lower leaves are hidden from view.

Plants can grow for many years undisturbed, but if a clump becomes overcrowded, or if you want to increase your stock, lift and divide the clumps in early spring, or in fall in mild climates. When replanting, set the divisions at the same depth at which the parents grew.

FUNDAMENTAL FACTS

ATTRIBUTES	Tall plants with large pink or white flowers; for the back of the border
SEASON OF INTEREST	Midsummer to fall
FAVORITES	Pink-flowered 'Atropurpureum', smaller 'Gateway', white 'Bartered Bride'
QUIRKS	For compact growth, cut plants back by one-third in late spring
GOOD NEIGHBORS	Daylilies, goldenrod, garden phlox, rudbeckia, ornamental grasses
WHERE IT GROWS BEST	Damp soil and full sun
POTENTIAL PROBLEMS	Fungal powdery mildew, leaf spot; grasshoppers, flea beetles
RENEWING PLANTS	Lives for years; divide crowded clumps 5–6 years in spring or fall
CRITTER RESISTANCE	Good
SOURCE	Bedding plants, division
DIMENSIONS	1.2–2 m (4–7 ft) tall, 1–1.2 m (3–4 ft) wide

LADY'S MANTLE

Alchemilla mollis

HARDINESS:
Zone 4

PREFERRED SOIL pH:
Neutral

PREFERRED SOIL TYPE:
Moist, well-drained, average

PREFERRED LIGHT:
Partial shade

Lady's Mantle in the Landscape

How often do you find a versatile beauty that is as easy to please as it is elegant? The large, rounded leaves of the lady's mantle are soft apple green and velvety to the touch, with edges that look as if they were cut by pinking shears. Before they fully open, the leaves are pleated, resembling an old-fashioned lady's cape. The leaves catch and hold drops of rain or morning dew, which bead up like teardrops along their surface. It was once a popular and romantic notion that a lady who washed her face in the morning dew that had collected on the leaves would have youthful skin.

Because lady's mantle is a low, mounding plant, standing at most 0.6 m (2 ft) tall and wide, it deserves a front-row position in a flower border. Its primary asset is its attractive display of foliage all season, although lady's mantle also produces clusters of diminutive chartreuse flowers on slender stems in spring and early summer. The clouds of fine-textured color are a perfect complement for blue and purple blossoms, such as those of catmint

From late spring to early summer, lady's mantle issues a cloud of bright chartreuse blooms.

and lavender, which flower at the same time. In flower arrangements, lady's-mantle flowers hold well for a week or longer.

Potted Splendor

Lady's mantle looks elegant when grown in containers and is versatile enough to blend with pots of terra-cotta, lead, or stone. Its neutral leaves and bright flowers work equally well in a colorfully decorated ceramic pot. Grow it solo or slip in a few bright-colored annuals, such as pansies, primroses, and coleus to keep the color coming from spring to fall.

This adaptable perennial can survive the fickle watering that pots receive, because it tolerates drought as well as rainstorms. When potting it, give lady's mantle fertile soil and make certain the container has ample drainage. As a guide to watering, stick your index finger into the soil up to the first knuckle. It's time to water when the soil feels dry.

Growing Lady's Mantle

Lady's mantle is at its best when it is growing in well-drained, fertile soil in partial shade, but it tolerates sun and average growing conditions. Set out new plants in early spring and add a thin layer of organic mulch to keep weeds at bay, reduce the need for water, and allow the plants to thrive in sun. Avoid planting in wet soil, or the roots will rot.

Although lady's mantle is for the most part pest free, beware of slugs and snails if it is growing in the shade. These night-feeding mollusks can riddle the handsome foliage with holes. To prevent or control the problem, set out shallow dishes of beer to attract and drown them.

Dig up and divide lady's mantel in spring about every 3 years, when the

The pleated leaves collect raindrops and dew, which glisten like jewels on a cape.

centers of clumps are crowded and have reduced flowering, or when you want to increase your stock. When replanting, set the divisions at the same depth at which the parents grew. Also keep your eyes open for volunteer seedlings, which can be gently transplanted in spring.

FUNDAMENTAL FACTS

ATTRIBUTES	Large leaves, airy chartreuse flowers; for beds, herb gardens, pots
SEASON OF INTEREST	Flowers from late spring to early summer; foliage spring to fall
FAVORITES	*A. mollis*
QUIRKS	Roots grow better when cooled by organic mulch
GOOD NEIGHBORS	Astilbe, catmint, lavender, Siberian iris
WHERE IT GROWS BEST	Fertile soil in partial shade
POTENTIAL PROBLEMS	Slugs and snails
RENEWING PLANTS	Lives several years; divide crowded clumps in early spring
CRITTER RESISTANCE	Good
SOURCE	Bedding plants, division
DIMENSIONS	0.6 m (2 ft) tall and equally wide

LAMB'S EARS

Stachys byzantina

HARDINESS:
Zone 3

PREFERRED SOIL pH:
Neutral

PREFERRED SOIL TYPE:
Average, well-drained

PREFERRED LIGHT:
Sun to partial shade

Lamb's Ears in the Landscape

Velvety to the touch, lamb's ears is a groundcover or edging plant that can be counted on to fill in wherever it is needed. The silvery gray leaves are a calming influence on hot-colored flowers, including everything from ruby red poppies to orange zinnias. Lamb's ears is one of the few plants that can keep company with hard-to-match magenta flowers, such as those of rose campion or hot pink dianthus. Yet it casts a soft glow in the company of pastel flowers.

Maybe it's the soft texture of the leaves, or the plant's informal habit, but lamb's ears naturally make a garden look comfortable. Grown along a walkway or driveway, or skirting a line of shrubs or roses, this plant blurs hard lines. And because it establishes itself quickly, it makes a newly planted garden look less stiff and bare.

Before you rush out to buy a flat, however, bear in mind the plant's size and habit. Individual plants reach 30 cm (12 in) or more in height and width, and they do spread and sprawl, so allow some room for future expansion when planting. If you encourage lamb's ears to follow its natural growth patterns, a single plant will form a pool of luminous silvery leaves in only one season.

Look Out for Flowers

While lamb's ears is prized for its foliage, it does have flowers. In late spring, woolly stalks carrying small,

'Silver Carpet' has particularly luminous, velvety leaves but produces no flowers.

Clumps of fast-growing lamb's ears can form a dense groundcover in a single year.

lavender blossoms emerge from the clump and shoot up to twice the plant's height. If you want an informal cottage-garden effect, or if nearby plants that bear clashing flowers are not yet in bloom, you may welcome these understated flowers, which attract bees in droves. However, some gardeners feel the flower stalks detract from the foliage and look unkempt, so they clip them off. To eliminate the chore of removing flower stalks, you can plant the nonflowering cultivars 'Silver Carpet' and 'Helene von Stein'.

Growing Lamb's Ears

Lamb's ears grows best in average, well-drained soil. Full sun is preferable, but the plants also adapt to partial shade. In areas with long, hot summers, plant them where they'll receive afternoon shade. But even with shade, the foliage may decline after a long spate of humid nights. In hot climates, grow heat-tolerant cultivars, such as 'Big Ears', which has leaves twice the size of the species. Avoid heavy watering and fertilizing, which can lead to lanky growth that is unattractive and vulnerable to rot. Also avoid getting the leaves wet when watering.

In early spring, you can dig new plantlets that pop up between older plants and move them to where you want them to grow. Use a sharp knife to cut out a small circle of soil and roots around the new plantlet, and lift it from beneath without pulling on the plant itself. When planting, set it at the same depth at which the parent plant grew, and keep the soil moist for several weeks to encourage fast rooting. Lamb's ears are remarkably pest free and are even unappealing to deer.

FUNDAMENTAL FACTS

ATTRIBUTES	Soft, fuzzy silver-gray leaves; for edging or ground cover
SEASON OF INTEREST	Spring and summer
FAVORITES	Nonflowering 'Silver Carpet', 'Helene von Stein'; 'Big Ears' for heat
QUIRKS	Plants may die back in hot, humid conditions
GOOD NEIGHBORS	Herbs, iris, roses, salvia, lavender
WHERE IT GROWS BEST	Well-drained soil in sun to partial shade
POTENTIAL PROBLEMS	Crown rot in poorly drained soil
RENEWING PLANTS	Lives many years; divide crowded clumps
CRITTER RESISTANCE	Excellent
SOURCE	Bedding plants, division
DIMENSIONS	30–60 cm (12–24 in) tall and equally wide

Lamb's ears provide a cooling presence when massed as an edging or groundcover.

Fragrant lavender spikes beg to be snipped and dried for use in sachets and wands.

LAVENDER

Lavandula spp.

HARDINESS:
Zone 5 unless otherwise indicated

PREFERRED SOIL pH:
Neutral to slightly alkaline

PREFERRED SOIL TYPE:
Infertile, well-drained

PREFERRED LIGHT:
Sun

Lavender in the Landscape

The clean, refreshing fragrance of lavender is one of the most popular scents in the world, used in perfumes, soaps, sachets, and thousands of other items. Luckily for gardeners, lavender looks as good as it smells. Although grown as a perennial, it is actually a small shrub with grayish evergreen

The flower spikes of *L. stoechas* are topped with bracts resembling little rabbit ears.

leaves that appear needlelike yet are soft to the touch. When crushed, the leaves release a soft scent. The purple or lavender flower spikes that appear in late spring or early summer release the perfume with intoxicating clarity.

Lavender naturally possesses a neat, mounding form, growing about as wide as it is tall. Compact types make an aromatic pathway edging and are even grown as lawns in arid regions, while larger types work well as a low hedge. You can keep a single large mound as a specimen in the border or grow it in a pot. Always plant lavender in a sunny, dry location, because heat helps release its fragrance. Grow it near fragrant roses for a double punch of perfume, or pair it with aromatic creeping thyme or sweet-scented annuals, such as sweet alyssum.

The most popular lavender, widely grown because it is moderately cold hardy, is English lavender (*Lavandula angustifolia*). Two excellent cultivars are the dark purple-flowered 'Hidcote', at 60 cm (24 in) tall, and medium purple 'Munstead', at 35 cm (14 in) tall. Called French or Spanish lavender, *L. stoechas* is hardy to Zone 8 and may survive in Zone 7 if it is planted in a place protected from winter wind, such as near a wall or building. Growing nearly 1 m (3 ft) tall, it produces flower spikes topped by tufted bracts in late spring and summer.

Growing Lavender

Good drainage, lean soil, sun, and heat will ensure success with lavender. Be stingy with fertilizer or you'll get leaves at the expense of flowers. Set out new plants in early spring, and clip off spent flowers to prolong the bloom time. Where lavender is not hardy, grow it in pots and bring them indoors for winter. Cut the plants back by half their size when you bring them inside in late fall, and keep them cool and dry through winter. Then shift them back outdoors first thing in the spring.

In areas where lavender can be grown outdoors, it will prosper for years with little care beyond annual pruning if pleased with the conditions. Wait until spring to trim back old stems, which shelter the plant's roots and low buds through winter.

The best way to propagate lavender is to root 15 cm (6 in) long stem cuttings taken from plants in the late summer. Remove leaves from the lower half of the stems, and dip the cut ends into rooting powder and insert them into damp sand up to half their length. Cuttings root in about

6 weeks. Lavender is so pest free that it is often dried and included in insect-repelling sachets to tuck into drawers filled with linens and woolens.

FUNDAMENTAL FACTS

ATTRIBUTES	Fragrant purple flowers, evergreen foliage; for beds, pots, dried flowers
SEASON OF INTEREST	Spring to fall
FAVORITES	*L. angustifolia* 'Hidcote', 'Munstead'; *L. stoechas* in warm climates
QUIRKS	Cannot tolerate excessive soil moisture or extreme winter cold
GOOD NEIGHBORS	Artemisia, coreopsis, dianthus, roses, thyme
WHERE IT GROWS BEST	Sun; infertile, well-drained soil
POTENTIAL PROBLEMS	Root rot in wet soil
RENEWING PLANTS	Lives years; prune severely in late winter; start plants from cuttings
CRITTER RESISTANCE	Excellent
SOURCE	Bedding plants, stem cuttings in late summer
DIMENSIONS	30–90 cm (12–36 in) tall and wide

'Hidcote' has deep purple flowers, which contrast beautifully with the silvery foliage.

'Dora Bielefeld' has faintly spotted leaves, but its handsome flowers turn from pink to violet.

LUNGWORT

Pulmonaria spp.

HARDINESS:
Zone 4

PREFERRED SOIL pH:
Neutral

PREFERRED SOIL TYPE:
Fertile, moist, well-drained

PREFERRED LIGHT:
Partial to full shade

Lungwort in the Landscape

If you have a shady spot to fill and want an elegant, exciting plant to put there, consider lungwort, also commonly called pulmonaria. This is an ideal plant for growing under trees and shrubs or on the north side of a building. Even in deep shade, lungwort forms a broad, dense swath of handsome variegated foliage that blocks out weeds and forms a novel, eye-catching groundcover.

With pale green leaves and pink flowers, 'Mrs. Moon' is a shade-garden mainstay.

The slightly hairy leaves range in length from 15–30 cm (6–12 in) and can be speckled, streaked, or flushed with white or silver. When massed, the plants become a luminous carpet, with the spots creating little pools of light that glow in the shady places that lungwort likes to frequent. So pretty are lungwort's leaves that gardeners like to scatter the plants throughout a woodland garden or use them to line shady steps and paths. Lungwort is also a great addition to a spring bulb bed, flattering the flowers of daffodils, tulips, and grape hyacinths while they last and hiding the bulbs' foliage as it fades.

Fairy-Tale Flowers

While the leaves are still small and tender in spring, lungwort rushes to produce flowers that linger for only a few weeks. Loose clusters of buds open to pink, violet-blue, or white bells that remind some gardeners of little fairy caps. *Pulmonaria saccharata* 'Mrs. Moon', an old favorite, has pink flowers that age to blue atop silver-dappled leaves. For bright raspberry flowers atop foliage splashed with cream, try 'Berries and Cream'. 'Excalibur', which has pinkish red buds and blue flowers, boasts long, metallic silver leaves with green hems. 'White Wings' is a long-blooming type with pure white flowers.

Growing Lungwort

Because the plants rise and shine so early in the spring, fall is the best time to plant lungwort. These plants thrive in classic woodland conditions: partial to full shade in moist, loose-textured soil. Take special care with lungworts that have predominantly white leaves; these need more shade than those with mostly green leaves.

If the soil seems infertile, dig in some compost or other organic matter before planting and spread a thin layer of compost over the area early each spring. For a dense groundcover, set the plants 30 cm (12 in) apart. Always water lungwort generously and regularly when it's newly planted, and furnish water as needed to keep the soil moist. Lungwort doesn't fare well in overly dry conditions. When stressed, it wilts.

Lungwort is prone to powdery mildew, a disfiguring fungal infection, where days are warm and moist and nights are cool, or when it is grown in cool, damp sites or areas with poor air circulation. Luckily, many new hybrids, such as 'Excalibur', have good resistance to this problem. If mildew does strike, clip off and dispose of any foliage covered with powdery white patches. New leaves will sprout afresh and last through the season.

Pests seldom bother lungwort. Night-feeding slugs and snails will occasionally visit plants growing in deep shade. Set out saucers of beer to lure and drown these pests. Deer may nibble lungworts growing in naturalized gardens. Tuck bars of strong-smelling deodorant-formula bath soap among plantings to repel them, or apply commercial repellents as directed on the label.

FUNDAMENTAL FACTS

ATTRIBUTES	Broad leaves variegated with white or silver; for beds, woodland gardens
SEASON OF INTEREST	Spring into summer
FAVORITES	'Berries and Cream', 'Mrs. Moon'; mildew-resistant 'Excalibur'
QUIRKS	Will wilt and may burn in dry, sunny conditions
GOOD NEIGHBORS	Bleeding heart, daffodil, dogwood, forsythia, iris
WHERE IT GROWS BEST	Under deciduous trees or in a northern exposure
POTENTIAL PROBLEMS	Powdery mildew in cool, damp sites
RENEWING PLANTS	Lives many years; divide crowded clumps
CRITTER RESISTANCE	Good except for deer, slugs and snails
SOURCE	Bedding plants, division
DIMENSIONS	15–30 cm (6–12 in) high, 30–60 cm (1–2 ft) wide

MEADOW RUE

Thalictrum spp.

HARDINESS:
Zone 5

PREFERRED SOIL pH:
Neutral to slightly acid

PREFERRED SOIL TYPE:
Fertile, moist

PREFERRED LIGHT:
Partial shade

Meadow Rue in the Landscape

Meadow rue is a graceful plant with the texture of a maidenhair fern and a bonus of airy pastel flowers. As the name implies, this is a fine plant for meadows but it's also ideal for the edges of woodlands and for flower gardens. Standing 1–1.8 m (3–6 ft) tall, meadow rue has presence when set in the background, while its attractive foliage and powder-puff flowers invite close scrutiny.

Shade-tolerant meadow rue combines well with hosta, columbine, and Solomon's seal. Its delicate green foliage, which appears in midspring, makes it ideal for combining with ephemeral spring-flowering woodland plants, such as Virginia bluebells, bleeding heart, and trillium, filling the site where their leaves fade away in early summer.

Flowers with a Watercolor Palette

Once appreciated only by wildflower enthusiasts, meadow rue has recently caught the interest of nursery professionals. *Thalictrum rochebrunianum* 'Lavender Mist' reaches the impressive height of 1.8 m (6 ft) and has clusters of puffball-like purple flowers on wiry purple stems. Plant it in front of dark evergreens for contrast, with a front edge of tulips, bleeding hearts, hostas, and columbines. Also compelling are two species that stand 1 m (3 ft) tall: *T. flavum* ssp. *glaucum* (formerly *T. speciosissimum*), with airy, pale yellow flowers and gray-green leaves, and *T. aquilegifolium*, with white, lavender, or pink blossoms. For a shorter thalictrum, try *T. kiusianum* from Japan. At only 15 cm (6 in) tall with a spread of up to 60 cm (2 ft), it produces lavender flower puffs and is delightful for edging a woodland path or shady walkway.

Growing Meadow Rue

Plant meadow rue in fertile, moist, well-drained soil, in a location that receives partial shade to sun. Plants growing in hot climates especially appreciate afternoon shade. To make a strong statement, group 3–5 plants, spacing them 35–40 cm (14–16 in) apart. Each spring, apply a 2.5 cm (1 in) layer of composted manure at the base of the plants to keep the roots fertilized, cool, and moist.

In midsummer, if the leaves begin to decline after blooming ceases, you can prune the foliage back to the ground to force fresh new leaves. Pruning off the seed heads also prevents this wildflower from reseeding.

Most species can be started from seeds sown outdoors in late summer. Cover the seeds with 0.3 cm (1/8 in) of soil and keep them moist until seedlings are established. To increase your stock, take stem cuttings in spring and root them in moist soil. You can also divide mature plants in early spring. But, unless your stand becomes too dense, you can safely leave these insect- and pest-free plants undisturbed for years.

Plant *T. aquilegifolium* in the middle of the bed, for a good view of its fuzzy pink flowers.

The fluffy yellow blooms of *T. flavum* ssp. *glaucum* contrast with gray-green leaves.

FUNDAMENTAL FACTS

ATTRIBUTES	Feathery rose, purple, white, or yellow flowers, ferny foliage; for beds
SEASON OF INTEREST	Spring and summer
FAVORITES	*T. rochebrunianum* 'Lavender Mist'; *T. aquilegifolium*; *T. kiusianum*
QUIRKS	May be semi-evergreen from Zone 8
GOOD NEIGHBORS	Bleeding heart, bloodroot, columbine, hosta, lobelia, Solomon's seal
WHERE IT GROWS BEST	The edges of wooded areas; in partial shade and moist soil
POTENTIAL PROBLEMS	Staking may be needed in fertile soil, which causes spindly growth
RENEWING PLANTS	Lives many years; divide crowded clumps
CRITTER RESISTANCE	Excellent
SOURCE	Seeds, division, stem cuttings
DIMENSIONS	15 cm–1.8 m (6 in–6 ft) tall, 30 cm (12 in) wide

A. *napellus* forms a field of blue in summer and offers pretty, deeply cut foliage all season.

MONKSHOOD

Aconitum spp.

HARDINESS:
Zone 3 unless otherwise indicated

PREFERRED SOIL pH:
Neutral to slightly acid

PREFERRED SOIL TYPE:
Fertile, moist, well-drained

PREFERRED LIGHT:
Sun to partial shade

Monkshood in the Landscape

If you've lusted after the tall blue spires of delphiniums but found that they are too finicky to grow, try the far less fussy monkshood. This native of mountains and alpine meadows stands 1–1.2 m (3–4 ft) tall and sends up spikes of blue, pink, yellow, or white-and-blue hooded blossoms between midsummer and early fall. The dark green foliage is deeply divided and clothes the base of the plants with a skirt of lush greenery.

Monkshood is an old-fashioned flower perfectly suited to cottage gardens or casual borders. It should be placed at the back of the border because of its height and also because it should be kept away from children and pets who might be tempted to take a bite of its poisonous leaves, stems, and flowers. Some good companions of comparable size with similar bloom times include rudbeckia, cohosh, obedient plant, purple coneflower, and sneezeweed.

A healthy monkshood will brandish several spires of flowers arranged all around the stem that open from the top down. Each blossom has an unusual shape, with the uppermost petal forming a helmet or hood, hence the common name. The plants may become so heavily laden with blossoms that they need to be staked. Use inconspicuous plastic or bamboo stakes and fasten the stems to them with soft green twine, raffia, or yarn. If carefully installed, the stakes will be scarcely visible.

Beyond Blue Hues

The monkshood family has a number of worthwhile relatives that expand the color range beyond the fetching azure found in the traditional monkshoods, *Aconitum napellus* (Z5) and its equally well known cousin, *A. carmichaelii*. There's a white-flowered cultivar, *A. napellus* ssp. *vulgare* 'Album', and two pink versions: 'Carneum' in salmon and 'Roseum' in shell pink. *A. lycotonum* ssp. *neapolitanum* (Z5) has abundant yellow flowers, while 'Ivorine' (Z4) has pale ivory-yellow blossoms. For a charming color combination, try *A.* × *cammarum* 'Bicolor' or 'Eleanor', both of which have white flowers edged in blue.

Growing Monkshood

Where it is happy, monkshood is as care-free as it is stunning. It excels in areas with cool summer weather but flags where hot, humid summers are the rule. In warm climates, grow monkshood in partial shade and mulch to keep roots cool and moist.

Monkshood demands well-drained and fertile soil, so dig in plenty of compost or other organic matter prior to planting. The roots of all monkshoods are poisonous; be sure to handle plants with gloves when planting. Position plants in a permanent home, because monkshood roots are brittle and rarely survive disturbance. It is best not to divide them.

Monkshood is prone to two diseases linked to poor soil drainage.

Monkshood gets its name from the arched upper petals that create a helmet, or hood.

Crown rot causes leaf yellowing and brown streaks in the foliage; verticillium wilt causes yellowing on one side of the plant only. To prevent these problems, allow soil to dry between waterings and plant in a well-drained location. Because of its toxicity, monkshood is virtually pest free.

FUNDAMENTAL FACTS

ATTRIBUTES	Spikes of blue, pink, yellow, white, or blue-and-white flowers; for beds
SEASON OF INTEREST	Midsummer to early fall
FAVORITES	*A. napellus* and cultivars, *A. carmichaelii*, *A.* × *cammarum* 'Bicolor'
QUIRKS	All plant parts are poisonous if eaten
GOOD NEIGHBORS	Purple coneflower, rudbeckia, sneezeweed
WHERE IT GROWS BEST	In well-drained, fertile soil; areas with warm days and cool nights
POTENTIAL PROBLEMS	Root rot, verticillium wilt when grown in wet soil
RENEWING PLANTS	Lives several years; do not divide
CRITTER RESISTANCE	Good
SOURCE	Seeds
DIMENSIONS	1–1.2 m (3–4 ft) tall, 0.6–1 m (2–3 ft) wide

OBEDIENT PLANT

Physostegia virginiana

HARDINESS:
Zone 3

PREFERRED SOIL pH:
Neutral to slightly acid

PREFERRED SOIL TYPE:
Moist, well-drained, average

PREFERRED LIGHT:
Sun to partial shade

Obedient Plant in the Landscape

A real problem-solving plant for areas with damp soil, obedient plant thrives with its roots sunk into soggy under-pinnings. It offers plenty of luminous rose pink or white flowers that coordinate with nearly everything else you might want to grow. Obedient plant is

Obedient plant quickly fills a damp site and faithfully produces masses of pink blooms.

The cream-edged leaves of 'Varie-gata' play up the pink blooms.

doubly appreciated because it develops its wands of trumpet-shaped blossoms in late summer, when little else is in flower, and the blooms linger long into fall. Because of its height, it's best suited to the back of a flower border, a meadow garden, or even the edges of a streambed. Obedient plant stands a stately 1–1.2 m (3–4 ft) tall with sparse, pointed foliage, which makes it best displayed en masse.

Obedient plant is a good neighbor for late-blooming asters, moisture-loving meadow rue, and clumps of ornamental grasses or sedges. For a daring pink display, grow it in the company of pink-flowered garden phlox. Just bear in mind that obedient plant spreads by means of creeping roots that travel far and fast. This characteristic makes it a handful for anyone who values strict discipline in a plant or who gardens in small spaces. But the obedient plant's meandering ways are an asset in more informal garden schemes where it can express its natural exuberance.

Playful Plants

The obedient plant's common name refers to the unique way that the individual flowers, when nudged left or right, will remain pointed in that direction until you realign them. This characteristic makes it a fun-filled addition to a child's garden.

All cultivars make good cut flowers, but 'Bouquet Rose' is particularly valued for its 1–1.5 m (3–5 ft) tall rose pink spikes. 'Vivid', the most popular garden variety, has hot pink flowers on shorter, 38 cm (15 in) stems. Or you might prefer the pure white 'Summer Snow', which has a less aggressive personality than its relatives. Better behaved still is a new introduction called 'Miss Manners', which forms clumps rather than running about, and it produces white flowers atop 1 m (3 ft) tall stems. The cultivar 'Variegata' not only offers abundant lavender pink flowers but also has gray-green leaves, which are edged in milky white.

Growing Obedient Plant

Luxuriating in damp soil, obedient plants will be grateful if you find a soggy spot when setting out young plants in late spring or early fall. The site shouldn't be overly fertile, and there's no need for further feeding, as too much fertility leads to weak stems that fall over easily. Obedient plant can tolerate dry soil, which can help to curtail its tendency to wander, but lack of water will also diminish its height and profusion of flowers.

To get this perennial off to a running start, tuck it into a roomy hole and backfill thoroughly, tamping the soil down to eliminate air pockets. Water it well and spread a thin layer of grass clippings or straw as a mulch, just enough to keep weeds at bay and retain moisture around the roots. Unless there is ample natural dampness, water every few days until the plants begin to produce new growth. To enjoy more flowers on shorter plants, prune back the tallest, earliest stems in early summer. The pruned stems will form several branches all topped with blossoms.

Obedient plant is virtually pest and disease free, and needs to be divided only to control its growth or to increase plantings. Dig and divide plants in the spring, cutting through rhizomes to separate plantlets from the parent. Set plantlets at the same depth at which the parent plant grew, watering as needed to keep the soil moist until plantlets are established.

FUNDAMENTAL FACTS

ATTRIBUTES	Pink or white flowers, green or variegated leaves; for beds
SEASON OF INTEREST	Late summer into fall
FAVORITES	'Bouquet Rose', 'Vivid', 'Summer Snow', 'Miss Manners', 'Variegata'
QUIRKS	Stems retain curves when bent or twisted
GOOD NEIGHBORS	Asters, garden phlox, goldenrod, meadow rue, ornamental grasses
WHERE IT GROWS BEST	In a sunny site, and in damp soil
POTENTIAL PROBLEMS	Spreads rapidly; uproot unwanted plants
RENEWING PLANTS	Lives many years; divide every 3 years and discard weak plants
CRITTER RESISTANCE	Good
SOURCE	Bedding plant, division
DIMENSIONS	0.2–1.2 m (2–4 ft) tall, 0.3–1 m (1–3 ft) wide

ORIENTAL POPPY

Papaver orientale

HARDINESS:
Zone 3

PREFERRED SOIL pH:
Near neutral

PREFERRED SOIL TYPE:
Fertile, well-drained

PREFERRED LIGHT:
Sun to partial shade

Oriental Poppy in the Landscape

Foretelling summer, Oriental poppies infuse late spring with a blast of pure, bright color. The 12 cm (5 in) wide cup-shaped flowers have petals with the texture of crepe paper in fabulous shades of red, wine, orange, pink, and white. When the setting sun strikes their big translucent petals, they seem to light up the garden.

New foliage appears early in spring, with divided leaves about 30 cm (12 in) tall emerging from

The pure white petals of 'Perry's White' are intensified by the violet-black flower's center.

'Prinzessin Victoria Louise' flowers in a soft shade of salmon touched with rose.

central rosettes with long taproots. Soon thereafter, straight 1–1.2 m (3–4 ft) tall flowering stalks appear in time to bloom along with bearded iris, continuing for about 2 weeks. Then the leaves slowly brown and vanish in midsummer. Do not be concerned, as new foliage will magically appear in fall, and the period of dormancy helps the plants survive summer heat. As a result, Oriental poppies live for many years with little care.

Oriental poppies are gorgeous when planted against a fence or wall or anywhere that breezes can stir the long-stemmed flowers. You can also use them to punctuate the back of a mixed perennial border. It is best to plant them singly, because you'll have a gap in midsummer when they go dormant. Place a plant close by that will swallow up the space, such as baby's breath or obedient plant.

Color Is the Key

The old-fashioned Oriental poppies usually have shiny red flowers, and

there are many red cultivars, from 'Brilliant' to 'Prince of Orange.' Variations that offer dramatic texture with their ruffled and deeply fringed petals are 'Türkenlouis', in a rich red, and 'Curlilocks' in an orange-red.

If you prefer subtler, softer colors, Oriental poppies are happy to comply. 'Helen Elizabeth' has salmon petals set off by purplish black centers, and 'Raspberry Queen' blooms in a luscious sherbet shade. 'Royal Wedding' and 'Perry's White' both have white petals with central black blotches.

To help these fabulous flower colors stay fresh in arrangements for several days, cut stems in the morning, quickly sear the base of the stems over a flame, and condition them by submerging the stems for several hours in deep, cool water before arranging.

Growing Oriental Poppy

Set out purchased plants in spring, in fertile, deeply dug soil, in sun in the cool-summer climates or in slight afternoon shade in warm regions. Once they are established, leave these perennials undisturbed, adding a 2.5 cm (1 in) thick layer of compost or well-rotted manure as a top-dressing each fall. Fertilize only in

With its fringed petals, 'Curlilocks' offers a charming variation on the usual red bloom.

spring and fall while leaves are growing. And don't overwater; Oriental poppies are adapted to dry conditions. For neatness, remove the stems, either before seed heads ripen or after. The round, smooth pods can be dried and used in flower arrangements.

Pests rarely bother this tough perennial. If sap-sucking aphids or spider mites occasionally stipple leaves with small pale spots, simply wash them off the plant with a forceful spray of water.

Increasing the Bounty

Propagate Oriental poppies by division, which is best done in summer after the foliage dies back. Dig deeply to remove the entire taproot of each plantlet. Seeds are also an option, although seedlings will not necessarily look exactly like their parents.

FUNDAMENTAL FACTS

ATTRIBUTES	Big, textured flowers in orange, red, pink, and white; for beds
SEASON OF INTEREST	Late spring
FAVORITES	'Helen Elizabeth', 'Raspberry Queen', 'Perry's White', 'Türkenlouis'
QUIRKS	Plants go dormant in midsummer
GOOD NEIGHBORS	Bearded iris, centaurea, gypsophila, obedient plant, peony
WHERE IT GROWS BEST	Sun and fertile soil in cool-summer climates
POTENTIAL PROBLEMS	Occasionally aphids or spider mites
RENEWING PLANTS	Lives many years; divide overcrowded roots after flowering in summer
CRITTER RESISTANCE	Good
SOURCE	Division, seeds
DIMENSIONS	In bloom, 1–1.2 m (3–4 ft) tall, 0.6 m (2 ft) wide

Bright, tough, and colorful, *Tanacetum coccineum* 'James Galway' is a must in a border.

PAINTED DAISY

Tanacetum coccineum

HARDINESS:
Zone 5

PREFERRED SOIL pH:
Neutral

PREFERRED SOIL TYPE:
Well-drained, sandy

PREFERRED LIGHT:
Full sun to partial shade

Painted Daisy in the Landscape

Invaluable for cutting, these bright, tough plants, also known as pyrethrums, are a must for the border. The lacy dark green foliage forms a neat mound, almost as attractive as the flowers, emerging in spring as a bright green froth and darkening with age. In midsummer, wiry stems arise, each carrying one daisylike flower of red, pink, or white and up to 8 cm (3 in) in diameter. Single flowers have brightly colored petals around the outside, with bright yellow, small tubular flowers forming a central disk. In double flowers, the central disk is mounded with larger tubular flowers in the same or a contrasting color.

Plants vary in height and range from 45 cm (18 in) to 90 cm (3 ft), depending on the variety. The taller ones may need staking, but are the best for cutting. Blooms last a long time as a cut flower, and it is widely used by commercial florists for this reason. This plant is the source of the botanical insecticide pyrethrum.

Pick a Painted Daisy

Painted daisies can be grown from seeds obtained from the larger seed houses, but these plants are generally not as good as the named forms, although the resulting seedlings should give you a selection of colors. Robinson's Strain is a superior seed-grown form that is often separated out into individual colors, the plants divided, and sold as color selections. Far better, however, are the named varieties like the red single 'Crimson Giant', 'Brenda' with cerise pink flowers around a yellow disk, 'Eileen May Robinson' a salmon pink, or the white 'Avalanche'. If you prefer double flowers, look for 'Pink Bouquet', rose pink with a silvery center, 'Sensation', a bright red, or 'Venus', pure white.

Growing Painted Daisy

Set out container-grown plants in spring, preferably in groups of 3 of the same variety, about 30 cm (1 ft) apart. Make sure the drainage is good as plants are short-lived in heavy wet soil and may not survive over winter. Cut flower stems back to the base as soon as flowering is finished to encourage repeat bloom. Keep plants watered during periods of extended drought. In fall, protect the crowns with a mulch of a fluffy material, such as evergreen boughs, which hold the snow and help prevent heaving due to frost action, especially near the limits of hardiness or where midwinter thaws are common. Plants may be attacked by aphids or spider mites. Aphids excrete a sticky liquid that makes the leaves shiny and, if not controlled, can weaken the plants. Spray them with insecticidal soap. Mites feed mainly on the underside of the leaves and cause a pale stippling; wash them off with a strong spray of water.

New Plants from Old

Painted daisies tend to be fairly short-lived if left to their own devices and need to be divided every 3–4 years to keep them from going into a decline. This is the way to increase named forms, which will not come true from seeds. Saving seeds and starting new plants this way will generally result in poor colors and often give plants with deformed flowers. Wait until new growth has started in spring, so you can see where the growing points will be, then lift plants and gently tease them apart into several smaller clumps. Try to get pieces with three or four shoots on each. Discard the middle of the old clump as this will have become hard and woody and will not grow well. Improve the soil in the planting area by digging in an 8–10 cm (3–4 in) layer of well-rotted compost, then replant at the same depth as the original plant. It is also helpful to water with a fertilizer with a high middle number (often sold as "plant starter") as this encourages root production.

FUNDAMENTAL FACTS

ATTRIBUTES	Much divided foliage, individual flowers on wiry stems, good for cutting
SEASON OF INTEREST	Midsummer flowers, attractive foliage all summer
FAVORITES	'Crimson Giant', 'Brenda', 'Pink Bouquet', 'Venus'
QUIRKS	Not hardy on the Prairies, requires well-drained soil
GOOD NEIGHBORS	Flowering annuals, peonies, ornemental grasses, black-eyed Susan
WHERE IT GROWS BEST	In sun to partial shade and well-drained soil
POTENTIAL PROBLEMS	Aphids, mites, winter heaving
RENEWING PLANTS	Divide every 3–4 years
CRITTER RESISTANCE	Good
SOURCE	Garden centers, division
DIMENSIONS	45–90 cm (18–36 in) tall, 45 cm (18 in) wide

'Festiva Maxima' is a classic, with fragrant white double flowers streaked subtly in scarlet.

PEONY
Paeonia hybrids

HARDINESS:
Zone 2

PREFERRED SOIL pH:
Near neutral

PREFERRED SOIL TYPE:
Well-drained, average

PREFERRED LIGHT:
Sun, afternoon shade

Peony in the Landscape

No other perennial welcomes spring as sensationally as peonies do. These long-lived, care-free plants emerge from dormancy in late winter, and by spring their reddish spears grow rapidly into shrub-sized mounds of deep green foliage. Their buttonlike buds are deceptively small at first but soon swell and burst into single, semi-double, or double flowers up to 25 cm (10 in) in diameter, which remain in glory for a couple of weeks. During that time, peonies make impressive cut flowers, lasting 10 days in a vase if gathered while still in bud. After the flowers pass, the glossy, lobed leaves remains an asset all season.

Peonies can be interspersed among fellow perennials, such as iris and dianthus in a flower bed, and they also mesh well with roses, vines, and ornamental grasses. When grouped by themselves, they make a strong statement flanking a doorway, anchoring the foundation of a house, or forming a seasonal hedge.

A Garden Classic

Many of the most popular peonies grown today are old hybrids of *Paeonia lactiflora*, the Chinese peony. These fragrant, time-honored favorites bloom in white, pink, and red; some have cupped petals around fluffy golden centers, while others form pompons of ruffled petals. The finest white is 'Festiva Maxima', which issues globes of snowy petals streaked subtly with scarlet on the inside. 'Sarah Bernhardt' is a prized pink, with fluttery petals the color of apple blossoms, while 'Félix Crousse' is carmine with an even darker red center.

Planting and Growing Peony

Plant peonies in early fall so that the roots become established and the plants experience the period of cold essential for blooming in spring. Peonies often flourish for 75 years or more when grown in a hospitable site, and resent disturbance once they've found a home, so place them carefully. Choose a sunny spot with well-drained but moisture-retentive organic soil.

Proper planting depth is crucial: If peonies are planted too deep, they will grow but not bloom. In cold-winter climates, place the plant so that the dormant growing points, or "eyes," of the thick, tuberous roots are buried beneath 5 cm (2 in) of soil. However, in mild-winter areas, plant so that the eyes are barely covered with soil. When planting peonies in groups, space them 1–1.2 m (3–4 ft) apart. Surround plants in spring with commercial wire peony hoops to support the flowers, which can weigh down the stems.

Peonies are untroubled by pests. The ants that often crawl over the blossoms do no harm; just shake them

Peonies fit handsomely in the garden or can be massed as a foundation planting.

off before bringing cut flowers into the house. Peonies can, however, contract the fungal disease botrytis, which browns buds and spots leaves. Spray plants with a copper-based fungicide as directed on the label before buds open. After a hard frost, cut foliage to the ground and dispose of it to get rid of fungal spores.

'Sarah Bernhardt' fills the garden stage with scented, ruffled double flowers in soft pink.

FUNDAMENTAL FACTS

ATTRIBUTES	Large flowers, neat mounding foliage; for beds, seasonal hedges
SEASON OF INTEREST	Blooms spring to early summer
FAVORITES	White 'Festiva Maxima', pink 'Sarah Bernhardt', red 'Félix Crousse'
QUIRKS	Plants need a period of winter chilling in order to produce flower buds
GOOD NEIGHBORS	Astilbe, clematis, dianthus, iris, ornamental grasses, poppies, roses
WHERE IT GROWS BEST	Sun to partial shade; well-drained, organic soil
POTENTIAL PROBLEMS	Heavy flowers can bend stems to the ground
RENEWING PLANTS	Lives for decades; rarely needed, but crowded plants can be divided
CRITTER RESISTANCE	Good
SOURCE	Bedding plants, division
DIMENSIONS	Plants 0.6–1 m (2–3 ft) tall and equally wide; flowers 10–25 cm (4–10 in) in diameter

Like many varieties, 'Europe' has an "eye." The pink spot peers out from white blooms.

PHLOX (GARDEN)
Phlox paniculata

HARDINESS:
Zone 3

PREFERRED SOIL pH:
Slightly acid

PREFERRED SOIL TYPE:
Organically rich

PREFERRED LIGHT:
Sun to partial shade

Garden Phlox in the Landscape

In midsummer, when many flowering plants go dormant and butterflies have a harder time finding nectar, garden phlox emerges and becomes a meeting place for winged creatures. A North American native, garden phlox are tall, upright plants that inhabit woodland clearings near streams and rivers. Cultivars have been developed for garden performance that bloom more heavily than the wild species. These stand 1–1.5 m (3–5 ft) tall and produce rounded flower clusters composed of dozens of 1.3 cm (1/2 in) wide fragrant pink, white, lavender, and rose blossoms. The oval leaves are medium green but tend to be a bit darker when plants are well fed and grown in partial shade.

Garden phlox likes plenty of sun and fresh air around its top growth but wants its roots to be cool and moist. In cold climates grow garden phlox in sun and keep it well mulched at all times. Where summers are hot, garden phlox will bloom much stronger and longer if the plants are shaded in the afternoon and topped with an organic mulch.

The Healthiest Beauties

Plant breeders have had great success coaxing beautiful colors out of pink-blooming ancestral strains, resulting in cultivars, such as 'Franz Schubert', which has soft lilac flowers, each accented by a white center. Flowers in red shades are available, as are some varieties with variegated foliage, but these unusual types tend to be smaller and less vigorous than the white-, pink-, or lavender-blooming cultivars.

In recent years the nursery industry has promoted garden phlox with good resistance to powdery mildew, a fungal disease that strikes when days are warm and humid and nights are cool, causing unsightly white patches on leaves but not killing the plants. Cultivars with superior mildew resistance include the pure white 'David', the pure pink 'Robert Poore', and 'Eva Cullum', which bears pink flowers with an almost red central eye. In areas prone to powdery mildew, thin plants to increase air circulation and avoid wetting the leaves when irrigating to help prevent the disease.

Insect pests rarely visit phlox, but sap-sucking spider mites may give leaves a pale, stippled appearance. They are most active during droughts and can be eradicated by hosing off foliage early in the day so that it dries before evening, when mildew problems are likely to develop. If leaves show holes left by beetlelike phlox bugs or other chewing pests, spray plants with a botanical insecticide as directed on the label.

Growing Phlox

Set out purchased plants in early spring. Sprinkle compost or other organic matter into each planting hole and set the plants so that the roots are covered with 2.5 cm (1 in) of soil topped by another 5 cm (2 in) of organic mulch. Keep the roots evenly moist during the first summer after planting. To prolong flowering for many weeks, cut off old flower clusters to encourage new buds to form. Cut stems back close to the ground in winter, after plants become dormant.

Fertilize garden phlox in spring with an organic or controlled-release fertilizer. Every 3 years, or when plants become crowded, dig up the clump in early spring, separate individual plants, and replant them after renewing the site by digging in organic matter, such as compost.

FUNDAMENTAL FACTS

ATTRIBUTES	Long-lasting white or pastel flowers on tall plants; for beds, woodlands
SEASON OF INTEREST	Midsummer through fall
FAVORITES	Mildew-resistant 'David', 'Robert Poore'; bicolored 'Eva Cullum'
QUIRKS	Produces second crop of flowers if cut back when initial flowers fade
GOOD NEIGHBORS	Ageratum, artemisia, daylily, obedient plant
WHERE IT GROWS BEST	Fertile soil with morning sun and afternoon shade
POTENTIAL PROBLEMS	Powdery mildew; spider mites, phlox bugs
RENEWING PLANTS	Lives many years; divide crowded clumps every 3 years
CRITTER RESISTANCE	Good
SOURCE	Bedding plants, division
DIMENSIONS	0.6–1.2 m (2–4 ft) tall, mature clumps 0.6–1.2 m (2–4 ft) wide

Garden phlox forms rounded clusters of flat, fragrant flowers that last through the summer.

PHLOX (OTHER)

Phlox divaricata; P. subulata

HARDINESS:
Zone 3 unless otherwise indicated

PREFERRED SOIL pH:
Slightly acid

PREFERRED SOIL TYPE:
Fertile, moist

PREFERRED LIGHT:
Partial shade

Woodland and Moss Phlox in the Landscape

The shady slopes of eastern North American woodlands harbor many native plant riches, including dainty spring-blooming phlox. Similar to the tall garden phlox only in the size and form of the individual blossoms, woodland phlox are small plants never more than 30 cm (12 in) tall. They

'McDaniel's Cushion' is a particularly vigorous moss phlox with deep pink blooms.

grow into casual colonies, covering the ground and lighting up the shade with their blue, pink, and lavender blossoms. Some selections are fragrant, and all reappear each year with no effort on the part of the gardeners who grow them. Blooming begins in concert with daffodils, tulips, and other spring-flowering bulbs, and the plants all but disappear by the time summer heat arrives. In sites that become deeply shaded after trees leaf out, hardy ferns make particularly good companions, hiding the thin, fading foliage of the phlox.

Phlox subulata forms low-growing mounds of mossy foliage covered in spring with blooms.

Colorful Carpets

Several native species fall into the woodland phlox category, but the most widely planted one is blue phlox (*Phlox divaricata* [Z4]), a matchless choice for open glens framed by tall shade trees. Moss phlox (*P. subulata*) is a related species with ground-hugging mossy foliage. This petite plant is typically grown on sunny slopes and completely covers itself with pink, white, or lavender blossoms in early spring.

In filtered shade, grow *P. divaricata* 'Clouds of Perfume', which forms 30 cm (12 in) tall plants covered with fragrant blue blossoms, or 'Chattahoochee', which has violet-blue flowers with magenta eyes. Where sun is more limited, try 15 cm (6 in) tall 'Fuller's White' or 'Sherwood Purple', or mix them for an eye-popping duet.

For sunnier areas, choose *P. subulata*. 'Candy Stripe' is remarkable for its pink-and-white flowers with perky magenta markings in the center of each little flower.

Growing Phlox

Set out plants in fall or spring in any soil that is well drained and has a neutral to slightly acid pH. Amend sand or heavy clay with organic matter before planting and water well when plants are in place. The shade-tolerant species usually face little competition from weeds, but you will probably need to pluck out invaders from new plantings of moss phlox.

After woodland phlox blooms in spring, let it shed seeds before clipping it back in midsummer. You can also cut down a large planting with the lawn mower, raising the blade to its highest setting to protect the basal growth. Leave the area undisturbed, and new growth will appear from fall through winter, ready to bloom next spring. Moss phlox needs no special care beyond fertilizing in early summer and occasional watering in severe droughts. It is less prone to insects and the fungal disease powdery mildew than its cousin, garden phlox.

P. subulata 'Amazing Grace' is amazingly dainty, with pale pink pinwheel blooms.

FUNDAMENTAL FACTS

ATTRIBUTES	Petite plants; blue, white, or pink flowers; for beds, groundcover, edging
SEASON OF INTEREST	Spring
FAVORITES	*P. divaricata* 'Clouds of Perfume', 'Chattahoochee' for partial shade; 'Fuller's White', 'Sherwood Purple' for shade; *P. subulata* 'Candy Stripe' for sun
QUIRKS	Prefers slightly acid soil
GOOD NEIGHBORS	Candytuft, deciduous trees, pansies, spring bulbs, shrubs
WHERE IT GROWS BEST	Humus-rich soil in open woodlands
POTENTIAL PROBLEMS	Rare
RENEWING PLANTS	Lives many years; seldom needed if plants reseed
CRITTER RESISTANCE	Good
SOURCE	Bedding plants, division
DIMENSIONS	15–30 cm (6–12 in) tall and equally wide

Pin-shaped stamens, shown in *Scabiosa* 'Butterfly Blue', explain the common name.

PINCUSHION FLOWER

Scabiosa spp.

Prolific *S.* 'Pink Mist' sends up hundreds of buttonlike flowers all season.

S. graminifolia has grassy, silvery foliage, a pretty background for the pink blooms.

HARDINESS:
Zone 4

PREFERRED SOIL pH:
Neutral to slightly alkaline

PREFERRED SOIL TYPE:
Fertile, well-drained

PREFERRED LIGHT:
Sun to very light shade

Pincushion Flower in the Landscape

These pretty plants should be front and center in the garden. The foliage forms neat mounds, and the nectar-rich flowers, which draw butterflies like magnets, bloom continuously from late spring to fall, staying fresh even in high heat. Flower colors range from true blue and pink to soft yellow and cream. Each lacy, button-shaped blossom, 5 cm (2 in) across, is composed of tightly massed little florets and held on a wiry stem that's about 30 cm (1 ft) long. White-tipped stamens peeking above the petals look like tiny pins stuck into the flower, hence the common name. Each flower lasts several days, which is ideal for use in bouquets. The finely divided gray-green foliage stays low and compact, making this care-free perennial suitable for edging borders and paths.

All in the Family

Scabiosa 'Butterfly Blue' has stronger growth and more blooms per season than other pincushion flower. It grows 30 cm (1 ft) tall, needs no staking, and produces hundreds of care-free lavender-blue flowers per plant. Its sister, 'Pink Mist', is equally prolific and has bright pink flowers.

S. ochreleuca, a drought-tolerant perennial that's great for rock gardens, produces soft butter yellow flowers from spring through fall. *S. caucasica* 'Alba' holds its many white flowers on 60 cm (2 ft) stems. For a lush effect, grow this taller pincushion flower behind 'Butterfly Blue' and 'Pink Mist'. *S. graminifolia* forms mats of slightly silvery grasslike leaves and has rose pink to lilac flowers.

Growing Pincushion Flower

Grow pincushion flowers in full sun or bright partial shade, in near neutral soil amended with organic matter. Container-grown plants can be set out anytime, but spring is best. Set plants at the same depth at which they grew in their containers, and keep the soil lightly moist after planting and for the rest of the summer. A thin mulch of rotted leaves, shredded bark, or other organic material will help keep the soil cool and moist, the way pincushion flowers like it.

To keep the plants flowering as long as possible, gather blossoms for bouquets and remove faded flowers. The more you cut, the more buds will develop. A deep drench with a liquid all-purpose plant food in midsummer will help keep plants in bloom longer into the fall. Healthy, well-fed pincushion flowers rarely have problems with pests or diseases.

Although they may look unsightly, do not cut plants back after they turn brown in winter, because the stems will help shelter the crowns from ice, snow, and frigid winds. Do clip off the old foliage first thing in spring before new foliage emerges.

To propagate pincushion flowers, dig and divide plants in early spring. Or, take 15 cm (6 in) long stem cuttings in midspring, remove leaves from the lower halves of the stems, and set them in moist soil to half their length. Keep the soil moist until they are rooted and growing and can be planted in the garden.

FUNDAMENTAL FACTS

ATTRIBUTES	Gray-green leaves; blue, pink, yellow, or cream flowers; for beds, cutting
SEASON OF INTEREST	Late spring to fall
FAVORITES	'Butterfly Blue', 'Pink Mist' for nonstop flowers
QUIRKS	Needs to retain browned foliage through winter
GOOD NEIGHBORS	Artemisia, butterfly flower, catmint, dianthus, dusty miller, lilies
WHERE IT GROWS BEST	In sun and fertile, well-drained, slightly alkaline soil
POTENTIAL PROBLEMS	Poor soil drainage in winter leads to root rot
RENEWING PLANTS	Lives many years; divide crowded clumps
CRITTER RESISTANCE	Excellent
SOURCE	Division, stem cuttings, seeds
DIMENSIONS	30 cm (12 in) tall and equally wide

PRIMROSE
Primula spp.

HARDINESS:
Zones as indicated

PREFERRED SOIL pH:
Slightly acid

PREFERRED SOIL TYPE:
Fertile, moist

PREFERRED LIGHT:
Partial shade

Primroses in the Landscape

When planted in the right spot, primroses are easy to grow. Not every garden, however, can offer their preferred conditions. These old-fashioned beauties need a climate that is neither too hot nor too cold, partial shade, and a humus-rich, acidic, moist soil. If that doesn't sound like your garden, primroses are best used as niche plants for growing alongside shaded water features or enjoying in containers or window boxes as a sign of spring. They can also be grown as annuals.

Primroses are petite, ranging in height from 20–60 cm (8–24 in)

Polyanthus primroses are strong bloomers that create a colorful carpet in early spring.

Japanese primrose blooms in late spring with tall tiers of white, pink, or red flowers.

when in bloom. Before and after flowering, a low-lying basal rosette of crinkled leaves is the only evidence of their presence. Because of their small size, place primroses where they can be appreciated up close.

Categorizing Primroses

The genus *Primula* includes hundreds of species, but if you want care-free primroses, it is enough to know only a few names. Polyanthus primroses (Z5) are a large, popular group of easily grown hybrids with blooms ranging from bright white to dark purple. Japanese primrose (*P. japonica* [Z3]) has a terrific thirst, but as long as moisture is abundant, varieties like 'Postford White' are hardy and dependable. Because of its globe-shaped clusters of fragrant lilac-colored blossoms, drumstick primrose (*P. denticulata* [Z2]) is worth its untidy foliage. If you want a primrose for the shade garden, try cowslips (*P. veris* [Z4]), which settle in easily to form colonies studded with small yellow flowers in spring.

Growing Primroses

If you're just getting started with primroses, begin by setting out pur-

chased plants first thing in spring. Prepare the site the previous fall if possible, because plants are eager to bloom soon after the soil becomes workable in spring. Dig in peat moss or another acidic form of organic matter, and make sure the site is convenient to water. In areas where winters are mild, provide primroses with good soil drainage, because waterlogged roots are susceptible to fatal root rot in winter.

Expect the plants to flower for several weeks and then persist as green rosettes until about midsummer. At that point they may seemingly melt away or go dormant, or they may hold a few of their leaves if they are

P. vulgaris is an English wildflower beloved for the simple charm of its pastel flowers.

protected from sun by nearby plants or the tree canopy.

Although primroses can be started from seed, they are slow to grow. The easiest way to obtain more plants is through division. Simply dig an established plant in spring and use a small knife to separate the leaf rosettes. Replant each one individually, along with a piece of root, in a container filled with a potting mix composed of soil and peat moss. Set the plantlets at the same depth at which the mother plant grew. Starting the divisions in containers improves survival, as you can give them closer attention, then shift them to the garden after they have developed a mass of new roots.

Primrose leaves and flower petals can be tattered by night-feeding slugs and snails. Set out saucers of beer to attract and drown them, or collect and dispose of them at twilight.

FUNDAMENTAL FACTS

ATTRIBUTES	Petite plants with showy, colorful flowers; for damp sites, pots
SEASON OF INTEREST	Spring
FAVORITES	Polyanthus primroses, *P. denticulata*, *P. japonica* 'Postford White', cowslips
QUIRKS	Often goes dormant in midsummer
GOOD NEIGHBORS	Deciduous trees, spring bulbs, rhododendron
WHERE IT GROWS BEST	Shaded, damp, humus-rich, acidic soil
POTENTIAL PROBLEMS	Cold-winter injury; root rot in wet soil during mild winters
RENEWING PLANTS	Lives to 5 years; divide every 3–4 years
CRITTER RESISTANCE	Occasionally slugs and snails
SOURCE	Bedding plants, division
DIMENSIONS	10–60 cm (4–24 in) tall, 15 cm (6 in) wide

A mass of red-tinged 'Bright Star' brings the care-free look of a meadow to the garden.

PURPLE CONEFLOWER

Echinacea purpurea

HARDINESS:
Zone 3

PREFERRED SOIL pH:
Near neutral

PREFERRED SOIL TYPE:
Average, well-drained

PREFERRED LIGHT:
Sun to partial shade

Dusky pink petals droop from a central cone on this popular wildflower.

Purple Coneflower in the Landscape

No native wildflower has won as many gardeners' hearts as purple coneflower has. Large and long-limbed, at 1 m (3 ft) tall, the plants produce a dramatic show of long-lasting flowers in summer. Each daisy-like bloom consists of a prominent cone-shaped orange flower center surrounded by rosy, downward-slanted petals. The flowers are at once wild and elegant, making this perennial a must-have for arrangements. Purple coneflower also attracts benefi-cial wildlife, notably butterflies in summer and goldfinches in fall.

As with many native plants, there is quite a bit of variation in terms of flower size, color, and shape. These subtle differences add to this flower's interest when it's grown in wildflower meadows. But more refined selections are worth pursuing for a perennial border, where purple coneflower should always hold a prominent place on the strength of its late-summer and fall performance. Unlike some of its wild ancestors, which have petals that sweep back from the cone, the award-winning variety 'Magnus' has big flowers with petals that don't droop, so the flower really asserts its daisylike look. For coneflowers of a different color, try the creamy 'White Swan' or the reddish 'Crimson Star'. The 'Nana' cultivar is a little shorter, making it possible to invite purple coneflower to the front of flower gardens, where it can be enjoyed up close.

Not surprisingly, some of purple coneflower's most successful associ-ates share its wild heritage, among them blanket flower, coreopsis, gold-enrod, and rudbeckia.

Patience Pays Off

Don't expect purple coneflower to be an instant hit, as plants need 2–3 years to reach their full glory. Sun helps them grow quickly, although some gardeners prefer the slightly relaxed habit the plants develop when grown in partial shade. To create instant impact, set plants in groupings of 3–5, so that sparse blossoms appear to be more numerous. By the time the plants attain maturity, you will have plenty of flowers to admire and enjoy.

Growing Purple Coneflower

Unlike many plants native to central and eastern North America, purple coneflower prefers neutral soil. If your soil is acidic clay, modify its texture and pH by amending each planting site with sand and garden lime added according to package directions. Set out plants in spring around the time of your last frost. Water during dry spells in the first summer, but do not fertilize. Heavy-handed feeding leads to green growth at the expense of flowers. Thereafter purple coneflowers do a good job of fending for them-selves. They tolerate drought, succumb to root rot only when grown in soggy soil, and are rarely bothered by pests except rabbits and groundhogs.

Established plants seldom require dividing, but division is the best way to propagate and rejuvenate a plant that has lost stamina because of old age. In fall or early spring, while the plants are dormant, dig them up and shake the soil off the roots. Then use your hands and a small knife to untangle roots and cut apart the crowns, or growing points, taking care not to break off the delicate roots. Replant them immediately, at the same depth at which they previ-ously grew, and water well until the divisions are established.

FUNDAMENTAL FACTS

ATTRIBUTES	Dusty pink flowers with dark centers; for wild-flower meadows, beds
SEASON OF INTEREST	Summer
FAVORITES	'Magnus' for upright petals, 'White Swan', 'Crimson Star', 'Nana'
QUIRKS	Must have soil with good drainage
GOOD NEIGHBORS	Blanket flower, coreopsis, ornamental grasses, rudbeckia
WHERE IT GROWS BEST	Full sun; average, well-drained soil
POTENTIAL PROBLEMS	Root rot in overly wet soil conditions
RENEWING PLANTS	Lives for years; divide every 4–5 years
CRITTER RESISTANCE	Good except rabbits and groundhogs
SOURCE	Bedding plants, division
DIMENSIONS	0.6–1.2 m (2–4 ft) tall, up to 60 cm (2 ft) wide

RED-HOT POKER

Kniphofia cvs.

HARDINESS:
Zone 6

PREFERRED SOIL pH:
Near neutral

PREFERRED SOIL TYPE:
Fertile, well-drained, fertile

PREFERRED LIGHT:
Sun

The strong, sturdy flower stems rarely need staking, even when laden with blooms.

Red-Hot Poker in the Landscape

When you want strong lines and fiery color, reach for red-hot poker. This plant has straight, sturdy, 1–1.2 m (3–4 ft) flower stems jutting from grasslike foliage. The unique flower spikes are composed of slender, tubular, 2.5 cm (1 in) long blossoms. The lower ones are creamy yellow, while those at the tip are scarlet to orange, a combination that creates the illusion of a poker just pulled from the fire.

To get this exciting performance, plant red-hot poker in sun and well-drained, organically rich soil. Make sure that the soil never dries out, particularly when flowers are poised to bloom. Otherwise, there is no need to pamper this resilient, care-free plant.

Though dramatic, red-hot pokers blend right into a perennial garden. They combine well with everything from white foxgloves and yellow coreopsis to lavender catmint or purple verbena.

Cooling the Fire

The shocking flower shades are fun, but red-hot pokers are also available in softer colors. 'Primrose Beauty' is a mellow yellow, while 'Ada' is tawny gold and 'Buttercup' has green buds that open to clear yellow. Aptly named 'Vanilla' is creamy white, and 'Little Maid' is similarly hued but with longer spikes on a 60 cm (2 ft) tall plant. Reblooming red-hot pokers are also available. For rebloom as well as reliable hardiness, go for the orange-red 'Alcazar', coral 'Earliest of All', and 'Royal Standard', which has yellow and vermilion flowers.

Growing Red-Hot Poker

In areas with long, hot summers, site red-hot pokers where they get some afternoon sun. Elsewhere, let them bake in the sun. The main require-ment is well-drained, organically rich soil. If the ground dries as the season progresses, apply an 8 cm (3 in) layer of organic mulch or water as needed to keep the soil barely moist. Good drainage is especially critical in the winter. Red-hot-pokers subjected to sodden winter soil will fail.

Plants need a little help to survive the winter in cold climates. Mulch with hay or leaves snuggled close to the stem. Rather than cut the foliage back in fall, leave it intact and tie it together to protect the central crown from collected water and ice damage.

Although red-hot pokers become hefty plants, be patient. New plants grow slowly, and the flower spectacle won't occur until the second or even third season. Nudge plants along with an application of a balanced fertilizer or compost each spring.

Red-hot-pokers resent dividing. To increase your supply, dig small divisions from the outside of the clump in spring, being careful not to damage roots. Plant divisions at the same depth at which the parent plant grows. This is a plant that's virtually pest and disease free. Even deer will nibble it only if desperately hungry.

'Buttercup' is a "cooler" poker, with green-ish buds that open to a soft clear yellow.

Not all red-hot pokers are red. Tangerine-flowered 'Brimstone' glows in sunlight.

FUNDAMENTAL FACTS

ATTRIBUTES	Red, orange, or yellow flower spikes; grassy leaves; for beds, accents
SEASON OF INTEREST	Spring to fall
FAVORITES	'Primrose Beauty', 'Ada', 'Vanilla', 'Little Maid' for color; 'Royal Standard', 'Alcazar' for rebloom
QUIRKS	Slow to establish, mulch first winter
GOOD NEIGHBORS	Catmint, coreopsis, foxglove, verbena
WHERE IT GROWS BEST	Sun and organically rich, well-drained soil
POTENTIAL PROBLEMS	Roots may rot in wet soil; thrips may mottle foliage
RENEWING PLANTS	Lives 6 years or more; plants resent division
CRITTER RESISTANCE	Good except for deer (rare)
SOURCE	Bedding plants, small divisions
DIMENSIONS	0.6–1.2 m (2–4 ft) tall, 60 cm (2 ft) wide

The strong magenta flowers of rose campion are quieted by silvery-gray, felted foliage.

ROSE CAMPION

Lychnis coronaria

HARDINESS:
Zone 3

PREFERRED SOIL pH:
Adaptable

PREFERRED SOIL TYPE:
Average to poor

PREFERRED LIGHT:
Sun

Rose Campion in the Landscape

Famous as a fixture in farmyards and cottage gardens, rose campion is a lovely addition to any flower garden. The hue of rose in the flowers is actually a shocking magenta, which perfectly suits the plants' frosty gray, felted foliage. But quieter colors are available as well. Easy to grow and always willing to self-sow, rose campion features 2.5 cm (1 in) wide, flat, velvety flowers held aloft on stiff, angular branches. Best of all, rose campion has a modest appetite and easily withstands drought and neglect. Blooming in summer, rose campion thrives in sun but adapts easily to partial shade where summers are very hot.

Rose campion plays well with other silvery foliage plants that have a lacier texture, such as artemisia or dusty miller. Or use it in a pastel border of campanulas, lavender, catmint, and yarrows to liven up the scene. The right shade of pink petunia will echo the color of rose campion, helping it flow through the garden in style. It also looks particularly fine lined up single file where its stems can be silhouetted against evergreen shrubs or a dark-colored fence or building.

Toned-Down Toughness

There's good news for those who'd like to capitalize on rose campion's toughness but find the magenta flowers too shocking. There is the soft-hued 'Alba', with its little white flowers and sage-gray foliage. 'Angel's Blush' is similar, but each flower has a center of light blushing pink. And, if you want to see an array of shades and are willing to start from seed, try 'Diamonds and Rubies', a grab-bag seed mix of several flower colors.

Growing Rose Campion

Choose a spot with well-drained soil that gets morning sun. Light, sandy soil of poor quality is certainly an option. You can sow seeds where you want them to grow, barely covering them with soil; start seeds indoors in winter; or purchase seedlings. Set plants out early, while the seedlings are small, because rose campion hates to have its roots cramped in containers. Seedlings started early that are well chilled by late-spring frosts often bloom their first year in the garden.

After transplanting, rose campion needs water to get started, but then you can let it take care of itself. There is seldom a need to mulch or fertilize. Excessive water is its only enemy, so be careful if you've chosen to combine rose campion with plants that require irrigation.

Individual plants pass away after three or four seasons, or sometimes sooner where summers are very warm and humid, and dividing mature plants does more harm than good. But a family of "pups," or plantlets, invariably surrounds the mother plant. Indeed, at the limits of hardiness, rose campion acts like a hardy annual, reseeding itself perpetually, with volunteer seedlings that popped up the previous fall producing flowers. Insect and four-footed pests are unheard of where this plant is concerned.

FUNDAMENTAL FACTS

ATTRIBUTES	Magenta, pink, or white flowers; felted gray foliage; for beds
SEASON OF INTEREST	Early summer for flowers; all season for foliage
FAVORITES	White 'Alba', pale pink 'Angel's Blush', 'Diamond and Rubies' mix
QUIRKS	Does not grow well if its roots are cramped in a container
GOOD NEIGHBORS	Artemisia, shrub roses, pink-flowered zinnias, white or pink petunias
WHERE IT GROWS BEST	Average to infertile soil in areas with warm summer temperatures
POTENTIAL PROBLEMS	Constantly wet soil leads to root rot
RENEWING PLANTS	Lives 2–3 years; allow to reseed; divisions have poor survival rate
CRITTER RESISTANCE	Good
SOURCE	Bedding plants, seeds
DIMENSIONS	0.6–1 m (2–3 ft) tall, 0.3–0.6 m (1–2 ft) wide

The Oculata Group rose campions have white flowers with hot pink eyes.

Providing months of black-eyed blooms, rudbeckias are great for gardens or meadows.

RUDBECKIA

Rudbeckia spp.

HARDINESS:
Zone 3 unless otherwise indicated

PREFERRED SOIL pH:
Neutral to slightly acid

PREFERRED SOIL TYPE:
Average to moist, well-drained

PREFERRED LIGHT:
Sun

Rudbeckia in the Landscape

Best known as black-eyed Susans, rudbeckias reward minimal effort with a 3-month outpouring of flowers that few other perennials can match. Turn rudbeckias loose in a sunny meadow, where they'll supply a splash of bright yellow all summer, or plant a mass alongside a wooden fence for a casual, colorful display. Rudbeckia's appearance is neat enough to be included in a perennial border, preferably in a spot where it can grow tall and full.

Unlike some daisy relatives, rudbeckias have sturdy stems. No matter how many flowers they generate, the plants never flop or need staking. The stiff stems make rudbeckias ideal for arrangements, especially if you cut stems early in the morning, before they've been stressed by sun.

Selecting Susans

Rudbeckias are native to the North American Midwest and South, and some of the best cultivars are crosses of species that have stood the test of time. The 60 cm (2 ft) tall 'Goldsturm' cultivar, which is propagated by division, is one of the best for longevity and all-around garden performance.

There are numerous other rudbeckias to try from either plants or seed. Cutleaf coneflowers (*Rudbeckia laciniata*) make a stunning show in late summer, producing a riot of yellow flowers with green centers atop 1.8 m (6 ft) tall plants. For double flowers, go for the shaggy, many-petaled 'Goldquelle'. Three-lobed coneflower (*R. triloba* [Z5]) can tolerate some shade and spews out dozens of button-sized, black-eyed yellow daisies on 1 m (3 ft) tall plants.

When they are pleased with their site, rudbeckias develop into vigorous clumps. But they also have a talent for adapting their growth pattern to the climate in which they are grown. In hot, humid climates, plants may flourish for only two years or so, during which time they shed seeds that sprout in either fall or early spring. So, even if a parent perishes unexpectedly, you should find plenty of adoptable

Compact and vigorous, 'Goldsturm' produces extra large flowers from summer to fall.

volunteers that are easily dug and moved to where you want them to grow and flower.

Growing Rudbeckia

Grow rudbeckias in well-drained, moderately fertile soil to get them off to a strong start. Set out plants in early spring, or in the fall where winters are mild. If the site is naturally moist, you'll need to water less. If you want to increase your stock, dig and divide mature plants in the spring, replanting them at the same depth at which they previously grew.

Late in the season you may see whitish patches of powdery mildew on the leaves. By this time the flowers are on the wane, and it's fine to cut the plants back to 15 cm (6 in) from the ground to nip this unsightly, but never fatal, fungal disease in the bud. While most pests shun rudbeckias, you may spot sap-sucking aphids on tender new growth. Knock them off with a strong stream of water, or apply insecticidal soap according to label directions. If food is scarce, deer may browse the plants. Tuck bars of deodorant-formula bath soap among plantings to repel them, or apply a commercial repellent according to package directions.

FUNDAMENTAL FACTS

ATTRIBUTES	Prolific yellow daisies on robust plants; for meadows, beds
SEASON OF INTEREST	Early summer to fall
FAVORITES	'Goldsturm', 'Goldquelle'; *R. laciniata*; *R. triloba*
QUIRKS	Sometimes short-lived, but renews itself by self-seeding readily
GOOD NEIGHBORS	Joe Pye weed, ornamental grasses, purple coneflower, Russian sage
WHERE IT GROWS BEST	In sun and moist, well-drained soil
POTENTIAL PROBLEMS	Powdery mildew in late summer; aphids
RENEWING PLANTS	Individual plants last 2–3 years; divide when flowering diminishes
CRITTER RESISTANCE	Good except for deer (occasionally)
SOURCE	Bedding plants, division
DIMENSIONS	0.6–1 m (2–3 ft) tall or more, 0.6–1 m (2–3 ft) wide; varies by species

RUSSIAN SAGE

Perovskia atriplicifolia

HARDINESS:
Zone 5

PREFERRED SOIL pH:
Adaptable

PREFERRED SOIL TYPE:
Average, well-drained

PREFERRED LIGHT:
Sun

Russian Sage in the Landscape

There's a time during the hottest part of the summer when most perennials take a breather and stop blooming. That's when Russian sage steps in, just in time to cool down the heat with its frosty gray-green leaves and cool lavender flower spikes. Growing rapidly to 1 m (3 ft) tall or more, Russian sage makes a statement with its foliage early in the season. But it's in midsummer that the willowy stems are crowned with sprays of lavender

Flowers form on small branches, creating tiered fans of cool lavender in midsummer.

Russian sage is care-free in every way: hardy, drought-tolerant, and neatly shaped.

blooms that can linger for 2 months. Russian sage bursts on the scene just as the flowers of daylilies and other early-summer bloomers recede. And it remains handsome as the flowers of late-blooming perennials, such as Joe Pye weed, sedum, and garden phlox start to open. The fanlike flowering stems, picked when the flowers on the lower third of the spire are opening, provide a wonderful addition to homegrown bouquets.

A single plant of Russian sage spreads out to a girth that can reach 1 m (3 ft) across, so one robust specimen can anchor a corner or light up the back of a border. If you encourage branching by lightly pruning the plant early in summer, Russian sage forms a very broad swath of color.

There are a few named cultivars, such as dainty 'Blue Spire', a strongly upright grower with lacy, finely cut leaves. For a more compact plant with flower spires of a lighter violet color, opt for 'Longin', whose leaves are not as serrated as those of the species. Or,

if you prefer a lacier look with baby blue blossoms, try 'Filigran'.

Tough Beauty

Though not technically a sage, Russian sage has many of the same virtues. The soft, gray-green leaves emit a light herbal scent when brushed, and the plant's robust root system helps it withstand long, hot summers and dry spells. Because it rarely wilts in heat, mulching is not necessary. The plant is, however, a bit lax, so site it where it can flop gracefully or set it behind perennials that can help support it. Russian sage is naturally durable and easily weathers winters.

Growing Russian Sage

A sunny spot in well-drained soil is all this plant asks. Boggy soil is fatal, leading to a slow death from root rot. Also avoid shady locations, which will cause Russian sage to stretch out, reaching for the sun. Early spring is the best time to set out purchased

FUNDAMENTAL FACTS

ATTRIBUTES	Silvery, divided foliage; spikes of lavender flowers; for beds, cutting
SEASON OF INTEREST	Early summer to fall
FAVORITES	'Blue Spire', 'Longin', 'Filigran'
QUIRKS	Performs best when subjected to cold winters and hot summers
GOOD NEIGHBORS	Daylilies, garden phlox, ornamental grasses, sedum, veronica, yarrow
WHERE IT GROWS BEST	In sun and well-drained soil
POTENTIAL PROBLEMS	Prolonged wet soil causes fatal root rot
RENEWING PLANTS	Lives many years; cut back to 30 cm (12 in) in early spring
CRITTER RESISTANCE	Excellent
SOURCE	Stem cuttings, division
DIMENSIONS	1–1.2 m (3–4 ft) tall, 1 m (3 ft) wide

plants. After their first year in the garden, cut them back to 30 cm (12 in) in early spring so that the new season's growth will arise from the roots rather than from old stems. Plants will grow happily for several years in hospitable sites. If plants become overcrowded over time, divide them and replant the divisions.

Once you have one plant, you will probably want a few more. Stem cuttings taken in midspring are easy to root in containers filled with a mixture of sand and damp peat moss kept in partial shade until rooting occurs. You will know that roots have formed, and that the cuttings can be planted in the garden, when new growth begins to show on the stems.

This naturally aromatic plant repels insects and four-footed pests. Diseases are practically unheard of.

To support sneezeweed stems that are heavy with blooms, plant it among taller plants.

SNEEZEWEED

Helenium cvs.

The petals of 'Golden Youth' and other sneezeweeds fall back from a center button.

HARDINESS:
Zone 3

PREFERRED SOIL pH:
Neutral

PREFERRED SOIL TYPE:
Moist, well-drained

PREFERRED LIGHT:
Sun

Sneezeweed in the Landscape

Don't let the common name daunt you. Sneezeweed will not torment allergy sufferers. But this profuse-flowering plant is native to fields and meadows, often growing beside and blooming simultaneously with ragweed, which is the real culprit. Not far removed from their wildflower roots, the 1–1.2 m (3–4 ft) tall garden varieties of sneezeweed retain an ability to adapt to a variety of settings, making them suitable for formal and informal perennial beds as well as cutting gardens. You'll find sneezeweeds issuing their yellow, copper, bronze,

'Bruno' provides rich red blooms late in the season, later than most other sneezeweeds.

red, burgundy, and often multicolored blooms in mid to late summer, pumping out flowers for 10 weeks or more, till fall frost finally slows them down.

Fiery Flowers

Each flower has a buttonlike center that is usually yellow, and they have slightly drooping petals. An old favorite is 'Moerheim Beauty', which has a golden center and bronze red petals that age to burnt orange. 'Bruno' is bright red, 'Crimson Beauty' is mahogany red, and 'Coppelia' is a dark bronze red. Grow sneezeweed in masses to enjoy the range of flower colors. Or contrast them with late-season, blue-flowered bloomers, such as Russian sage and anise hyssop.

The daisylike flowers of sneezeweed are carried generously on small-leaved, multibranched stems, which make an especially full display. The branches are profuse but often not strong enough to hold their heavy burden of bloom, so sneezeweed usually requires staking. Once the plants achieve their full height, install 4–6 slender stakes around the clump and weave soft twine between the stakes and stems to give gentle support so you don't have to bully the plants into standing straight when they flower.

Nothing to Sneeze At

To look their best and flower profusely, sneezeweed should be planted in spring or fall in moist, well-drained soil. If the chosen spot tends toward dryness, incorporate some moisture-retaining compost into the soil before planting, apply an 8 cm (3 in) thick layer of organic mulch to reduce evaporation, and water as needed to keep plants from wilting. These hungry plants also like soil amended with a generous amount of nutrient-rich

compost as well as a dose of balanced, controlled-release fertilizer applied as directed on the package each spring when new growth begins. Sneezeweeds can become lanky, especially in hot-summer regions. You can produce compact growth without inhibiting flowering by cutting them back to 30 cm (12 in) in early summer.

While virtually pest-free, sneezeweeds can develop a leaf-disfiguring fungal disease, powdery mildew, in late summer. Pinch off and dispose of infected leaves, or cut badly infected plants to 30 cm (12 in) to encourage healthy new growth. To keep plants vigorous, divide them every other year and apply a 15 cm (6 in) layer of loose mulch, such as straw or evergreen boughs, after the first freeze, and remove it in spring.

FUNDAMENTAL FACTS

ATTRIBUTES	Tall plants with flowers in yellow, bronze, red, burgundy; for beds
SEASON OF INTEREST	Midsummer through fall
FAVORITES	'Moerheim Beauty', 'Bruno', 'Crimson Beauty', 'Coppelia'
QUIRKS	Needs staking and irrigation during dry periods to prevent wilt
GOOD NEIGHBORS	Garden phlox, goldenrod, ornamental grasses, bee balm, Russian sage
WHERE IT GROWS BEST	In sun and moist, well-drained soil
POTENTIAL PROBLEMS	Powdery mildew in late summer
RENEWING PLANTS	Lives several years; divide every other year to promote flowering
CRITTER RESISTANCE	Good
SOURCE	Bedding plants, division
DIMENSIONS	1–1.2 m (3–4 ft) tall, 60 cm (2 ft) wide

SOLOMON'S SEAL

Polygonatum spp.

HARDINESS:
Zone 4 unless otherwise indicated

PREFERRED SOIL pH:
Near neutral

PREFERRED SOIL TYPE:
Moist, crumbly

PREFERRED LIGHT:
Full to partial shade

P. odoratum 'Variegatum' has green leaves delicately edged with creamy streaks.

Solomon's seal stems will stretch toward light, creating an elegant arch over shorter plants.

Solomon's Seal in the Landscape

One of the most graceful plants for the shade garden, Solomon's seal is also one of the toughest. It can withstand total neglect and tolerates both frigid cold and humid heat. Solomon's seal grows from a fleshy root, which sends up several long stems that arch elegantly toward the light. Along the length of each stem, either green or variegated green-and-cream leaves line up in opposite pairs in perfect order. In spring, Solomon's seal puts on a brief floral show, with dainty bell-shaped white blossoms dangling from the stems. In fall a crop of blueberry-like fruits may appear before the foliage turns a soft yellow and goes dormant for the winter.

Solomon's Seal in All Sizes

A favorite among shade gardeners because it reflects light, variegated Solomon's seal (*Polygonatum odoratum* 'Variegatum') has leaves edged with delicate creamy white streaks resembling brushstrokes. It grows 0.6–1 m

The leaves of *P. x hybridum* are slightly wavy, and the blooms are tipped in green.

(2–3 ft) tall. Plant three to five among shorter-growing shade-lovers and let them arch dramatically overhead. Or try growing them in a larger group, edged with a skirt of the silvery leaved dead nettle 'White Nancy' or of silver-speckled lungwort.

The North American native *P. biflorum* (Z3) ranges in height from 1–1.8 m (3–6 ft) and is also known as great Solomon's seal. A sizable clump is very impressive when framed with ferns or large, bold-leaved hostas.

P. x hybridum, which reaches to 1.2 m (4 ft), often features wavy leaves, either green or variegated with cream, and has green-rimmed flowers. Use it as an accent or scatter clumps among trillium and woodland phlox.

Growing Solomon's Seal

Prepare soil in a shady spot by mixing in organic matter to improve its texture and ability to hold moisture while also providing good drainage. Solomon's seal is at home growing near seasonal streams or in a woodland garden. Set out container-grown plants in spring or plant dormant roots as soon as they can be procured in late winter or early spring. You can always tell the top of the rhizome from the bottom because the tips from which new growth will arise point upward. Be careful not to snap off these delicate tips. Cover the

rhizomes with 2.5 cm (1 in) of soil topped with 2.5 cm (1 in) of rich organic mulch.

Solomon's seal spreads to form very long-lived colonies, especially if it likes the conditions. When colonies get thick, use a digging fork to unearth plants in early spring before growth begins. Cut apart the rhizomes, which resemble ginger root, and replant sections large enough to contain both roots and growth points where you want more of these graceful plants. Set the new plants in the soil at the same depth at which the parent plants grew.

The only pests that seem to bother Solomon's seal are night-feeding slugs and snails, which chew smooth-edged holes in the leaves. Control them by removing garden debris, handpicking them at dusk, or setting out saucers of beer to attract and drown them.

FUNDAMENTAL FACTS

ATTRIBUTES	Arching stems with attractive leaves; for beds
SEASON OF INTEREST	Spring to late fall
FAVORITES	*P. odoratum* 'Variegatum', *P. biflorum*, *P. x hybridum*
QUIRKS	Stems arch toward the available light
GOOD NEIGHBORS	Dead nettle, epimedium, ferns, hosta, lungwort, woodland phlox
WHERE IT GROWS BEST	Light shade; moist, crumbly soil
POTENTIAL PROBLEMS	Snails and slugs
RENEWING PLANTS	Plants live many years; divide crowded clumps and replant in spring
CRITTER RESISTANCE	Excellent
SOURCE	Bedding plants, division
DIMENSIONS	0.6–1.8 m (2–6 ft) tall and equally wide

Spiderwort's little cloverleafs of color seem to float atop loose stands of straplike foliage.

SPIDERWORT

Tradescantia spp.

HARDINESS:
Zone 3

PREFERRED SOIL pH:
Near neutral

PREFERRED SOIL TYPE:
Average, moist

PREFERRED LIGHT:
Sun to partial shade

Spiderwort in the Landscape

This pretty North American native plant grows with vigor and ease in most parts of the country. Adaptable to variable conditions, spiderwort is at its best in warm-summer sites and moist soil. A strongly upright plant that bears lilac blue 3-petaled flowers over a 2-month period, spiderwort is a natural choice for sunny flower gardens in cool-summer climates or shady areas in warm regions. The tri-

The triangular blooms are short-lived, but new buds open each morning in summer.

angular flowers appear in small clusters at the stem tips and close at night, with new buds opening every day.

Spiderwort is ideal for filling low spots in gardens or wild meadows. In a long flower border that is partly in sun and partly in shade, use it as a "repeat" plant to tie the border together. Spiderwort thrives in deeply dug, well-drained beds, but it can also tolerate wet-soil conditions that give other flowering plants trouble with root rot.

Spiderwort Opportunities

Glistening, intensely saturated flower color in late spring through summer is spiderwort's main charm. Most plants sold for the garden are hybrids between several species. The cultivar 'Purple Profusion' grows 45 cm (18 in) tall with a long season of bluish purple flowers set off by yellow stamens. 'Zwanenburg Blue' offers flowers of a rare royal blue and foliage veined in purple, while 'Pauline' has large pink flowers. A white form, 'Snowcap', provides sparkling contrast when paired with blue cultivars.

There are also compact spiderworts, at 25 cm (10 in) tall, which are ideal for smaller gardens. These include 'Bilberry Ice', which has two-toned flowers with lavender streaks, and rose-flowered 'Red Cloud'.

Growing Spiderworts

Set plants out in early spring, 30 cm (12 in) apart. Plant them at the same depth they occupied in their nursery pots and water as needed to keep soil moist for a few weeks until they show signs of growth. Ideally, soil should be moist and loamy, but spiderwort can also adapt to drier conditions after its first year in the garden. Fertilize plants each spring with a deep drench of liquid all-purpose plant food, mixed according to label directions.

In summer, after the plants have finished blooming and the straplike foliage becomes yellowed, cut plants back to 5 cm (2 in) from the ground. Abundant rainfall, or irrigation, will often coax a second flush of foliage and flowers. However, more often the plants will simply go dormant until the following spring.

Increasing the Bounty

Every 4–5 years in early spring, dig and divide clumps. Look for points of narrow foliage poking through the soil's surface at about the time early daffodils bloom. Use a spade or a sharp knife to cut the large mass into smaller clumps, each of which should have 3 or more crowns. Transplant individual clumps to their new locations and water immediately. In mild-winter climates, you can also dig and divide large clumps in the fall. When grown in spots they like, spiderworts self-sow easily. You can dig and move seedlings in spring in colder regions, and in spring or fall in mild climates. These stalwart natives are rarely if ever visited by pests or diseases.

FUNDAMENTAL FACTS

ATTRIBUTES	Upright plants with blue, pink, or white flowers; for beds, meadow gardens
SEASON OF INTEREST	Late spring through summer
FAVORITES	'Purple Profusion', 'Snowcap', 'Zwanenburg Blue'
QUIRKS	Flowers last only a day, but new ones open daily
GOOD NEIGHBORS	Columbine, daylily, ferns, foxglove, ornamental grasses, hosta, iris
WHERE IT GROWS BEST	In partial shade and moist, average soil
POTENTIAL PROBLEMS	In favorable sites and climates it can become moderately invasive
RENEWING PLANTS	Lives many years; divide crowded clumps in early spring every 4–5 years
CRITTER RESISTANCE	Good
SOURCE	Division, self-seeds
DIMENSIONS	25–60 cm (10–24 in) tall, 25–45 cm (10–18 in) wide

STONECROP
Sedum spectabile

HARDINESS:
Zone 4

PREFERRED SOIL pH:
Neutral

PREFERRED SOIL TYPE:
Average, well-drained

PREFERRED LIGHT:
Sun to partial shade

Stonecrop in the Landscape

These hardy perennials boast thick, succulent foliage that emerges as handsome rosettes in spring. Stonecrops are virtually care-free throughout the summer and brandish domed clusters of white, pink, or salmon blossoms in late summer into fall. In winter, the dried, russet-toned flowers remain intact, adding color to the garden when you most appreciate it, and hold caps of snow.

While stonecrops enhance flower beds, these versatile plants have a tough constitution for difficult sites. As long as there is good drainage, they tolerate a variety of soils. They adjust to growing in sand and gravel with good humor and persevere during

'Brilliant' bursts into flower with deep pink blooms atop yellowish green foliage.

The domed clusters that bloom so brightly in summer turn to soft russet shades in fall.

droughts. Stonecrops are also exceptionally salt tolerant and grow with abandon in coastal gardens. And they can edge parched paths or hot curbs and adjust to conditions in containers.

More of a Good Thing

The best-known stonecrop is the hybrid 'Autumn Joy'. It has plump, juicy green leaves and large, flat clusters of pink blossoms that emerge on 50–60 cm (20–24 in) stems in late summer and darken to a rosy russet by season's end.

Other stonecrops to invite into your garden include the enchanting 'Stardust', with nearly white flowers atop tall, 45 cm (18 in) stems clad in pale blue-green leaves. 'Matrona' has smoky pink flowers on 45–60 cm (18–24 in) stems, with gray-green leaves edged with pink-purple. 'Brilliant' lives up to its name with bright rose blooms.

For colorful sedum foliage, 'Variegatum' creates a tapestry effect with yellow-and-green leaves topped with

bright pink flowers. 'Frosty Morn' has pale gray-green leaves rimmed in icy white and pink to white flowers.

Growing Stonecrop

In most climates stonecrops perform best in sun, but if your summers are searing, plant them where they will receive afternoon shade. Don't fertilize, and water only when a serious drought is in progress. Pinch back the plants several times before midsummer to encourage bushier growth and more flowers. Stonecrops need to be

With its frosty flowers, 'Iceberg' looks refreshing on sultry late-summer days.

divided only when the centers of aging clumps begin to grow and flower less vigorously.

Because of their tough, thick leaves, stonecrops are not pestered by insects or diseases, with the exception of the potentially fatal root or stem rot caused by soggy soil or overfertilizing. During droughts, deer may browse plants. Tuck bars of deodorant bath soap into plantings as a deterrent, or use commercial repellents according to label directions.

Increasing the Bounty

It is easy to root stem cuttings taken in early summer. Take 15 cm (6 in) long stem cuttings, remove the leaves from the lower third of the stems, and insert them halfway into moistened, well-drained potting soil. Place the cuttings in a shady spot and keep the soil barely moist until roots form.

FUNDAMENTAL FACTS

ATTRIBUTES	Succulent leaves, pink or white flower clusters; for groundcover, beds, pots
SEASON OF INTEREST	Year-round; blooms late summer to fall
FAVORITES	'Autumn Joy', 'Stardust', 'Matrona', 'Variegatum', 'Frosty Morn', 'Brilliant'
QUIRKS	Needs well-drained soil
GOOD NEIGHBORS	Blanket flower, coreopsis, ornamental grasses, Russian sage, salvias
WHERE IT GROWS BEST	A sunny, well-drained site with average soil
POTENTIAL PROBLEMS	Stem rot when soil is wet and humidity high
RENEWING PLANTS	Lives 4 years or longer; divide crowded clumps every 3–5 years
CRITTER RESISTANCE	Good except for deer (occasionally)
SOURCE	Bedding plants, cuttings
DIMENSIONS	30–60 cm (12–2? tall and equa?l

The blossoms resemble little roses, in sun-kissed colors, such as gold, peach, and red.

SUN ROSE

Helianthemum hybrids

HARDINESS:
Zone 6 unless otherwise indicated

PREFERRED SOIL pH:
Neutral to slightly alkaline

PREFERRED SOIL TYPE:
Sandy with added organic matter, well-drained

PREFERRED LIGHT:
Sun

Sun Rose in the Landscape

Sun rose offers multitudes of fresh-looking, 2.5 cm (1 in) wide, single or double roselike flowers that cover the low-growing, shrublike plants in late spring to early summer. Flowers in clear, bright colors, including yel-... white, peach, red, and orange top ...lothed with small, gray-green ...metimes called rock rose, ...elights in tumbling over ... mainstay in sunny ...because of its short ...lso delightful as

an informal edging plant or an accent at the front of a border. In container gardens, display sun rose alongside hens and chicks in broad, shallow clay pots and troughs.

Sun Roses Galore

Popular hybrids are a mix of *Helianthemum nummularium*, which is also called frostweed, and several other species that hail from high altitudes and exposed, rocky outcrops. In mild-winter climates the plants are often evergreen and can spread twice as wide as the same varieties grown in colder climates, where they become dormant in winter. Hardiness varies slightly with each variety.

For a sun rose with fire-engine red flowers, consider 'Henfield Brilliant', which grows well, particularly on the West Coast. Plants reach about 25 cm (10 in) tall and 50 cm (20 in) wide. For a hardier plant, try 'Raspberry Ripple'. It's a good bet in Zone 5, with attractive gray-green leaves and red-and-white flowers. Other good

choices include 'Cerise Queen', which has double cherry red flowers; 'Annabel', which has double pink flowers; and 'Ben Nevis', which blooms with buttery yellow flowers.

Growing Sun Rose

Sun roses prefer a lean, well-drained, neutral to slightly alkaline soil. If your soil is heavy clay, amend it with sand and organic matter to lighten it. For acidic soil, add garden lime according to package directions. Set out potted plants in spring, or in fall where winters are mild. Allow 60 cm (2 ft) between plants so they will have room to sprawl as they mature. Keep the soil barely moist for a few weeks until the plants show signs of growth. Shear them back by half their height after they have finished flowering in early summer and expect a second flush of flowers in late summer or fall.

Sun roses benefit from protection from cold winter winds and accumulated ice or snow. In early winter,

Let low-growing sun rose flow through the garden to create a stream of color in late spring.

FUNDAMENTAL FACTS	
ATTRIBUTES	Small, rose-shaped flowers on low plants; for dry sites, rock gardens
SEASON OF INTEREST	Spring to fall
FAVORITES	'Henfield Brilliant', 'Ben Nevis', 'Annabel', 'Raspberry Ripple'
QUIRKS	Remains evergreen in mild-winter climates
GOOD NEIGHBORS	Candytuft, hens and chicks, moss phlox, stonecrop, veronica
WHERE IT GROWS BEST	In sun and gritty or rocky, well-drained soil
POTENTIAL PROBLEMS	Grows poorly in extreme heat or wet soil
RENEWING PLANTS	Lives many years in mild climates; root stem cuttings in late summer
CRITTER RESISTANCE	Good
SOURCE	Bedding plants, cuttings
DIMENSIONS	20–30 cm (8–12 in) tall, to 1 m (3 ft) wide

cover them with evergreen boughs loosely piled over the crowns, or growing points, and remove the boughs first thing in spring.

Increasing the Bounty

Sun roses tend to be short-lived, especially in regions with cold, wet winters, such as along the Atlantic Coast. Take 8 cm (3 in) long stem cuttings in late summer and root them in moist soil under fluorescent lights indoors or in a partly shaded cold frame outdoors. After cuttings root, keep them fairly dry through winter and hold them in a cold frame, or in an indoor space that remains above freezing, until spring.

Tough-leaved sun roses are nearly impervious to pests and diseases, with the exception of fungal root rot when they are grown in cold, wet soil.

SWEET WOODRUFF

Galium odoratum

HARDINESS:
Zone 4

PREFERRED SOIL pH:
Slightly acid

PREFERRED SOIL TYPE:
Moist, fertile, well-drained

PREFERRED LIGHT:
Partial shade

Tiny, vanilla-scented flowers appear in spring, above stiff, starlike green leaves.

Sweet Woodruff in the Landscape

This dainty-looking plant is actually a durable and vigorous groundcover. For success with sweet woodruff, let it do what it does best: cover broad areas of ground in semishady spots. Once established it excludes weeds, so it's wonderful for carpeting a slope, filling in underneath trees and spring-flowering shrubs, or prettying up a ravine or equally difficult spot. All it really requires is moderately damp soil, but be careful not to mire the roots in boggy ground, which can induce fatal root rot.

The apple green leaves of sweet woodruff are tiny, thin, and borne in starlike whorls around brittle stems that poke up only 10–12 cm (4–5 in) above the soil. The airy-looking leaves provide a welcome lightness and delicacy that other shady groundcovers fail to provide. The sprightly 2.5 cm (1 in) diameter white flowers appear in great numbers, like a froth covering the plants in spring, and last for a few weeks. Both the leaves and the flowers exude a soft, spicy scent that adds to the plant's appeal. The fragrance is even more pronounced when the leaves and blossoms are dried for potpourris and sachets.

Tapestry of Flowers

Thanks to its tendency to spread into mats, sweet woodruff is a great addition to a spring flower display. It emerges slightly later than most spring bulbs, allowing them to show off their charms solo and then covering up their foliage as it yellows and dies. The petite white starry flowers mix well with everything from white-flowered daffodils to tulips of almost any hue. Think of sweet woodruff as a filler, like baby's breath, in a living spring bouquet.

With a little planning, you can spice up your sweet woodruff planting by interspersing other spring bloomers. Sprinkle in some woodland phlox, or plant sweet woodruff in a skirt around ferns, Solomon's seal, or

Sweet woodruff is at its best when allowed to roam and form a carpet in partial shade.

hellebores. Just don't crowd any of these bedfellows; allow about 30 cm (12 in) on all sides at planting time, then watch the tapestry emerge as the plants mature. Sweet woodruff doesn't give the impression of being a fast traveler, yet it does cover an impressive spread of ground in a fairly short time. If it grows where it's unwanted, just pull it up by the roots.

Growing Sweet Woodruff

Buy flats of sweet woodruff from a garden center in springtime. It takes quite a few plants to make an impressive initial display. Choose a spot in partial shade, such as under tall trees. Plants in strong light may bleach to a lighter shade of green or turn yellow. Soil should be moist and enriched with acidic peat moss or partially composted leaves. Space the plants 30 cm (12 in) apart. In late winter, fertilize dormant sweet woodruff with a 5 cm (2 in) deep mulch of composted manure or a commercial controlled-release fertilizer. Plants undergoing long droughts or high heat may go dormant in summer.

While rarely bothered by pests or diseases, the plants can attract hungry deer. If you discover deer browsing your sweet woodruff, tuck deodorant-bath soap into plantings to deter them, or use commercial deer repellent applied per package directions.

FUNDAMENTAL FACTS

ATTRIBUTES	A low, spreading plant with tiny white fragrant flowers; for groundcover
SEASON OF INTEREST	Spring, summer
FAVORITES	Species; sold by species or common name
QUIRKS	Leaves fade in too much sun; plants go dormant in drought or high heat
GOOD NEIGHBORS	Daffodils, hyacinths, tulips, woodland phlox
WHERE IT GROWS BEST	Under deciduous trees in moist, fertile soil
POTENTIAL PROBLEMS	If soil is not sufficiently fertile, plants yellow and begin to die out
RENEWING PLANTS	Persists indefinitely; divide only to increase plantings
CRITTER RESISTANCE	Good except for deer
SOURCE	Bedding plants, division
DIMENSIONS	10–30 cm (4–12 in) tall and equally wide

THYME

Thymus spp.

HARDINESS:
Zone 5

PREFERRED SOIL pH:
Neutral to slightly alkaline

PREFERRED SOIL TYPE:
Crumbly, well-drained

PREFERRED LIGHT:
Sun

In early summer, the leaves of *T. serpyllum* var. *albus* are covered in white flowers.

Thyme in the Landscape

Brush against or tread upon a planting of thyme and a pungent aroma wafts upward. This fragrant herb, used for centuries in the kitchen, is a care-free charmer in the garden, withstanding drought, heat, strong sun, and even light foot traffic. Its leaves always look tidy and become smothered under tiny flowers for several weeks in late spring and early summer.

Varying in height from 5–20 cm (2–8 in), thyme can serve many purposes. The smallest grow easily between paving stones, cascade over the edges of containers, or fit in the crevices of a sunny stone wall. The more upright varieties form little mounds of foliage that are perfect for edging a sunny bed of other herbs, flowers, or even roses.

The Colors and Scents of Thyme

Thyme leaves may be golden, green, blue-gray, bronze, or silver and they smell like everything from woodsy nutmeg to refreshing lemon. The flowers are often pastels, in white, pink, or lavender, although some varieties bloom in hot pink or red.

Woolly thyme (*Thymus pseudolanuginosus*) forms a dense carpet of fuzzy gray-green foliage with white flowers. The popular creeping thyme (*T. serpyllum*), also called mother-of-thyme, forms a 10 cm (4 in) tall groundcover with olive leaves and pink or purple flowers. One cultivar, 'Coccineus', spreads a dull crimson layer of flowers over its deep green leaves. Lemon thyme (*T.* × *citriodorus*) stands a little taller, reaching 15 cm (6 in), with variegated green-and-yellow lemon-scented leaves topped by tiny white or lilac flowers. The thyme commonly used in cooking, *T. vulgaris*, is a wiry 20 cm (8 in) tall plant with lavender flowers. The cultivar 'Argentus' has green leaves edged in silver, while those of 'Aureus' are rimmed in gold.

Growing Thyme

Because thyme is slow to mature from seedlings, it is best to purchase starter plants in spring. Once established, thyme travels quickly by sending out runners, so set plants 30 cm (12 in) apart in a well-drained, sandy soil. Until plantlets show signs of new growth, keep the soil barely moist. Thyme can contract the fatal fungal disease root rot when grown in soggy soil, so if your soil is clay, amend it with sand and organic matter to improve drainage, or grow thyme in containers of fast-draining soil.

After flowers fade, trim old growth to encourage new shoots. In harsh winter areas, mulch with evergreen boughs after the ground freezes to prevent wind and cold damage. In spring or fall, you can easily divide plants by digging and transplanting

T. serpyllum 'Coccineus' is a creeping variety with deep pink to crimson flowers.

rooted chunks into prepared soil at the same depth at which they grew.

Thyme is pest free except for occasional visits from cottony, sap-sucking mealybugs, which can be controlled by rinsing them off the foliage with a forceful spray of water from a hose.

FUNDAMENTAL FACTS

ATTRIBUTES	Fragrant creeping herb; white, pink, or lavender flowers; for groundcover
SEASON OF INTEREST	Spring through fall
FAVORITES	*T. serpyllum* 'Coccineus'; *T. vulgaris* 'Argentus', 'Aureus'; *T.* x *citriodorus*
QUIRKS	Seed-grown plants mature slowly and vary in looks and flavor
GOOD NEIGHBORS	Achillea, alyssum, poppy, rosemary, lavender, salvia, most herbs
WHERE IT GROWS BEST	Sun in sandy, well-drained soil
POTENTIAL PROBLEMS	Soggy soil in any season encourages deadly fungal root-rot disease
RENEWING PLANTS	Lives years; divide every 2 years to maintain vigor
CRITTER RESISTANCE	Good except for mealybugs
SOURCE	Bedding plants, division
DIMENSIONS	5–20 cm (2–8 in) tall, to 30 cm (12 in) wide

Common thyme, the type most used in cooking, is a mounding plant with lavender blooms.

The "tri-" in trillium refers to the three-petaled flowers that rise above clusters of three leaves.

T. grandiflorum has relatively large blooms, which open white and age to pink.

The flowers of *T. erectum* nod over large, pale green, diamond-shaped leaves.

TRILLIUM
Trillium spp.

HARDINESS:
Zones as indicated

PREFERRED SOIL pH:
Neutral to slightly acid

PREFERRED SOIL TYPE:
Moist, fertile

PREFERRED LIGHT:
Partial shade

Trillium in the Landscape
The genus *Trillium* is a precious part of the natural heritage of North America. Most of these natives are concentrated in the East, but a handful are native to the Midwest and West. Once you've seen these wildlings growing in the forest, you'll want them to grow in a woodland garden.

The "tri-" in the name trillium refers to the fact that plants have clusters of three leaves and three-petaled flowers. The leaves may be mottled in silver, bronze, purple, or shades of green, and the flowers range from white and pale yellow to a deep ruby red. Plant these natural beauties in drifts among asarum, Solomon's seal, ferns, and woodland phlox. Trilliums bloom in the spring and become dormant by midsummer.

Treasured Trilliums
Trilliums are too delicate to ship, and many are protected in the wild, which means you should buy them only from a reputable local plant nursery. For the eastern parts, great white trillium (*T. grandiflorum* [Z4]) is a good choice. This species has large showy flowers, usually white to pale pink, with highly recurved petals. 'Flore Pleno' is a double-flowered form, while 'Rosea' is pink. Westerners should consider *T. ovatum* (Z6), which has smaller leaves and flowers with petals that are not recurved. No matter where you live, follow the advice of wildflower experts in your area when adding to your trillium collection. Many nurseries propagate favorite selections that show remarkable vigor under local growing conditions.

Growing Trillium
To keep trilliums happy, duplicate their native habitat by giving them moist, shady, woodland conditions. Set out container-grown plants in late winter or early spring and keep the soil moist. Expect little from new plantings the first year and leave the site undisturbed after the plants go dormant in summer. They will emerge first thing the next spring, ready to bask in late-winter sun and flower before the trees leaf out.

Dividing trilliums is tricky and best left to professionals. The procedure involves nicking the root while the parent plant is still in the ground, which coaxes it to separate into two plants, and after several months cutting them apart and replanting them. Under the best conditions trilliums take two years or more after division to attain flowering size.

Try not to move trilliums once they are planted. There is no such thing as a crowded trillium colony, because the plants look most attractive when several stems are clustered close together. If transplanting becomes necessary because of a shift in your garden's location, dig and transplant trilliums in early spring. Move the plant with the soil packed around the roots to minimize trauma.

This otherwise tough native is nearly impervious to pests or diseases but can be nibbled by slugs and snails. Handpick and dispose of these night-feeding pests at dusk or set saucers of beer nearby to lure and drown them.

FUNDAMENTAL FACTS

ATTRIBUTES	Unusual, three-part foliage and flowers; for woodland gardens
SEASON OF INTEREST	Spring
FAVORITES	*T. grandiflorum*; *T. g.* 'Flore Pleno', 'Rosea'; *T. ovatum*
QUIRKS	Plant naturally goes dormant in summer
GOOD NEIGHBORS	Asarum, ferns, Solomon's seal, woodland phlox
WHERE IT GROWS BEST	Moist woodlands
POTENTIAL PROBLEMS	Slugs or snails may chew plants in damp sites
RENEWING PLANTS	Plants live many years; never need rejuvenating
CRITTER RESISTANCE	Good
SOURCE	Bedding plants, root division
DIMENSIONS	30–45 cm (12–18 in) tall and wide

Turtleheads are a care-free source of pink blooms in wet sites in mid to late summer.

TURTLEHEAD

Chelone lyonii

True to the plant's common name, the flowers really do resemble small turtle heads.

HARDINESS:
Zone 3

PREFERRED SOIL pH:
Near neutral

PREFERRED SOIL TYPE:
Moist

PREFERRED LIGHT:
Sun to partial shade

Turtlehead in the Landscape

Naturally damp areas in sun to partial shade are among the hardest sites to landscape. You want to grow plants that will add color to the area, but you want to avoid having to slog through the wet soil to groom, fertilize, stake, weed, or otherwise fuss with the plants. Look no further: turtleheads are the solution to such a dilemma.

Native from Newfoundland to the southern Appalachians and west to Minnesota, easygoing turtleheads are medium-sized perennials, no more than 1.2 m (4 ft) high and half as wide. Tolerant of very wet soil, they will thrive in moist conditions just as well, spreading slowly with little or no attention. The thickly stacked mint green leaves are topped in mid to late summer by pink tubular flowers that bear a whimsical resemblance to turtle heads, all with mouths agape. Butterflies find them irresistible.

'Hot Lips', a new sensation, is a variety whose foliage emerges bronze with a purple tinge, and matures to green with red stems. By late summer, rose pink flowers appear on short spires crowning the plants. 'Hot Lips' is a bit shorter than its parents, topping out between 0.6–1 m (2–3 ft).

While you wait a year or two for a handful of plants to establish, or if you just want to give the site season-long interest, try interspersing turtleheads with early bloomers, such as bleeding heart and columbine. Fellow late-season performers, such as garden phlox and ferns, will help showcase turtleheads when they reach their peak in late summer.

Growing Turtlehead

In nature, these perky plants enjoy the damp, fertile soil found in ditches, along the sides of streams and ponds, and in low-lying meadows, and they do well in similar garden conditions. They are less fussy about exposure than soil and moisture. Sun or partial shade are tolerated with equal good humor. However, when grown in full sun or in hot-summer regions, a 5 cm (2 in) deep mulch of rotted leaves and judicious watering will keep the soil from drying out during midsummer droughts and provide all the nutrients the plants need. If grown in dense shade or overfertilized, stems that normally don't require staking can become floppy. When air circulation is stagnant, fungal mildew can mar the foliage with gray or white patches. Thin affected plants to increase air circulation and dispose of infected leaves. Otherwise, turtleheads are untroubled by pests or diseases.

Increasing the Bounty

Divide the plants in spring by cutting pieces of roots with a few new stems attached and plopping the pieces into the ground where you want them to grow. Or take 10 cm (4 in) long stem cuttings in early summer, rooting them in moist soil or a glass of water and transplanting them as soon as roots show. Or sow seeds in fall directly on soil in any moist site.

FUNDAMENTAL FACTS

ATTRIBUTES	Pink flower spikes on mint green foliage; for damp areas, pond sides
SEASON OF INTEREST	Mid to late summer
FAVORITES	Rose pink-flowered 'Hot Lips'
QUIRKS	Needs some shade in hot-summer climates
GOOD NEIGHBORS	Bleeding heart, columbine, garden phlox, Joe Pye weed, grasses
WHERE IT GROWS BEST	Damp soil in full sun to partial shade
POTENTIAL PROBLEMS	Drought stress; fungal mildew due to crowding, poor air circulation
RENEWING PLANTS	Plants live many years; remove older plants to relieve crowding
CRITTER RESISTANCE	Good
SOURCE	Plants, division, cuttings
DIMENSIONS	0.6–1.2 m (2–4 ft) tall, 0.3–0.6 m (1–2 ft) wide

Spiking types are spectacular en masse and mix well with flat flowers, such as coreopsis.

VERONICA

Veronica spp.

HARDINESS:
Zones as indicated

PREFERRED SOIL pH:
Near neutral

PREFERRED SOIL TYPE:
Moist, fertile, well-drained

PREFERRED LIGHT:
Sun to partial shade

Veronica in the Landscape

Also known as speedwell, veronica is a beloved old perennial that may have an upright form, with spiky flowers, or be a low-growing, mounding creeper. Both types bloom in blue, as well as pink, white, lavender, and rose, in late spring and summer.

Give upright-growing veronicas one of the best spots your garden has to offer. The plants produce dozens of 45 cm (18 in) long flower spikes, which can be cut regularly to prolong flowering. Any flower with flat blossoms, such as coreopsis or purple coneflower, looks great with upright veronica. Creeping veronicas are dainty little plants to grow near the bases of shrubs or small trees or as edging in beds and containers. They bloom in spring and occasionally produce more flowers during the summer. After blooming, the plants persist as compact green groundcovers.

The Showiest Speedwells

There are many well-known veronica cultivars with superb qualities. 'Sunny Border Blue' (Z4) and 'Crater Lake Blue' (Z5) are outstanding upright veronicas that provide a constant parade of blue flower spikes from early to late summer. Try 'Red Fox' (Z3) for pink flowers and 'Icicle' (Z3) for white.

Among creeping types, 'Waterperry' (Z5) grows only 12 cm (5 in) tall, and each plant spreads to 30 cm (12 in) wide. It blooms heavily in spring, covering itself with purple-blue blossoms, followed by a few flowers later in summer. The foliage turns bronze in the fall. 'Trehane' (Z4) has golden foliage that contrasts beautifully with its purplish blue flowers.

Growing Veronica

Veronicas need moist, fertile soil, and at least 4 hours of sun per day. Amend planting holes with compost and after planting add an 8 cm (3 in) layer of mulch to help keep the soil moist. If planted in reasonably fertile soil there is no need to fertilize; too much fertilizer can cause stems to flop. The key to keeping the upright veronicas in bloom is regular deadheading. Remove spikes as they fade, and new flowers will keep coming.

In late summer when days are hot and nights are cool and damp, the disfiguring fungal disease powdery mildew can make white, powdery patches appear on leaves. Pick off and dispose of infected leaves and avoid splashing water on the plants when irrigating. If the disease continues to spread, cut plants to within several centimeters (a few inches) of the soil to encourage healthy new growth.

Pests are rare, but if small, pear-shaped sap-sucking insect aphids appear on stem tips, knock them off with a strong stream of water from a hose. Hand pick and dispose of any caterpillars you find nibbling on leaves or treat plants with BT, a commercial biological insecticide, as directed on the label.

Increasing the Bounty

Divide upright veronicas by cutting off rooted shoots from the outer edges of the clump in spring or fall. Propagate spreading veronicas by slicing some rooted stems from the edge of an existing planting with a spade. Replant, setting the plantlets in prepared holes at the same depth at which the parent plants grew.

FUNDAMENTAL FACTS

ATTRIBUTES	Spikes or mats of blue, pink, or white flowers; for beds, pots, edging
SEASON OF INTEREST	Late spring through late summer
FAVORITES	Upright 'Sunny Border Blue', 'Red Fox', 'Icicle'; creeping 'Waterperry'
QUIRKS	Remove faded flowers to prolong flowering
GOOD NEIGHBORS	Artemisia, coreopsis, daylily, gypsophila, purple coneflower, rose
WHERE IT GROWS BEST	Moist, well-drained, fertile soil in sun to partial shade
POTENTIAL PROBLEMS	Powdery mildew in late summer; occasionally aphids or caterpillars
RENEWING PLANTS	Plants live many years; divide to increase plantings as needed
CRITTER RESISTANCE	Excellent
SOURCE	Bedding plants, division
DIMENSIONS	12–60 cm (5–24 in) tall, 30–45 cm (12–18 in) wide

Most veronicas feature blue flowers, ranging from pale blue to deep violet or navy.

YARROW

Achillea spp.

HARDINESS:
Zone 3

PREFERRED SOIL pH:
Adaptable

PREFERRED SOIL TYPE:
Average, well-drained

PREFERRED LIGHT:
Sun

Yarrow in the Landscape

Stalwart and care-free, yarrow is a boon to any sunny garden with well-drained soil. This drought-tolerant plant has ferny green foliage that adds soft texture to the garden and can remain evergreen in mild winters. The long-lasting blooms, formed in domed clusters, are composed of many small flowers that attract butterflies and beneficial insects.

The most vigorous form, *Achillea millefolium*, is a spreading plant that sends out runners just below the soil. These develop root buds that break through the soil to form new plants. 'Summer Pastels' produces clouds of

Yarrow is famed for its yellow flowers, which range from pale cream to vibrant chrome.

Some flower varieties change color, progressing from soft yellow buds to rich pink blooms.

flowers in cream, light yellow, pink, orange, and lilac. These 60 cm (2 ft) tall plants are ideal to grow beside paved surfaces that heat up in summer or as a blooming groundcover in dry areas that are difficult to water.

Upright-growing *A. filipendulina* produces rich yellow flower clusters on stiff stems up to 1 m (3 ft) tall. This yarrow tends to stay put, growing in tight clumps that are ideal for the middle or back of borders.

The best varieties are propagated by division rather than seeds, so start with purchased, named plants. Try 'Coronation Gold' in hot-summer areas and 'Moonshine' for silvery gray foliage. Other good choices are pink-flowering 'Appleblossom', brick red 'Fireland', and 'The Pearl', which has abundant little white flowers.

Durable Beauty

For a continuous show of color, deadhead plants by clipping off the spent blooms. Yarrows bloom longer in cool weather, but you can maximize flowering in hot weather by cutting back the plants to right above the soil in midsummer, after their first flush of flowers fades. They will rebound and provide a repeat performance by fall. The flower heads make superb cut flowers, or you can gather and dry them for use in dried bouquets.

Growing Yarrow

All species are easy to start from seed indoors 4 weeks before the last spring frost or in the garden after frosts pass. The seeds need light to germinate, so sprinkle them on the surface of moistened soil. If growing indoors, place the pots on a windowsill or under fluorescent lights, and keep the soil moist and at room temperature for 10–15 days. After sprouting, seedlings can be grown at temperatures as low as 10°C (50°F). Transplant seedlings into individual pots when they have several sets of mature leaves, and plant outside after the soil warms in spring.

Young yarrow plants require water when first planted, but need little care after they produce new growth. Avoid mulching, which can cause stem rot, as can chronic soil dampness or too much shade. Once spreading types get going, you may need to sever the runners of plants that wander too far.

A. filipendulina benefits from division every 3 years, when the centers of clumps begin to flower poorly. Dividing and thinning plants also improves air circulation, which helps prevent fungal leaf diseases like rust, recognized by rusty spots on leaf undersides. If problems occur, trim off and dispose of infected foliage. Add gritty gravel or compost to heavy clay soil at planting time to discourage root rot. Problem-free, pungently scented yarrow repels both insects and deer.

FUNDAMENTAL FACTS

ATTRIBUTES	Long-lasting pastel or red flowers on ferny plants; for beds, cutting, drying
SEASON OF INTEREST	From early summer to frost, with a lull in flower production in midsummer
FAVORITES	'Appleblossom', 'Coronation Gold', 'Fireland', 'Moonshine', 'Summer Pastels', 'The Pearl'
QUIRKS	Wet soil and mulch may lead to stem or root rot
GOOD NEIGHBORS	Balloon flower, campanula, iris, peony,
WHERE IT GROWS BEST	Sun and well-drained soil of average fertility
POTENTIAL PROBLEMS	Fungal leaf disease or root rot under damp or crowded conditions
RENEWING PLANTS	Individual plants live up to 4 years; divide when clumps cease flowering
CRITTER RESISTANCE	Excellent
SOURCE	Plants, division, seeds
DIMENSIONS	0.6–1 m (2–3 ft) tall, 0.3–0.6 m (1–2 ft) wide

Yucca makes a bold statement in the garden, especially when in bloom.

YUCCA

Yucca spp.

HARDINESS:
Zone 4

PREFERRED SOIL pH:
Adaptable

PREFERRED SOIL TYPE:
Average

PREFERRED LIGHT:
Sun to partial shade

Yucca in the Landscape

With their erect, swordlike leaves radiating in all directions from the plant's base, yuccas are associated with the American Southwest, but they can find a place in any garden. These architectural garden plants are incredibly easy to grow and have many attractive features. The broad, stiff, evergreen leaves are usually green and may have loose filaments along the edges that shred into interesting curlicues. Some fancy cultivars boast leaves variegated in cream, white, or gold. *Yucca filamentosa* 'Garland's Gold' is banded with yellow, and *Y. flaccida* 'Golden Sword' has yellow stripes. Most yuccas grow several feet tall and make a statement even before they send up flower stalks in summer that reach 1.8 m (6 ft). For small gardens, there are scaled-down cultivars that stand a mere 60 cm (2 ft) tall, such as *Y. filamentosa* 'Bright Edge', whose green leaves have broad yellow edges.

Yuccas tolerate almost any soil and weather conditions, including sand and salt spray near well-traveled roads and the seashore. Because of their drought tolerance, yuccas are perfect for garden spots that are out of hose and sprinkler range, and their ability to make do with what nature dishes out makes them ideal for weekend gardeners. They excel in large pots, surviving for several hot summer days without watering. And their evergreen foliage will mark the end of a path or driveway even in snowy winter. But because the leaf tips are pointed, make sure yuccas are spaced a comfortable distance from high-traffic areas.

Pair yuccas with other plants that love heat, drought, and sun. White-flowered zinnias combined with green-and-white variegated yuccas make a striking match. Yuccas with leaves striped in yellow combine well with chartreuse-flowered euphorbias. Use a line of yuccas as a hedge or low, prickly barrier to discourage human or animal intruders or mix them in foundation plantings under windows.

Growing Yuccas

Yuccas form tough, long-lived plants that send up leaves from a central base, or crown. In spring, just as new growth begins, plant yuccas 1 m (3 ft) apart in full sun, in very well drained soil. Excellent drainage is important because root rot, which develops in soggy soil, is one of the few problems to pester yuccas. Dig the planting hole as deep as the nursery container and twice as wide. When planting in heavy clay soil, improve the drainage in the planting hole by digging in enough coarse sand and organic matter, such as compost, to make the soil crumbly.

Plant in groups of 3–5 to make the plants a focal point in a landscape. In a small garden, however, a single plant will serve as an accent. To establish new plants quickly, water and fertilize with a balanced fertilizer according to package directions, but after initial pampering, leave yuccas growing in the ground untended.

For a neat appearance, remove old, discolored leaves and old flowering stalks while wearing heavy gloves to protect against the pointed leaves. If plants become overcrowded after several years, thin them in spring or fall, wearing protective goggles and gloves. The thick, prickly leaves of yucca effectively repel pests of both insect and four-footed varieties.

FUNDAMENTAL FACTS

ATTRIBUTES	Spiked leaves, spires of white flowers; for beds or as an accent plant
SEASON OF INTEREST	Year-round; blooms in summer
FAVORITES	'Garland's Gold', 'Golden Sword'; dwarf 'Bright Edge'
QUIRKS	Sharp leaves can injure; wear gloves and goggles when tending plants
GOOD NEIGHBORS	Artemisia, butterfly flower, coreopsis, euphorbia, rudbeckia, sedum
WHERE IT GROWS BEST	Sun, in dry or well-drained soil
POTENTIAL PROBLEMS	Root rot in soggy soil
RENEWING PLANTS	Plants live many years; divide crowded clumps and remove old plants
CRITTER RESISTANCE	Excellent
SOURCE	Bedding plants, division
DIMENSIONS	Plants 1 m (3 ft) tall and wide; flower stalks to 1.8 m (6 ft) tall

The gold-striped leaves of 'Golden Sword' arch slightly, softening its appearance.

In summer, small, cream-colored, bell-shaped flowers emit a fragrance at night.

CHAPTER NINE

CARE-FREE VINES

Easy to grow and able to solve perplexing landscape problems, vines deserve liberal use in the care-free garden. Employ a roaming vine to disguise a chain-link fence or hide a tree stump, or use a vine-covered trellis to add instant height to any scene. Vines may be annual or perennial, evergreen or deciduous, and grown for flowers or foliage alone. Vines vary in how they cling and climb. Most twine around a support, twisting their way skyward. Boston ivy and climbing hydrangea attach to a wall or tree trunk by means of little aerial roots called hold-fasts. Some, such as clematis, ascend using twisting leaf stems, while others cling with curling tendrils.

Perennial vines may seem like a major commitment, but they aren't the only route for those who want to try a rambler. Start with an annual vine like morning glory or sweet pea that adds beautiful flowers to the scene for a season, then allows you to change your mind next year. When you find a spot that seems incomplete without a vine, consider a permanent perennial species. Vines are available for almost any garden situation, whether sunny or shaded. Some can reach for the sun they require. In fact, the "roots in the shade and head in the sun" description suits several vines, particularly clematis, honeysuckles, and sweet peas. Climbing roses and wisteria need more sun, while others like Boston ivy need a half day of shade. You can use sun-loving vines to create shade by training them to grow overhead on a pergola or arbor to create a shady summer seating area on a patio.

While vines often do need pruning to show them the way you want them to grow or to control their size, they are basically low-maintenance. As you study this section, look for vines that will thrive in the areas you have to offer. Also consider scale, because the most successful way to grow vines is to fit them to the site. You'll find that the contributions care-free vines make to your garden will soon have you looking for places to grow more.

Akebia is a strong, twining climber that can easily scramble a height of two stories.

AKEBIA
Akebia spp.

HARDINESS:
Zone 5 unless otherwise indicated

PREFERRED SOIL pH:
Adaptable

PREFERRED SOIL TYPE:
Fertile, moist, well-drained

PREFERRED LIGHT:
Sun to partial shade

Akebia in the Landscape

Vigorous enough to scramble up walls, fences, pergolas, and other large structures, akebia is a twining perennial vine that's in a hurry. Also known as chocolate vine, this plant is one of a large number of climbers that ascend by coiling their stems around a porch column, fence post, trellis, or any ver-tical support. Akebia's rampant growth makes it useful for screening out an unattractive view, concealing compost heaps or trash cans, covering a blank wall or fence, and even for creating shade on a terrace. Akebias can climb to 9 m (30 ft) or more, but they are also content to weave themselves over a low fence or tree stump, building up multiple layers to form a thick, lush mound of foliage.

Of Foliage and Flowers

Handsome, thick foliage is the main reason to grow this vine. Five-leaf akebia (*Akebia quinata*) has leaf clusters with 5 leaflets, each one rounded, light green, and 5 cm (2 in) long. *A. trifoliata* (Z6) is similar, but the leaflets are in clusters of 3 and can reach 10 cm (4 in) long. When viewed from the distance, the vine gives the overall effect of a soft, finely textured curtain. And because five-leaf akebia performs as an evergreen or semievergreen in mild climates, these lucky gardeners can enjoy the foliage nearly year-round.

In spring akebias produce attractive drooping clusters of flowers, which release a faint vanilla scent, especially at night. The buds dangle like little lavender cherries, then open into male and female flowers on the same stem. The larger, reddish or purplish brown flowers at the base are female, while the pale purple ones that hang from the tips are male. If pollinated, akebia may produce 8 cm (3 in) long grayish purple fruits that split open to reveal black seeds. But fruit production is uncommon outside of the plant's homelands of Japan, China, and Korea.

Growing Akebia

Akebias are remarkably unfussy. While they prefer fertile, moist, well-drained soil, they do just as well in average soil. While they need sun, they can also tolerate partial shade. The only thing akebias resent is having their roots disturbed. So select a permanent site carefully and leave the vine alone once it has been planted.

Set out container-grown plants in either spring or fall, allowing at least 6–8 weeks for the new plants to settle in before the onset of extreme summer heat or winter cold. Young plants may need protection to survive their first winter. Spread a 10 cm (4 in) deep layer of a fluffy mulch, such as dried leaves or evergreen boughs, over the root zone after the first hard freeze in fall.

Young stems may need help to start twining. Let them grow a little and watch their natural habit to see if they coil clockwise or counterclockwise. Then tie the stems loosely to the support with soft green twine or yarn following their inclination. If the stems can't yet reach the support, place bamboo stakes around the plant that reach the base of the support. Tie the stems onto the stakes, and they'll soon start climbing up to the support.

The flowers of fiveleaf akebia dangle amid little leaf clusters composed of five leaflets.

FUNDAMENTAL FACTS

ATTRIBUTES	Vigorous vine with fragrant flowers; for shade, screening, or privacy
SEASON OF INTEREST	Spring through fall
TYPE OF VINE	Semievergreen perennial; climbs by twining
FAVORITES	Two species: Five-leaf akebia (*A. quinata*) and *A. trifoliata*
QUIRKS	Plants resent root disturbance and will not grow well if transplanted
GOOD NEIGHBORS	Grow as a background for perennials or annuals
WHERE IT GROWS BEST	Widely adaptable to soils and sites with sun to partial shade
POTENTIAL PROBLEMS	Will outgrow a small, confined space
RENEWING PLANTS	Lives many years; prune to the ground in late winter to rejuvenate
CRITTER RESISTANCE	Excellent
SOURCE	Bedding plants
DIMENSIONS	To 9 m (30 ft) long

Established plants often need to be pruned back to control their wandering tendencies. Pruning may be done at any time of the year, although early summer, after the flowers fade, is the preferred time. Prune only as needed to control the size of the vine and to train it so that it will expand into places where you want it to grow. In mild climates, a plant that has grown out of control can be reined in if you cut it back to the ground in late winter or in early spring.

Akebia has no serious insect pests, is untroubled by diseases, and needs fertilizer only in poor soils. If foliage becomes sparse and turns light green, it's time to apply an all-purpose controlled-release commercial fertilizer according to label directions.

BOSTON IVY

Parthenocissus tricuspidata

HARDINESS:
Zone 5 unless otherwise indicated

PREFERRED SOIL pH:
Slightly acid

PREFERRED SOIL TYPE:
Average

PREFERRED LIGHT:
Partial shade

Boston Ivy in the Landscape

No vine provides coverage comparable to Boston ivy, making it unsurpassed for covering large, blank masonry walls. Native to China and Japan, this perennial vine is grown for its glossy green, sharply lobed leaves, which are arranged in overlapping tiers so dense that the support behind them disappears. The leaves of some varieties are purplish when young and may become veined or edged in pink as they mature. In fall Boston ivy turns brilliant red, and in winter the leafless stems draw interest with the lines they trace, stretching ever upward until they reach 18 m (60 ft) in length.

Boston ivy fastens itself to a surface with adhesive, suckerlike pads called holdfasts. They cause no harm to brick, stone, or stucco, but can hold moisture against wood surfaces, contributing to its decay. And, should you need to pull the vine down to paint a wooden structure, substantial work is involved in removing holdfasts and their residue from the wall.

Focused Fall Color

Several cultivars show special characteristics. Both 'Beverley Brooks' and 'Lowii' have smaller leaves than the species and grow a bit shorter. On the other end of the scale is 'Robusta', an especially vigorous, large-leaved cultivar. For maximum color, try 'Veitchii'

The deeply lobed leaves of Boston ivy are often outlined, veined, or flushed with red.

or 'Atropurpurea'. These start and end the growing season with reddish purple leaves that are green in summer.

All in the Family

The North American native counterpart to Boston ivy is Virginia creeper (*Parthenocissus quinquefolia* [Z2]). With 5 slender leaflets splayed out like the fingers of a hand, Virginia creeper foliage is less glossy than that of Boston ivy but also turns bright red in fall. Vigorous but not dense, this carefree native vine is just right for informal natural areas or as a groundcover.

Growing Boston Ivy

Plant Boston ivy in spring, in a partially shaded site. It is not fussy about soil but grows vigorously in fertile soil high in organic matter, so amend the planting hole with leaf mold, compost, or dried manure if your soil has a lot of clay or sand. Keep the roots barely moist throughout the first growing season, and in subsequent years when rainfall is lacking. Young vines may need some training to get them to climb until the holdfasts unfurl from the stems and touch the support. Press the stems against the growing surface by propping them behind a brick, or a similar object. The stems will soon send out holdfasts to grab the wall on contact.

Boston ivy goes out in flames in fall, creating a solid curtain of brilliant crimson.

Don't let this vigorous vine, which grows several feet each year, get out of control. Prune in any season to keep the vines away from eaves and window or door frames, and to contain size. Its thick leaves are an adequate deterrent to pests and diseases.

FUNDAMENTAL FACTS

ATTRIBUTES	Shade-tolerant vine with lobed leaves and fall color; for covering walls
SEASON OF INTEREST	Spring to late fall
TYPE OF VINE	Deciduous perennial; climbs with adhesive holdfasts
FAVORITES	Compact 'Lowii; vigorous 'Robusta'; 'Veitchii' for foliage color
QUIRKS	Can attach to almost any surface; very vigorous
GOOD NEIGHBORS	Provides a textured, colorful backdrop for any shade-tolerant plant
WHERE IT GROWS BEST	Fertile, moist soil in partial shade
POTENTIAL PROBLEMS	Can cause structural damage to wood surfaces and roofs
RENEWING PLANTS	Lives for years; renewal not necessary
CRITTER RESISTANCE	Excellent
SOURCE	Bedding plants
DIMENSIONS	To 18 m (60 ft)

The foliage grows in dense, overlapping tiers, eventually concealing the support behind it.

C. x jackmanii is a classic that produces velvety violet flowers from summer into fall.

CLEMATIS
Clematis spp.

HARDINESS:
Zones as indicated

PREFERRED SOIL pH:
Near neutral

PREFERRED SOIL TYPE:
Moist, fertile, well-drained

PREFERRED LIGHT:
Foliage in sun, roots in shade

Clematis in the Landscape

Boasting some of the most beautiful flowers of any vine, clematis produces abundant blossoms in a range of colors, including blue, purple, red, pink, yellow, and white. The most commonly grown types are the large-flowered types of clematis, which have showy star-shaped flowers up to 20 cm (8 in) in diameter.

Clematis vines climb by looping little leaf stalks, or tendrils, around a neighboring branch, wire, stake, trellis, or other thin support. The plants can also be trained to drape over a fence, porch railing, or lamppost. You can even grow clematis in a large container outfitted with a willow-pole tepee. When the plant is not in flower, the leaves make a lovely screen.

Large-flowered Clematis

These are the ones most people think of when clematis are mentioned, and with their showy flowers, this is not surprising. Most varieties have flowers 15–20 cm (6–8 in) across that are really eye-catching. A large number have been around for many years and are old favorites. *Clematis × jackmanii* (Z2) has abundant purple flowers for much of the summer, while 'Henryi' (Z4) lights up the garden with snow white flowers ribbed in cream. These should both be pruned almost to the ground in spring. Another older variety is 'Nelly Moser' (Z3), with blooms of the palest pink striped down the center of each petal with a broad rose pink band. This does not need cutting back hard, just remove any old wood that does not show signs of growth in spring. 'Ville de Lyon' (Z3) has bright carmine flowers and, if not pruned too hard in spring, will reward you with two flushes of flowers, the first about 15 cm (6 in) across and the second around 10 cm (4 in), but both freely produced. Another interesting large-flowered variety that flowers twice is 'Proteus' (Z4). Here, the flowers are double or semi-double in the first flush of blooms, and single in the second set, but are full-sized each time. This variety does not need any pruning.

Other popular large-flowered clematis include 'Ernest Markham' with petunia red petals that are rounded at the tip, rather than

Leaves with a bronze cast enhance the pure white flowers of clematis cultivar 'Henryi'.

pointed, and yellow stamens in the center. 'Hagley Hybrid' is also sold as Pink Chiffon and has shell pink, cup-shaped flowers with brown stamens, while 'Gipsy Queen' is violet-purple with a velvety sheen and purple stamens. All these are hardy to Zone 3 and need to be cut back hard in spring. In Zone 4 you can also try the Canadian introduction 'Blue Ravine' with large mid-blue flowers from early summer onward. This variety thrives on heat and should be planted in full sun. 'Rouge Cardinal' is another fairly new introduction, this time from France, with crimson petals and buff-colored stamens. 'Marie Boisellot' is another variety with two names and is sometimes sold as 'Madame le Coultre'. Whatever the name, it is a stunning sight in full flower. The flowers open a very pale pink and fade to white with age. It is exceptionally free flowering. Most of these large-flowered varieties will grow to about 4 m (12 ft) in height.

Small-flowered Clematis

Spectacular as the large-flowered varieties are, they are hard-pressed to equal the floral display put on by some of the small-flowered varieties. Although the individual flowers may be smaller, generally 5–10 cm (2–4 in) across, they are produced in such numbers that they completely hide the foliage at times. While most clematis have six petals, some of these have only four, which gives them a more open, star-shaped appearance. 'Abundance' is one of these, with wine red flowers, petals that twist slightly at the tips, and greenish central stamens. The occasional flower has five or six petals, just to confuse things. The number of petals varies as well in 'Polish Spirit', although six is the average. Flowers open a plum purple with a red-purple stripe down each petal, and fade with age to a mauve-pink. These are hardy to Zones 3 and 2 respectively and flower in summer. You don't have to grow clematis on a trellis; plant these where they can climb into a tree or large shrub to enjoy their beauty in a new way. They will climb about 4 m (12 ft) into a crab apple for example, and their mid-summer flowers bring color between the apple flowers and the ripe fruit. Prune these hard in spring, cutting them back to about 15 cm (6 in) from the soil.

For early-summer bloom, try varieties of *C. macropetala*. These have nodding, bell-like blooms that look almost double because the inner

'Nelly Moser' blooms twice, flowering in early summer and again in late summer.

Wine red 'Abundance' puts on a stunning display of plentiful star-shaped, small flowers.

petals are nearly as long as the outer ones. The species is native to northern China and Siberia, which accounts for its hardiness to Zone 3. 'Blue Bird' has slate blue flowers with twisted petals, and 'Rosy O'Grady' is similar but with pale rose colored flowers. Both will give some repeat blooming later in the summer and were introduced by Dr. Skinner in Dropmore, Manitoba. These do not need pruning except to remove any stems that don't show signs of new growth.

Clematis for Spring

There are two excellent clematis species that flower in spring, and each has varieties in different colors. The alpine clematis (C. *alpina*) is hardy to Zone 4 and has small, nodding flowers that last for several weeks. The flowers are like little bells, often white, but capped with four long, pointed petals in various colors that are the showy part of the flower and open to about 8 cm (3 in) wide. Flowers open as soon as the weather warms a little and are produced in great quantities. 'Pink Flamingo' is a bright pink, 'Willie' a pale pink, 'Francis Rivis' a lavender blue, and 'Pamela Jackman' a darker blue.

The mountain clematis (C. *montana*) is not as hardy and only grows to Zone 6, but where it will survive it

puts on a spectacular display. This can climb into tall trees or up the side of brick buildings and covers itself with white or pink flowers in late spring. While the alpine clematis grows to about 3 m (10 ft) and is suitable for quite small trellises, this species can climb 14 m (45 ft), so be cautious where you plant it. 'Alexander' has cream flowers, 'Mayleen' is deep pink and has bronzy foliage, and 'Tetrarose' has pinkish mauve flowers.

Clematis for Fall

While the large-flowered clematis bloom through the summer, they do not generally continue flowering into fall, but there are some species with smaller flowers that will continue to give a good display up to quite severe frosts. The Texas clematis (C. *texensis*) is hardier than its name suggests and will thrive in Zone 4 and the following hybrids are hardy to Zone 2. The flowers are like little bells, 5 cm (2 in) long, that may be pendent or upright, and with petals that curve back to reveal the central yellow stamens. Flowering starts in summer and continues well into fall on plants that will reach almost 3 m (10 ft). 'Duchess of Albany' is a bright pink with darker bands down the middle of each petal, and 'Gravetye Beauty' is a bright red

with flowers like miniature lily-flowered tulips.

The Russian virgin's bower (C. *tangutica*) brings a new color into clematis. The flowers are bright yellow nodding bells about 4 cm (1 in) wide that give rise to fluffy seed heads that last well into winter and are most attractive when coated with frost. This is probably the hardiest of all clematis and will survive in Zone 1. It is a very vigorous plant that quickly covers an arbor or fence and will grow up to 6 m (20 ft) in a single summer. C.×*fargesoides* 'Paul Farges' has open, white, 4 cm (1 in), star-shaped flowers with fluffy stamens. Unlike the previous fall-flowering clematis that have flowers on individual stems, these grow on branched stems with several blooms on each stalk, making the display very noticeable. It is a vigorous plant that can reach 8.5 m (28 ft) and is hardy to Zone 2. The sweet autumn clematis is now called C. *terniflora* but it is still listed in some catalogs as C. *paniculata*. The hawthorn-scented, white, star-like flowers appear from September onward in a frothy mass that can transform a fence into a breathtaking sight. Grow this close to the house where you can appreciate

C. 'Duchess of Albany' is a bright pink with darker bands down each petal.

C. *montana* 'Mayleen' can climb 14 m (45 ft), so be careful where you plant it.

the fragrance, rather than on a trellis at the bottom of the garden. It is also hardy to Zone 2. All these fall-flowering species should be cut back hard in spring.

FUNDAMENTAL FACTS

ATTRIBUTES	Blue, purple, red, pink, yellow, or white flowers; for trellises, thin supports
SEASON OF INTEREST	Spring through fall
TYPE OF VINE	Deciduous perennial; climbs by clinging with twining tendrils
FAVORITES	C. x *jackmanii*, 'Henryi', 'Nelly Moser', C. *terniflora*
QUIRKS	Grows best with foliage in sun and roots in shade
GOOD NEIGHBORS	Azaleas, hydrangeas, bulbs, evergreen shrubs, roses, small trees
WHERE IT GROWS BEST	In sunny sites with moist, organically rich soil
POTENTIAL PROBLEMS	Clematis wilt, a soil-borne disease that enters plants through injuries
RENEWING PLANTS	Vines live many years; prune in summer or winter, depending on variety
CRITTER RESISTANCE	Good
SOURCE	Bedding plants, cuttings
DIMENSIONS	1.8–8.5 m (6–28 ft); flowers to 20 cm (8 in)

Dense-growing Dutchman's pipe vine is ideal for covering a wall quickly or creating shade.

DUTCHMAN'S PIPE

Aristolochia macrophylla

The flowers open to form a shape that resembles an old-fashioned smoker's pipe.

HARDINESS:
Zone 5

PREFERRED SOIL pH:
Neutral to slightly acid

PREFERRED SOIL TYPE:
Moist, fertile, well-drained

PREFERRED LIGHT:
Partial shade to sun

Dutchman's Pipe in the Landscape

Dutchman's pipe gets its common name from its curious 8 cm (3 in) long, brownish yellow, U-shaped blooms, which look like miniature versions of an old-fashioned smoker's pipe. Unfortunately, the charming flowers are often hidden behind the 25 cm (10 in) wide, heart-shaped leaves, which are arranged in dense, overlapping layers, like shingles.

The lush growth of this twining vine makes it useful for framing attractive views or for blocking out less desirable ones. It's also a favorite porch vine, providing shade in summertime. But be prepared to accommodate it. Growing at least 4.5–9 m (15–30 ft) in length, this vigorous vine needs plenty of room and a sturdy support to bear its weight.

The best options are strong wires strung over masonry or a wrought-iron trellis. If you're growing the vine on a porch, run wires between screw-eye bolts fastened into framing. If you use a wooden trellis, choose one made of a rot-resistant wood, such as cedar, because the dense growth will hold moisture against its support.

Growing Dutchman's Pipe

Plant Dutchman's pipe in spring. A site with partial shade will suit this adaptable woodland native. Dig a roomy hole and add a 5 cm (2 in) layer of organic matter, such as well-rotted manure, compost, or leaf mold to improve drainage, as this vine doesn't like soggy soil. Bury the vine's stem no deeper than it grew in the nursery container. Fill the hole, water it well, and then mulch. Water as needed to keep the roots moist through the first season after planting. Irrigate established plants as needed to keep soil from drying out during droughts, because Dutchman's pipe grows poorly in dry conditions.

Do not be misled by slow growth the first couple of years after planting this vine. Once established, Dutchman's pipe needs heavy pruning at least twice in the summer to keep it within bounds. Pinching vine tips during the growing season encourages branching, leading to bushier growth.

Tender shoots may be visited by sap-sucking insect aphids or spider mites. Knock them off plants with a strong stream of water from a hose.

Increasing the Bounty

Often there's hardly room for one vine, let alone several, but if you want more, gather and sow seeds when in fall. Provide 4°C (40°F) for 3 months. Or, take 10 cm (4 in) long softwood cuttings in midsummer when growth is mature but not yet woody. Apply rooting hormone to the cut, insert cutting by half its length into moist soil, and provide bottom warmth and partial shade until rooted.

FUNDAMENTAL FACTS

ATTRIBUTES	Bold foliage and yellow pipe-shaped blooms; for shade, privacy
SEASON OF INTEREST	Spring to fall
TYPE OF VINE	Woody perennial vine; climbs by twining
FAVORITES	Available by species name only
QUIRKS	Needs ample water, but dislikes soggy soil
GOOD NEIGHBORS	This is a stand-alone plant, or use as a background for perennials
WHERE IT GROWS BEST	In partial shade and moist soil enriched with organic matter
POTENTIAL PROBLEMS	So vigorous it can crush a trellis that is not sturdy
RENEWING PLANTS	Lives years; if needed, cut back in spring
CRITTER RESISTANCE	Good except aphids or spider mites
SOURCE	Bedding plants
DIMENSIONS	4.5–9 m (15–30 ft) long

'Brant' has deliciously sweet black grapes and handsome lobed leaves that turn red in fall.

GRAPE

Vitis spp. and cvs.

HARDINESS:
Zone 6 unless otherwise indicated

PREFERRED SOIL pH:
Neutral to slightly alkaline

PREFERRED SOIL TYPE:
Fertile, well-drained

PREFERRED LIGHT:
Sun to partial shade

Grapevines in the Landscape

There's no reason grapevines should be confined to vineyards. Although grapes grown for appearance may produce little fruit, the gnarled, woody trunks and stems clothed in 15 cm (6 in) wide leaves make these vines versatile in the landscape. They are easy to grow, offer summer shade, and can be trained and pruned to fit a variety of sturdy trellises. Pergolas and arbors are especially suited to growing grape vines, because these plants like nothing better than establishing themselves with thick, treelike trunks

topped by fruiting vines that cling to their supports with twining tendrils.

Choosing Good Grapes

If you want to have pretty plants as well as juicy grapes, the best place to start is your local nursery. Like other fruits, grape cultivars vary in their

V. vinifera 'Purpurea', a variety of the wine grape, has plum leaves that darken in fall.

need for winter chilling and their resistance to pests and diseases that may be prevalent in your region. Local sources can steer you toward the best choices for your area.

Grape species native to North America are numerous and make fine garden plants, particularly in informal areas where you can let them ramble over fences. Perhaps the most ornamental grape is the fast-growing crimson vine (*Vitis coignetiae* [Z5]), which makes an excellent screen and boasts brilliant red foliage in fall. Muscadine grape (*V. rotundifolia*) is a close second, with nearly round 12 cm (5 in) wide leaves that turn yellow in fall. The riverbank grape (*V. riparia* [Z4]) is a vigorous vine with three-lobed leaves, sweetly scented flowers and almost black fruits with a strange taste.

Growing Grapevines

Grapes are easy to grow in any sunny, well-drained site. Buy plants in early spring, when they are just emerging from dormancy, and plant them in soil enriched with organic matter, such as leaf mold, compost, or well-aged manure. Unless you want abundant foliage, do not fertilize these plants. Train the vines where you want them to grow the first year and monitor them for problems.

Commercially grown grapes are prone to numerous diseases that cause leaves to discolor and wither, but these are seldom a problem in home landscapes. If your vines display disfiguring leaf spots, apply a sulphur-based fungicide registered for use on grapes, according to package directions. Japanese beetles may chew holes in the leaves, seriously weakening young plants. Deer may also browse grapes. Hang bars of a strong-smelling deodorant-formula bath soap among vines to deter them or apply

FUNDAMENTAL FACTS

ATTRIBUTES	Summer and fall foliage, fruits, and woody trunks; for shade, privacy
SEASON OF INTEREST	Year-round
TYPE OF VINE	Woody deciduous perennial; climbs by clinging with tendrils
FAVORITES	Seek locally adapted cultivars
QUIRKS	Aged trunks have a tree-like quality
GOOD NEIGHBORS	Bugleweed or astilbe as a groundcover beneath the vines
WHERE IT GROWS BEST	In sun and fertile, well-drained soil
POTENTIAL PROBLEMS	Fungal leaf spot diseases; Japanese beetles
RENEWING PLANTS	Vines live many years; prune back to the main trunk in early spring
CRITTER RESISTANCE	Good except for deer
SOURCE	Bedding plants, cuttings
DIMENSIONS	To 15 m (50 ft) long; leaves to 30 cm (12 in)

commercial repellents as directed on the label.

Little pruning is needed the first year, but once vines are established they should be cut back in late winter, just before the buds swell in spring. If you are growing grapes as ornamental vines, prune them as needed to control their size and eliminate weak growth. Because the main trunk is attractive year-round, allow it to grow as tall as you like and cut back the lateral branches to only a few buds. Grapes can also be trimmed in summer, which encourages them to produce a pretty flush of new, light green leaves. To propagate, pin a trailing vine to the ground and cover it with soil. When rooted, sever the rooted vine and plant it as directed above.

Honeysuckle is a vigorous vine that quickly fills a trellis with fragrant, colorful blooms.

HONEYSUCKLE

Lonicera spp.

L. sempervirens 'Sulphurea' has yellow flowers and yellow berries that later turn red.

HARDINESS:
Zones as indicated

PREFERRED SOIL pH:
Slightly acid

PREFERRED SOIL TYPE:
Average

PREFERRED LIGHT:
Partial shade to sun

Honeysuckle in the Landscape

Because of its sweet scent, honeysuckle is always welcome when grown near a terrace, porch, or any outdoor living area where you can drink in the fragrance. Or let honeysuckle ramble over an old tree stump, cover an arbor or pergola, or trail over a fence, where its colorful flowers can enliven the landscape.

Hummingbirds enjoy the nectar of this old-fashioned flowering vine, as do butterflies. Many cultivars of honeysuckle perform best in partial shade, although they can handle more sun in cool-summer areas. Honeysuckle, which twines around any support, is ideal for growing on a mailbox or lamppost, or you can install a trellis to help it cover a wall. Because cultivars vary in size and vigor, be sure to choose one that fits the space you want to fill.

All in the Family

Scarlet trumpet honeysuckle (L. × *brownii* 'Dropmore Scarlet' [Z2]) is a vigorous, long-flowering vine with bright red flowers, yellow inside, that grows to 4 m (12 ft) tall. More fragrant and willing to bloom intermittently from spring until late fall is salmon-flowered L. × *heckrottii* 'Goldflame' (Z5), which grows 3.5 m (12 ft) long and is a top performer for porch pillars. Heavy-blooming and highly fragrant, cultivars of L. *periclymenum* (Z4) will bloom repeatedly with proper care. Look for the 9 m (30 ft) long, yellow-flowered 'Graham Thomas' or the 4.5 m (15 ft) long, red-and-white 'Serotina'.

Growing Honeysuckle

Plant honeysuckles in spring, but where winters are mild you can also set them out in the fall. Honeysuckle thrives where its roots are shaded, but the vines can climb into sunlight.

Loosen the soil to a depth of 45 cm (18 in) and work in an 8 cm (3 in) layer of organic matter, such as composted manure. Set plants at the same depth at which they grew in their containers and cut them back to 30 cm (12 in) to encourage branching. Water as needed to keep the soil barely moist for the first growing season and mulch with a 5 cm (2 in) layer of shredded bark, dried leaves, or pine needles to help keep the soil around the roots cool and moist.

Fertilize established vines each spring with an all-purpose controlled-release fertilizer according to label directions. To encourage reblooming, drench the roots in midsummer with a balanced-formula liquid fertilizer as directed on the label.

Remove older shoots in spring. Spring pruning encourages later flowering. If earlier flowering is desired, wait to prune until after the plants bloom in late spring or early summer. With reblooming cultivars, prune plants lightly after any flush of flowers to help force out new growth. These vigorous vines are rarely if ever bothered by either pests or diseases.

FUNDAMENTAL FACTS

ATTRIBUTES	Fragrant, trumpet-shaped flowers in red, yellow, white, pink; for trellises
SEASON OF INTEREST	Spring to fall
TYPE OF VINE	Deciduous or evergreen perennial; climbs by twining
FAVORITES	L. × *heckrottii* 'Goldflame', L. *periclymenum* 'Serotina'
QUIRKS	Reblooming depends on pruning and culture
GOOD NEIGHBORS	Makes a good background for sun-loving perennials
WHERE IT GROWS BEST	Sites where roots are in shade and the foliage is in partial shade or sun
POTENTIAL PROBLEMS	Neglected vines may overgrow their supports
RENEWING PLANTS	Vines live many years; prune back hard in midsummer or early spring
CRITTER RESISTANCE	Excellent
SOURCE	Bedding plants
DIMENSIONS	3–14 m (10–45 ft) long

The orange-red flowers of *L. sempervirens* are especially inviting to hummingbirds.

HOPS
Humulus spp.

HARDINESS:
Zone 4 unless otherwise indicated

PREFERRED SOIL pH:
Near neutral

PREFERRED SOIL TYPE:
Fertile, well-drained

PREFERRED LIGHT:
Partial shade to sun

Hops in the Landscape

Humulus lupulus is the vine whose fruits are used in making beer. While the species holds little interest in the garden, the gold-leaved cultivar 'Aureus' is a striking accent for partial shade. Established plants send their twining shoots climbing 4.5 m (15 ft) in a single season, even in cold climates where frosts cut the stems to the ground in winter. Fragrant flowers

H. lupulus 'Aureus' is a golden accent that mixes well with pink and purple flowers.

appear in midsummer, enlarging to form 2.5–5 cm (1–2 in) long, greenish white, papery cones, or "hops," that mature to brown color. They make lovely cut flowers and have a fresh, woodsy smell.

The female flowers enlarge into papery, pale green cones that can be used in making beer.

Another garden-worthy variety is the variegated Japanese hop (*H. japonicus* 'Variegatus' [Z5]). With lobed green leaves streaked in white, it is a perennial often grown as an annual that reaches 7.5 m (25 ft) long. Use either vine to camouflage buildings or grow it anywhere a vigorous vine is wanted. Hops can be interplanted with other flowering vines, such as annual morning glory or cardinal climber for a dense screen with colorful accents.

Growing Hop Vines

Sow seeds in spring directly in the garden. Or start seeds indoors 6 weeks before your last frost, sowing them over moist soil and pressing them in lightly. Keep the soil evenly moist and at about 21°C (70°F) until the vines are established. Then plant them outdoors after danger of frost has passed.

Set out container-grown vines in spring. Choose a site with partial shade, because the leaves have the best color when they receive some shade in summer. Before planting, have a support in place that can hold this big vine. A sturdy wooden trellis, an arbor, or a well-secured piece of landscape netting tacked to a wall will do. Prepare a planting hole enriched with compost, and set the plant at the same depth at which it grew in the pot.

Gently train by winding young stems around the support. To prevent wilting, water as needed, which may be twice a week in hot weather. In winter, trim off dead shoots. To identify live stems, gently scrape the bark with your thumbnail. Live shoots are green beneath the bark; dead shoots will be brown and brittle. In early spring, fertilize with a balanced granular fertilizer as directed on the label.

While hops are largely trouble free, Japanese beetles will chew the leaves. The beetles prefer feeding in

FUNDAMENTAL FACTS

ATTRIBUTES	Vigorous vine with lobed foliage and fragrant flowers; for trellises
SEASON OF INTEREST	Spring to fall
TYPE OF VINE	Herbaceous perennial; climbs by twining around a support
FAVORITES	Gold-leaved *H. lupulus* 'Aureus', variegated *H. japonicus* 'Variegata'
QUIRKS	Can be slow to establish its first year
GOOD NEIGHBORS	Cardinal climber, morning glory, orange- or red-flowered perennials
WHERE IT GROWS BEST	Light shade with fertile, moist, well-drained soil
POTENTIAL PROBLEMS	Japanese beetles
RENEWING PLANTS	*H. lupulus* lives more than 5 years; cut back to the ground in fall
CRITTER RESISTANCE	Excellent except for Japanese beetles
SOURCE	Bedding plants
DIMENSIONS	Twining up to 7.5 m (25 ft)

full sun, so planting hops in partial shade is a deterrent. A small, shiny flea beetle can also feed on the foliage, eating small holes and giving the appearance of being peppered with buckshots. While unsightly, it does not weaken these vigorous vines.

Increasing the Bounty

Take cuttings in midsummer, taking shoots with 5–7 pairs of leaves. Remove foliage from the lower half of the shoot, dip the cut tip in commercial rooting powder, and insert the leafless portion of shoot into a damp mixture of sand and peat moss. Shoots will also root in a vase of water. When the cutting develops new growth it can be planted in the garden.

HYACINTH BEAN

Lablab purpureus

HARDINESS:
Tender

PREFERRED SOIL pH:
Acid

PREFERRED SOIL TYPE:
Fertile, moist

PREFERRED LIGHT:
Sun

The shiny seedpods, in a deep red-violet, accent the maroon-tinged leaves.

Hyacinth Bean in the Landscape

A fast-growing vine with handsome foliage, flowers, and seedpods, hyacinth bean is grown as a food plant in India, where both the young pods and the fresh seeds are eaten. In this country, hyacinth bean is usually grown for its good looks, particularly in areas where summers are hot. 'Giganteus' is a cultivar with exceptionally large white flowers; 'Ruby Moon' has lilac-colored flowers. This energetic climber is clad in large, segmented reddish leaves that make an attractive

Hyacinth bean vine grows to 5.5 m (18 ft) in a season, cladding its support in rich color.

display throughout the growing season. By midsummer, the ornamental leaves are accented by clusters of fragrant purple or white flowers resembling those of sweet pea. After the blossoms fade, they are followed by large, flat, red-violet seedpods as shiny as patent leather. New flowers open, and beans form until summer's end.

Hyacinth bean is a vigorous vine that is able to climb several different types of trellises. The twining vines will wind themselves through chain-link fencing, scramble over a tripod of poles, or turn strings or bird netting into a lush green screen. They can even climb up the stalks of tall sunflowers or any other sturdy neighbor tall enough to shoulder a vine that tops out somewhere between 3–5.5 m (10–18 ft). Shrubs and small trees are particularly suitable for the job.

Growing Hyacinth Bean

Hyacinth bean is easy to raise from seed. Where the growing season is short, start seeds indoors a month before the last frost. Soak the seeds overnight in warm water. Plant one

seed to each 10 cm (4 in) pot of moistened potting soil, barely covering the seeds with soil. Place the pots on a sunny windowsill, and keep the soil moist and at room temperature until the seedlings are sturdy and it is warm enough to plant them outdoors in the garden.

Seeds can also be sown directly in the garden when the soil warms. Loosen the soil and dig in a 5 cm (4 in) thick layer of compost or leaf mold. Incorporate a low-nitrogen fertilizer, such as a 5-10-10 formula, according to package directions. Set the seeds 30 cm (12 in) apart and barely cover them with soil. Keep the soil constantly moist until the seedlings are sturdy.

When grown in warm temperatures and provided with water as needed to prevent wilting, hyacinth bean grows with lightning speed, rapidly twining as much as 5.5 m (18 ft) in length, so make sure the supports are already in place at planting time. Apply an 8 cm (3 in) thick mulch of chopped leaves or compost, and fertilize monthly with a granular

low-nitrogen fertilizer high in phosphorus and potash, such as 5-10-10, applied at half strength, to promote vigorous growth.

Care-free hyacinth beans have tiny sharp hairs on their leaves that effectively defend them from most insect pests, and disease problems, other than root rot when grown in soggy soil, are almost nonexistent. Rabbits may nibble young plants. If so, cover seedlings with pest-excluding floating row cover, a nonwoven fabric, or bird netting until mature leaves form.

After fall frosts kill the vines, pull them out of the garden and compost them. In mild winter climates, where hyacinth bean may live from year to year, it will benefit from occasional pruning to manage its shape and size.

FUNDAMENTAL FACTS

ATTRIBUTES	Reddish foliage; lilac or white flowers, red-violet pods; for trellises
SEASON OF INTEREST	Summer to frost; it is evergreen in warm-winter climates
TYPE OF VINE	Tender perennial; climbs by twining around its support
FAVORITES	'Giganteus' for large white flowers; 'Ruby Moon' for lilac flowers
QUIRKS	Grows poorly in soggy soil and cool summers
GOOD NEIGHBORS	Marigolds, petunias, salvia, shrubs, small trees, sunflowers
WHERE IT GROWS BEST	Sun in fertile, warm, moist soil
POTENTIAL PROBLEMS	Fatal root rot when grown in wet soil
RENEWING PLANTS	If evergreen, cut back in spring; otherwise reseed
CRITTER RESISTANCE	Good except for rabbits
SOURCE	Bedding plants
DIMENSIONS	To 5.5 m (18 ft) long

The flowers form in loose, lacy clusters, with larger florets dangling from the edges.

HYDRANGEA CLIMBING
Hydrangea petiolaris

This vine is breathtaking in bloom, brightening the garden with spots of snow white.

HARDINESS:
Zone 5

PREFERRED SOIL pH:
Acid

PREFERRED SOIL TYPE:
Fertile, moist

PREFERRED LIGHT:
Partial shade

Climbing Hydrangea in the Landscape

Gardeners with shady spots are fortunate, because they can grow climbing hydrangea, one of the loveliest and most care-free vines. This plant grows from shaggy-barked, woody stems clothed from spring to fall in glossy, dark green, heart-shaped leaves that turn a glowing golden yellow in fall. In summer, 20 cm (8 in) wide clusters of snowflake-shaped white flowers persist for several weeks.

Strong aerial rootlets help climbing hydrangea attach itself to trees, walls, or buildings. The rootlets will not harm masonry, but make sure there are no existing cracks where roots can invade. Because the thick vines and foliage retain moisture and can cause wooden walls to rot, put up a sturdy trellis 30 cm (1 ft) or more from a wooden wall to allow air to circulate behind the vine. And select a permanent site with plenty of room, as climbing hydrangea reaches a mature height of 20 m (65 ft).

Growing Climbing Hydrangea

Easy to plant and care for, climbing hydrangea will repay a good start. A site in full sun is acceptable in cool-summer climates, if the soil is moist. Partial shade is better in hot areas. This vine is a natural for a woodland garden where leaf litter creates a slightly acid soil pH. Alkaline soil causes leaves to yellow and keeps the vine from thriving. If your soil is alkaline, add garden sulphur according to the package label to create a slightly acidic soil pH before planting; test the soil annually and reapply as needed. Prepare a hole in spring, making it as deep as the vine's nursery container and twice as wide. Add a balanced, controlled-release fertilizer at the rate suggested on the package. Set the plant in, fill around it with soil, and water.

You'll need to help vines climb for the first year or two, until the aerial roots grab the support. For a masonry surface, pound in "rose nails," which have a soft metal head that you can bend around a stem to hold it to the support. Tie the stems to a trellis with soft twine. Water as needed to keep the soil moist during the growing season and apply an 8 cm (3 in) thick mulch of organic matter, such as chopped oak leaves, to retain moisture. This thick-leaved vine is virtually untroubled by either pests or diseases. Climbing hydrangea needs little pruning. At the limits of hardiness, it grows best on an east-facing wall.

Increasing the Bounty

Climbing hydrangea is easy to propagate from cuttings. Early in the growing season, take 15 cm (6 in) long tip cuttings from unwanted branches that are not attached to a support. Remove leaves from the bottom half of the cuttings and insert each halfway into moist sand or a well-drained potting soil. Keep the soil moist and set the cuttings in a shady site. Move the pots into a cold frame or to a room that remains above freezing through the winter. The following spring, plant the cuttings outdoors where they are to grow.

FUNDAMENTAL FACTS	
ATTRIBUTES	Deep green foliage and lacy white flower clusters; for walls, buildings, trees
SEASON OF INTEREST	Year-round
TYPE OF VINE	Deciduous woody perennial; climbs by clinging with aerial rootlets
FAVORITES	*H. petiolaris*
QUIRKS	May not bloom for several seasons after planting; needs early training
GOOD NEIGHBORS	Rhododendron, azalea, perennial geranium, iris, ornamental grasses
WHERE IT GROWS BEST	Partial shade in acid soil high in organic matter
POTENTIAL PROBLEMS	Yellowing leaves when grown in alkaline soil
RENEWING PLANTS	Vines live many years without rejuvenation
CRITTER RESISTANCE	Excellent
SOURCE	Bedding plants
DIMENSIONS	Up to 20 m (65 ft) long

Morning glories form trumpet-shaped blossoms that open each morning and close at noon.

'Heavenly Blue', an old-fashioned variety, features sky blue flowers with white centers.

MORNING GLORY

Ipomoea spp.

HARDINESS:
Tender

PREFERRED SOIL pH:
Neutral

PREFERRED SOIL TYPE:
Average to poor

PREFERRED LIGHT:
Sun

Morning Glory in the Landscape

Morning glory has been a favorite in the summer garden since the 1930s, when *Ipomoea tricolor* 'Heavenly Blue', with its sky blue, trumpet-shaped flowers, came on the market. This early-flowering beauty opened the way for hybrids with 8 cm (3 in) wide blossoms in a rainbow of colors, such as white 'Pearly Gates', purple 'Grandpa Ott's', rose 'Scarlett O'Hara', and red 'Crimson Rambler'. Morning glories are named for the fact that the flowers open in early morning and close by noon, with new buds opening daily. Newer cultivars have been bred to stay open longer.

Grow these vines on a trellis or fence, or let them twine around strings stretched from the ground to the edge of a porch roof. Few other vines work as well as morning glories for disguising a chain-link fence.

All in the Family

Moonflower (*I. alba*) is grown for its large, sweet-scented, white flowers, which unfurl at dusk to reveal saucerlike, 15 cm (6 in) wide blossoms. This rapid grower can climb to 3 m (10 ft) in a growing season and reach 12 m (40 ft) in frost-free areas.

Japanese morning glories (*I. × imperialis*) climb to only 1–1.2 m (3–4 ft). They have funnel-shaped flowers up to 15 cm (6 in) across in a lovely range of colors from pale pink to deep maroon, often with a white edging. Many varieties also have leaves variegated with white flecks and splashes. They're easy to grow and particularly stunning when combined with flowering annuals in containers.

Growing Morning Glory

Morning glories are easy to raise from seeds planted in garden soil after the last frost has passed. To improve sprouting, scratch through the hard covering, or seed coat, which helps the seeds soak up water. Rub the large seeds over coarse sandpaper or nick them with a nail file, just until you see flecks of white beneath the dark seed coat. Drop the seeds into a cup of tepid water and soak them overnight. In the morning, drain and plant the seeds according to packet directions.

Grow morning glories in sun and warm soil of average to poor fertility. Growing them in rich soil or feeding heavily while growing results in excessive foliage and few flowers. Space seeds 8 cm (3 in) apart and cover them with 1.5 cm (1/2 in) of soil. Keep the soil moist until plants are up and growing. Thin seedlings to 25 cm (10 in) apart when they are 10 cm (4 in) tall and fertilize them once with a balanced fertilizer, such as 10-10-10, as directed on the package.

Mostly care-free, this vine can be chewed by night-flying beetles, which cause temporary cosmetic damage. Day-feeding Japanese beetles are more serious. Pick them off early in the morning, when they are sluggish, or control them with a botanical insecticide as directed on the label.

FUNDAMENTAL FACTS

ATTRIBUTES	Fast-growing foliage, and trumpet-shaped flowers; for trellises, fences
SEASON OF INTEREST	Summer
TYPE OF VINE	Annual or tender perennial; climbs by twining
FAVORITES	'Heavenly Blue', 'Scarlett O'Hara', 'Pearly Gates'; *I. alba*, *I. × imperialis*
QUIRKS	Flowers open in the morning and close by midafternoon
GOOD NEIGHBORS	Makes a good background for flowering annuals and perennials
WHERE IT GROWS BEST	Sun and well-drained, average to poor soil
POTENTIAL PROBLEMS	Beetles, blooms poorly when grown in shade
RENEWING PLANTS	Sow seeds in spring
CRITTER RESISTANCE	Good
SOURCE	Seeds
DIMENSIONS	1–4.5 m (3–15 ft) long

ROSE CLIMBING
Rosa spp.

HARDINESS:
Zone 6

PREFERRED SOIL pH:
Neutral to slightly acid

PREFERRED SOIL TYPE:
Average, well-drained

PREFERRED LIGHT:
Sun

Climbing Rose in the Landscape

Climbing roses lend a romantic touch to any garden. Many different roses of mixed ancestry are called climbers, and all tend to bloom heavily in early summer on long canes that grew the season before. Modern hybrids often rebloom in fall when given good care.

Climbing roses need a sturdy trellis, wall, or arbor to shoulder their weighty canes. At the bases of these beauties you can plant small daffodils or other spring-flowering bulbs. But plant larger companions far enough away to let air circulate around the canes, discouraging fungal infections.

The extremely hardy 'Zéphirine Drouhin' is a thornless climber with fragrant pink roses.

'Blaze' is a prolific bloomer, producing red flowers for most of the growing season.

The cool blue flowers of catmint are a classic companion for roses, as is clematis, which discreetly intertwines with rose canes and blooms in midsummer, when rose flowers fade.

Fine Climbers

Visit display gardens in your area to see locally adapted cultivars. Pink-flowered 'America' and 'New Dawn', red 'Blaze', and yellow 'Golden Showers' are all modern classics, but some older cultivars, such as the fragrant, pink, thornless 'Zéphirine Drouhin' and the red 'Dortmund', are worth seeking out. In cold climates, grow the climbing Explorer Series roses, which will survive to Zone 3 without winter protection. Look for pale pink 'John Davis', mid-pink 'Louis Jolliet', or red 'Henry Kelsey'.

Growing Climbing Rose

Plant climbing roses in spring, just as they are emerging from dormancy. Dig a planting hole 45 cm (18 in) wide and deep and mix in an 8 cm (3 in) deep layer of compost or other organic matter. Plant container-grown roses that are growing on their own roots at the same depth at which they grew in their container. Plant grafted roses, which have a knobby lump called a graft union at the bottom of the primary cane, by setting the graft union 5–10 cm (2–4 in) below soil level if you live in cold areas; the colder the zone, the deeper the graft union should go.

When planting a bare-root rose, such as those from mail-order nurseries, build a cone of soil in the hole, making the cone tall enough to allow the graft union to be placed as described above. Carefully spread the roots over the cone and cover with soil. After planting either type, water well and keep the soil barely moist the first season. Spread an 8 cm (3 in) thick mulch of compost to retain soil moisture and act as a barrier to prevent soil-borne fungal-disease spores from splashing onto foliage.

Prune climbing roses to enhance sun exposure on new growth while eliminating old branches, which are at risk for developing disease. After the first year, prune back old canes after they bloom, but don't be too aggressive with reblooming cultivars. Cut canes just above a leaf with 5, never 3, leaflets and cut at a 45° angle so that rainwater will run off, and not rot the cut ends. Flower buds will develop on the canes at these points.

Climbing roses do not actually climb but lean on their support, so tie the canes to the support with a soft, stretchy material, such as old pantyhose. Fertilize climbing roses in the spring and again in midsummer, using a rose fertilizer at the rate given on the package label. In Zone 5, mound 30–45 cm (12–18 in) of soil or rotted manure over the base of the rose in early winter to insulate it, and remove the material in spring.

The same diseases that plague other roses can weaken climbers. To deter leaf-disfiguring fungal diseases, such as powdery mildew and blackspot, choose a sunny location with good air circulation. To water, use soaker hoses with the holes pointing down rather than the oscillating type of sprinkler, to reduce the spread of blackspot. Japanese beetles are serious pests. Use a botanical insecticide on plants. Roses attract deer. Tuck bars of deodorant-formula bath soap among canes to deter them or apply a commercial repellent according to label directions.

FUNDAMENTAL FACTS

ATTRIBUTES	Stately plants with red, pink, yellow, or white flowers; for trellises
SEASON OF INTEREST	Late spring to early summer, often with repeat bloom in late summer
TYPE OF VINE	Deciduous, long-limbed shrub grown as climber
FAVORITES	'Golden Showers', 'Blaze', 'America', 'Dortmund', 'John Davis'
QUIRKS	Canes don't actually climb, and must be tied to a support
GOOD NEIGHBORS	Catmint, clematis, daffodils and other bulbs, perennials
WHERE IT GROWS BEST	Fertile, well-drained sites in sun
POTENTIAL PROBLEMS	Blackspot, powdery mildew; Japanese beetles
RENEWING PLANTS	Lives many years; prune annually to maintain plant health and size
CRITTER RESISTANCE	Good except for deer
SOURCE	Nursery plants
DIMENSIONS	2–6 m (7–20 ft) tall, 1.2–3 m (4–10 ft) wide

Scarlet runner beans climb quickly, making an ornamental screen for the vegetable garden.

SCARLET RUNNER BEAN

Phaseolus coccineus

HARDINESS:
Tender

PREFERRED SOIL pH:
Neutral to slightly alkaline

PREFERRED SOIL TYPE:
Average, well-drained

PREFERRED LIGHT:
Sun

Varieties such as 'Painted Lady' have bicolored blossoms, creating a softer look.

Scarlet Runner Bean in the Landscape

With scarlet runner bean, you can have your ornamental vine and eat it, too. This vine produces colorful flowers followed by edible green snap beans, and the more beans you pick, the more flowers the vine will produce. Grow scarlet runner beans on a fence to bring a decorative touch to the vegetable garden, or give them a string trellis and let them become temporary summer sunscreens for porches or decks. Or create a tepee of bamboo poles and train scarlet runner beans into a summer playhouse for young children. You can even push a tripod of thin stakes into a large container for a portable plant show. And as a bonus, you can expect to attract the interest of hummingbirds when scarlet runners begin to bloom.

Variations in Red

Loose clusters of deep orange-red flowers give this vine its common name, but several cultivars offer slightly different variations on the scarlet theme. 'Scarlet Emperor' is prized for both the flavor of its beans and the rich color of its blossoms, which appear along 1.8 m (6 ft) vines. Grown since Colonial times, 'Painted Lady' bears bicolored red-and-white blossoms on 2.4 m (8 ft) vines. A pure white-flowered version, 'Albus', is also available from some mail-order nurseries that carry heirloom varieties. A newer variety, the 55 cm (22 in) tall 'Dwarf Bees', is a scarlet runner in compact bush form that's ideal for pots or baskets.

Growing Scarlet Runner Bean

Like other beans, scarlet runner bean vines grow best in warm, well-drained soil. Wait until after the last spring frost before planting. Sow the large seeds in pairs in the garden, spacing each pair 15–20 cm (6–8 in) away from the next pair. Plant the seeds 2.5 cm (1 in) deep and about 8 cm (3 in) away from their support, whether poles, a wire fence, or strings attached to a porch roof. After they grow upward for 45 cm (18 in) or so, the vines may be trained horizontally, if desired, onto a lower fence, a stump, or other support.

In cold climates you may want to start seed indoors in spring to give young plants a head start. Don't rush, because the seedlings will grow very quickly and be ready to transplant within 3 weeks of sowing. Plant 2 seeds to a 10 cm (4 in) pot, and snip off the weaker one when the seedlings sprout. When transplanting, disturb the roots as little as possible.

Soils that are high in nitrogen can result in very leafy vines and few flowers, so be somewhat stingy when it comes to using fertilizer. Allow some of the broad, flat pods to mature to a mahogany color, then dry, shell, and save the seeds for planting next year.

Four-footed pests like rabbits, woodchucks, and deer relish these vines. The best defense is growing them inside a fence, patrolling the garden with a dog, or applying a commercial repellent as per label.

The blossoms resemble the flowers of peas and are usually colored a vivid orange-red.

FUNDAMENTAL FACTS

ATTRIBUTES	Fast grower with scarlet blooms, edible beans; for fences, trellises, pots
SEASON OF INTEREST	Summer
TYPE OF VINE	Tender perennial; climbs by twining
FAVORITES	'Scarlet Emperor', 'Painted Lady', 'Albus', 'Dwarf Bees'
QUIRKS	May temporarily stop blooming in very hot weather
GOOD NEIGHBORS	Blue-flowered ageratum, white begonia, white sweet alyssum
WHERE IT GROWS BEST	In sun and moderately fertile soil
POTENTIAL PROBLEMS	Seeds will rot if planted in cold, wet soil
RENEWING PLANTS	Grown as an annual; sow seed in spring
CRITTER RESISTANCE	Poor; plants vulnerable to rabbits, deer, and woodchucks
SOURCE	Seeds
DIMENSIONS	0.6–4 m (2–12 ft); pods to 30 cm (12 in)

Sweet peas bloom with winged flowers that range in color from pastels to jewel tones.

SWEET PEA

Lathyrus odoratus

HARDINESS:
Tender

PREFERRED SOIL pH:
Near neutral

PREFERRED SOIL TYPE:
Fertile, moist

PREFERRED LIGHT:
Sun to partial shade

Sweet Pea in the Landscape

Popular for centuries as fragrant cut flowers as well as sumptuous garden vines, sweet pea vines bear elegant pocketbook-shaped blossoms in colors including white, yellow, pink, red, purple, and blue, and bicolors. Old-fashioned types, such as Old Spice hybrids, have the headiest perfume but usually fewer and smaller blossoms. Modern types boast long wands of fluttery flowers in luminous shades but aren't as aromatic as old varieties. Most grow 1.2–1.8 m (4–6 ft) tall and usually have stiff, upright stems if given the support of a string or net trellis. There are also bush varieties sufficiently compact to use at the garden's edge or in containers.

Sweet peas require cool weather, and young plants are surprisingly hardy.

All in the Family

While regular sweet peas grow and flower poorly in hot weather, the perennial pea (*Lathyrus latifolius*) can take the heat. This vigorous vine, which grows to 3 m (10 ft), produces pink or white blossoms that resemble sweet peas but do not have their scent. Perennial sweet peas are dependably hardy to Zone 4 and flower through the hottest summers. Spring vetchling (*L. vernus* [Z4]) is a non-climbing, mound-shaped plant with mauve to pink flowers in early spring. It needs a semi-shaded location where it is protected from the fierce heat of summer.

Growing Sweet Pea

Soak seeds overnight in water and plant them 5 cm (2 in) deep in cool garden soil that has been deeply dug and amended with organic matter, such as compost. Time planting to take advantage of cool weather. Plant as soon as the soil can be worked in cool regions. Cold-climate gardeners can also jump-start the season by sowing seeds indoors in late winter, using individual peat pots. Keep the soil barely moist and grow the seedlings on a sunny, cool windowsill. Transplant them into the garden 2 weeks before your last frost date, after hardening off. Handle seedlings gently, planting peat pot and all, and disturb the roots as little as possible. Be sure to completely bury the peat pots or they evaporate water from below soil level.

Mulch the soil around the roots with an 8 cm (3 in) thick layer of chopped dried leaves, straw, or shredded bark to keep the roots cool and moist. Install a trellis early on and help the young plants find the support if their own search falters.

Pick off spent flowers to encourage continued flowering. If you see the small, pear-shaped, sap-sucking insects known as aphids clustered on the leaf undersides of new growth, knock them off the plant with a forceful spray of water. Or apply insecticidal soap according to the package directions. Four-footed pests, including deer, rabbits, and woodchucks, nibble sweet peas. Fencing them is the best defense, but applications of a commercial repellent used as directed on the label is somewhat effective.

FUNDAMENTAL FACTS

ATTRIBUTES	Delicate foliage; dainty, fragrant flowers; for trellises, cut flowers
SEASON OF INTEREST	Spring to summer
TYPE OF VINE	Tender annual; climbs by clinging with tendrils
FAVORITES	'Winter Elegance' for hot climates; Old Spice hybrids for fragrance
QUIRKS	Sweet peas expire in hot weather and fail to thrive in dry soil
GOOD NEIGHBORS	Lobelia, pansies, or sweet alyssum
WHERE IT GROWS BEST	Areas with mild winters, cool springs, or consistently cool summer nights
POTENTIAL PROBLEMS	Heat stress, aphids
RENEWING PLANTS	Reseed each year
CRITTER RESISTANCE	Poor; shoots vulnerable to deer, rabbits, and woodchucks
SOURCE	Seeds
DIMENSIONS	Annual 1.2–1.8 m (4–6 ft); perennial 3 m (10 ft)

Sweet peas prefer cool weather, mixing well with early spring bloomers such as pansies.

TRUMPET VINE

Campsis radicans

HARDINESS:
Zone 5 unless otherwise indicated

PREFERRED SOIL pH:
Neutral to slightly acid

PREFERRED SOIL TYPE:
Average

PREFERRED LIGHT:
Sun to partial shade

C. radicans 'Flava' has buttery blooms that combine well with other garden flowers.

'Madame Galen' is a dependable hybrid with deep apricot blossoms veined in red.

Trumpet Vine in the Landscape

This care-free woody perennial vine needs room to romp. A spirited North American native, trumpet vine willingly covers everything from stumps to brick walls. It cascades over a steep bank, swarms up tall trees, and scrambles over a masonry shed or garage roof with ease, but you can also discipline it with pruning shears and use it to cover a pergola. However, because this vine fastens itself to its support with aerial rootlets, it is not a good choice for growing on wooden buildings, where it can hold moisture against the wood, inviting rot. Both hummingbirds and humans enjoy trumpet vine's clusters of orange-red funnel-shaped flowers, which bedeck the roaming branches of this vine from midsummer into autumn. New leaves mature to a glossy green color before turning yellow in the fall.

All in the Family

Often seen growing in woodlands of the Southeast, trumpet vine makes a fine addition to any garden that has ample room to support its ambitious size, which can top out at 9 m (30 ft). A lovely yellow-flowered cultivar, 'Flava', is often available at nurseries, and its soft color is easy to combine with other garden flowers.

Cultivars of the hybrid *C. × tagliabuana* (Z6) are shrubbier and more compact in habit and offer larger flowers produced over a longer period than the species. Two excellent choices are 'Madame Galen', with dark apricot flowers veined with red, and bright red-flowered 'Coccinea'.

The showiest member of the family is Chinese trumpet vine (*C. grandiflora*). Hardy to Zone 8, it has large, loose clusters of flowers, each opening to about 8 cm (3 in) wide in late summer. Chinese trumpet vine is an excellent cover for a wooden pillar or a rustic fence, although its stems, which are heavy when flowering, may need to be tied to a support.

Growing Trumpet Vine

Spring is generally the best time to plant trumpet vine. Choose a site that gets at least a half day of sun, because sun leads to ambitious flowering. Take the time to amend the planting hole with an 8–10 cm (3–4 in) layer of compost, dried manure, or leaf mold.

Young vines often need assistance, so tie them to a string to help them to begin their first season's climb. Once they attach to a support, they quickly take off. The vines tend to produce suckers, which are shoots that can emerge from roots several feet from the main plant. Remove them with a sharp spade to control the size of the planting. You can plant the suckers in a new location, if desired. The plants may also shed seeds, but mowing usually keeps both suckers and seedlings in bounds.

Prune established vines in late winter or early spring to control their size. It does no harm to let branches run into trees. Overgrown vines may be cut back to within a few centimeters (inches) of the soil in late winter; leave only 2–3 buds on the stem. Trumpet vines rarely need fertilization and are naturally free of pests and diseases.

FUNDAMENTAL FACTS

ATTRIBUTES	Trumpet-shaped flowers in yellow or red; for trellises, pillars, walls
SEASON OF INTEREST	Spring to fall
TYPE OF VINE	Woody perennial; climbs by clinging with aerial rootlets
FAVORITES	C. radicans 'Flava'; 'Madame Galen', 'Coccinea'; C. grandiflora
QUIRKS	With age, can become top-heavy, with bare stems at the base
GOOD NEIGHBORS	Blanket flower, butter daisy, coreopsis
WHERE IT GROWS BEST	At the edge of wooded areas or in a partly shaded garden
POTENTIAL PROBLEMS	Suckers can become invasive if not controlled
RENEWING PLANTS	Lives many years; prune overgrown vines in late winter to 2–3 buds
CRITTER RESISTANCE	Excellent
SOURCE	Nursery plants
DIMENSIONS	To 9 m (30 ft)

Trumpet vine, also known as trumpet creeper, is a robust vine that thrives in partial shade.

Japanese wisteria is a free-flowering vine that engulfs an arbor with color and fragrance.

WISTERIA

Wisteria spp.

HARDINESS:
Zone 6 unless otherwise indicated

PREFERRED SOIL pH:
Slightly acid

PREFERRED SOIL TYPE:
Average

PREFERRED LIGHT:
Sun

Wisteria in the Landscape

This hardy vine has it all: statuesque woody stems, feathery leaflets, and long clusters of fragrant lilac, pink, or white pea-shaped flowers in spring. Give this heavy vine something substantial to ramble over, such as a 2.5 m (8 ft) tall arbor held aloft on stout posts. Or let it scramble into large trees, as it does in the wild. Where space is limited, you can still enjoy wisteria by pruning it into an umbrella shape on a single treelike trunk, a form called a standard.

All in the Family

Japanese wisteria (*Wisteria floribunda*) produces the best show of flowers and is available with blue, pink, or white flowers. Once Japanese wisterias are old enough to bloom, pruning is

American wisteria blooms in midspring producing short, dense, lilac flower clusters.

needed to control their exuberant growth. Wait 2–4 weeks after flowering and then cut side branches back hard, to within 3–6 buds of the main trunk. A second pruning, in late winter, may also be necessary. If flowering is poor, give this winter pruning by shortening new shoots back to 2–3 buds.

American wisteria (*W. frutescens*) is less vigorous than Japanese wisteria and better suited to small gardens. Its cultivar 'Magnifica' has blue flowers; 'Nivea' has white flowers. Because this species flowers on new wood, prune established vines heavily in winter. The show begins in midspring and is followed by a growth spurt and a second flush of bloom in early summer, and possibly a third in late summer.

An excellent alternative, Kentucky wisteria (*W. macrostachya* [Z7]) produces lilac purple flowers on new growth in early summer and is best pruned in winter.

Chinese wisteria (*W. sinensis*) is a popular choice for gardens along the West Coast. It has shorter flower clusters than Japanese wisteria, and rather than opening gradually, the clusters pop open all at once, often with an explosion of fragrance. It blooms in late spring and can repeat in summer.

Growing Wisteria

Begin with wisteria grown from cuttings or grafted plants, which will flower in a couple of years. Plant in spring in deeply dug, well-drained soil enriched with organic matter. Beginning a year after planting, fertilize in spring with high-phosphorus fertilizer, such as a 5-10-5 formula. Wisterias are pest and disease free, and need little care other than irrigating as needed to keep the soil moist while vines are flowering. If your wisteria refuses to bloom and it's still

W. floribunda 'Alba' drips with long, fragrant clusters of white flowers in late spring.

small enough to handle, digging it up and replanting it can sometimes trigger the vine to flower.

FUNDAMENTAL FACTS

ATTRIBUTES	Fragrant, drooping flower clusters; for trellises, arbors
SEASON OF INTEREST	Late spring to early summer
TYPE OF VINE	Hardy woody perennial; climbs by twining around a support
FAVORITES	*W. floribunda*, *W. frutescens*, *W. sinensis*
QUIRKS	Vines on some species twine clockwise, others twine counterclockwise
GOOD NEIGHBORS	Wisteria is best grown as a specimen plant
WHERE IT GROWS BEST	In sun and slightly acid, well-drained soil
POTENTIAL PROBLEMS	Vines can grow out of control or bloom poorly if not pruned regularly
RENEWING PLANTS	Lives for decades; prune back overgrown vines with a saw
CRITTER RESISTANCE	Excellent
SOURCE	Nursery plants
DIMENSIONS	Vines 9 m (30 ft) long; clusters 0.6 m (2 ft) long

CARE-FREE BULBS

Bulbs are a cinch to grow because Mother Nature does most of the work. Daffodils, tulips, and many others store food reserves from year to year in weighty roots, making them very adaptable. Only true bulbs have a special type of storage root that makes them different from similar-growing plants with underground storage parts called tubers, corms, or rhizomes. But to the gardener these differences are of little consequence. What's important, and more fun, is stocking your landscape with "bulbs" for all seasons.

Bulbs are often grouped according to flowering time. Spring-flowering bulbs are usually very cold hardy, and include daffodils, tulips, hyacinths, and small species, such as crocus and squill. They are usually planted in the fall, and although they do not show green tips or flower buds until spring, they need a long start because they need a period of cold before they will start to grow. Some bulbs, especially daffodils, make considerable root growth in late fall and, if not planted until the soil is cold, may not flower at all. Summer-flowering bulbs, such as alstroemerias, gladiolus, and cannas are not tolerant of cold, and many need to be dug and stored indoors over winter in cold areas, or grown as annuals.

Except for cannas, calla lilies, some irises, and a few others, bulbs grow poorly in wet soil, so choose a site with good soil drainage. Some bulbs are so bumpy or oddly shaped that it's difficult to tell which side is up, but don't worry. Even bulbs planted upside-down send their shoots up and roots down. Many bulbs have a dormant period, so remember to let the leaves yellow and die back naturally to allow time for them to store nutrients for the next year.

Study each entry of this section to find out if a particular bulb will thrive in your garden. Then combine it with other plants having similar needs, and the results will be a personal palette of care-free plants for your garden.

Alstroemeria have freckled blooms mostly in yellow or orange, but also in softer colors.

ALSTROEMERIA

Alstroemeria spp. and hybrids

HARDINESS:
Zone 7

PREFERRED SOIL pH:
Slightly acid

PREFERRED SOIL TYPE:
Well-drained

PREFERRED LIGHT:
Sun to partial shade

Alstroemeria in the Landscape

Most gardeners meet alstroemeria for the first time in restaurants, where the cut flowers are frequently used as table ornaments. Because the freckled tubular blossoms can last more than 2 weeks in a vase, alstroemerias are often the flower of choice in public places and are included in many florists' bouquets. Also known as Peruvian lilies, these beauties have been grown little outside of very

Alstroemeria look like miniature lilies, and combine well with flowering perennials.

warm climates, as most older cultivars suffered badly from cold winters and were too tall and rangy to make good container plants. In the last few years, however, both of these limitations have been overcome. New varieties, such as the yellow-flowered 'Sweet Laura', are hardy enough to survive in Zone 7, and compact versions, such as Meyer's Hybrids and 'Compact Red' fit in roomy pots or small raised beds.

When planted in the garden, alstroemerias grow 75 cm (30 in) tall, with the bulk of the flowers rising on thin, sturdy stems in early summer. The alstroemerias that grow well in a wide range of climates have flowers that are either yellow or deep orange, though it is possible to find varieties with purple, white, lavender, or pink flowers. Alstroemeria leaves are narrow, slightly twisted, and usually medium green. When grown near perennials that like similar growing conditions, such as gypsophila or lavender, alstroemerias can become garden standouts.

Alstroemeria Basics

Alstroemeria is a member of the lily family, and its trumpetlike blossoms do resemble those of the lily. However, rather than growing from true bulbs, alstroemerias grow from thick, brittle roots. In the garden the roots spread outward, forming colonies. If left untended the plants can become weedy looking, but this is easily avoided by clipping off old flowers and foliage in midsummer. This grooming is really the only maintenance that alstroemerias require.

Like other lilies, alstroemerias need excellent drainage. Plant in deep, loamy soil that holds moisture well in spring and early summer and dries out almost completely in the fall. If your soil is heavy clay, it is best to grow these flowers in raised beds.

Growing Alstroemeria

Set out container-grown plants in fall, even though they may look ragged or dormant. Carefully set the fleshy roots in well-dug beds, covering them with 15 cm (6 in) of soil. The plants will not emerge until spring and may not bloom well until the following year. After alstroemerias are planted, it is best to leave them alone, because digging and dividing always reduces flowering for at least a year, and the brittle roots are easily damaged.

After the first hard freeze of autumn, pile a fluffy, insulating mulch, such as evergreen boughs or straw, over alstroemerias at least 10 cm (4 in) deep. As long as the soil does not freeze hard to the depth at which the roots are planted, the plants will endure a cold winter. Cold injury caused by shallow planting or prolonged freezing is the main problem you are likely to have with these durable plants. They are otherwise untroubled by pests or diseases.

FUNDAMENTAL FACTS

ATTRIBUTES	Speckled lilylike blossoms in many colors; for beds, cutting, pots
SEASON OF INTEREST	Early summer
FAVORITES	Yellow-flowered 'Sweet Laura'; 'Compact Red'
QUIRKS	Foliage dies back after flowers fade
GOOD NEIGHBORS	Gypsophila, lavender, lilies
WHERE IT GROWS BEST	Widely adaptable to soils and sites with sun to partial shade
POTENTIAL PROBLEMS	Root injury in subfreezing winters
RENEWING PLANTS	Lives for years; dividing not recommended
CRITTER RESISTANCE	Good
PLANTING DEPTH	15–20 cm (6–8 in)
SOURCE	Bare root plants
DIMENSIONS	0.6–1.5 m (2–5 ft) tall, mature clumps often 1 m (3 ft) wide

Caladiums are grown for their large leaves, which are colorfully ribbed and spotted.

CALADIUM

Caladium bicolor

HARDINESS:
Tender

PREFERRED SOIL pH:
Slightly acid

PREFERRED SOIL TYPE:
Moist, well-drained

PREFERRED LIGHT:
Partial to full shade

Caladium in the Landscape

For a look of tropical luxuriance in the shade garden, nothing beats caladiums. Their large, heart-shaped leaves, splashed or veined with red, pink, white, and green, create a colorful rain-forest ambiance. Caladiums can be used to edge a path or encircle a birdbath and they mingle well with ferns, impatiens, or other shade-loving plants. You can easily create a container that's made for the shade by combining caladiums with upright or trailing annuals that thrive in low light, such as coleus and fuchsias. Choose caladiums in colors that complement their surroundings. 'Candidum', which boasts white leaves edged in green, lights up any shady spot and mixes with other plants. 'Freida Hempel', whose large red leaves are edged in green and ribbed in crimson, works better as an accent. Because caladiums are often sold in 10 cm (4 in) pots with a few leaves, it's easy to select them by color.

Smaller caladiums with elongated leaves are the best choice for containers. A favorite is 'Miss Muffet', a dwarf whose creamy white leaves are dotted with rose and edged in apple green. 'Rosalie', with carmine leaves edged in dull green, is another option.

Growing Caladium

Hailing from tropical South America, caladiums cannot survive conditions much below room temperature, and thrive in warm, humid conditions. They need a head start indoors in spring to get them up and growing. Most gardeners buy plants at garden centers, but you can buy the dormant tubers and start them in a warm indoor room. Plant the tubers, with the bumpy sides up, 5 cm (2 in) deep in sterile soilless planting mix. Keep the containers at a warm room temperature and keep the planting mix constantly moist.

Plant caladiums outdoors, spacing them 20–30 cm (8–12 in) apart, when night temperatures warm to 16°C (60°F). In summer, water as needed to keep the soil moist, and fertilize the plants every 2–3 weeks with a balanced soluble fertilizer, applied according to package directions. If the leaves develop holes and slimy trails, suspect slugs or snails. Control these night-feeding mollusks by setting out saucers of beer to lure and drown the pests. If the foliage is pale and stippled, sap-sucking spider mites may be feeding on leaf undersides. Rinse them off with water from a hose or apply insecticidal soap per label.

To save them overwinter, you need to stop watering a month before the first frost, so that the soil and tubers dry. Lift dry tubers before frost hits the plants. Remove leaves and air-dry the tubers for a few days. Store them through winter in a box or paper bag filled with dry peat moss kept at a temperature above 21°C (70°F). Check monthly, and if the tubers are beginning to shrivel, mist them with tepid water.

Increasing the Bounty

Where summers are long and warm enough for caladiums to develop large tubers, you can divide clumps in early spring and replant. In most areas of Canada, caladiums lose vigor each year, despite care, making them unsuitable to propagate.

FUNDAMENTAL FACTS

ATTRIBUTES	Large multicolored leaves in white, pink, red, and green; for beds, pots
SEASON OF INTEREST	Summer
FAVORITES	'Candidum', 'Freida Hempel', 'Miss Muffet', 'Rosalie'
QUIRKS	Flowers are insignificant and are usually removed
GOOD NEIGHBORS	Ferns, hosta, impatiens, coleus, fuchsia
WHERE IT GROWS BEST	Moist, fertile soil in partial shade
POTENTIAL PROBLEMS	Cold injury; spider mites, slugs and snails
RENEWING PLANTS	Lives several years; divide clumps of tubers in spring
CRITTER RESISTANCE	Excellent
PLANTING DEPTH	5 cm (2 in)
SOURCE	Tubers, bedding plants
DIMENSIONS	20–90 cm (8 in–3 ft) tall, to 60 cm (2 ft) wide; leaves 30 cm (12 in)

Caladiums, available in a dazzling array of colors, bring an exotic look to the landscape.

Shaped like softly rolled cornucopias, calla lily flowers are a stunning garden accent.

CALLA LILY

Zantedeschia spp.

HARDINESS:
Zone 9

PREFERRED SOIL pH:
Slightly acid

PREFERRED SOIL TYPE:
Fertile, moist

PREFERRED LIGHT:
Partial shade to sun

'Black-eyed Beauty' bears creamy white flowers marked in maroon at the throat.

Calla Lily in the Landscape

Famed for their elegant appearance, calla lilies can be a special indulgence in the summer garden. Shaped like softly rolled cornucopias, the flowers make a stunning accent when grown in either beds or containers. The large, deep green, arrow-shaped leaves are a graceful backdrop for a flower border. You can also accent a turning point in the garden by tucking a clump of calla lilies into the bend of a path. No matter where you grow them, these South African natives always make an impact. And, once they come into bloom in late summer, calla lilies also make superb cut flowers.

The traditional calla lily grows 1–1.2 m (3–4 ft) tall, with big creamy white flowers and large leaves that are often speckled with white. Modern hybrids are a more manageable size, with some reaching only 20–60 cm (8–24 in) in height, and blooming in soft yellow, peach, deep pink, or rose, often with a darker throat. Tuck a few into a shady border for a tropical look, use them in a pot, or, best of all, plant them in a damp place near a pond or stream, using them as a water-garden accent.

All in the Family

Zantedeschia aethiopica is the traditional calla lily, with 25 cm (10 in) long white flowers atop 1.2 m (4 ft) long stems. Its cultivar 'Green Goddess' has white flowers marked in green. *Z. albomaculata* also bears white flowers but is a smaller plant and boasts white-spotted, dark green leaves. *Z. rhemanii* grows to 30 cm (1 ft) and has small pink to rose flowers. *Z. elliottiana* is 60 cm (2 ft) tall and has white-spotted leaves and yellow blossoms.

Among varieties, seek fiery red-flowered 'Flame', peach 'Cameo', and 'Black-eyed Beauty', which has cream flowers with maroon throats.

Growing Calla Lily

Calla lilies are perennial and can grow outdoors year-round in Zone 9. But they are frost sensitive, so in colder climates wait until the weather is warm to plant them in the garden. Choose a site with fertile soil in partial shade or sun and set the rhizomes about 10 cm (4 in) deep and 30 cm (12 in) apart. Or get a head start by planting dormant tubers indoors a month before your last spring frost date, planting one per 15 cm (6 in) pot. Put the pots on a sunny windowsill and keep the soil evenly moist until new growth appears and it's warm enough to plant them outside.

Calla lilies love moisture, so surround them with moisture-retentive organic mulch, and water as needed to keep the soil from drying out. Fertilize them once a month with a water soluble, all-purpose balanced plant food. When cold weather approaches, withhold water so that the soil dries out and dig the tubers before the first frost, trimming away the leaves. Allow the tubers to air-dry for a few days and then store them in a paper bag filled with dry peat moss at about 10°–13°C (50°–55°F). Before planting in spring, divide clumps by breaking them apart into individual tubers.

Should leaves look pale and exhibit faint webbing, spider mites are the culprits. Knock them off the plants with a strong spray of cold water.

'Green Goddess' is elegantly subtle, with white blossoms flushed with green.

FUNDAMENTAL FACTS

ATTRIBUTES	Large, tropical-looking leaves and flowers; for pots, beds, cutting
SEASON OF INTEREST	Summer
FAVORITES	*Z. aethiopica* 'Green Goddess'; 'Black-eyed Beauty', 'Cameo', 'Flame'
QUIRKS	Thrives in wet soil
GOOD NEIGHBORS	Caladiums, ferns, hosta, impatiens, iris
WHERE IT GROWS BEST	Moist, fertile soil in partial shade
POTENTIAL PROBLEMS	Cold injury; spider mites
RENEWING PLANTS	Lives several years; divide large clumps by breaking tubers apart
CRITTER RESISTANCE	Excellent
PLANTING DEPTH	10 cm (4 in)
SOURCE	Tubers, nursery plants
DIMENSIONS	20–120 cm (8–48 in) tall, 35 cm (14 in) wide

'Rosamund Cole' produces large golden blossoms suffused with scarlet.

CANNA

Canna x generalis cvs.

HARDINESS:
Tender

PREFERRED SOIL pH:
Adaptable

PREFERRED SOIL TYPE:
Moist to wet

PREFERRED LIGHT:
Sun

Canna in the Landscape

These vibrantly flowered Victorian favorites are back by popular demand. Cannas' arrow-shaped upright leaves, up to 60 cm (2 ft) long, can be green, golden, or bronze or have multicolored stripes. Their crowning glory is their flamboyant, trumpet-shaped flowers in scarlet, yellow, salmon, or orange, which appear in midsummer. Cannas can grow in average garden soil, but because they prefer damp conditions, they are ideal for the edge of a pond or poorly drained spots. Few perennials can match cannas'

endurance in sultry summers. They are also striking plants for growing in big containers, combining them with petunias, sweet potato vine, and other annuals.

All in the Family

Cannas have both showy foliage and exotic flowers. Fancy-leaved cultivars include 'Pretoria', which has yellow-and-green-striped leaves; 'Tropicana', with leaves striped in orange-red, peach, and green; and 'Wyoming', which is famed for its rich bronze foliage. If you want to focus on flowers, try 'Cleopatra', which has unusual red-freckled yellow flowers; 'Chinese Coral', with peach-colored blossoms; orange-red 'Lucifer'; and pale yellow 'Madame Butterfly'. A related canna with a less dramatic look is *C. indica*, or Indian shot. The flowers are smaller and usually red marked with yellow, while the green leaves may be stained with bronze or purple.

Growing Cannas

Cannas thrive in hot weather but cannot tolerate the cold. Plant cannas in spring after the last frost has passed.

C. indica is a less dramatic species with daylily-like flowers in red flushed with yellow.

Lay the rhizomes on their sides about 5 cm (2 in) below the soil's surface, 30–45 cm (12–18 in) apart. Keep the soil moist until they sprout.

Occasionally small caterpillars, including canna leaf roller and corn earworms may chew holes in new leaves before they unfurl, creating a row of perforations when the leaves open. Overlook light damage or trim off damaged leaves. If the problem is severe, apply the biological insecticide Bt (*Bacillus thuringiensis*) as directed to control the caterpillars.

The roots must be lifted and stored for winter. Dig them up after a hard frost has blackened the leaves and shake off any loose soil. Cut off old stems and let the rhizomes air-dry in a warm place. Pack the rhizomes in paper bags filled with dry peat moss, and store them for the winter at 4°–10°C (40°–50°F). Replant in spring as soon as the weather is settled and mild. In warm parts of British Columbia, they may survive winter if heavily mulched.

Increasing the Bounty

Cannas are easy to increase by division. Separate rhizomes in spring

With bronze-tinged leaves and orange-red blooms, 'Wyoming' packs a double punch.

before planting. Replant at the same depth at which the rhizomes previously grew.

They are vigorous plants and a single rhizome planted in spring will normally spread rapidly to give many rhizomes by fall.

FUNDAMENTAL FACTS

ATTRIBUTES	Large, colorful leaves and showy flowers; for beds, pots
SEASON OF INTEREST	Summer
FAVORITES	Large, colorful leaves and showy flowers; for beds, pots
QUIRKS	Thrives in damp or wet soil and humid heat
GOOD NEIGHBORS	Butter daisy, castor bean, crocosmia, daylily
WHERE IT GROWS BEST	Warm, humid climates in a sunny location
POTENTIAL PROBLEMS	Canna leaf roller, corn earworms
RENEWING PLANTS	Lives many years; divide crowded rhizomes in spring or early summer
CRITTER RESISTANCE	Good
PLANTING DEPTH	5–8 cm (2–3 in)
SOURCE	Tubers, nursery plants
DIMENSIONS	0.6–1.8 m (2–6 ft) tall; clumps to 1.8 m (6 ft) across

'Lucifer', which blooms in vibrant flame red, is perhaps the best known crocosmia.

CROCOSMIA

Crocosmia spp.

HARDINESS:
Zone 5

PREFERRED SOIL pH:
Near neutral

PREFERRED SOIL TYPE:
Average

PREFERRED LIGHT:
Sun

Crocosmia in the Landscape

When the show from your spring-flowering bulbs is long gone, you'll never miss them when the brilliant summer blossoms of crocosmia take center stage. Imagine arching flower spikes holding rows of vibrant trumpet-shaped florets that open gradually over several weeks, extending the show into early fall. Most often seen with bright red flowers, crocosmias also have yellow, orange, or bicolored blossoms. All are easy to grow and provide excellent cut flowers.

Crocosmias look best when grown in a grouping of several plants at least 60 cm (2 ft) wide. The flat, pointed, sword-shaped leaves don't look spindly when grouped, and a sizable planting also provides the scale needed for these 1–1.2 m (3–4 ft) tall, narrow plants. Because crocosmias bloom in such hot colors, they are best grown in the company of plants with quieter flowers. Summer annuals, such as white petunias, blue ageratum, or yellow zinnias make a fine frame for crocosmias and calm their fiery flowers. Crocosmias also make good partners for yellow-flowered daylilies and fall-blooming asters.

All in the Family

The saturated red flowers of 'Lucifer' is nearly synonymous with crocosmia, and it may be the hardiest and most care-free variety. 'Lucifer' is an old, reliable hybrid, as are yellow-flowered 'Jenny Bloom' and 'George Davidson'. Other good choices are 'Aurora' for orange flowers, 'Solfaterre' for apricot blooms, and 'His Majesty' for large red flowers with yellow centers.

The red-and-orange flowers of *Crocosmia masonorum*, which grow on 70 cm (28 in) tall stems, are particularly eye-catching. The individual flowers face upward, and look like summer-blooming daffodils.

Growing Crocosmia

Plant dormant crocosmia corms in early spring in a sunny, well-drained site. The corms are flattened disks with a slightly raised, pointed bud on the top of each one. Plant 5 corms per square foot (about 0.1 m²) and set them 12 cm (5 in) deep. Add organic matter if needed to improve the soil's texture, but don't worry about fussing over these plants. For best results, fertilize with a controlled-release, all-purpose plant food in early summer,

FUNDAMENTAL FACTS

ATTRIBUTES	Vivid flowers atop graceful, sword-shaped leaves; for beds, cutting
SEASON OF INTEREST	Summer to early fall
FAVORITES	'Lucifer', 'Jenny Bloom', 'George Davidson', 'Aurora'; *C. masonorum*
QUIRKS	Flower spikes arch, and the individual florets face to the sides
GOOD NEIGHBORS	Ageratum, daylilies, petunias, zinnias
WHERE IT GROWS BEST	In sunny, well-drained locations
POTENTIAL PROBLEMS	Sparse blooms due to overcrowding; yellow leaves due to poor soil
RENEWING PLANTS	Lives up to 5 years; divide: discard old corms and replant young ones
CRITTER RESISTANCE	Excellent
PLANTING DEPTH	13 cm (5 in)
SOURCE	Corms
DIMENSIONS	1–1.2 m (3–4 ft) tall, 30 cm (12 in) wide

following label directions. The leaves will yellow if soil nutrients are lacking. After the first freeze in late fall, snip off foliage at ground level and dispose of the leaves. In Zones 5 and 6, spread 10 cm (4 in) of straw, leaves, or other organic mulch over the dormant corms after the first freeze to insulate them from the ravages of winter.

Dig, divide, and replant every 4–5 years in early spring to avoid overcrowding, which leads to decreased flowering. When you lift the corms, you will see new ones atop the old ones. Break off the old, woody corms and replant only the young ones. They will bloom heavily the second year after division. Pests and diseases seldom trouble these care-free beauties.

Crocosmia is a very narrow plant and is shown to best advantage when grown in groups.

Large-flowered Dutch crocus are a welcome sight in spring, flowering despite snow.

CROCUS
Crocus spp.

HARDINESS:
Zone 4

PREFERRED SOIL pH:
Adaptable

PREFERRED SOIL TYPE:
Average

PREFERRED LIGHT:
Sun to partial shade

'Cream Beauty' is an early-blooming crocus with small, round flowers of creamy yellow.

Crocus in the Landscape

Few sights are as welcome as the first crocus of the season poking their heads through patches of melting snow. The small, ground-hugging, cup-shaped flowers open during the first sunny days of spring, and are clad in gay hues of purple, yellow, and white. Some have petals veined in contrasting shades, some are subtle pastels, and others are bright hues, but all enliven the landscape when few other plants are in bloom. These diminutive heralds of spring can grow almost anywhere, but because they stand just a few inches above the soil, it's important to place them where you won't miss them. Group them in a bed, sprinkle them throughout the lawn, or use them to line a walkway or accent a rock garden.

Crocuses do most of their growing while hardy perennials remain dormant, so they make excellent companions for peonies, lilies, and plants that wait until summer to gain size, such as balloon flowers. Crocuses also paint a delightful picture when informally grouped at the bases of deciduous shrubs and trees.

All in the Family

Often called the snow crocus because it blooms so early, *Crocus chrysanthus* is available in several cultivars whose names reveal their colors, the best being 'Blue Pearl', 'Cream Beauty', and 'Goldilocks'. If you'd like larger flowers, try Dutch crocuses, such as purple 'Remembrance', lilac-striped white 'Pickwick', golden 'Mammoth Yellow', and white 'Jeanne d'Arc'.

Not all crocus bloom in spring. *C. speciosus* opens its lavender blossoms in fall, as does a similar-looking plant, *Colchicum speciosum*, often called autumn crocus. The large violet flowers of autumn crocus make fall feel like a second spring, and the blooms are followed by grassy green foliage that persists through winter in warm areas.

Growing Crocus

Crocuses grow from small, bulblike corms sold in autumn. Plant the corms after the soil cools in the fall, in a sunny, protected spot. Set crocus corms 8 cm (3 in) deep, pointed end up, and 5 cm (2 in) apart. The most impressive display comes when crocus are planted in groups of 10 or more, so that they look as if they were planted by Mother Nature herself.

After the blossoms fade, it's important to allow crocus to keep their leaves until they naturally fade away, because they will continue to photosynthesize and nourish the old corms as well as the new ones that are constantly developing underground. The foliage is easily camouflaged by planting crocus among leafy perennials. In the lawn, crocus leaves blend into green grass. Should crocus become so crowded that they stop blooming, dig and separate the corms as the leaves begin to yellow in late spring. Lift and separate the corms and replant them without delay. Spring-blooming crocus need to be divided every 5 years or so, but autumn crocus can be left untouched for many years.

Crocus emerges so early that it is virtually trouble-free. It blossoms and goes dormant before most pests and diseases pose a threat. Rodents, however, relish the corms. To protect corms, encase them in a cage of wire screening or in commercial wire bulb baskets at planting time. You can also cover corms with coarse, gravel before filling the planting holes with soil to discourage digging rodents.

FUNDAMENTAL FACTS

ATTRIBUTES	Small, cup-shaped white, yellow, or lilac flowers; for beds, naturalizing
SEASON OF INTEREST	Spring or fall
FAVORITES	'Blue Pearl', 'Goldilocks'; 'Remembrance', 'Pickwick'; *C. speciosus*
QUIRKS	Needs winter chilling to initiate flowering
GOOD NEIGHBORS	Lawn grass, peonies, lilies, spring-flowering shrubs, balloon flower
WHERE IT GROWS BEST	In full sun and well-drained soil
POTENTIAL PROBLEMS	After several years, overcrowding reduces flowers
RENEWING PLANTS	Lives years; divide big clumps and replant corms every 5 years
CRITTER RESISTANCE	Poor; corms are vulnerable to rodents, rabbits, and deer
PLANTING DEPTH	8 cm (3 in)
SOURCE	Corms
DIMENSIONS	*C. chrysanthus* 5–10 cm (2–4 in) tall, 5 cm (2 in) wide; Dutch crocus 13 cm (5 in) tall, 10 cm (4 in) wide

CYCLAMEN

Cyclamen spp.

HARDINESS:
Zones as indicated

PREFERRED SOIL pH:
Neutral to slightly acid

PREFERRED SOIL TYPE:
Fertile, well-drained

PREFERRED LIGHT:
Partial shade

Cyclamen in the Landscape

You're probably familiar with the florist's cyclamen (*Cyclamen persicum*), which is tender and is a popular winter houseplant because of its colorful blossoms. But there are also smaller, hardier, garden-worthy species that thrive in humus-rich soil, blooming in cool autumn weather, when little else is in flower. These dainty plants, with heart-shaped leaves and pink, rose, or white flowers that resemble shooting stars, make a unique accent for shady spots. Nestle a few against the roots of a large tree or tuck them into the curve of a path. When pleased with their location, hardy cyclamen will grow into lovely naturalized colonies.

Seasonal Cyclamen

You can extend cyclamen bloom time by growing different species. Hardy to Zone 7, ivy-leaved cyclamen (*C. hederifolium*) blooms in late summer to early fall with white or pink flowers held on 15 cm (6 in) stems. A few weeks after the flowers fade, dark green ivy-shaped leaves emerge, each marked with silver. The foliage lasts through winter, then the plants go dormant from spring to late summer.

The leaves of *C. coum* (Z5) appear in fall; the magenta or fuchsia pink flow-

C. persicum is tender and often sold as a houseplant. It can grow outdoors in Zone 9.

Ivy-leaved cyclamen have small flowers that emerge before the leaves in late summer.

ers appear on 10 cm (4 in) stems in early spring. *C. coum* also goes dormant in summer, but tolerates hot weather better than ivy-leaved cyclamen.

Growing Cyclamens

Cyclamens are sold as potted plants or dormant tuber-corms. The tuber-corms, which have some characteristics of both tubers and corms, look like smooth, rounded, somewhat flattened brown cookies. Small nubbins of growth indicate "this side up" when planting. Plant tuber-corms in summer and set out container-grown plants in early fall.

Before planting, amend soil with organic matter in the form of compost or leaf mold. Good drainage is crucial, because cyclamens grow poorly or rot in wet soil. Set tuber-corms 2.5 cm (1 in) below the soil's surface and after planting, mulch lightly with dried, chopped leaves.

When cyclamens are established, fertilize with a balanced organic or controlled-release fertilizer when new growth appears. Flower buds that appear crinkled and fail to open have likely been damaged by cyclamen mites, a minute spiderlike pest. Remove faded foliage in early summer to interrupt the life cycle of this pest.

C. coum 'Album' is a white-flowered variety that is suited to warm climates.

The next fall, apply a commercial miticide labeled for use on cyclamen, according to package directions, as the flowers and foliage appear. Gaps in a planting can often be attributed to mice, which can eat the tubers.

FUNDAMENTAL FACTS

ATTRIBUTES	Heart-shaped leaves and dainty flowers; for beds, woodland gardens
SEASON OF INTEREST	Fall through spring
FAVORITES	*C. hederifolium* and *C. coum*
QUIRKS	Needs good soil drainage in summer
GOOD NEIGHBORS	Bugleweed, ferns, hosta, Solomon's seal
WHERE IT GROWS BEST	In open woods beneath tall trees
POTENTIAL PROBLEMS	Cyclamen mites, mice
RENEWING PLANTS	Lives for many years; does not need to be rejuvenated
CRITTER RESISTANCE	Fair; mice can seriously damage young plants
PLANTING DEPTH	2.5 cm (1 in)
SOURCE	Tubercorms, nursery
DIMENSIONS	10–15 cm (4–6 in) tall, spreads up to 30 cm (12 in) wide

'Dutch Master' bears the scalloped central trumpet, in golden yellow, of the classic daffodil.

DAFFODIL

Narcissus spp.

HARDINESS:
Zone 4

PREFERRED SOIL pH:
Adaptable

PREFERRED SOIL TYPE:
Average, well-drained

PREFERRED LIGHT:
Sun to partial shade

Daffodil in the Landscape

Daffodils are versatile bulbs, as comfortable in formal landscapes as in meadows or open woodlands. By growing varieties with different flowering times, you can enjoy the parade of yellow, salmon, white, or orange flowers from early spring to early summer. Some varieties, such as 'Cragford', also emit a fragrance that is forever associated with spring.

All in the Family

There are many types of daffodil, with flower shapes ranging from the classic trumpet to ruffled puffs. Because the bulbs are inexpensive and readily available, it's easy to stock grow whatever types you like. The trumpet daffodil stands 35–50 cm (14–20 in) tall and has a long central floral tube framed by a star of petals. Cultivars number in the hundreds and include yellow 'Dutch Master' and white 'Mount Hood'.

Large-cupped daffodils are the same size but have a flattened central cup. 'Ice Follies' has white petals and a yellow cup that turns white with age. It performs better in mild-winter areas than do many other daffodils, yet is hardy enough for cold climates.

Petite cyclamineus daffodils are ideal for planting in pots, beneath small trees that drop their leaves in fall or near spring-flowering shrubs, such as forsythia. Only 18–35 cm (7–14 in) tall with dramatically back-swept petals, this type includes such old favorites as 'February Gold', 'Tête-à-tête', and 'Jack Snipe'.

Growing Daffodil

Plant firm, dormant daffodil bulbs in fall, with pointed ends up, in groupings of 10 or more. Dig holes wide enough for several bulbs and mix 5 cm (2 in) of compost into the soil at the bottom of the hole. Set bulbs 20 cm (8 in) deep and 15 cm (6 in) apart, then fill the hole with soil.

As soon as new foliage emerges in spring, fertilize daffodils with a commercial bulb fertilizer according to package directions or apply a top-dressing of compost. There is no need to protect daffodil foliage from late freezes, because it is very hardy.

After daffodils flower, let leaves remain to nourish the bulbs for next year's flowers. The emerging leaves of perennials such as peony, daylily, Siberian iris, and hosta will hide the daffodils' yellowing leaves. If you're careful not to dig so deeply that you damage the bulbs, you can plant shallow-rooted annuals over them after the daffodil leaves shrivel.

Daffodils are so critter resistant that they can be planted near tulips and crocus to help repel rodents, who find these other bulbs tasty. Although they are virtually indestructible, daffodil bulbs can rot if planted in poorly drained soil, so plant only in well-drained locations. They can also fall prey to the bulb-eating larvae of narcissus bulb fly. To avoid problems, discard bulbs with soft or discolored spots. If a patch of bulbs is affected, do not replant in the same area, because soil can harbor pest eggs. Plant bulbs in a new location.

Increasing the Bounty

Daffodils make offsets, which nestle against the mother bulb. Over the years they can become so crowded that flowering diminishes. If this happens, dig up the clump as the leaves fade in early summer. Separate and replant bulbs immediately. The largest will flower next spring. Smaller ones will bloom in subsequent years.

The large, pale yellow flower cups of 'Ice Follies' magically turn white as they age.

FUNDAMENTAL FACTS

ATTRIBUTES	Straplike foliage, colorful flowers; for beds, woodlands, naturalizing, pots
SEASON OF INTEREST	Early spring to early summer
FAVORITES	'Dutch Master', 'Ice Follies', 'February Gold', 'Jack Snipe', 'Cragford'
QUIRKS	Bulbs need winter chilling; plants must retain fading foliage
GOOD NEIGHBORS	Daylilies, hosta, iris, ornamental shrubs, pansies, peonies, small trees
WHERE IT GROWS BEST	Well-drained soil in sun to partial shade
POTENTIAL PROBLEMS	Overcrowding, bulb rot, narcissus bulb fly
RENEWING PLANTS	Lives for years; divide overcrowded clumps
CRITTER RESISTANCE	Excellent
PLANTING DEPTH	20 cm (8 in)
SOURCE	Bulbs
DIMENSIONS	18–50 cm (7–20 in) tall, 15 cm (6 in) wide

Tall-growing hybrids are available in a remarkable range of colors and bicolors.

GLADIOLUS
Gladiolus spp. and hybrids

HARDINESS:
Tender or as indicated

PREFERRED SOIL pH:
Neutral

PREFERRED SOIL TYPE:
Average

PREFERRED LIGHT:
Sun

Gladiolus in the Landscape

Topping out at 1.2 m (4 ft), with bold, colorful spikes of funnel-shaped flowers atop leaf blades, gladiolus are like exclamation points for the garden. These inexpensive, easy-to-grow bulbs bloom in lovely colors and bicolors ranging from pure white to dark red and provide outstanding cut flowers for summer bouquets. Cut gladiolus when the first flowers at the bottom of the spike are open; the others will quickly unfurl in the vase.

Because of their lanky physique, glads can be awkward in the landscape. For the best effect, grow them in groups at the back of the border or station the tall spires against a fence or building, letting the structure act as a backdrop while blocking wind and helping to support the plants.

All in the Family

The common summer-flowering gladiolus are hybrids that are usually tender. In the mildest parts of British Columbia, they may survive outdoors if protected with a 10 cm (4 in) mulch in late fall, especially if planted close to a wall. But there are other types that withstand more cold. *G. communis* ssp. *byzantinus* is hardy to Zone 5 and grows 0.6–1 m (2–3 ft), with purple-red flowers often striped in white. Plant gladiolus in groups of 5 or more for a care-free display of color from late summer onward.

Growing Gladiolus

Gladiolus bloom about 10 weeks after planting. By planting the corms every 2 weeks from early spring through midsummer, you'll enjoy a succession of blossoms all season. Choose a sunny, well-drained spot and mix an all-purpose granular fertilizer, such as 10-10-10 into the soil as you dig, allowing about 1 tablespoon of fertilizer per corm. Plant the corms 10–15 cm (4–6 in) deep and 10 cm (4 in) apart. The small nubbin of new growth indicates the top of the corm and should point up.

Gladiolus grow so tall and slender that they need to be planted in groups of 5 or more and staked with bamboo canes and some soft garden twine to inconspicuously "corset" the group. Water only if the soil becomes very dry, as gladiolus hate wet soil and can develop root rot. Provide plants with a second helping of balanced fertilizer when flower spikes appear. In midsummer, watch for signs of thrips. These nearly invisible, sap-sucking insects make silvery streaks in leaves and distort flowers. Control thrips with a commercial insecticide labeled for this use, as directed.

Funnel-shaped flowers open from the bottom of the spike to its top.

FUNDAMENTAL FACTS

ATTRIBUTES	Tall spikes of dramatic flowers in many colors; for beds, cutting
SEASON OF INTEREST	Late spring to summer
FAVORITES	Choose hybrids by color; *G.* x *colvillei*, *G. communis* ssp. *byzantinus*
QUIRKS	In warm climates, corms can overpopulate if left in the ground over winter
GOOD NEIGHBORS	Celosia, gomphrena, lavatera, marigold, zinnia
WHERE IT GROWS BEST	In sunny, well-drained sites protected from wind
POTENTIAL PROBLEMS	Thrips; root rot in overly wet soil
RENEWING PLANTS	Lives many years; divide overgrown clumps
CRITTER RESISTANCE	Good
PLANTING DEPTH	10–15 cm (4–6 in)
SOURCE	Corms
DIMENSIONS	Hybrids to 1.2 m (4 ft) tall; hardy types 0.6–1 m (2–3 ft) tall; flowers to 10 cm (4 in) wide

In areas where gladiolus are not hardy, dig the corms when the leaves begin to yellow in late summer and trim the leaves to 2.5 cm (1 in) from the corm. Brush away loose soil and store corms in a paper bag of peat moss in a cool, dry, dark place, such as an unheated room or a garage that remains above freezing. Many gardeners in warmer climate Zones dig and store the corms, too, to keep plants from growing small, weedy offspring called cormlets. Cormlets reach flowering size in about 3 years, but because the mature corms are inexpensive, there is little reason to nurture cormlets.

GRAPE HYACINTH

Muscari spp.

HARDINESS:
Zones 3 to 8

PREFERRED SOIL pH:
Adaptable

PREFERRED SOIL TYPE:
Average

PREFERRED LIGHT:
Sun to partial shade

M. latifolium is easy to recognize by its dark purple flowers topped by a lighter tuft.

Grape Hyacinth in the Landscape

Named for their grapelike clusters of tiny urn-shaped blue, white, or pink blossoms, grape hyacinths are adaptable, comely little plants that can be scattered almost anywhere in the landscape. They are just right for nestling up against tree trunks or

M. armeniacum is the most commonly grown species. It spreads reliably into colonies.

planting beneath spring-flowering shrubs. Or use grape hyacinths in the perennial border in combination with the emerging shoots of peonies or as companions to other spring bulbs. In lawns that already include crocus, daffodils, or other small flowers, grape hyacinths are a welcome addition. Because grape hyacinths grow leaves from fall through winter, they are handy to use as markers to remind you where daffodils and other bulbs, which don't emerge till spring, are planted. And the blossoms also make dainty but fleeting cut flowers.

All in the Family

Most grape hyacinth reach 15–30 cm (6–12 in) tall and flower on leafless stems that jut from clumps of slender, grassy leaves. They are all hardy, carefree, dependable spring bloomers and vary only in intensity of color and fragrance.

Muscari armeniacum has fragrant dark blue-violet flowers accented by a thin white edge. The 'Blue Spike' cultivar

has a denser cluster of double blue blossoms and makes a long-lasting cut flower. 'Cantab' has light blue flowers that appear later than most other types. M. *botryoides* is a centuries-old favorite with sky blue flowers that smell of plums. To add contrast to naturalized drifts of grape hyacinth, combine it with the pure white variety, 'Album', and the pink 'Carneum'. The flower spikes of M. *latifolium* feature dark violet-black flowers on the lower portion of the stem and lighter, blue-violet flowers toward the tip.

An unusual species is the tassel hyacinth (M. *comosum*), which grows to 45 cm (18 in) and produces shaggy, tasseled flowers in blue-violet. However, it can't be counted on for long-term performance and may flower well only the first year after planting.

Growing Grape Hyacinth

Plant grape hyacinths in early fall, spacing bulbs 5 cm (2 in) apart and 10 cm (4 in) deep in groups of 10 or more. Grape hyacinths are so easy-

going that you can plant them simply by pounding a piece of 2.5 cm (1 in) diameter pipe into the ground 10 cm (4 in) deep, pulling out the plug of soil, dropping in the bulb, and then filling in the hole.

Thin gray-green leaves will appear a few weeks after planting and persist all winter. After the blooming show in spring, grape hyacinths slip into a summer slumber and will disappear altogether, remaining in a state of dormancy until fall.

Virtually pest- and disease-free grape hyacinths increase freely with little attention and can make colonies in only a few years. Should they become overcrowded, dig up clumps and move the bulbs in fall, when the new leaves appear.

FUNDAMENTAL FACTS

ATTRIBUTES	Clusters of blue, white, or pink flowers; for beds, woodlands, naturalizing
SEASON OF INTEREST	Spring
FAVORITES	M. armeniacum 'Blue Spike', M. botryoides 'Album', M. latifolium
QUIRKS	Needs 6 weeks minimum winter chilling; leaves grow from fall to spring
GOOD NEIGHBORS	Daffodils, hyacinths, pansies, peonies, shrubs, trees
WHERE IT GROWS BEST	Anywhere except extremely dry sites
POTENTIAL PROBLEMS	Can be invasive; dig out unwanted plants
RENEWING PLANTS	Lives many years; dig crowded clumps, separate, and replant in fall
CRITTER RESISTANCE	Excellent
PLANTING DEPTH	10 cm (4 in)
SOURCE	Bulbs
DIMENSIONS	15–45 cm (6–18 in) tall

HYACINTH

Hyacinthus orientalis

HARDINESS:
Zone 4

PREFERRED SOIL pH:
Neutral to slightly alkaline

PREFERRED SOIL TYPE:
Average

PREFERRED LIGHT:
Sun to partial shade

'Carnegie' is one of the finest white varieties, with particularly dense flower spikes.

Hyacinth in the Landscape

Hyacinths are among the most elegant spring-flowering bulbs, with a sweet perfume that is the essence of spring. Their 15–20 cm (6–8 in) tall flower spikes are crowded with bell-shaped blossoms that have jaunty, curled-back petals. Hyacinths bloom year after year, but the spikes often become slightly longer and less densely packed with blossoms after their debut. This change softens their appearance, making them less soldierly, but the fragrance remains as strong as ever. Hyacinths are available with flowers in a wide range of soft colors from whites to soft yellows and pinks, plus many shades of blue from light lavender to deep purple.

Use hyacinths in a formal flower border, as an edging for foundation shrubs, or even as container plants. Combined with pansies and primroses in beds or half-barrels, hyacinths become a feast for the eyes. And if you follow the show with marigolds and zinnias, the 15 cm (6 in) tall browning leaves will be well camouflaged into summer. But outdoor performance is not your only option with hyacinths. Potted up in the fall and kept in a place that's cool but remains above freezing, or in a refrigerator, for 12–14 weeks, hyacinths will eagerly bloom indoors while winter still holds sway in the garden.

Colors Old and New

With a color range that increases all the time, hyacinths are available in numerous cultivars. Some favorites include the apricot-salmon 'Gypsy Queen', maroon 'Distinction', purple 'Bismarck', blue-lilac 'Delft Blue', pink 'Anne Marie', and gleaming white 'Carnegie'. Varieties treasured since Victorian times include the primrose yellow 'City of Haarlem', purple 'General Kohler', pink 'Chestnut Flower', and ivory 'L'Innocence'.

Growing Hyacinth

Blessed with an easy-to-please personality, hyacinths are gratifying bulbs for any gardener. Buy and plant bulbs in the fall, choosing plump, firm specimens. The bigger the bulb, the larger the flower spike will be. Plant bulbs with the pointed ends up, 20 cm (8 in) deep and 8–10 cm (3–4 in) apart in groupings of 5 or more. Your chosen site should be in sun to partial shade, with rich, loose soil and good drainage. Water after planting and then apply a 5 cm (2 in) thick layer of loose mulch, such as shredded bark, especially in colder zones.

In spring, the flowers begin as clusters of light green buds and then shoot out into flowers in a matter of days. After the blooms fade, cut off the flower stem and allow the leaves to grow until they turn yellow before removing them.

Take precautions when handling hyacinth bulbs, because they can irritate your skin or eyes if you touch your hands to your eyes. As a precaution, wear gloves when planting the bulbs and keep the bulbs out of the hands of children. Hyacinths bloom so early in spring that there are rarely any insects or diseases present to cause them problems.

FUNDAMENTAL FACTS

ATTRIBUTES	Fragrant spring flowers in a wide range of colors; for beds, pots
SEASON OF INTEREST	Spring
FAVORITES	'Gypsy Queen', 'City of Haarlem', 'Anne Marie', 'Bismarck', 'Delft Blue'
QUIRKS	Needs 8 weeks minimum winter chilling; bulbs can irritate skin on contact
GOOD NEIGHBORS	Candytuft, daffodil, pansy, primrose, snapdragon, tulip
WHERE IT GROWS BEST	In sun and well-drained soil in cool climates
POTENTIAL PROBLEMS	Wet soil in winter can induce root rot
RENEWING PLANTS	Lives up to 5 years; replace old, poorly flowering bulbs in fall
CRITTER RESISTANCE	Good
PLANTING DEPTH	20 cm (8 in)
SOURCE	Bulbs
DIMENSIONS	30 cm (12 in) tall, 10 cm (4 in) wide

'Pink Pearl' was introduced in 1922 and is still treasured for its rich fuchsia pink blossoms.

LILY

Lilium spp.

HARDINESS:
Zone 3 unless otherwise indicated

PREFERRED SOIL pH:
Neutral to acid

PREFERRED SOIL TYPE:
Fertile, well-drained

PREFERRED LIGHT:
Sun to partial shade

Lily in the Landscape

Their sometimes fragrant, trumpet-shaped, large blossoms in white, pink, yellow, and orange have earned lilies the nickname "queen of the bulbs." With an upright habit, lilies mingle easily with shrubs, roses, perennials, and annuals. Site them prominently in a bed, pot, or by a walk, where you can enjoy the blossoms all summer.

All in the Family

Most modern lilies are hybrids and are organized into groups. Oriental lilies

'Enchantment' is one of the best known lilies, ideal for pots or beds.

(Z4), have huge, fragrant blossoms and grow to 1.5 m (5 ft). Asiatic lilies grow 1 m (3 ft) tall and produce smaller flowers over a long period. Trumpet lilies reach 1.5–1.8 m (5–6 ft) tall, have smaller but more numerous flowers, and grow into vigorous clumps in a few years.

Among the species there is the Easter lily (*Lilium longiflorum*), which blooms in spring with long white trumpets but is hardy only to Zone 7. A good choice for the back of the

border is the 2.4 m (8 ft) tall Turk's-cap lily (*L. superbum* [Z4]), whose freckled orange petals are folded back into little turbans. A garden standout is the gold-band lily (*L. auratum* [Z5]), a late-season bloomer with white flowers streaked in gold and spotted with crimson.

Growing Lily

Sold in both spring and fall, lily bulbs should be planted promptly, as they remain dormant for only a short time. Choose a sunny site with fertile, very well drained soil amended with rotted manure or other organic matter. Dig a hole 3 times as deep as the bulb is high, gently set the bulbs 15–20 cm (6–8 in) apart, and cover with soil. Lilies are also sold in pots. Plant them as you would any perennial, setting them in the hole at the same depth they occupied in the pot.

Fertilize lilies soon after they emerge in spring with an organic or low-nitrogen granular fertilizer, such as 5-10-10, applied as directed on the label. Stake tall types as the stems develop to keep them from toppling in the wind. When cutting the flowers, take short stems and leave the remaining foliage to nourish the bulb. Clip off spent flowers to keep energy from going into producing seeds.

Tiny sap-sucking, pear-shaped insects called aphids may congregate on tender shoots and buds. Knock them off with a forceful spray of water. An increasingly common pest is the bright red European lily beetle. Inspect plants daily, especially in spring, and squash the beetles when found. Look for egg masses on the backs of leaves and sluglike grubs. If left unchecked, they quickly defoliate and kill plants. Protect against deer by planting in well-traveled areas near your house or put a fence around your lilies.

Increasing the Bounty

Most lilies multiply into clumps that may need dividing every 5 years or when the plants produce few flowers. In fall, or early spring in cold areas, dig up a clump, break it into smaller pieces, and replant them immediately.

One of the best known varieties, 'Star Gazer' is a richly scented Oriental lily.

FUNDAMENTAL FACTS

ATTRIBUTES	Large, many colored flowers; for beds, pots, cut-flower arrangements
SEASON OF INTEREST	Summer
FAVORITES	Asiatic, Oriental, trumpet lilies; *L. longiflorum*, *L. superbum*, *L. auratum*
QUIRKS	Needs a minimum of 6 weeks chilling below 4°C (40°F)
GOOD NEIGHBORS	Ajuga, sedum, midsized ornamental grasses, roses, small shrubs
WHERE IT GROWS BEST	In sun and fertile, well-drained soil; may need light afternoon shade
POTENTIAL PROBLEMS	Aphids; European lily beetle
RENEWING PLANTS	Lives up to 5 years; divide in fall or in early spring in cold climates
CRITTER RESISTANCE	Poor; vulnerable to deer, woodchucks, rabbits, mice, and voles
PLANTING DEPTH	3 times as deep as the bulb is high
SOURCE	Bulbs
DIMENSIONS	1–2.5 m (3–8 ft) tall, 30 cm (12 in) wide

Speckled orange turbans dangle from towering stems on Turk's-cap lilies in summer.

MAGIC LILY

Lycoris squamigera

HARDINESS:
Zone 5 unless otherwise indicated

PREFERRED SOIL pH:
Acid to nearly neutral

PREFERRED SOIL TYPE:
Average

PREFERRED LIGHT:
Sun to partial shade

Spider lily blooms have dozens of slender stamens that give rise to the common name.

The lilac-pink blooms of magic lily blend beautifully with deep pink flowers, such as roses.

Magic Lily in the Landscape

Picture this: less than a week after a late-summer rainstorm, 0.6 m (2 ft) tall, leafless stems of lilac-pink, fragrant, lilylike flowers appear like magic. If it sounds like a sorcerer has been at work in your garden, now you know why a couple of the common names of lycoris are magic lily and surprise lily. These tough flowering bulbs make an elegant addition to the woodland garden, where they fit in nicely with other shade-tolerant perennials. If you plant them near deciduous trees, they receive sun when they need it in early spring to grow leaves, but will be shaded in late summer, when the flowers appear.

The straplike leaves of magic lily take up quite a bit of space in the spring garden and often become floppy and disheveled with age. They need the same spring-to-summer growing schedule as daffodils and tulips, so leave the foliage undisturbed until it yellows. Consider combining them with large leafy perennials, such as hostas or ornamental grasses that can hide their aging leaves and fill the gap until flowering time. They also look fine growing in rows, such as along the edge of a lawn. The fragrant blossoms make excellent cut flowers.

All in the Family

Magic lily has a close relative, spider lily (*Lycoris radiata*), which is hardy only to Zone 8. Popular on the West Coast, spider lilies have thin, rosy red, curled-back petals with long, spidery stamens atop straight green stems. The variety 'Alba' blooms in white. Like magic lilies, spider lilies send up flowers following a rain shower in late summer or early fall. However, the dark green foliage of spider lilies grows from fall to spring and completely disappears by summer. Another relative is golden spider lily (*L. aurea*), which has 8 cm (3 in) long orange-yellow blossoms at the end of the season. Also hardy to Zone 8, it can be grown in a container.

Growing Magic Lily

In many areas magic lilies are called "pass-along" plants, because they multiply and are handed over the garden fence from neighbor to neighbor, but bulbs can also be obtained from mail-order nurseries in the fall. Magic lilies don't like to be disturbed, so decide where you want them to grow, plant them, and then leave them. Space the bulbs 20–25 cm (8–10 in) apart in 15 cm (6 in) deep holes. A group of 3–5 bulbs will make a nice initial showing and eventually fill in. Patience is necessary, because magic lilies do not bloom the first, or sometimes even the second, year after planting. In times of serious drought, you may need to encourage magic lilies to bloom by slowly watering them with a drip hose in late summer until the ground is saturated.

After 8 or 9 years, clumps of bulbs may become crowded and need to be divided. This is best done in early summer, just as the leaves are dying back. These tough plants are virtually impervious to pests and diseases.

Magic lilies flower in late summer after a rain, springing up on tall, leafless stalks.

FUNDAMENTAL FACTS

ATTRIBUTES	Large pink, red, or yellow trumpet-shaped flowers; for beds, pots
SEASON OF INTEREST	Late summer to early fall
FAVORITES	*L. squamigera, L. radiata* and *L. radiata* 'Alba', *L. aurea*
QUIRKS	Needs 6 weeks minimum winter chilling; may not bloom the first year
GOOD NEIGHBORS	Caladiums, hostas, small ornamental grasses
WHERE IT GROWS BEST	Sites that are moist in spring and late summer but dry in summer
POTENTIAL PROBLEMS	Failure to bloom due to overcrowding or extreme summer drought
RENEWING PLANTS	Lives for many years; dig up and divide in early summer
CRITTER RESISTANCE	Excellent
PLANTING DEPTH	15 cm (6 in)
SOURCE	Bulbs
DIMENSIONS	60 cm (24 in) tall, 30–50 cm (12–20 in) wide

A. hollandicum 'Purple Sensation' creates a forest of rich violet globes in late spring.

ORNAMENTAL ONION

Allium spp.

HARDINESS:
Zones 4 to 8

PREFERRED SOIL pH:
Near neutral

PREFERRED SOIL TYPE:
Fertile, well-drained

PREFERRED LIGHT:
Sun

Ornamental Onion in the Landscape

If you think of onions as bulbs that make you weep, think again. Ornamental onions have but a faint onion scent and only if leaves are crushed. What they offer instead is beautiful flowers in shades of purple, lavender, mauve, and white. Individual flowers are clustered together atop sturdy stems, where they open in unison to create an impressive globe or an open

A group planting of alliums will become a virtual sea of blue when they are in flower.

starburst. Ornamental onions make great accent plants in the perennial border from late spring to summer, when most reach their pinnacle of beauty. And the flowers, both fresh and dried, are good for bouquets.

All in the Family

One of the easiest ornamental onions to grow is *Allium hollandicum* 'Purple Sensation'. The 1 m (3 ft) tall plant produces a dense, 10 cm (4 in) wide cluster of rich violet flowers. Because the leaves are skimpy, combine it with a full-foliaged bedfellow, such as yarrow or zinnia.

With its 15–25 cm (6–10 in) diameter flower clusters on 30–60 cm (12–24 in) tall stems, star of Persia (*A. christophii*) is suitable for the front of the border. Purple flowers with a silvery metallic sheen appear in late spring. Another big-flowered species is giant onion (*A. giganteum*), which has dense, 15 cm (6 in) purple clusters atop stems that can reach 1.2 m (4 ft).

Most ornamental onions have plain grassy foliage, but *A. karataviense* has wide, arching, lightly pleated blue-green leaves. Its mauve-pink flowers blend with everything from silver-leaved artemisia to hardy geraniums. Stems grow to about 20 cm (8 in) tall, topped by 8 cm (3 in) wide flower clusters. *A. senescens* also has attractive foliage. The gray-green leaves are loosely twisted and grow in a whorled clump, from which 60 cm (2 ft) tall stems of mauve flowers emerge in late summer.

Another easy-to-grow allium, drumstick allium (*A. sphaerocephalum*), produces its 5 cm (2 in) wide oblong clusters of reddish purple flowers on 1 m (3 ft) tall stems that sway in the breeze in early summer.

Growing Ornamental Onion

Plant allium bulbs in the fall in a sunny site with good drainage, otherwise the bulbs may rot. Dig a hole about 12 cm (5 in) deep for small bulbs, such as those of 'Purple Sensation', and 20 cm (8 in) deep for larger bulbs. Set bulbs in soil with the

pointed ends up, in groupings of 3–5 for the smaller alliums or individually for the larger ones. Ornamental onions produce sulphur, the source of the characteristic onion scent, which naturally repels insect and four-footed pests. In fact, growing any member of the onion family near plants that usually attract pests can offer protection to the companions.

Alliums do not multiply quickly from bulbs, but some reseed. Seedlings look like grass and take several years to flower. If you don't want volunteers, cut off and dispose of old flowers as they fade to keep them from setting seed. Better yet, cut the flowers as they open for a bouquet.

FUNDAMENTAL FACTS	
ATTRIBUTES	Clusters of white, mauve, or purple flowers; for beds, cutting
SEASON OF INTEREST	Late spring to early summer and late summer
FAVORITES	A. hollandicum 'Purple Sensation', A. christophii, A. karataviense
QUIRKS	Requires cold winter dormancy period to initiate flowering
GOOD NEIGHBORS	Artemisia, hardy geranium, ornamental grasses, yarrow
WHERE IT GROWS BEST	Sunny, well-drained sites in regions with dry summers
POTENTIAL PROBLEMS	Wet soil rots the bulbs
RENEWING PLANTS	Lives many years; rejuvenation is generally unnecessary
CRITTER RESISTANCE	Excellent
PLANTING DEPTH	12–20 cm (5–8 in) depending on species
SOURCE	Bulbs
DIMENSIONS	20–90 cm (8–36 in) tall; flowers to 25 cm (10 in) in diameter

Each snowdrop produces only one flower, so group plants in drifts for the greatest impact.

SNOWDROPS

Galanthus spp.

HARDINESS:
Zone 4

PREFERRED SOIL pH:
Slightly acid

PREFERRED SOIL TYPE:
Average

PREFERRED LIGHT:
Partial shade to shade

G. nivalis 'Pusey Green Tip' has double flowers with green markings on the tips.

Snowdrops are one of the earliest bloomers, suddenly bringing the landscape to life.

Snowdrop in the Landscape

One of the earliest flowers to bloom in the garden, snowdrops are a welcome sign that winter is ending. These early risers have dainty white flowers composed of 3 waxy, oblong petals around a small center cup accented by green markings. Like a lantern, each flower is suspended from a grasslike stalk that stands 8–25 cm (3–10 in) above a few narrow leaves. When cold weather cuts their growing spree short, snowdrops hug the earth and are easily buried under late-season snow. They may look delicate, but snowdrops are very hardy.

The plants like shade, especially as soil heats up in summer. Grow them under trees and shrubs or let them poke up among the leaves of an evergreen ground covers. Not many plants bloom as early as snowdrops, but they mix well with other spring-flowering plants, such as hellebore, crocus, and *Cyclamen coum*. To disguise their resting place when snowdrops go dormant in late spring, plant them among leafy shade lovers such as ferns and hostas.

All in the Family

The common snowdrop (*Galanthus nivalis*) has a honey-scented white flower with the typical green markings between petals. Collectors who enjoy expanding on the theme should try the cultivar 'Viridiapicis', whose flowers have additional green markings on the tips of the 3 petals. In 'Flore Pleno', the petals are doubled, resembling a starched petticoat.

Though still small, giant snowdrop (*G. elwesii*) grows taller than the other species, has longer leaves, and sports green markings at the base and tips of the petals. It is not as easy to find at garden centers as the common snowdrop.

Growing Snowdrop

Snowdrops grow from small bulbs that can dry out if they are held too long before planting, so purchase and plant them as soon as they are available in autumn. Since each small bulb sends up similarly diminutive leaves and produces only one 3-petaled flower, plant the bulbs in groupings of 10–25 for an eye-catching display. Set the bulbs 8 cm (3 in) deep and 5 cm (2 in) apart. Water after planting and continue watering if less than 2.5 cm (1 in) of rain falls per week in late autumn.

Increasing the Bounty

About 2–3 years after planting, snowdrops begin to multiply by producing small bulbs, called offsets, and multiply until some bulbs are pushed out of the soil. Dig the bulbs while the leaves are still green but after flowers fade. Separate and replant promptly. Bulbs moved in early summer, while the foliage is still green, establish themselves more quickly than dormant bulbs planted in fall. Snowdrops are trouble free, as they go dormant before pests and diseases are active.

FUNDAMENTAL FACTS	
ATTRIBUTES	Dainty white flowers that bloom very early; for beds, naturalizing
SEASON OF INTEREST	Late winter to early spring
FAVORITES	*G. nivalis* and cultivars 'Viridiapicis', 'Flore Pleno'; *G. elwesii*
QUIRKS	Needs 6 weeks minimum winter chilling; grows poorly in hot climates
GOOD NEIGHBORS	Ferns, hosta, primrose, vinca minor, woodland phlox, hellebore, crocus
WHERE IT GROWS BEST	Moderate shade in cool climates
POTENTIAL PROBLEMS	Overcrowded bulbs push out of the soil and fail to bloom
RENEWING PLANTS	Lives for decades; divide and replant overcrowded clumps after flowering
CRITTER RESISTANCE	Good
PLANTING DEPTH	8 cm (3 in)
SOURCE	Bulbs
DIMENSIONS	8–25 cm (3–10 in) tall, 2.5–5 cm (1–2 in) wide

SQUILL

Various spp.

HARDINESS:
Zone 3 unless otherwise indicated

PREFERRED SOIL pH:
Slightly acid

PREFERRED SOIL TYPE:
Average, well-drained

PREFERRED LIGHT:
Sun to partial shade

Squill brightens the dull soil of early spring with star-shaped blossoms of purest blue.

Squill in the Landscape

If true blue color appeals to you, you will love the variety of dainty spring-flowering bulbs that are known as squill. Siberian squill (*Scilla siberica*), striped squill (*Puschkinia scilloides*), and Italian squill (*Hyacinthoides italica* [Z5]) all produce charming starlike flowers in shades of blue in early spring, creating pools of color in the woods, under shrubs and trees, or in the perennial bed or rock garden.

You can pair squill with small, early-blooming tulips, such as the Kaufmanniana and Greigii tulips, or let them form a carpet under tall-stemmed tulips. Use groups of 50 or more squill to every 10 tulips, planting the squill together so that the tulips appear to float over a wave of blue flowers. You can also scatter bulbs under early-flowering shrubs, such as azalea or viburnum. These little bulbs are so sturdy that they can even be planted in a lawn, provided you are willing to wait until the bulbs' leaves wither before you mow.

An Extended Family

These bulbs grow approximately 15 cm (6 in) tall and have short, iris-like foliage. Siberian squill has nodding, deep electric blue flowers that hang like bells from leafless stems. Striped squill has pale, almost translucent blue flowers with a dark blue line penciled down the center of each petal. They grow in dense clusters along the end of the flower stem, resembling small hyacinth blossoms. Italian squill has fragrant, violet-blue flowers that form little rounded clusters at the top of its flower stems.

Growing Squill

Squill bulbs are inexpensive, making it affordable to plant them in large numbers. Informal drifts look more natural and have more impact than lines or circles. Plant squill bulbs in early fall, before planting hyacinths or other big bulbs, in a sunny location in well-drained soil. To plant dozens of bulbs quickly, use a hand tool called a bulb planter, which pulls out circular plugs of soil about 10 cm (4 in) in diameter and equally deep. Make holes 5–10 cm (2–4 in) apart, drop in the bulbs so that the pointed ends are pointing up, and cover them with the excavated soil. You can also dig a large hole and gently scatter the bulbs in it, making sure they are spaced 5–10 cm (2–4 in) apart.

The following spring, after the leaves emerge, water the new planting to keep the soil moist if rainfall is lacking. To make sure the bulbs have stored plenty of nourishment for next year's flowers, do not mow or otherwise remove the leaves until they turn yellow in late spring.

Unfortunately, squill do not thrive in heat and may flower well for only a few years in regions with consistently hot summers, but it is affordable to replant as needed. On the other hand, they laugh at the cold, making them care-free choices for areas with deep freezes in the winter.

Increasing the Bounty

These bulbs increase by self-sowing. Fledglings can be encouraged with a dose of balanced liquid fertilizer applied according to package label in spring, while squill are actively growing. To divide congested colonies, dig some bulbs after they've flowered, separate them, and replant promptly. Like other early-blooming bulbs, squill remains disease- and pest-free because it goes dormant before most pests and diseases become active.

FUNDAMENTAL FACTS

ATTRIBUTES	Cold-hardy plants with dainty blue flowers; for naturalizing, beds, lawns
SEASON OF INTEREST	Early spring
FAVORITES	*Scilla siberica, Pushkinia scilloides, Hyacinthoides italica*
QUIRKS	Needs a minimum of 8 weeks below 4°C (40°F); short-lived in hot climates
GOOD NEIGHBORS	Crocus, daffodils, tulips, spring-flowering shrubs and trees
WHERE IT GROWS BEST	Slightly acid, well-drained soil
POTENTIAL PROBLEMS	Hot weather cuts short the life cycle, weakening the bulbs
RENEWING PLANTS	Lives many years in cold climates; divide crowded clumps in late spring
CRITTER RESISTANCE	Excellent
PLANTING DEPTH	10 cm (4 in)
SOURCE	Bulbs
DIMENSIONS	15 cm (6 in) tall

The electric blue flowers of Siberian squill nod gracefully over short, straplike leaves.

'Oxford' is a Darwin tulip with slightly ruffled scarlet petals flushed with deep red.

TULIP

Tulipa spp.

HARDINESS:
Zone 4

PREFERRED SOIL pH:
Neutral to slightly alkaline

PREFERRED SOIL TYPE:
Average, well-drained

PREFERRED LIGHT:
Sun

Tulip in the Landscape

Tulips are the quintessential spring bulb, available in a range of sizes, shapes, and colors to suit any landscape. And by selecting varieties with different flowering times, you can guarantee a steady display of color from early to late spring. The low-growing, early-flowering tulips look lovely planted in clusters beside walkways or at the front of a flower garden. Taller, mid- to late-season tulips are excellent massed in beds, with pansies planted at their bases. They can also be grown for long-lasting cut flowers.

Kaufmanniana tulips hold white or yellow petals marked in red atop short stems.

All in the Family

There are hundreds of hybrid tulips, grouped by size and flower shape. Darwin and Triumph tulips have cup-shaped flowers on 38–60 cm (15–24 in) tall stems in mid to late spring. They are best for cutting and bringing strong color to the garden, although the bulbs last only a few years. For fancy flowers, try Parrot tulips, whose petals are fringed, and Double Late tulips, with peonylike flowers. Both bloom in mid to late spring on 45–60 cm (18–24 in) stems.

Smaller tulips that bloom from early to mid spring usually live the longest, and in cold Zones can reproduce and grow into clumps. At 30–45 cm (12–18 in) tall, Fosteriana tulips are gold, orange, or red. The 25 cm (10 in) Greigii tulips have chocolate-striped green leaves and red or yellow pointed flowers. Even smaller, at 10–20 cm (4–8 in) tall, are the Kaufmanniana tulips, with flowers that resemble water lilies in red-streaked with white or yellow.

Growing Tulips

Plant tulips in mid to late fall. Bulbs need 8 weeks of soil temperatures below 4°C (40°F) to induce flowering. Many varieties can be potted and forced into winter flowering if given a suitable cold period. Choose a sunny site, as tulips will turn toward the sun if they don't get enough light. Plant small tulips 12 cm (5 in) deep and larger types 20 cm (8 in) deep. Space bulbs 8 cm (3 in) apart with the pointed ends up.

After the spring show is over, clip off spent flower heads and fertilize the bulbs by sprinkling bone meal or commercial bulb food, as directed, on the soil around the bases of the plants to encourage leaf growth. But even with the best care, many varieties will not flower well 2 or 3 years after planting. In hot-summer areas, high humidity can cause bulbs to rot. While insect and disease problems are few, tulips are a delicacy for chipmunks, voles, and mice. For protection, enclose bulbs loosely in chicken wire when planting. To discourage deer, rabbits, and woodchucks, either fence the plants in or grow them in containers near the house.

FUNDAMENTAL FACTS	
ATTRIBUTES	Bold blooms in many colors, shapes, and sizes; for beds, pots, cutting
SEASON OF INTEREST	Spring
FAVORITES	Darwin, Triumph, Parrot, Double Late, Fosteriana, Greigii, Kaufmanniana
QUIRKS	Needs 8 weeks minimum winter chilling; blooms decrease after 2–3 years
GOOD NEIGHBORS	Candytuft, daylily, forget-me-not, primrose
WHERE IT GROWS BEST	Sunny, well-drained sites with long, cool springs
POTENTIAL PROBLEMS	Bulb rot in wet soil or humid areas
RENEWING PLANTS	Most live 3 years; replenish with new bulbs; grow long-lived species tulips
CRITTER RESISTANCE	Poor; vulnerable to deer, woodchucks, rabbits, chipmunks, mice, voles
PLANTING DEPTH	Small bulbs 12 cm (5 in); large bulbs 20 cm (8 in)
SOURCE	Bulbs
DIMENSIONS	10–60 cm (4–24 in) tall, depending on type

The large, chalice-shaped blossoms of Darwin tulips are perfect for formal spring displays.

Wood hyacinths are among the few shade-tolerant bulbs, ideal for coloring woodlands.

WOOD HYACINTH

Hyacinthoides hispanica

HARDINESS:
Zone 4

PREFERRED SOIL pH:
Neutral to slightly acid

PREFERRED SOIL TYPE:
Moist, organically rich

PREFERRED LIGHT:
Partial shade

Wood Hyacinth in the Landscape

An excellent choice for the woodland garden, wood hyacinths grow into robust clumps that bear loose spikes of blue, pink, or white flowers in mid to late spring. The bell-shaped flowers, also called Spanish bluebells, can be cut for bouquets, adding a touch of the woods to the scenery indoors.

Plant wood hyacinths beneath large trees in partial shade, and combine them with other shade-tolerant perennials, such as ferns, hostas, and woodland phlox. They are also lovely mingling with evergreen groundcovers, such as periwinkle (*Vinca minor*) or pachysandra. Or plant them at the bases of colorful spring-flowering shrubs, such as azalea and forsythia.

Often found in nursery catalogs under one of their older names, *Scilla campanulata* or *Endymion hispanicus*, wood hyacinths have been reclassified as *Hyacinthoides hispanica*. The new name is apt because of the plants' resemblance to true hyacinths. Although their fragrance is light compared with that of traditional garden hyacinths, wood hyacinths are much more vigorous and willing to persist and increase year after year.

Wood hyacinth bulbs are most often available with flowers in violet-blue or in mixtures of blue, pink, and white. A few named varieties do exist. 'Danube' is a dark blue variety that is particularly abundant, 'Excelsior' is violet-blue with a dark blue stripe, 'Rose Queen' is sparkling pink, and 'Alba' is snowy white.

Growing Wood Hyacinth

Wood hyacinths are care-free bulbs that you can plant and forget. Handle them carefully before planting them in fall and plant them as soon as possible, because the bulbs dry out easily. Plant in small colonies of 10–25 bulbs, in a natural-looking drift.

Wood hyacinth bulbs have both flattened bases and tops. To tell which end is up, look for scales folded around each other; this indicates the top and should face up. It's no disaster if you make a mistake; bulbs planted upside down will straighten themselves out and grow just fine.

Before planting, amend the soil with compost, leaf mold, or rotted manure. Set bulbs 12 cm (5 in) deep and 10 cm (4 in) apart, and water them in as you fill the planting hole. Add a 10 cm (4 in) layer of bark

Also known as Spanish bluebells, wood hyacinths bloom in frilled bells of deep blue.

chips, evergreen boughs, straw, or other fluffy organic mulch to insulate the plantings. Each spring, clip off old flowers and let the leaves ripen through midsummer, when they turn yellow and die back. Pest and disease problems are rare.

Increasing the Bounty

Wood hyacinths produce seed and develop offsets. Scattered seedlings can be numerous, but you will see few if you cut off the flowers before they set seed. To increase your supply, dig, divide, and replant young bulbs in early summer, while the leaves are still green. Wood hyacinths pull themselves deeper into the ground over time, so be prepared to dig.

FUNDAMENTAL FACTS	
ATTRIBUTES	Spikes of blue, pink, and white flowers; for beds, woodland gardens
SEASON OF INTEREST	Mid to late spring
FAVORITES	*H. hispanica* and cultivars 'Blue Danube', 'Rose Queen', 'Excelsior', 'Alba'
QUIRKS	Needs 8 weeks minimum winter chilling; bulbs settle into the soil over time
GOOD NEIGHBORS	Azalea, dogwood, evergreen groundcovers, ferns, hosta
WHERE IT GROWS BEST	Shaded sites with organically rich soil
POTENTIAL PROBLEMS	Occasionally invasive if allowed to reseed
RENEWING PLANTS	Lives for decades; rarely needs rejuvenation; divide to increase stock
CRITTER RESISTANCE	Excellent
PLANTING DEPTH	12 cm (5 in)
SOURCE	Bulbs
DIMENSIONS	30–38 cm (12–15 in) tall, mature clumps 30–60 cm (12–24 in) wide

CARE-FREE SHRUBS

Long-lived and resilient, shrubs add structure to the landscape and create a backdrop for garden beds. Diverse species exhibit a range of qualities, including showy flowers, fragrance, fall color, and food and shelter for wildlife. Well-placed shrubs can be the most care-free plants in the garden, needing little attention once they become established.

Shrubs have something to offer year-round. Azaleas, rhododendrons, and bridal wreath spiraea ring in spring with an explosion of early flowers. As the mercury rises, warm breezes bear the heavenly scent of lilacs, giving way to that of roses and clethra. Berried shrubs including holly and viburnum are examples of the bounty of autumn, a season when other shrubs, such as winged euonymus display their brightest foliage colors. Broad-leaved and needled evergreen shrubs carry the garden through winter. As the new year begins, the carmine bark of red-osier dogwood shows its richest color, and witch hazel defies nature by blooming during the coldest season of the year.

Use shrubs to fill out the space under trees or to feather the edge between wooded and open areas. A shrub grouping requires little care, and can take the place of trees in small gardens. Almost every house appears more anchored with a few shrubs around its foundation, and farther from the house shrubs can frame desirable views, screen out undesirable ones, or soften the look of walls or fences. Some, such as hydrangeas, even thrive in containers.

To grow shrubs successfully, you must find the right match for your situation. The plant's requirements must come first, because a shrub that's unhealthy from being grown in an inappropriate spot will never live up to its potential. The entries that follow provide all this information and more. The shrubs presented here are easy to establish and maintain. Some require no fertilizing or pruning, and rarely need watering once established, because the root system grows deep and extensive, and has no trouble finding nutrients and moisture.

Azaleas announce spring with flowers of yellow, orange, red, lavender, and pink.

AZALEA

Rhododendron spp. and hybrids

HARDINESS:
Zones as indicated

PREFERRED SOIL pH:
Acid

PREFERRED SOIL TYPE:
Moist, loamy, well-drained

PREFERRED LIGHT:
Partial to full shade

Azalea in the Landscape

The signature shrub of springtime in many parts of the country, azaleas come in an array of sizes, flower colors, and growth habits. Some are hardy to Zone 4, although evergreen types are generally hardy only to Zone 7. Related to rhododendrons, azaleas are distinguished from them by their smaller, oval leaves, tubular flowers, and usually shorter, twiggier stature.

Azaleas cover themselves in white, pink, lavender, yellow, orange, or red blossoms in spring. They range from 60 cm (2 ft) tall dwarfs to 6 m (20 ft) giants. Smaller azaleas are often used as foundation shrubs, because they thrive in the part-day shade cast by buildings. They also grow well in pots and flower beds and make an elegant path edging, while the taller types are substantial enough to mix into a border of shrubs or stand beneath trees. Some varieties are deliciously fragrant.

'George Tabor' is an evergreen hybrid suited to hot summers and mild winters.

All in the Family

It's always safest to buy azaleas locally, because nurseries sell plants adapted to local conditions. Where winters are cold, look for Minnesota-bred Northern Lights hybrids, which can tolerate temperatures as low as -34°C (-30°F). Deciduous hybrids from Europe, such as the popular Exbury and Knap Hill azaleas, are hardy to Zone 5. In warm climates, look for evergreen azaleas bred in the southeastern states, often called Indian hybrids, of which the pink-flowered 'George Tabor' is a popular example. There are also new reblooming evergreen azaleas, such as the Encore hybrids (Z7), which bloom in spring and again in fall.

Native North American species are easy to grow and provide decades of pleasure, often outlasting the hybrids. In cold climates, try the spice-scented white swamp azalea (*R. viscosum*) or pink pinxterbloom azalea (*R. periclymenoides*), both hardy to Zone 5. Good choices for warm-summer, mild-winter areas include flame azalea (*R. calendulaceum* [Z5]), with yellow-orange flowers, and plumleaf azalea (*R. prunifolium* [Z7]), with crimson blooms that open in midsummer. Western gardeners can grow the Western azalea (*R. occidentale* [Z6]), which has creamy pink flowers.

Azaleas bloom brilliantly in spring, and some also offer fall color, or are evergreen.

FUNDAMENTAL FACTS

ATTRIBUTES	Tubular flowers in a range of colors; for beds, woodland gardens, pots
SEASON OF INTEREST	Spring to early summer for flowers; year-round for evergreen types
FAVORITES	All native species; Knap Hill, Northern Lights, Indian, Encore hybrids
QUIRKS	Prefers shallow planting and acid soil with a pH of 4.5–6.0
GOOD NEIGHBORS	Dogwood, ferns, hosta, holly, pines, serviceberry, silverbell, spring bulbs
WHERE IT GROWS BEST	Open woodland settings
POTENTIAL PROBLEMS	Root rot; lace bugs
PRUNING	Remove damaged wood or shape plants after flowering
CRITTER RESISTANCE	Good
SOURCE	Nursery plants
DIMENSIONS	0.6–6 m (2–20 ft) tall, 0.6–3.7 m (2–12 ft) wide

Growing Azalea

Plant azaleas where they'll be shaded from summer sun, and in fertile, moist, well-drained soil. To prevent root rot, barely cover their roots with soil. In poorly drained areas build a berm of soil about 30 cm (1 ft) high to plant them on. Water well and mulch with an 8 cm (3 in) layer of organic mulch to retain moisture. Fertilize plants every spring with a formula designed to maintain soil acidity. Prune only to remove damaged or dead wood or to control plant size, preferably after the flowers fade in early summer.

Leaves that look bleached may have fallen victim to lace bugs, small sucking insects that can be found on leaf undersides. Control them by applying insecticidal soap per label directions.

'Crimson Pygmy' is a favorite dwarf shrub with purplish red leaves and red berries.

BARBERRY

Berberis spp.

HARDINESS:
Zone 4 unless otherwise indicated

PREFERRED SOIL pH:
Neutral to slightly acid

PREFERRED SOIL TYPE:
Moist, well-drained

PREFERRED LIGHT:
Sun to partial shade

Barberry in the Landscape

Barberries are a large group of evergreen and deciduous shrubs that get their name from their barblike spined branches. The evergreen types maintain a presence in the landscape year-round whether they are grown as hedges, foundation plants, or specimens in a bed. The deciduous barberries add bright color to the fall scene, and both types produce berries in autumn. Because some species are a host to a serious disease of wheat, the cultivation of many barberry species is banned in Canada. Those described here are not affected.

All in the Family

Wintergreen barberry (*Berberis julianae*) is a dense, vigorous shrub with glossy leaves that are tinted copper when young. Growing into an impenetrable mass 1.8 m (6 ft) tall and wide, wintergreen barberry produces yellow flowers in spring, followed by small, blue-black berries. Normally evergreen to Zone 6, the leaves blush red in fall, and the plant sometimes sheds its leaves in extreme cold. However, healthy new foliage will appear first thing in spring.

Japanese barberry (*B. thunbergii*) is deciduous and usually grows less than 1.2 m (4 ft) tall and wide. The green leaves turn scarlet in fall, blending with red berries that last through the winter. Many cultivars have purplish red leaves that intensify in summer sun. These include 'Crimson Pygmy', a compact bush that grows less than 1 m (3 ft) tall and wide, and 'Rose Glow', which can reach 1.5 m (5 ft) tall and wide and has young leaves mottled in silver and pink. These dark-leaved barberries look dazzling when paired with plants that have chartreuse leaves, such as 'Marguerite' sweet potato vine or a sun-tolerant chartreuse coleus. There is also a Japanese barberry with golden yellow foliage named 'Aurea'.

These two species have been hybridized to create mentor barberry (*B. × mentorensis*), which has the vigor of one parent and vibrant foliage of the other. It grows to 2 m (7 ft) tall and 3 m (10 ft) wide and withstands dry conditions like a champ.

Growing Barberry

At nurseries, you will usually find barberries sold in containers. Set them out in either spring or fall, in planting holes twice as wide and as deep as the root ball. Plant them at the same depth at which the plants grew in their containers. Water well and cover the root zone with an 8 cm (3 in) thick layer of organic mulch to help maintain soil moisture. Most barberries transplant very easily, show excellent disease resistance, and are seldom bothered by insect or animal pests.

Many varieties of Japanese barberry glow with brilliant crimson foliage in the fall.

Prune barberries only to shape the plants or remove damaged branches. If plants are leggy or misshapen because of old age or storm damage, severe pruning in early spring will force vigorous new growth.

FUNDAMENTAL FACTS

ATTRIBUTES	Green, red-purple, or gold foliage; fall berries; for beds, hedges
SEASON OF INTEREST	Spring to fall; year-round for evergreens
FAVORITES	*B. julianae; B. thunbergii* 'Crimson Pygmy', 'Rose Glow'; *B. × mentorensis*
QUIRKS	Strong sun intensifies leaf coloring
GOOD NEIGHBORS	Euonymus, holly, foliage plants with chartreuse or burgundy leaves, juniper
WHERE IT GROWS BEST	Full sun in fertile, well-drained soil
POTENTIAL PROBLEMS	Plant may grow poorly and colored leaves may revert to green in shade
PRUNING	Prune in early spring to remove damaged wood, control size, or renew
CRITTER RESISTANCE	Excellent
SOURCE	Nursery plants
DIMENSIONS	1–2 m (3–7 ft) tall and equally wide

Wintergreen barberry produces clusters of yellow flowers, followed by blue-black berries.

BLUEBEARD

Caryopteris x clandonensis

HARDINESS:
Zone 6

PREFERRED SOIL pH:
Slightly acid

PREFERRED SOIL TYPE:
Average

PREFERRED LIGHT:
Sun to partial shade

The leaves of 'Worcester Gold' are flushed with gold, contrasting with its blue flowers.

Bluebeard in the Landscape

When summer sets in and the color rush of late spring begins to fade, bluebeard fills the void and complements neighbors with abundant, dependable blue blossoms that appear until fall. A light and airy-looking 1 m (3 ft) tall shrub with small, pointed, gray-green leaves lined by clusters of flowers, bluebeard more resembles a bushy perennial than a shrub. Silhouette bluebeard against a weathered wooden barn or fence, let it spread beside a rock outcrop, or plant it in long rows backed by dark green conifers. Or put bluebeard's soft color and texture to work neutralizing brighter bloomers in a mixed bed.

Even before bluebeard begins its midsummer blossoming, the white-backed leaves add a silvery effect to the garden and are dense enough for bluebeard to be used as a formal hedge or path edging. And, should you brush against bluebeard on a warm, sunny day, a pleasant herbal fragrance, reminiscent of sage, will be your reward.

Luring Butterflies

Beyond being beautiful and dependable, bluebeard also attracts bees and butterflies. Its blue blossoms are among the most powerful butterfly magnets in the garden. Place bluebeard within easy view of seating areas, where you can spend summer afternoons watching butterflies romancing the blossoms.

Choosing the Blues

Different cultivars boast a variety of blue hues, so you can choose cultivars with a favorite color or mix different shades. Most cultivars have flowers that are a medium shade of blue, such as those of 'Arthur Simmonds', which ranks among the best performers. In fact, 'Arthur Simmonds' is often the plant you get when nursery plants are simply labeled "caryopteris" or "bluebeard." If dark blue-purple flowers are your goal, 'Dark Knight' or 'Kew Blue' can provide them. With golden rather than gray-green foliage contrasting against the blossoms, 'Worcester Gold' presents a very different picture. And if you want a dwarf growth habit, opt for 60 cm (2 ft) tall 'Heavenly Blue', whose flowers are a bright blue.

These cultivars are all derived from a hybrid between *Caryopteris incana* and *C. mongolica*. One parent, *C. incana*, is definitely garden worthy in Zones 8 or warmer. It is slightly taller and less refined in habit than the hybrids, but its large dark blue flowers are worth finding a place for in the border.

Growing Bluebeard

This is one of the easiest shrubs to grow in a sunny location with well-drained soil. Pests ignore it, but chronically wet soil can cause root rot. A willing transplanter, bluebeard shows new growth a few weeks after planting, if you add a sparse handful of a balanced fertilizer, and occasionally irrigate. Leave the brown flower bracts intact for winter interest, then prune plants back hard first thing in the spring so that only a few inches of woody stem remain above ground to initiate new growth. Bluebeard flowers on new wood, so spring pruning encourages flower and foliage density as well as removing any frost injury. Given a long growing season, light pruning in midsummer stimulates a second flush of flowers.

FUNDAMENTAL FACTS

ATTRIBUTES	Blue flowers that attract butterflies, gray-green foliage; for beds, hedges
SEASON OF INTEREST	Early summer to fall
FAVORITES	'Arthur Simmonds', 'Dark Knight', 'Heavenly Blue', 'Worcester Gold'
QUIRKS	Grows like a hardy perennial where winters are cold
GOOD NEIGHBORS	Aster, chrysanthemum, daylily, purple coneflower, rose, rudbeckia
WHERE IT GROWS BEST	Sun in any average garden soil
POTENTIAL PROBLEMS	Root rot where drainage is poor
PRUNING	Prune in early spring; in mild climates, prune again in midsummer
CRITTER RESISTANCE	Excellent
SOURCE	Nursery plants
DIMENSIONS	0.6–1 m (2–3 ft) tall and equally wide

The silver leaves and blue flowers of Bluebeard calm its fiery-flowered garden companions.

Boxwood, which has a naturally rounded form, is often sheared into precise shapes.

BOXWOOD

Buxus spp.

HARDINESS:
Zone 5

PREFERRED SOIL pH:
Neutral to slightly acid

PREFERRED SOIL TYPE:
Fertile, well-drained

PREFERRED LIGHT:
Sun to partial shade

Boxwood in the Landscape

Boxwood is a widely grown evergreen that deserves its popularity. Dwarf forms can be used to anchor flower beds or edge walkways, while larger types fit well into foundation plantings. Boxwoods make an excellent backdrop for bulbs or perennials with light foliage and add a background for sitting areas or entryways. Be careful when digging around boxwood roots. Injured roots are entry points for soilborne, fungal root-rot diseases.

Typically slow-growing, boxwood will endure for centuries. Its only limitation is poor tolerance of extreme cold. While there are cultivars suited to every area, common boxwood (*Buxus sempervirens*) is usually hardy to Zone 6, while littleleaf boxwood (*B. microphylla*) is hardy to Zone 5 and tolerates summer heat better.

Boxwoods Old and New

Cultivars of common boxwood offer many variations in size and shape. 'Myrtifolia', grown since the 1700s, is a 1.2 m (4 ft) shrub with narrow leaves. The dark green 'Handworthensis', grown since the 1870s, is strongly upright, as is 'Graham Blandy', which becomes a column reaching 3.5 m (12 ft) tall. 'Vardar Valley', a relative newcomer from the 1950s, takes cold in stride and forms a mounding shape to 2 ft (0.6 m) high and 3–4 ft (1–1.2 m) wide. Often called edging box, 'Suffruticosa' is another old variety that seldom grows taller than 60 cm (2 ft), making it good for a low hedge.

Littleleaf boxwood is generally smaller in leaf and stature than common boxwood. 'Green Pillow' has a spreading habit, reaching only 38 cm (15 in) tall but 1 m (3 ft) wide. 'Curly Locks' is an upright grower, to 60 cm (2 ft), with slightly twisted branches. A very slow-growing variety known as Korean boxwood (*B. m. var. koreana*) tolerates both heat and cold well but may still brown in winter. 'Green Mountain' and 'Green Gem' overcome this defect, remaining green all winter and reaching 60 cm–1 m (2–3 ft) tall and wide.

Growing Boxwood

Prepare planting holes by working in a 10 cm (4 in) deep layer of compost or other organic matter, as well as sharp sand if the site catches runoff water. Set out plants in either spring or fall and expect to see little new growth the first year. Boxwoods often do not reach full size for 5–8 years.

Boxwoods have a naturally neat look, but you can prune them if you prefer a tight shape. Avoid pruning in late summer. The resulting growth is easily injured by freezing weather.

Most cultivars offer good disease resistance, but boxwood can have problems with scale, tiny immobile

Tiny scented flowers emerge in spring amid the glossy leaves of common boxwood.

aphid relatives that hide on leaf undersides and suck plant juices, causing leaves to turn pale. Control by spraying with dormant oil in late winter. When entire plants or major sections turn brown, the problem is likely root rot. Remove plants promptly and replace with a moisture-tolerant species.

With its short stature and slow growth, boxwood makes a low, care-free hedge.

FUNDAMENTAL FACTS

ATTRIBUTES	Slow-growing evergreens with small leaves; for beds, edging, hedges
SEASON OF INTEREST	Year-round
FAVORITES	'Myrtifolia', 'Vardar Valley', 'Curly Locks', 'Green Gem'
QUIRKS	Shallow roots are easily injured by cultivation
GOOD NEIGHBORS	English ivy, liriope, magic lily, rose, tulip
WHERE IT GROWS BEST	In fertile, well-drained soil where winters are not severe
POTENTIAL PROBLEMS	Scale; root rot
PRUNING	Prune or shear any time from late winter to early summer
CRITTER RESISTANCE	Good
SOURCE	Nursery plants
DIMENSIONS	0.3–3.5 m (1–12 ft) tall, 0.3–1.2 m (1–4 ft) wide; leaves to 2.5 cm (1 in)

'Pink Sensation' becomes a mass of rosy lilac flowers that are a magnet for butterflies.

BUDDLEIA

Buddleja davidii

HARDINESS:
Zone 5

PREFERRED SOIL pH:
Neutral to slightly acid

PREFERRED SOIL TYPE:
Average

PREFERRED LIGHT:
Sun

Buddleia in the Landscape

In midsummer, when it's almost too hot to garden, it's time to relax and enjoy the floral show put on by buddleia, also known as butterfly bush. This tall, deciduous flowering shrub, and the many butterflies, bees, and other insects that visit its nectar-rich blossoms, are a focal point in any summer garden. Extremely versatile,

'White Profusion' produces hundreds of flowers, which turn into russet seed heads.

these shrubs complement medium-sized flowering perennials, such as rudbeckia and purple coneflowers, and harmonize with ornamental grasses. Buddleias can combine with other shrubs, or even grow in pots.

The long, slender leaves range from 10–25 cm (4–10 in) long, with green upper surfaces and silvery gray undersides, a combination that makes this shrub beautiful to behold even before it flowers. The cones of white, yellow, pink, blue, or purple flowers, up to 30 cm (1 ft) long, begin to open in early summer and will keep blooming until fall if spent flowers are clipped off every couple of weeks. In Zones 8 and 9, don't be surprised if your butterfly bush survives some winters as an evergreen.

A Haven for Butterflies

Butterfly bush is enjoying a well-deserved surge in popularity because of the magic spell it casts on butterflies and the availability of colorful new cultivars. All cultivars attract butterflies, but the pink 'Pink Delight' and purple 'Nanho Purple' are top picks if attracting butterflies is your main mission. Other colors will tempt you as well, particularly the rich purple of 'Dartmoor', vibrant lilac of 'Empire Blue', red-violet of 'Royal Red', and white of 'White Bouquet'.

Although *Buddleja davidii* is the most popular type for cold regions, a few similar species are equally easy to grow in Zones 8 and 9. For distinctive yellow flowers there is *B.globosa*. *B. lindleyana* produces pendulous violet flower clusters up to 25 cm(10 in) in length.

Buddleia sends out numerous sprays of tiny flowers that can reach 30 cm (1 ft) long and last from summer to fall.

FUNDAMENTAL FACTS

ATTRIBUTES	Fragrant flowers in white, blue, pink, purple, and yellow; for beds, pots
SEASON OF INTEREST	Late spring through early fall; evergreen in mild climates
FAVORITES	'Pink Delight', 'Nanho Purple', 'Empire Blue', 'Dartmoor', 'Royal Red'
QUIRKS	Holds some leaves through winter in Zones 7 to 9
GOOD NEIGHBORS	Daylily, purple cone-flower, rose, rudbeckia, ornamental grasses
WHERE IT GROWS BEST	Any sunny location
POTENTIAL PROBLEMS	Unpruned plants become long-limbed and weak
PRUNING	Prune in late winter or early spring, before new growth begins
CRITTER RESISTANCE	Good
SOURCE	Nursery plants
DIMENSIONS	1.8–2 m (6–7 ft) tall, 1.2–1.5 m (4–5 ft) wide; flowers to 30 cm (1 ft)

Growing Buddleia

As long as they can bask in the sun and are anchored in well-drained soil, buddleia thrive on neglect. They laugh at drought and rarely wilt. Container-grown plants demand regular watering and fertilizing with a balanced fertilizer to remain at their healthiest.

To ensure continuous flowers on attractive bushes, prune the whole plant back to 30–60 cm (1–2 ft) tall in late winter or early spring. Butterfly bushes quickly recover and grow 1.8–2 m (6–7 ft) tall by fall. To encourage reblooming, remove spent flowers. Established plants are satisfied by a springtime half-strength application of organic or timed-release, balanced fertilizer. Buddleia has no serious problems with insects or disease.

The single, slightly ruffled crimson blossoms of 'Alexander Hunter' resemble roses.

CAMELLIA
Camellia spp.

HARDINESS:
Zones 7 or 8

PREFERRED SOIL pH:
Acid

PREFERRED SOIL TYPE:
Moist, humus-rich

PREFERRED LIGHT:
Partial to full shade

Camellia in the Landscape

Camellias are shade-garden treasures for mild-winter climates. They have been cherished in Asian gardens for thousands of years and for centuries in North America, were they are also grown in cool rooms indoors in cold-winter areas. Set off by glossy evergreen leaves, the rose-shaped flowers may be single, semidouble, or double and come in white, pink, red, or also bicolor combinations. Camellias will bloom from fall to spring, depending on your climate and the cultivar.

Because all camellias need shade, and many benefit from protection

'Narumi-gata' is treasured for its large single white flowers tinged with pink.

from wind, they can be planted around a house foundation, where they thrive in the part-day shadows, or planted under a high canopy of trees. The new hardy camellias, adapted to Zone 7, should be given similar protection from winter wind, as well as from morning sun, which can damage flower buds that have been frosted and need to thaw gradually. Where cold weather is not a concern, the shrubs can be grown as a hedge or screen.

Camellias make beautiful cut flowers. Snip a short woody stem with a blossom and a pair of leaves and float it in a glass bowl, a popular indoor display technique for these flowers.

All in the Family

Durable and long-lived, common camellia (*Camellia japonica*) produces the most magnificent flowers of all. These are usually grafted plants, growing on the hardier rootstocks of related plants. They grow into pyramidal bushes 6–7.5 m (20–25 ft) tall, bloom from fall to spring, and are hardy in Zones 8 and 9. Good choices among the thousands of cultivars include the crimson 'Alexander Hunter', pink 'Debutante', white

'Purity', and 'Donckelaeri', which is red marbled with white.

Sasanqua camellias (*C. sasanqua*) grow on their own roots and bloom in late fall to winter. These tough 1.8–3 m (6–10 ft) tall shrubs can tolerate a half day of sun, and many are hardy to Zone 8. Look for bright red 'Crimson King', rose 'Hugh Evans', and pink-tinged white 'Narumi-gata'. Gardeners in Zone 7 should watch for the new hybrids created by crossing *C. sasanqua* with a Chinese species, such as the medium pink 'Winter's Charm' and light blush pink 'Winter's Star'.

Growing Camellia

Before setting out a container-grown plant, dig a planting hole 3 times the width of the container and mix in a 10 cm (4 in) deep layer of compost or peat moss. Also add garden sulphur if needed to create an acid soil with a pH of 4.5–6.0. Set the plant high in the hole so that the top of the root ball is 5 cm (2 in) above the soil line. As the soil settles, the plant will sink, ending up only slightly raised. Keep the soil over the roots mulched year-round with an 8 cm (3 in) thick layer of shredded bark or pine needles. When properly planted, camellias need little fertilizer or pruning.

In freezing Zones, grow camellias in pots and bring them into a chilly room, such as a porch or garage, as temperatures approach freezing. When they bloom, bring them indoors or cut the flowers for arrangements.

Camellias are relatively pest free, but sap-sucking scale insects, which look like small immobile oval bumps, sometimes colonize stems and leaves. To smother and kill scale, spray commercial horticultural oil, in late winter according to label directions. Squirrels, which are very hard to control, may eat flower buds.

Japanese camellias are resilient evergreens with glossy leaves and prolific blossoms.

FUNDAMENTAL FACTS

ATTRIBUTES	Glossy evergreen foliage, single or double flowers; for beds, pots, specimens
SEASON OF INTEREST	Year-round; flowers appear in fall, winter, or spring
FAVORITES	*C. japonica, C. sasanqua* and their cultivars; hardy 'Winter's Charm'
QUIRKS	Blooms in winter
GOOD NEIGHBORS	Azaleas, ferns, hosta, Japanese anemone, primrose, pulmonaria
WHERE IT GROWS BEST	Partial shade in warm climates
POTENTIAL PROBLEMS	Frost damage to the blossoms; scale
PRUNING	Prune off damaged stems, spent flowers
CRITTER RESISTANCE	Good except for squirrels
SOURCE	Nursery plants
DIMENSIONS	*C. japonica* 6–7.5 m (20–25 ft) tall, 2.4 m (8 ft) wide; *C. sasanqua* 1.8–2.4 m (6–8 ft) tall, 1.2 m (4 ft) wide; flowers to 20 cm (8 in)

CLETHRA
Clethra alnifolia

HARDINESS:
Zone 5

PREFERRED SOIL pH:
Acid to neutral

PREFERRED SOIL TYPE:
Moist, loamy

PREFERRED LIGHT:
Sun to partial shade

Clethra in the Landscape

Commonly known as summersweet or sweet pepperbush, clethra is an essential shrub for gardeners who crave fragrance. The 10 cm (4 in) long bottlebrush-shaped flower spikes appear in mid to late summer and last into fall, filling the air with their spicy-sweet perfume and attracting bees and butterflies. Not only are the blossoms welcome at a time when little else is in bloom, but the foliage is lovely all season. Ribbed and lightly toothed, the oval green leaves are downy when young and turn a clear yellow in autumn.

Clethra is native to the eastern woodlands of North America, where it usually grows as an understory tree. When given good garden soil and at least a half day of sun, it grows into a robust, naturally rounded bush up to 2.4 m (8 ft) tall. Clethra's growth habit is also affected by soil moisture. An ideal shrub for damp locations, clethra transforms an abundant water supply into numerous leafy stems. In drier sites, it is more likely to grow tall with a lean profile.

Grow it along a woodland edge with other shade-tolerant plants, such as serviceberry, hydrangea, or dog-

Clethra's spikes of white flowers release a strong spicy-sweet perfume in late summer to fall.

wood. Or use it as a specimen plant at the back of a border that receives partial shade, mixing it with such companions as Japanese anemone, cohosh, perennial geranium, and ornamental grasses. Clethra also makes a fine freestanding shrub when used to define the edges of a lawn, and smaller cultivars can mark an informal path. The shrubs withstand salt spray, so are useful for seashore sites, and tolerate the shade of buildings when planted around foundations. And because it leafs out late in spring, clethra is a good shrub to underplant with any number of spring-flowering bulbs.

Spectacular Summersweets

Clethra is undergoing a revival of interest because many new forms are available in an array of sizes and colors. Check plant tags carefully, because new cultivars vary in their mature size. If you want a large shrub, look for either the species, which bears white flowers that may be pinkish in bud, or the 1.8 m (6 ft) tall 'Ruby Spice', which has dark pink flowers. 'Rosea' and 'Pink Spires' are

smaller varieties, seldom growing more than 1.2 m (4 ft) tall, with soft pink flowers. 'Paniculata' has slightly arching branches and larger flowers than the species. For tight spots, look for the petite, white-flowered 'Hummingbird', which grows only 1 m (3 ft) tall and wide but has the same sweet fragrance of other clethras.

Growing Clethra

One of the most attractive attributes of clethra is that it takes care of itself. Set out plants as promptly as possible in early spring to give them time to establish before summer. They like soil with a pH of 4.5–7.0. If you have alkaline soil, add garden sulphur as per package label to adjust the pH. Keep the soil constantly moist for the first 2 months after planting by watering regularly and maintaining a 5 cm (2 in) deep organic mulch. Although clethras prefer moist conditions, after they develop extensive roots they are surprisingly drought tolerant. They need little or no fertilizer.

Clethras can be left unpruned, although most gardeners prefer to remove old flower spikes in winter or early spring, before new growth begins. If clethras outgrow their welcome, they respond well to pruning at almost any time of year. In Zones 5 and 6, mulch over the root zone, applying a 15 cm (6 in) thick layer of fluffy evergreen boughs, dried leaves, or straw after the ground freezes to protect the shallow roots from damage.

Although problems are rare, many of the insects attracted by clethra's fragrant blossoms also sample the leaves. Small holes in leaves are usually the work of night-flying beetles that do not cause serious injury. In dry, hot weather, sap-sucking spider mites may cling to leaf undersides, causing leaves to look bleached. Knock them off with water from a hose and keep the soil moist to repel them. If Clethra attracts deer, tuck deodorant bar soap among shrubs or apply a commercial repellent as directed.

FUNDAMENTAL FACTS

ATTRIBUTES	Fragrant flowers in white or pink; for beds, edgings, specimens
SEASON OF INTEREST	Summer
FAVORITES	'Ruby Spice', 'Rosea', 'Pink Spires', 'Hummingbird', 'Paniculata'
QUIRKS	Thrives in soggy soils
GOOD NEIGHBORS	Azalea, serviceberry, hydrangea, Japanese anemone, spring bulbs
WHERE IT GROWS BEST	Moist woodland settings
POTENTIAL PROBLEMS	Beetles, spider mites
PRUNING	Clip off old seed heads in early spring
CRITTER RESISTANCE	Good
SOURCE	Nursery plants
DIMENSIONS	1–2.4 m (3–8 ft) tall and 1.2–1.8 m (4–6 ft) wide

Rockspray cotoneaster is perfectly content spilling its branches over a rock, wall, or slope.

COTONEASTER

Cotoneaster spp.

Ground-hugging rockspray cotoneaster is distinguished by its stiff, "fishbone" stems.

HARDINESS:
Zone 4 unless otherwise indicated

PREFERRED SOIL pH:
Adaptable

PREFERRED SOIL TYPE:
Average, well-drained

PREFERRED LIGHT:
Sun

Cotoneaster in the Landscape

If you have a dry, sloping, or otherwise difficult spot in sun, there is a cotoneaster to cover it. These sprawling shrubs come in various sizes and shapes, from large fountain-shaped bushes to groundcovers. Most provide interest over several seasons, with tiny white or pink flowers in spring, dense foliage in summer, bright leaf color in fall, and berries that last into winter. Where winters are mild, some species are reliably evergreen. All cotoneasters have small leaves and leggy branches. They are best grown in masses of three or more, so that they form a thicket of stems and foliage. Feel free to plant them in awkward, hard-to-reach places, as cotoneasters require no pruning and are drought tolerant once established.

All in the Family

Tough cotoneasters can survive winter cold, although heat tolerance varies with the species. For a quick cover, bearberry cotoneaster (*Cotoneaster dammeri*) grows less than 1 m (3 ft) tall and grows up to 1.8 m (6 ft) wide. Closer to the ground, creeping cotoneaster (*C. adpressus*) is a fine-textured groundcover. Plants grow 30–45 cm (12–18 in) tall, yet spread up to 1.8 m (6 ft) wide. Easily distinguished by its stiff, angular branches, 60 cm (2 ft) tall rockspray cotoneaster (*C. horizontalis* [Z5]) can be trained to grow on walls or allowed to spill over rocky slopes. At 1 m (3 ft) in height, cranberry cotoneaster (*C. apiculatus*) grows in similar terrain and, like most cotoneasters, produces abundant, vibrant red berries.

Growing Cotoneaster

Cotoneasters transplant best when set out in spring. Space plants almost as far apart as they are expected to spread and apply mulch between them to suppress weeds for two full seasons, the usual time it takes for plants to grow into a tight mat. On slopes, spread landscaping fabric over the site, cut holes in it for each plant, and cover the fabric around the plants with a thick blanket of mulch.

Fertilize established cotoneasters growing in poor soil with a balanced controlled-release fertilizer in spring. The plants need little other care. Prun-

Many cotoneasters produce crimson berries in fall, providing food for wildlife.

ing is done only to rejuvenate overgrown plantings. Sheared back to 5 cm (2 in) stubs in late winter, elderly cotoneasters will rebound with vigorous new growth in a single season.

Sap-sucking spider mites occasionally make leaves appear pale. Knock pests off plants with a strong stream of water from a hose or apply insecticidal soap as directed on the label.

FUNDAMENTAL FACTS

ATTRIBUTES	Spreading semievergreen plants with four-season interest; for groundcover
SEASON OF INTEREST	Spring through winter
FAVORITES	C. dammeri, C. adpressus, C. horizontalis, C. apiculatus
QUIRKS	Grows wider than it is tall
GOOD NEIGHBORS	Best grown in masses
WHERE IT GROWS BEST	Slopes and other well-drained spots
POTENTIAL PROBLEMS	Spider mites
PRUNING	Rarely needed; prune overgrown plants hard in winter or early spring
CRITTER RESISTANCE	Good
SOURCE	Nursery plants
DIMENSIONS	Groundcover species to 1 m (3 ft) tall and 1.8 m (6 ft) wide

The vivid fall foliage of winged euonymus gives rise to its nickname of burning bush.

'Emerald 'n' Gold' is a popular foundation shrub that pairs well with dark evergreens.

E. fortunei 'Emerald Gaiety' is a bushy, spreading plant with white-margined leaves.

EUONYMUS
Euonymus spp.

HARDINESS:
Zones as indicated

PREFERRED SOIL pH:
Neutral to slightly acid

PREFERRED SOIL TYPE:
Fertile, well-drained

PREFERRED LIGHT:
Sun to partial shade

Euonymus in the Landscape

A number of very different shrubs, with different uses in the landscape, are known by the common name of euonymus. Winged euonymus (*Euonymus alatus*), so named because of the winglike ridges on the woody stems, is a stiff, vaselike shrub that can reach 3.5 m (12 ft) tall and 1.8–2.4 m (6–8 ft) wide. Sometimes called burning bush because of its intense red fall foliage, this naturally neat plant is a fine choice for boundary plantings or a dense hedge that never needs pruning. To make the color really glow, plant winged euonymus against an evergreen background, which will also highlight its bare winter silhouette. It is hardy to Zone 3.

Evergreen euonymus (*E. japonicus*) is a 4.5 m (15 ft) tall shrub with large, lustrous leaves. Hardy to Zone 5, it is popular in warm climates for foundation plantings and specimens in beds. Wintercreeper (*E. fortunei*) is a low-growing or vinelike shrub often used as groundcover or allowed to creep up walls or fences. Bushy varieties reach 1–1.2 m (3–4 ft), and the stems of vining types can grow to 3 m (10 ft). Hardy to Zone 5, and usually evergreen in Zones 6 to 9, this plant has waxy leaves that stand out against junipers and other green conifers.

All in the Family

'Compactus' is a smaller, more globe-shaped version of winged euonymus, though it is hardly compact at 3 m (10 ft) tall. It has purplish red fall foliage, while the leaves of 'October Glory' are an even brighter crimson than those of the species.

Evergreen euonymous offers a number of variegated cultivars. The leaves of 'Aureus' are splashed boldly with gold, those of 'Silver King' are edged in white, and 'Tricolor' has yellow leaves marked with green and pink. 'Microphyllus', called box-leaf euonymus, has the narrow leaves and compact habit of a boxwood.

Wintercreeper also offers colorful cultivars. 'Emerald 'n' Gold' has leaves variegated in green and deep yellow, while 'Emerald Gaiety' has silver-rimmed leaves. The leaves of 'Coloratus' turn purplish red in fall.

Growing Euonymus

Set out purchased plants in early spring, in holes twice as wide and deep as the plant's nursery container. Work a 5 cm (2 in) layer of compost into each hole to improve drainage, set plants in, fill around them and water well. Euonymus transplant with ease and should show new growth within a few weeks of planting.

Winged euonymus rarely has problems of any kind. Other euonymus can be damaged by scale, which are tiny immobile sap-sucking insects that congregate on stems and leaf undersides. Spray infested plants with dormant oil applied in the winter as directed by the label. In damp areas, euonymus can contract powdery mildew, a disfiguring fungal disease that deposits white, powdery patches on leaves. Severely prune plants in late winter or early spring to control it.

FUNDAMENTAL FACTS

ATTRIBUTES	Colorful variegated or fall foliage; for beds, groundcover
SEASON OF INTEREST	Spring through fall
FAVORITES	*E. alatus, E. japonicus, E. fortunei* and their cultivars
QUIRKS	Plants produce best coloration when grown in full sun
GOOD NEIGHBORS	Boxwood, juniper, magnolia, wax myrtle
WHERE IT GROWS BEST	In sun and fertile soil
POTENTIAL PROBLEMS	Rare for winged euonymus; scale and powdery mildew on other species
PRUNING	Prune in early spring to remove diseased stems and rejuvenate plants
CRITTER RESISTANCE	Good
SOURCE	Nursery plants
DIMENSIONS	*E. alatus* to 3.5 m (12 ft) tall, 2.4 m (8 ft) wide; *E. japonicus* to 4.5 m (15 ft) tall, 3 m (10 ft) wide; *E. fortunei* 1–3 m (3–10 ft) tall and wide

'Spring Glory' is an old-fashioned prolific bloomer with large, rich yellow flowers.

FORSYTHIA

Forsythia spp. and hybrids

HARDINESS:
Zones as indicated

PREFERRED SOIL pH:
Neutral to slightly acid

PREFERRED SOIL TYPE:
Average

PREFERRED LIGHT:
Sun to partial shade

Forsythia in the Landscape

The dazzling stems of forsythia, laden end to end with small, bell-shaped, golden flowers, signal us that spring has indeed arrived. Because flowers appear before leaves, forsythias are aflame with color, often for several weeks. For a preview of the show, cut stems as the buds swell and bring them indoors to bloom in a vase.

Growing 1.8–2.4 m (6–8 ft) tall and equally wide, forsythias are often used as specimen shrubs in lawns or planted along boundaries as an informal hedge. You can also combine versatile forsythias with other shrubs, place a single one at the back of a flower border, or underplant them with spring bulbs. Even when forsythias are not in flower, the arching stems of older varieties and the upright stems of newer ones appear graceful and refined. In fall the long pointed leaves turn bronzy red, prolonging this plant's season of interest.

Forsythias for Every Garden

Even though the flowers are surprisingly tolerant of light frosts, it's important to choose cultivars suited to your climate to avoid frost damage to the buds and flowers. In Zones 3 and 4, 'Ottawa' is a good choice because its buds will open even after they have been exposed to freezes. 'Northern Gold' is another cold-hardy variety. In Zones 5 to 9, 'Spring Glory' blooms so heavily that the stems appear to have been dipped in gold. Two old-fashioned heavy bloomers for Zones 6 to 9 are 'Spectabilis' and 'Lynwood'. New cultivars are ideal for small gardens or as a showy groundcover, ideal for a slope. 'Gold Tide' is one that only reaches 50 cm (20 in) tall, but it spreads to 1.2 m (4 ft) wide.

Growing Forsythia

Plant out container-grown plants at anytime from late winter to early summer. When purchased in spring, forsythias will often bloom in their pots, which makes it easy to shop for an eye-catching plant. Space them so that at least half of their mature width is left between plants. You can fill in the spaces with spring-blooming bulbs. Except for irrigating as needed

to keep the soil moist during the first season, forsythias require little care and are resistant to pests and diseases.

Poor flowering is usually the result of improper pruning. Avoid pruning forsythia aggressively and shaping them into tight balls. For the best show, let forsythia follow its natural growth pattern, in which long stems arise from the base of the plant, sometimes arching over to the ground when they become heavy with leaves.

To promote next year's flowers, each spring, after the flowers have faded, use lopping shears to cut off one-third of the largest, oldest, and least floriferous stems to the ground. Also remove any dead or damaged stems. But to preserve flower buds do not cut stem tips unless they crowd into walkways or other high-traffic areas. It is usually necessary to thin old stems only every 2–3 years to encourage flower production.

FUNDAMENTAL FACTS

ATTRIBUTES	Graceful shrubs with profuse yellow blossoms; for beds, hedges, specimens
SEASON OF INTEREST	Spring to fall
FAVORITES	'Ottawa', 'Northern Gold', 'Spring Glory', 'Lynwood', 'Gold Tide'
QUIRKS	Improper pruning reduces flowering
GOOD NEIGHBORS	Flowering cherry, lilac, spring-flowering bulbs
WHERE IT GROWS BEST	In sun and average garden soil
POTENTIAL PROBLEMS	Poor flowering due to aggressive pruning
PRUNING	Every 2–3 years, remove up to one-third of the oldest stems after blooming
CRITTER RESISTANCE	Good
SOURCE	Nursery plants
DIMENSIONS	0.6–2.4 m (2–8 ft) tall, 1.2–2.4 m (4–8 ft) wide

For the best display, resist shaping and allow forsythia to follow its natural growth pattern.

HOLLY
Ilex spp.

HARDINESS:
Zones as indicated

PREFERRED SOIL pH:
Slightly acid

PREFERRED SOIL TYPE:
Average, well-drained

PREFERRED LIGHT:
Sun to partial shade

Holly in the Landscape

Fast-growing and easy to please, hollies are among the best shrubs to plant along the foundation of a house. And hollies with spiny leaves naturally deter traffic, making them excellent screening shrubs for boundaries. Modern cultivars are predictable in their sizes and shapes, so it is easy to choose hollies that fit into any spot and rarely need pruning. Although many do have prickly foliage, some species boast small, smooth leaves and are easy to include in a mixed border. The most popular hollies are evergreen, enriching the landscape with their glossy foliage year-round.

Hollies are also valued for their colorful berries in red, black, or yellow. However, for good fruit set, you will usually need at least one male plant for every six females. The sex of the plant is given on plant tags or often reflected in the cultivar name, such as 'Blue Boy' and 'Blue Girl'.

Sorting Through Hollies

There are hundreds of hollies, and while they are a vigorous, care-free group, it's best to select a variety suited to your region. English holly (*Ilex aquifolium*) does best in cool, moist

Chinese holly is a heat-tolerant type that has wavy, spiny leaves and red berries.

climates, and its range is limited to Zones 7 to 9. Most have the classic wavy oval leaves with sharp spines and bright red or yellow berries, and plants usually grow to a height of 4.6 m (15 ft). A few cultivars, such as 'Silver Beauty' and 'Golden Milkmaid', have variegated leaves.

Meserve hollies (*I.* × *meserveae*) are very cold tolerant, being hardy from Zone 5. Also called blue hollies, these hybrids have glossy, spiny, blue-green foliage. Look for such cultivars as 'Blue Angel', 'Blue Prince', and 'Blue Girl', which all grow 1.8 m (6 ft) tall

and 1.5 m (5 ft) wide. In hot, dry areas, look for the densely branched Chinese holly (*I. cornuta*), which grows from Zones 7 to 9. Many varieties grow to 3 m (10 ft), but 'Dwarf Burford' and 'Rotunda' are naturally rounded in shape and grow into tight mounds only 1.2–1.5 m (4–5 ft) tall and wide. Lusterleaf holly (*I. latifolia*), hardy from Zone 7, is another good choice for hot climates. It has large, elegant, leathery leaves and grows to 7.5 m (25 ft) tall.

With small, smooth leaves that bring a fine texture to the landscape, Japanese holly (*I. crenata*) looks a lot like boxwood. Evergreen in Zones 6 to 9, this species needs moist soil and will not survive prolonged drought. The gracefully mounding 'Helleri', at only 45 cm (18 in) tall and 1 m (3 ft) wide, is a popular cultivar.

For damp, acid soil, look to two North American natives. Inkberry (*I. glabra*) is an evergreen with black fruits that grows 1.5–1.8 m (5–6 ft) and is hardy to Zone 5. Winterberry (*I. verticillata*) is deciduous, hardy to Zone 4, and grows up to 4.5 m (15 ft) tall and 3 m (10 ft) wide. 'Red

The mounding shape and fine texture of *I. crenata* 'Helleri' make it a good companion.

FUNDAMENTAL FACTS

ATTRIBUTES	Lustrous leaves, berries; for beds, specimens
SEASON OF INTEREST	Year-round for evergreens
FAVORITES	*I. aquifolium, I. cornuta, I. crenata, I. glabra, I.* × *meserveae, I. verticillata*
QUIRKS	Both male and female plants needed for fruit set
GOOD NEIGHBORS	Boxwood, euonymus, juniper, spirea
WHERE IT GROWS BEST	Any soil and at least a half day of sun
POTENTIAL PROBLEMS	Spider mites, scale
PRUNING	To shape plants, prune anytime from early spring to midsummer
CRITTER RESISTANCE	Good
SOURCE	Nursery plants
DIMENSIONS	45 cm–7.5 m (18 in–25 ft) tall, 1–3.5 m (3–12 ft) wide

Sprite' and 'Winter Red' have especially colorful and attractive berries.

Growing Holly

Hollies can be planted in spring or early fall, or even in summer if you are willing to water them regularly. They should show vigorous growth the second season after planting and reach full size in 5–6 years.

Their tough, thick leaves are protection against most pests and diseases. Occasionally, minute sapsucking spider mites or scale insects may attack, creating a pale stippled appearance on leaves. Knock mites off plants with a strong stream of water from a hose or apply insecticidal soap or a commercial miticide labeled for use on hollies according to label directions. Control scale with horticultural oil applied as directed.

In neutral soil, *H. macrophylla* 'Générale Vicomtesse de Vibraye' produces pink blooms.

Mophead hydrangeas form large globes of starlike flowers that range from pink to blue.

White flowers highlight the cream-edged leaves of *H. macrophylla* 'Quadricolor'.

HYDRANGEA

Hydrangea spp.

HARDINESS:
Zones as indicated

PREFERRED SOIL pH:
Slightly alkaline to slightly acid

PREFERRED SOIL TYPE:
Rich, moist, well-drained

PREFERRED LIGHT:
Sun to partial shade

Hydrangea in the Landscape

Adaptable and long-lived, hydrangeas are deciduous shrubs smothered under their immense heads of papery florets from summer till fall. The handsome flower clusters, excellent for cutting and drying, appear on the tips of upright stems clothed in deep green, sometimes variegated leaves.

Plant hydrangeas around house foundations or integrate them into flower beds. They are also stunning specimens in the lawn and make a colorful boundary border, mixing well with many other shrubs. Smaller cultivars are even suited to large pots.

Chameleon Flowers

The most common species is bigleaf hydrangea (*H. macrophylla*), which grows 1.2–1.8 m (4–6 ft) tall and is hardy to Zone 6. The flowers of mophead, or hortensia, types produce big globes of star-shaped petals, while the lacecap types have flatter flowerheads with frilly blossoms in the center and larger florets around the edges.

Flower colors range from pink to blue but can be altered by changing soil acidity. The lower the pH, the deeper the blue. For blue flowers, apply aluminum sulphate or a commercial "bluing" compound. For pink flowers, add a high-phosphorus fertilizer or garden lime. Use any amendment according to package directions.

All in the Family

The smooth hydrangea (*H. arborescens*) is a North American native that is hardy to Zone 3 and produces white, snowball-like flower clusters that can reach up to 30 cm (1 ft) in diameter. Another care-free native, the oakleaf hydrangea (*H. quercifolia* [Z5]) has large conical white flowers that age to purple, and its lobed leaves turn yellow and red in fall. It reaches 2.5 m (8 ft) tall and wide and tolerates shade.

The peegee hydrangea (*H. paniculata* 'Grandiflora') reaches 4.5 m (15 ft) tall and spends most of the summer covered in dense clusters of creamy flowers that resemble cotton candy. Peegees prefer partial shade and fertile soil and are hardy to Zone 3.

Growing Hydrangea

Plant hydrangeas in spring or fall at the same depth at which they grew in the nursery pot. Keep the soil moist

The peegee hydrangea is smothered under large cones of white flowers in summer.

the first growing season and water during dry spells thereafter. Add an 8 cm (3 in) layer of organic mulch to retain soil moisture. Shape the plant and remove any damaged or weak branches right after flowering by cutting stems back to a strong set of leaves. Prune old, woody stems to the ground every 2–3 years in late winter.

Hydrangeas aren't troubled by pests or diseases and don't need any winter protection in cold climates.

FUNDAMENTAL FACTS

ATTRIBUTES	Handsome deep green leaves; large clusters of white, pink, blue flowers
SEASON OF INTEREST	Early summer to fall
FAVORITES	*H. macrophylla, H. quercifolia, H. arborescens, H. paniculata*
QUIRKS	Flower color can change
GOOD NEIGHBORS	Azalea, mountain laurel, rhododendron
WHERE IT GROWS BEST	In fertile, moist, well-drained soil
POTENTIAL PROBLEMS	Soil pH above 7.0 can cause leaf yellowing
PRUNING	Prune plants right after flowering
CRITTER RESISTANCE	Excellent
SOURCE	Nursery plants
DIMENSIONS	1–4.5 m (3–15 ft) tall and wide

Groundcover junipers like 'Tamariscifolia' make excellent no-mow groundcovers for slopes.

'Plumosa Aurea' has yellow-green foliage that turns purple-brown in winter.

JUNIPER
Juniperus spp.

HARDINESS:
Zone 2 but variable

PREFERRED SOIL pH:
Adaptable

PREFERRED SOIL TYPE:
Average, well-drained

PREFERRED LIGHT:
Full sun

Juniper in the Landscape

Some type of juniper eventually wins a place in every care-free landscape. Adaptable and hardy, junipers ask only for sun and good soil drainage. They'll thrive for many years without pruning, watering, or other maintenance. These reliable evergreens endure cold winters with ease, many being hardy to climates as cold as those in Zone 3. And junipers come in so many forms and colors that there's bound to be exactly the right one for any site you have in mind.

Considering how tough they are, the gentle elegance that junipers bring to the landscape is nothing short of amazing. Although the scalelike evergreen foliage is scratchy to the touch, its density and fine texture combine to give junipers a soft appearance. Large, vase-shaped junipers will form a beautiful dark green backdrop for flowering perennials; compact cultivars can be used in foundation plantings. Low-growing junipers will knit themselves together into a lush, weed-resistant groundcover that's an ideal no-mow covering for slopes. In addition, there are upright columnar and pyramidal junipers that grow to tree size, providing wind breaks, or strong vertical structure for small spaces.

Getting to Know Junipers

With most garden plants, it makes sense to begin the selection process on the basis of plant names. However, this can lead to unnecessary confusion with junipers, because several major species compare closely in terms of hardiness, diversity of form, and practical use in the landscape. So, rather than sorting through hundreds of cultivar names, it's better to decide on a size, shape, and color, and then shop around to see what's available.

Depending on selection, junipers may be blackish green, medium grass green, blue-green, gray-green, or have bold chartreuse leaf tips. In cold climates where few other evergreens are present in the garden, dark-colored junipers are often preferred because of the rich green color they bring to the winter landscape. In areas where

J. procumbens 'Nana' is a a slow-growing, small shrub that thrives in dry, sandy soil.

other evergreens are easily grown, gray-green or blue-green junipers are often used as accent plants. Be careful with gold-tipped junipers, however. Although they are an easy way to light up a green landscape, a little of their intense color usually goes a long way.

Sizing Up Junipers

The nursery industry does an excellent job of labeling junipers. Plant tags often include all the information you need to make a good selection. In the language of the trade, a vase-shaped plant grows into an inverted triangular shape, with stems that arch up and away from a central base. Those that grow less than 1.2 m (4 ft) tall and wide are top candidates for use as foundation shrubs, while larger vase-shaped junipers are best used as accent shrubs or grouped into a hedge for a sunny lawn.

Dozens of junipers exhibit what is called a spreading habit. These plants may grow less than 1 m (3 ft) tall, yet spread as wide as 3 m (10 ft). Their mature size can be difficult to imagine when you are looking at a small plant in a pot, but trust what the tag has to say. Spreading junipers can be used to

'Blue Chip' is a spreading juniper that holds its excellent blue-green color all year long.

flank walkways or cover gentle slopes, or stand alone as broad pools of evergreen color in an open lawn.

Groundcover junipers generally grow to less than 30 cm (12 in) tall, but each plant may spread to 3 m (10 ft) wide. There is much variation among cultivars in foliage color and winter hardiness, so it is wise to listen to advice on cultivars from local nursery experts. Excellent vigor is important, because stressed groundcover junipers may do a poor job of suppressing weeds. For example, fine-textured 'Blue Pacific' shore juniper tolerates salty soil, but it suffers from winter cold north of Zone 7. By comparison, 'Bar Harbor' trades its summer green for bronze red in winter and is hardy to Zone 2.

Upright junipers can be sorted into two shapes: straight columnar plants, which are often very narrow and up to 3 m (10 ft) tall, or symmetrical, pyramidal shapes that resemble Christmas trees. Unlike most evergreen trees, however, pyramidal junipers, such as bright green 'Hetzii Columnaris' or gray-green 'Silver Spreader', seldom exceed 4.5 m (15 ft) in height, making it easy to fit them into small landscapes. Columnar

junipers are so narrow that they can be used at the back of a flower border or planted near the corner of a house without interfering with traffic.

Growing Junipers

Junipers are easy to transplant in spring. Where winters are mild, you can also set them out in fall. To encourage the development of new

roots, dig planting holes about twice as wide as the nursery container and at the same depth. After planting, provide water during dry spells as needed to keep the soil moist the first season. When planting spreading or groundcover junipers, surround plants with a broad, thick mulch, such as bark chips or compost, to control weeds until they reach mature size. Hand-weed as needed, and refresh the mulch every few months to support this process.

Prune junipers only to remove damaged stems. The plants look best when allowed to follow their natural growth patterns, and severe pruning can result in brown patches that never fill out with fresh green growth.

Keeping Junipers Healthy

Most junipers grow for many years with no pest problems, but occasionally you may notice brown lantern-shaped twiggy sacs hanging from stems. These are the cocoonlike dwellings of the bagworm, a caterpil-

Junipers with golden foliage like 'Carbery Gold' are best used to accent green gardens.

lar that eats juniper foliage. Remove and dispose of the bags by hand as soon as you spot them. Rarely, a fungal disease called twig blight causes stem tips to turn brown and die. Prune off and dispose of discolored branches. If the problem continues, spray plants with a commercial fungicide labeled for use on junipers. Bright orange, plum-like growths in winter are rust disease fruiting bodies. Prune off and destroy as soon as noticed. Juniper scale are tiny insects that hide and feed inside branch crevices, weakening the branches until they turn yellow. Less than 1.5 cm (1/2 in) long, and oval in shape, scale are usually white or light brown. Spray affected plants in late spring with a commercial garden insecticide labeled for use for scale on junipers. Apply as directed on the package labels.

FUNDAMENTAL FACTS

ATTRIBUTES	Hardy evergreens to use as foundation shrubs, accents, groundcovers
SEASON OF INTEREST	Year-round
FAVORITES	Choose locally adapted cultivars by size, shape, and color
QUIRKS	Grows poorly in wet soil
GOOD NEIGHBORS	Candytuft, daylily, spring-flowering bulbs
WHERE IT GROWS BEST	Full sun in any well-drained site
POTENTIAL PROBLEMS	Twig blight, bagworm, scale, rust
PRUNING	Plants live decades; prune only to remove damaged branches
CRITTER RESISTANCE	Excellent
SOURCE	Nursery plants
DIMENSIONS	Varies with type, from 15 cm (6 in) to 4.5 m (15 ft) high, and 1–3.7 m (3–12 ft) wide

'Mme. Lemoine' has been popular since the 1890s for its double, white flowers.

LILAC
Syringa spp.

HARDINESS:
Zone 2

PREFERRED SOIL pH:
Neutral to slightly acid

PREFERRED SOIL TYPE:
Well-drained sandy loam

PREFERRED LIGHT:
Sun

Lilac in the Landscape

Lilacs, like roses, linger in the romantic hearts and memories of gardeners. Often found in older gardens, these long-lived plants with tough constitutions are cherished for their spectacular trusses of fragrant spring flowers. Hundreds of cultivars exist, featuring single or double flowers in deep purple, blue, pink, yellow, and white.

Lilacs are excellent plants to locate at doorways or along paths, where the sweet fragrance will greet passersby. Or place them along the edge of the lawn, where they can be planted close enough together to form a hedge. Compact dwarf types can be worked into mixed flower borders or included in foundation groupings with other shrubs on the sunny side of a house.

World-Class Lilacs

The most fragrant of all lilacs is the common lilac (*Syringa vulgaris*), whose flowers are usually the pale purple color that gives this shrub its common name. It grows to about 3 m (10 ft) tall and has numerous cultivars, ranging from the old-fashioned double white 'Mme. Lemoine' to the dark violet 'Night'. Some have bicolored blossoms, such as 'Sensation', whose purple-red florets are edged in white.

Common lilac requires a period of winter freezing to set flower buds, and seldom flowers well in areas with hot, humid summers and mild winters. But two lilacs developed from Chinese species show better heat tolerance. *S. meyeri* 'Palibin' is a slow grower with dense trusses of lilac-pink blossoms. *S. patula* 'Miss Kim' has fragrant flowers that are purple in bud and fade to a blue-tinged white. Both grow less than 1.2 m (4 ft) tall and bloom well in southern Ontario. In climates with cold winters, look for cultivars of *S. × hyacinthiflora*, such as 'Blanche Sweet' and 'Esther Staley'. These bloom early in spring with a distinct sweet fragrance, are resistant to powdery mildew disease and boring insects. Another hybrid that has made a big splash in cold-climate gardens is the 3–3.5 m (10–12 ft) tall *S. × prestoniae*, represented by the bright pink-flowered 'Miss Canada' and claret-colored 'Redwine'. Developed in Canada, these are equally hardy.

Growing Lilac

Select a site that receives at least 6 hours of sun daily and has good air circulation. These are both important conditions for limiting problems with fungal leaf diseases, which erupt in damp, stagnant air. Plant container-grown or bare-root plants in late winter or early spring. Container-grown plants set out after they have emerged from dormancy need attentive watering to keep the soil around the roots moist if their first summer in the garden is a dry one.

Once established, lilacs respond to fertilizing with a balanced, timed-release commercial product, or top-

FUNDAMENTAL FACTS

ATTRIBUTES	Fragrant white, pink, yellow, or purple flowers; for specimens, hedges
SEASON OF INTEREST	Late spring to fall
FAVORITES	'Ester Staley', 'Blanche Sweet', 'Sensation', 'Palibin', 'Miss Kim'
QUIRKS	Flowers on old wood
GOOD NEIGHBORS	Azalea, candytuft, crocus, daffodil, forsythia, tulip, perennials
WHERE IT GROWS BEST	In sun, well-drained soil, and cool climates
POTENTIAL PROBLEMS	Powdery mildew, lilac borers
PRUNING	Lives for decades; cut one-fourth of old stems to ground level in winter
CRITTER RESISTANCE	Good
SOURCE	Nursery plants
DIMENSIONS	1.2–4.5 m (4–15 ft) tall and equally wide

dressing of compost in spring. In acid soils, it is also helpful to sprinkle garden lime on the soil above the roots, according to package directions, every 3–4 years to neutralize the pH.

Prune lilacs to improve flowering, promote good air circulation, and discourage powdery mildew and boring insects, which weaken the plants. Remove damaged or diseased stems as soon as you notice them. In midwinter, cut out about one-fourth of the oldest, largest stems as close to the ground as possible. Also snap off any suckers, which are stems growing up from the base of the plant.

Branches that have small holes with sawdust around the openings harbor boring caterpillars; in summer, they cause stems to wither and die. Cut the stem 2.5 cm (1 in) below the hole and dispose of it, or insert a thin wire into each hole to kill the pests.

Common lilac bears conical blooms up to 20 cm (8 in) long, usually in pale purple.

MAHONIA
Mahonia spp.

HARDINESS:
Zone 5 unless otherwise indicated

PREFERRED SOIL pH:
Slightly acid

PREFERRED SOIL TYPE:
Fertile, moist, well-drained

PREFERRED LIGHT:
Partial shade

Mahonia leaves are glossy and edged with spines, much like those of many hollies.

Mahonia in the Landscape

It is the beauty of mahonia's large, blue-green, hollylike leaves that makes this shrub so useful in the landscape. A group of mahonias, or a single one, flanked by azaleas or ferns makes a dramatic picture. And adding to this shrub's appeal are its early flowers and berries. Yellow flower clusters open in early spring, weeks ahead of daffodils, and develop over summer months into bunches of dark blue berries that persist until birds snap them up.

Mahonias perform best if you find a shady, sheltered spot where they won't be scorched by sun or whipped by winter winds. Place them along a house foundation, in front of a hedge, or near a wall where they'll receive a few hours of morning sun but shade from midday onward. Nestle these stiffly upright plants among other shrubs, such as barberry and camellia, or with shade-loving perennials, such as ferns and hostas. Mahonias are also stunning when underplanted with pachysandra, lamium, or other shade-tolerant groundcovers.

Mahonias Large and Small

The most popular species is Oregon grape holly (*Mahonia aquifolium*), native to the forests of the Pacific Northwest. Its new spring leaves have a reddish cast, and the bronze coloring often returns with winter's cold. Growing 1–1.5 m (3–5 ft) tall, this species spreads by underground stems into a broad clump. Yet it's far from invasive, and routine thinning of old canes in winter will maintain its size.

Lending a strong architectural presence to the landscape, leatherleaf mahonia (*M. japonica* 'Bealei') grows 2.4–3 m (8–10 ft) tall and about 1.8 m (6 ft) wide. Its large leaves, composed of 9–15 spined leaflets, are held at a stiffly horizontal angle from the stems. It is hardy to Zone 7.

Growing Mahonia

Plant container-grown plants in either fall or spring, in holes that are the same depth as the nursery containers but twice as wide. Enrich the soil in the hole with compost or leaf mold, set plants at the same depth at which they grew in their containers, fill in the hole, and water well. Mulch with a 5 cm (2 in) layer of shredded bark or pine needles to keep the soil moist.

Mahonias have an upright form that adds a structural element to the landscape.

After their first season, mahonias become drought tolerant.

These tough plants have few pest or disease problems but may need pruning every other year to help maintain their vigor. In winter, lop off the oldest canes, cutting them close to the ground. You can remove up to one-third of the canes at a time. Never prune mahonia by cutting off the stem tips, or you will remove the best

Leaves of Oregon grape holly turn bronze in fall, with some stems glowing bright red.

foliage along with flower buds and all chances of seeing fruit develop.

FUNDAMENTAL FACTS

ATTRIBUTES	Hollylike leaves, yellow flowers, blue berries; for beds, foundations
SEASON OF INTEREST	Year-round
FAVORITES	Oregon grape holly, leatherleaf mahonia, and their cultivars
QUIRKS	Very sensitive to sunburn and windburn
GOOD NEIGHBORS	Azalea, barberry, ferns, hosta, pachysandra, lamium, epimedium
WHERE IT GROWS BEST	Partial shade with wind protection
POTENTIAL PROBLEMS	Parched leaves from excessive sun
PRUNING	Lives many years; cut out oldest canes at ground level in winter
CRITTER RESISTANCE	Good
SOURCE	Nursery plants
DIMENSIONS	1–2.4 m (3–8 ft) tall, 1–1.8 m (3–6 ft) wide

The red-spotted pink blossoms of 'Olympic Fire' burst open from deep crimson buds.

MOUNTAIN LAUREL

Kalmia latifolia

HARDINESS:
Zone 5

PREFERRED SOIL pH:
Acid

PREFERRED SOIL TYPE:
Fertile, moist, organic

PREFERRED LIGHT:
Partial shade

Mountain Laurel in the Landscape

Mountain laurel is one of the most beautiful native North American shrubs. Blooming in late spring or early summer, it sends out clusters of white, pink, or red, cup-shaped blossoms, each marked with darker spots or splashes. The shrub's nickname,

Even cultivated forms of mountain laurel have an informal look suited to woodlands.

calico bush, refers to these colorful splattered and splotched petals.

With its long, leathery, narrow leaves, mountain laurel looks elegant at the edge of a wood, especially in the company of azaleas, rhododendrons, and oakleaf hydrangea. It also makes a beautiful accent shrub for shady rock gardens or foundation plantings. This evergreen can tolerate a half day of sun, which often improves its flowering, but in hot-summer climates, the plants are healthier when grown mostly in shade.

Mountain Laurels Old and New

The wild species grow slowly into large, contorted, rangy plants with woody stems shaped by the light and wind patterns of the site. The pink flower buds open to white blossoms with dark pink markings. However, plant breeders in the United States have introduced a whole raft of named varieties in recent years and they now come in tones from white to dark red, as well as several bicolored forms.

When adding mountain laurels to a more structured garden, choose the modern cultivars that have been developed for diverse flower colors, faster growth, and compact growth habit. If you want a large shrub with richly colored flowers, consider 'Bullseye'. It bears white blossoms flushed with maroon on plants that eventually reach 1.8–2.4 m (6–8 ft) tall. 'Olympic Fire' is smaller at 1.2–1.8 m (4–6 ft) tall but no less striking. The buds are bright crimson and open to pale pink flowers speckled in red. A dwarf cultivar, 'Elf', grows less than 1 m (3 ft) tall but spreads 1.2–1.5 m (4–5 ft) and bears shell pink buds that open to white flowers. Smaller still is the deep pink 'Tiddlywinks', which barely reaches 60 cm (2 ft) tall and an equal width at maturity.

Growing Mountain Laurel

Choose a site with good drainage and prepare planting holes by working in an 8 cm (3 in) deep layer of compost, leaf mold, or peat moss. Set plants slightly higher than they grew in their containers, water well, and cover the root zone with a 5 cm (2 in) layer of organic mulch, such as shredded bark or compost. Keep the root zone barely moist for 2 months after planting, but allow it to become nearly dry between waterings. Soggy soil leads to fatal root rot.

Fertilize established mountain laurels each summer. Apply a granular fertilizer designed to maintain soil acidity at half the rate recommended on the label, or apply garden sulphur as needed to achieve a pH of 4.5–5.8. Limit pruning to trimming off dead twigs. Never cut stem tips, which will keep the plant from flowering.

By late summer, you may see a few fungal leaf spots. Pick off unsightly leaves. The plants will endure this natural stress and grow replacements.

FUNDAMENTAL FACTS

ATTRIBUTES	Clusters of cuplike flowers; for foundations, woodland gardens
SEASON OF INTEREST	Year-round for foliage; blooms late spring to early summer
FAVORITES	Standard 'Bullseye', 'Olympic Fire'; dwarf 'Elf', 'Tiddlywinks'
QUIRKS	May develop root rot and languish or die in poorly drained soil
GOOD NEIGHBORS	Azalea, hydrangea, dogwood, rhododendron, winterberry holly, ferns
WHERE IT GROWS BEST	Rocky woodland areas with cold winters and mild summers
POTENTIAL PROBLEMS	Leaf spot, root rot
PRUNING	Lives many years; prune rarely, only to remove dead twigs
CRITTER RESISTANCE	Good
SOURCE	Nursery plants
DIMENSIONS	Wild species 2.4–3.5 m (8–12 ft) tall, 2.5 m (8 ft) wide; cultivated forms 0.6–2.5 m (2–8 ft) tall, 0.6–1.8 m (2–6 ft) wide; leaves 12 cm (5 in) long

Mugo pine ranges in size from a small tree to dwarf shrubs sized to fit into containers.

MUGO PINE

Pinus mugo

HARDINESS:
Zone 2

PREFERRED SOIL pH:
Adaptable

PREFERRED SOIL TYPE:
Average

PREFERRED LIGHT:
Sun to partial shade

Mugo Pine in the Landscape

Botanically speaking, mugo pine is a tree, but it is very successful when grown as a shrub. Its extreme hardiness exceeds that of even juniper, so it is among the few evergreens that will succeed for gardeners in the coldest of climates. And, because of mugo pine's ability to withstand strong sun, it is equally at home in hot, arid landscapes, or anywhere in between.

The stocky, upright branches are clothed in 2.5–5 cm (1–2 in) long deep green needles and feature upright new stem tips, called candles, in late spring. This is a pine that rarely manages to grow more than 1.5 m (5 ft) above the ground, but its width can equal its height.

Mugo pine is often used as a specimen plant in places that are difficult to irrigate, such as near streets, or at driveway entrances, or along the outer edges of a large lawn. But its compact size also makes it a good choice for rock gardens, small beds, and foundation plantings. It's a good neighbor to medium-sized, sun-loving perennials and creates a pleasing combination of textures when planted along with ornamental grasses. There are even cultivars, such as the 30 cm (12 in) tall and 45 cm (18 in) wide 'Slowmound', that are small enough to be used in containers or troughs.

Modern Mugos

For many years mugo pines were propagated from seed, which led to substantial variation in the size and growth habit of plants available at nurseries. Inexpensive mugos are still grown from seed, so even plants of respected varieties, such as 'Compacta', may look a little different from one another as they mature. Happily, nurseries have recently begun propagating mugos from cuttings, making it possible to create more uniform plants. As part of this development, new named cultivars are beginning to appear for sale, including the 1 m (3 ft) tall 'White Bud', which sports nearly white branch tips, or candles, and the bushy 'Big Tuna', which grows 1.5 m (5 ft) tall and equally wide. Also look for dwarfs, such as 'Winter Gold' and 'Ophir', whose foliage turns from deep green to golden yellow during the winter.

Growing Mugo Pine

Set out container-grown plants in spring in cold climates or anytime except midwinter in Zones 8 and 9. Dig a hole as deep as the nursery container and twice as wide. Although the plants can adapt to any type of soil, get the roots off to a good start by amending the soil with organic matter. Fill the hole and top it off with a 5 cm (2 in) thick layer of organic mulch to retain soil moisture and suppress weeds. Expect to see only modest growth the first year after planting, followed by faster development in succeeding seasons.

Mugo pines do not need pruning, but should they threaten to grow too tall for their site, the upward growth can be stopped by breaking off the candles in early spring. This is seldom necessary with newer cultivars. Unlike many other pines, mugos shed very few needles. It is their habit to hold needles for up to 5 years. Don't worry if up to one-fourth of the needles drop in late fall; they will quickly be replaced by a new crop.

A pest called pine sawfly occasionally feeds on the new growing tips in mid to late spring. Control these small caterpillars with red heads by applying insecticidal soap according to directions. Treat promptly, because an uncontrolled infestation often results in a larger, more damaging population the following year.

FUNDAMENTAL FACTS

ATTRIBUTES	Attractive mounding shape, green needles
SEASON OF INTEREST	Year-round
FAVORITES	'White Bud', 'Big Tuna', 'Winter Gold', 'Ophir'
QUIRKS	Seed-grown plants may lack uniformity and not resemble the parents
GOOD NEIGHBORS	Ornamental grasses, sun-loving perennials
WHERE IT GROWS BEST	Sun in a wide range of climates
POTENTIAL PROBLEMS	Pine sawfly
PRUNING	Lives for decades; to control size, snap off candles in late spring
CRITTER RESISTANCE	Excellent
SOURCE	Nursery plants
DIMENSIONS	0.6–1.5 m (2–5 ft) tall, 1–1.5 m (3–5 ft) wide

'Winter Gold' is a dwarf, spreading shrub whose needles turn golden in cold weather.

Red-osier dogwood produces fuzzy clusters of white flowers in the spring.

The shrubs form clumps of glossy stems that turn bright red during cold temperatures.

The golden stems of 'Flaviramea' stand out when displayed against dark evergreens.

RED-OSIER DOGWOOD

Cornus stolonifera

HARDINESS:
Zone 2 unless otherwise indicated

PREFERRED SOIL pH:
Slightly acid

PREFERRED SOIL TYPE:
Average, moist

PREFERRED LIGHT:
Sun to partial shade

Red-Osier Dogwood in the Landscape

When the sap rises in late winter, the stems of red-osier dogwood turn from purplish brown to vibrant red, lending much-appreciated color to the landscape. Also called red-twig dogwood, this species grows into a many-stemmed, shrubby clump that welcomes spring with small, yellowish white flowers and oval green leaves. White berries emerge in summer, which birds relish and harvest before the leaves drop in fall.

Although an individual plant is attractive, a mass planting makes a dramatic, unusual statement when the stems color up in cold weather. You can set this plant off to best advantage by growing it against a backdrop of evergreen trees or shrubs, or underplanting it with an evergreen groundcover, such as ivy. It is just the right size for combining with clumps of ornamental grasses. Because it spreads by suckers, or shoots growing up from the roots, red-osier dogwood is also a good choice for controlling erosion on hillsides or stream banks.

For real winter drama, mix the species with cultivars that have different stem colors. 'Flaviramea' has golden yellow stems in winter, while those of 'Kelseyi' are yellow-green tipped in red. All varieties will tolerate shade, but the stem color is much improved when grown in sun. In many varieties, cold temperatures bring out the brightest colors. 'Cardinal', for example, shows striking cherry red stems when grown where winters are cold but is yellow-orange when mild.

To vary the look during the growing season, you can also mix in a variety with colorful foliage. The green leaves of 'White Gold' have broad white margins.

All in the Family

Several other dogwoods also produce colorful stems in winter. Tartarian dogwood (*Cornus alba*) is similar to red-osier dogwood, though a little slower to spread. The 'Sibirica' and 'Bloodgood' cultivars have red stems that rival those of true red-osiers. This species is also hardy to Zone 2.

Other good choices include the 'Corallina' cultivar of the pagoda dogwood (*C. alternifolia*) and blood-twig dogwood (*C. sanguinea*), especially 'Winter Beauty', which has yellow-orange stems tipped in red. These are both hardy to Zone 4.

Growing Red-Osier Dogwood

Set out plants in spring so they will be well rooted by winter. Keep the soil slightly moist and mulch with 5 cm (2 in) of compost or other organic mulch. Each spring sprinkle a light application of balanced timed-release fertilizer to encourage vigorous new growth and more spectacular stem color the following winter.

FUNDAMENTAL FACTS

ATTRIBUTES	Vivid red or yellow stems in winter; for specimens, hedges, slopes
SEASON OF INTEREST	Year-round
FAVORITES	'Flaviramea', 'Kelseyi', 'Cardinal', 'Sibirica', *C. sanguinea*, 'White Gold'
QUIRKS	Cold temperatures improve stem color
GOOD NEIGHBORS	Holly, juniper, mahonia, mugo pine, ornamental grasses, ivy
WHERE IT GROWS BEST	In sun and cold climates
POTENTIAL PROBLEMS	Powdery mildew, leaf spots in damp, stagnant air
PRUNING	Lives for decades; thin stems or prune back severely in late winter
CRITTER RESISTANCE	Good
SOURCE	Nursery plants
DIMENSIONS	1.2–3 m (4–10 ft) tall and equally wide

While red-osiers can reach 2.5–3 m (8–10 ft) in height, pruning techniques that stimulate colorful new stems will also control plant size. In late winter, either cut the oldest one-third of the stems to ground level annually or cut all of them back to the ground every 3 years. The first method will result in tall, symmetrical shrubs, while the second approach is best when growing red-osier dogwood as a hedge.

Potential problems include powdery mildew and other fungal leaf diseases, but they usually cause only cosmetic damage. Should severe problems develop, prune plants back hard in winter and destroy the prunings. Newer varieties often show improved disease resistance. Planting in an airy site and keeping irrigation water off leaves discourages fungal diseases.

'Yaku Princess' is regal, forming elegant mounds of dense flowers in apple blossom pink.

RHODODENDRON

Rhododendron spp.

HARDINESS:
Zones as indicated

PREFERRED SOIL pH:
Acid

PREFERRED SOIL TYPE:
Moist, humus-rich, well-drained

PREFERRED LIGHT:
Partial to full shade

Rhododendron in the Landscape

Rhododendrons bring beauty to the spring garden. Their thick, leathery, evergreen leaves vary from 8–15 cm (3–6 in) long and are carried on woody branches that form elegant tiers. In late spring to summer, trusses of large, tubular flowers adorn the stem tips, each set off by a frame of green leaves. Flower colors include purple, red, white, yellow, and pink.

Mass large rhododendrons for a privacy screen or boundary marker and use compact types along paths or in foundation plantings. Site them

'Blue Peter' flowers freely, with large globes of lavender-blue marked with a maroon ray.

carefully, so that their brittle limbs won't spread into high-traffic areas. Fill the foreground of the plantings with a shade-loving groundcover, such as ferns or lamium. Rhododendrons also enjoy the company of their fellow woodland plants, including dogwood and mountain laurel.

Selecting Rhododendrons

There are thousands of species and cultivars, ranging in height from 60 cm (2 ft) to 2.4–3 m (8–10 ft). Most are hardy from Zone 6, although some Ironclad hybrids are hardy to Zone 4. The best way to find a rhododendron is to visit a local nursery, which will have plants that are adapted to your area. You can select from the plants they carry by size and color.

Among smaller types, look for Yako rhododendrons (*R. yakushimanum* [Z5]), a Japanese native that forms a rounded plant with felted young leaves. Two good North American species are the Carolina (*R. carolinianum* [Z5]) and catawba rhododendrons (*R. catawbiense* [Z4]), both with purplish flowers.

The 'P.J.M.' hybrid (Z4) is popular for its lavender-pink blossoms and leaves that turn burgundy in the fall. Other favorite hybrids are the lavender blue 'Blue Peter' (Z8), red 'Nova Zembla' (Z4), creamy yellow 'Unique', and white 'Boule de Neige' (Z5).

Growing Rhododendron

Select a site with filtered shade, or one with morning sun and afternoon shade. Plants growing in deep shade may grow leggy and flower poorly, while those in sun will show scorched leaves. Protect them from strong wind, which can shred the leaves.

Rhododendrons need loose, moist soil with a pH of 4.5–6.0, so prepare a roomy planting hole amended with acidic leaf mold or peat moss. Plant in spring and set plants high, so that the topmost roots are barely covered with soil. Spread 8 cm (3 in) of compost, bark chips, or other organic mulch over the roots. Water only as needed to keep the soil barely moist. Too much water leads to incurable root rot. Occasional problems with dieback, which causes branch tips to

Yako rhododendrons have unusual bell-shaped white flowers flushed with pink.

blacken and die, are caused by burrowing caterpillars called borers and by fungal disease. Cut back affected stems to healthy wood and dispose of the damaged portions.

If you see yellow splotches on leaf surfaces and insect excrement on leaf undersides, suspect lacebug. Spray plants with insecticidal soap per label and dispose of fallen leaves to remove the insects' nesting places.

FUNDAMENTAL FACTS

ATTRIBUTES	Large flowers, leathery leaves; for specimens, foundations, beds
SEASON OF INTEREST	Year-round; blooms late spring to summer
FAVORITES	Choose varieties suited to local conditions by size and flower color
QUIRKS	Leaves temporarily droop and curl as a protective response to cold weather
GOOD NEIGHBORS	Azalea, fern, mountain laurel, hydrangea, mahonia, dogwood, holly
WHERE IT GROWS BEST	Partial shade in moist, organically rich soil
POTENTIAL PROBLEMS	Dieback, lacebug, root rot
PRUNING	Lives for decades; prune only to remove dead or damaged wood
CRITTER RESISTANCE	Good
SOURCE	Nursery plants
DIMENSIONS	1–3 m (3–10 ft) tall, 1.2–4.5 m (4–15 ft) wide

The pink blooms of 'Fragrant Delight' contrast with its red stems and bronze new leaves.

ROSES

Rosa spp.

HARDINESS:
Zones 2 to 6, depending on type

PREFERRED SOIL pH:
Near neutral

PREFERRED SOIL TYPE:
Fertile, loamy

PREFERRED LIGHT:
Sun

Rose in the Landscape

Roses have been cherished as garden plants for centuries. Although modern roses are more tolerant of disease than their ancestors are, these beauties remain somewhat demanding. However, with careful attention to plant selection, planting site, pruning, and fertilization, anyone can grow at least a few roses without having to constantly ward off problems.

Roses are often grown in rose beds, so that their growing requirements can be easily met, or they may

Vigorous 'Stanwell Perpetual' blooms early and often repeats later in the season.

be mixed with a few annuals or low-growing perennials. Many roses, however, can be grown in a perennial border, where they blend magnificently with bluebeard, catmint, and lavender. Other types can be massed as groundcovers, grown as hedges, or showcased as specimens. Small roses can even be grown in containers.

The Language of Roses

Roses are divided into a number of types based on their ancestry, growth habits, flower form, and uses in the landscape. And although some types are easily identified, such as the long-stemmed roses known as hybrid teas, modern "landscape" roses are difficult to categorize. Any gardener who has fallen in love with roses will eventually acquire a specialized vocabulary to better understand these intriguing plants, but most gardeners can get by with a few terms.

Landscape rose is a broad category used to identify roses developed within the last 15 years or so that are disease resistant and usually require only casual pruning. Varieties such as 'Simplicity', 'Flower Carpet', and 'Carefree Wonder' are in this category. Landscape roses often have little fragrance and their flowers tend to be small, but the plants can be counted on to bloom over a very long season.

English rose describes a large group of roses that combine the fragrance and flower form of old roses with the disease tolerance of modern types. These are typically vigorous, bushy plants that bloom heavily in late spring and lightly in summer or fall, provided they are pruned and fertilized between flower flushes. When disease problems arise on English roses, such as 'Heritage', prompt removal of the affected leaves can usually preserve the plants' health.

Rugosa roses are a species with tough, quilted leaves that are naturally resistant to insects, disease, and even salt spray. Rugosas have been used to breed varieties that tolerate both disease and extreme cold. In cold climates, the most dependable roses are rugosa varieties such as the white 'Blanc Double de Coubert' and deep pink 'Hansa'. If old flowers are not pruned off, rugosa roses produce colorful hips that are rich in vitamin C, providing food for birds in winter.

Floribunda roses load up with large clusters of flowers in late spring, with sporadic blooming thereafter. Fragrant and beautiful, floribundas, such as the white 'Iceberg' and red 'Europeana', are the best roses for planting along a fence, although problems with fungal leaf diseases such as blackspot or powdery mildew often follow prolonged damp spells.

Hybrid tea roses are prone to every rose malady, but gardeners forgive these flaws because of the beauty and fragrance of the flowers. Cultivars number in the thousands and include the revered red-flowered 'Mr. Lincoln' and coral red 'Fragrant Cloud'. If you cannot resist dabbling in these temperamental beauties, consult a rose society or display garden in your area to learn which varieties grow especially well under local conditions.

Growing Roses

Select a sunny site where you will have easy access to care for the plants. You can set out dormant bare-root roses, which are usually offered by mail-order nurseries, in early spring, before the first leaves appear. Later in the season, after the plants have begun

'Fire Princess' grows only 30 cm (1 ft) tall, excellent for containers and flower beds.

active growth, plant only container-grown roses. These can be planted all summer, providing the soil around their roots is kept moist afterward. Roses begin developing new roots at the same time that they grow new leaves, so early planting gives them an entire season to become established.

To prepare for planting, dig a hole 45 cm (18 in) deep and wide and enrich the soil with compost, well-rotted manure, or peat moss. Mix in a timed-release fertilizer or a commercial plant food developed for roses according to package directions.

Next, look at the main stem. Many roses are grafted, which means the stems of a desired variety have been attached to the roots of a hardier rose. This forms a callused bump just above the roots, which is called the graft union. It can be injured by cold, so in Zones 2 to 6 this bulge should be 2.5–10 cm (1–4 in) below the soil line; the colder the winter, the deeper it should be. Where winters are mild, set plants higher, with the graft union about 2.5 cm (1 in) above the soil.

If you are planting a container-grown rose, adjust the depth of the hole with soil so that the graft union

'Iceberg' is a spectacular floribunda, with large, double white, very fragrant blooms.

will be at the desired level. Slide the plant gently from the pot, set it in the hole, and fill around it with soil. If you are planting a bare-root rose, create a cone-shaped mound of soil in the center of the hole at the height required for the graft union to be at the desired level. Set the plant atop the mound and spread the roots out around the cone's sides. Fill the hole around the cone carefully with soil.

Water the plants in well and spread 5–8 cm (2–3 in) of compost or other organic mulch. If there is no rain, water every third day with a deep, slow soaking, taking care not to wet the foliage. Once roses are established, they need 2.5 cm (1 in) of water weekly. Fertilize established roses at least twice each season, in spring and early summer, with a balanced timed-release fertilizer or one formulated for roses. In Zones 8 and 9, where hybrid tea roses may rebloom in the fall, feed them a third time in late summer.

Prune roses in early spring to remove dead stems and thin out the canes, which improves air circulation and discourages fungal infections. To help plants rebloom, prune off old flowers as they fade, cutting just above a leaf that has 5 leaflets.

From Zone 6 northward, insulate the base of plants from extreme cold by piling a 30 cm (12 in) deep cone of soil and mulch around plants in late fall, after they go dormant. Even if buds higher up on the plants are killed, those protected beneath the mulch will survive and form the first branches on the next season's plants.

The Trouble with Roses

The list of every problem a rose might have would be long indeed, but the three most common ones are blackspot, powdery mildew, and Japanese

beetles. Blackspot is a fungal disease and the primary problem that weakens roses. In arid climates blackspot is uncommon, but wherever nights are humid you can expect to see black spots appear on the leaves, which eventually wither and fall. Healthy plants with good natural resistance will survive small outbreaks, but highly susceptible plants need to be sprayed with a commercial rose fungicide as directed on the label.

A rose fungicide usually treats or prevents powdery mildew as well. This fungal disease causes gray or white patches to develop on leaves in a wide range of climates, usually in late summer when days are warm and humid and nights are cool. Roses are usually more resistant to this disease than to blackspot.

Several types of beetles eat rose leaves, but iridescent green Japanese beetles, prevalent in the eastern part of the continent, make short work of whole plants, blossoms and all. Hand-pick and dispose of beetles early in the morning when they are sluggish, or spray plants regularly with a botanical insecticide as directed on the package. Rose leaves and flowers are

Vivid flowers and low-growing habit make 'Flower Carpet' an ideal groundcover.

'Gertrude Jekyll' is an English rose bearing generous clusters of double pink blooms.

also a treat for browsing deer and rabbits. The best critter defense is a fence, but you can tuck bars of deodorant-formula bar soap among plants or apply a commercial repellent as directed on the label. Or switch to trouble-free rugosa roses, which are more resistant to all these problems.

FUNDAMENTAL FACTS

ATTRIBUTES	Beautiful, fragrant flowers; for specimens, beds, groundcovers, hedges
SEASON OF INTEREST	Late spring to fall
FAVORITES	Landscape, English, rugosa, floribunda, and hybrid tea roses
QUIRKS	Plants will rebloom if deadheaded and fertilized after each flowering
GOOD NEIGHBORS	Allium, bluebeard, candytuft, catmint, lavender, petunia, sweet alyssum
WHERE IT GROWS BEST	Sunny, well-drained sites with moderate winters
POTENTIAL PROBLEMS	Blackspot, powdery mildew; Japanese beetles
PRUNING	Lives for decades; prune in late winter to remove dead wood
CRITTER RESISTANCE	Fair; vulnerable to deer and rabbits
SOURCE	Nursery plants
DIMENSIONS	1–1.8 m (3–6 ft) tall, 0.6–1.5 m (2–5 ft) wide

Smokebush can grow to the size of a small tree, providing a bold expanse of plum color.

SMOKEBUSH
Cotinus coggygria

The foliage of all smokebush varieties turns a burnished purple-red when fall arrives.

The plum leaves of 'Royal Purple' have scarlet margins, foreshadowing its fall color.

HARDINESS:
Zone 5

PREFERRED SOIL pH:
Acid to neutral

PREFERRED SOIL TYPE:
Average

PREFERRED LIGHT:
Sun to partial shade

Smokebush in the Landscape

When allowed to follow its natural inclinations, this unusual shrub grows into a 4.5 m (15 ft) tall tree, hence the confusion between its common names of smokebush and smoke tree. But even in its treelike form, smokebush is small enough to fit in with other large shrubs or to serve as a focal point in the lawn, at the corner of a house, or near a drive or walkway. Wherever it is planted, smokebush always commands attention because of its unusual airy, rounded flower plumes, which resemble puffs of purple smoke. These plumes appear in summer and persist until fall.

Sorting Out Smokebush

The species has green leaves that are often tinged pinkish bronze when young, feature a red midrib and edges through the summer, and turn yellow and red in fall. The 25 cm (10 in) long flower plumes are tawny green and so profuse that the shrub's leaves are barely visible.

As beautiful as the species is, many gardeners prefer the purple-leaved cultivars, such as 'Velvet Cloak', 'Royal Purple', and 'Purpureus'. The Rubrifolius group includes a variety of plants whose leaf color ranges from claret to plum. The flowers for all of them are a smoky pinkish purple, and the leaves turn red in autumn.

You can spotlight the dark leaves by pairing smokebush with high-contrast companions, such as Russian sage, artemisia, or other plants with gray foliage. Plants with golden leaves or pink flowers will also intensify smokebush. A particularly striking combination is smokebush under-planted with coleus and New Guinea impatiens that exhibit shades of purple, chartreuse, and pink.

Growing Smokebush

While smokebush tolerates sites with some shade, growing it in full sun deepens the leaf colors, which provides a beautiful frame for the fluffy flower panicles. So select a site where the shrub will get plenty of light. Set out new plants in early spring and provide water during droughts the first season after planting. Because smokebush has fast-growing, fibrous roots, it becomes established quickly and is soon very drought tolerant.

Plants of any age rarely have pest problems and require no special care beyond a light application of fertilizer every spring. Use an organic or timed-release, balanced fertilizer applied at half strength according to package directions. Smokebush prefers a soil pH of 5.5–6.8, and leaf color will be poor if it grows in overly fertile or very acid soil. If necessary, neutralize the soil with garden lime in fall, applied per package directions.

When grown as a shrub, smokebush needs little pruning. Prune only to remove damaged wood or to shape the plant in spring. Aggressive pruning results in long, unattractive, poor-flowering branches. You can keep shrubs compact and short by pruning back to 15 cm (6 in) every 2–3 years. This treatment turns smokebush into a leafy, rounded shrub. Flowering will be sparse, but no other shrub can equal the purple foliage.

FUNDAMENTAL FACTS

ATTRIBUTES	Airy flower clusters, colorful foliage; for specimens, beds, foundations
SEASON OF INTEREST	Late spring through fall
FAVORITES	'Velvet Cloak', 'Royal Purple', 'Purpureus', Rubrifolius group
QUIRKS	Rich or very acid soil leads to poor flowering
GOOD NEIGHBORS	Artemisia, Russian sage, dusty miller, new Guinea impatiens, coleus
WHERE IT GROWS BEST	Adapts to many climates and soils
POTENTIAL PROBLEMS	Usually trouble-free
PRUNING	Lives for decades; prune to shape plant or remove damaged branches
CRITTER RESISTANCE	Excellent
SOURCE	Nursery plants
DIMENSIONS	3–4.5 m (10–15 ft) tall and equally wide

S. japonica 'Nana' is a heavy-blooming dwarf that can be used as a groundcover.

SPIREA

Spiraea spp.

HARDINESS:
Zones as indicated

PREFERRED SOIL pH:
Adaptable

PREFERRED SOIL TYPE:
Average

PREFERRED LIGHT:
Sun to partial shade

Spirea in the Landscape

Spireas are a varied group of plants grown for their attractive foliage, graceful habit, and charming flower clusters, which have small, slightly fuzzy flowers in white, pink, and red. While there are many species and cultivars, there are basically only two types: those that bloom in spring to early summer and those that bloom in summer. Both share a care-free nature and are very easy to grow.

Spireas are also easy to use in the landscape. They make a valuable addition to foundation groupings, especially when planted among shrubs with dark foliage, which highlights spireas' soft flower colors. Mound-forming types make a neatly shaped filler for shrub and flower borders or can be massed as a groundcover. Those with arching habits make graceful specimens and are dense enough to be grouped into a hedge.

Sorting Through Spireas

Two spring bloomers have been popular for centuries because of their elegant fountain shape and profuse flowers. Both bridalwreath (*Spiraea prunifolia*) and Vanhoutte spirea (*S. × vanhouttei*) have 1.5–1.8 m (5–6 ft) long arched stems studded with white flowers. They are also quite cold tolerant, being hardy to Zone 4.

The leading summer bloomer is Japanese spirea (*S. japonica*), a compact, mounding shrub that usually grows 1–1.2 m (3–4 ft) tall and equally wide. The plants are covered with airy clusters of dusty pink flowers framed by pointed, 8 cm (3 in) long leaves with serrated edges.

Varieties grown for their flowers include 'Anthony Waterer', a favorite with crimson blossoms, and 'Shirobana', which produces white and rose flowers in the same cluster. Other Japanese spirea are valued for their foliage. 'Goldflame' has yellow leaves contrasting with pink flowers. All are hardy to Zone 3.

Growing Spirea

Spireas grow quickly when planted in early spring. Amend planting holes with organic matter, such as compost or leaf mold, and set plants at the same depth at which they grew in their containers. In alkaline soils, also work a small handful of garden sulphur into planting holes. Spireas need slightly acidic conditions; if the pH is too high, green-leaved types will develop yellow leaves. After planting, cover the root area with an 8 cm (3 in) layer of mulch to retard evaporation from soil. Water as needed to keep it barely moist the first season.

Once they are established, bridalwreath types need no special care. Japanese spirea benefits from a light feeding with an organic or timed-release balanced fertilizer each spring. Aphids may occasionally infest plants, but these sap-sucking insects can be

FUNDAMENTAL FACTS

ATTRIBUTES	Graceful white, pink, or red flowers; for specimens, hedges, beds
SEASON OF INTEREST	Spring to fall
FAVORITES	Bridalwreath, Vanhoutte spirea; *S. japonica* 'Shibori', 'Goldflame'
QUIRKS	Plants can bounce back from winter damage, neglect, and overpruning
GOOD NEIGHBORS	Azalea, euonymus, iris, juniper
WHERE IT GROWS BEST	Thrives in a range of climates and soils
POTENTIAL PROBLEMS	Occasionally aphids
PRUNING	Lives for decades; type and time of pruning depends on variety
CRITTER RESISTANCE	Good
SOURCE	Nursery plants
DIMENSIONS	1–1.5 m (3–5 ft) tall and equally wide

knocked off foliage with a strong spray of water or apply insecticidal soap as directed on the label.

Pruning in Season

Neither type of spirea demands attentive pruning, but it's important to preserve flower buds when grooming the plants. Spring bloomers set flowers on old wood, so the best time to prune is after the flowering period has ended. To maintain the natural arching shape, prune out old woody stems near the base of the plant. Then thin crowded stems by cutting them back to various lengths for a more natural appearance.

Japanese spirea blooms on new wood, so you can prune as much or as little as you like in early spring, just as the plants begin to develop new leaves. In cold climates, prune stems damaged over winter to the ground.

Japanese spireas form mounding plants that fit easily in a flower garden or shrub border.

The snowball flowers of Korean spice viburnum release an intense spicy sweet fragrance.

VIBURNUM
Viburnum spp.

HARDINESS:
Zones as indicated

PREFERRED SOIL pH:
Slightly acid

PREFERRED SOIL TYPE:
Fertile, well-drained

PREFERRED LIGHT:
Sun to partial shade

Viburnum in the Landscape

Viburnums are custom-made for care-free landscapes. There are 150 species, and at least that many garden-worthy cultivars, including both evergreen and deciduous plants with a range of sizes, silhouettes, and flower types. Viburnums have it all: attractive foliage in various shapes that turns colors in fall, graceful flowers in white and pink, and prolific yellow,

Korean spice viburnum is covered in spring with large globes of waxy white flowers.

blue, black, or red berries that feed birds in the cold months. It is easy to find one that fits your site and design needs, even if it's difficult to choose from all the plant possibilities.

Viburnums are showy enough to be specimens but also join comfortably with others in a shrub border or foundation planting. In fact, the larger varieties are a beautiful way to soften house corners. Compact plants can be incorporated into flower beds, and evergreens can be massed to create an informal hedge or screen. Note that if you are growing viburnums for their berries, having more than one plant usually improves fruit set.

Sun Lovers for Cold Climates

Hardy to Zone 2, 3.5 m (12 ft) tall cranberry bush viburnums are top choices for sunny sites in cold climates. Both the European cranberry (*Viburnum opulus*) and American cranberry bush (*V. trilobum*) have flattened, white flower clusters in late spring, maplelike leaves that turn to red in fall, and heavy crops of red berries.

European cranberry bush can attract aphids by late summer. You can take advantage of the superior aphid tolerance and smaller size of American cranberry bush cultivars. 'Wentworth' grows quickly to 2.4 m (8 ft) tall and wide, has excellent fall foliage color, and bears large, red edible fruits. 'Compactum' grows into a dense 1.8 m (6 ft) tall bush, making it ideal for hedge planting. 'Xanthocarpum' has yellow fruits that glow in the sun.

Viburnums for Borders and Boundaries

Two sun-loving, fragrant species thrive when grown in moist, fertile soil in Zones 5 and 6 respectively. Beginning in spring, the spicy sweet aroma of Korean spice viburnum (*V. carlesii*) beckons. Clusters of pink buds open to nearly white, 8 cm (3 in) balls of fragrant flowers. Unlike most viburnums, this spicy favorite prefers soil with a neutral pH, so you will need to add garden lime according to package directions when planting it in acid soil. At 1.8 m (6 ft) tall and wide, the species is an excellent deciduous viburnum for boundaries or screening, but look for the dwarf, 1 m (3 ft) tall 'Compactum' cultivar when using Korean spice viburnum in foundation groupings.

'Cayuga' has a multitude of pink buds that open to give fragrant white flowers. This variety is also much more resistant to fungal leaf spots and mildew than other species.

While not as fragrant as Korean spice viburnum, Burkwood viburnum (*V. × burkwoodii*) is a workhorse among fragrant shrubs and is easier to grow in poorly drained and acid soils. It blooms in spring, with pink buds opening to white, and has glossy, semievergreen leaves with felted undersides. 'Mohawk' has clove-scented flowers followed by a good crop of red fruits that ripen to black.

If you're willing to trade spring fragrance for fall color, the linden viburnum (*V. dilatatum*) is an incredibly trouble-free shrub for Zone 5. Planted in any sunny, well-drained spot, it will mature into a 2.4 m (8 ft) tall mounded shrub with lovely white spring flowers followed by abundant black berries that persist well into winter. The fall foliage color is usually a strong bronze red, which serves as a beautiful backdrop for the immature berries. Bright red fruit that turns pink following frost is displayed by 'Erie', while 'Catskill' is smaller growing but wide spreading, with good fall color and dark red fruits that last well into winter. 'Oneida' is more upright and noteworthy for its repeat blooming during the summer following the spring display. 'Michael Dodge' is a cultivar that is literally covered with yellow fruits in fall.

A species known for its foliage is leatherleaf viburnum (*V. rhytidophyllum*). Its oblong semievergreen leaves reach up to 18 cm (7 in) long. Reaching 4.5 m (15 ft) tall, this fast-growing plant blooms with small, fuzzy clusters of cream flowers in late spring and bears plentiful fruits that change from red to black. The leatherleaf viburnum looks like a dense rhododendron, and is perfect for boundaries, screens, hedges, and foundation plantings. It is hardy to Zone 5. A good choice for the West Coast is laurustinus (*V. tinus*), which has glossy leaves, white flowers that open from pink buds, and egg-shaped metallic blue fruits that ripen to black. Hardy to Zone 7, this species makes an attractive informal hedge.

Desirable Doublefiles

For gardeners whose want spectacular flowers, few shrubs can compete with the doublefile viburnum (*V. plicatum* f. *tomentosum*). Mature specimens are at least 3 m (10 ft) tall, and may grow twice as wide, and feature strong horizontal branching. Double rows of showy, bright white, flower clusters appear in late spring, creating a tiered effect. The bright green leaves turn reddish purple in fall. Best in light filtered shade from Zone 6, this deciduous viburnum is without peer for balancing the vertical lines of a house.

Burkwood viburnum blooms open from pink buds to form flattened, perfumed clusters.

Cultivars of doublefile viburnum each have their own special charm. 'Mariesii' is the best-known full-sized doublefile, growing 2.5 m (8 ft) tall and wide, while 'Shasta' is popular for its less imposing 1.8 m (6 ft) size. Both 'Roseum' and 'Pink Beauty' have white flowers that age to pink.

Other Viburnums Worth Growing

Another hybrid, 'Alleghany', has dark green, leathery leaves that may stay over winter in mild climates and shows off creamy white flowers in spring. Clusters of brilliant red fruits brighten the landscape in early fall and turn almost black as they mature and invite the birds to feast. This is hardy to Zone 5 as is 'Seneca', a selection of a Japanese species (*V. sieboldii*). It has wide spreading branches with large heads of creamy flowers in spring. In fall, pendant heads of bright red fruits last for several months.

While many viburnums are fragrant, fragrant viburnum (its botanical name used to be *V. fragrans* but has been changed to *V. farreri*), hardy from Zone 6, has sweetly scented flowers that open in early spring before the leaves unfurl. It needs a sheltered location to protect the early blooms, which can be forced into flowering indoors if cut. The foliage is slightly bronzed and turns maroon red in fall.

Growing Viburnum

Viburnums are tough, pest-resistant plants that ask for little beyond a hospitable site that has moist, well-drained soil, usually with a nearly neutral soil pH of 5.0–6.5. Plant out container-grown viburnums in spring, just as they are emerging from dormancy. Prepare planting holes by digging in an 8 cm (3 in) thick layer of organic matter, such as compost or leaf mold. Set the plants

Blooming in spring, burkwood viburnum is a valuable addition to a shrub border.

at the same depth they occupied in their nursery containers, fill the hole around the plants with soil, firm it, and water in well. Top the root zone with an 8 cm (3 in) thick organic mulch to keep insect- and disease-carrying mud from splashing onto leaves during heavy rains and to help retain soil moisture. Each spring, apply an organic or timed-release, balanced fertilizer at the rate recommended on the package label.

Extremely hot, humid, or rainy summer weather can cause outbreaks of fungal leaf spot diseases. Don't worry if some of the leaves wither and fall. These resilient plants will recover on their own and be ready to bloom enthusiastically the following spring.

Viburnums need little pruning. Trim them only to remove dead wood or shape the plants. Prune evergreen types in spring and deciduous viburnums right after they flower.

FUNDAMENTAL FACTS

ATTRIBUTES	Lovely flowers, colorful berries, fall foliage; for beds, hedges, specimens
SEASON OF INTEREST	Spring through late fall; year-round for evergreens
FAVORITES	Choose cultivars matched to your climate and site
QUIRKS	Fruit set is heaviest when multiple plants are grown
GOOD NEIGHBORS	Bluebeard, euonymus, forsythia, juniper, lilac, spirea, summersweet
WHERE IT GROWS BEST	Growing conditions depend on the cultivar
POTENTIAL PROBLEMS	Aphids; fungal leaf spot diseases
PRUNING	Lives for years; prune in spring or after flowering, depending on type
CRITTER RESISTANCE	Good
SOURCE	Nursery plants
DIMENSIONS	1–6 m (3–20 ft) tall and wide

WEIGELA
Weigela spp. and cvs.

HARDINESS:
Zone 5 unless otherwise indicated

PREFERRED SOIL pH:
Neutral

PREFERRED SOIL TYPE:
Well-drained

PREFERRED LIGHT:
Full sun

Weigela in the Landscape

For a splash of color in early summer, the bright red varieties of weigela are hard to beat. The majority of weigela grown in gardens are named varieties that resulted from crossing different species. As a result their color ranges from white, through many shades of pink, to bright and dark red, often with a different color inside the flower. In addition, one species, *Weigela middendorfiana*, has yellow flowers with orange or red markings in the throat. Weigela hybrids are versatile shrubs that come in many different sizes and are thus able to fill different roles in the garden. Dwarf varieties like dark pink 'Minuet' or red 'Tango' grow only 60–75 cm

W. middendorfiana's elegant, funnel-shaped blossoms appear in early summer.

(24–30 in) high, and can be used as a low hedge to define a garden area without cutting off the view. Both are hardy to Zone 4. At the other end of the scale are the white 'Candida' and pale pink 'Carnaval', which will grow to 2.5 m (8 ft) and are best suited for the back of a mixed border where their light green foliage will show off later blooming perennials.

Foliage also needs to be taken into consideration because not all weigelas are green. 'Looymansii Aurea' has bright yellow leaves that are edged in red when they first open, although this fades in the sun. Both *W. florida* and *W. praecox* have variegated forms with leaves that are edged in cream at first, becoming white with age. 'Foliis Purpureis' has pink flowers over purple-tinged leaves.

Welcoming Weigelas

For many years 'Newport Red' was the best of the bright red forms but this has dwindled in popularity and been replaced with the newer and brighter 'Red Prince'. This has flowers that don't fade as they age, and often re-blooms in late summer. It is more upright in shape and grows 1.5–2 m (5–6 ft) tall. A recent introduction from the Central Experimental Farm in Ottawa is 'Rumba', which is hardy to the southern parts of Zone 3. This is a more spreading shrub, growing 1 m (3 ft) tall, with yellow-green leaves edged in purple, dark red flowers with a yellow throat, and flowering from June to September. 'Bristol Ruby' is another readily available variety with ruby red flowers, freely produced in early summer, and an upright habit to 2 m (7 ft).

Pink and white varieties are not as common but 'Polka', another Ottawa introduction, has pink flowers that are yellow inside on a long-

The profusion of pink blossoms of *W. praecox* 'Variegata' are especially handsome.

blooming plant with dark green leaves. This grows about 1.2 m (4 ft) tall and wide. 'Dropmore Pink', introduced from Morden, Manitoba, is also pink but taller, at 2 m (6 ft), and hardy to Zone 3. Midnight Wine is a recent introduction with dark burgundy leaves and deep pink flowers on a dwarf 30 cm (12 in) plant that can be used at the front of a mixed border. The white form of 'Bristol Ruby' is called 'Bristol Snowflake' and has white flowers flushed with pink on a similar sized plant.

Growing Weigelas

Plant container-grown plants in spring and set them out half their eventual height away from other plants in roomy planting holes that have been modestly amended with organic matter. In spring, once growth has started, prune off any shoots that have been winter killed and don't show new growth.

Established plants will grow well and the older wood should be pruned out every 3–4 years. If pruning becomes necessary, it should be done as soon as flowers fade, since blooms develop on short

shoots from previous year's growth. There are no serious pest or disease problems.

FUNDAMENTAL FACTS

ATTRIBUTES	Free-flowering shrubs of varying heights and colors
SEASON OF INTEREST	Early summer, with re-bloom in some varieties
FAVORITES	'Red Prince', 'Minuet', 'Polka', *W. praecox* 'Variegata'
QUIRKS	Flowers often have yellow throats
GOOD NEIGHBORS	Forsythia, flowering cherries, most sun-loving perennials
WHERE IT GROWS BEST	Full sun and well-drained soil
POTENTIAL PROBLEMS	Few, some winter kill but rarely severe except at limits of hardiness
PRUNING	Occasionally remove some older shoots after flowering
CRITTER RESISTANCE	Good
SOURCE	Nurseries and garden centers
DIMENSIONS	30 cm–2.5 m (12 in–8 ft) tall, 45 cm–1.8 m (18 in–6 ft) wide

WITCH HAZEL

Hamamelis spp.

HARDINESS:
Zones as indicated

PREFERRED SOIL pH:
Slightly acid

PREFERRED SOIL TYPE:
Average

PREFERRED LIGHT:
Partial shade

Witch Hazel in the Landscape

In winter, when they're least expected, witch hazel's clusters of crinkled yellow or coppery red blooms burst forth on bare stems like off-season fireworks. Although the blooms last less than a month and are small and shaggy, fragrant witch hazel flowers inspire winter-weary gardens and the gardeners who keep them.

Witch hazel is valuable enough for its early-season blooms, which shrug off cold. But these deciduous shrubs also boasts outstanding fall color, with the wavy-toothed leaves turning yellow, orange, and red. To make sure you don't miss the cheer this humble shrub has to offer, place it where you can enjoy it: near a driveway or in front of a window. The flowers are particularly stunning when backlit by winter sun, becoming a soft haze of color. An evergreen backdrop helps show off the confetti-like blossoms, which are also pretty companions for bulbs that bloom early in spring.

Wild and Wonderful Witch Hazels

Growing to 6 m (20 ft) tall and 4.5 m (15 ft) wide, hybrid witch hazel (*Hamamelis × intermedia*) is derived from Chinese and Japanese species. Its cultivars are usually grafted onto the hardy roots of a North American native species and have large, very fragrant flower clusters. 'Arnold Promise' has abundant golden yellow flowers and a fruity perfume, while the flowers of

'Winter Beauty' are tangerine. Red-blooming cultivars are often less fragrant than the others but just as beautiful. Try 'Diane' and 'Jelena' for copper-red flowers and 'Carmine Red' for deep bronze red. These are hardy from Zone 6.

'Pallida' is a popular Chinese witch hazel (*H. mollis*) grown for its abundant soft yellow flowers on slightly furry branches. Growing to about 3 m (10 ft), it is hardy to Zone 5 and is a good choice for warmer climates. A little hardier is 'Goldcrest', whose golden blossoms are stained with purplish red at the base.

Vernal witch hazel (*H. vernalis*), a North American native, has less showy flowers than others, but is still worth growing. Hardy to Zone 5, it has a handsome vase shape and small, apricot, highly scented flowers that curl back up in extreme cold. Another native is common witch hazel (*H. virginiana*), the source of the medicinal astringent. At 4.5 m (15 ft) tall and wide, with golden yellow flowers in fall, it is excellent for Zone 4.

Growing Witch Hazel

Plants are sold either in containers or with their rootballs wrapped in burlap. Either way, set them out while they are dormant, in fall or late winter. Set plants at the same depth at which they grew in the field or pot and water them in well. Witch hazels prefer moist soil but will adapt to just about any site. Be sure to allow plenty of room for them to spread.

Witch hazels rarely have problems with pests or diseases and need pruning only to shape the plants or remove damaged branches. Many varieties send out suckers, or underground shoots. Pull them off as soon as they appear, to preserve hybrid plants and stop the spread of native species.

Witch hazel blooms are spidery, with many slender petals forming a shaggy cluster.

The flowers of 'Jelena' are flushed with coppery red and appear in dense clusters.

FUNDAMENTAL FACTS

ATTRIBUTES	Fragrant crinkled flowers; for beds, foundations, woodland gardens
SEASON OF INTEREST	Winter to early spring and fall
FAVORITES	'Arnold Promise', 'Diane', 'Carmine Red'; 'Pallida'; *H. vernalis*; *H. virginiana*
QUIRKS	Some plants retain brown leaves in winter
GOOD NEIGHBORS	Azalea, holly, mahonia, rhododendron
WHERE IT GROWS BEST	Open woodlands or woodland edges
POTENTIAL PROBLEMS	Essentially problem free
PRUNING	Lives for years; prune to shape plant; remove suckers
CRITTER RESISTANCE	Excellent
SOURCE	Nursery plants
DIMENSIONS	3–6 m (10–20 ft) tall and 2.4–3.7 m (8–12 ft) wide

Witch hazels are large, spreading shrubs that thrive along the edges of woodlands.

CARE-FREE TREES

Trees are undoubtedly the largest and most long-lived plants in the landscape. Everything in your garden, including you and your family, are affected by the height of trees, the shade they cast, and even the area of your yard that is bordered by their spreading branches. Choosing just the right tree, and placing it carefully, will reward you year after year as the tree grows to maturity. While smaller plants are adaptable enough to allow you to dig and move them to find the best site, trees are deeply rooted in place. Because of this basic fact of tree life, before planting, you must look to the future, imagining how the tree and your garden will appear years from now.

As part of this process, be sure to envision the mature size of a new tree. Most of the trees described in this chapter are well suited to fitting the scale of most houses. Very tall trees, such as white pines, are best planted in large, open spaces where their massive size won't make a house seem tiny in comparison. Also consider the shade patterns a new tree will cast over your garden or your house, and how those patterns will change with the seasons and with the years. A specimen tree may seem expensive at first, but in time it can grow to be more valuable than all of your other plants combined. The tree that you plant today also is one of the few plants in your garden that may outlive you, and perhaps outlive your grandchildren. Of course, a tree cannot work these wonders unless it is a good match for the site. Because tree roots are extensive, it's impossible to modify the soil to make it suit the needs of a certain tree. Instead, you must choose species that will accept your garden's soil, sunlight, and wind without complaint.

The trees described here are generally easy to please provided their site requirements are met. Their roots are as hard and tenacious as their trunks, so they are extremely trustworthy plants. Choose the right trees and plant them with care, and you will be making a wise lifetime investment.

Sargent cherry is extremely cold hardy and combines spectacular flowers with fall color.

CHERRY FLOWERING

Prunus spp.

HARDINESS:
Zones as indicated

PREFERRED SOIL pH:
Neutral to slightly acid

PREFERRED SOIL TYPE:
Average, moist, well-drained

PREFERRED LIGHT:
Sun

Suited to small yards, the easy-to-grow Higan cherries are short, bushy trees.

Flowering Cherry in the Landscape

Flowering cherries are among the most ornamental trees in the spring landscape. Ranging in height from 3.5–15 m (12–50 ft), these small trees may stand upright in columns, spread out into broad canopies, or have arching, or weeping, branches. The flower colors are limited to white and pink, but the flowers can have flat profiles, open cups, or frilly puffs of petals. And the soft pastel flower colors contrast beautifully with the red-streaked bark and bronze tint of young leaves. In fall, many cherry trees offer handsome foliage in shades of red, orange, and yellow.

'Okame' is a fruitless flowering cherry that can be planted near patios and driveways.

Flowering cherries make a colorful statement wherever they are planted. Let them rise over a drift of spring-flowering bulbs or perennials. Plant them in the lawn or beside a path, where the faded spring blossoms will drop to the surface in a confetti of dainty petals. Or place one in a foundation grouping, where the flowers will enliven the green of foliage.

Selecting Flowering Cherries

Some cherries are such delicate beauties that they are difficult to grow. But there are plenty of choices among care-free trees. One of the best is Sargent cherry (*Prunus sargentii*), a classic that stands above the rest at a height of 15 m (50 ft). Hardy to Zone 5, it displays single pink flowers on a rounded crown, has crimson fall foliage, and richly hued bark marked with horizontal stripes. If your yard doesn't have room for the Sargent's broad branches, try 'Columnaris' or 'Rancho', two flowering varieties with narrow, upright shapes.

Higan cherry (*P. × subhirtella*) and its many cultivars offer a range of easy-to-grow trees. 'Autumnalis' is an unusual plant in that it bears long-lasting semidouble white flowers intermittently from fall to spring, depending on the climate. Most Higan cherries are bushy plants that reach 7.5–9 m (25–30 ft) tall and are hardy to Zone 7. Several cultivars are smaller and have been grafted to produce a weeping habit. 'Pendula', 'Pendula Rosea', and 'Pendular Rubra' are slender trees with big mushroom-shaped crowns of drooping branches that are smothered with flowers in varying shades of pink. Slightly more cold sensitive than the species, they grow 3.5–4.5 m (12–15 ft) tall. A famous flowering relative is the Yoshino cherry (*P. × yedoensis*), the

species of the famous trees planted in Washington, D.C. The slightly arching branches of Yoshino bears almond-scented white flowers and form a flat-crowned plant 12 m (40 ft) tall.

Growing Flowering Cherry

Plant cherries in spring in well-drained but moisture-retentive soil. Keep the soil moist the first year after planting, as drought-stressed trees can fall victim to borers. These pests are grubs that bore holes into the trunk, which "bleed" a sticky sap. Borers can rapidly kill young trees, but trees three or more years old can survive untreated. Replace young trees that show signs of borer damage.

Prune young cherries in late winter to remove broken limbs, thin out crowded branches, and help the tree grow into a strong, balanced shape. After 5 years, pruning should be limited to removing damaged limbs.

FUNDAMENTAL FACTS

ATTRIBUTES	White or pink spring flowers, fall foliage, attractive bark; for specimens
SEASON OF INTEREST	Spring to fall
FAVORITES	Sargent cherry, Higan cherry, Yoshino cherry and cultivars
QUIRKS	Many ornamental cherry trees are short lived
GOOD NEIGHBORS	Spring-flowering bulbs and perennials, azalea, hydrangea, lilac
WHERE IT GROWS BEST	Average garden conditions in sun
LONGEVITY	Lives 20 to 50 years
POTENTIAL PROBLEMS	Trunk borers can attack drought-stressed trees
SOURCE	Nursery plants
DIMENSIONS	Sargent cherry, 3.5–15 m (12–50 ft) tall, to 9 m (30 ft) wide

In spring, native flowering dogwood lights up the landscape with pink, or white flowers.

DOGWOOD

Cornus spp.

HARDINESS:
Zones as indicated

PREFERRED SOIL pH:
Acid

PREFERRED SOIL TYPE:
Moist, well-drained

PREFERRED LIGHT:
Partial shade

Dogwood in the Landscape

In spring and early summer the buds of dogwood trees pop open into showy white or pink bracts that light up the landscape for weeks. The trees put on a second show in fall, when their leaves turn a rich red. Finally, after the last leaves flutter to the ground, the trees continue to draw interest with textured tan bark and red fruits, which birds eat in winter.

Dogwoods are native woodland trees that shine in such a setting. Stand them before a forest of dark evergreens, pair them with serviceberry or redbud, or underplant them with spring-flowering bulbs or dwarf azaleas. These small trees are also at home in foundation plantings, at the corner of a house, or alongside a driveway.

Selecting Dogwoods

Flowering dogwood (*Cornus florida*) is an excellent North American native. At 9 m (30 ft) tall, with branches arranged in layers, flowering dogwood has saucerlike blossoms. It is available in many varieties offering a range of flower and leaf colors and is hardy from Zone 6. 'Cloud Nine' has large white flowers that float on the branch tips, while 'Cherokee Chief' bears bright, deep rose blossoms. Both 'Rainbow' and 'Welchii' have leaves variegated in cream to yellow and red. Flowering dogwoods in the wild are prone to anthracnose, a serious fungal disease. They are less susceptible in a home landscape, but consequently, a similar but disease-resistant Asian species has become a popular substitute. Kousa dogwood (*C. kousa*), also Zone 6, blooms later and has white blossoms with pointed petals on erect branches. Reaching 7.5 m (25 ft), it is more tolerant of dry soil and is often grown as a multitrunked tree. Another reliable North American native is the Pacific dogwood (*C. nuttallii*), which can reach 15 m (50 ft). This hefty, pyramidal tree, hardy to Zone 7, does best in a cool, moist site and needs frequent watering when grown in sun.

Growing Dogwood

Dogwoods are so irresistible that you might be tempted to buy one no matter what conditions exist in your yard. But select a site where the roots will be cool and shaded, in well-drained, acid soil, while the foliage receives light and good air circulation. Plant in spring and set the tree in a hole no deeper than it grew in the nursery container. Water as needed to keep the soil moist during drought and spread an 8 cm (3 in) thick layer of leaf mold or other organic mulch over the root zone to conserve water. Dogwoods are slow to develop and bloom, so be patient. Flowering dogwoods grown in deep shade with poor air circulation are at risk for anthracnose, which causes dark spots to form on leaves and weakens the tree. Those stressed by dry soil and excessive sun may be attacked by dogwood borers, which girdle trees by chewing small holes in the trunk. Both problems can be prevented by planting dogwoods in partial shade in a spot that is easy to irrigate.

FUNDAMENTAL FACTS	
ATTRIBUTES	White or pink flowers, fall color, red fruits; for woodlands, specimens
SEASON OF INTEREST	Spring and fall
FAVORITES	Flowering dogwood, Kousa dogwood, Pacific dogwood, and cultivars
QUIRKS	Young trees are slow to develop and flower
GOOD NEIGHBORS	Azalea, hellebore, redbud, serviceberry, spring-flowering bulbs
WHERE IT GROWS BEST	In slightly acidic soil and partial shade with good air circulation
LONGEVITY	Lives 100 years or more
POTENTIAL PROBLEMS	Anthracnose, dogwood borers
SOURCE	Nursery plants
DIMENSIONS	9–15 m (30–50 ft) tall, to 9 m (30 ft) wide

Prune off dead branches, below borer holes, and dispose of them. Give the tree two seasons to regain its strength; replace a tree that is obviously dying. Dogwoods require no other pruning and are otherwise maintenance-free.

Kousa dogwood blooms later than flowering dogwood, and has bigger flowers.

FALSE CYPRESS

Chamaecyparis spp.

HARDINESS:
Zones as indicated

PREFERRED SOIL pH:
Neutral to slightly acid

PREFERRED SOIL TYPE:
Fertile, moist

PREFERRED LIGHT:
Sun

False Cypress in the Landscape

No matter where you live, there is probably a false cypress well suited to your garden. Most of these long-lived evergreens grow into columns or cones that spread a bit with age and have flat, scaly foliage colored from golden yellow to apple green to soft blue-gray. The larger trees, which can eventually reach 30 m (100 ft), are ideal for screens, boundary markers, and backdrops for shrubs and smaller trees. The slow-growing dwarfs, up to 1.8 m (6 ft), are fit for foundation plantings, terrace edgings, shrub borders, and rock gardens. And some varieties are so graceful that you'll want to show them off as specimens.

All in the Family

Nootka cypress (*Chamaecyparis nootkatensis*) is very long-lived, growing for up to 1,000 years. Native to the Pacific Northwest, this species is hardy to Zone 5, prefers a moist climate, and resists damage from ice, winds, and occasional flooding. While most form a stiff pyramid, the dwarf 'Compacta' forms a globe, and 'Lutea' takes on the

C. lawsoniana 'Aurea Densa' is a bushy tree with stiff branches and golden needles.

shape of a yellow-green cone. The most elegant is the 9 m (30 ft) tall 'Pendula', whose weeping foliage hangs in long streamers.

Lawson's cypress (*C. lawsoniana*), native to western North America, is widely grown in moderate to mild climates. The 1.8 m (6 ft) 'Aurea Densa' is a compact cone of gold leaves. 'Ellwoodii', a slow-growing tree, matures to a 9 m (30 ft) column of gray-green that turns blue in cold weather. Most Lawson's cypress are hardy to Zone 6 but they may need protection from winter wind.

Two popular Asian natives have many cultivars that vary in foliage color, leaf shape, size, and silhouette. Hinoki false cypress (*C. obtusa*), hardy to Zone 5, is a conical tree with horizontal branches carrying thick sprays of deep green foliage. Look for 'Nana Gracilis', a slow-growing variety with dark green, slightly curving leaves that grows to 3.5 m (12 ft). Sawara false cypress (*C. pisifera*) forms a narrow

pyramid but is a looser, more open plant than other types. Two varieties with golden leaves that have a strong presence in the landscape are 'Gold Spangle' and the feathery 'Plumosa Aurea'. Both are hardy to Zone 4 and reach about 6 m (20 ft).

Growing False Cypress

Plant small specimens, keeping the soil ball intact to avoid root injury. Keep the soil around the roots moist the first year; plants should endure drought thereafter. Apply an 8 cm (3 in) layer of organic mulch to retard evaporation from the soil. In warm climates, site plants on a northern exposure or plant in partial shade.

False cypress are virtually pest- and disease-free. Sap-sucking spider mites occasionally infest them in hot, dry weather, causing inner foliage to die. Dislodge damaged leaves and mites with a strong water spray from a hose.

FUNDAMENTAL FACTS

ATTRIBUTES	Graceful coniferous evergreens with colorful foliage; for accents
SEASON OF INTEREST	Year-round
FAVORITES	Nootka, Lawson's, Sawara, Hinoki false cypress
QUIRKS	Leaves mature from a narrow, pointed wedge to a flat, scaly spray
GOOD NEIGHBORS	Red-osier dogwood, river birch, serviceberry, winterberry holly
WHERE IT GROWS BEST	Moist sites in climates with a cool summer
LONGEVITY	Can live more than 1,000 years
POTENTIAL PROBLEMS	Spider mites
SOURCE	Nursery plants
DIMENSIONS	1.8–30 m (6–100 ft) tall and wide, depending on species or cultivar

C. nootkatensis 'Pendula' is one of the most graceful varieties, with weeping branches.

C. lawsoniana 'Ellwoodii' forms a gray-green column that turns steely blue in cold.

With its broad, rounded canopy, the golden-rain tree is ideal for casting shade in summer.

GOLDEN-RAIN TREE
Koelreuteria paniculata

HARDINESS:
Zone 7

PREFERRED SOIL pH:
Acid to alkaline

PREFERRED SOIL TYPE:
Adaptable, well-drained

PREFERRED LIGHT:
Sun to partial shade

Golden-Rain Tree in the Landscape

This is one of the most remarkable flowering trees of summer. Golden-rain tree has so many unique qualities that many gardeners looking for a yard-sized shade tree put it at the top of their list. With a mature size of up to 12 m (40 ft) tall, and a rounded canopy of up to 9 m (30 ft) wide,

Golden-rain tree pours out clusters of yellow blossoms that last 2–3 weeks in summer.

golden-rain tree is easy to fit into most landscapes. It is beautiful as a lawn or patio specimen, where the sun can strike the flowers, making them glow. And because it has deep roots that are not invasive, you can put it in a garden and underplant it with any perennial, annual, ground-cover, or bulb that will tolerate shade. Golden-rain tree thrives in heat and shrugs off cold, although young trees can be damaged by low temperatures.

Small trees grow slowly at first and then quickly gain size after the third year. But even young trees display all the features that make golden-rain tree so popular. The feathery green leaves are divided and arranged in neat pairs, giving the tree a fluffy texture. The foliage often turns yellow in fall, where it's displayed against the dark bark and picturesque branching.

During the first heat wave of summer the tree produces yellow flowers in showy clusters that are 30–38 cm (12–15 in) long. They add vibrant color to the landscape for 2–3 weeks. Once the flowers fade, hollow, papery, 3-sided seedpods emerge, looking like little lanterns. They are subtle pale green, then progress through pale yellow and pinkish tones to a warm chocolate brown. The seedpods often persist into winter, producing a pleasant rustling sound in the wind.

All in the Family

Most gardeners grow the species, and while there are a few cultivars, they are proving to be less hardy and will probably only survive in coastal British Columbia. 'September' blooms later in summer, and 'Fastigiata' grows slowly into a narrowly upright tree, 7.5 m (25 ft) tall and 1 m (3 ft) wide. Other species are excellent ornamentals for warm climates. Chinese flame tree (*K. bipinnata*), hardy to Zone 9, is bigger all around. It grows to 18 m (60 ft), has larger golden flowers, and sends out 5 cm (2 in) long rosy salmon seedpods.

Growing Golden-Rain Tree

Golden-rain tree will grow in any type of soil as long as the site has good drainage. In all but the mildest climates, plant in early spring, as trees set out in fall are more prone to cold-weather injury. Small, container-grown specimens are preferred to those whose roots are wrapped in burlap, because they are less likely to suffer root injury while being handled. When planting, take care to keep the soil ball intact and set the tree at the same depth it occupied in the nursery container. Water as needed to keep the soil moist the first year, but after that golden-rain trees become drought tolerant.

Golden-rain tree has an undeserved reputation for suffering storm damage. The branching pattern is structurally sound enough to protect the tree from wind or the weight of ice. Still, it pays to prune young trees to eliminate narrow limb crotches and remove weak or crowded branches. After 5 years, it should need no pruning, and the tree seldom, if ever, has problems with pests or diseases.

FUNDAMENTAL FACTS

ATTRIBUTES	Deciduous tree with yellow flowers, decorative seedpods; for specimens
SEASON OF INTEREST	Spring to fall
FAVORITES	*K. paniculata*
QUIRKS	Trees planted in fall may fail in cold climates
GOOD NEIGHBORS	False cypress, lacebark pine, star magnolia, bulbs, groundcovers
WHERE IT GROWS BEST	Sunny site with well-drained soil
LONGEVITY	Lives for many years; becomes more attractive with age
POTENTIAL PROBLEMS	If unpruned, limbs may suffer wind damage
SOURCE	Nursery plants
DIMENSIONS	12–18 m (40–60 ft) tall and equally wide

'J.C. van Tol' has shiny, nearly spineless leaves and plentiful crops of red berries.

HOLLY

Ilex opaca

HARDINESS:
Zone 6

PREFERRED SOIL pH:
Acid

PREFERRED SOIL TYPE:
Average, well-drained

PREFERRED LIGHT:
Sun to partial shade

American Holly in the Landscape

When other trees are bare in winter, evergreen hollies laden with bright berries bring much appreciated beauty to the garden. There are many holly species in cultivation, but none can match the native American holly for its combination of classic cone shape, hardiness, and longevity.

American hollies have spiny, leathery green leaves, persistent red berries, and smooth gray bark. It grows slowly, but this species can reach 15 m (50 ft) in height after several decades, and it may live for centuries. American hollies eventually need space to spread, but you can surround them in foundation groups or borders with shrubs of more modest proportions, such as hydrangea, witch hazel, rhododendron, and clethra.

Sex and the Single Holly

Because hollies produce male and female flowers on separate plants, the berry-producing females need a male nearby for pollination. The sex of the plant is listed on the nursery tags, simplifying your search for the right one. A little pollen literally goes a long way when bees carry it, so one male plant growing within a few blocks of a group of females is usually sufficient. Find an out-of-the-way place in your landscape for a good pollinator which will have attractive foliage, but no berries, such as 'Jersey Knight' or 'Isaiah'. To avoid an unbalanced look when planting hollies in groups, make them all the same gender. In addition to producing berries, some females are a bit hardier. Look for 'Amy', 'Cardinal', 'Merry Christmas', and 'Old Heavyberry' if you garden in Zone 6, at the northern edge of American holly's hardiness range.

Other Care-Free Hollies

English holly (*Ilex aquifolium*) looks similar to American holly but is hardy only to Zone 7 and does best in cool, moist climates. While many varieties are grown as shrubs, 'Green Pillar' is an especially handsome upright tree, with dark green, spiny leaves and clusters of red berries. Because it needs little pruning, it is suitable for hedges, although it is also an excellent stand-alone specimen. 'J.C. van Tol' is an unusual variety with spineless leaves and it does not need a pollinator to produce berries.

For warm climates, try Altaclara holly (*I. × altaclarensis*), hardy to Zone 7. This vigorous grower tolerates heat, wind, drought, and salt spray and can grow 4.5–6 m (15–20 ft) tall. Its thick, glossy, nearly smooth leaves and heavy crops of red berries make this a valuable specimen tree.

Growing American Holly

Even though holly grows slowly, select a small specimen, which will do a better job of establishing itself in your yard for a long, happy life. Set plants out in early spring in a well-drained site that is also protected from winter weather, especially winds, which can cause leaves to brown. Hollies must be transplanted with a generous soil ball, so take care to keep it intact to prevent damaging the roots.

American holly has a classic conical shape.

American hollies are occasionally bothered by leaf miners, which are small caterpillars that tunnel into leaves, disfiguring them with trails. Snip off and dispose of affected leaves and remove fallen, infested leaves to solve the problem. If green berries fail to turn red, they may be infested with holly midges. Prune off and destroy infested berries, and if problems persist, switch to a cultivar that escapes damage by blooming later in spring.

Despite its name, 'Silver Queen' is a male whose broad leaves are edged in cream.

FUNDAMENTAL FACTS

ATTRIBUTES	Evergreen foliage and abundant red fruits; for specimens
SEASON OF INTEREST	Year-round; berries in winter
FAVORITES	'Cardinal', 'Merry Christmas', 'Old Heavyberry' for berry production
QUIRKS	Female trees need a male pollinator to set berries
GOOD NEIGHBORS	Clethra, hydrangea, pine, rhododendron, witch hazel
WHERE IT GROWS BEST	Sun or open shade in well-drained, acid soil
LONGEVITY	Lives for centuries
POTENTIAL PROBLEMS	Leaf browning from winter exposure; leaf miners, holly midges
SOURCE	Nursery plants
DIMENSIONS	To 15 m (50 ft) tall and 7.5 m (25 ft) wide

Hop hornbeam has a spreading habit and strong structure that withstands strong winds.

HORNBEAM

Carpinus caroliniana, C. betulus, Ostrya virginiana

HARDINESS:
Zone 3 unless otherwise indicated

PREFERRED SOIL pH:
Neutral to slightly acid

PREFERRED SOIL TYPE:
Moist to well-drained

PREFERRED LIGHT:
Sun to shade

Hornbeam in the Landscape

American hornbeam (*Carpinus caroliniana*) is a sinewy tree also known as ironwood or blue beech. The names refer to its hard wood, bluish gray bark, and resemblance to a beech tree. Its cousin the hop hornbeam (*Ostrya virginiana*) also has strong wood and the same tough constitution. These trees have a small stature and a neat habit with spreading limbs. These undemanding species grow slowly to 9 m (30 ft), and they can be tucked into a border or foundation grouping without fear that they will outstrip their spaces anytime soon.

The two species may share several characteristics, but there are differences. American hornbeam has smooth bark covering subtle ripples in the trunk, like skin stretched tightly

The flattened fruit clusters of hop hornbeam dangle from the branches in summer.

over muscles. Hop hornbeam has the same fluted appearance, but the bark is rough and has a shredded texture. American hornbeam flowers are inconspicuous catkins that appear in spring and are followed by a fall crop of nutlike seeds that birds relish. Hop hornbeam has showy fruit clusters in summer that dangle from branch tips and look like the flowers of hops. American hornbeam turns either yellow-orange or maroon in fall, while hop hornbeam has golden fall color.

Other Care-Free Hornbeams

American hornbeam and hop hornbeam are eastern North American natives with very large natural ranges. European hornbeam (*C. betulus*) is similar and popular for hedges, because it withstands shearing well. 'Fastigiata' is a strongly upright variety that spreads out a bit with age and is often available at nurseries. It grows to 15 m (50 ft) and makes an excellent landscape tree from Zone 5.

Growing Hornbeam

For best results, select a site that mimics the hornbeams' natural habitats. American hornbeam is a lowland tree happiest in a moist, shady place, while hop hornbeam grows best on higher ground in sun or partial shade. Hornbeams are tough to transplant, so don't plan to move one after it's in the ground. Choose a tree in a large nursery container or a balled tree with a big soil ball. Plant in spring and be careful not to plant too deeply, as burying the lower section of the trunk can lead to problems with disease.

Hornbeams are susceptible to damage by gypsy moth larvae, which eat the leaves in midsummer. However, not every caterpillar is a pest. American hornbeams are important food for the larvae of tiger swallowtail and other butterflies. So you may want to ignore the casual feeding by caterpillars with smooth skins, which are likely to be butterfly larvae, and step in with the biological control Bt (*Bacillus thuringiensis*), used as directed on the label, if dark, hairy gypsy moth caterpillars feed in large numbers.

FUNDAMENTAL FACTS	
ATTRIBUTES	Deciduous tree with attractive bark; for specimens, foundations
SEASON OF INTEREST	Spring to fall; *C. caroliniana* blooms in spring, *O. virginiana* in summer
FAVORITES	*C. caroliniana*, *C. betulus* and 'Fastigiata', *O. virginiana*
QUIRKS	Plants have very tough wood and are difficult to transplant
GOOD NEIGHBORS	Blends well with many trees and shrubs
WHERE IT GROWS BEST	*C. caroliniana* in moist soil, *O. virginiana* in well-drained soil
LONGEVITY	Lives up to 150 years
POTENTIAL PROBLEMS	Gypsy moths
SOURCE	Nursery plants
DIMENSIONS	To 9 m (30 ft) tall and wide

C. betulus 'Fastigiata' grows strongly upright and is useful as a hedge or screen.

The young branches of 'Sango-kaku' are coral red, blending with its bright fall foliage.

JAPANESE MAPLE

Acer palmatum

HARDINESS:
Zone 6

PREFERRED SOIL pH:
Slightly acid

PREFERRED SOIL TYPE:
Fertile

PREFERRED LIGHT:
Partial shade

Japanese Maple in the Landscape

Delicate in appearance and artistic in habit, Japanese maples offer a range of attractive features for the landscape. Most have smooth, grayish brown bark and branches that naturally form graceful layers or interesting, contorted shapes. Some grow into fluffy, billowing mounds, while others shoot asymmetrically into the air. The leaves are beautifully shaped and may be green, bronze, red, purple, or bicolored. In fall, the foliage is burnished in gold, russet, orange, and crimson.

Japanese maples quickly become focal points in the landscape and are often the tree of choice for small yards, because they seldom grow taller than 7.5 m (25 ft). They do best with a few hours of shade daily, so feel free to plant them at an entryway or near the house foundation. Their well-behaved roots make them suitable for including in flower beds or underplanting with bulbs, ground-

A. palmatum var. *dissectum* is famed for its finely cut leaves, which flutter in the wind.

covers, or shallow-rooted annuals. Dwarf cultivars, which grow to 1.8 m (6 ft), can edge patios and walkways but give the trees room to spread as wide as their mature height. The green-leaf types are easy to blend with other plants; those with colored leaves make striking specimens.

Many Choices and Virtues

The best way to choose a Japanese maple is to visit a nursery and select a plant personally. Check plant tags for mature size and wait until the trees leaf out so that you can see the foliage shape or color before buying.

There are two main leaf forms: divided and lobed. Varieties labeled cut-leaf or thread-leaf maple (*A. palmatum* var. *dissectum*) have very lacy, finely divided leaves and gracefully drooping branches. While some have green leaves that turn yellow or red in autumn, 'Ornatum' is one of several Japanese maples with bronze-red foliage that turns crimson in fall.

Among trees whose leaves have 5 or 7 lobes, a favorite is the red-leaved 'Atropurpureum', which retains its wine color during most of the growing season. 'Bloodgood' is reddish purple in summer, then turns bright red in fall. Several unusual cultivars boast variegated leaves. 'Butterfly' has

The leaves of 'Crimson Queen' are deeply divided and colored reddish purple.

FUNDAMENTAL FACTS

ATTRIBUTES	Deciduous trees with graceful form and leaves; for specimens, beds
SEASON OF INTEREST	Year-round
FAVORITES	'Ornatum', 'Bloodgood', 'Atropurpureum', 'Sango-kaku', 'Butterfly'
QUIRKS	Branches on some varieties form attractive contorted shapes
GOOD NEIGHBORS	Birches and other, taller trees; bulbs; perennials; groundcovers
WHERE IT GROWS BEST	Organically rich soil in partial shade
LONGEVITY	Lives many decades
POTENTIAL PROBLEMS	Rare; can suffer in prolonged droughts
SOURCE	Nursery plants
DIMENSIONS	1.8–7.5 m (6–25 ft) tall and equally wide

green leaves rimmed in pink and cream, while 'Shigitatsu Sawa' has yellow-green leaves veined in dark green. 'Sango-kaku' has coral young branches, which glow against its yellow and orange fall foliage.

Growing Japanese Maple

Plant Japanese maples in spring except in warm climates, where fall planting gives them a head start before the following summer's heat. These trees have shallow roots that benefit from good soil, so enrich a very broad planting hole with organic matter before setting in the tree. Keep the soil moist the first year and fertilize young trees each spring with an organic or controlled-release, balanced fertilizer according to package directions. An 8 cm (3 in) layer of organic mulch over the root zone year-round helps retain moisture and discourage weeds. Aside from the risk of drought stress, this tree is virtually trouble-free.

LACEBARK PINE

Pinus bungeana; other species

HARDINESS:
Zone 5 unless otherwise indicated

PREFERRED SOIL pH:
Acid to slightly alkaline

PREFERRED SOIL TYPE:
Average, well-drained

PREFERRED LIGHT:
Sun

Lacebark pine's lower branches are often pruned off to show the multistemmed trunk.

Lacebark Pine in the Landscape

Lacebark pine is a multitrunked evergreen tree native to China that is grown primarily for its colorful peeling bark. The gray outer bark flakes off in irregular patches, revealing blotches of cream, purple, yellow, and green. This marbled pattern is framed by the rigid, gray-green, 5–10 cm (2–4 in) long needles, which are held in groups of three.

Plant lacebark pine in a prominent, sunny place, such as near a terrace, pathway, or house window, where you can view the patterns of its bark. As the tree develops, you can prune off the lower branches so that its lovely bark and multiple trunks become more visible. Or you can group several unpruned lacebarks to form a handsome windbreak, screen, or background planting in the garden.

Unlike some conifers, lacebark pine does not lose its green color in extreme low temperatures. In winter, it makes quite a statement when grown alongside other trees with ornamental bark, such as river birch and serviceberry.

Slow and Steady

Lacebark pine takes its time to reach maturity, but it attains a height of 1.8 m (6 ft) in 10 years, 4.3 m (14 ft) in 20 years, and 10.5–12 m (35–40 ft) within 50 years. As the tree ages, its shape begins to open up and then spread out, and the bark begins to peel. The colorful bark is most prominent on the large, sprawling limbs of older trees.

Other Care-Free Pines

Several other medium-sized pine species also exhibit ornamental bark. Chilgoza pine (*Pinus gerardiana*) is a close relative from the Himalayas with a rounded canopy, silvery bark that peels

Lacebark pine earned its name from the patterns formed by its peeling outer bark.

off in plates, and long needles. It is hardy in Zone 7. Both Japanese red pine (*P. densiflora*) and American red pine (*P. resinosa*) earn their common names from their rust-colored bark. On older branches, the thick, scaly outer layer cracks to show gray inner bark. Hardy to Zone 5, the Japanese species has one particularly graceful variety. 'Umbraculifera' grows slowly into a densely branched umbrella shape that rarely exceeds 3.5 m (12 ft) in height. The American red pine grows robustly north into Zone 2, becoming a 30 m (100 ft) tall tree.

Bosnian pine (*P. heldreichii*) has ash gray bark that splits, revealing yellow patches beneath. This egg-shaped tree grows slowly to 7.5 m (25 ft), is hardy to Zone 6, and is tolerant of dry, alkaline soil. Montezuma pine (*P. montezumae*) is hardy only to Zone 7, but it makes a striking columnar specimen for warmer climates. The rough reddish brown bark develops fissures that contrast with drooping, 20–25 cm (8–10 in) long, blue-green needles. Seek these species at specialty nurseries and from mail-order sources.

Growing Lacebark Pine

Select a site where lacebark pine can bask in the sun. It grows best in well-drained soil, and will thrive in dry sites with poor soil and without supplemental irrigation. The trees transplant easily if they have a substantial root ball.

Pruning should be done selectively, a little at a time as the tree ages, to provide a view of the attractive bark. Cut back unwanted branches when they are still small to minimize the size of the pruning scar. Limbs can be pruned in any season.

Lacebark pine is resistant to many insects and diseases but not to the European pine shoot moth. Its larvae tunnel into tips of new stems, causing them to turn brown and die. Prune off and destroy damaged branches as you find them. Spray trees with a commercial insecticide that is labeled for controlling this pest on lacebark pine trees, applying it as directed on the package label.

FUNDAMENTAL FACTS

ATTRIBUTES	Peeling bark, multi-stemmed trunk; for screens, specimens
SEASON OF INTEREST	Year-round
FAVORITES	Lacebark pine is sold by species name
QUIRKS	Grows very slowly
GOOD NEIGHBORS	River birch, serviceberry, and other trees with ornamental bark
WHERE IT GROWS BEST	In a site with sun and well-drained soil
LONGEVITY	Lives 100 years or more
POTENTIAL PROBLEMS	European pine shoot moth larvae
SOURCE	Nursery plants
DIMENSIONS	To 12 m (40 ft) tall and equally wide; needles to 10 cm (4 in)

The blossoms of southern magnolia form waxy cream bowls with a rich fragrance.

MAGNOLIA
Magnolia spp.

HARDINESS:
Zones as indicated

PREFERRED SOIL pH:
Acid

PREFERRED SOIL TYPE:
Well-drained, otherwise adaptable

PREFERRED LIGHT:
Sun to partial shade

Magnolia in the Landscape

One of the most beloved of all trees, magnolias delight the senses with their glossy foliage, fragrant blossoms, and majestic shape. This is a diverse group of trees, with giant species that reach heights up to 25 m (80 ft) and have leaves up to 60 cm (2 ft) long, as well as more manageable types that grow 4.5 m (15 ft) high.

Large magnolias are often grown as specimens in the lawn or near the corner of a house. Smaller magnolia trees are lovely planted in groupings along the edge of a driveway or as part of a border. Because the large leaves block so much light and the shallow roots resent disturbance, grass and groundcovers should not be grown beneath magnolias. Besides, most species look best when the lower branches sweep the ground, where the flowers and conelike fruits are clearly visible.

More Cold, Less Space

The famed magnolia of the Southeast is the evergreen southern magnolia (*Magnolia grandiflora*), which has 20 cm (8 in) long leaves and scented, waxy, 25 cm (10 in) wide, creamy white blossoms in early summer. The species is hardy to Zone 7, as is 'Little Gem', a columnar variety reaching 9 m (30 ft) that is ideal for hedges and smaller gardens. The cultivars 'Edith Bogue', 'Victoria', and '24-Below' will survive in southern Zone 6.

Even hardier is the sweet bay magnolia (M. *virginiana*), which will survive in Zone 6 and tolerates shade and wet soil. It is evergreen in warm climates and has round, ivory blossoms. The saucer magnolia (M. x *soulangeana*), hardy to Zone 5, produces large, cup-shaped flowers in white, pink, or lavender before the leaves appear in spring. It reaches 4.5 m (15 ft) high and equally wide. There are many lovely cultivars, including the rose-flushed 'Alexandrina', purple-stained 'Lennei', and rose-purple 'Burgundy'.

Growing Magnolia

Magnolias thrive in sun to partial shade and slightly acid soil with average to good drainage. In Zones 6 and 7, be careful to avoid planting in low spots, called frost pockets, where cold air settles in winter and can damage flower buds in spring. Also select a protected site where winter winds can't shred the leaves.

Trees less than 2.4 m (8 ft) tall are easier to transplant than large ones.

Plant magnolias in the spring in Zones 5 and 6, and from fall to early spring in other zones. Dig a wide planting hole and settle the tree at the same depth at which it grew in its container or in the field. Fill the hole around it with soil, water thoroughly, and spread an 8 cm (3 in) thick mulch of shredded bark on the soil above the root zone to maintain soil moisture in hot weather. Should a drought strike the first summer after the tree is planted, water the tree weekly by slowly dripping water onto the root zone for an hour or longer each time you irrigate.

Magnolias need no pruning and have no serious pest problems, but they can be damaged by winter ice storms. Prune away dead or damaged limbs in late winter and the tree will usually recover after a year or two.

FUNDAMENTAL FACTS

ATTRIBUTES	Glossy leaves, fragrant flowers, conelike fruits; for specimens
SEASON OF INTEREST	Evergreens year-round; deciduous spring to fall
FAVORITES	M. grandiflora, M. virginiana, M. x soulangeana and cultivars
QUIRKS	Shallow roots are easily damaged by tilling
GOOD NEIGHBORS	River birch, hollies, pines
WHERE IT GROWS BEST	Sun to partial shade; large leaves need protection from wind
LONGEVITY	Lives 100 years or more
POTENTIAL PROBLEMS	Splintered limbs and crowns from ice storms
SOURCE	Nursery plants
DIMENSIONS	4.5–25 m (15–80 ft) tall, to 12 m (40 ft) wide

The majestic southern magnolia can reach 25 m (80 ft) tall and 12 m (40 ft) wide.

Parrotia often grows into a broad, rounded tree that spreads as wide as its mature height.

PARROTIA

Parrotia persica

HARDINESS:
Zone 7

PREFERRED SOIL pH:
Acid to near neutral

PREFERRED SOIL TYPE:
Average, well-drained

PREFERRED LIGHT:
Sun to partial shade

Parrotia's toothed oval leaves turn from glossy green to crimson very early in fall.

Parrotia in the Landscape

If you want a small tree that showcases the colors of autumn, look no further than parrotia. Native to Iran and often called Persian parrotia, this rounded tree with colorful fall foliage and dramatic peeling bark tops out at 12 m (40 ft) tall with an equal spread. In early fall, while most trees are still green, parrotia begins to attire itself in an array of bright colors. Starting from the top and working down through the crown as days pass, parrotia's colorful display of yellow, orange, and red ranks among the most brilliant of the season.

With strongly horizontal limbs that may begin at ground level, parrotia may be grown either as a large shrub or a small tree with multiple trunks. Parrotia's gray bark cracks and peels as the tree matures, revealing a mottled patchwork of green, brown, cream, and pink beneath. To better see the bark, most gardeners prune away the lower limbs, making the trunk visible in all seasons. But be sure to retain enough of the low branches to keep the fall color display at eye level.

Although autumn color is parrotia's hallmark, it is really beautiful year-round. In spring, before the 10 cm (4 in) shiny, oval leaves develop, small flowers with showy red stamens appear. If the tree is grown close to a window or a walkway, the diminutive flowers can be appreciated as a very early sign of spring.

A Tree of Many Shapes

Parrotia comes in a variety of treetop, or crown, shapes. Depending on the tree's early training in nursery fields, you might encounter very upright specimens with a few spreading limbs near the top or bushier plants with numerous broad, horizontal limbs. 'Pendula' is a smaller variety with a dome-shaped top and weeping branches. Since parrotia transplants easily, the best approach when buying is to view plants at a nursery that are big enough to reveal their branching habit, then select the shape you prefer.

Parrotia has a close relative (*Parrotiopsis jacquemontiana*) from the Himalayas. Hardy to Zone 7, it has smooth gray bark and bright yellow fall color, and it grows under similar conditions.

Growing Parrotia

Plant parrotia in the spring in fertile, well-drained soil. Parrotia displays its best autumn color when grown in acid soil, but it also accepts a near neutral soil pH. This tree prefers partial shade, especially in hot-summer areas, but grows more compact and striking and provides its best fall colors if grown in sun in cool-summer areas. Water deeply during droughts the first year after planting.

In late winter, prune as needed to reveal the attractive bark. Though rarely pestered by insects, Japanese beetles can cause minor damage to leaves. Pick them off and dispose of

P. persica 'Pendula' exhibits intense fall color and handsome weeping branches.

them in the morning, when they are sluggish. Or spray with insecticidal soap following the directions on the container.

FUNDAMENTAL FACTS

ATTRIBUTES	Vibrant fall color, peeling bark, spring blossoms; for specimens
SEASON OF INTEREST	Year-round
FAVORITES	*Parrotia persica* and 'Pendula'; *Parrotiopsis jacquemontiana*
QUIRKS	Fall color progresses from top to bottom of tree
GOOD NEIGHBORS	Lacebark pine, red buckeye, stewartia, witch hazel
WHERE IT GROWS BEST	Average soil in sun or partial shade
LONGEVITY	Lives at least 50 years
POTENTIAL PROBLEMS	Japanese beetles
SOURCE	Nursery plants
DIMENSIONS	To 12 m (40 ft) tall and wide

RED BUCKEYE

Aesculus pavia; other species

HARDINESS:
Zone 5

PREFERRED SOIL pH:
Acid to neutral

PREFERRED SOIL TYPE:
Average

PREFERRED LIGHT:
Partial shade

In late spring, red buckeye is covered with long clusters of trumpet-shaped blossoms.

Red Buckeye in the Landscape

The first North American native trees to leaf out in spring, red buckeyes are surprisingly tolerant of late frosts. Since they produce leaves so early, a defense is necessary to protect the foliage from hungry herbivores. Red buckeyes have a toxic sap that deters pests from munching the star-shaped, deeply veined, reddish leaves.

In nature, buckeyes become squat, round-topped, understory trees in moist forests. But in the home landscape they are valued as 7.5 m (25 ft) tall shade trees that produce clusters of red flowers in late spring; hence the common name of red or scarlet buckeye. The variety 'Atrosanguinea' has even deeper red flowers. Clusters of trumpet-shaped flowers attract bees and hummingbirds in large numbers. More curious than beautiful, the clusters of large nuts that develop in late summer eventually drop to the ground. The nuts are toxic if eaten.

Red buckeyes like moist, shady conditions and will even tolerate occasional flooding, but their shallow roots cause them to be easily drought-stressed. Planting in a shady location helps, but red buckeyes will also grow in sun if soil moisture is adequate. In such a location, the trees' dense growth and spectacular red flowers make a terrific display. Red buckeyes are at their best when grown beside stately trees that stand bolt upright.

Other Care-Free Buckeyes

California buckeye (*A. californica*) is a West Coast native with a multi-stemmed trunk and fragrant white to pink flowers that reaches 6–12 m (20–40 ft) tall. It is hardy in Zone 8 and tolerates dry, hot conditions. Yellow buckeye (*A. flava*), with yellow flowers and colorful fall foliage, is a larger tree that is native to the Southeast and is hardy from Zone 4.

Growing Red Buckeye

Red buckeyes and their near relatives should be transplanted carefully, keeping the soil ball intact, to avoid damaging roots, in very early spring. Set them at the same depth they occupied in their nursery pots or in the ground, fill the hole around the root ball with soil and water well. The trees often drop their leaves by summer's end, but if they receive ample moisture through summer they will retain their foliage later into fall. This characteristic can be used to advantage by planting red buckeyes where their early dormancy will reveal the fall colors of

'Atrosanguinea' is a variety with flowers that are a darker red than those of the species.

companion trees. Buckeyes form a broad, many-branched shape, so prune only to remove dead wood.

The fungal disease rust, which deposits a brownish powdery residue on leaves, occasionally troubles buckeyes. The disease weakens trees and slows their growth but does not kill them. To interrupt the disease cycle, rake up and dispose of fallen leaves.

FUNDAMENTAL FACTS

ATTRIBUTES	Early spring foliage, red flowers in late spring; for woodland gardens
SEASON OF INTEREST	Spring through summer
FAVORITES	*A. pavia* and 'Atrosanguinea', *A. californica*, *A. flava*
QUIRKS	Leaves drop in late summer; leaves and fruits are toxic if eaten
GOOD NEIGHBORS	Parrotia, stewartia, white pine, witch hazel
WHERE IT GROWS BEST	Average to wet conditions in partial shade
LONGEVITY	Lives several decades
POTENTIAL PROBLEMS	Susceptible to drought stress and fungal rust leaf disease
SOURCE	Nursery plants
DIMENSIONS	To 7.5 m (25 ft) tall and equally wide

REDBUD

Cercis canadensis; other species

HARDINESS:
Zone 5

PREFERRED SOIL pH:
Widely adaptable

PREFERRED SOIL TYPE:
Moist, fertile, well-drained

PREFERRED LIGHT:
Partial shade

European redbud is densely clothed with rosy lilac flowers that appear in spring.

Redbud in the Landscape

In the woods of eastern North America, redbud is usually second among the trees that flower in early spring, blooming just after serviceberries and right before dogwoods. In the home landscape, the lavender-pink blossoms of the redbud flower in concert with early crocuses and daffodils. Redbuds bloom prolifically before their leaves unfurl, covering their branches with tiny flowers from the tips of their twigs all the way to the main trunk. Flowers sometimes even push their way right through the bark of old limbs, though blossoming is often heaviest on 2-year-old branches.

The rest of the year, redbud is a small, muscular-looking tree with broad, heart-shaped leaves. It produces long, yellow-green seedpods that turn brown, and the leaves go yellow in fall. Redbud grows about 4.5–6 m (15–20 ft) tall and wide. For it to enjoy a long life, redbud needs moist, well-drained soil in a partly shaded site, a situation often found along the edges of yards or near the corners of houses. It transplants best when small, and grows quickly the first 5 to 10 years after planting. Thereafter this tree maintains a steady size but often declines after 20 years.

Other Care-Free Redbuds

Several color variants are available. Sometimes called whitebud, *Cercis canadensis* 'Alba' has pure white flowers, while those of 'Ruby Atkinson' are pale pink. These pastel-flowered types are often easier to blend into the vibrant spring garden color scheme. For a vivid statement, there is 'Flame' and 'Double Flame', both with magenta flowers, and 'Forest Pansy', which has wine red leaves.

Another native is western redbud (*C. occidentalis*), which looks similar to its eastern cousin but is more drought tolerant and hardy to Zone 8. Nurseries in hot, dry regions may also stock redbuds adapted to local conditions, such as *C. mexicana*, *C. reniformis*, or *C. texensis*. *C. reniformis* 'Oklahoma' is a particularly profuse bloomer.

The European redbud (*C. siliquastrum*), also called Judas tree, is a slightly larger tree than the native redbud. The spring flowers are a darker shade of rose, and the seedpods are purple. It is hardy to Zone 7.

Growing Redbud

Redbuds have rangy roots that were not designed with transplanting in mind. Balled-and-burlapped trees are fine if you plant them while they are small, but look for container-grown plants when setting out larger redbuds to reduce transplant shock. Provide water to keep the soil barely moist the first season after transplanting. Young trees quickly grow into an open, irregular, vase-shape that requires no pruning. As they age, redbuds may lean toward the most abundant light, which gives them an even more interesting shape.

Redbuds can slowly fall victim to several life-shortening diseases. Trunk canker causes branches to die, and verticillium wilt, a soil-borne fungal disease, also causes parts of redbud trees to wilt and die. Ultimately, most elderly redbuds succumb to heartwood rot, dying from the inside out. When a redbud more than 20 years old shows consistent signs of decline, you should make plans to plant a replacement tree nearby.

Redbud blooms early in the season, mixing with azaleas and a variety of spring bulbs.

FUNDAMENTAL FACTS

ATTRIBUTES	Pink flowers in spring, yellow leaves in fall; for specimens, woodlands
SEASON OF INTEREST	Spring through fall
FAVORITES	*C. canadensis* and cultivars; *C. reniformis* 'Oklahoma'; *C. siliquastrum*
QUIRKS	Tends to lean toward the sun as it grows older
GOOD NEIGHBORS	Dogwood, azalea, serviceberry, silverbell, spring bulbs
WHERE IT GROWS BEST	Moist, fertile soil in partial shade
LONGEVITY	Lives 10–20 years
POTENTIAL PROBLEMS	Trunk canker, verticillium wilt, heartwood rot
SOURCE	Nursery plants
DIMENSIONS	4.5–6 m (15–20 ft) tall and wide

European white birch, a river birch relative, has silvery white peeling bark when young.

RIVER BIRCH

Betula nigra; other species

HARDINESS:
Zone 3

PREFERRED SOIL pH:
Acid

PREFERRED SOIL TYPE:
Moist, sandy soil

PREFERRED LIGHT:
Sun

River Birch in the Landscape

A highly desirable landscape tree, river birch is famous for its ridged, ruddy brown bark that peels, revealing shaggy, salmon flakes. It also has a rounded crown, topping out at 12–21 m (40–70 ft). Its small, diamond-shaped, green leaves flutter in the breeze, creating a light, airy effect. In fact, the canopy is so open that you'll have no trouble growing bulbs, annuals, and groundcovers at its base, where they'll receive ample light.

As its common name suggests, river birch is found in lowland areas where the soil is often saturated. Its adaptability to poorly aerated sites also gives it an advantage in gardens with compacted soil. Hardy from Zone 3, river birch equally at home in extreme summer heat. This is the perfect tree for urban areas or a new garden where fast growth and sun tolerance are important. River birch makes a lovely specimen or a graceful marker at the corner of a house.

Popular River Birches

For added drama, look for the variety 'Heritage', whose bark peels in large, tawny orange patches instead of small, curly flakes. It is also tolerant of dry soil and resistant to pests. 'Heritage' is very easy to find and is often the only river birch carried at nurseries. A classy dwarf called 'Little King' is also becoming popular. Standing 6–7.5 m (20–25 ft) tall, this variety develops a tapered trunk and is in scale with small landscapes.

Other Care-Free Birches

Another birch with peeling bark is paper birch (*B. papyrifera*), which grows to 30 m (100 ft). This birch earned its name from the silvery to creamy white bark that curls into little tubes, like rolls of paper. Hardy to Zone 2, it is not dependable in extreme summer heat, which also makes it vulnerable to pests. European white birch (*B. pendula*), has silvery white peeling bark when young, but the trunk turns dark with age. The branches are droopy, creating a soft crown atop a 12 m (40 ft) tall tree. It tolerates drier, less acid soil than other birches and is hardy to Zone 2. 'Purpurea' and 'Purple Splendor' have purplish leaves, and 'Youngii' is a smaller, weeping variety with a mushroom shape.

Growing River Birch

Transplant river birch in early spring. It will establish quickly, growing up to 1 m (3 ft) annually in loose, sandy, acid soil if kept moist in droughts. Yellowing leaves indicate alkaline soil. Amend soil with garden sulphur, per label, to neutralize the soil pH. Dry soil reduces vigor, making trees susceptible to borers, which are small caterpillars that bore holes into the trunk, seriously weakening the plants. It pays to irrigate as needed and lay an 8 cm (3 in) layer of mulch to reduce evaporation from the soil.

River birch requires no pruning, but it drops small twigs and leaves, which do require periodic raking. Occasionally river birches become infested with sap-sucking insect aphids. Spray aphids off foliage with water from a hose, or apply an insecticidal soap formula that also contains citrus compounds, per label.

FUNDAMENTAL FACTS

ATTRIBUTES	Attractive bark, open canopy; for specimens, foundation plantings
SEASON OF INTEREST	Year-round
FAVORITES	*B. nigra* 'Heritage', 'Little King'; *B. papyrifera*; *B. pendula*
QUIRKS	Drops small twigs and leaves that require raking
GOOD NEIGHBORS	False cypress, pines, red-osier dogwood, winterberry holly, viburnums
WHERE IT GROWS BEST	Moist soil and full sun
LONGEVITY	Lives many years
POTENTIAL PROBLEMS	Aphids, borers; leaves turn yellow when trees are grown in alkaline soil
SOURCE	Nursery plants
DIMENSIONS	12–21 m (40–70 ft) tall and to 9 m (30 ft) wide

The round, open canopy of river birch tops limbs whose bark peels in small, curly flakes.

Serviceberries are shrubby, multitrunked trees that are smothered in white flowers in spring.

SERVICEBERRY

Amelanchier spp.

HARDINESS:
Zone 4

PREFERRED SOIL pH:
Acid

PREFERRED SOIL TYPE:
Moist to average

PREFERRED LIGHT:
Sun to partial shade

Serviceberry in the Landscape

These are an outstanding group of landscape plants, many native to North America and well suited to small gardens and woodlands. Serviceberries form shrubby, multi-trunked trees that usually grow no taller than 10 m (35 ft). All have snow-white flowers in early spring,

Serviceberries develop purplish red berries in summer that are a delicacy for birds.

sometimes with a touch of apple-blossom pink, followed by reddish purple fruits in early summer that rank at the top of the menu for many

birds. Most have terrific fall foliage color and silver-gray bark that shines all through winter.

Serviceberries are compact enough to include in a shrub border or foundation grouping. They make a graceful contribution to the edge of a woodland, mixing well with dogwood and redbud. Smaller specimens combine well with twiggy shrubs, such as clethra, hydrangea, witch hazel, and red-osier dogwood.

Selecting Serviceberries

Allegheny serviceberry (*Amelanchier laevis*) is the largest species used in home gardens, reaching about 9–10 m (30–35 ft) in height. 'Prince Charles' is desirable for its vigorous growth, abundant blossoms, and red-orange fall foliage. Apple serviceberry (*A. × grandiflora*) is slightly smaller, at 7.5 m (25 ft), but has larger flowers and its young leaves are bronze. There are many cultivars including 'Autumn Brilliance', which have exceptional leaf color in autumn; 'Robin Hill' has pink buds that open to pale pink flowers that fade to white. 'Strata' has a horizontal branching habit.

A. lamarckii is a bushy, spreading tree with coppery new leaves that mature to green. While the species has prolific white blossoms, 'Rubescens' has soft pink flowers that open from purple-pink buds. Another is the shadblow or downy serviceberry (*A. canadensis*). In the wild, the species can grow to 18 m (60 ft), but most varieties available for gardens grow no more than 4.5–6 m (15–20 ft) tall. 'Prince William' and 'Springtyme' are smaller, at 3.5 m (12 ft).

A good choice for the Northwest is alder-leaf serviceberry (*A. alnifolia*), which has slightly furry young branches and toothed leaves. The variety 'Alta Glow' forms a column

up to 6 m (20 ft) tall and has yellow to burgundy leaves in autumn.

Growing Serviceberry

Plant in early spring, with the soil ball intact. All species will grow in ordinary soil provided they are watered during drought, especially their first year. Spread an 8 cm (3 in) thick layer of organic mulch to retain soil moisture. Growing serviceberries in partial shade lessens the need for supplemental water, but flowering and fall foliage color will be reduced.

Serviceberries have few pest or disease problems in cold climates, but in warm, humid areas they can contract fungal leaf diseases, which dilute the fall color display but do not kill the trees. Occasionally trees stressed by wet soil are attacked by boring insects. If needed, apply a general-purpose insecticide registered for this tree and borers, according to label directions. Pruning is seldom necessary.

FUNDAMENTAL FACTS

ATTRIBUTES	Spring flowers, colorful berries, showy fall foliage; for borders
SEASON OF INTEREST	Spring to fall
FAVORITES	A. laevis, A. x grandiflora, A. lamarckii, A. canadensis, A. alnifolia
QUIRKS	Grows poorly in wet soil or during severe drought
GOOD NEIGHBORS	Dogwood, mountain laurel, pine, redbud, winterberry holly, witch hazel
WHERE IT GROWS BEST	Fertile garden soil with good drainage
LONGEVITY	Lives many years
POTENTIAL PROBLEMS	Foliar fungal diseases in warm humid weather; borers
SOURCE	Nursery plants
DIMENSIONS	To 9–10.5 m (30–35 ft) tall and to 6 m (20 ft) wide

Silverbell develops a round canopy, which is accentuated by profuse white flowers.

SILVERBELL

Halesia carolina

HARDINESS:
Zone 4 unless otherwise indicated

PREFERRED SOIL pH:
Acid

PREFERRED SOIL TYPE:
Well-drained, fertile, organic

PREFERRED LIGHT:
Sun to partial shade

Silverbell in the Landscape

Popularly known as Carolina silverbell, this medium-sized tree makes a charming specimen, especially if you grow it where you can appreciate the rows of bell-shaped white or pale pink flowers that line the branches in late spring. While silverbell is valued primarily for its blossoms, this North American native has other ornamental features. On young trees, the dark gray bark is striped with what looks like white frost nestled between ridges. As the plant matures, the bark flakes slightly, revealing patches of gray and brown. Little egg-shaped, winged fruits appear in fall, turning from green to tan and often clinging to the branches into winter.

Sites for Silverbell

The secret of placing a silverbell in the garden is to find a spot where you can view the flowers either at eye level or from above. When grown in a home landscape, silverbell will reach 9 m (30 ft) tall and 6 m (20 ft) wide. This is large enough for the tree to be a specimen in the lawn but still compact enough to not take over a yard. Silverbells can mark the end of a path, line a driveway, or create a backdrop for a shrub border, joining beautifully with rhododendron, mountain laurel, and azalea. Because the tree prefers partial shade, especially in the afternoon, it is a good choice for the edge of a wooded backdrop, where its dainty flowers will stand out against the larger forest trees and evergreens. Silverbell will not grow well in a hot, dry location or along a busy street, where it can be poisoned by airborne pollutants. Also avoid siting these trees where they will be exposed to strong winds, which can damage branches.

Other Care-Free Silverbells

There are two other species of silverbell available for the home garden. The major differences between the three species, from a landscaping perspective, is size. These are hardy to Zones 5 and 6 respectively.

A taller tree growing to 21 m (70 ft) or more, mountain silverbell (*Halesia monticola*) is a tree that grows in the higher elevations of the Southeast. The variety 'Rosea' has pale rose blossoms, while *H. monticola* var. *vestita* has larger flowers than the species, up to 2.5 cm (1 in) across and they are sometimes flushed with pink.

The two-winged silverbell (*H. diptera*) is a smaller, spreading tree, with only 2 wings on the fruits instead of the usual 4. *H. diptera* var. *magniflora* is a variety with prolific flowers that reach more than 2.5 cm (1 in) in width.

Growing Silverbell

Silverbell transplants easily in either spring or fall. Select a site in sun or partial shade with slightly acid, moist, well-drained soil. Alkaline soil will cause the leaves to yellow. Sprinkle garden sulphur in the planting hole, if needed, to adjust the soil pH, following package directions. Disturb the roots as little as possible during planting and set the tree at the same depth at which it grew in the nursery pot.

In spring, a multitude of dainty white bells dangle in neat rows from the branches.

Water well to eliminate any air pockets around the roots and spread an 8 cm (3 in) thick layer of organic mulch to reduce evaporation from the soil. Water as needed the first year after planting to keep the soil from drying out. Silverbell grows moderately, and it may take 3 years or more for the tree to reach its mature spread. Once established, however, silverbell needs no special care, has virtually no problems with pests or diseases, and needs pruning only to remove dead or damaged limbs.

FUNDAMENTAL FACTS

ATTRIBUTES	Bell-shaped flowers in pink or white; for specimens, woodlands
SEASON OF INTEREST	Spring to fall
FAVORITES	*H. tetraptera, H. monticola, H. diptera*
QUIRKS	Bark begins to flake on older trees
GOOD NEIGHBORS	Azalea, rhododendron, mountain laurel, viburnum, witch hazel
WHERE IT GROWS BEST	In moist, well-drained soil in partial shade
LONGEVITY	Usually lives more than 40 years
POTENTIAL PROBLEMS	Ice damage to small limbs
SOURCE	Nursery plants
DIMENSIONS	9 m (30 ft) tall and 6 m (20 ft) wide

Snowbell is an understory tree with broad, rounded leaves that hide fragrant flowers.

SNOWBELL

Styrax spp.

HARDINESS:
Zone 5 unless otherwise indicated

PREFERRED SOIL pH:
Acid

PREFERRED SOIL TYPE:
Well-drained, fertile, organic

PREFERRED LIGHT:
Sun to partial shade

Snowbell in the Landscape

While most trees are regarded as plants that preside over a section of your yard, snowbell is a small tree that's most at home in a garden. This little wonder needs rich, deeply dug, fertile soil, just as many perennials do, but once planted it asks for little in terms of maintenance. Instead, expect to spend time enjoying snowbell's bell-shaped white blossoms, which dangle below the branches in late spring or early summer.

This little tree, which stays under 9 m (30 ft) tall, lives life to the fullest. It is one of the first woody plants to leaf out in spring, and one of the last to give up for the season in late fall. Thereafter, it displays its interesting branching pattern and peeling bark until it impatiently sends out its textured green leaves again at the first opportunity next spring.

Plant snowbell anywhere you can view the flowers, such as by a path or driveway, near a window, or at the edge of a flower border or lawn. It likes the partial shade along the edge of a woodland and the companionship of other shade plants, such as rhododendron, azalea, and mountain laurel. Any groundcover that tolerates shade, such as pachysandra, can be planted at its feet, although snowbell also looks handsome with a skirt of dark mulch. In colder climates, you can tuck snowbell along the house foundation or near a wall for protection from freezing wind, or give it a northern exposure, so that leaves that are covered by spring frosts have time to thaw before being hit by sun.

All in the Family

The most popular and reliable species is the Japanese snowbell (*Styrax japonica*). The branches spread wide in horizontal fans to form a rounded canopy of narrow oval leaves. The flowers hang from long stems, their little yellow stamens clearly visible when viewed from below. 'Pink Chimes' produces prolific pink flowers that are darker at the base.

As the name indicates, fragrant snowbell (*S. obassia*) has sweet-scented flowers on short stems that are almost hidden among the broad, rounded leaves. Both Japanese and fragrant snowbell take their time reaching a mature size of 6–9 m (20–30 ft) tall and 3–6 m (10–20 ft) wide, and both are hardy enough to survive in well-protected spots in Zone 5.

There are two species native to the southeastern part of the continent. *S. americanus*, hardy to Zone 6, and *S. grandifolius*, hardy to Zone 8, have equally nice flowers but are shrubby, growing only 3 m (10 ft) high and wide. These snowbells like moist conditions and tolerate flooding for short periods.

Growing Snowbell

Snowbells have moderate needs including average moisture, light, and soil fertility. They should be transplanted when fairly small, because they don't survive transplanting when older. Plant them in spring, keeping the soil ball intact to avoid damaging roots. Water well, and keep the soil moist during droughts. Spread a thick 8 cm (3 in) layer of organic mulch over the root zone to retard evaporation from the soil. Snowbells are not bothered by insects or disease and don't need pruning.

FUNDAMENTAL FACTS

ATTRIBUTES	Dainty, bell-shaped white flowers, attractive branching; for woodlands
SEASON OF INTEREST	Spring to fall
FAVORITES	*S. japonica* and 'Pink Chimes', *S. obassia*
QUIRKS	Frost can damage the foliage, which emerges early in spring
GOOD NEIGHBORS	Pachysandra, rhododendron, azalea, mountain laurel, viburnum
WHERE IT GROWS BEST	Deep, fertile, moist, well-drained soil where protected from winter wind
LONGEVITY	Lives for 30 years or more in good conditions
POTENTIAL PROBLEMS	A poorly sited plant will not perform well
SOURCE	Nursery plants
DIMENSIONS	To 9 m (30 ft) tall and to 6 m (20 ft) wide

Japanese snowbell keeps its narrow leaves until late in fall and leafs out early in spring.

'Waterlily' is cherished for its long, slender, white petals that unfurl from pink buds.

STAR MAGNOLIA

Magnolia stellata

HARDINESS:
Zone 5 unless otherwise indicated

PREFERRED SOIL pH:
Slightly acid

PREFERRED SOIL TYPE:
Fertile, moist, well-drained

PREFERRED LIGHT:
Sun or light shade

Star Magnolia in the Landscape

A classic harbinger of spring, star magnolia blooms early in the season and, unlike some of its fellows, early in its life. Even plants that are only a few years old unfold their white or pink flowers, with up to 18 petals arranged in a loose star shape. They emerge on bare branches, before the shiny, deep-green, oblong leaves appear, during the last gasp of winter. The flowers look stunning when viewed in bright light against a dark background of pines, junipers, or broadleaf evergreens.

Seldom more than 4.5 m (15 ft) tall and wide, star magnolia is a tree that fits easily into almost any size of yard. It is small enough to plant near driveways and entryways, in foundation plantings, and at the back of shrub borders. In cold climates, protect the buds by siting star magolias on the north or east side of a wall, fence, or building, so that the flowers open more slowly and are less likely to be damaged by frost. At the limits of hardiness, they are often grown as shrubs.

Several cultivars are available. 'Centennial' has up to 32 white petals in each flower. 'Royal Star', with up to 30 white petals, is a vigorous tree that blooms about 10 days later than other magnolias, which is an asset in colder locations where frosts may threaten the blossoms. 'Waterlily' has especially fragrant white blossoms with long, slender petals. 'Rose King', 'Dawn', and 'Rubra' all have pink flowers that sometimes fade to white.

Other Care-Free Magnolias

Several other small, equally hardy magnolias can stand in for or join a grouping of star magnolias. Growing quickly to 9 m (30 ft) in height and width, Loebner magnolia (*Magnolia* × *loebneri*) has fragrant starlike flowers with fewer petals than star magnolias, and blooms later, making it a better choice in cold areas. 'Merrill' and 'Ballerina' are excellent white-flowered varieties, while 'Leonard Messel' has pastel lilac-pink blossoms.

Small magnolias with goblet-shaped flowers include Yulan magnolia (*Magnolia denudata*), which grows to 12 m (40 ft), but it has a graceful presence in the landscape, and produces large, fragrant white blossoms. 'Elizabeth' is famous for its copper-tinged leaves and fragrant flower goblets of primrose yellow. It blooms in midspring and is hardy to Zone 6. 'Butterflies' is similar, but has double yellow flowers and is hardy to Zone 5. 'Galaxy', 'Betty', and 'Heaven Scent' are hybrids with pink flowers.

Growing Star Magnolia

Star magnolias have tender roots that do not respond well if transplanted in fall. Plant them in early spring, taking care to keep the soil ball intact. Provide water during droughts until they are well established. Cover the root zone year-round with an 8 cm (3 in) thick layer of organic mulch.

Frosts that ruins blossoms just as they open in spring are star magnolia's biggest problem. They can also experience decay around pruning wounds and winter-damaged tissue in spring. Prune only to remove damaged limbs and to balance the canopy, and do the job in late winter, while the plants are still dormant.

FUNDAMENTAL FACTS

ATTRIBUTES	Starlike white or pink flowers, shrubby habit; for specimen, borders
SEASON OF INTEREST	Early spring to fall
FAVORITES	*M. stellata* 'Royal Star', 'Centennial', 'Waterlily', 'Dawn', 'Rose King'
QUIRKS	Flowers appear early in spring and may be damaged by frost
GOOD NEIGHBORS	Broadleaf and needle evergreens, spring bulbs, other small magnolias
WHERE IT GROWS BEST	Fertile, well-drained, acid soil in a site protected from wind
LONGEVITY	Lives many years
POTENTIAL PROBLEMS	Decay following winter damaged or wind-torn branches
SOURCE	Nursery plants
DIMENSIONS	To 4.5 m (15 ft) tall and wide

Star magnolia is an early bloomer, unfurling its star-shaped flowers at winter's end.

STEWARTIA
Stewartia spp.

HARDINESS:
Zone 5 unless otherwise indicated

PREFERRED SOIL pH:
Acid

PREFERRED SOIL TYPE:
Well-drained, fertile, organic

PREFERRED LIGHT:
Partial shade

Stewartia in the Landscape

Some trees, if given extra care, can tolerate many different habitats, even if they don't perform at their best. Not so with stewartias. If the habitat meets their needs, no extra care is necessary. But if conditions aren't right, no extra care will help them to adapt. If you do have a suitable spot, with fertile, well-drained, acid soil and partial shade, use it to grow a spectacular stewartia, which easily becomes the focus of any landscape in which it grows.

This is truly a tree for all seasons. In spring, it is clothed in lustrous, oval, slightly ribbed leaves. Related to camellias, stewartias boast a profusion of delicate, cup-shaped white flowers that open over several weeks in summer. After the leaves turn red and drop in fall, the peeling bark of the trunk is revealed. This trait becomes more dramatic as the tree matures.

You'll want to show off your stewartia as a stand-alone specimen, perhaps at the edge of the lawn, by a path, or at the edge of a wooded area. It will draw attention at the back of a shrub border, but keep its companions, such as azaleas and viburnums, short so that the trunk is visible. Stewartias also look striking rising from a

These small trees have white flowers in summer and abundant leaves that turn red in fall.

swath of shade-tolerant groundcover, such as ferns, asarum, or periwinkle.

Selecting Stewartias

All stewartias have the same attractive features, which vary only slightly from one species to another. The most popular is Japanese stewartia (*Stewartia pseudocamellia*), which tops out at 18 m (60 ft) in the wild but usually grows 9–12 m (30–40 ft) in the garden. Its flowers are 5–8 cm (2–3 in) wide, the reddish bark flakes in large plates, and the fall foliage color is reddish purple. Its close relative, Korean stewartia (*S. pteropetiolata* var. *koreana*), has bright reddish orange fall foliage, is

hardy to Zone 6 and has wider spreading flowers. It grows to 12 m (40 ft). The tall stewartia (*S. monadelpha*) can reach 18 m (60 ft) under ideal conditions, with an informal habit and smaller flowers. It is also hardy to Zone 6.

Two stewartias are native to the southeastern part of the continent. Showy stewartia (*S. ovata* var. *grandiflora*) has particularly large flowers, up to 10 cm (4 in) wide, and orange to scarlet fall foliage. It grows to about 4.5 m (15 ft). Virginia stewartia (*S. malacodendron*) also has a compact size and large flowers, but the blossoms emerge from leaf clusters and

may be hidden by them. Both of these natives do well in hot climates, but are hardy only from Zone 7.

Growing Stewartia

Select a shady, protected site with well-drained, acid soil amended with organic matter. Stewartias transplant poorly and should be planted in their permanent location while still small. Plant in early spring with the soil ball intact to avoid damaging roots, and keep the soil moist the first season. Cover the root zone with an 8 cm (3 in) thick layer of organic mulch and water during droughts by letting a hose drip slowly onto the soil above the roots for several hours. A young tree will grow slowly for a few years and then gain 30–60 cm (12–24 in) of height annually until it reaches full size.

Stewartias are untroubled by pests and diseases. Pruning is unnecessary except to repair damaged limbs.

FUNDAMENTAL FACTS

ATTRIBUTES	White flowers, colorful fall foliage, flaking bark; for specimens
SEASON OF INTEREST	Year-round
FAVORITES	All species; select by size, hardiness, flower size, and fall leaf color
QUIRKS	Thrives only in preferred growing conditions
GOOD NEIGHBORS	Azalea, viburnum, ferns, groundcovers
WHERE IT GROWS BEST	In fertile, organic soil and afternoon shade
LONGEVITY	Lives at least 40 years when properly sited
POTENTIAL PROBLEMS	Quickly shows stress if grown in infertile, dry, or soggy soil
SOURCE	Nursery plants
DIMENSIONS	4.5–18 m (15–60 ft) tall, to 9 m (30 ft) wide

WHITE PINE

Pinus strobus, P. monticola

HARDINESS:
Zone 3

PREFERRED SOIL pH:
Acid to nearly neutral

PREFERRED SOIL TYPE:
Average

PREFERRED LIGHT:
Sun to partial shade

Eastern white pine forms a pyramid that takes on an open shape in shady locations.

White Pine in the Landscape

The white pines are outstanding, aromatic landscape trees native to large areas of North America. The Eastern white pine (*Pinus strobus*) is among the tallest trees on the eastern part of the continent, reaching about 7.5 m (25 ft) in 20 years and eventually reaching 45 m (150 ft) at maturity. It is also one of the most beautiful. The tree grows into an irregular pyramid, and has 12 cm (5 in) long green needles with a bluish tint. The needles are soft to the touch, making this a choice pine tree to grow where people will be walking nearby.

While eastern white pine cannot tolerate salt or air pollution, it does tolerate up to a half day of shade, which means it can grow happily alongside flowering dogwoods, serviceberries, and rhododendrons. It can also adapt to many types of soil as long as the site has good drainage.

Western white pine (*P. monticola*), which is native to the Pacific coast, is similar, although it forms a narrower, more symmetrical pyramid that tops out at 27 m (90 ft). The needles are brighter green and grow 10 cm (4 in) long. The western white pine is ideal for specimens, groupings, and screens, and is hardy from Zone 7.

Selecting White Pines

There are numerous varieties of white pines, offering different sizes, colors, and growth habits. Among the eastern white pines, 'Nana' is a dense, round dwarf useful for rock gardens and edging. 'Pendula' is a weeping form, while 'Fastigiata' grows upright. 'Blue Shag' has blue foliage, and 'Nivea' has bluish needles tipped in white. Several western white pines also have pronounced blue foliage including the slender 'Skyline', vigorous 'Ammerland', and dwarf 'Minima.'

Growing White Pine

Plant white pine in spring or early fall in well-drained soil, keeping the soil ball intact to prevent root damage. If the root ball is skimpy, it may be

With its dense but soft foliage, eastern white pine is excellent for massing as a screen.

necessary to stake young trees to secure them against strong wind. Expect newly planted trees to grow slowly for 2 to 3 years, then suddenly gain size. Until new growth is vigorous, water during droughts by soaking the root zone every 7–10 days.

Nurseries often force white pines to produce dense branches by clipping back the "candles", or growth tips, by about half in early summer. But this can cause double leaders to form at the crown, which are weak compared to a single leader. In the landscape, it is best to leave white pines unpruned unless you want to remove low branches to make it possible to walk or sit under the trees. Do this job in spring, while the trees are young, to limit the number of bumpy calluses that form on the main trunk.

Unlike other pines, white pine is not very susceptible to the pine-wilt nematode that slowly kills trees. It is also more resistant to sawflies, tip blights, and other common needle diseases. Occasionally white pine aphids attack, evidenced by splatters of white residue on the bark. Treat this insect pest with an garden insecticide labeled for white pine and the pest, applying as directed on the label.

FUNDAMENTAL FACTS

ATTRIBUTES	Soft, aromatic foliage; pyramidal form; for specimen, screens
SEASON OF INTEREST	Year-round
FAVORITES	Eastern white pine, western white pine, and their cultivars
QUIRKS	Grows slowly for several years after planting, then swiftly gains size
GOOD NEIGHBORS	Dogwood, rhododendron, serviceberry, star magnolia, witch hazel
WHERE IT GROWS BEST	Well-drained soil in sun to partial shade
LONGEVITY	Lives 100 years or more
POTENTIAL PROBLEMS	White pine aphids; grows poorly in soggy soil
SOURCE	Nursery plants
DIMENSIONS	27–45 m (90–150 ft) tall and 12 m (40 ft) wide

An ideal shade tree, yellowwood spreads its branches wide to form a feathery canopy.

YELLOWWOOD

Cladrastis spp.

HARDINESS:
Zone 4 unless otherwise indicated

PREFERRED SOIL pH:
Neutral to alkaline

PREFERRED SOIL TYPE:
Fertile, well-drained

PREFERRED LIGHT:
Sun to partial shade

Yellowwood in the Landscape

Yellowwood is the perfect shade tree for yards where lack of space is a consideration. Growing about 30 cm

Yellowwood has smooth gray bark that wraps itself into the folds of old trunks.

(12 in) per year until it reaches 12–15 m (40–50 ft) at maturity, this tree has attractive, spreading branches and feathery leaves that together form a full, round canopy. The light green, oval leaves turn yellow in autumn, contrasting with the smooth gray bark that wraps itself into folds and crevices of the trunks of old trees. The fall color is all the more striking when the tree is showcased against a brick building or backed by dark, dense evergreens, such as pine trees.

Yellowwood flowers in late spring or early summer, after the peak bloom of many other trees and after the danger of frost has passed. Young trees bloom sparsely, if at all, and a mature tree may produce blossoms only every 2–3 years. Ironically, yellowwood flowers more often when it is stressed by drought. When it does flower, the effect is thrilling. The cascades of white blossoms, resembling those of wisteria, drip from the branches, often reaching 38 cm (15 in) long.

Selecting Yellowwoods

The American yellowwood (*Cladrastis kentukea*), native to the Southeast, adapts easily to many climates and growing conditions. There is one variety, 'Rosea', which has pink flowers.

The Japanese yellowwood (*C. platycarpa*) blooms a little later than the North American native, and the white flowers, which are marked with yellow, grow only 25 cm (10 in) long. For a slightly different flowering form, look for Chinese yellowwood (*C. sinensis*). This species has narrower, finely textured leaflets, and the pink-flushed flowers stand in erect pyramids. It is not quite as hardy as is American yellowwood, but it makes a distinctive specimen from Zone 6.

FUNDAMENTAL FACTS

ATTRIBUTES	White or pink flowers, yellow fall foliage; for specimen
SEASON OF INTEREST	Spring to fall
FAVORITES	*C. kentukea* and pink-flowered 'Rosea', *C. platycarpa*, *C. sinensis*
QUIRKS	Doesn't bloom every year; flowers in droughts
GOOD NEIGHBORS	Japanese maple, lace-bark pine, red-osier dogwood, pine, false cypress
WHERE IT GROWS BEST	Average, well-drained soil, either in sun or partial shade
LONGEVITY	Lives more than 50 years
POTENTIAL PROBLEMS	Can develop weak branches that break during ice storms
SOURCE	Nursery plants
DIMENSIONS	12–15 m (40–50 ft) tall, about 9 m (30 ft) wide

Growing Yellowwood

Plant yellowwood in early spring, keeping the soil ball intact to avoid root damage. Yellowwood grows poorly in soggy soil, but will spread its deep fibrous roots readily in most other soil types.

In open situations, where it does not have to struggle for light, yellowwood spreads its branches to a width of 9 m (30 ft). Prune away any that form a narrow angle or that may be weak and easily snapped off in icy weather. This is important, because the botanical name of the genus means "brittle branch." If pruning is needed, do it in late summer or early fall while the target branches are still small. Avoid pruning in late winter or early spring to minimize excessive sap flow from cuts. Yellowwood is not troubled by any pests or diseases.

CHAPTER THIRTEEN

CARE-FREE CONTAINERS

Every home, regardless of its size, has special spots that can be enlivened with beautiful plants grown in containers. There are literally hundreds of plants that are not only willing but eager to grow in the confined spaces of pots, baskets, window boxes, and planting boxes. Pair these container-compatible plants with the growing conditions they prefer, and you can enrich virtually any space in your yard with pleasing splashes of color and texture.

The most alluring attribute of containers is their versatility. In addition to the obvious places you might station pots of flowering plants, such as on your deck or patio, or flanking an entryway or steps, special containers are available for mounting on fences, straddling porch rails, or attaching to windowsills. And, because many containers can be picked up and moved at a moment's notice, you can have instant color when and where you want it. Best of all, by changing plants, you can change a color scheme or create seasonal displays.

Two aspects of container gardening that take time and attention are watering and fertilizing. Plants in containers don't have the luxury of sending out roots to forage for moisture and nutrients, so strive to keep container-grown plants where they can be reached easily with a hose or watering can. It's a happy coincidence, however, that potted plants used to decorate outdoor rooms are usually convenient to water and fertilize. Most flourish if fertilized at every other watering with a balanced, water-soluble fertilizer applied at half strength.

In this chapter you'll discover invaluable tips for combining plants to make colorful container gardens, and you'll learn shortcuts for preparing soil mixes and filling containers and tricky-to-plant wire baskets. You'll find tips for using containers to bring color to difficult places, such as a shady spot where it's hard to coax plants to flower or a site with poor, dry soil. Consult the plant encyclopedia entries for care-free shrubs, vines, perennials, and annuals that thrive in containers, and you'll soon enjoy container gardens in every season of the year.

A few potted plants can turn a plain setting of any size, such as a small balcony, into a welcoming garden.

Getting Creative with Containers

A container garden offers countless opportunities for creativity in the landscape. You can enhance a house entryway with an elegant hanging basket and enliven a barren terrace with pots of greenery. You can screen an unattractive view and highlight a special landscape feature. Potted plants can hide a homely house foundation, soften the hard architecture of a balcony, and transform a blank wall into a kaleidoscope of color.

Containers can be great problem solvers, too. They make it possible to grow plants where the soil is poor, shallow, or dominated by large rocks. You can even grow plants where there is no soil at all, such as on paved walkways, patios, porches, and steps. If you have a sun-baked yard, you can tuck a few of your favorite shade-loving plants into pots set under a tree. Conversely, gardeners who contend with too much shade can give sun-seeking plants the conditions they need by moving potted specimens as the light changes through the day. If wildlife likes to nibble your garden, you can protect plants that need to be pampered by putting them into containers and siting them close to the house.

Containers are ideal for impatient, restless, and experimental gardeners. With a few flowers and a few minutes, you can turn a basket or urn into an instant garden. If you like to change the look of your landscape with the seasons, containers make it easy to create different designs to suit your mood or the calendar. And when you're ready to push the limits of your talents with new plant combinations or temperamental specimens, container gardens are an inexpensive way to test your ideas on a small scale.

COLOR IN CONTAINERS

Colorful container plants can serve as strong punctuation points in the garden, creating contrast and drama, or as a unifying element, drawing together separate spaces. For example, pots of red impatiens would bring striking spots of color to the beginning and end of a shady, ivy-lined path. Pots of pink petunias could be parked at an entry gate, around the front door, by a fountain, and throughout the landscape to become a repeating color theme.

Because containers offer such concentrated color, you may need to use a few tricks to tame rowdy combinations or give the eye a rest. For example, "neutral" plants, such as gray-leaved dusty miller and white-flowered sweet alyssum work wonders at turning down the heat of potted red geraniums. Foliage plants, such as hosta and vinca, offer welcome relief from a visual overdose of blooms. Conversely, you can sprinkle pots of white caladiums or pastel impatiens in quiet, shady places that need a boost or station a large urn of dramatically patterned coleus on a pedestal to color a bed of ferns.

CARE-FREE SECRETS

Pot Up Extra Bedders

When you buy annual flowers to use in outdoor beds, buy a few extras to plant in pots. Keep one or two container-grown plants to replace any that fail after being set out in beds. Combine others in large pots to create "container bouquets."

CLOSE-UP WITH CONTAINERS

When plants are kept close to outdoor activity areas, including patios, decks, and porches, it's easier to admire their colors and textures than it is when you grow the same plants farther away in a bed. This is especially true of flowering plants with intricate color patterns, such as impatiens with patterned petals or dark-veined balloon flowers, and it's also true of plants with striking foliage, such as bronze-leaved ornamental grasses or silvery leaved heucheras.

Because plants growing in containers located only a few steps from your door are so convenient to maintain, they present an excellent opportunity to grow showy varieties that need a little extra attention to maintain their good looks. Vigorous bedding geraniums famed for their huge clusters of double flowers, for example, need regular deadheading and fertilizing. When these and other showy plants are kept in containers on a patio or deck, the small amount of extra effort they require seems more like a privilege than a chore. Living close to containers also means that you can monitor them for emerging pest and disease problems easily and treat them before the pests can cause damage. In fact, container plants are often healthier than those growing in the open garden, because the sterile, free-draining soil used in pots reduces risk of disease, and elevated containers discourage invasion from many pests who prefer to stay close to the ground.

MOBILE BEAUTIES

Containers are invaluable when you must move beloved plants to a new home. Should you need to relocate plants, especially over a long distance, they will fare better if you can get them accustomed to life in pots several weeks before moving day. Afterward, they will wait patiently in their containers while you get settled and prepare a more permanent location for them.

But containers are most often used to provide a permanent home for a plant, which is especially good news for apartment and condominium dwellers whose gardening space is limited to a terrace or patio. Given proper care, even trees and shrubs can live happily in containers for many years.

If your yard is large enough to provide an out-of-the-way nursery area, you can shuffle pots so that each container can be moved to a place where it will be fully appreciated as it reaches its peak. Don't worry if that spot is shady, because sun-loving flowers, such as petunias, geraniums, and globe amaranth are often grateful for temporary shade when they have reached the blooming stage.

If your own mobility is limited, container gardens make it easy to enjoy plants. Pots and boxes can be raised to a convenient height, eliminating the need to bend or stoop, and they can be moved or arranged to accommodate the special needs of the gardener. And because container gardens are usually smaller in scale, they are less taxing to care for.

PUSHING HARDINESS

Containers offer the easiest way to grow bulbs, perennials, and even shrubs that are tender in your area. Instead of digging them up at the end of the season

Provide an out-of-the-way nursery area for growing replacement plants, such as hostas, in pots.

Where space is limited, small trees, such as a Japanese maple, can live for many years in a pot.

or watching them succumb to cold, simply move the entire pot to a sheltered spot, such as an unheated garage or storage area, or anywhere the plants will not be exposed to freezing temperatures. This maneuver works beautifully with caladiums, calla lilies, and cannas, and where winters are short, even vigorous petunias and geraniums can be maintained through winter this way.

When growing small, hardy shrubs in containers, sometimes careful placement of the pots is all that is needed to give those plants the edge they need to survive the frigid weather in good condition. Snuggle evergreen azaleas, camellias, and hydrangeas against a sunny wall, which will absorb the sun's warmth and protect them from wind, and they may well make it through the winter with no trouble, even if they are marginally hardy in your area.

Choosing Containers

Gardeners can choose from a vast selection of plant containers, ranging from classic clay flowerpots to whimsical wire baskets to items rescued from the trash bin, such as worn boots or leaky wagons. The single feature every plant container must have is one or more drainage holes, so that excess water can escape rather than pool up around plant roots. When buying containers, always check for drainage holes, because it can be difficult or impossible to drill holes in certain materials, such as glazed ceramic, without cracking or destroying the pot.

PICKING THE RIGHT POT

The first consideration when selecting a container is function, or what you want the pot to do. The most important and practical issue is size. Make sure that the container is large enough for the plants you want to grow. The pot should allow sufficient room for roots to spread and the pot should look in balance with the mature height of the plant. Generally, a pot should be one third the height of a mature plant.

A shallow bowl works well for low-growing lobelia or bulbs, for instance, but could not balance tall, rangy cosmos or trailing ivy vines. Conversely, diminutive plants, such as sweet alyssum, would be dwarfed in a large urn, while tall gladiolus stems would look just right. Don't overdo it, however. While it's tempting to put a small plant in a large pot that will support its mature size, it will grow poorly in the beginning. It's better to start with a small pot that's in proportion to the plant's size, then transplant it to slightly larger containers as it grows.

Round pots with tapering sides are classic and more practical for planting and transplanting than elaborate containers with handles or narrow necks. Long, rectangular troughs are useful for narrow spots, such as along a path or a window ledge. Half-moon-shaped pots and wire mangers, which have flat backs, are designed to hang on a wall.

Also think about weight and drainage. If you plan to move the containers frequently or are growing plants on a balcony, select lightweight foam or fiber-glass pots. If you need a pot that won't topple in a stiff wind, a heavy concrete or stone planter is best.

Don't worry if a container you like seems to have too many drainage holes. You can easily slow the flow of water and prevent seepage of the potting soil by placing a piece of porous cloth or landscape fabric in the base of the pot, or covering it with a layer of small stones or pot shards.

DREAMING OF DESIGN

After you've thought about practical concerns, you can dream about the design possibilities offered by the nearly limitless array of containers. Pots are made from so many materials and are available in so many shapes, size, and colors that it is difficult to choose.

Narrow your options by considering the style of your home and landscape. Traditional urns and pots with classical swag decorations, for example, would suit a Colonial or Victorian house. Splint baskets or half-barrels have a rustic feel suited to a informal or rustic house. They would lend charm to a casual grouping of pansies, petunias, or browallia.

Containers come in such an array of sizes, shapes, colors, and materials, that it can be hard to choose.

If needed, you can drill extra drainage holes into the bases of most pots (left). Clay shards placed over the holes slow drainage and reduce erosion (center). Raising pots aids drainage and discourages pests (right).

TYPES OF CONTAINERS

Use the information here as a guide when shopping for containers. If you are buying plants and containers at the same time, it's easy to see how well the combination works before you buy.

MATERIALS	CHARACTERISTICS	BEST USES	CARE TIPS
Terra-cotta and other ceramics	Available in many sizes and shapes; some have colorful glazed exteriors. Unglazed pots allow soil to dry quickly.	For summering plants. Heavy and stable enough for shrubs and small trees. Glazed pots should be used in protected locations.	Either empty pots or allow soil to dry completely before storing indoors in cold winters, because frozen soil can cause the material to crack.
Concrete and stone	Heavy and stable. Porous material allows soil to dry out quickly. Pots may lack drainage holes. Wind and weather resistant.	For tough, resilient shrubs, herbs, and flowers that tolerate dry soil, such as typical rock-garden plants.	Because of their weight, these containers are seldom moved and must be cleaned in place. They are safe to leave out over cold winters.
Plastic	Lightweight and inexpensive. Slows water evaporation from the soil. Black pots heat up quickly and can injure plant roots.	For plants that are left outdoors through winter in mild climates. Also use as liners for more decorative containers.	Clean and store indoors, away from cold and bright light, which causes plastic to become brittle.
Wooden planters and half-barrels	Handsome, versatile, and sturdy. Can be stained or painted. Weather resistant.	Large types for ornamental grasses, shrubs, and trees. Small types for window boxes and porch rails. Use with plastic liners to protect wood.	Clean and dry before storing through winter to preserve joints and finishes. Can be left outside in winter if covered with plastic sheeting.
Wire baskets and mangers	Lightweight and available in many ornamental shapes. Wire may be plain or coated. Must be lined with moss or coconut fiber to retain soil. Fairly weather resistant.	For displaying plants on a wall, fence, or windowsill, or use as a hanging basket. Ideal for summer annuals and winter arrangements.	Clean and dry before storing through winter. Check for rust spots in spring and repaint as needed.
Fiberglass and molded foam	Lightweight containers designed to resemble concrete, stone, wood, or clay. Materials hold moisture and insulate plant roots well. Weather resistant.	For porch boxes, window boxes, and patio planters filled with any type of plant.	Empty and clean at least every other year. Containers last longer if cleaned thoroughly between uses and stored in a dry place through winter. Can be left outdoors over winter, and foam pots provide good root insulation.

A container should be broad and tall enough to look in balance with the plants you grow in it.

When considering pot color, look first to the background. A terra-cotta pot practically disappears if placed against a brick wall, while a glazed ceramic container in blue would stand out handsomely. Next, consider what plants you want to use, making a nice marriage between the colors of the flowers, foliage, and the container.

The point of view is also important, so think about where you will place containers and how they will be viewed. Plants that are viewed from above, such as hens and chicks, look attractive in a broad, low container. A dwarf Japanese maple, on the other hand, which would be seen from the side, would be best in a sculptural pot, such as an urn.

STANDS AND SAUCERS

There are two accessories often used with containers. Saucers fit under pots to collect water that escapes from the drain holes. These are useful for pots standing on decks, where you want to avoid water stains on the wood, and also under hanging baskets to prevent drips onto outdoor furniture or porch floors. Many plastic pots come with saucers attached, but you will usually need to add saucers to other types of containers. Select one in the same material as the container and in a size that is in proportion to the pot and fits comfortably under the base. While saucers do a good job of minimizing stains to a surface, they do need to be drained if they fill with water, because plant roots that wick up water constantly from below are in danger of root rot.

Handy accessories that are new to the scene are terra-cotta "feet," which lift the pot slightly above the ground to promote good drainage. You'll need three or four per pot, and you can choose from plain blocks or fanciful designs, such as frogs and lion's paws. Keep in mind that water seeping from drain holes can stain the surface underneath the pot.

Great Plants for Containers

As with other types of gardens, the first step in creating a container garden is deciding on the result you want to achieve and how much time you are willing to invest in the project. All plants grown in containers require regular watering and feeding, but additional upkeep, such as pinching, pruning, training, and repotting, varies greatly from plant to plant.

From the beginning, be realistic about how much care you are willing to give your container garden, and choose plants, containers, and locations accordingly. Many plants that need full sun will grow in containers, but a sunny exposure also increases the amount of watering you must do to keep your plants from being chronically thirsty. Lanky, long-stemmed plants that are supported in the garden by their neighbors may need to be staked, as will plants grown in windy locations. Flowering perennials that put on a brilliant show for a brief period, such as lilies and balloon flowers, may need to be moved to a less conspicuous location once their blossoms have faded and replaced with other plants.

Also bear in mind that growing plants in containers can be a short-term or long-term adventure. For example, a pot of tulip bulbs planted in the fall will develop in spring to dazzle your deck for a few weeks, but then the show will be over. However, a shapely juniper or Japanese maple may grace your patio for many years. Keeping at least one small shrub or tree in a container is rewarding, but because cold penetrates from the sides, making the soil extra cold, it must be at least two zones hardier than where you live.

You can grow any type of garden plant in a container, including annuals, perennials, vines, groundcovers, bulbs, shrubs, and trees. Those listed here always do well when grown in pots, but check the plant profiles in the encyclopedia section to see if a plant that interests you is known to grow well in containers. Frequently, specific cultivars are preferred for container culture because they possess characteristics needed for potting. Also study displays at local nurseries and garden centers to see what varieties are used in hanging baskets and other containers or are recommended for use in containers. You may also find certain varieties particularly suited to container gardening listed in garden catalogs.

Sweet pea is a cool-weather favorite for its wispy tendrils, fragrant flowers, and compact size.

THE CHARACTERISTICS THAT COUNT

When choosing plants for containers, look for those that possess these special attributes:

- Long period of bloom or bloom period that fills a seasonal niche
- Attractive, persistent foliage
- Tendency to branch well without frequent pinching
- Pleasing silhouette
- Good tolerance for dry soil
- Sturdy stems that don't need staking
- Ability to recover quickly from transplanting
- Ornamental features, such as seedheads or berries that prolong visual interest
- "Self-cleaning" flowers that don't need to be manually removed once they fade

CLASSIC CONTAINER PLANTS

Whether you grow them in individual pots or in combination, these care-free plants adapt easily to life in containers:

Annuals: Ageratum, begonia, browallia, chrysanthemum, coleus, cosmos, dusty miller, fan flower, flowering tobacco, fuchsia, geranium, globe amaranth, impatiens, lantana, licorice plant, lobelia, nasturtium, ornamental grasses, pansy, periwinkle, petunia, portulaca, salvia, snapdragon, stock, Swan

Succulent plants make excellent hanging basket specimens because they can tolerate dry soil.

River daisy, sweet alyssum, sweet potato vine, and verbena all shine when grown in containers.

Perennials: Artemisia, astilbe, balloon flower, bergenia, bugleweed, candytuft, coreopsis, daylily, deadnettle, dianthus, euphorbia, ferns, hens and chicks, heuchera, hosta, lady's mantle, lamb's ears, lavender, lily, lungwort, ornamental grasses, phormium, primrose, rose campion, stonecrop, sun rose, and thyme all make good container specimens.

Vines: Clematis, scarlet runner bean, sweet pea, and wisteria can all be grown in roomy containers.

Bulbs: Caladium, calla lily, canna, crocus, daffodil, hyacinth, and tulip are good seasonal pot plants.

Shrubs: Azalea, bluebeard, boxwood, camellia, hydrangea, juniper, mugo pine, rose, and viburnum are compact enough to grow in pots.

Trees: Flowering cherry, Japanese maple, and snowbell can be grown in half barrels or big pots.

Groundcovers: Ivy, liriope, and vinca are handsome cascading plants for pot.

STARTING OFF RIGHT

While it's always important to buy healthy plants, this is especially true of specimens intended for containers. Pots are subject to more stress than open gardens, and because the season for containers is often limited, there is no time to waste nursing sub-standard, struggling plants. You want vigorous youngsters that will quickly mature into strong adults without needing extraordinary care while they grow.

Look for starter plants with fresh green leaves unmarred by spotting or yellowing and sturdy, stocky stems lined with foliage. Make sure the plants are well developed overall, not full on one side but bare on another. Select small plants with robust growth and a good number of buds, rather than larger plants in full flower; younger plants often adapt more quickly and grow more readily in a new location.

Also check the base of the pot. If roots are growing rampantly out of the drain holes, the plant has become "potbound" and may not establish easily when transplanted. Fresh, whitish roots should just be emerging from or visible around the drain holes.

CONTAINER COMMUNITIES

To keep your container collection care-free, place plants together that have similar preferences for light, fertilizer, and water. For example, plants that tolerate hot, dry conditions, such as portulaca, hens and chicks, stonecrop, and sun rose, make a fine container community for sun-drenched decks. And it's easy to satisfy the needs of thirsty shade lovers, such as caladiums, ferns, and impatiens, if they are growing near one another.

Cluster together plants that need training or regular deadheading. You will be much more likely to steer sweet peas toward their trellis or pinch off old blossoms from nasturtiums or pansies if the plants are grown in close quarters. When planning containers for distant places in your landscape, such as near your mailbox or as accents for a rear entry gate, use low-maintenance plants, such as ornamental grasses, sweet potato vine, or juniper.

CHANGING WITH THE SEASONS

Container gardens are an ideal way to celebrate the changing seasons, because it takes little time or effort to change the plants to seasonal favorites. And, because containers can be kept in protected places, you can often push the growing season a little bit. For example, if you pot up pansies as soon as they are available in late winter and keep them on a deck, sheltered from wind, they'll bloom before the last

snow has passed. Ornamental cabbage and kale will provide rich color through the short days of autumn and become even more colorful in winter.

Some traditional container plants, such as spring hyacinths and summer impatiens, fade quickly after they bloom heavily for several weeks. Rather than lamenting their passing, relegate the faded plants to the compost heap and replace them with plants suited for the coming season.

Hens and chicks thrive in containers, and are best placed where they can be viewed from above.

Group plants with similar needs, such as marguerites and Swan River daisies, for easier care.

Combinations for Containers

A pot teeming with petunias or a basket bursting with verbena is beautiful in its own way, and many gardeners like the unified look that comes from using one type of plant, often in one color, in a container. But combining different plant varieties in containers is easy and fun and never fails to satisfy the creative itch that all gardeners share. These days, container combinations, also called container bouquets, are very much in style, as you can see by visiting any botanical garden or garden center. Creating container bouquets is not at all difficult, because the design guidelines for success are simple to understand and put into action.

You can place as many different plants together as you like, but it's usually best to begin by combining only two or three plant varieties. When only two plants are involved, the goal is to create a pleasing partnership of form, texture, and color. This is easily accomplished by pairing a tall or upright plant with a smaller one that has a mounding or cascading growth habit, which creates a sense of balance and fullness. Another important consideration is that the two plants share similar preferences for sun and soil; this is essential to assure good health for both plants. Finally, plants that form the strongest duets must look good at more or less the same time. Long-blooming plants are better choices than those that bloom all at once and then must be replaced.

Use the list that follows as a starting place for can't-miss partnerships between care-free plants. Then experiment with other possibilities of your own devising. When you find yourself wondering if two plants will make handsome companions, it's easy to try the liaison on for size by growing them first in individual containers placed side by side.

A well-balanced arrangement is structured with tall plants in the back of the container and bushy fillers in the middle.

TEN CAN'T-MISS, TWO-WAY PARTNERSHIPS

- Zonal geranium and petunia
- Caladium and impatiens
- Rose campion and ivy-leaved geranium
- Salvia and sweet alyssum
- Petunia and lobelia
- Fan flower and narrow-leaf zinnia
- Tulip and pansy
- Globe amaranth and portulaca
- Ornamental grass and sweet potato vine
- Japanese maple and English ivy

WORKING IN THREES

Combining three or more plants in a container is a bit like flower arranging, in that you begin with a tall, upright plant to structure the design, add a second plant that will fill out the picture with foliage and color, and connect the arrangement to the container with a cascading plant that will gently spill over the edges. Creating container bouquets in this manner is tremendously rewarding, although it is also full of surprises.

The lists below sorts 50 popular care-free plants into uprights, fillers, and cascading plants, but there is substantial crossover between categories because of the crowded nature of container combinations. When several plants are packed into a container, their roots compete for moisture and nutrients, and above the surface, the leaves and stems compete for light. As a result, stems are often somewhat lax and rangy, which is usually a blessing. For example, although you may not like to see coreopsis or rose campion flopping over in your garden, when the same thing happens in a container the effect softens the edges of the container. Still, to maintain the height needed to keep a container combination balanced, it may be necessary to stake the tallest plants.

Shade is often a factor in container combinations, because window boxes and other containers placed close to the house usually receive a maximum of a half day of sun. Light limitations often cause otherwise compact plants to stretch out, becoming much more vinelike or trailing in habit. This often happens with nasturtiums and petunias, making them do double duty as cascading plants. Vining plants, such as English ivy, vinca, and sweet potato vine, always cascade, and their foliage persists all season.

Uprights: Caladium, calla lily, canna, clematis, coreopsis, cosmos, flowering tobacco, geranium, globe amaranth, hydrangea, liriope, ornamental grasses, phormium, rose campion, salvia, scarlet runner bean, snapdragon, sweet pea, and yucca provide height.

Fillers: Ageratum, artemisia, begonia, browallia, coleus, dianthus, dusty miller, fan flower, heuchera, impatiens, lady's mantle, lantana, nasturtium, pansy, periwinkle, petunia, portulaca, rose campion, Swan River daisy, and verbena soften pot edges.

Cascading plants: Candytuft, dead nettle, English ivy, licorice plant, lobelia, petunia, sun rose, sweet alyssum, sweet potato vine, thyme, and vinca will trail gracefully over pot edges.

CONTAINER CREATIVITY

Much of the fun in creating container bouquets is letting your imagination run wild, and the longer you garden, the more combinations you'll want to try. As you continue to grow as a container gardener,

A well-designed container bouquet should include a mixture of upright plants and trailing ones.

keep in mind a few simple guidelines that will help you devise pleasing plant pictures in small spaces, where every element counts.

One of the easiest ways to achieve a harmonious design is to use plants with the same or similar colors. A pot with all red plants, or plants in red and gold, can be striking in its simplicity. You can also go for a bold contrast, combining frosty blue flowers with fiery yellow ones. Remember that "hot" colors appear to advance, while "cool" colors recede. So place red, orange, and yellow toward the back of the container and the blue, purple, and green in front to balance the arrangement.

Also take into account the size, shape, and texture of the flowers and foliage. Big, bold leaves can easily overpower companions plants that have delicately cut or feathery looking foliage, just as large trumpet or saucer-shaped flowers will overwhelm neighbors with dainty little pompon or starlike blossoms. Contrast adds interest, as long as the various elements share a common theme or are balanced visually. A tall, spiky phormium, for example, would pot-hugging dwarf sweet alyssum but the phormium would provide drama and look balanced when it is paired with heuchera, begonia, or any other plant with equally prominent foliage.

PLANTING CONTAINER BOUQUETS

The tallest plants in a container combination usually have correspondingly large root masses, so it's best to set them in place first, and then to surround them with the smaller and easier to handle plants. The angle that the container will be viewed from ultimately determines where these plants will all be placed. If the container will be viewed from all sides, such as when it's displayed on a table or when it is hanging from a porch, you will want to place the tallest plants in the center of the container. If the pot will be placed against a wall, hedge, or other background, then you can set the tallest plants toward the rear of the container, and fill in around the sides and front with shorter plants.

Plant the fillers next, allowing sufficient room for these medium-height, bushy plants to spread out as they grow and mature. Because you want these filler plants to be very bushy, consider pinching them back

Using Neutral Colors

Use plants with soft, neutral colors, such as gray-leaved dusty miller, white-flowered sweet alyssum, or vinca *(Vinca major)*, to tame fiery-colored companions, such as red geraniums or bright yellow marigolds. Neutral plants also add a light-reflecting twinkle to patio container combinations that are intended to be viewed in the evening.

lightly after transplanting, by snipping off stem tips, even if this delays flowering by a few weeks.

Finally, you should tuck cascading plants just inside the rim of the container. Your aim is to create a lush, overflowing floral bouquet, but you should not completely cover up the pot. Fine-textured cascading plants, such as lobelia or sweet alyssum, form such flowery masses that you may need only one or two to balance a container planting. When using plants that grow into long, sparse tendrils, such as licorice plant or vinca, plan to include three or more of them in your masterpiece.

If a pot is viewed from all sides, center the tall plants, and edge the pot with cascading plants.

Treating Container Plants Right

It's tempting to think of container gardening as instant gardening because the planting process is so fast and easy. Choose a container and the plants you want to grow, add potting soil and water, and you're ready to go. However, plants grown in containers do have several special needs, because the small space and volume of soil in which the roots grow limit the amount of nutrients and water available. To help your container plants grow their best, it is important to use high-quality potting soil that allows for vigorous root growth, appropriate fertilizer to encourage healthy foliage and abundant flowering, and proper watering techniques that never leave plants parched and dry or drown them.

POTTING SOILS

Plants growing in containers need quick-draining, fluffy, light soil. Garden soil and commercial topsoil intended for use in garden beds are too heavy, and plant roots will not thrive in them. The easiest route is to buy container potting soil, although you can also mix it yourself.

Packaged potting soil is readily available and is sold in bags ranging from 2–25 kg (5–50 lb). There are differences in quality and price among brands, but you should buy the best you can afford. Begin at a nursery or garden center, and ask for the best potting soil available. Try out a small bag. When you find a product you like, you can buy it in larger quantities, usually at a discount.

Whether you buy it or mix your own, the potting soil should be a fine-tuned mixture of peat moss, compost, and a little sand, with small amounts of puffy white perlite or flaky vermiculite added to lighten the mix and aid drainage. Some warning signs of poor-quality potting soil are a clumping, claylike consistency, numerous wood chips or sticks, an extremely gritty feel, and color that is either gray or light brown rather than dark brown to black.

In recent years, many potting-soil manufacturers have begun adding fertilizer to their mixes. Potting soils that include fertilizer simplify the planting process, because you don't need to mix in fertilizer as you plant or begin feeding plants for several weeks after planting. However, potting soils without added fertilizers are still a good value, and it's easy to sprinkle in small amounts of a balanced granular fertilizer as you fill pots with potting soil or begin fertilizing after planting with a water-soluble formula.

If you want to mix your own potting soil, fill a large bucket or wheelbarrow with two-thirds compost that has been screened to remove sticks, stones, and clumps. The remaining one-third should be a combination of peat moss and either perlite or vermiculite, which are available at any garden center or nursery (wear a dust mask when mixing in these dusty ingredients). Stir the mixture together to combine all ingredients and you're ready to plant.

Spread a layer of pebbles or pot shards over the drain holes of a container to keep soil in while letting excess water drain out. Then add soil until the pot is about three-quarters full. Shake or rock the pot gently to help settle the soil, and place the root balls of your plants on the soil, building it up as needed so that the base of each plant is just below the rim of the pot. Continue filling soil in around the plants and shaking until the soil reaches 2.5 cm (1 in) from the pot rim; if you plan to top the soil with an ornamental mulch, fill to 5 cm (2 in) of the rim. The soil should not "shrink" too much if you've shaken the pot and covered the drain holes properly. Large containers should be placed in their final position before being filled, so that they won't have to be moved when heavy with soil. Some gardeners also like to soak terra-cotta, stone, or cement planters in water before filling them, so that the container does not wick moisture out of the soil.

The proper soil, watering, and fertilizer will ensure healthy, robust plants that need minimum care.

Yellowing leaves may indicate a lack of nutrients. Balanced liquid fertilizer aids quick color recovery.

When filling a wire basket, layer in moss, coconut fiber, or other liner before adding soil (left). Plants rolled in paper stay clean while potting (center). Remove paper, add soil, and upright plants to finish the container.

FEEDING CONTAINER PLANTS

The roots of container-grown plants cannot wander far and wide in search of nutrients, so it's up to you to supply them. Even if you start with potting soil that contains fertilizer, those nutrients will be gone in a matter of weeks. Plants will use some of them, and the rest will be flushed out when you water.

There are two easy ways to keep container-grown plants well fed. You can dose them with water-soluble plant food, which is a liquid or granular food that is mixed into the water used to irrigate plants. Apply this liquid fertilizer full strength according to the package directions, usually every 10–14 days. Some gardeners prefer to use the fertilizer at half the strength but twice as often.

You can also scratch small amounts of a balanced organic fertilizer into the soil surface every 6–8 weeks. For plants that will remain in the containers for a long time, as opposed to seasonal displays, use a commercial controlled-release fertilizer, which has a coating that breaks down gradually depending on temperature and moisture.

Plants vary in their nutritional needs, so there is no fixed feeding schedule that suits all plants. However, because container plants are easy to monitor, you can usually tell when they are not getting enough nutrients. Slow growth, yellow leaves, and poor flowering are the most common signs of nutritional deficiency. If plants quickly improve after being drenched with a liquid fertilizer, you will know for certain that you underestimated their appetites. Still, be careful not to overdo it, or your plants may develop browned leaf edges, a symptom of fertilizer burn. To safeguard against this problem, never exceed the application rates given on the fertilizer label.

WATERING STRATEGIES

All plants grown in containers require regular watering, and their need for water increases as they gain size. When plants are small, you can usually do a good job of watering them with a watering can equipped with a sprinkle head, or rose, or a hose equipped with a watering wand. These perforated watering heads reduce water pressure while breaking up the stream into a gentle flow that soaks into the soil without dislodging delicate plants. But after the root system becomes extensive, watering becomes more challenging. Instead of soaking into the soil around the roots, water may run over the top of the soil and seep down through a gap that often develops between the soil and the pot. Sometimes it runs off the surface of the soil, so that even though you water, the root ball may remain dry. It is a common mistake to think that the plant does not need water when this happens. You can tell when this is happening by watching how much water seeps through the drain holes and by testing the pot for weight. If you tip the pot and it seems no heavier than before you watered, it's time to take action. The best way to know for sure, however, is to stick your finger into the soil. If the soil feels dry up to the first knuckle on your finger, then the soil definitely needs to be well watered.

The first remedy is to water with warm water, which soaks into dry soil much faster than cold. Then poke small holes into the soil's surface with an ice pick, pencil, or screwdriver. Water thoroughly, sprinkle in enough fresh potting soil to fill the gap just inside the rim of the pot, and water again.

Another solution is to place the pot into a large tub and fill with warm water up to the pot rim. Let the soil soak up water from beneath for about a half hour, then drain. This is often the best way to revive plants that have dried out completely. If the problem persists despite your efforts, you will need to repot the plant into a larger container.

A watering can with a rose allows you to water without disturbing soil or injuring delicate plants.

Grouping plants with like needs and placing them in a frequently visited location makes maintenance easy.

Container Garden Maintenance

When container-grown plants receive the right amount of light, moisture, and nutrients, they are usually among the most care-free plants in your garden. Because we keep them in places where we see them often and interact with them daily as we check their needs for water, small problems can be spotted quickly and fixed straightaway.

One problem that's unique to plants grown in pots is salt buildup in the soil, evidenced by whitish deposits on the rim of the pot and sometimes on the soil's surface as well. Some salts are always present in municipal water supplies, and if potting soil becomes too salty, the plants will not be able to take up the moisture and nutrients they need. Accumulated salts can also burn stems and leaves.

To correct this problem, make a habit of flushing containers every few weeks by flooding them with water; drench them again an hour or so later. Like a cleansing bath, this operation dissolves accumulated soil salts, although you may still see residue on containers. In winter or whenever containers are empty, take the time to scrub away crystallized salt deposits with warm water and a stiff brush.

PINCHING AND GROOMING

Every blossom counts in the small world of a container garden, so it's important to do everything you can to encourage the development of bud-bearing stems. With annual flowers, pinching or clipping off old blossoms is crucial to prolonging their flowering. And, when entire stems appear to have borne their last bud, clipping them off will often force out a new flowering stem.

When deadheading old blossoms or removing old stems, always use scissors or pruning shears rather than tugging at the plants with your fingers. Even modest pulling can injure roots, particularly when plants are growing in containers filled with light-textured potting soil.

Also, don't be afraid to control the shape of your plants when you discover ways that pruning might make a plant healthier or more attractive. Many gardeners elevate this process into a true art form, as seen in tightly sculpted topiary and in dramatic bonsai. If you like working with long-lived vines, shrubs, and trees, the same pruning methods used for plants growing in the ground, such as thinning, heading back, and shearing, can be used to shape plants growing in containers. In addition, it's not always practical to move a plant into a larger pot. To save space in the garden, as plants become rootbound, they can be unpotted and root pruned, then potted up in the same container again.

MONITORING ROOTS

Large plants grown in containers seldom attain full size because their root area is restricted. While most of the best plants for containers willingly accept this limitation, it's important to unpot the plant and check its roots when it seems unable to take up water or simply stops growing. Crowded roots are the most common problem, but occasionally insects or diseases are to blame.

Remove spent flowers to promote new buds (left). When roots overtake the soil, it's time to trim them and repot the plant (center). Healthy young plants will have a vigorous, white root system and plenty of soil (right).

In mild climates, simply nestle container plants near the house to shield them from winter winds.

To look at the roots of a container-grown plant, allow the soil in the pot to dry out, then lay the pot on its side and tap it gently. Jiggle the plant to remove it from the container without pulling too hard on the main stem. If the roots are badly matted, spiraled around the inside of the pot into a tight mass, or so thick that you can hardly see the potting soil, it's time to repot the plant.

If you are "potting on," or repotting in a new, larger container, select a pot slightly larger than the existing one but still in proportion to the plant's size. Fill the pot with fresh soil, loosen the plant roots by teasing them away from the soil ball, and continue planting as you would with a new specimen.

If you want to put the plant back in the same container, you'll need to trim the roots. Lay the plant on a bed of newspaper or a plastic sheet. Gently pull away some of the soil, hold the plant upright, and slice from top to bottom with a sharp knife all around the outside of the root ball to cut off old roots and stimulate new growth. Fill the pot with fresh soil and replant as you would a new specimen.

Missing roots indicate that a soil-borne disease has invaded, and there is usually no cure. Dispose of the plant and soil in the garbage, thoroughly clean the container by scrubbing with a solution of warm, soapy water and household bleach, rinse the pot, and start over by filling the pot with commercial, sterile potting mix and setting in a healthy plant.

WHEN WINTER COMES

The first few autumn frosts spell the end for most annuals grown in containers. They are best dumped onto the compost heap, potting soil and all. Then give the empty pots a good scrubbing with solution of soapy water and household bleach, and let them dry before storing them for winter. Ideally, you should store the pots in a place where they will not freeze, but pots that are kept dry and protected from ice and snow usually withstand cold without cracking or splitting.

If you have been growing potted hardy perennials, trim back the dead foliage with sharp pruning shears and move the containers to a place where it is cool enough to foster dormancy but not where plants are subject to constant freezing and thawing. Depending on your climate, it may be sufficient to place the pots against a wall of your house or beneath a bench, where they'll be protected from wind. If your storage space is limited to a deck or a patio, place dormant potted perennials in an insulated foam picnic cooler tucked into a protected corner and cover the pots with several centimeters (inches) of loose, fluffy mulch, such as evergreen boughs. You can also use plastic bubble wrap as pot insulation. Wrap it around the outside of individual, planted pots and secure it with a water-resistant tape, or stuff the bubble wrap between and over the top of a group of stored containers and secure it with tape.

Hardy shrubs and trees usually need to remain outdoors in winter, because prolonged exposure to warm, dry indoor air is as stressful for them as hard freezes. Move them to a place where they won't be tortured by winds and be prepared to move them indoors for short periods of time in extreme cold. Even if light levels are low, it's usually better to store hardy evergreens in a cool garage or storage building over winter than it is to bring them into heated indoor spaces in the winter. Keep the soil around the roots lightly moist, by watering once a month, but do not apply fertilizer to these or any other dormant plants until early the following spring, just as they begin to send up new leaves.

Give similar treatment to hardy bulbs that you pot up in the fall. Most daffodils, hyacinths, and tulips need at least 6 weeks of chilling in early winter, after which they can be moved to a less frigid place as they commence growth. Wait until you see green shoots poking through the soil before you shift them to a spot on a warm windowsill indoors.

CARE-FREE LAWNS

A beautiful lawn works magic in the landscape. Its fine texture and vibrant green color contrast with the broader leaves of shrubs, trees, and perennials, framing and unifying the plantings bordering its edges. A broad, flat swath of grass also creates a rest for the eye, letting your attention flow from its uncluttered expanse to busier looking plantings and landscape features, and back again. Think of your lawn as a carpeted floor for your garden, enhancing the landscape in the same way attractive flooring flatters indoor rooms.

A lawn also serves practical purposes. It provides space for outdoor activities, such as ball games with the kids, entertaining friends, and relaxing. Grass can also be a hardworking walkway between beds or a buffer zone between your house and the street. These two jobs are what lawns do best. If you find yourself spending many hours maintaining large areas of turf that do not serve these purposes, you might be growing too much grass. The strategies on the following pages will help you make your lawn attractive, care-free, and will help you decide what is just the right size.

Lawns are composed of turf grasses, and different grass species have specific preferences for soil, sunlight, and climate. Good care can bring out the best in any turf grass, but you may find that the reason your lawn fails to respond to your efforts is that the grass simply does not fit the site. Switching to a different grass species or blend of several species that is better adapted to your yard may be the answer, or you can plant groundcovers in areas that are too shady, too dry, or too steep for grass to thrive. Groundcovers are also invaluable for filling spaces that are awkward to mow, and for reducing the size of your lawn and its maintenance, while preserving its lush, green look. The care-free grasses and groundcovers described in this chapter can be used to create attractive green garden floors in any site.

A slight slope helps water drain, preventing it from pooling on the grass where it can invite fungal disease.

Creating the Care-Free Lawn

Whether you are improving a lawn or planning a new one, the first step toward a care-free lawn is to assess your site. In all climates, lawn grasses grow best where there is a slight slope to facilitate drainage and where they receive at least a half day of sun.

A slight slope is built into most home landscapes, because one of the last steps in house construction is grading the area around the foundation so that rainwater will naturally flow away from the building. But if the grade of your yard is so steep that mowing is difficult, planting the area with any of the care-free, soil-retaining groundcovers listed at the end of this chapter is usually the best, least expensive solution. Another option is to build a low retaining wall that divides the slope into two or more manageable levels containing graded soil.

If shade from large trees confounds your efforts to grow a lush lawn, the first step is to prune off low-hanging tree branches, removing all branches within 3–3.5 m (10–12 ft) of the ground. Even if this technique, called "limbing up," is insufficient to make the site bright enough for lawn grasses, it will at least make the area hospitable to shade-tolerant groundcovers.

If dense shade is inevitable, an alternative is to encourage moss. Moss grows naturally in moist, cool shade and can create an a velvety, green "lawn" that tolerates foot traffic. Moss can go dormant during dry spells, requiring no irrigation, and it springs back after the first rainfall. You may need to pull a few weeds, but moss requires no other maintenance.

Just don't jump to the conclusion that you should eliminate trees in order to have a better lawn. Instead, work out ways to help stately trees and shrubs grow in happy harmony with your lawn. This is not at all difficult and will result in a handsome landscape.

DESIGNING A CARE-FREE LAWN

Any time is a good time to design a care-free lawn. Begin by determining which parts of your yard do the best job of supporting turf grass. This is probably something you already know if you have lived in your home for more than a year, because good sites for grass are revealed each time you mow.

The next step is to determine how much lawn you actually need. Compared to other landscape plants, such as shrubs or groundcovers, thirsty and fertilizer-hungry lawns are a high-maintenance way to cover soil, and it's easy to end up with much more lawn than your landscape requires. If sections of turf grass are not performing one of the functions listed below, move on to the care-free strategies suggested in this chapter for lawn alternatives.

FRONT-YARD FUNDAMENTALS

There is no reason to keep up a huge front lawn devoted solely to grass. Consider growing just enough grass, or a combination of lawn and groundcover, to fulfill the following three needs.

OPENING THE ENTRY. Lawn areas that adjoin narrow front walkways magically make the area seem wide and spacious. Sections of grass planted near entryways also impart a neat, manicured appearance that frames the house.

A lawn adjoining the front walkway makes the house entry look spacious and welcoming.

ENLARGING SMALL SPACES. If your front yard is small, a flowing swath of grass will make it seem larger. Even a very small area devoted to lawn can pull off this trick, which also has the happy effect of making a small house appear larger.

FRAMING FOUNDATION SHRUBS. The ornamental plants growing around the foundation of your house will appear more interesting when the foreground is paved with the fine, even texture of lawn grass. For maximum visual impact, you can add an edging or a mowing strip to create a tailored dividing line between lawn areas and mulched beds of trees, shrubs, and flowering plants.

BACKYARD BASICS

The backyard is naturally a more private, personal area of the landscape than the outward-facing front lawn. So understandably, your backyard lawn should make it easier to pursue the things you enjoy doing outdoors, but just like the front yard, it is an important visual element that enhances your home.

EXPANDING ACTIVITY SPACE. Lawns that adjoin patios and decks enlarge the area available for outdoor dining, entertaining, and relaxing. If you have active children, a long, narrow lawn provides better running space than a small square.

SOFTENING THE HARDSCAPE. If your backyard is heavy on hard surfaces, such as a deck, patio, walkway, or paved drive, use a patch of grass to create a soft, inviting green counterpoint.

OPENING THE VISTA. Lawns make even cramped yards feel more spacious by visually separating flower or shrub borders, vegetable gardens, or wooded areas from the house.

LINKING DIVERSE AREAS. For backyards that are busy with a variety of features, such as a terrace, freestanding planting beds, a sitting area, and foundation plantings, a lawn can link the different spaces and create visual unity.

FLATTERING FOCAL POINTS. Special landscape features, such as a fountain or pool, pergola, or beautiful specimen tree, can be framed with grass to make them more prominent. A focal point should be easily seen, and there's no better way to clear the view than with a low, flat carpet of grass.

CARE-FREE SECRETS
Set Aside Trees

When redesigning your lawn, separate trees from lawn by blanketing the area beneath the trees with an organic mulch or a shade-tolerant groundcover. Besides looking good, a defined buffer zone of attractive mulch or ground-hugging plants prevents accidental injuries to tree trunks caused by lawn mowers or string trimmers.

The backyard lawn allows space for outdoor activity and creates a visual buffer between house and garden.

Good Shapes for Lawns

The trickiest part of mowing a lawn is negotiating curves and corners, whether they are found at property boundaries, along a walkway or garden bed, or at the edge of a house, patio, or deck. Having to turn or back up the mower every few minutes makes the job slower and more tiring. Keep these mowing pitfalls in mind when deciding on a shape for your lawn and "design out" awkward spots.

You can sculpt your lawn into several practical and attractive shapes. Square or rectangular panels of grass are most commonly seen, but you can soften the sharp corners by drawing out the edges of adjoining foundation or garden beds into gentle curves. Doing so maintains a planned, orderly appearance, but also gives a lawn an informal and inviting appearance. The curves create more space for lower-maintenance perennial plants and shrubs, reduces the square meterage (footage) of lawn, and eliminates tight angles that add time and effort to mowing.

Circular or oblong lawns do an amazing job of opening up small yards and allow lots of room out-

A mowing strip set flush with the soil maintains a lawn edge and eliminates the need to trim.

side the circle for shrubs and flowers. They are especially well suited to formal design schemes. An asymmetrical shape will also work, providing it has broad, flowing curves rather than tight squiggles. Such irregular shapes work best in large areas and can create a pleasing sense of movement.

To map out a new shape, you can use your mower to cut lines in an existing lawn. You can also lay down a board to serve as a straight edge when defining straight lines or a garden hose to plot the contours for curving ones. Spray the outline on the grass with a white or brightly colored paint or sprinkle flour to mark the shape as a guide when removing old turf or planting a new area.

ADDING A FRAME

There are several low-maintenance ways to keep lawn edges that abut mulched beds or patches of groundcover looking tidy without constant trimming and edging. A lasting solution is to install a mowing strip of bricks, flat stones, landscape timbers, or concrete pavers. This type of edging is set

A circular lawn is well suited to a formal landscape and is easy to mow, thanks to its gentle curves.

into the ground with the surface of the paving flush with the soil, so that the wheels of your mower roll over it. A mowing strip adds an attractive visual element to the landscape and lets you achieve a clean cut without the need to follow up with an edger or string trimmer.

For a less visible barrier, you can pound thin, hard plastic, rubber, or metal edging into the ground along the edge of the turf, leaving just the very top sticking above the soil. Some edging material requires you to dig a narrow trench or at least loosen the soil with a sharp spade. Others, however, are designed to penetrate the soil when pounded in with a rubber mallet. If the edging heaves out of the ground as the soil freezes and thaws in late winter, simply pound it back in when the soil is moist. These edgings are particularly useful in discouraging enthusiastic grasses with running stems, such as Kentucky bluegrass, from creeping into adjoining beds, as well as preventing aggressive groundcovers or perennial plants from sneaking into the lawn.

Whether you choose a paver or the pound-in edging, be sure to leave a thin strip of mulch on the side opposite the grass. This bare area prevents damage to plantings from the mower.

In some lighting situations, you may not need any type of lawn edging. If the dividing line between the lawn and a flower bed or a patch of groundcover coincides with a break between sunlight and shade, the sun-loving lawn grass will naturally retreat from

Grass paths create a sense of movement and continuity, leading eyes as well as feet to garden beds.

Lawns that abut mulched beds need to be trimmed regularly and edged yearly to keep a neat shape.

the shaded area, and the shade-tolerant perennial, annual, and groundcover plants won't send runners or young plants into the bright light.

KEEPING THE EDGE

If you don't install a paved mowing strip or other type of barrier, you'll need to maintain the lawn edge by cutting into the soil. This usually needs to be done at least once a year, in spring.

It's easy with the proper tools. You can use a sharp spade or a special edging tool that has a half-moon blade with a flattened top and foot rest, where you press down with the ball of your foot. Keeping the tool vertical, use it to slice down into the soil to the top of the edger, or about 10 cm (4 in) deep if using a spade. Draw the blade straight up or rock it slightly side to side to keep from disturbing the soil and to leave a clean line.

Trimming Tools

Lawns that border a wall, raised planting bed, or paved area may be difficult to mow, so you will need to trim them to keep the grass looking manicured. Long-handled shears or string trimmers that cut the grass blades without digging into the soil work best for this purpose.

Maintaining a Care-Free Lawn

Lawn grasses are by nature tough, resilient plants, yet they do require ongoing care. The most important lawn-keeping tasks are fertilizing, watering, mowing, preventing pests and diseases, and weeding. If you think of lawn grasses as low-growing foliage plants, valued for their leaves, it's easy to work with their natural growth cycles.

THE NEED TO FEED

Unlike deeply rooted perennials, shrubs, and trees, grass roots seldom venture far into the soil, which limits their access to nutrients and water buried deep below the soil surface. At the same time, their crowns are constantly growing, producing new leaves. This rapid growth depletes nutrients that are naturally available in the topsoil, where the root are, so regular fertilizing is necessary to keep the lawn strong, healthy, and free of weeds.

All grasses crave nitrogen, the nutrient that powers the growth of new leaves. However, too much nitrogen creates a quick flush of green top growth without supplying other nutrients needed for root growth or to support the plants. Grasses perform best when given a slow, steady supply of a fertilizer that contains all three primary nutrients: nitrogen, phosphorus, and potassium. Such a balanced fertilizer promotes top growth, root development, disease resistance, and hardiness.

One of the best ways to fertilize the lawn is to use a mulching mower. These rotary mowers pulverize the nitrogen-rich clipped blades into tiny pieces and spread them back into the soil, where organisms break them down to release nutrients. Don't worry about leaving ugly clumps of cut grass on the lawn; clippings from mulching mowers are so small that they sink invisibly between the blades. If you don't have a mulching mower, you can use a regular mower without a bag. If you cut as often as needed to remove no more than one-third of the top growth, the small clippings will disappear.

When selecting a commercial fertilizer, look for a formula designed especially for lawns, such as an 8-2-2 formulation. Stay away from spray-on liquid fertilizers, which supply a blast of nitrogen that is used up quickly or may even run off before plants can use it. A granular fertilizer, especially one that acts slowly, is best. Organic fertilizers are preferred, not only because they release their nutrients gradually but also because they will not chemically burn grass, or cause it to turn brown, with an overdose. They also encourage the beneficial organisms that break down organic matter in the soil, releasing nutrients in a soluble form that grass roots can absorb.

It's important not to fertilize grass too much or too often. Twice a year is usually sufficient, using a fertilizer designed for blade development before plants start their active growth and using one designed for root development before plants go into dormancy. In cold climates, fertilize in spring and fall. In warm climates, fertilize in early and late summer. Read the package directions for recommendations on the proper amount to apply.

Use a sprinkler early in the day, so that grass can dry before nightfall and won't burn in midday sun.

To ensure even coverage, invest in a drop spreader. This handy piece of equipment has a hopper set between wheels that releases fertilizer in a fixed amount as you roll it over the lawn and is very easy to use. Most fertilizer packages will tell you how to calibrate the spreader opening so that you apply exactly the right amount.

WATERING WISDOM

Like every plant, grass needs water. But you really want to water the soil, which is the reservoir for the roots, rather than the blades themselves. Sprinkling the grass lightly every few days does more harm than good, because water never has a chance to sink deep into the soil. As grass roots rise to the surface to seek water rather than reaching deeply into the soil, the lawn quickly succumbs to drought and summer heat.

Lawns need at least 2.5 cm (1 in) of water per week (for measuring water, see p. 324). Let the soil, light, and climate be your guide. Heavy clay soil holds moisture longer than sandy soil, which lets

A drop spreader makes short work of applying fertilizer and is easily calibrated for different products.

Criss-Cross Lawn Fertilizing

To get complete coverage with lawn fertilizer, apply it in a criss-cross pattern across your lawn. Read the package to find out how much fertilizer you need for the size of your yard. Apply half that amount by pushing a loaded drop spreader over the lawn in parallel north-south rows. Then apply the other half while working in an east-west direction.

water pass right through. And lawns in light shade or cool climates will stay moist longer than those baking in sun in a warm climate. It's time to irrigate when the blades wilt or lose their springiness when you step on them. You can also check the need for water by digging up a little plug of turf. If the soil is moist, there's no need to water, and you can simply push the plug back into its hole. If it's dry, apply water.

Lawn sprinklers are the most convenient way to cover large areas. Automatic impulse systems are the most efficient but are expensive to install and may not be necessary in regions that usually have plentiful rainfall. If you have a portable surface sprinkler that revolves or oscillates, make sure it is in good condition so that the coverage is as even as possible.

Whatever type you use, the goal is to water slowly and deeply, so that moisture has a chance to sink to the roots, about 10–15 cm (4–6 in) deep, without running off or pooling. Water early in the morning on a still day, so that grass blades can dry off before sunset and water is not blown away from its target. Never water at midday, when much of the moisture is lost to evaporation before it hits the soil and wet grass can burn in the sun. To gauge the amount of water reaching the lawn, scatter several small cans beneath the sprinkler, each marked with a line 2.5 cm (1 in) up from the bottom of the can. Note how long the sprinkler must run to fill the can to the line. That's the amount of time you should run the sprinkler when watering in the future.

During drought, when municipal ordinances often prohibit lawn watering, don't worry. Most grasses simply go dormant and will spring back to life when moisture returns. In arid regions, where every drop of water is precious, consider planting a drought-tolerant grass species, such as buffalo grass. You can also cover as much space as desired with drought-tolerant groundcovers, such as low-growing shrubs, perennials, or even herbs, such as thyme or lavender, which thrive in arid places.

KNOW HOW TO MOW

Proper mowing keeps grass height under control, encourages root growth, and discourages weed growth and disease. The optimum height depends on the species as well as the lawn use. Fine-bladed grasses used for display lawns do best at about 2.5 cm (1 in). Coarse-textured grasses are used for high-traffic lawns and many grasses recommended for cool climates should grow to 8 cm (3 in) or more, especially during the hot summer months.

The basic rule for mowing height is to take off no more than one-third of the blade each time you mow. If the ideal height for your grass species is 5 cm (2 in), mow when it reaches 8 cm (3 in). Taking off a small portion of the blades causes the least shock to the plants and leaves plenty of blades to make food for the roots. If blades are cut too short and can't supply enough food, the roots will grow

Drought-Survival Strategies

When drought-stressed lawns can't be relieved because of municipal water restrictions, you can still help your struggling lawn survive. Stop mowing or mow very high, because tall grass blades shade the soil, keep it cool, and reduce evaporation. Also avoid walking on the grass, to prevent the soil from being packed down, and don't fertilize, so that grass can go dormant and conserve its resources.

poorly and weaken the plant, allowing disease to take hold. Longer blades also shade out weed seedlings, and the vigorous roots that result will keep most weeds from getting a foothold.

The ideal height can vary according to season. When grasses are growing actively, you can keep the blades a little shorter, about 5 cm (2 in). Active growth occurs in spring and fall in cold climates. During periods of stress from drought or heat, cut the blades higher. Grass growing in shade also should be allowed to grow 2.5 cm (1 in) longer than the same grass grown in sun, so that it has more surface exposed to light to help it manufacture energy.

If your climate is dry, replace some lawn with colorful, drought-tolerant groundcover perennials and herbs.

A healthy, well-maintained lawn will naturally crowd out weeds and repel pests and diseases.

PREVENTING DISEASES AND PESTS

Fungal infections can sometimes crop up in lawns, such as brown patch and leaf spot, which usually appear as brown patches or dead spots in the lawn. Lingering dampness contributes to the problem, so correcting drainage problems that allow water to stand on the lawn helps prevent many diseases. Over-fertilization can also contribute to disease, because a lawn that grows too lush and thick holds morning dew for several hours. Also avoid evening watering to reduce the amount of time that your lawn is wet, because many fungal spores become active in the cool, damp hours of evening.

A healthy lawn will tolerate light insect feeding by common pests including sod webworms and chinch bugs. But in areas where June beetles or Japanese beetles are numerous, their larvae can seriously weaken lawns as they feed on grass roots in spring. The larvae of both types of beetles are small whitish grubs, easily found by digging up a patch of troubled grass in spring. For long-term control, apply parasitic nematodes, which multiply in the soil and feed on the developing larvae. Where winters are cold, the nematodes do not survive and must be reapplied if the problem returns.

KEEPING OUT WEEDS

Weeds interfere visually with the uniform carpet effect that lawns provide. A few invaders do little harm, but large patches of weeds rob water and nutrients from the grass, weakening the lawn. Healthy, vigorous lawns are naturally resistant to weeds. If you fertilize properly, water deeply, and mow high, the grass will grow so thick that weeds won't have a chance. However, stressed lawns are vulnerable to dozens of weed species. Some, such as chickweed and crabgrass, are shallow-rooted annuals that die back after setting seed. Others, such as plantain and dandelion, are tenacious, deep-rooted perennials and will return year after year.

To halt the spread of annual weeds, you need to stop adult plants from dropping seeds and stop seeds from sprouting. Pull up annual weeds before they can set seed. If seedheads are already visible, use a bag attachment when mowing and compost the clippings, because compost piles often become hot enough during decomposition to destroy the seeds.

If seeds drop, you can spread a commercial pre-emergent herbicide, which is a substance that prevents the seeds from developing. There are several broad-spectrum granular pre-emergents available at garden centers that you can broadcast with a fertilizer spreader. An organic pre-emergent derived from corn is also now available from garden suppliers. Because crabgrass is so common, there is a pre-emergent designed just to control this weed.

Apply weed preventers according to package directions at the right time, which is shortly before weed seeds are germinating in your region. You will not be able to spread grass seed for the length of time designated on the package label after applying a pre-emergent weed preventer, because it will also keep grass seed from sprouting.

Perennial weeds must be dug out, roots and all. The easiest time to do this is when plants are young, with small roots, and after a rain, when the soil is soft. Be sure you take out the entire root, especially of deep-rooted weeds, such as dandelion or those with spreading, fibrous roots, such as violets.

You can also apply an herbicide for perennial weed control, which is usually a liquid that you can either spray on individual weeds or spread on a large area with a hose-end sprayer. No one product destroys all types of weeds or is safe for all grasses, so read the label carefully and use according to package directions. To be most effective, these herbicides should be applied when the perennial weed is actively growing, usually just after the plant flowers. Weeds should begin to shrivel and die in about 10 days.

It is important to follow safety practices when spraying herbicides. Notify your neighbors that you will be spraying. Spray on a still day, so that wind won't carry it onto desirable plants. Wear long-sleeved and long-legged clothing, socks, and protective gear, including a respirator, goggles, and gloves. Do not eat, drink, or touch your hands to your face while spraying and bathe immediately after applying the product. For information on storing and disposing herbicides safely and handling a spill or accidental poisoning, see the Maintenance chapter.

Maintaining Good Health

To keep your lawn in peak condition, you can perform a few easy tricks used by professionals. Depending on the growing conditions on your property, these techniques should be done every 1–3 years.

One of the easiest and best treatments for your lawn is top-dressing, which you can do in fall. Simply sprinkle a 1.5 cm (1/2 in) thick layer of screened, dry compost or very well-rotted manure over the grass, where it will release nutrients, encourage earthworm activity, and condition the soil. Spread any clumps evenly with the back of a metal rake and water it thoroughly. You can also use a mixture of topsoil, sand, and peat moss instead of compost, which will help to make soil friable.

Even in the healthiest lawns, stems, shallow roots, and other wiry plant parts can knit together into a tight mat known as thatch, which keeps water and fertilizer from penetrating the soil. This tough vegetation is slow to decompose, but you can help it break down by encouraging earthworms and soil organisms to do their jobs. Grow grass to the optimum height for the species, cut no more than one-third of the blade at a time, and let the clippings fall back into the lawn for beneficial soil organisms to recycle into nutrients. Use a balanced organic fertilizer and limit use of herbicides or fungicides. Keep in mind that vigorous, mat-forming grasses are more prone to developing thatch.

If thatch builds up thicker than 1.5 cm (1/2 in), it must be removed. Simply probe with your fingers around the base of grass plants to determine how thick the layer is. You can remove thatch manually by raking vigorously with a special thatch rake. For large lawns, rent a power dethatcher, often called a power rake, which cuts through the layer and lifts it so it can be raked up. Dethatch in spring and fertilize afterward to help the grass recover quickly.

Soil must be crumbly, or friable, enough for air, water, and fertilizer to move through it freely to the roots of grass. Lawns grown in clay soil or in soil that has been compacted by heavy foot or vehicle traffic lose vigor and are easy prey for diseases. To break up heavy or compacted soil, pierce the surface with numerous tiny holes. In very small areas, you can do this by sinking in a garden fork straight down, then wiggling it back and forth to enlarge

For small areas, use a metal tool called a thatch rake to slice through the thatch and pull it up.

the holes. For large lawns, you can rent a machine called a lawn aerator, which pulls up plugs of soil and leaves them on the grass. Don't bother to remove the plugs; they break down in about a week.

Aerate your lawn in early spring, when the soil is moist, and spread fertilizer when you've finished to promote new growth. You can also spread gypsum at the rate recommended on the package label. Gypsum is a soil conditioner that helps to break up sticky clay soil particles and it improves water and air circulation around the roots of grass plants.

A lawn aerator pulls up plugs of compacted or heavy soil to let water, air, and nutrients penetrate.

A power rake cuts through the thatch layer and lifts it from the soil so that it can be removed easily.

Select grass suited to the lawn's purpose. A medium- or coarse-textured species supports traffic in a play area.

Planting a Care-Free Lawn

As with other plants, the various grass species differ in their growth habits and hardiness. The specific preferences of nine lawn grasses are given on the following pages. Simply find the types that are likely to do well in your climate, and you'll be on the way to growing a care-free lawn, whether you are nurturing an established lawn or planting a new one. Also check with local garden centers for varieties they recommended for your area.

SELECTING GRASSES

Grasses are divided into two groups—cool season and warm season—based on the type of weather they prefer. Cool-season grasses, such as bluegrass and fine fescues, grow best in temperatures of 15–24°C (60–75°F) and often go dormant or semi-dormant in hot weather. Warm-season grasses, including St. Augustine and Bermuda grass, grow in temperatures of 26–35°C (80–95°F) and always go

dormant in winter. Most of Canada grows the cool-season varieties, but the warm-season grasses can also be grown in the warmest parts of Ontario.

Grasses are also classified by appearance. Fine-bladed grasses, such as cool-season bentgrass, have blades less than 6 mm (1/4 in) wide. These usually can't tolerate heavy traffic and are used to create a display lawn as velvety as a putting green. Grasses that can stand more traffic have blades ranging from medium to coarse and are best suited to children's play spaces, garden paths, and other heavily used lawn areas.

GROWTH HABITS OF GRASSES

Different species of lawn grass vary in their growth habits. Spreading, or sod-forming, grasses send out stems called rhizomes that creep either slightly above or below ground level, forming a new plant wherever they root. These grasses, including cool-season bluegrass and warm-season zoysia, eventually knit together tightly into a thick turf.

Bunch grasses grow only from the crown and form upright tufts, yet the individual plants grow so close together that they appear to be joined even though they are not. Common tuft-forming grasses include tall fescue, which is becoming increasingly popular because of its hard-wearing capability. Cool-season perennial ryegrass and transition-zone buffalo grass are primarily tuft-forming grasses, although they do spread modestly after becoming established.

Sod-forming grasses can be planted by installing individual sprigs or small plantlets called plugs, but this is rarely done in Canada. Most lawns are started from sod, which is rolled-up sheets of ready-to-plant grass with roots intact, which is harvested fresh from special local sod farms. Tuft-forming grasses are

Solarizing Weeds

If there's a concentrated patch of weeds in the lawn, spread a sheet of clear plastic over the area and weight the cover down with stones. In about 8 weeks, heat from the sun will kill weeds, weed seeds, and most insects and diseases in the upper few centimeters (inches) of soil, in a process called solarization. Afterward, you can simply rake up and dispose of the dead weeds before preparing the soil for new grass.

usually planted from seed, although they are also often available as sod.

STARTING FROM SCRATCH

When you're planting a new lawn area or replacing a section of damaged lawn, it pays to prepare the soil well. Dig up samples of soil from various parts of the proposed lawn area and test it with an over-the-counter kit from a garden center or send soil samples to a local agricultural college or independent soil-testing laboratory (look in the yellow pages of your telephone directory under "laboratories").

If your soil is infertile, spread a commercial balanced granular fertilizer designed for starting lawns, such as a 7-21-7 formulation. If the test shows that the soil is too acid or alkaline, you'll need to adjust the pH, or the level of acidity or alkalinity as measured on the recognized pH scale. Grass prefers a pH around 7.0, or neutral, the level at which it can take up nutrients most efficiently. To decrease acidity, indicated by a number below 7.0, add garden lime; to decrease alkalinity, indicated by a number above 7.0, add garden sulphur. Apply the amendments according to package directions and work them into the soil before planting.

This is also the time to correct soil structure to create a loose, well-drained home for grass roots. In soils that are more than 60–70 percent clay or sand, spread a 5–8 cm (2–3 in) thick layer of compost or well-rotted manure over the soil and work it in to a depth of 15 cm (6 in). Adding compost will also improve fertility and help neutralize the pH of soil. For large areas, you should rent a heavy-duty rototiller to prepare the bed, then rake the surface smooth

with the back of an iron rake and tamp it down moderately with your feet or a board.

PLANTING OPTIONS

Sod is the fastest way to start a lawn, but it requires careful handling and precision, so if you are covering a large area, it's best left to professionals. For smaller areas, start on one edge, laying the individual sods like bricks, with the joints alternating. Work from the freshly laid sod by standing on a plank and laying the new sod in front of the existing row.

Sowing seed is the easiest and least expensive way to start a patch of grass or an entire lawn. In warm climates, sow seed in late spring. In cold climates, seeds sown in early fall is most successful, because warm soil, cool nights, and usually plentiful moisture create ideal growing conditions. You can also plant in early spring, although plants will start more slowly in the cold soil, and you may have to water the young, shallow-rooted plants in summer to keep them strong.

Select a grass species that fits your yard and the kind of traffic it receives, and then purchase fresh, weed-free seed suited for your climate from a rep-

Use a rototiller to incorporate compost and other amendments into the soil before planting grass.

A Fast Patch

If your grass is a creeping, sod-forming type, you can be sure of an exact match when patching it, if you transplant plugs taken from other parts of your own yard. When patching a tuft-forming grass with seed, check the package label to make sure the seed you buy has a high germination rate, more than 80 percent.

utable garden center. Rough up prepared soil by drawing a sturdy metal rake lightly over the surface and sow the seeds evenly by hand or in a drop spreader according to the rate listed on the package. Rake the surface gently with a flexible leaf rake so that the seeds make good contact with the soil, then water lightly. Mist the soil daily as needed to keep the soil moist, which is very important for germination. You should see a covering of fine-bladed grass seedlings in 7–14 days. Once the grass reaches 5–8 cm (2–3 in) tall, mow it to 2.5 cm (1 in).

REPAIRING AND REFRESHING TURF

Sooner or later you will have to patch a section of lawn, whether it was dug up accidentally by a car tire, was overtaken by weeds, or worn out from excess foot traffic. The lawn may also grow thin with age or because of increased shade as nearby trees grow larger. To restore its vigor, you can overseed, which means spreading seed on an established lawn.

Mow the existing grass in the area to 2.5 cm (1 in) and rake vigorously with a flexible spring rake to remove as much of the clippings, old grass, and thatch as possible. Also make sure you pull out any weeds. Rough up the soil with an iron rake and sprinkle a 1.5 cm (1/2 in) deep layer of topsoil or compost over the spot. Level the surface with the back of a sturdy metal rake, if needed, then rough it lightly with a flexible spring rake to accept seed.

Broadcast the seed over the area by hand or with a drop spreader, water lightly, and keep the soil moist by misting it as often as needed with a hose fitted with a spray nozzle until the seeds germinate. You can mow the new grass after it reaches 5–8 cm (2–3 in) in height.

Lawn Grasses

In most of Canada, grasses must be hardy enough to survive freezing winters beautifully, even with no protective layer of snow. Although they are stressed by hot-summer weather, they should remain lush and green if watered, or peacefully go dormant during a drought and then green up again in the cooler temperatures and rainy days of autumn.

BLUEGRASS
Poa pratensis

The undisputed queen of lawn grasses is bluegrass, also called Kentucky bluegrass. This is a sod-forming type of grass with fine, dark green blades. It tolerates cold, heat, and rain but does not grow well in shady or damp conditions. Because bluegrass grows vigorously and quickly, it may need more water than other grass species. If you have a fertile, sunny site, bluegrass is the first grass to consider for creating a classic lawn.

There are many named varieties of bluegrass that show good disease resistance including 'Adelphi' and 'Glade'. Most packaged bluegrass seed and sod are actually mixtures of several species of grasses, including some shade-tolerant types that work together to grow a dense, luxurious lawn. Mow bluegrass to a height of 6–8 cm (2 1/2–3 in).

FINE FESCUE
Festuca rubra

Fine fescues, also called red fescues, are seldom grown as a primary lawn grass, but they are often included in seed blends because they tolerate shade, drought, and poor soil. They also show good disease resistance.

There are several kinds of fine fescue, all with very fine leaf blades. Creeping fescue is a sod-forming grass that spreads rapidly into a soft cushion of turf. It is good for cool, humid areas and acid soil. Look for 'Pennlawn', 'Dawson', and 'Flyer'. Chewings fescue is a tufting, upright grass that grows very well in shade. Good varieties for a dense turf include 'Jamestown' and 'Highlight'. Mow fine fescues to a height of 6–8 cm (2 1/2–3 in) in.

PERENNIAL RYEGRASS
Lolium perenne

Plant breeders have made big improvements in this grass species, which grows quickly from seed. It is often included in seed blends, because its fast germination helps retard soil erosion while slow-germinating grasses become established. Older varieties were strictly tuft forming, but several of the new ones are sod forming. Good choices include 'Manhattan II', 'Citation II', and 'Pennfine'.

The greatest shortcoming of perennial ryegrass is that it has shallow roots and can be killed by three consecutive weeks of hot, dry weather. One of its greatest assets is that it often stays green through winter, particularly in the warmer zones of its hardiness range. It is also resistant to heavy traffic and a number of lawn diseases. Mow perennial ryegrass to 5–6.5 cm (2–2 1/2 in) tall.

Many garden lawns are sown from a blend of grass seeds designed to grow in sun and shade.

LAWN SEED BLENDS

Many lawns in colder zones are a mixture of bluegrass, fine fescues, and perennial ryegrass, which can grow together without competing for moisture or nutrients. When a blend is sown, the perennial ryegrass germinates quickly and holds the soil in place, giving the slower-growing bluegrass a chance to become established. The fine fescues will fill in shady spots or pockets in a lawn where bluegrass shows weak growth due to low soil fertility. Over a period of about three years, the bluegrass will gradually take over, except in areas where the other two species are better adapted.

LAWN GRASSES

NAME	HARDINESS	PREFERRED SOIL pH	PREFERRED SOIL TYPE	PREFERRED LIGHT
BLUEGRASS *Poa pratensis*	Zone 3	Neutral	Fertile, well-drained	Sun
FINE FESCUES *Festuca rubra*	Zone 3	Neutral to slightly acid	Fertile, well-drained	Sun to partial shade
PERENNIAL RYEGRASS *Lolium perenne*	Zone 3	Neutral to slightly acid	Any well-drained soil	Sun to partial shade

Care-Free Grasses

While the typical blue-grass lawn does an excellent job of showing off the flowers and shrubs, it is fairly high maintenance and needs regular and frequent mowing to look its best. There are other grasses that, while they may not look quite as lush and green, are hard wearing, and need less attention. They are becoming increasingly popular as more gardeners discover their benefits, less frequent mowing, quicker recovery from drought, and less need for expensive fertilizers.

TALL FESCUE
Festuca arundinacea

Tall fescue features unusually deep roots, so it tolerates summer heat and drought better than many other species. This tuft-forming grass gets its coarse texture from thousands of individual plants growing side by side, which also means it withstands heavy traffic. It has a wide blade that accounts for its somewhat rough and coarse appearance close up. Tall fescue is a very hard wearing care-free grass, making it a good choice for gardens where young children will be playing.

Tall fescue is a light feeder, so you can fertilize as usual in fall and lightly or not at all in spring. Irrigating during droughts in summer will help keep it from browning too badly, but expect this grass to appear somewhat ragged in the hottest part of summer.

Look for newer tall fescue varieties, such as 'Apache', 'Falcon', and 'Rebel II'. Mow to a height of 10 cm (4 in), which helps increase the grass's tolerance to heat. Tall fescues make good lawns in Zone 4 and warmer.

BUFFALO GRASS
Buchloe dactyloides

A native plant of the North American Great Plains, buffalo grass is a relative newcomer to home lawns.

Because it tolerates climate and soil extremes, it is a natural choice for western lawns. A sod-forming grass with excellent tolerance to cold (Zone 3), buffalo grass excels in dry, neutral to alkaline soil where other lawn grasses fail. It has a fine texture, needs water only until it becomes established, grows slowly, and remains short, requiring infrequent mowing. You can sometimes get by with mowing it only once or twice a season.

The species has prickly seed heads, but newer varieties produce few of these, which are easily controlled through routine mowing. In addition, improved varieties, such as 'Prairie', creep a little after becoming mature clumps. These varieties can be grown from either sod or plugs planted from mid spring to early summer.

Buffalo grass needs only one light feeding in early summer and should be cut to a height of 6–8 cm (2 1/2–3 in).

BLUE GRAMA GRASS
Bouteloua gracilis

Also native to the Great Plains, from Manitoba to Texas, this grass is becoming increasingly used for home lawns, especially where summer droughts are common. Although it may go dormant during prolonged periods of drought, it recovers quickly and, since its roots can go down 2.5 m (7 ft), it can withstand moderate periods of drought without going dormant at all.

It prefers neutral to alkaline soils and will also thrive on slightly saline ones where other grasses will not grow. Hardy to Zone 3, it will grow on a wide range of soils, from sandy to moderately clayey, providing they are not acidic.

Sod-forming in our climate, it has a fine texture and needs watering only until established. This grass grows only 30–45 cm (12–18 in) tall, but may be only 15 cm (6 in) where rainfall is sparse and is a good candidate for a wildflower meadow where its attractive seed-heads, like little curved combs, add to the autumn scene.

In the garden, once established, it can be cut to 8 cm (3 in) and should be given a light feed in early summer. This grass is best grown from seed sown while the soil is still warm in fall.

Where summers are hot and winters are cold, tall fescue makes a hard-wearing lawn.

Care-Free Groundcovers

Any plant that carpets the ground with foliage, stays under 30 cm (12 in) in height, and grows so thickly that it naturally chokes out weeds qualifies as a groundcover. If you think of lawn grass as only one type of groundcover, it becomes easier to imagine using other plants to replace patches of turf in parts of your landscape.

Dozens of plants, including shrubs, ornamental grasses, perennials, and herbs, make hard-working groundcovers when planted in a site that allows them to spread into broad mats of foliage. They require less water and care than lawn grass, making them excellent choices for arid regions and gardeners who want low-maintenance landscapes. A few shrubs commonly used as groundcovers, including cotoneaster, also produce berries, and a number of spreading perennials, such as bugleweed and lamb's ears, add flowers to the show.

There are basically two types of groundcovers: deciduous, which loses its foliage in winter, and evergreen, which retains its foliage year-round. Deciduous groundcovers, when planted in broad bands or drifts, are a great way to fill small nooks that are difficult to mow. Or you can use them to cover difficult slopes, bring lively color to shade, or put them to work as a visual transition between lawn and paved areas. Deciduous groundcovers require a little more attention, because they cannot shade out weeds year-round the way evergreens do, but they still demand less upkeep than a grass lawn.

Groundcovers that are evergreen or semievergreen, meaning that they retain their foliage except in the coldest winters, work all year in partnership with your lawn or in place of it. Where winters are very cold, your choices may be limited to spreading juniper or periwinkle, but gardeners in mild-winter climates have many more choices.

GROUNDCOVER CHOICES

You will find many of the following care-free groundcovers described fully in the encyclopedia section of this book.

Sun-loving shrubs that spread into care-free groundcovers include low-growing cultivars of:

- cotoneaster
- euonymus
- juniper
- Russian arborvitae

Shade-loving perennial groundcovers include:

- asarum
- dead nettle
- epimedium
- fern
- hellebore
- lungwort
- periwinkle
- sweet woodruff

Where at least a half day of sun is available, select from among these perennials:

- bugleweed
- dianthus
- lamb's ear
- creeping phlox
- thyme
- spreading veronica

Naturally low-growing blue fescue makes a handsome groundcover for a sunny yard.

GROWING GROUNDCOVERS

For long-term success with fast-growing perennial groundcovers, take the time to prepare the planting site well, as plants will be living in their new home for many years. Dig the soil at least 15 cm (6 in) deep and mix in compost or other organic matter to improve the texture, or build a shallow berm of improved soil. When setting out slow-growing groundcover shrubs, however, prepare individual planting holes in unimproved soil, because cultivating soil unnecessarily often triggers an explosion of germinating weed seeds.

Make sure you have enough plants, which may be more than you think. Perennial groundcover starter plants are usually planted 15–30 cm (6–12 in) apart in all directions, and closer spacing results in faster coverage. When planting a large area or a steep slope with spreading shrubs, it is often wise to stretch a sheet of landscaping fabric over the prepared soil, then cut holes in it where you need to set in the plants. When finished, top with 8 cm (3 in) of an ornamental mulch, such as shredded bark or bark chips. Besides suppressing weeds, this "double mulch" retains soil moisture. After planting, irrigate groundcovers as needed to keep the soil moist the first season to help them become established.

While groundcovers are filling in, you can sprinkle a pre-emergent herbicide, which prevents weed seed from sprouting, on the soil around them. It will not harm groundcover plants, as this product only affects seeds. Even so, some hand weeding is usually necessary before plants start to spread. Pull out weeds when they are young, so that you disturb the soil as little as possible and prevent the weeds from robbing water and nutrients from the groundcover. After two seasons, the weed population will drop sharply as the groundcovers take over, blocking the light that weeds need to grow.

MAINTAINING GROUNDCOVERS

Groundcovers can do a much better job of blanketing the ground when they are adequately fertilized. In early spring, spread a balanced, commercial, slow-release or organic fertilizer at the rate recommended on the package. You can also spread 5 cm (2 in) of compost or well-rotted manure.

Watch for signs of trouble. Tiny, stationary tan or brown discs attached to plant stems are a sign of scale, which is not an unusual insect pest to discover lurking in groundcovers. Trim back badly infested stems and destroy the clippings. You can treat moderate outbreaks with commercial dormant oil or a pesticide labeled for use on the plant species with the scale problem. Use according to label directions.

Just as grass requires routine mowing, groundcovers may need regular edging and cutting back. Hard edging materials, such as bricks or flat stones, can reduce the frequently of this chore, but you may still will need to use pruners, garden shears, or a mower to keep spreading groundcovers from moving into areas where they are not wanted.

If, after a hard winter, your groundcover plants have brown and tattered foliage, you can renew them in early spring by cutting them back nearly to the ground using a string trimmer or mower set at a high setting. Within a few weeks, they will produce fresh, healthy new foliage.

REJUVENATING OLD PLANTINGS

After several years, some groundcovers become so crowded and overgrown that their health deteriorates. The method of rejuvenation depends on the type of plant you are growing. Flowering perennials often need to be dug and divided, and shrubs, except for juniper, can be pruned back severely. Some spreading groundcovers, such as liriope, can be sheared back to 10 cm (4 in) with a string trimmer or a mower with its blade set at its highest setting in late winter or early spring. Rake out the debris and then apply fertilizer and a 5 cm (2 in) layer of an organic mulch. By early summer, the planting should be covered with fresh new growth.

EVERGREEN GROUNDCOVERS

Vigorous and durable, evergreen groundcovers are top plants for framing a lawn, masking the bases of trees, or planting on slopes. They usually cannot withstand foot traffic, but they do an excellent job of edging walkways or other hard surfaces provided you are willing to trim them back from time to time. You can also put them to work near deciduous shrubs or combine them with spring-flowering bulbs. Some

of the most popular, effective, and care-free evergreen groundcovers are listed here.

IVY

Hedera spp.

English ivy (*Hedera helix*) has a well-deserved reputation for growing with such exuberance that it climbs trees and buildings, sometimes overwhelming them. However, when planted as a groundcover and trimmed two or three times a year to keep its edges neat, English ivy is well behaved. The same can be said of English ivy's large-leaved and tender cousin, Canary ivy (*H. canariensis*), which grows from Zone 8. Because they are so persistent and deeply rooted, these ivies are the best evergreen groundcovers for planting beneath trees that have extensive surface roots.

The best varieties for groundcover use have broad, dark green foliage, not small, divided "bird's foot" leaves. These and the types that have variegated leaves are nice for filling small areas in shady places and growing in containers, but they seldom give the thick coverage needed to control weeds.

Every 6 weeks or so, check to make sure that the ivy is not growing on trees. If it is already clinging to the trunks, pull off the stems and trim them back to about 15 cm (6 in) from the base of the tree. Fertilize ivy lightly in early spring with a balanced commercial fertilizer, such as 10-10-10, applied

according to package directions, and shear back plantings damaged by severe winter weather.

Few pests or diseases other than sap-sucking scale insects bother established ivy. Control these pests by spraying commercial dormant oil as directed on the package label. Leaves are sometimes infected with fungal diseases that cause them to develop spots before turning yellow and dropping off. This does not require treatment, because the leaves are quickly replaced by vibrant new growth.

LIRIOPE

Liriope muscari, L. spicata

Often known as lily turf, this easy-to-grow groundcover has handsome grasslike foliage and purple flower spikes in late summer. The most common species, blue lily turf (*Liriope muscari*), grows into bigger and prettier clumps year after year. Creeping liriope (*L. spicata*) spreads via short creeping stems, so it is the best type for covering a large space. Plant liriope in broad bands or use it as an edging between the lawn and a shrub bed or foundation grouping.

Plant liriope 15 cm (6 in) apart; it usually fills in within 2 years. Liriope seldom needs fertilizing, but it does look better in spring if the old leaves are trimmed off before the new growth begins. In late winter, use hedge clippers or even a lawn mower set at the highest setting to remove the winter-ravaged leaves just above the plants' crowns.

EVERGREEN GROUNDCOVERS				
NAME	**HARDINESS**	**PREFERRED SOIL pH**	**PREFERRED SOIL TYPE**	**PREFERRED LIGHT**
IVY *Hedera* spp.	Zone 6 (a few to Zone 5)	Neutral to slightly acid	Well-drained	Winter sun, summer shade
LIRIOPE *Liriope muscari,* *L. spicata*	Zone 7 Zone 6	Slightly acid	Average	Partial shade
PACHYSANDRA *Pachysandra terminalis*	Zone 3	Acid	Rich, fertile, moist	Partial to full shade
PERIWINKLE *Vinca* spp.	Zone 3	Acid to neutral	Well-drained	Partial to full shade

You can dig and divide liriope to increase your supply, but it is not necessary for plant health. Few pests or diseases ever bother these plants.

PACHYSANDRA
Pachysandra terminalis

Pachysandra, also commonly known as Japanese spurge, demands a shady site, soil of average fertility, and regular moisture. When given the conditions it prefers, pachysandra is truly the queen of evergreen groundcovers, willing to spread into an ankle-deep blanket of green whorled leaves. Variegated forms are not as vigorous as the green-leaved types, but they are beautiful when put to work filling in between azaleas, rhododendrons, and other shade-tolerant shrubs.

Before planting pachysandra in spring, work in an 8 cm (3 in) thick layer of compost or rotted manure. Set plants 15 cm (6 in) apart and mulch between them to help keep the soil moist. Fertilize established plantings in spring and midsummer, using an organic or balanced, controlled-release fertilizer, such as 5-10-10. A soaker hose, snaked between the plants, and concealed by them, is the easiest way to provide water during dry spells.

In fall, be sure to rake off fallen tree leaves. They promote damp conditions that can lead to problems with leaf blight, a fungal disease, which makes the leaves turn black. Treat badly affected areas with a fungicide labeled for use on pachysandra, applied according to package directions. If harsh winter weather leaves pachysandra foliage ragged and yellow, trim back the top 5 cm (2 in) of foliage first thing in spring. This will help force out new branches, restoring the handsome blanket of green.

PERIWINKLE
Vinca spp.

Periwinkle features glossy, dark green or variegated leaves and starry blue flowers in spring. This vining groundcover spreads by sending out long stems that develop roots wherever they touch the ground. It is an excellent choice for growing on slopes or beneath large shrubs and can be planted with small daffodils and other spring bulbs. *Vinca minor* is hardy to Zone 3 and stays evergreen even in cold climates. A larger

Ivy is a classic evergreen groundcover, ideal for edging a path and surrounding trees in a lawn.

cousin, *V. major*, is hardy to Zone 6 and makes a taller, coarser-looking groundcover.

Periwinkle requires at least partial shade and will turn yellow or simply refuse to grow in searing sun. When planted near walkways or other hard surfaces, it needs regular trimming to keep the edges neat. This is a wonderful groundcover to grow beneath deciduous trees, as it cannot climb up tree trunks the way ivy does. However, you will need to gently rake off leaves in fall, because periwinkle thrives on winter sunshine.

Set out plants in spring, spacing them 30 cm (12 in) apart. Expect two years to pass before the groundcover fills in. Except for a tendency to become invaded by weeds, such as tree seedlings, care-free periwinkle rarely suffers from pest problems.

CARE-FREE SECRETS
Think Big When Planting Groundcover

When it comes to groundcovers, the more space they cover, the greater their visual impact, and the more care-free your landscape will become. Instead of using small dabs of groundcovers here and there, put these plants to work covering large areas that you don't need for outdoor living or don't want to mow.

Drought-Tolerant Woody Plants

Although plants for dry soils were covered briefly on pages 18 and 19, they were mostly perennials with fairly shallow roots, and still need occasional watering during the summer. The plants described here are trees and shrubs that provide the framework of the garden and, by casting shade, provide different conditions that support a wider range of other plants.

With severe droughts becoming increasingly common, plants that are able to survive without additional watering may be the wave of the future. As more and more municipalities impose watering bans during the summer, and country dwellers are scared to risk running their wells dry, having plants that can survive without additional water can make the difference between having a colorful garden or a brown one.

GROWING WOODY PLANTS

All plants need water for the first little while after being planted, even these drought-tolerant ones. It makes sense to plant in early spring before watering bans are in place, so that you can give them a good start with sufficient water to get them established. The larger the plant, the longer the period that it takes to produce a good root system, and the longer the period that watering is essential. While large plants give "instant gardens" it is often wiser to plant smaller plants that need less water. Trees and shrubs require additional watering longer than annuals and perennials. If necessary, one can always use "gray water", baby's bath water for example (after it has cooled), to keep these woody plants alive during their first summer.

After planting, don't try and grow grass under woody plants, it only competes for the available moisture. Instead, cover the area out to the edge of the branches with a mulch of shredded bark, bark nuggets, or coarse compost, and extend this each spring as the plants grow larger.

WOODY PLANTS IN THE LANDSCAPE

Russian olive (*Elaeagnus angustifolia*) is a small tree or large shrub with silvery foliage that makes a good accent plant and is hardy to Zone 2. The bright yellow flowers scent the air in spring and give edible, though slightly mealy, yellowish fruits that are used as a food in its native Russia. It is a good choice for poor soils because the roots can obtain nitrogen from the air. On the downside, the wood is brittle, so exposed locations should be avoided.

The closely related native silverberry (*E. commutata*) is equally hardy, has silvery fruits, and equally fragrant flowers. It does not make as good a specimen plant because it spreads by suckers, but is a good choice for stabilizing sandy soils or banks. Another good choice for poor soils is the black locust (*Robinia pseudoacacia*). This is also able to fix atmospheric nitrogen and survive where other trees would perish. Long chains of fragrant white flowers garland the branches in spring and are sought by bees. The wood is very hard, resists rot, and is much used for fence posts. This tree is prone to borers, but these don't seem to kill the tree and even branches riddled with borer holes keep on growing and flowering. If cut down close to the ground, it will regrow from the base. The variety 'Frisia' is similar but with yellow foliage. Both are hardy to Zone 4.

Distinctive because it is the only maple with fragrant flowers, the Amur maple (*Acer tataricum* ssp. *ginnala*) comes from the Amur River basin in northern Russia, which accounts for its Zone 1 hardiness. The pale cream flowers in early spring give typical maple keys in summer but these are flushed with red and look like flowers from a distance. In fall, the leaves turn a flame red that lights the landscape until hard frost put an end to the display. This is normally grown

The leaves of *P. coronarius* 'Variegatus' (mock orange) have broad, creamy white edges.

The clusters of semidouble flowers of *P. coronarius* have a rich, persuasive scent.

as a tall shrub reaching about 7 m (20 ft) and useful as a windbreak, but can also be trained into a small tree with a single stem.

With their snow-white blooms and fragrant flowers, mock orange (*Philadelphus*) deserve a place in every garden; the fact that they are drought-tolerant is a bonus. Most are hybrids, the results of crosses made between the various species, and they vary in size from 0.6–2.5 m (2–8 ft), so be sure you purchase the right size for the location.

All hardy to Zone 3: 'Snowdwarf' grows 60 cm (2 ft) tall and has semidouble flowers. 'Buckleys Quill' is twice this height and has flowers with narrow quill-like petals. 'Minnesota Snowflake' and 'Virginal' are popular varieties that grow to 2.5 m (8 ft), both with double flowers, but are vigorous growers that need pruning immediately after flowering every third year. There are two varieties of the common mock orange (*P. coronarius*) that are commonly grown: 'Variegatus' has white-edged leaves and 'Aureus' the golden leaved form that keeps its color well. They only have single flowers, but the perfume still drifts across the garden to let you know they're blooming.

CHAPTER FIFTEEN

CARE-FREE MAINTENANCE

When you create a garden of care-free plants, you are automatically taking steps toward reducing garden maintenance. When well sited, with the type of soil and exposure they prefer, the plants described in this book will thrive with little attention beyond minimal feeding, weeding, and watering. The plant combinations in Part 1 will help you match their cultural needs to sites where these plants grow best. The profiles in Part 2 will give you the names of many species and cultivars that are especially well adapted to various climates and growing conditions. In this chapter we'll share tips for providing your plants with the minimal care they deserve, and we'll also help you time your efforts to the season when your care will do the most good.

This chapter includes information on getting more plant performance for less effort. You'll also find advice on warding off problems when buying, planting, feeding, and watering plants, as well as tips for the minimal weed control and pruning that these plants require to maintain their health and good looks. Discover easy methods for multiplying your plants. Despite the natural resistance of these plants, the occasional flying or four-footed pest will visit your garden, so we'll also describe methods of repelling and controlling these pests. A helpful Calendar of Care is a seasonal checklist for timing your maintenance tasks so that they don't get out of hand.

No one wants a landscape that's a source of tiresome work, and although some maintenance is unavoidable, here you'll find ways to make it more enjoyable. Experienced gardeners wait for good weather and favorite times of the day to work in their gardens, whether they are doing things they enjoy, such as setting out new plants, or more formidable tasks, such as mowing the lawn. In a garden stocked with care-free plants, you have plenty of opportunities to pick and choose the green-thumb activities in keeping with your mood and what you want to accomplish on any given day.

In any season, shop early while the selection is good, so that you can be assured of healthy plant specimens.

Start With the Best

When you begin with the best-quality care-free plants you can find, you can look forward to excellent results from your efforts in the garden. It is wise to buy plants in the proper season, which is spring for most annuals, perennials, shrubs, and trees in most parts of the country, although in areas with mild, rainy winters or hot, dry summers, many plants are best set out in the fall. In any season, shop early, when the selection is good, even though you may be buying plants that are just emerging from, or going into winter dormancy. Purchasing plants that have already gone dormant, and planting them in early spring, is a smart investment. As plants begin their most active season of aboveground growth, they are also poised to develop vigorous new roots over the long, upcoming growing season, and a strong root system will carry them safely through their first winter in the ground.

Study plant tags carefully before making your selection, because the tags often contain useful information about plant size, spacing, and requirements for sun or shade. Plants that are purchased from mail-order catalogs or on-line catalogs often come packaged with detailed instructions for planting and care. Set aside a place in your home where you can keep all your plant tags or instruction sheets so that you can refer to them in the future, should you need to order more of the same variety, or review the cultural information.

Waste no time in getting your new plants planted in the ground. If you must make your plants wait for a few days, set them in a sheltered outdoor spot, out of blazing sun or drying wind, and make sure that their roots do not dry out. When rainy weather forces you to delay planting of dormant bare-root plants or hardy bulbs, make room for them in your refrigerator if you can, or put them in an unheated garage or basement. Cool temperatures help to keep these plants dormant until you are ready to plant them in your garden.

BUYING HEALTHY PLANTS

Annual bedding plants and many perennials will be actively growing when you buy them, which makes it easy to select strong plants. Here are some shopping details worth checking.

LEAF COLOR. Look for plants with healthy looking green leaves that have no signs of yellowing, which is the most common symptom of plants that have been stressed by a lack of fertilizer and water. The only time this rule does not apply is if you are examining golden-leaved varieties, which will be labeled as having chartreuse leaves.

CARE-FREE SECRETS

Shielding the Sun

To help ease plants into their new home, and reduce wilting, transplant them on a cloudy day. If you can't avoid planting in sunny weather, cover newly planted flowers with cardboard boxes, upside-down flowerpots, or small pails for the sunniest part of the day, for three days to shield them from strong sun.

ROOTS. A few small roots growing out of drainage holes are a sign of a strong root system. Avoid plants that have been held in pots for so long that roots have grown into thick tangles near the bottoms of the containers or are emerging from drain holes.

BUDS AND FLOWERS. Flowering plants that show a blossom or two are young and vigorous with a long flowering life ahead of them, but bypass those that appear to have been in bloom for several weeks. Annuals may be stressed and "bloomed out," and perennials that are already in bloom may transplant successfully, but usually will not bloom heavily in your garden until the following year.

COMFORTING COMPOST

Substances that you mix into soil to improve its texture and overall hospitality to plant roots are called soil amendments. The most useful and versatile soil amendment is compost, which is made by mixing together various organic materials, such as kitchen vegetable scraps, lawn clippings, and dried leaves, so that they decompose within a few months into a

Study plant tags carefully; they often provide information about plant size, hardiness, and culture.

dark, crumbly material that is also called humus. Mixing compost into soil enhances the soil's ability to retain both water and air, and provides it with a crumbly texture that roots can easily penetrate. In addition, compost contains enzymes and micronutrients that benefit plants by boosting their immune system. The neutralizing effect that compost has on soil pH helps plant roots absorb nutrients from the soil. Compost should not be considered a fertilizer, because compost usually contains only a little nitrogen, the nutrient most needed by growing plants, and the nutrient that is abundant in most fertilizers.

You can make your own compost by piling together plant debris, soil, grass clippings, shredded leaves, and vegetable materials, and then adding enough water to keep the mass moderately moist. Turning the pile speeds the decomposition process, which is always faster in warm weather, and probably stops entirely in winter. And while composting is a convenient way to recycle garden refuse, if you are planting numerous plants you will probably need to buy extra compost.

Compost is sold in bags at garden supply stores, or you can buy it by the truckload from farmers who turn out batches made from sources ranging from rotten hay and stable litter to spent mushroom-growing medium. And, many towns and cities now compost yard waste and make the material available to residents at a very reasonable cost. Because compost is so variable in content and nutrients, it is often wise to buy a small amount from any given source, try it, and then decide if you want more.

ACIDIC AMENDMENTS

Plants that require acidic soil, such as ferns, azaleas, and rhododendrons, benefit from being mulched and having their planting holes amended with acidifying humus, such as peat moss, pine needles, or oak leaves. Peat moss has the added advantage of being a poor medium for soil-borne fungi, so it is also good to use in situations where root rot is to be avoided at all costs. For example, a mixture of peat moss and sand makes a good rooting medium for soft-stem cuttings.

Leaf mold is nothing more than composted, or rotted leaves. Fully composted leaves will be nearly

Compost is made by mixing garden waste and kitchen scraps and allowing them to decompose.

neutral in pH, but if you use partially decomposed acidic leaves like oak leaves, it will be slightly acidic. Leaf mold is seldom sold, but it is easily made. Simply pile leaves in a shady place where they will be regularly dampened by rain, and forget about them for two years. That's how long it takes for tree leaves to decompose into a material that, when stirred lightly with a digging fork, breaks apart into dark brown, crumbly leaf mold.

PLANT AT THE RIGHT DEPTH

As a general rule, it is best to set plants in the soil at the same depth at which they grew in their containers. Be especially attentive to planting depth when setting out shrubs and trees, which have the highest transplant survival rate when their roots are disturbed as little as possible. It is usually better to dig a broad planting hole than a very deep one, because most new roots grow outward rather than straight down. Also bear in mind that when you place a plant into a hole with several centimeters (inches) of cultivated soil at the bottom of it, the plant will sink deeper as the soil settles and becomes compacted. For this reason, setting plants slightly high in the prepared hole, so that the soil over their topmost roots forms a small mound, makes a good start. After several weeks, the soil around the plant usually settles until it is even with the surrounding soil.

Wise Watering

New plants benefit from watering often enough to keep the soil barely moist during their first season in the ground, because they are growing on skimpy roots. After a few weeks or months, depending on the growth rate of the plants, you can water less frequently. Plants with mature, extensive root systems usually do a good job of finding the water they need deep within the soil. And plants that are mulched during the growing season need minimal supplemental water, because the mulch shades the soil, keeping it cool and reducing evaporation of moisture just below the soil's surface.

Whether you are watering young plants or established ones, it's important that the water you provide soaks deeply into the soil. When only the top few centimeters (inches) are dampened, roots will gravitate toward the soil's surface, and plants with extensive surface roots dry out more quickly during droughts than those with deep, water-seeking roots. For this reason, providing a small trickle of water over several hours is usually better for plants than watering them with a strong shower for a few minutes.

But you need not spend hours watering your plants. Most garden centers and discount stores sell soaker hoses, which are inexpensive, perforated hoses with tiny holes so that they slowly drip water along the length of the hose into the soil. You can snake soaker hoses between your plants and disguise them by covering them with mulch. Soaker hoses made from recycled tires are weatherproof and can be left in the garden all year long. There are only a couple of tricks to using soaker hoses. The first is to turn the water pressure on very low, so that the water weeps out evenly along the entire length of the hose. And, where possible, lay the hose on an incline so that the end is below the height of the faucet, so that gravity will help the water drain from it efficiently.

SPRINKLERS AND NOZZLES

When your whole yard is parched by dry weather, and the plants that wilted in the midday sun the day before are still drooping first thing the following morning, they are in dire need of irrigation.

If water use is not restricted in your community, running a sprinkler is the easiest solution. However, watering by hand may be your only alternative. Garden supply stores stock an array of special adjustable garden-hose nozzles, which will allow you to change the force and stream of water in keeping with the task at hand, making it possible to switch from a gentle shower to a misty spray without having to turn off the water.

If you keep a number of plants in containers, you will love what's called a watering wand. This is a sprinkler-type of nozzle with a long handle that screws onto the end of your hose. A watering wand

A watering wand is a nozzle with a long handle that makes it easy to reach hanging baskets.

makes it easy to reach plants growing in high hanging baskets and other hard-to-reach areas.

CARE-FREE WATERING

Whenever you water your garden plants, your objective should always be to soak the root zone rather than the foliage. Fungi that cause leaf-spot diseases become active when leaves are damp, so keeping leaves dry helps to prevent these problems. For this reason, it is often best to water early in the morning, so that water will soak into the soil before temperatures rise, and wet leaves can dry before the cool hours of evening. In arid climates, where disease is not a problem, water in the evening to reduce evaporation, and plants have all night to soak up water before facing dry wind or hot sun the following day.

CARE-FREE SECRETS
Measuring Water

Gardeners are usually advised to provide plants with 2.5 cm (1 in) of water per week during droughts. It may seem odd to measure liquid in centimeters (inches), but it is easily accomplished. Draw a line 2.5 cm (1 in) from the bottom of a shallow container, such as an empty margarine tub or tuna can. Set the container where sprinkler water falls into it when you run the sprinkler. When the water in the container reaches a height of 2.5 cm (1 in), move your sprinkler and the emptied can to a new area and repeat the process until the garden is covered.

Snake soaker hoses between your plants for an easy, water-conserving method of irrigation.

Fertilizing Your Plants

Except for large shrubs and trees, nearly every plant in your garden will benefit from being fertilized at the right time, with the right kind and amount of fertilizer. And almost all plants need nutrients most at that time of the year when they are in their most active period of green growth or are producing flower buds.

UNDERSTANDING FERTILIZERS

Sorting through fertilizers presents a bit more of a challenge. Fertilizer and plant food are two ways of saying the same thing, and it's easy to be overwhelmed by the product choices that await you at any garden center or discount store. Yet choosing and using fertilizers need not be complicated. Depending on the type of garden you have, you will probably need only a few products to meet the nutritional needs of all of your plants. Every box or bag of fertilizer lists three numbers on the label, which represent how much of the three primary plant nutrients, nitrogen, phosphorus, and potassium, are contained in the bag, box, or bottle. The first number represents nitrogen, the second phosphorus, and the third stands for potassium. Nitrogen contributes primarily to the development of healthy green leaves and stems. Phosphorus contributes to the growth of roots, flowers, and fruit. Potassium also aids in flower and fruit production, but in addition, it promotes plant health and resistance to disease and environmental stress.

When one or more numbers in a fertilizer analysis are higher than the others, it indicates that there is more of one nutrient, as in 14-4-4, which is a formulation that is high in nitrogen. If you relate this to the description of nitrogen, above, you can see that this formulation would be a good one to use on a green lawn, or to fertilize green, leafy garden plants. High numbers, such as 20-20-20, simply show that a fertilizer product is very concentrated and potent and will require a great deal of dilution before being applied, whereas low numbers, such as 4-4-4, indicate lesser amounts of the same nutrients and less dilution is needed. However, you do not have to be a mathematician to figure out how much of any fertilizer to use. Instead, simply follow the application rates given on the package label.

Because they are so concentrated, manufactured fertilizers usually have high analysis numbers, so you will use a small amount of them with each application. Organic fertilizers, which may be made from manure, alfalfa meal, feather meal, and many other natural ingredients, have comparatively low analysis numbers, so more of an organic fertilizer is required to accomplish the same end. Not surprisingly, potent synthetic fertilizers usually cost more per pound than their bulkier organic counterparts. And manufactured fertilizers, unless they are slow-release formulas, usually work faster than organic ones, which release their nutrients slowly over several months. In most cases, it is advantageous to apply fertilizers that release nutrients slowly enough for plants to absorb them, to reduce runoff and waste.

STOCKING YOUR GARDEN PANTRY

Two types of plants, lawn grasses and acid-loving plants, such as azaleas and rhododendrons, require special types of fertilizer. Details on lawn fertilizers,

Fertilizer packages list 3 numbers. This formula represents how much of the 3 primary plant ingredients, nitrogen, phosphorus, and potassium that it contains.

which are generally high in nitrogen content, are given in Chapter 7. Most garden centers sell boxes of clearly labeled azalea or acidifying fertilizer, which help maintain the acid soil pH these plants need, while also supplying the plants with the nutrients that they require.

For most other plants, look for products that claim to be all-purpose plant foods or all-purpose fertilizers. With this type of fertilizer, the three numbers in the analysis are usually identical (or nearly so), so they are also called "balanced" fertilizers. For example, a couple of top-selling manufactured granular, dry fertilizers have an analysis of 13-13-13 and 14-14-14, while a leading balanced organic fertilizer has an analysis of 5-5-5. Any of these will do for routine plant feeding. To apply a granular, dry fertilizer, either mix it into the planting hole along with a little soil prior to planting, or scatter it over the surface of the soil above the root zone of an established plant. Then use a hand cultivator to lightly scratch the fertilizer into the soil so it will not wash or blow away before rain can dissolve it and carry the nutrients into the soil in a form that plant roots can absorb.

Dry fertilizers are convenient to use, and they usually supply nutrients to plants for several weeks or even months, depending on the formulation. But sometimes you may need very fast results, which is what you get with liquid or powdered soluble plant foods that are mixed with water and then poured onto the soil surrounding the plants. When treated with a soluble fertilizer, struggling plants with yellowing leaves often show improved leaf color within a day. And, there is no better way to fertilize container plants than to treat them to half-strength helpings of soluble fertilizer on a weekly basis.

Organic mulches, such as bark nuggets, cool the soil in summer, reduce evaporation, and smother weeds.

The Magic of Mulch

Each time you set out a plant, the final planting step is usually to cover the ground around it with a blanket of mulch. Mulches are organic or inorganic materials that retard evaporation from the soil, smother weeds, and insulate the root zone of plants, keeping them cool in summer and protecting them from frost damage in winter. Organic mulches have the added benefit of attracting beneficial earthworms, which aerate the soil and contribute plant nutrients.

Mulches also give the garden a clean, well-managed appearance, and to a degree, you can even color-coordinate some mulches, such as choosing reddish or dark brown wood chips, or earthy-looking rich, black compost to fine-tune the color scheme.

You can buy many types of mulch at garden centers and discount stores, either in bags or by the truckload. Some of the most common organic mulches include bark nuggets, shredded wood chips, and pine needles, which are often sold in neatly bound bales. For these or any other mulch to be effective, they should be spread on the ground about 8 cm (3 in) thick. You should expect them to pack down in time, and also expect the organic ones to gradually decompose, becoming a thinner layer after a few months. When this happens, simply spread more mulch over the old.

Be careful not to pile mulch right against the trunks of trees, or to smother the bases of shrubs or perennials. With woody plants, it is usually best to leave 5 cm (2 in) of open space between the trunk or stem and the blanket of mulch, to avoid holding moisture next to the trunk, which is a situation that invites disease and insect infestation.

MULCHING FOR WINTER PROTECTION

Mulches help cool soil temperatures during the growing season, and you can also depend on mulch to reduce the negative impact of cold winter weather on dormant plants. In many areas, the problem is not due to prolonged freezing, but to repeated freezing and thawing of the soil, which causes plant roots to break, and can actually heave plants out of the soil exposing their roots to frost damage. In cold-winter areas, piling on a double layer of fluffy organic mulch after the soil freezes, helps keep plants safe from these destructive changes in the weather.

Where winters are usually mild, sudden cold snaps can damage plants that hold tender green growth through the winter. An extra layer of winter mulch composed of a fluffy material, such as straw or evergreen boughs, safeguards shallow roots and green shoots from frost damage, without smothering the crowns of the plants. To protect young shrubs

In winter, piling on a double layer of fluffy organic mulch insulates plants against frost damage.

from hungry rabbits and deer, enclose the plants in a protective cage made from wire fencing and put insulating mulch inside the cage.

OUTWITTING WEEDS

Attentive mulching will go a long way toward preventing weed problems, but in every garden some weeds invariably find places to grow. Weeds are always most troublesome in open, cultivated soil that receives abundant sunshine, but even shade gardens can become targets for vining weeds and unwanted tree seedlings.

Beds filled with flowering plants often must be weeded by hand, which can be a pleasant chore if done when the soil is moist so that weeds pull free with ease. Wear comfortable, close-fitting gloves, and make use of a kneeling pad. But don't rest when your bed is clean. Instead, mulch the weeded space immediately to frustrate weedy replacements, which will certainly appear if the area is left unmulched.

Where you have more space to work, a sharp hoe can make quick work of eliminating young weeds, which will quickly wither in the sun when they are sliced off just below the soil's surface. You may need a pair of pliers to pull and twist out woody weeds, which have extremely tough, tenacious roots. When woody tree or shrub seedlings are simply cut off at ground level, they will often resprout from the roots left behind.

To control the worst weeds, cover the ground with a commercial nonwoven fabric weed barrier, and then cover the fabric with an attractive organic mulch. This is the best way to keep weeds out of new groundcover plantings or shrub groupings until they reach mature size, which often take two years. After that, they will effectively shade out weeds.

NO-SWEAT METHODS

Keep a Sharp Edge

A slicing instrument like a hoe does a much better job of cutting through weeds when it has a sharp edge. Use a metal file or whetstone to sharpen your hoe after every time you use it. To make digging easier, sharpen your spade every few weeks during the growing season as well.

Supporting Your Plants

Almost all vines require some type of trellis, and you can be endlessly creative as you devise or purchase arches, iron or wood trellises, or panels of wooden lattice that will hold wandering stems aloft. Single upright pillars and openwork obelisks tend to become unstable after they become heavy with plants, so it is crucial that they be deeply and firmly anchored in the ground. Arches are less likely to topple, but if you live in a windy area, it may be best to grow vines on wooden trellises that are securely attached to walls.

Many bushy and upright perennials also benefit from support, which should be tailored to the growth habit of each plant. For example, tall hollyhocks, lilies, and snapdragons can be loosely tied to thin wooden or bamboo stakes pushed into the ground near the base of the plants. It is best to use three twine-wrapped stakes to surround each plant, so that the plant will be able to sway in the wind, but will not snap off at the point where it would be tied to a single stake.

In order to hold up bushier perennials, such as peonies, that tend to flop over when they become heavy with blossoms, you should invest in metal plant supports fashioned into hoops or grids. If you can't find acceptable products at retail stores, check the huge selection of plant supports sold by garden mail-order catalogs. Whether you choose interlocking links, circular grow-through supports, or upright metal stakes with "arms" that bend, you will find them invaluable for keeping your favorite flowers high and dry. And, what could be easier than placing a support ring over a peony when it is just beginning to grow in spring, marking its spot while

Almost all vines require some type of trellis or arbor to support the length of their climbing stems.

bracing new stems against the forces of wind and rain? Other flowers that benefit from circular or grow-through plant supports include balloon flower, foxglove, gladiolus, gypsophila, larkspur, rudbeckia, sneezeweed, and tithonia.

CARE-FREE SECRETS

Marking Special Spots

When you're not using metal support hoops to support plants, put them, or even off-season tomato cages, to work marking places where dormant plants are at rest. In winter, these wire supports also can be used to hold mulches in place around roses and other marginally hardy plants.

Cutting flowers for a bouquet encourages plants to produce new blossoms, extending the flowering season.

Grooming Your Plants

Trimming off withered blossoms and tattered stems does much more than make your garden appear neatly groomed. It also coaxes plants to produce more stems and blossoms, extending the flowering time of many plants. While most perennials and shrubs will bloom all at once no matter what you do, and some plants can shed their old flowers without aid, most annuals and a few perennials depend on you to relieve them of old flowers. When deprived of the opportunity to produce seeds, annuals have no choice but to flower again and again, in an attempt to set seeds.

Often called deadheading, this operation is best undertaken with a sharp pair of handheld pruning shears. Scissors work well, too, provided the stems are not extremely woody or tough. The objective is to make swift, clean cuts without twisting or pulling on the plant. Gather your trimmings in a small pail, along with any leaves that appear yellow, spotted, or brown around the edges. If they appear old and tattered add them to your compost pile; if any leaves appear to be diseased or insect infested, dispose of them in the trash.

THE ART OF SMART PRUNING

Many gardeners are entirely too eager to prune shrubs and trees, which is a way of inventing unnecessary work. And, while most woody plants do benefit from pruning at some time in their lives, you should always have a clear purpose before you embark on a pruning campaign. Until you have a definite objective in mind, it is usually best to content yourself with observing the plant a while longer. Then, begin pruning when you know exactly what you hope to accomplish, such as removing crossed or damaged branches or shaping the plant, and it is important to prune at the right time of the year to prevent winter frost damage to new growth initiated by pruning in the fall, or to keep from cutting off next year's flower buds.

There are many good reasons to prune, and in fact some plants can never reach their peak of health and beauty without regular, thoughtful pruning. Consider the following valid reasons to prune, and compare them to the pruning needs you see in your yard. Then choose from the techniques described in this section to do the job right.

REMOVING dead or diseased plant parts. Any time is a good time to relieve plants of stems or branches

Trimming off withered blossoms and tattered stems is an operation that gardeners call deadheading.

that have died or seem to be in the process of doing so. By midspring you should be able to identify plant parts killed by winter's cold. An easy way to determine if a branch is dead is to scrape away a small piece of bark. If there is a layer of green tissue just beneath the bark, and the branch is flexible and not brittle, the branch is alive.

SHAPING a plant to improve its structural strength. This is the real purpose behind pruning young trees, and you can also prune some shrubs to bring out the best in their natural shapes. However, every young tree does not need this type of pruning. Only those with branches that cross or rub against each other, causing wounds that are entry points for disease; those with very acute crotch angles (which tend to split in storms), or trees in which you wish to eliminate low-hanging branches, or dense shrubs that need to be opened up, such as a rose, to allow light and air to reach the center where it will discourage fungal infections. Opening up a mature tree is called creating windows in the canopy, and it is a natural-looking way to admit light into a garden area or to allow homeowners to enjoy a view without losing their tree. Structural pruning of shrubs is usually done for artistic reasons, for example training an azalea to look like a small tree, or accentuating the sinewy curving trunks often found on rhododendron, smokebush, and witch hazel.

PRUNING to promote better flowering. When left to their own devices, many shrubs will grow foliage so dense that flowering suffers. Roses are an excellent example, particularly reblooming roses, such as hybrid teas. Other reblooming shrubs, such as bluebeard and buddleia also flower more and longer when old branches are headed back. Yet this pruning goal is not limited to reblooming plants. Thinning out old branches from forsythia, hydrangea, lilac, and mahonia greatly improves the vigor and flowering performance of the healthier branches that remain on the shrubs. Up to a third of the branches can be removed from a shrub each year without affecting its appearance or health.

PRUNING to rejuvenate old plants. Old age is relative where plants are concerned. Young or old, bluebeard grows best when it is cut back nearly to the ground each spring, and buddleia grows back best from a 30–60 cm (1–2 ft) tall stump. With red-osier dogwood, the best stem color develops on 1- and 2-year-old stems, and cutting out old ones is the best way to keep plenty of new ones coming on. As for huge old shrubs that need large-scale renewal, the best approach is to thin out old branches gradually, over a period of 2–3 years.

ELIMINATING hiding places for pests and diseases. Do not hesitate to prune off limbs or branches that are riddled with holes that are oozing sap, or are surrounded by sawdust, which are made by boring caterpillars. Plant tissues that are badly damaged by these pests seldom recover completely, so there is little reason to prolong the plant's suffering. Also trim off and dispose of branches that are disfigured with corky looking galls, or any that appear hopelessly lost to mildew or fungal leaf spot diseases.

PRUNING TECHNIQUES

There are three basic techniques for pruning plants: thinning, heading back, and shearing. It's important to understand the difference between these techniques, because the easiest method, heading back, is seldom the best.

THINNING is what you do when you follow a branch or stem back to where it sprouts, and prune it at its point of origin. With trees, this is usually where it emerges from a larger branch or the trunk. But in the case of long-limbed shrubs, such as forsythia and mahonia, most stems originate right at the ground. Spend a few minutes studying where branches originate and you will know exactly how to do this type of pruning. Always make pruning cuts at an angle to the stem to allow water to drain from the cut surface to keep it from rotting. Although

Thinning removes up to a third of the oldest shrub branches to promote colorful new growth.

Most pruning tasks can be accomplished with a pruning saw, pruning shear, and lopping shear.

Long-handled hedge trimmers can be used to shear back flowering perennials and groundcovers.

thinning is often a slow and awkward way to prune, it is the best way to preserve the natural shape of any woody plant.

HEADING BACK a technique that involves pruning off the tips of branches, which causes buds farther down the branch to develop into new stems and flowers. This type of pruning increases the number of branches, making a plant bushier. It is used mostly for plants that bloom on stem tips, such as buddleia, rose, and most perennial vines. Deadheading, or removing the spent flowers, of annuals and perennials uses this same principle. Because heading back is easy compared to thinning, many gardeners mistakenly head back azaleas, forsythia, and hydrangea, robbing the plants of their natural beauty as well as many future flowers.

SHEARING is wholesale heading back, and its use should be limited to plants you wish to grow as dense hedges, for example barberry, boxwood, holly, and other shrubs that have a tight, compact form. Yet do keep in mind that just because a shrub can be sheared does not mean that this is necessary. When dwarf cultivars of shrubs are chosen, often little or no pruning of any kind is needed to keep them shapely and attractive.

PLANT PRUNER'S TOOLBOX

Pruning cuts should always be smooth rather than having ragged edges, so sharp tools are essential. The following four tools can handle most pruning jobs in a home landscape.

PRUNING SHEARS use a scissors action to cut through stems less than 1 cm (1/2 in) thick. Light thinning and heading back, including deadheading of flowers, can usually be done with pruning shears. There are two styles, anvil pruners and bypass pruners. Anvil pruners have one blade that presses a branch against an "anvil," and cuts through it. Anvil pruners are often less expensive than bypass pruners, but if you use them, you run the risk of damaging a branch by crushing the cut edge, leaving an unattractive cut that is open to disease. Bypass pruners are generally preferred, because they have two cutting blades that work together like a pair of scissors to make a sharp, clean cut.

LOPPERS are long-handled pruning shears that can cut through woody stems up to 2 cm (3/4 in) thick. They are the tools of choice for thinning branches from shrubs or for removing long suckers that often emerge from the bases of trees.

A PRUNING SAW is needed to cut through woody tree limbs, or to prune shrub branches more than 2.5 cm (1 in) thick. This saw is also available in a long-handled version for cutting tree branches that are beyond a gardener's reach. Handle with care, because pruning saws have deep, sharp teeth.

HEDGE TRIMMERS make fast work of shearing plants. Hand-operated hedge trimmers are fine for small jobs, but if you maintain a large hedge you will find electric or rechargeable, battery operated models a true joy to use.

HOW TO PRUNE HEAVY TREE LIMBS

If you look closely at the place where one tree branch joins a larger one, including the trunk, you will see a wrinkled raised collar of bark. Strive to make pruning cuts just outside this collar, without cutting into it. This is because the collar contains chemicals that the tree uses to wall off the injury (your pruning cut), making it naturally impervious to invasion by pests and diseases. Tree experts no longer recommend painting a pruning wound with tar or paint, which can trap moisture, inviting rot and disease.

If the limb is a large one, begin by cutting it off about 15 cm (6 in) from the branch collar. To keep the weight of the limb from binding the saw blade, first make a small cut on the underside of the branch. Then cut off the limb starting from the top edge of the branch, about 2 cm (1 in) beyond the cut on the branch underside.

Remove the stub by making a single downward cut just outside the branch collar.

To keep the weight of a branch from binding the saw blade, remove it in stages.

After making the first cut halfway through the branch, make another, cutting downward.

Look where the branch joins the trunk, and you will see a wrinkled raised collar. Cut outside the collar.

Preserve the branch collar, which contains chemicals that will naturally heal the pruning wound.

When dividing perennials, insert two garden forks into a clump, back to back, and lever the roots apart.

Propagating Plants

The vast majority of plants can be grown from seed, and starting your own seeds, or buying commercially grown seedlings, are often the best ways to begin when you are growing annuals. However, several other methods of propagating plants provide faster and better ways of increasing your supply of perennials, bulbs, and sometimes even shrubs. Modern nurseries sometimes use high-tech tissue-culture methods to propagate plants, in which a cluster of cells is nurtured into a plant grown in a test tube. This has become an inexpensive way to produce disease-free, identical plant cultivars, but it can only be done in a laboratory setting. At home you can use more time-tested methods, such as dividing or rooting cuttings to increase your supply of plants.

Plants that naturally reproduce, expanding into thick clumps are prime candidates to propagate by digging and dividing. Indeed, some plants grow with such vigor that they must be divided every few years to keep them from becoming so crowded that they fail to bloom well. Early spring, when plants are emerging from dormancy, is usually the best time to dig and divide them, although spring-flowering bulbs are best dug in early fall, and iris are best propagated in late summer. The plant profiles in Part 2 of this book describe the best times to divide specific plants, or you can consult the Care-Free Garden Calendar at the end of this chapter.

DIGGING AND DIVIDING

Before you dig up crowded plants, prepare a bed so that you can replant the best divisions right away. Also water the old planting if needed, preferably the day before you dig, because digging is always easier, and fewer roots are broken, when you dig in soil that is slightly moist.

Use a digging fork to loosen the soil on the outside of the clump, gradually working to the center of the clump. As you encounter the root mass, try to get the fork beneath it, lifting it intact if you can. This is easily accomplished with a crowded clump of spring-flowering bulbs or plants with shallow roots, such as bee balm or lamb's ears. But because the roots are so heavy, it may not be practical to actually lift a huge clump of daylilies or hostas onto a tarp where you can meticulously divide the crowns. Instead, use a sharp spade to cut straight down through the root mass, cutting it into halves or fourths. Then lift the smaller chunks, and discard severely damaged roots and the crowns attached to them. Pry apart smaller clumps by inserting two garden forks, back to back, and levering the roots apart. You should still have plenty of healthy small clumps that you can divide for replanting.

ROOTING CUTTINGS

Both luck and skill are required to coax 10 cm (4 in) softwood cuttings to root. Take them from healthy stem tips in early to midsummer and insert them into a pot of damp rooting medium, which is usually sterile, soilless commercial potting medium, or a mixture of clean sand and peat moss. Numerous plants are willing to be propagated this way, including dusty miller, artemisia, Russian sage, and even some shrubs including buddleia and bluebeard.

To reduce wilting, pinch off all but the top tuft of two or four leaves from each cutting. Then dip the cut ends into water and then into commercial rooting powder, which is available at garden centers, before tucking them into a pot filled with damp rooting medium. To maintain a high level of humidity, enclose each container in a roomy plastic bag. When kept in a warm, shady place, with close monitoring to ensure that the soil never dries out, at least half of the cuttings should root in 4 to 6 weeks. Some can even be rooted in a jar of water on a sunny windowsill. At the first sign of new growth, gently transplant the cuttings to containers of fresh potting soil, and pamper them in pots for another month or two before planting them in the garden.

Few things are more rewarding than watching stem cuttings develop roots in a jar of water.

When grown where they receive adequate light and air, plants rarely succumb to pests and diseases.

Pests and Diseases

When well-sited, any plant will be healthier and more resistant to problems, and the plants in this book have been chosen because they are naturally healthy and pest and disease resistant. But in any garden pest problems will pop up sooner or later. Whether those problems are due to insects or diseases, prompt intervention greatly improves your chances of saving plants from unnecessary suffering. Check your garden plants often for signs of trouble, and be prepared to administer first aid right when the need arises.

It may be comforting to know that a pest or disease problem on one plant seldom poses a serious risk to neighboring plants of a different species. With few exceptions, notably slugs, snails, grasshoppers, and Japanese beetles, each species of insect and disease-causing microorganism specialize in a narrow range of plants. In other words, aphids that cluster on your roses are unlikely to colonize lilacs, because their physiology is such that they cannot digest the juices from lilac plants. The same is true of many diseases, including those that cause dark spots or light patches to form on leaves. So, when a zinnia suffers from powdery mildew, it is not likely that your marigolds will be similarly affected. Translated into a practical plan of attack, this means that you can focus on pest and disease problems as rather isolated incidents when your landscape is comprised of a diverse collection of plants.

GENTLE INTERVENTIONS

When you first notice a pest problem, simply removing and disposing of the affected plant part is sound practice, especially when the problem is a disease, most of which are caused by microscopic fungi. Yet this is impractical when the problem is more widespread, as when spider mites have colonized the leaf undersides of a large shrub. Instead, spraying plants thoroughly and often with a strong spray of water from a hose will dislodge and disable these and other fragile sucking insects like aphids. If more serious treatment is indicated, apply insecticidal soap or horticultural oil, both of which are available as concentrates at most garden centers. Insecticidal soap kills small insects by corroding their bodies with fatty acids, and horticultural oil smothers them, leading to their rapid decline. Use these and other pest-products according to label directions only on plants listed on the label and for insects listed on the label.

If more aggressive measures are needed to control an insect pest, look for a general-purpose commercial garden pesticide labeled for use on the plant and the pest that you want to control. In addition, a botanical pesticide derived from the bark of the neem tree, azadirachtin, controls a number of common insects and suppresses some diseases, as does pyrethrum, which is derived from natural plant toxins, and its synthetic equivalent, pyrethrin. Neem has the added benefit of repelling insects for a limited amount of time after application, but its availability is limited in Canada.

WHEN A FUNGICIDE IS NEEDED

Fungal leaf and root-rot diseases are usually most active in humid weather and in wet soil. They can often be avoided by siting plants in an area with good air circulation, pruning plants to allow sun and air to circulate to inner branches, and planting in soil that is naturally well drained, amending soil with compost to improve drainage, or building shallow berms or raised beds so that plants can be set above the surrounding soil.

But, often in late summer when days are humid and nights are cool, spores of disfiguring leaf diseases like powdery and sooty mildew can erupt. Unfortunately, there is no one-size-fits-all fungicide that will control all fungal plant diseases. Instead, you must check product labels to see if the affected plant is listed. You can do more harm than good to a plant by treating it with a fungicide that it cannot tolerate, or by mixing the concentrate at a stronger rate than is recommended on the label. Also, be very careful when using fungicides near water, because many of them are toxic to fish and other aquatic animals. Warnings of any environmental dangers will be listed on all product labels.

For fungicides to work well, you must get excellent coverage with the spray. Many fungi colonize leaf undersides, so spraying from the bottom up as well as from the top down is always wise. Avoid spraying just before rain is expected, as the product may be washed off before it has a chance to work.

SAFE STORAGE

Before you purchase a pesticide or herbicide, read the label carefully. Check to see that it is labeled (registered) for use on the pest, disease, or weed that you want to treat, and that it is also labeled for safe use on the plant that you want to apply it to. Do not use a pesticide on a plant or pest for which it is not labeled. Study the product label for guidelines about protective clothing and application; what is the best season, time of day, and weather for application. For instance, you should never apply such products on a windy day to avoid damaging nearby plants, and also to avoid having the pesticide drift from your yard into a neighboring one. You also should avoid applying pesticides before rain is expected, and you should apply them when the temperatures are between 18°C (65°F) and 29°C (85°F).

 CONSULT A PHYSICIAN before spraying to be sure that you have no medical conditions that should pre-

vent you from spraying. If you are in doubt, hire a professional licensed applicator.

 KEEP CHILDREN AND PETS AWAY from the area during and after application, for as long as the label instructs, and inform neighbors that you will spray.

 MEASURE AND MIX CHEMICALS in a well-ventilated area and precisely as directed on the product label. Applying a stronger-than-recommended solution is illegal, and may harm plants. Wear old clothing with long sleeves and long legs and dispose of it, or wash it separately and store it with the product. Do not touch your face or eat or drink until you finish the task and then bathe thoroughly.

 MANY GARDEN PESTICIDES REMAIN VIABLE for years when stored in a cool, dry place. In the interest of safety, store lawn and garden chemicals in their original containers, in a locked cabinet out of reach of children and pets, and label the cabinet door with its contents.

 IF YOU EXPERIENCE A CHEMICAL SPILL or suspect pesticide poisoning, consult the product label for first-aid action, or a hot-line phone number. Also, telephone 911, your physician, or a poison-control center (the number should appear at the front of your telephone directory). Keep the product nearby

so that you can read the active ingredients, which are listed on the label, to the help-line person who answers the telephone.

THE FALL CLEAN-UP

When the first blasts of winter cold cause leaves to flutter down and perennials to die back and become dormant, you have an excellent opportunity to interrupt the life cycles of many pests and diseases by cleaning up your garden. Many fungal plant diseases overwinter in old fallen leaves and stems, and some insects find safe harbor in plant debris as well.

Before winter makes working outdoors uncomfortable, gather dead plant material that lies on the ground and pull up withered annuals, roots and all. Gloved hands and a stiff rake will be your primary tools, though you may also need pruning shears to snip off the stems of perennials flush with the soil. Before traces of their presence disappears, mark the locations of plants you intend to divide or move in spring. After the first hard freeze, apply a thick, fluffy mulch of straw or evergreen boughs to insulate marginally hardy plants against damage from freezing and thawing. Then, when the new season begins, you will be ready to sail into it quickly.

Interrupt the life cycles of many pests and diseases by cleaning up your garden in fall.

CARE-FREE GARDEN CALENDAR

Summer is the high activity season in the garden, but if you plan ahead, you will have plenty of time during the summer to admire your garden rather than toiling in it. A fundamental care-free strategy is to do as much maintenance as you can during the "off seasons" of early spring and fall. Where winters are mild, winter is actually the first active gardening and maintenance season of the year. The following calendar is organized by season and by type of plant to help your care-free plants perform at their peak, year-round.

PLANTS	LATE WINTER	SPRING	EARLY SUMMER
ANNUALS	Plant cold-tolerant flowering annuals including larkspur and poppies in all Zones. Remove mulch from overwintered pansies in cold areas.	Set out bedding plants of cold-tolerant flowering annuals including calendula, dusty miller, forget-me-not, lobelia, snapdragon, and stocks in early spring. Plant containers with spring-flowering plant combinations. After the soil warms, sow seeds in the garden for marigolds, nasturtiums, and zinnias. Set out warm-season annuals like begonias and annual geraniums after the last frost has passed.	Deadhead annuals regularly to prolong their flowering time, and pinch back coleus and plectranthus to increase the number of branches. Begin fertilizing annuals being grown in containers on a biweekly basis. Plant heat-tolerant annuals including fan flower, lantana, sweet potato vine, and tithonia.
PERENNIALS	Look for the emergence of early bloomers like hellebores. Where the soil is not frozen, set out dormant perennials that have thick, heavy roots, such as goatsbeard, gypsophila, and peony. As winter winds down, gradually rake back mulch used to cover dormant perennials, and topdress the root zones with a 2 cm (1 in) blanket of compost. Prune back ornamental grasses to just above the crowns, or growing points.	Set out potted and bare-root perennials as early as possible, just as they are emerging from dormancy. Dig and divide asters, bee balm, lamb's ears, and other perennials that have become crowded. When new growth shows on established plants, fertilize them with an organic or controlled release fertilizer. Stake or support tall and bushy perennials while they are still small so that they hide the supports as they grow.	Trim spent flowers from early bloomers, such as candytuft and woodland phlox. Set out late bloomers such as asters, goldenrod, and sneezeweed. Lightly fertilize ferns and other woodland perennials. Weed and mulch established perennials, and provide stakes or other supports for tall and floppy plants.
VINES	Repair trellises if needed. Prune grapes. Plant sweet peas and other cool-season annuals.	Prune winter damage from large perennial vines like climbing roses and clematis, and erect or repair trellises. Fertilize established vines. Plant seeds of annual vines in the garden, such as hyacinth bean, morning glory, and scarlet runner bean.	Guide new stems of clematis, honeysuckle, and climbing rose toward their support, and tie them loosely if needed. Prune wisteria to control its size. Cut or deadhead sweet pea flowers to encourage new buds.
BULBS	Look for green growing tips of spring-flowering crocus, cyclamen, daffodils, hyacinths, snowdrops, squill, and tulips.	After the flowers wither, fertilize spring-flowering bulbs with commercial bulb fertilizer or bone meal according to label. Leave the foliage intact until it begins to yellow. Fertilize crocosmia and lilies with an all-purpose fertilizer, as soon as new growth appears. After the last frost passes, plant caladiums, callas, cannas, and gladiolus.	Mark the locations of spring-flowering bulbs that you want to dig and divide in the fall. Set out more gladiolus. Fertilize caladiums, especially those growing in containers.
SHRUBS	Check stems for signs of small, oval immobile scale insects on branches and spray with dormant oil if needed. Prune back bluebeard and buddleia severely.	Prune away branches that appear dead or diseased. Plant all types of evergreen and deciduous shrubs. After the flowers fade, thin old branches from forsythia, lilac, and other spring-blooming shrubs. Fertilize young shrubs with an organic or controlled-release, all-purpose fertilizer. Renew mulches.	When pruning shrubs that have already bloomed, retain berry-bearing branches as much as possible. Continue setting out container-grown plants except in very hot summer areas. Provide water as needed to young shrubs planted in the spring.
TREES	Now's the time to plant hardy evergreens, such as false cypress and pines.	Set out new trees just as they are emerging from dormancy. Fertilize young trees with an organic or controlled release, balanced fertilizer applied according to package directions. Prune dead branches from established trees.	Hand weed around the bases of trees, and prune off any small suckers that emerge from the lower trunk.
LAWNS AND GROUNDCOVERS	In cold climates, rake up plant debris as soon as the snow melts. Cut back old leaves from liriope, and shear back ivy, pachysandra, and other groundcovers that need rejuvenation.	Fertilize lawns and apply a crabgrass preventer if desired. Set out new groundcover plants.	Plant seed or sod in areas that need repair. Mow often, removing only one-third of the grass blades' length as you mow. Fertilize established groundcovers with an organic or timed-release fertilizer.

PLANTS	LATE SUMMER	FALL	EARLY WINTER
ANNUALS	Pull up spring-planted annuals like pansies that are bloomed out. Give other annuals a deep drench with a soluble fertilizer. Shear back petunia and sweet alyssum to rejuvenate the plants. Set out flowering cabbage and kale, pansies, and chrysanthemums.	Expect many summer-weary annuals to make a strong comeback after nights become longer and cooler. In mild-winter regions, continue planting hardy pansies and ornamental cabbage and kale, plant larkspur and poppies outdoors from seed, and set out bedding plants of dusty miller, annual dianthus, forget-me-not, and snapdragon, if they will survive.	Where frosts are not severe, lightly mulch over over-wintering pansies with a fluffy mulch of straw or evergreens.
PERENNIALS	Cut old flowering stems from all perennials that have already bloomed. Dig and divide bearded iris. Plant offsets from bugleweed and hens and chicks. Stake tall asters.	In Zones 7 to 9, you can save time in spring by dividing many perennials in fall, such as bee balm, bugleweed, daylilys, dianthus, obedient plants, and yarrows. In other areas, trim off dead foliage and renew mulches around plants as cold weather descends.	After the ground freezes, mulch over dormant perennials with a thick fluffy organic mulch like straw to keep the soil from thawing and refreezing. Where winters are milder, check plants often to see if any have been heaved out of the ground. Gently push them back down if needed.
VINES	Trim honeysuckles, climbing hydrangeas, and other big vines as needed to control their size. Pull up sweet peas when flowering subsides. Fertilize climbing roses that rebloom in the fall.	After frost kills annual vines, gather up the dead stems and foliage and compost them.	Repair wobbly trellises.
BULBS	If the weather is good, begin digging and dividing crowded clumps of crocuses and daffodils.	Plant spring-flowering bulbs of all types. Dig, dry, and store tender bulbs including caladiums and gladioli.	Where the ground is not frozen, spring flowering bulbs may be planted until mid-December.
SHRUBS	Check plants for problems with insect aphids or spider mites, and treat infestations promptly. Shear hedge plants for the last time. Fertilize reblooming roses.	As deciduous shrubs shed their leaves, rake them up and compost them. Inspect stems for signs of insect scale and spray with horticultural oil according to package directions, if needed.	Evergreen shrubs may be planted where winters are not too severe.
TREES	If the weather is very dry, provide deep drenches of water to trees planted earlier in the season.	Enjoy the fall show of colorful foliage, and then rake up leaves to interrupt the life cycles of tree-eating pests that lay eggs in fallen leaves. Deposit the leaves in a compost pile where they will turn to leaf mold, an excellent acidifying mulch.	Renew mulches beneath young trees to help moderate soil conditions. Remember to keep mulches from touching the trunks of trees to allow air to circulate and reduce chances of disease and insect infestation.
LAWNS AND GROUNDCOVER	Where winters are cold, fertilize lawns with a low-nitrogen, high-potash fertilizer. Trim edges of groundcover plantings.	Rake leaves that pack down on lawns and groundcovers, blocking the light and health-giving air circulation that these plants require. Reduce mower height for the last few mowings to lessen the chance of damage from snow-mold fungus that is more common on long grass.	Do not walk on lawns that are frozen but not covered with snow.

GLOSSARY

A

Acclimatization The adaptation of a plant to a site or to a change in climate.

Acid soil Soil with a pH value less than 7.0, also sometimes called "sour" soil. See pH, pH scale.

Adhesive disks On some climbing vines, a circular, flattened organ at the end of a tendril used by the plant to attach itself to a support. Example: Virginia creeper.

Aeration The act of supplying oxygen to the soil, in a garden by digging or in a lawn by using a spiked tool to punch holes through the sod and thatch into soil.

Aerial roots On some vines, above-ground, root-like appendages on the stem, used by the plant to attach itself to a support. Example: English ivy.

Alkaline soil Soil with a pH value more than 7.0, also sometimes called "sweet" soil. See pH, pH scale.

Amendment A material that is added to the soil to improve its condition, usually being an organic or mineral substance, such as compost, sand, or limestone.

Annual A plant that completes its life cycle, from seed to the flowering stage and setting seed again, all within a single season.

Antitranspirant A waxy material applied to foliage to temporarily prevent water loss.

Aphid Any of the over 4,000 species of small, soft-bodied, pear-shaped insects with mouth parts especially adapted to piercing and sucking sap from the tender tissues of a plant. Also called plant louse.

Average soil Generally, a loam soil. See loam.

B

Bacteria Microorganisms that live in soil, water, plants, and other organic matter that can cause diseases.

Bactericide Any pesticide that kills bacteria.

Balanced fertilizer Any fertilizer that contains balanced amounts of nitrogen, phosphorus, and potassium, the three major plant nutrients. Example: 10-10-10 formulation.

Balled-and-burlapped Term used to describe a nursery plant with its root ball and some soil wrapped in burlap for protection during transport or shipping.

Bare-root Term used to describe a dormant nursery plant sold without soil around its roots.

Bedding plant A flowering or foliage plant used for garden display, sold as a small, young plant, most commonly an annual.

Beneficials Insects, amphibians, or plants that control harmful insects, increase the productivity or fertility of plants, or attract other beneficials or wildlife.

Biennial A plant requiring two seasons to complete its life cycle; leaves are formed the first year, flowers and seeds the following season. Example: foxglove.

Biological control Any living or biologically derived agent that controls garden pests and/or diseases. Examples: ladybird beetles eating aphids or BT controlling cabbage worms. See BT.

Blight A disease that causes plants to wither and die without rotting.

Borers Worm-like larvae of beetles or clearwing moths that damage both woody and herbaceous plants by boring into and tunneling beneath the bark of tree and shrub trunks and twigs or within the stems of herbaceous plants, often killing the host plant.

Bract A modified structure found at the base of a flower or flower cluster, usually leaf-like or scaly in appearance but in some plants, such as the dogwood, extremely colorful and showy.

Branch collar The thickened ring in the area of a tree where a main branch joins the trunk.

Broadcast To scatter seeds or fertilizer evenly over a wide area of soil.

Broad-leaf Term used to describe a plant having broad, flat leaves as opposed to the needlelike leaves of conifers; usually, but not always, deciduous. Examples: Dandelion, Rhododendron.

BT (Bacillus thuringiensis) Any of approximately 30 different bacterial diseases that infect, sicken, and kill insect pests, with different varieties of the bacteria infecting different and very specific pests. Often used to control caterpillars.

Bulb A swollen underground stem where food is stored during a plant's dormant period. Example: tulip bulb.

C

Calcareous A term used to describe alkaline soils containing limestone.

Caliche A hard, alkaline soil or soil crust containing white calcium carbonate. It can be found in arid western regions.

Cane A slender woody stem, such as those of rose, raspberry and blackberry bushes.

Canker A lesion of usually sunken, decayed tissue found most often on plant stems or branches.

Canopy The uppermost crown of leaves in a tree.

Chlorosis An unseasonable yellowing of leaves generally caused by disease, nutrient deficiency, or a soil pH imbalance.

Clay soil Soil composed of very small particles that make it sticky, heavy, and hard to dig. Often compacted and slow-draining. Heavy soil.

Cold frame A bottomless box with a hinged, clear or translucent, plastic or glass top used to harden off and protect plants from the cold.

Compaction Soil that has become so dense that air and water cannot penetrate, usually caused by foot or vehicular traffic.

Complete fertilizer Any fertilizer containing nitrogen, phosphorus, and potassium.

Compost Organic matter, usually vegetative, that has decomposed; used as a soil conditioner, mulch, and disease inhibitor.

Conifer A cone-bearing tree or shrub; usually refers to evergreen plants.

Contact pesticide A pesticide that kills insects or other pests on contact.

Controlled-release (slow-release) fertilizer A fertilizer in which the fertilizer particles are coated with a material that dissolves slowly, thus providing fertilizer to a plant over a long period of time.

Corm An underground bulblike stem that bears roots and nourishes a plant. Example: gladiolus.

Crown (1) The basal part of herbaceous perennials from which both the stems and roots grow. (2) The uppermost branches of a tree.

Cultivar (abbr.: cv.) A named plant variety selected from the wild or a garden and cultivated by controlled propagation to preserve certain characteristics. Distinguished in a plant's name by the use of single quotation marks. Example: *Thuja occidentalis* 'Gold King'.

Cutting A leaf, shoot, root, or bud cut from a parent plant for use in propagation.

D

Damping off A fungal disease linked to poor air circulation, which usually attacks seedlings, causing them to collapse and die.

Deadhead The removal of faded flowers to prevent seeding and to encourage more vigorous blooming.

Deciduous Trees and shrubs that shed their leaves at

the end of the growing season and grow new foliage at the start of the next season.

Diatomaceous earth Abrasive powder made of the ground, fossilized shells of aquatic diatoms that damages soft-bodied pests, such as snails and slugs, when they crawl over it.

Dieback The death of stems beginning at the tip, caused by disease, damage, or stress.

Direct seeding, direct sowing To sow seeds directly on the soil outdoors where they will sprout.

Division The process of propagating a plant by separating its roots, crown, bulbs, or rhizomes.

Dormancy A period when a plant temporarily stops growing, usually in winter or in dry weather.

Dormant oil A refined petroleum product sprayed on dormant plants as a pesticide to smother insects.

Drench Application of a pesticide or fertilizer to the soil around the roots of a plant.

Drip line An imaginary line around the outer circumference of a tree's canopy, used as a guide in applying fertilizer, mulch, or for planting.

E

Espalier (1) A tree or shrub pruned and trained to grow flat against a wall, trellis, or fence. (2) The training or support of such a plant.

Evergreen A plant that retains its foliage throughout the year. Example: pine.

Exposure A description of the variation, intensity, and duration of sunlight, wind, and temperature of a site.

Eye (1) A growth bud, such as the eye of a potato. (2) The center of a flower, especially when it is of a contrasting color.

F

Family Botanically, a group of plant genera having overall similar characteristics.

Fertilizer Any of the numerous organic or synthetic materials containing one or more of the minerals necessary for plant nourishment.

F1 hybrid A plant bred from two pure-breeding parents to produce a hardier and more productive offspring; will not breed true in the next generation.

Friable Easily crumbled, as in loam soil. See loam.

Frost hardy A term used in referring to a plant that is capable of withstanding barely freezing temperatures; usually refers to annuals or tender perennials.

Fungicide Any substance used to kill or inhibit fungi.

Fungus A plant organism without chlorophyll that reproduces by spores that can cause diseases.

G

Gall An abnormal outgrowth on a plant cause by insects, bacteria, mites, or fungi.

Genus (plural: genera) Botanically, a group of plant species generally similar in flower form, appearance, and growth habit. The first word of a plant's botanical name denotes the genus.

Germinate To begin to grow; to sprout from seed.

Grafting A method of plant propagation in which a bud or shoot from one plant is joined to the roots or a shoot of another. See Graft union, Rootstock, Scion.

Graft union The place on a grafted plant where the bud or shoot and rootstock join. See Grafting.

Green manure A fast-growing crop, such as alfalfa, that is dug into the soil while still growing to increase the organic content, normally in the same growing season.

Greensand A pulverized rock powder of sandy clay that is used to supply potassium, magnesium, and trace minerals to plants.

Groundcover A low-growing plant that spreads quickly to form dense colonies, often used to prevent soil erosion or cover shaded areas. Example: pachysandra.

Growing on Growing young plants indoors to a size suitable for planting out.

H

Habit The characteristic growth pattern of a plant.

Half-hardy A term used to describe a plant that can tolerate some cold temperatures or a light frost, but will not overwinter outdoors without protection.

Hardening off The process of gradually acclimatizing a plant that has been grown indoors to outdoor conditions prior to transplanting. See Acclimatization.

Hardiness The ability of a plant to survive over a range of hot or cold climactic conditions.

Hardiness zone map A map based on the average annual minimum temperature range, frost-free period, and precipitation for a specific geographic region.

Hardpan A hard, dense lower layer of soil formed when minerals leach down and bind with soil particles, blocking drainage and inhibiting root penetration of the soil.

Hardy Term used to describe a plant that can survive freezing temperatures without protection.

Heaving The pushing of plants out of the soil through the action of alternate freezing and thawing of the soil.

Heavy soil A common term sometimes used when referring to clay soil.

Heeling in To plant in a temporary location.

Herbaceous Any plant that has soft or tender upper growth rather than woody growth, specifically, an annual, biennial, or perennial.

Herbicide A product used to control or kill weeds.

Holdfast A term most commonly used to refer to the aerial roots or discs of vines by which they attach themselves to supports; also may sometimes be used in referring to tendrils and twining leafstalks.

Honeydew A viscous liquid excreted by aphids and other sucking insects that acts as a growth medium for certain molds and as a food source for ants.

Horticultural oil A refined oil that, when mixed with water, is used as a pesticidal spray; a general term that includes both dormant oil and summer oil.

Humus Decayed or partially decayed organic matter derived from the natural decomposition of vegetable matter, which is used as a soil amendment, and it may contain plant nutrients.

Hybrid A plant bred from the cross-fertilization of two or more genetically different parents, whether between different plants in a species, between different species of the same genus, or between plants in different genera.

I

Inorganic fertilizer A synthetic fertilizer that provides nutrients to encourage plant growth.

Inorganic mulch A mulch made from an inorganic substance, such as plastic sheeting or gravel. See Mulch.

Insecticidal soap An insecticide, either homemade or commercially prepared, made from the salts of fatty acid in soap.

Insecticide Any substance that kills insects.

Interplant To plant two or more types of plants with different bloom times or growth habits together.

L

Landscaping fabric Any of a wide variety of modern woven or bonded synthetic materials that allow water and air to pass through. Used for frost and pest protection, shading plants, mulch, and erosion control.

Larva (plural: larvae) The immature growth stage of many insects, such as caterpillars or grubs.

Last frost date Not an absolute date, but an average of

the various dates on which the last frost of winter historically has occurred in a specific geographic area.

Leaf spot (1) Name given to any of numerous viral or bacterial diseases, the main symptom of which is discolored spots on plant foliage. (2) A symptom of such a disease on a leaf.

Leggy Word used to describe a spindly plant with leafless stems, abnormally elongated stems, or with leaves spaced abnormally far apart on the stem.

Lime One of several compounds containing calcium and derived from limestone; used in powdered form sprinkled on the ground to provide plants with calcium and to make the soil more alkaline.

Loam A fertile, well-drained soil that has a relatively equal balance of sand, silt, and clay and is also usually rich in humus. Friable, or crumbly, soil.

M

Mealybug Small, soft-bodied, oval insects covered with powdery white filaments. Mealybugs attach themselves to the axils, or crotches, of leaves, pierce the stems, and suck sap from the plant, producing honeydew in the process, upon which sooty mold grows.

Medium The term used for a soil or soilless mix in which plants are grown, potted, or propagated. It is also called growing medium.

Microclimate A small area where the climate differs from that of the surrounding area.

Micronutrients Minerals, such as boron, necessary in small amounts for proper plant growth, also called trace, or minor, elements.

Milky spore disease A bacterial disease deadly to Japanese beetle grubs, which is used as a pesticide against them. Also sometimes called milky disease.

Miticide A pesticide, or acaricide, that kills mites.

Mother plant (parent plant) Any plant from which divisions and/or cuttings are taken for plant propagation, or the seed parent in a hybrid cross.

Mulch A protective organic or inorganic material applied to the soil's surface to provide weed or pest control, conserve moisture, or keep soil cooler in summer and warmer in winter.

N

Neem (1) A tall, usually evergreen tree, the neem tree (*Azadirachta indica*), which is native to East India. (2) An organic botanical, low toxicity commercial insect repellent and insecticide with long-lasting effects,

which is extracted from the seeds of the neem tree.

Nematode A microscopic worm that lives in soil, plants, or water, with some being beneficial to plants and others being harmful.

Neutral soil Soil with a pH value of 7.0. See pH and pH scale.

Nitrogen A major nutrient essential for plant growth.

NPK Chemical symbols for nitrogen, phosphorus, and potassium, the three major nutrients in fertilizer.

Nutrient Any element necessary for plant growth.

O

Organic fertilizer Any substance of plant, animal, or mineral origin, such as compost, manure, or greensand, containing plant nutrients, used as a fertilizer.

Organic matter Any substance derived from decomposed plant or animal material.

Organic mulch A mulch made from an organic plant material, such as shredded bark. See Mulch.

Overseeding A lawn renovation technique in which a lawn or an area of a lawn is reseeded after mowing, raking, and dethatching.

Overwinter (1) To live through the winter, usually in a dormant state. (2) To shelter marginally hardy plants outdoors or indoors during the winter.

P

Peat moss Partially decayed sphagnum moss used in potting media, soil amendments, and as a mulch.

Perennial (1) A flower that dies down to dormant roots over the winter and resumes new growth in spring. (2) A nonwoody plant that lives several seasons.

Perlite Granular volcanic rock used to improve aeration in a growing medium.

Pesticide A substance used to control and destroy insects, fungi, bacterial, mites, weeds, and other pests.

Phosphorus A major nutrient essential for plant growth. Sometimes also referred to phosphate.

pH The degree of acidity or alkalinity in the soil, measured numerically; pH that is too high or too low can impede the absorption of soluble nutrients from the soil by plant roots.

pH scale A scale graded from 0 (pure acid) to 14 (pure lye) used to measure acidity or alkalinity. From the neutral point (7.0) the numbers increase or decrease geometrically; thus pH 5 is 10 times more acid than pH 6; pH 4 is 100 times more acid.

Pinch To remove a stem's soft growing tip to promote

production of side shoots or flowers. Also called pinching out and pinching back.

Plantlet A new plant, complete with leaves and, usually, roots, arising from the roots, runners, rhizomes, or stems of another plant. Also, a new small plant created by division.

Post-emergent herbicide An herbicide used to control or destroy established plants.

Potassium A major nutrient essential to plant growth. Sometimes also referred to as potash.

Potting soil Any soil mixture or soilless medium created specifically for growing plants in containers.

Powdery mildew (1) Any of several fungi which produce a white powdery coating on a plant's surface, particularly leaves. (2) A plant disease caused by said fungi.

Pre-emergent herbicide An herbicide that acts to control plants before or during germination.

Propagate To grow new plants from parent stock.

Prune To cut back the growth of a plant to maintain its vigor, retain its shape, or encourage new growth.

R

Resistant Term applied to a plant that is not likely to be affected by a specific stressor, such as disease, insects, pests, or drought.

Rhizome A swollen underground plant stem that stores food and produces shoots and root formation.

Root ball The roots and accompanying soil visible when a plant is taken from its site and transported.

Rooting hormone, rooting powder A substance used in propagation to encourage rooting.

Rootknot nematode A minute worm that inhabits the soil and causes extensive damage to the roots of plants.

Rootstock The section of a plant onto which the shoot or bud of another plant is grafted.

Rosette (basal rosette) A cluster of leaves radiating from one stem in a compact circular arrangement at or near the surface of the soil. Example: dandelion.

Rots Diseases, characterized by decaying plant tissue, particularly root systems, caused by fungi or bacteria.

Row cover A light-weight woven or nonwoven, spun-bonded fabric placed over plants as protection from sunburn, frost or pests.

Runner A trailing, slender stem that grows along the ground and roots to produce a new plant.

Rust Any of several fungal diseases that cause disfiguring rusty-looking spots on stems or leaves, especially during cool, damp, late-summer weather.

S

Sandy soil A fast-draining granular soil made up of very large particles.

Sawfly larvae Caterpillar-like larvae that feed in masses on tree foliage, sometimes stripping entire branches or even trees before dropping to the ground to pupate.

Scab Any of several fungal diseases that create rough raised spots on a plant's leaves or fruit.

Scale Soft-bodied, sap-sucking insects that, as adults, attach themselves to the plant and form hard, waxy protective shields.

Scarify To nick, scratch, or apply a chemical treatment to a tough seed coat to induce speedier germination.

Scion A shoot or bud taken from one plant and grafted onto the rootstock of another. See Grafting.

Scorch Browning of the leaves along the veins or edges due to hot weather, too much or too little fertilizer, or damage from pesticides.

Self-sow The spontaneous, unassisted shedding of fertile seeds that will germinate and produce seedlings around or near the parent plant.

Semi-evergreen A plant whose leaves remain green for part, but not all, of the winter or on which some, but not all, of the foliage is retained in a green condition through the winter. Example: akebia

Sharp sand Course sand with sharp-edged grains, generally used as a soil amendment.

Shrub A woody plant with a number of branching stems, often coming from or near the plant's base, and having little or no main trunk.

Side-dress To spread or sprinkle fertilizer, compost, manure, or other nutrient-rich materials on the soil around the base of a plant or alongside a row.

Silty soil A soil with a powdery feel, less sticky than clay when wet and tending to be powdery when dry.

Soilless mix A potting medium that contains no soil; it is usually a combination of peat moss, perlite, or vermiculite, and sometimes fertilizer.

Sooty mold A harmless but unattractive blackish fungus found on the leaves of plants infested with sap-sucking, honeydew-producing insects, such as aphids, scales, and whiteflies.

Species (abbr.: sp. [singular] or spp. [plural]) Botanically, a group of plants sharing at least one distinct trait that sets them apart from all others; a unit of classification that ranks immediately below the genus; the second word in the Latin name of a plant. See Genus.

Spider mite Any of numerous species of tiny, spider-like pests that feed on and can seriously damage plant leaves, eventually weakening the host plant. Also sometimes called red mites or mites.

Spores The dustlike reproductive cells of flowerless plants like ferns, fungi, and mosses.

Stolon A spreading stem that grows along or under the ground and roots at the tip to produce a new plant.

Stratify To store seeds in a cool, dark, moist place for a certain period of time to promote germination.

Stress Any environmental or other factor, such as drought, insects, or diseases, that weakens a plant.

Succulents Plants that store water in their fleshy leaves or stems. Example: cacti.

Sucker An undesirable shoot arising from the roots, underground stems, or the rootstock of a grafted plant.

Sulphur (1) A dust or wettable powder used both as a fungicide and, when mixed with other substances, as a miticide and insecticide. (2) In granular form, a soil conditioner used to acidify alkaline soil.

Summer oil A refined petroleum product applied to growing plants to control and destroy insects.

Systemic Term used to describe a treatment that is absorbed by a plant; may be a fertilizer or an insecticide, fungicide, or a bactericide.

T

Taproot The main, downward-growing root, usually long and fleshy, that anchors a plant in the soil.

Tender Term used to refer to a plant that is susceptible to damage from cold.

Tendril On a vine, a coiling, thread-like growth used to attach it to a support. Example: nasturtium.

Thatch Undecomposed plant material that accumulates at the base of lawn grass.

Thinning To remove surplus seedlings, flowers, branches, or fruits so that the remaining ones grow more vigorously.

Thrips Tiny, slender, barely visible winged insects that feed on the sap from plant tissues, scraping the tissues with their rasping mouth parts to release the sap and causing significant damage, including scarred fruit and leaves, buds that turn brown and never open, and severely deformed flowers.

Tilth The friability of the top layer of soil.

Tolerant A term used to refer to a plant that can endure specific stressors without undue hardship, such as drought, diseases, pests, or cold.

Top dress To apply fresh soil, compost, or fertilizer to the soil's surface around the base of a plant without working it into the soil.

Topiary A tree or shrub pruned into an ornamental shape. Sometimes refers to vines growing on a moss-stuffed frame that has an ornamental shape.

Topsoil The topmost layer of soil, usually refers to nutrient-rich soil, but topsoil can be of poor quality.

Train To direct a plant to grow into a desired form.

Transplant To move a plant from one location to another, one pot to another, or from indoor flats to outdoor beds.

Tree A woody plant with one thickened main stem (trunk) generally topped by a distinct crown, or canopy, of branches and leaves.

Tuber A short, thickened, usually underground stem or root where food is stored. Example: potato.

V

Variegated In referring to plant leaves, those marked by striations or patterns in contrasting colors.

Variety (abbr.: var.) A distinct variation in a species, which is given a name of its own; often used interchangeably with cultivar.

Vermiculite A moisture-retaining mineral used to lighten soils and potting mixes.

Vine A plant with branches that either recline and trail along the ground or climb by twining their stems around a support or by attaching tendrils, aerial roots, or leaf stalks to a support.

Virus A primitive microorganism that infects living cells and can cause incurable plant diseases.

Volunteers Plants that grow from self-sown seeds.

W

Whiteflies Tiny, white, moth-like sucking insects that feed on leaves, weakening and stunting the host plant and often transmitting viral diseases between plants.

Wilts Any of a number of bacterial or fungal diseases, usually incurable and fatal, that cause leaves to wilt, turn yellow or brown, wither, and die.

Woody Word used to describe certain types of plants, specifically, trees and shrubs, with hard stems or trunks that do not die back in winter.

X

Xeriscaping Landscaping method based on the use of low-volume irrigation and drought-tolerant plants.

INDEX

Note: Page references in **boldface** indicate illustrations or photographs.

Zone map, *see endsheets*

CREDITS

Picture Research & Editing: Alexandra Truitt & Jerry Marshall (www.pictureresearching.com)

Front cover: © Ken Druse **Back cover:** © Ping Amranand **Pages: 2–3** © Neil Campbell-Sharp **6** © Carolyn Bucha **7** C © Carolyn Bucha; BR © Carolyn Bucha **8** L to R © Clive Nichols/The Old Vicarage, Norfolk; © Hans Reinhard/Reinhard-Tierfoto; © Susan A. Roth (Design: Landcraft Environments); © Derek Fell; © Pam Spaulding/Positive Images **9** L to R © Ping Amranand; © Photos Horticultural; © Reader's Digest Assoc.; © Ron Sutherland/Garden Picture Library; © Derek Fell **10** © Susan A. Roth (Design: Landcraft Environments) **12** © Carolyn Bucha **13** © Mayer/Le Scanff/Garden Picture Library **14** © Carolyn Bucha **15** © Neil Campbell-Sharp; BR © Dolores Santoliquido **16** © Carolyn Bucha **17** © Lynn Karlin **18** © Carolyn Bucha **19** © Jerry Pavia; BR © Dolores Santoliquido **20** © Carolyn Bucha **21** © Clive Nichols/Lower Hall, Shropshire; CR © Dolores Santoliquido **22** © Carolyn Bucha **23** © Steven Wooster/Garden Picture Library **24** © Ping Amranand **26** © Carolyn Bucha **27** © Photos Horticultural; CR © Dolores Santoliquido **28** © Carolyn Bucha **29** © Pam Spaulding/Positive Images **30** © Carolyn Bucha **31** © Pam Spaulding/Positive Images **32** © Carolyn Bucha **33** © Pam Spaulding/Positive Images; CR © Dolores Santoliquido **34** © Clive Nichols/The Old Vicarage, Norfolk **36** © Carolyn Bucha **37** © Lamontagne/Garden Picture Library **38** © Carolyn Bucha **39** © Karen Bussolini/Positive Images; CR © Dolores Santoliquido **40** © Clive Nichols/Coton Manor, Northamptonshire **42** © Carolyn Bucha **43** © Susan A. Roth (Design: Conni Cross) **44** © Carolyn Bucha **45** © Jerry Pavia; BR © Dolores Santoliquido **46** © Carolyn Bucha **47** © Gay Bumgarner/Positive Images **48** © Pam Spaulding/Positive Images **50** © Carolyn Bucha **51** © Roger Foley; BR © Dolores Santoliquido **52** © Carolyn Bucha **53** © 2001 Alan & Linda Detrick **54** © Carolyn Bucha **55** © Clive Nichols/Waterperry Gardens, Oxfordshire **56** © Carolyn Bucha **57** © Neil Campbell-Sharp **58** © Carolyn Bucha **59** © Brigitte Thomas/Garden Picture Library **60** © Carolyn Bucha **61** © Susan A. Roth (Design: Conni Cross) **62** © Clive Nichols **64** © Carolyn Bucha **65** © Derek Fell **66** © Carolyn Bucha **67** © Ben Phillips/Positive Images; BR © Dolores Santoliquido **68** © Photos Horticultural **70** TL © Derek Fell; BC © Reader's Digest Assoc. **71** CL © Reader's Digest Assoc.; TC © Reader's Digest Assoc.; BC © Reader's Digest Assoc. **72** BL © Reader's Digest Assoc.; TR © Derek Fell **73** TL © Reader's Digest Assoc.; BC © Derek Fell **74** TC © Derek Fell; BR © Derek Fell **75** CL © Reader's Digest Assoc.; TC © Chris Burrows/Garden Picture Library **76** BL © Derek Fell; TR © Derek Fell **77** TL © John Glover/Garden Picture Library; BL © Reader's Digest Assoc.; BR © Reader's Digest Assoc. **78** BL © Reader's Digest Assoc.; TC © Storey Communications, Inc.; BR © Reader's Digest Assoc. **79** TL © Reader's Digest Assoc.; CL © Reader's Digest Assoc.; TR © Reader's Digest Assoc. **80** TL © Reader's Digest Assoc.; BL © Reader's Digest Assoc. **81** TL © Derek Fell; BC © Derek Fell **82** TR © Reader's Digest Assoc.; BL © Reader's Digest Assoc. **83** TC © Marianne Majerus/Garden Picture Library; BR © Derek Fell **84** TL © Reader's Digest Assoc.; BC © Reader's Digest Assoc. **85** CL © Derek Fell; TC © Reader's Digest Assoc. **86** TL © Reader's Digest Assoc.; BC © Derek Fell **87** CL © Reader's Digest Assoc.; BC © Reader's Digest Assoc.; CR © Derek Fell **88** TC © All-America Selections; BR © Derek Fell **89** TL © Reader's Digest Assoc.; TR © Reader's Digest Assoc. **90** TR © Derek Fell; C inset © Derek Fell; BL © Howard Rice/Garden Picture Library **91** TL © Reader's Digest Assoc.; BR © Derek Fell **92** BL © Derek Fell; C inset © Derek Fell; TR © Reader's Digest Assoc. **93** TL © Reader's Digest Assoc.; CL © Reader's Digest Assoc.; BL © Reader's Digest Assoc. **94** TL © Reader's Digest Assoc.; BR © Reader's Digest Assoc. **95** BL © Reader's Digest Assoc.; TC © Derek Fell **96** TL © Reader's Digest Assoc.; BR © Reader's Digest Assoc. **97** BL © Derek Fell; TR © Derek Fell **98** CL © Derek Fell; BR © Derek Fell **99** TL © Reader's Digest

Assoc.; CL © Photos Horticultural; BL © Reader's Digest Assoc. **100** BL © Photos Horticultural; TC © Reader's Digest Assoc. **101** TL © Reader's Digest Assoc.; BR © Reader's Digest Assoc.; BR inset © Reader's Digest Assoc. **102** © Trevor Cole **103** BL © Derek Fell; CL © Reader's Digest Assoc.; TR © Derek Fell **104** BL © Reader's Digest Assoc.; BR © Derek Fell **105** TL © Reader's Digest Assoc.; BC © Reader's Digest Assoc.; TR © Reader's Digest Assoc. **106** BL © Reader's Digest Assoc.; CT © Reader's Digest Assoc.; CT inset © Reader's Digest Assoc. **107** CL © Reader's Digest Assoc.; TC © Reader's Digest Assoc.; BC © Derek Fell **108** TL © Derek Fell; BC © Derek Fell; C © Derek Fell **109** BL © Reader's Digest Assoc. **110** TR © Reader's Digest Assoc.; BC © Reader's Digest Assoc. **111** CL © Holt Studios International/Primrose Peacock; TC © Reader's Digest Assoc. **112** TL © Derek Fell; BC © Reader's Digest Assoc. **113** TC © Reader's Digest Assoc.; BR © Derek Fell **114** BL © Photos Horticultural; TR © Derek Fell **115** © Reader's Digest Assoc. **116** TL © Photos Horticultural; BC © Derek Fell **117** TC © Derek Fell; BR © Trevor Cole **118** TC © Derek Fell; BC © Reader's Digest Assoc. **119** CL © Reader's Digest Assoc.; TC © Reader's Digest Assoc. **120** BL © Derek Fell; TC © Derek Fell **121** TL © Michael Dodge and Assocs.; BR © Derek Fell **122** © Hans Reinhard/Reinhard-Tierfoto **124** TL © Derek Fell BC © Reader's Digest Assoc. **125** TC © Reader's Digest Assoc.; BL © Derek Fell; BC inset © Jerry Pavia **126** © Derek Fell **127** TL © Reader's Digest Assoc.; BC © Reader's Digest Assoc.; CR © Reader's Digest Assoc. **128** TL © Reader's Digest Assoc.; TC © Reader's Digest Assoc.; BC © Reader's Digest Assoc. **129** TC © Reader's Digest Assoc.; BR © Jerry Pavia; BR inset © Reader's Digest Assoc. **130** CL © David Goldberg; BC © Jerry Pavia; TR © Reader's Digest Assoc. **131** TL © Reader's Digest Assoc.; BC © Jerry Pavia **132** BL © Reader's Digest Assoc.; TC © Derek Fell **133** TL © Derek Fell; CL © Reader's Digest Assoc.; BL © Reader's Digest Assoc. **134** BL © Derek Fell; TC © Jerry Pavi **135** TL © Reader's Digest Assoc.; BR © Derek Fell **136** TC © Reader's Digest Assoc.; BL © Jerry Pavia **137** CL © Reader's Digest Assoc.; TC © Reader's Digest Assoc.; BC © Reader's Digest Assoc. **138** TR © Reader's Digest Assoc.; BC © Derek Fell **139** CL © Reader's Digest Assoc.; TR © Derek Fell **140** TL © Reader's Digest Assoc.; CL © Reader's Digest Assoc.; BL © Reader's Digest Assoc. **141** TL © Derek Fell; BL © Reader's Digest Assoc. **142** TL © Derek Fell; BC © Reader's Digest Assoc. **143** CL © David Goldberg; TR © Reader's Digest Assoc.; CR © Reader's Digest Assoc. **144** BL © Reader's Digest Assoc.; TC © Reader's Digest Assoc.; BR © Reader's Digest Assoc. **145** TL © Reader's Digest Assoc.; BC © Reader's Digest Assoc.; CR © Reader's Digest Assoc. **146** TL © Reader's Digest Assoc.; CT © Reader's Digest Assoc.; CB © Reader's Digest Assoc. **147** TL © Derek Fell; CL © Reader's Digest Assoc.; BL © Jerry Pavia **148** TL © Reader's Digest Assoc.; CL © Reader's Digest Assoc.; BL © Reader's Digest Assoc. **149** TL © Ron Evans/Garden Picture Library; CR © Reader's Digest Assoc.; BR © Reader's Digest Assoc. **150** BL © Reader's Digest Assoc.; CL inset © Howard Rice/Garden Picture Library; TC © Reader's Digest Assoc. **151** TL © Brigitte Thomas/Garden Picture Library; BC © Reader's Digest Assoc. **152** TL © Derek Fell; BL © Reader's Digest Assoc.; BR © Reader's Digest Assoc. **153** TL © Jerry Pavia; BC © Kathy Charlton/Garden Picture Library; TR © Reader's Digest Assoc. **154** TL © Reader's Digest Assoc.; BC © Reader's Digest Assoc. **155** CL © Derek Fell; BL © Jerry Pavia; TR © Derek Fell **156** TL © Reader's Digest Assoc.; BL © Jonathan Buckley; BR © Reader's Digest Assoc. **157** BL © Reader's Digest Assoc.; TR main © Jonathan Buckley; CR inset © Reader's Digest Assoc. **158** TL © Jerry Pavia; BC © Reader's Digest Assoc.; TR © Derek Fell **159** TC © Reader's Digest Assoc.; BR © Jerry Pavia **160** BL © Reader's Digest Assoc.; TC © Reader's Digest Assoc.; BC © Reader's Digest Assoc. **161** TL © Reader's Digest Assoc.; BC © Reader's Digest Assoc.; CR © Reader's Digest Assoc. **162** TL © Derek Fell; BL © Reader's Digest Assoc. **163** TL © Reader's Digest Assoc.; TC © Reader's Digest Assoc.; BR © Reader's Digest Assoc. **164** BL © Derek Fell; TC © Jerry Pavia; BR © Mike Lowe **165** TL © Derek Fell; CR © Derek Fell **166** TL © Reader's Digest Assoc.; BC © Derek Fell **167** BL © Reader's Digest Assoc.; TR © Reader's Digest Assoc. **168** BL © Derek Fell; TC © Reader's Digest Assoc.; CR © Reader's Digest Assoc. **169** TL © Reader's Digest Assoc.; TC © Reader's Digest Assoc.; BR © Reader's Digest Assoc. **170** TL © Reader's Digest Assoc.; C © Jerry Pavia **171** BL © Reader's Digest Assoc.; TR © Reader's Digest